CARLYLE

Carlyle, Thomas

CARLYLE

Selected Works, Reminiscences and Letters

EDITED BY

JULIAN SYMONS

HARVARD UNIVERSITY PRESS
CAMBRIDGE MASSACHUSETTS

SBN 674-79960-7
1970 Importation
Printed in Great Britain

Contents

 CONTENTS

LETTERS

Introduction

Few Victorian literary reputations have survived into the twentieth century more uncertainly than that of Thomas Carlyle. Those of his writings that were most topical appear, very naturally, most outdated; the industry that burrowed through a mass of rubbish to discern veritable facts about Cromwell and Frederick the Great seems almost ridiculous in face of the small army of assistants busy with card-indexes ranked behind the modern historian; the famous style that electrified his contemporaries stands forbidding as a road-block between Carlyle and modern readers. His philosophy, as far as it is understood, is likely to seem a blend of platitudes ('Work alone is noble') and of apologies for dictators.

None of the unfriendly criticisms made of Carlyle is without truth: yet, added together, they make a picture that is grotesquely inaccurate. To appreciate Carlyle the reader today must make a greater effort than is required of him by any other Victorian writer: but the rewards are correspondingly great. The style that seemed to bristle so formidably, when viewed from a too-respectful distance, proves to have a surprising resilience and friendliness once we have ventured into the midst of it: it has, indeed, less the effect of a *style* than of a man speaking to other men—stammeringly at times it may be, upon occasion finding difficulty in fitting words to the fiery shape of his ideas, but possessing unquestionable fine eloquence and passion. And the prophetic message that Carlyle felt himself destined to give to the world; that too has its meaning for those who live in the age of atomic power, though not quite in the form that Carlyle conceived it. More clear-sighted than any other British thinker of his century, he saw that the Age of Machinery (as he called the Industrial Revolution) spelled the doom of *laissez-faire* in politics and economics. He offered in opposition to the measured optimism about a slow but inevitable increase in human prosperity felt by Victorian Conservatives, Liberals and Radicals alike, a very different vision:

> In the days that are now passing-over us, even fools are arrested to ask the meaning of them; few of the generations of men have seen more impressive days. Days of endless calamity, disruption, dislocation, confusion worse confounded: if they are not days of endless hope too, then they are days of utter despair. For it is not a small hope that will suffice, the ruin being clearly, either in action or in prospect, universal. There must be a new world, if there is to be any world at all! That human things in our Europe can ever return to the old sorry routine, and proceed with any steadiness or continuance there; this small hope is not now a tenable one. These days of universal death must be days of universal newbirth, if the ruin is not to be total and final.

These words were written during years of revolutionary upsurge and social change: have they not some relevance to our own time also?

The selection made here from Carlyle's writings is designed to show the stages in which an unorthodox Radical thinker became an advocate of extreme authoritarian rule. Carlyle's roots were in Scottish Calvinism, a fact very forcibly shown in the memoir of his father James which begins on page 515. He wished to believe in a stern, and even savage, God who would rule mankind as they deserved. He had also a keen intellect, much sympathy with the oppressed and hatred of their oppressors, and an independence of mind that made him distrust all accepted ideas, even those of the Christian religion. Throughout his life he sought for a prophetic gospel to still the doubts about the nature of God and society that had been first revealed by his intellect.

'Signs of the Times', the first of Carlyle's writings printed here, is an attempt to blend faith and reason. Reason told Carlyle that this was the Age of Machinery: faith, that what he called here a 'Dynamic' spirit was needed to redress a purely mechanical conception of existence. The two must be co-ordinated, Reason informed by Dynamism, if the great social changes in prospect were to be fruitful and not disastrous. 'The thinking minds of all nations call for change. There is a deep-lying struggle in the whole fabric of society; a boundless, grinding collision of the New with the Old.' The New: that meant some better, juster state of society born necessarily—as it seemed to the man who had removed himself from the metropolis of Edinburgh to the lonely Scottish moors the better to understand the world—in violence and terror. It was the duty of the seer to ensure that the birth-pangs of the New Era were not too painful, nor too prolonged.

It was at lonely Craigenputtock that Carlyle conceived and wrote *Sartor Resartus*, that extraordinary profession of faith in a 'believing Radicalism'. The central character of the book, Teufelsdröckh, is Carlyle himself, 'a speculative Radical, and of the very darkest tinge', who has little use for 'the solemnities and paraphernalia of civilised Life', and loathes above all things the conventional and respectable. The book is a mixture of autobiography and social fable set down in a style that remains unique in English literature.

The origins of this style, with its fantastic blend of neologisms, nicknames and compound words, its elaborate metaphors mingled with homely colloquial phrases, lay partly in the speech of the Carlyle family, partly in other personal and literary influences. The reasons for its adoption, by a man who could write standard Johnsonian English, are made plain in a letter written by Carlyle to his friend John Sterling:

> If one has thoughts not hitherto uttered in English books, I see nothing for it but you must use words *not* found there, must *make* words, with moderation and discretion of course. . . . With whole ragged battalions of Scott's novel Scotch, with Irish, German, French, and even newspaper Cockney (where literature is little other than a newspaper) storming in on us, and the whole structure of our Johnsonian English breaking up from its foundations, revolution *there* is visible as everywhere else.

Revolution, indeed, Carlyle saw everywhere. 'Revolution on the back of revolution for a century yet?' *The French Revolution* was a perfect vehicle for such a style as Carlyle's: it was also a perfect medium in which to express his subconscious desire for violence. One of the extracts from the book printed here depicts most graphically the triumph of the extremists of the Mountain over the moderates of the Gironde: and in writing it Carlyle quite naturally identifies himself with the Mountain, and shows his contempt for Girondist moderation. But the feelings in him that were sympathetic to the disorder and overthrow of established ideas in the Revolution were checked always by the contrary desire for discipline and order. *The French Revolution* is the farthest he ever reached in the direction of Radicalism. Henceforth he is still, at least for a time, concerned with the well-being of the mass of people, still indignant at social injustice: but much more he is looking for a guide who will lead the people into the New Era, a guide whose heroic features slowly lose their benevolence through the years, until at last they take on the stern disciplinary look of the God revered by Carlyle's father.

Through *Chartism*, the lectures on heroes, *Past and Present* and the book on Cromwell, the search for a hero continues: and gradually Carlyle fixes his hope for the hero's appearance in the Aristocracy, in those whom he had called idlers, game-preservers, pheasant-shooters. In *Latter-day Pamphlets* the prophet's most savage irony and most bitter contempt are reserved for those friends of his early manhood, the philanthropists and intellectual Radicals, the improvers of mankind and the members of benevolent societies. In *Chartism* he had attacked the rich for thinking that the invention of the treadmill and the tightening of prison discipline could possibly improve social conditions: in *Latter-day Pamphlets* his hypothetical hero tells prisoners, whose lot Carlyle considers scandalously easy: 'Mark it, my diabolic friends, I mean to lay leather on the backs of you, collars round the necks of you; and will teach you, after the example of the gods, that this world is *not* your inheritance, or glad to see you in it.' Finally, in the enormously long, diffuse book about Frederick the Great that occupied thirteen years of his writing life, Carlyle identified the hero with the tyrant, forgot almost completely his ideas about social justice, and used his marvellous dramatic skill to describe merely a series of battles, and his rich comic sense to produce entertaining but ludicrously unjust pictures of all those figures in the story who were opposed to Frederick.

History, which he had once interpreted as the movement of masses seeking freedom, is now ordered by the ideas and actions of a single ruthless Godlike man.

The transformation is an interesting one: but it is less important than the fact that, from our vantage point in the middle of the twentieth century, we can understand that through the peculiar mixture of his heredity and early environment Carlyle had certain insights into the nature of society denied to other British thinkers. He understood (although in later life he forgot) that the opening of the first Mechanics' Institute was a more important event than the battle of Waterloo; that the 'rights' of men are not gracefully asked for and granted, but are obtained by one section of society at the expense of another; that the history of the world, for a period that he roughly estimated at two centuries, was likely to be violent, not peaceful. Much that Carlyle has to say, even in his later work, has a strikingly contemporaneous air: many of his observations might have been made in the nineteen fifties, instead of a century earlier. It is true that he attempted to justify all his ideas by reference back to a Creator who would see to it that right triumphed in the end: but that creator's earthly representative for the apportionment of right and wrong turned out to be Carlyle himself. Today we can separate Carlyle's ideas about society from the desperately-held faith with which he felt compelled to explain them: and when the separation has been made we can recognize him as the most original British thinker of his age.

It is less necessary, after the biographical attention paid both to Carlyle and his wife in recent years, to justify the space given to his reminiscences and letters. The semi-autobiographical memoirs of his father and his wife, which Carlyle wrote in the stress of emotion soon after their deaths, evoke scenes of his past life with a clarity and brilliance equal to anything in *The French Revolution*. The portrait of Jane Welsh Carlyle is partial, and too tender: but Carlyle shows himself with absolute fidelity as a man graceless and truculent but basically generous and humane, a wonderfully intelligent

Noble Savage trampling on the current conventional views of politics, life and literature. The letters reinforce this conception, although they have been chosen principally to show the course of Carlyle's ideas rather than his life.

The text used for this edition is, except for the *Reminiscences* and letters, that of the Centenary Edition published by Messrs. Chapman and Hall between 1896 and 1899. The first edition of the *Reminiscences* edited by J. A. Froude and published in 1881, was marked by many slight textual inaccuracies. The text used here is that edited by Charles Eliot Norton, and published in 1887. A further note on the background of the *Reminiscences,* and the circumstances in which they came to be published, will be found on page 514. The sources of the letters quoted are given on page 698.

JULIAN SYMONS

Chronological Table

1795	Thomas Carlyle born, on 4 December, at Ecclefechan.
1801	Jane Baillie Welsh born, on 14 July, at Haddington.
1806	Carlyle goes to Annan Academy.
1808	His first sight of Edward Irving, at the Academy.
1809	Sent to Edinburgh University.
1814	Appointed Teacher of Mathematics at Annan Academy.
1816	Moves from Annan to teach at the Burgh School of Kirkcaldy.
1818	Leaves Kirkcaldy, to live and work in Edinburgh.
1821	First meeting, at Haddington, with Jane Baillie Welsh.
1824	First visit to London, and first journey abroad, to Paris. Carlyle's translation of 'Wilhelm Meister's Apprenticeship' published.
1825	The *Life of Friedrich Schiller* published in book form. (It appeared originally in the *London Magazine* in 1823, under the title of 'Schiller's Life and Writings'.)
1826	Marries Jane Baillie Welsh, 17 October. They live in a house rented by her mother, 21 Comley Bank, Edinburgh.
1827	First contribution to the *Edinburgh Review*, *Jean Paul Friedrich Richter*, published. *German Romance* published.
1828	Move from Comley Bank to Craigenputtock.
1829	*Signs of the Times* published in the *Edinburgh Review*.
1831	*Characteristics* published in the *Edinburgh Review*. *Sartor Resartus* finished in July. Visits London in unsuccessful attempt to sell it. First meeting with John Stuart Mill.
1832	Death of his father, James Carlyle.
1833	Visited at Craigenputtock by Emerson. Publication of *Sartor Resartus* begun in *Fraser's Magazine*, at a specially reduced rate of payment.
1834	Moves from Craigenputtock to 5, Great Cheyne Row, Chelsea. Begins work on *The French Revolution*. Death of Irving.
1835	First book of *The French Revolution* is lent to Mill, and accidentally burned by his servant.
1837	*The French Revolution* published.

1838 *Sartor Resartus* published in book form. (An American edition with a preface by Emerson, had appeared in 1836.)

1839 *Critical and Miscellaneous Essays* published in four volumes. *Chartism* published in December.

1841 *On Heroes, Hero-Worship and the Heroic in History* published. This book was composed of six lectures given by Carlyle in 1840, with later emendations and additions.

1843 *Past and Present* published.

1845 *Oliver Cromwell's Letters and Speeches, with Elucidations*, published.

1850 *Latter-Day Pamphlets* published, first in pamphlet form, then as a book.

1851 *The Life of John Sterling* published.

1852 Work on *Frederick the Great* begun.

1853 Death of his mother, Margaret Carlyle. Publication of *Occasional Discourse on the Nigger Question.*

1858 First two volumes of the *History of Friedrich II of Prussia, called Frederick the Great*, published.

1863 Third volume of *Frederick the Great* published.

1864 Fourth volume of *Frederick the Great* published.

1865 Last two volumes of *Frederick the Great* published.

1866 Death of Jane Welsh Carlyle, on 21 April.

1867 *Shooting Niagara; and after?* published.

1872 Death of John Stuart Mill.

1875 *The Early Kings of Norway* published.

1881 Death of Carlyle, on 5 February, and burial at Ecclefechan.

Signs of the Times

Signs of the Times was written in 1829, and printed in the *Edinburgh Review*. Like all of Carlyle's writings before *The French Revolution* it was published anonymously; public acknowledgement of his authorship was made when the essay first appeared in book form, in the *Miscellanies* of 1839. This is the first essay to express quite openly Carlyle's views about the nature and movement of modern society; views which had been no more than implicit in his writings on German literature. The conclusions arrived at in *Signs of the Times* disturbed conventional Whigs and utilitarians, but gave pleasure to Radicals. The St. Simonian Society sent a friendly letter to him from Paris. Carlyle wrote to his mother: 'The people there seem to think me a very promising man, and that some good will come of me. Thus, a prophet is not without honour, save in his own country.'

Signs of the Times

It is no very good symptom either of nations or individuals, that they deal much in vaticination. Happy men are full of the present, for its bounty suffices them; and wise men also, for its duties engage them. Our grand business undoubtedly is, not to *see* what lies dimly at a distance, but to *do* what lies clearly at hand.

> Know'st thou *Yesterday*, its aim and reason;
> Work'st thou well *Today*, for worthy things?
> Calmly wait the *Morrow's* hidden season,
> Need'st not fear what hap soe'er it brings.

But man's 'large discourse of reason' *will* look 'before and after'; and, impatient of the 'ignorant present time,' will indulge in anticipation far more than profits him. Seldom can the unhappy be persuaded that the evil of the day is sufficient for it; and the ambitious will not be content with present splendour, but paints yet more glorious triumphs, on the cloud-curtain of the future.

The case, however, is still worse with nations. For here the prophets are not one, but many; and each incites and confirms the other; so that the fatidical fury spreads wider and wider, till at last even Saul must join in it. For there is still a real magic in the action and reaction of minds on one another. The casual deliration of a few becomes, by this mysterious reverberation, the frenzy of many; men lose the use, not only of their understandings, but of their bodily senses; while the most obdurate unbelieving hearts melt, like the rest, in the furnace where all are cast as victims and as fuel. It is grievous to think, that this noble omnipotence of Sympathy has been so rarely the Aaron's-rod of Truth and Virtue, and so often the Enchanter's-rod of Wickedness and Folly! No solitary miscreant, scarcely any solitary maniac, would venture on such actions and imaginations, as large communities of sane men have, in such circumstances, entertained as sound wisdom. Witness long scenes of the French Revolution, in these late times! Levity is no protection against such visitations, nor the utmost earnestness of character. The New-England Puritan burns witches, wrestles for months with the horrors of Satan's invisible world, and all ghastly phantasms, the daily and hourly precursors of the Last Day; then suddenly bethinks him that he is frantic, weeps bitterly, prays contritely, and the history of that gloomy season lies behind him like a frightful dream.

Old England too has had her share of such frenzies and panics; though happily, like other old maladies, they have grown milder of late: and since the days of Titus Oates have mostly passed without loss of men's lives; or indeed without much other loss than that of reason, for the time, in the sufferers. In this mitigated form, however, the distemper is of pretty regular recurrence; and may be reckoned on at intervals, like other natural visitations; so that reasonable men deal with it, as the Londoners do with their fogs,—go cautiously out into the groping crowd, and patiently carry lanterns at noon; knowing, by a well-grounded faith, that the sun is still in existence, and will one day reappear. How often have we heard, for the last fifty years, that the country was wrecked, and fast sinking; whereas, up to this date, the country is entire and afloat! The 'State in Danger' is a condition of things, which we have witnessed a hundred times; and as for the Church, it has seldom been out of 'danger' since we can remember it.

All men are aware that the present is a crisis of this sort; and why it has become so. The repeal of the Test Acts, and then of the Catholic disabilities, has struck many of their admirers with an indescribable astonishment. Those things seemed fixed and immovable; deep as the foundations of the world; and lo, in a moment they have vanished, and their place knows them no more! Our worthy friends mistook the slumbering Leviathan for an island; often as they had been assured, that Intolerance was, and could be nothing but a Monster; and so, mooring under the lee, they had anchored comfortably in his scaly rind, thinking to take good cheer; as for some space they did. But now their Leviathan has suddenly dived under; and they can no longer be fastened in the stream of time; but must drift forward on it, even like the rest of the world: no very appalling fate, we think, could they but understand it; which, however, they will not yet, for a season. Their little island is gone; sunk deep amid confused eddies; and what is left worth caring for in the universe? What is it to them that the great continents of the earth are still standing; and the polestar and all our load-stars, in the heavens, still shining and eternal? Their cherished little haven is gone, and they will not be comforted! And therefore, day after day, in all manner of periodical or perennial publications, the most lugubrious predictions are sent forth. The King has virtually abdicated; the Church is a widow, without jointure; public principle is gone; private honesty is going; society, in short, is fast falling in pieces; and a time of unmixed evil is come on us.

At such a period, it was to be expected that the rage of prophecy should be more than usually excited. Accordingly, the Millennarians have come forth on the right hand, and the Millites on the left. The Fifth-monarchy men prophesy from the Bible, and the Utilitarians from Bentham. The one announces that the last of the seals is to be opened, positively, in the year 1860; and the other assures us that 'the greatest-happiness principle' is to make a heaven of earth, in a still shorter time. We know these symptoms too well, to think it necessary or safe to interfere with them. Time and the hours will bring relief to all parties. The grand encourager of Delphic or other noises is—the Echo. Left to themselves, they will the sooner dissipate, and die away in space.

Meanwhile, we too admit that the present is an important time; as all present time necessarily is. The poorest Day that passes over us is the conflux of two Eternities; it is made up of currents that issue from the remotest Past, and flow onwards into the remotest Future. We were wise indeed, could we discern truly the signs of our own time; and by knowledge of its wants and advantages, wisely adjust our own position in it. Let us, instead of gazing idly into the obscure distance, look calmly around us, for a little, on the perplexed scene where we stand. Perhaps, on a more serious inspection, something of its perplexity will disappear, some of its distinctive characters and deeper tendencies more clearly reveal themselves; whereby our own relations to it, our own true aims and endeavours in it, may also become clearer.

Were we required to characterise this age of ours by any single epithet, we should be tempted to call it, not an Heroical, Devotional, Philosophical, or Moral Age, but, above all others, the Mechanical Age. It is the Age of Machinery, in every outward and inward sense of that word; the age which, with its whole undivided might, forwards, teaches and practises the great art of adapting means to ends. Nothing is now done directly, or by hand; all is by rule and calculated contrivance. For the simplest operation, some helps and accompaniments, some cunning abbreviating process is in readiness. Our old modes of exertion are all discredited, and thrown aside. On every hand, the living artisan is driven from his workshop, to make room for a speedier, inanimate one. The shuttle drops from the fingers of the weaver, and falls into iron fingers that ply it faster. The sailor furls his sail, and lays down his oar; and bids a strong, unwearied servant, on vaporous wings, bear him through the waters. Men have crossed oceans by steam; the Birmingham Fire-king has visited the fabulous East; and the genius of the Cape, were there any Camoens now to sing it, has again been alarmed, and with far stranger thunders than Gamas. There is no end to machinery. Even the horse is stripped of his harness, and finds a fleet fire-horse yoked in his stead. Nay, we have an artist that hatches chickens by steam; the very brood-hen is to be superseded! For all earthly, and for some unearthly purposes, we have machines and mechanic furtherances; for mincing our cabbages; for casting us into magnetic sleep. We remove mountains, and make seas our smooth highway; nothing can resist us. We war with rude

Nature; and, by our resistless engines, come off always victorious, and loaded with spoils.

What wonderful accessions have thus been made, and are still making, to the physical power of mankind; how much better fed, clothed, lodged and, in all outwards respects, accommodated men now are, or might be, by a given quantity of labour, is a grateful reflection which forces itself on every one. What changes, too, this addition of power is introducing into the Social System; how wealth has more and more increased, and at the same time gathered itself more and more into masses, strangely altering the old relations, and increasing the distance between the rich and the poor, will be a question for Political Economists, and a much more complex and important one than any they have yet engaged with.

But leaving these matters for the present, let us observe how the mechanical genius of our time has diffused itself into quite other provinces. Not the external and physical alone is now managed by machinery, but the internal and spiritual also. Here too nothing follows its spontaneous course, nothing is left to be accomplished by old natural methods. Everything has its cunningly devised implements, its prëestablished apparatus; it is not done by hand, but by machinery. Thus we have machines for Education: Lancastrian machines; Hamiltonian machines; monitors, maps and emblems. Instruction, that mysterious communing of Wisdom with Ignorance, is no longer an indefinable tentative process, requiring a study of individual aptitudes, and a perpetual variation of means and methods, to attain the same end; but a secure, universal, straightforward business, to be conducted in the gross, by proper mechanism, with such intellect as comes to hand. Then, we have Religious machines, of all imaginable varieties; the Bible-Society, professing a far higher and heavenly structure, is found, on inquiry, to be altogether an earthly contrivance: supported by collection of moneys, by fomenting of vanities, by puffing, intrigue and chicane; a machine for converting the Heathen. It is the same in all other departments. Has any man, or any society of men, a truth to speak, a piece of spiritual work to do; they can nowise proceed at once and with the mere natural organs, but must first call a public meeting, appoint committees, issue prospectuses, eat a public dinner; in a word, construct or borrow machinery, wherewith to speak it and do it. Without machinery they were hopeless, helpless; a colony of Hindoo weavers squatting in the heart of Lancashire. Mark, too, how every machine must have its moving power, in some of the great currents of society; every little sect among us, Unitarians, Utilitarians, Anabaptists, Phrenologists, must have its Periodical, its monthly or quarterly Magazine;—hanging out, like its windmill, into the *popularis aura*, to grind meal for the society.

With individuals, in like manner, natural strength avails little. No individual now hopes to accomplish the poorest enterprise single-handed and without mechanical aids; he must make interest with some existing corporation, and till his field with their oxen. In these days, more emphatically than ever, 'to live, signifies to unite with a party, or to make one.' Philosophy, Science, Art, Literature, all depend on machinery. No Newton, by silent meditation, now discovers the system of the world from the falling of an apple; but some quite other than Newton stands in his Museum, his Scientific Institution, and behind whole batteries of retorts, digesters, and galvanic piles imperatively 'interrogates Nature,'—who, however, shows no haste to answer. In defect of Raphaels, and Angelos, and Mozarts, we have Royal Academies of Painting, Sculpture, Music; whereby the languishing spirit of Art may be strengthened, as by the more generous diet of a Public Kitchen. Literature, too, has its Paternoster-row mechanism, its Trade-dinners, its Editorial conclaves, and huge subterranean, puffing bellows; so that books are not only printed, but, in a great measure, written and sold, by machinery.

National culture, spiritual benefit of all sorts, is under the same management. No Queen Christina, in these times, needs to send for her Descartes; no King Frederick for his Voltaire, and painfully nourish him with pensions and flattery: any sovereign of taste, who wishes to enlighten his people, has only to impose a new tax, and with the proceeds establish Philosophic Institutes. Hence the Royal and Imperial Societies, the Bibliothèques, Glypothèques, Technothèques, which front us in all capital cities; like so many well-finished hives, to which it is expected the stray agencies of Wisdom will swarm of their own accord, and hive and make honey. In like manner, among ourselves, when it is thought that religion is declining, we have only to vote half-a-million's worth of bricks and mortar, and build new churches. In Ireland it seems they have gone still farther, having actually established a 'Penny-a-Week Purgatory-Society'! Thus does the Genius of Mechanism stand by to help us in all difficulties and emergencies, and with his iron back bears all our burdens.

These things, which we state lightly enough here, are yet of deep import, and indicate a mighty change in our whole manner of existence. For the same habit regulates not our modes of action alone, but our modes of thought and feeling. Men are grown mechanical in head and in heart, as well as in hand. They have lost faith in individual endeavour, and in natural force, of any kind. Not for internal perfection, but for external combinations and arrangements, for institutions, constitutions,—for Mechanism of one sort or other, do they hope and struggle. Their whole efforts, attachments, opinions, turn on mechanism, and are of a mechanical character.

We may trace this tendency in all the great manifestations of our time; in its intellectual aspect, the studies it most favours and its manner of conducting them; in its practical aspects, its politics, arts, religion, morals; in the whole sources, and throughout the whole currents, of its spiritual, no less than its material activity.

Consider, for example, the state of Science generally, in Europe, at this period. It is admitted, on all sides, that the Metaphysical and Moral Sciences are falling into decay, while the Physical are engrossing, every day, more respect and attention. In most of the European nations there is now no such thing as a Science of Mind; only more or less advancement in the general science, or the special sciences, of matter. The

French were the first to desert Metaphysics; and though they have lately affected to revive their school, it has yet no signs of vitality. The land of Malebranche, Pascal, Descartes and Fénelon, has now only its Cousins and Villemains; while, in the department of Physics, it reckons far other names. Among ourselves, the Philosophy of Mind, after a rickety infancy, which never reached the vigour of manhood, fell suddenly into decay, languished and finally died out, with its last amiable cultivator, Professor Stewart. In no nation but Germany has any decisive effort been made in psychological science; not to speak of any decisive result. The science of the age, in short, is physical, chemical, physiological; in all shapes mechanical. Our favourite Mathematics, the highly prized exponent of all these other sciences, has also become more and more mechanical. Excellence in what is called its higher departments depends less on natural genius than on acquired expertness in wielding its machinery. Without undervaluing the wonderful results which a Lagrange or Laplace educes by means of it, we may remark, that their calculus, differential and integral, is little else than a more cunningly-constructed arithmetical mill; where the factors being put in, are, as it were, ground into the true product, under cover, and without other effort on our part than steady turning of the handle. We have more Mathematics than ever; but less Mathesis. Archimedes and Plato could not have read the *Mécanique Céleste*; but neither would the whole French Institute see aught in that saying, 'God geometrises!' but a sentimental rodomontade.

Nay, our whole Metaphysics itself, from Lock's time downwards, has been physical; not a spiritual philosophy, but a material one. The singular estimation in which his Essay was so long held as a scientific work (an estimation grounded, indeed, on the estimable character of the man) will one day be thought a curious indication of the spirit of these times. His whole doctrine is mechanical, in its aim and origin, in its method and its results. It is not a philosophy of the mind: it is a mere discussion concerning the origin of our consciousness, or ideas, or whatever else they are called; a genetic history of what we see *in* the mind. The grand secrets of Necessity and Freewill, of the Mind's vital or non-vital dependence on Matter, of our mysterious relations to Time and Space, to God, to the Universe, are not, in the faintest degree touched on in these inquiries; and seem not to have the smallest connexion with them.

The last class of our Scotch Metaphysicians had a dim notion that much of this was wrong; but they knew not how to right it. The school of Reid had also from the first taken a mechanical course, not seeing any other. The singular conclusions at which Hume, setting out from their admitted premises, was arriving, brought this school into being; they let loose Instinct, as an undiscriminating ban-dog, to guard them against these conclusions;—they tugged lustily at the logical chain by which Hume was so coldly towing them and the world into bottomless abysses of Atheism and Fatalism. But the chain somehow snapped between them; and the issue has been that nobody now cares about either,—any more than about Hartley's, Darwin's, or Priestley's contemporaneous doings in England. Hartley's vibrations and vibratiuncles, one would think, were material and mechanical enough; but our Continental neighbours have gone still farther. One of their philosophers has lately discovered, that 'as the liver secretes bile, so does the brain secrete thought'; which astonishing discovery Dr. Cabanis, more lately still, in his *Rapports du Physique et du Morale de l'Homme*, has pushed into its minutest developments.

The metaphysical philosophy of this last inquirer is certainly no shadowy or unsubstantial one. He fairly lays open our moral structure with his dissecting-knives and real metal probes; and exhibits it to the inspection of mankind, by Leuwenhoek microscopes, and inflation with the anatomical blowpipe. Thought, he is inclined to hold, is still secreted by the brain; but then Poetry and Religion (and it is really worth knowing) are 'a product of the smaller intestines'! We have the greatest admiration for this learned doctor: with what scientific stoicism he walks through the land of wonders, unwondering; like a wise man through some huge, gaudy, imposing

Vauxhall, whose fire-works, cascades and symphonies, the vulgar may enjoy and believe in,—but where he finds nothing real but the saltpetre, pasteboard and catgut. His book may be regarded as the ultimatum of mechanical metaphysics in our time; a remarkable realisation of what in Martinus Scriblerus was still only an idea, that 'as the jack had a meat-roasting quality, so had the body a thinking quality,'—upon the strength of which the Nurembergers were to build a wood-and-leather man, 'who should reason as well as most country parsons.' Vaucanson did indeed make a wooden duck, that seemed to eat and digest; but that bold scheme of the Nurembergers remained for a more modern virtuoso.

This condition of the two great departments of knowledge, —the outward, cultivated exclusively on mechanical principles; the inward, finally abandoned, because, cultivated on such principles, it is found to yield no result,—sufficiently indicates the intellectual bias of our time, its all-pervading disposition towards that line of inquiry. In fact, an inward persuasion has long been diffusing itself, and now and then even comes to utterance, That, except the external, there are no true sciences; that to the inward world (if there be any) our only conceivable road is through the outward; that, in short, what cannot be investigated and understood mechanically, cannot be investigated and understood at all. We advert the more particularly to these intellectual propensities, as to prominent symptoms of our age, because Opinion is at all times doubly related to Action, first as cause, then as effect; and the speculative tendency of any age will therefore give us, on the whole, the best indications of its practical tendency.

Nowhere, for example, is the deep, almost exclusive faith we have in Mechanism more visible than in the Politics of this time. Civil government does by its nature include much that is mechanical, and must be treated accordingly. We term it indeed, in ordinary language, the Machine of Society, and talk of it as the grand working wheel from which all private machines must derive, or to which they must adapt, their movements. Considered merely as a metaphor, all this is well enough; but here, as in so many other cases, the 'foam hardens itself into a shell,' and the shadow we have wantonly evoked stands terrible before us and will not depart at our bidding. Government includes much also that is not mechanical, and cannot be treated mechanically; of which latter truth, as appears to us, the political speculations and exertions of our time are taking less and less cognisance.

Nay, in the very outset, we might note the mighty interest taken in *mere political arrangements*, as itself the sign of a mechanical age. The whole discontent of Europe takes this direction. The deep, strong cry of all civilised nations,—a cry which, every one now sees, must and will be answered, is: Give us a reform of Government! A good structure of legislation, a proper check upon the executive, a wise arrangement of the judiciary, is *all* that is wanting for human happiness. The Philosopher of this age is not a Socrates, a Plato, a Hooker, or Taylor, who inculcates on men the necessity and infinite worth of moral goodness, the great truth that our happiness depends on the mind which is within us, and not on the circumstances which are without us; but a Smith, a De Lolme, a Bentham, who chiefly inculcates the reverse of this,—that our happiness depends entirely on external circumstances; nay, that the strength and dignity of the mind within us is itself the creature and consequence of these. Were the laws, the government, in good order, all were well with us; the rest would care for itself! Dissentients from this opinion, expressed or implied, are now rarely to be met with; widely and angrily as men differ in its application, the principle is admitted by all.

Equally mechanical, and of equal simplicity, are the methods proposed by both parties for completing or securing this all-sufficient perfection of arrangement. It is no longer the moral, religious, spiritual condition of the people that is our concern, but their physical, practical, economical condition, as regulated by public laws. Thus is the Body-politic more than ever worshipped and tendered; but the Soul-politic less than ever. Love of country, in any high or generous sense, in any other than an almost animal sense, or mere habit, has little importance attached to it in such reforms, or in the opposition shown them. Men are to be guided only by their self-interests. Good government is a good balancing of these; and, except a keen eye and appetite for self-interest, requires no virtue in any quarter. To both parties it is emphatically a machine: to the discontented, a 'taxing-machine'; to the contented, a 'machine for securing property.' Its duties and its faults are not those of a father, but of an active parish-constable.

Thus it is by the mere condition of the machine, by preserving it untouched, or else by reconstructing it, and oiling it anew, that man's salvation as a social being is to be ensured and indefinitely promoted. Contrive the fabric of law aright, and without farther effort on your part, that divine spirit of Freedom, which all hearts venerate and long for, will of herself come to inhabit it; and under her healing wings every noxious influence will wither, every good and salutary one more and more expand. Nay, so devoted are we to this principle, and at the same time so curiously mechanical, that a new trade, specially grounded on it, has arisen among us, under the name of 'Codification,' or codemaking in the abstract; whereby any people, for a reasonable consideration, may be accommodated with a patent code;—more easily than curious individuals with patent breeches, for the people does *not* need to be measured first.

To us who live in the midst of all this, and see continually the faith, hope and practice of every one founded on Mechanism of one kind or other, it is apt to seem quite natural, and as if it could never have been otherwise. Nevertheless, if we recollect or reflect a little, we shall find both that it has been, and might again be otherwise. The domain of Mechanism,—meaning thereby political, ecclesiastical or other outward establishments,—was once considered as embracing, and we are persuaded can at any time embrace, but a limited portion of man's interests, and by no means the highest portion.

To speak a little pedantically, there is a science of *Dynamics* in man's fortunes and nature, as well as of *Mechanics*. There is a science which treats of, and practically addresses, the primary, unmodified forces and energies of man, the mysterious springs of Love, and Fear, and Wonder, of Enthusiasm, Poetry, Religion, all which have a truly vital and *infinite* character; as well as a science which practically addresses the finite, modified developments of these, when they take the shape of immediate 'motives,' as hope of reward, or as fear of punishment.

Now it is certain, that in former times the wise men, the enlightened lovers of their kind, who appeared generally as Moralists, Poets or Priests, did, without neglecting the Mechanical province, deal chiefly with the Dynamical; applying themselves chiefly to regulate, increase and purify the inward primary powers of man; and fancying that herein lay the main difficulty, and the best service they could undertake. But a wide difference is manifest in our age. For the wise men, who now appear as Political Philosophers, deal exclusively with the Mechanical province; and occupying themselves in counting-up and estimating men's motives, strive by curious checking and balancing, and other adjustments of Profit and Loss, to guide them to their true advantage: while, unfortunately, those same 'motives' are so innumerable, and so variable in every individual, that no really useful conclusion can ever be drawn from their enumeration. But though Mechanism, wisely contrived, has done much for man in a social and moral point of view, we cannot be persuaded that it has ever been the chief source of his worth or happiness. Consider the great elements of human enjoyment, the attainments and possessions that exalt man's life to its present height, and see what part of these he owes to institutions, to Mechanism of any kind; and what to the instinctive, unbounded force, which Nature herself lent him, and still continues to him. Shall we say, for example, that Science and Art are indebted principally to the founders of Schools and Universities? Did not Science originate rather, and gain advancement, in the obscure closets of the Roger Bacons, Keplers, Newtons; in the workshops of the Fausts and the Watts; wherever, and in what guise soever Nature, from the first times downwards, had sent a gifted spirit upon the earth? Again, were Homer and Shakespeare members of any beneficed guild, or made Poets by means of it? Were Painting and Sculpture created by forethought, brought into the world by institutions for that end? No; Science and Art have, from first to last, been the free gift of Nature; an unsolicited, unexpected gift; often even a fatal one. These things rose up, as it were, by spontaneous growth, in the free soil and sunshine of Nature. They were not planted or grafted, nor even greatly multiplied or improved by the culture or manuring of institutions. Generally speaking, they have derived only partial help from these; often enough have suffered damage. They made constitutions for themselves. They originated in the Dynamical nature of man, not in his Mechanical nature.

Or, to take an infinitely higher instance, that of the Christian Religion, which, under every theory of it, in the believing or unbelieving mind, must ever be regarded as the crowning glory, or rather the life and soul, of our whole modern culture: How did Christianity arise and spread abroad among men? Was it by institutions, and establishments and well-arranged systems of mechanism? Not so; on the contrary, in all past and existing institutions for those ends, its divine spirit has invariably been found to languish and decay. It arose in the mystic deeps of man's soul; and was spread abroad by the 'preaching of the word,' by simple, altogether natural and individual efforts; and flew, like hallowed fire, from heart to heart, till all were purified and illuminated by it; and its heavenly light shone, as it still shines, and (as sun or star) will ever shine, through the whole dark destinies of man. Here again was no Mechanism; man's highest attainment was accomplished Dynamically, not Mechanically.

Nay, we will venture to say, that no high attainment, not even any far-extending movement among men, was ever accomplished otherwise. Strange as it may seem, if we read History with any degree of thoughtfulness, we shall find that the checks and balances of Profit and Loss have never been the grand agents with men; that they have never been roused into deep, thorough, all-pervading efforts by any computable prospect of Profit and Loss, for any visible, finite object; but always for some invisible and infinite one. The Crusades took their rise in Religion; their visible object was, commercially speaking, worth nothing. It was the boundless Invisible world that was laid bare in the imaginations of those men; and in its burning light, the visible shrunk as a scroll. Not mechanical, nor produced by mechanical means, was this vast movement. No dining at Freemasons' Tavern, with the other long train of modern machinery; no cunning reconciliation of 'vested interests,' was required here: only the passionate voice of one man, the rapt soul looking through the eyes of one man; and rugged, steel-clad Europe trembled beneath his words, and followed him whither he listed. In later ages it was still the same. The Reformation had an invisible, mystic and ideal aim; the result was indeed to be embodied in external things; but its spirit, its worth, was internal, invisible, infinite. Our English Revolution too originated in Religion. Men did battle, in those old days, not for Purse-sake, but for Conscience-sake. Nay, in our own days, it is no way different. The French Revolution itself had something higher in it than cheap bread and a Habeas-corpus act. Here too was an Idea; a Dynamic, not a Mechanic force. It was a struggle, though a blind and at last an insane one, for the infinite, divine nature of Right, of Freedom, of Country.

Thus does man, in every age, vindicate, consciously or unconsciously, his celestial birthright. Thus does Nature hold on her wondrous, unquestionable course; and all our systems and theories are but so many froth-eddies or sandbanks, which from time to time she casts up, and washes away. When we can drain the Ocean into mill-ponds, and bottle-up the Force of Gravity, to be sold by retail, in gas jars; then may we hope to comprehend the infinitudes of man's soul under formulas of Profit and Loss; and rule over this too, as over a patent engine, by checks, and valves, and balances.

Nay, even with regard to Government itself, can it be necessary to remind any one that Freedom, without which indeed all spiritual life is impossible, depends on infinitely more complex influences than either the extension or the curtailment of the 'democratic interest'? Who is there that, 'taking the high *priori* road,' shall point out what these influences are; what deep, subtle, inextricably entangled influences they have been and may be? For man is not the creature and product of Mechanism; but, in a far truer sense, its creator and producer: it is the noble People that makes the noble Government; rather than conversely. On the whole, Institutions are much; but they are not all. The freest and highest spirits of the world have often been found under strange outward circumstances: Saint Paul and his brother Apostles were politically slaves; Epictetus was personally one. Again, forget the influences of Chivalry and Religion, and ask: What countries produced Columbus and Las Casas? Or, descending from virtue and heroism to mere energy and spiritual talent: Cortes, Pizarro, Alba, Ximenes? The Spaniards of the sixteenth century were indisputably the noblest nation of Europe: yet they had the Inquisition and Philip II. They have the same government at this day; and are the lowest nation. The Dutch too have retained their old constitution; but no Siege of Leyden, no William the Silent, not even an Egmont or De Witt any longer appears among them. With ourselves also, where much has changed, effect has nowise followed cause as it should have done: two centuries ago, the Commons Speaker addressed Queen Elizabeth on bended knees, happy that the virago's foot did not even smite him; yet the people were then governed, not by a Castlereagh, but by a Burghley; they had their Shakspeare and Philip Sidney, where we have our Sheridan Knowles and Beau Brummel.

These and the like facts are so familiar, the truths which they preach so obvious, and have in all past times been so universally believed and acted on, that we should almost feel ashamed for repeating them; were it not that, on every hand, the memory of them seems to have passed away, or at best died into a faint tradition, of no value as a practical principle. To judge by the loud clamour of our Constitution-builders, Statists, Economists, directors, creators, reformers of Public

Societies; in a word, all manner of Mechanists, from the Cartwright up to the Code-maker; and by the nearly total silence of all Preachers and Teachers who should give a voice to Poetry, Religion and Morality, we might fancy either that man's Dynamical nature was, to all spiritual intents, extinct, or else so perfected that nothing more was to be made of it by the old means; and henceforth only in his Mechanical contrivances did any hope exist for him.

To define the limits of these two departments of man's activity, which work into one another, and by means of one another, so intricately and inseparably, were by its nature an impossible attempt. Their relative importance, even to the wisest mind, will vary in different times, according to the special wants and dispositions of those times. Meanwhile, it seems clear enough that only in the right coördination of the two, and the vigorous forwarding of *both*, does our true line of action lie. Undue cultivation of the inward or Dynamical province leads to idle, visionary, impracticable courses, and, especially in rude eras, to Superstition and Fanaticism, with their long train of baleful and well-known evils. Undue cultivation of the outward, again, though less immediately prejudicial, and even for the time productive of many palpable benefits, must, in the long-run, by destroying Moral Force, which is the parent of all other Force, prove not less certainly, and perhaps still more hopelessly, pernicious. This, we take it, is the grand characteristic of our age. By our skill in Mechanism, it has come to pass, that in the management of external things we excel all other ages; while in whatever respects the pure moral nature, in true dignity of soul and character, we are perhaps inferior to most civilised ages.

In fact, if we look deeper, we shall find that this faith in Mechanism has now struck its roots down into man's most intimate, primary sources of conviction; and is thence sending up, over his whole life and activity, innumerable stems,—fruit-bearing and poison-bearing. The truth is, men have lost their belief in the Invisible, and believe, and hope, and work only in the Visible; or, to speak it in other words: This is not a Religious age. Only the material, the immediately practical, not the divine and spiritual, is important to us. The infinite, absolute character of Virtue has passed into a finite, conditional one; it is no longer a worship of the Beautiful and Good; but a calculation of the Profitable. Worship, indeed, in any sense, is not recognised among us, or is mechanically explained into Fear of pain, or Hope of pleasure. Our true Deity is Mechanism. It has subdued external Nature for us, and we think it will do all other things. We are Giants in physical power: in a deeper than metaphorical sense, we are Titans, that strive, by heaping mountain on mountain, to conquer Heaven also.

The strong Mechanical character, so visible in the spiritual pursuits and methods of this age, may be traced much farther into the condition and prevailing disposition of our spiritual nature itself. Consider, for example, the general fashion of Intellect in this era. Intellect, the power man has of knowing and believing, is now nearly synonymous with Logic, or the mere power of arranging and communicating. Its implement is not Meditation, but Argument. 'Cause and effect' is almost the only category under which we look at, and work with, all Nature. Our first question with regard to any object is not, What is it? but, How is it? We are no longer instinctively driven to apprehend, and lay to heart, what is Good and Lovely, but rather to inquire, as onlookers, how it is produced, whence it comes, whither it goes. Our favourite Philosophers have no love and no hatred; they stand among us not to do, nor to create anything, but as a sort of Logic-mills, to grind out the true causes and effects of all that is done and created. To the eye of a Smith, a Hume or a Constant, all is well that works quietly. An Order of Ignatius Loyola, a Presbyterianism of John Knox, a Wickliffe or a Henry the Eighth, are simply so many mechanical phenomena, caused or causing.

The *Euphuist* of our day differs much from his pleasant predecessors. An intellectual dapperling of these times boasts chiefly of his irresistible perspicacity, his 'dwelling in the daylight of truth,' and so forth; which, on examination, turns out to be a dwelling in the *rush*-light of 'closet-logic,' and a deep unconsciousness that there is any other light to dwell in or any other objects to survey with it. Wonder, indeed, is, on all hands, dying out: it is the sign of uncultivation to wonder. Speak to any small man of a high, majestic Reformation, of a high majestic Luther; and forthwith he sets about 'accounting' for it; how the 'circumstances of the time' called for such a character, and found him, we suppose, standing girt and road-ready, to do its errand; how the 'circumstances of the time' created, fashioned, floated him quietly along into the result; how, in short, this small man, had he been there, could have performed the like himself! For it is the 'force of circumstances' that does everything; the force of one man can do nothing. Now all this is grounded on little more than a metaphor. We figure Society as a 'Machine,' and that mind is opposed to mind, as body is to body; whereby two, or at most ten, little minds must be stronger than one great mind. Notable absurdity! For the plain truth, very plain, we think is, that minds are opposed to minds in quite a different way; and *one* man that has a higher Wisdom, a hitherto unknown spiritual Truth in him, is stronger, not than ten men that have it not, or than ten thousand, but than *all* men that have it not; and stands among them with a quite ethereal, angelic power, as with a sword out of Heaven's own armory, sky-tempered, which no buckler, and no tower of brass, will finally withstand.

But to us, in these times, such considerations rarely occur. We enjoy, we see nothing by direct vision; but only by reflection, and in anatomical dismemberment. Like Sir Hudibras, for every Why we must have a Wherefore. We have our little *theory* on all human and divine things. Poetry, the workings of genius itself, which in all times, with one or another meaning, has been called Inspiration, and held to be mysterious and inscrutable, is no longer without its scientific exposition. The building of the lofty rhyme is like any other masonry or bricklaying; we have theories of its rise, height, decline and fall,—which latter, it would seem, is now near, among all people.

Of our 'Theories of Taste,' as they are called, wherein the deep, infinite, unspeakable Love of Wisdom and Beauty, which dwells in all men, is 'explained,' made mechanically visible, from 'Association' and the like, why should we say anything? Hume has written us a 'Natural History of Religion'; in which one Natural History all the rest are included. Strangely too does the general feeling coincide with Hume's in this wonderful problem; for whether his 'Natural History' be the right one or not, that Religion must have a Natural History, all of us, cleric and laic, seem to be agreed. He indeed regards it as a Disease, we again as Health; so far there is a difference; but in our first principle we are at one.

To what extent theological Unbelief, we mean intellectual dissent from the Church, in its view of Holy Writ, prevails at this day, would be a highly important, were it not, under any circumstances, an almost impossible inquiry. But the Unbelief, which is of a still more fundamental character, every man may see prevailing, with scarcely any but the faintest contradiction, all around him; even in the Pulpit itself. Religion in most countries, more or less in every country, is no longer what it was, and should be,—a thousand-voiced psalm from the heart of Man to his invisible Father, the fountain of all Goodness, Beauty, Truth, and revealed in every revelation of these; but for the most part, a wise prudential feeling grounded on mere calculation; a matter, as all others now are, of Expediency and Utility; whereby some smaller quantum of earthly enjoyment may be exchanged for a far larger quantum of celestial enjoyment. Thus Religion too is Profit, a working for wages; not Reverence, but vulgar Hope or Fear. Many, we know, very many we hope, are still religious in a far different sense; were it not so, our case were too desperate: but to witness that such is the temper of the times, we take any calm observant man, who agrees or disagrees in our feeling on the matter, and ask him whether our *view* of it is not in general well-founded.

Literature too, if we consider it, gives similar testimony. At no former era has Literature, the printed communication of Thought, been of such importance as it is now. We often hear that the Church is in danger; and truly so it is,—in a danger it seems not to know of: for, with its tithes in the most perfect safety, its functions are becoming more and more superseded. The true Church of England, at this moment, lies in the Editors of its Newspapers. These preach to the people daily, weekly; admonishing kings themselves; advising peace or war, with an authority which only the first Reformers, and a long-past class of Popes, were possessed of; inflicting moral censure; imparting moral encouragement, consolation, edification; in all ways diligently 'administering the Discipline of the Church.' It may be said too, that in private disposition the new Preachers somewhat resemble the Mendicant Friars of old times: outwardly full of holy zeal; inwardly not without stratagem, and hunger for terrestrial things. But omitting this class, and the boundless host of watery personages who pipe, as they are able, on so many scrannel straws, let us look at the higher regions of Literature, where, if anywhere, the pure melodies of Poesy and Wisdom should be heard. Of natural talent there is no deficiency: one or two richly-endowed individuals even give us a superiority in this respect. But what is the song they sing? Is it a tone of the Memnon Statue, breathing music as the *light* first touches it? A 'liquid wisdom,' disclosing to our sense the deep, infinite harmonies of Nature and man's soul? Alas, no! It is not a matin or vesper hymn to the Spirit of Beauty, but a fierce clashing of cymbals, and shouting of multitudes, as children pass through the fire to Moloch! Poetry itself has no eye for the Invisible. Beauty is no longer the god it worships, but some brute image of Strength; which we may call an idol, for true Strength is one and the same with Beauty, and its worship also is a hymn. The meek, silent Light can mould, create and purify all Nature; but the loud Whirlwind, the sign and product of Disunion, of Weakness, passes on, and is forgotten. How widely this veneration for the physically Strongest has spread itself through Literature, any one may judge who reads either criticism or poem. We praise a work, not as 'true,' but as 'strong'; our highest praise is that it has 'affected' us, has 'terrified' us. All this, it has been well observed, is the 'maximum of the Barbarous,' the symptom, not of vigorous refinement, but of luxurious corruption. It speaks much, too, for men's indestructible love of truth, that nothing of this kind will abide with them; that even the talent of a Byron cannot permanently seduce us into idol-worship; that he too, with all his wild siren charming, already begins to be disregarded and forgotten.

Again, with respect to our Moral condition: here also he who runs may read that the same physical, mechanical influences are everywhere busy. For the 'superior morality,' of which we hear so much, we too would desire to be thankful: at the same time, it were but blindness to deny that this 'superior morality' is properly rather an 'inferior criminality,' produced not by greater love of Virtue, but by greater perfection of Police; and of that far subtler and stronger Police, called Public Opinion. This last watches over us with its Argus eyes more keenly than ever; but the 'inward eye' seems heavy with sleep. Of any belief in invisible, divine things, we find as few traces in our Morality as elsewhere. It is by tangible, material considerations that we are guided, not by inward and spiritual. Self-denial, the parent of all virtue, in any true sense of that word, has perhaps seldom been rarer: so rare is it, that the most, even in their abstract speculations, regard its existence as a chimera. Virtue is Pleasure, is Profit; no celestial, but an earthly thing. Virtuous men, Philanthropists, Martyrs are happy accidents; their 'taste' lies the right way! In all senses, we worship and follow after Power; which may be called a physical pursuit. No man now loves Truth, as Truth must be loved, with an infinite love; but only with a finite love, and as it were *par amours*. Nay, properly speaking, he does not *believe* and know it, but only '*thinks*' it, and that 'there is every probability!' He preaches it aloud, and rushes courageously forth with it,—if there is a multitude huzzaing at his back; yet ever keeps looking over his shoulder, and the instant the huzzaing languishes, he too stops short.

In fact, what morality we have takes the shape of Ambition, of 'Honour': beyond money and money's worth, our only rational blessedness is Popularity. It were but a fool's trick to die for conscience. Only for 'character,' by duel, or in case of extremity, by suicide, is the wise man bound to die. By arguing on the 'force of circumstances,' we have argued away all force from ourselves; and stand leashed together, uniform in dress and movement, like the rowers of some boundless galley. This and that may be right and true; *but* we must not do it. Wonderful 'Force of Public Opinion'! We must act and walk in all points as it prescribes; follow the traffic it bids us, realise the sum of money, the degree of 'influence' it expects of us, *or* we shall be lightly esteemed; certain mouthfuls of articulate wind will be blown at us, and this what mortal courage can front? Thus, while civil liberty is more and more secured to us, our moral liberty is all but lost. Practically considered, our creed is Fatalism; and, free in hand and foot, we are shackled in heart and soul with far straiter than feudal chains. Truly may we say, with the Philosopher, 'the deep meaning of the Laws of Mechanism lies heavy on us'; and in the closet, in the market-place, in the temple, by the social hearth, encumbers the whole movements of our mind, and over our noblest faculties is spreading a nightmare sleep.

These dark features, we are aware, belong more or less to other ages, as well as to ours. This faith in Mechanism, in the all-importance of physical things, is in every age the common refuge of Weakness and blind Discontent; of all who believe, as many will ever do, that man's true good lies without him, not within. We are aware also, that, as applied to ourselves in all their aggravation, they form but half a picture; that in the whole picture there are bright lights as well as gloomy shadows. If we here dwell chiefly on the latter, let us not be blamed: it is in general more profitable to reckon up our defects than to boast of our attainments.

Neither, with all these evils more or less clearly before us, have we at any time despaired of the fortunes of society. Despair, or even despondency, in that respect, appears to us, in all cases, a groundless feeling. We have a faith in the imperishable dignity of man; in the high vocation to which, throughout this his earthly history, he has been appointed. However it may be with individual nations, whatever melancholic speculators may assert, it seems a well-ascertained fact, that in all times, reckoning even from those of the Heraclides and Pelasgi, the happiness and greatness of mankind at large have been continually progressive. Doubtless this age also is advancing. Its very unrest, its ceaseless activity, its discontent contains matter of promise. Knowledge, education are opening the eyes of the humblest; are increasing the number of thinking minds without limit. This is as it should be; for not in turning back, not in resisting, but only in resolutely struggling forward, does our life consist.

Nay, after all, our spiritual maladies are but of Opinion; we are but fettered by chains of our own forging, and which ourselves also can rend asunder. This deep, paralysed subjection to physical objects comes not from Nature, but from our own unwise mode of *viewing* Nature. Neither can we understand that man wants, at this hour, any faculty of heart, soul or body, that ever belonged to him. 'He, who has been born, has been a First Man'; has had lying before his young eyes, and as yet unhardened into scientific shapes, a world as plastic, infinite, divine, as lay before the eyes of Adam himself. If Mechanism, like some glass bell, encircles and imprisons us; if the soul looks forth on a fair heavenly country which it cannot reach, and pines, and in its scanty atmosphere is ready to perish,—yet the bell is but of glass; 'one bold stroke to break the bell in pieces, and thou art delivered!' Not the invisible world is wanting, for it dwells in man's soul, and this last is still here. Are the solemn temples, in which the Divinity was once visibly revealed among us, crumbling away? We can repair them, we can rebuild them. The wisdom, the heroic worth of our forefathers, which we have lost, we can recover. That admiration of old nobleness, which now so often shows itself as a faint *dilettantism*, will one day become a generous emulation, and man may again be all that he has been, and more than he has been. Nor are these the mere daydreams of fancy; they are clear possibilities; nay, in this time they are even assuming the character of hopes. Indications we do see in other countries and in our own, signs infinitely cheering to us, that Mechanism is not always to be our hard taskmaster, but one day to be our pliant, all-ministering servant; that a new and brighter spiritual era is slowly evolving itself for all men. But on these things our present course forbids us to enter.

Meanwhile, that great outward changes are in progress can be doubtful to no one. The time is sick and out of joint. Many things have reached their height; and it is a wise adage that tells us, 'the darkest hour is nearest the dawn.' Wherever we can gather indication of the public thought, whether from printed books, as in France or Germany, or from Carbonari rebellions and other political tumults, as in Spain, Portugal, Italy and Greece, the voice it utters is the same. The thinking minds of all nations call for change. There is a deep-lying struggle in the whole fabric of society; a boundless grinding collision of the New with the Old. The French Revolution, as is now visible enough, was not the parent of this mighty movement, but its offspring. Those two hostile influences, which always exist in human things, and on the constant intercommunion of which depends their health and safety, had lain in separate masses, accumulating through generations, and France was the scene of their fiercest explosion; but the final issue was not unfolded in that country: nay, it is not yet anywhere unfolded. Political freedom is hitherto the object of these efforts; but they will not and cannot stop there. It is towards a higher freedom than mere freedom from oppression by his fellow-mortal, that man dimly aims. Of this higher, heavenly freedom, which is 'man's reasonable service,' all his noble institutions, his faithful endeavours and loftiest attainments, are but the body, and more and more approximated emblem.

On the whole, as this wondrous planet, Earth, is journeying with its fellows through infinite Space, so are the wondrous destinies embarked on it journeying through infinite Time, under a higher guidance than ours. For the present, as our astronomy informs us, its path lies towards *Hercules*, the constellation of *Physical Power*: but that is not our most pressing concern. Go where it will, the deep HEAVEN will be around it. Therein let us have hope and sure faith. To reform a world, to reform a nation, no wise man will undertake; and all but foolish men know, that the only solid, though a far slower reformation, is what each begins and perfects on *himself*.

On History

On History was written in 1830, and published in *Fraser's Magazine*. It was included in the *Miscellanies* published in book form in 1839.

On History

Clio was figured by the ancients as the eldest daughter of Memory, and chief of the Muses; which dignity, whether we regard the essential qualities of her art, or its practice and acceptance among men, we shall still find to have been fitly bestowed. History, as it lies at the root of all science, is also the first distinct product of man's spiritual nature; his earliest expression of what can be called Thought. It is a looking both before and after; as, indeed, the coming Time already waits, unseen, yet definitely shaped, predetermined and inevitable, in the Time come; and only by the combination of both is the meaning of either completed. The Sibylline Books, though old, are not the oldest. Some nations have prophecy, some have not: but of all mankind, there is no tribe so rude that it has not attempted History, though several have not arithmetic enough to count Five. History has been written with quipo-threads, with feather-pictures, with wampum-belts; still oftener with earth-mounds and monumental stone-heaps, whether as pyramid or cairn; for the Celt and the Copt, the Red man as well as the White, lives between two eternities, and warring against Oblivion, he would fain unite himself in clear conscious relation, as in dim unconscious relation he is already united, with the whole Future, and the whole Past.

A talent for History may be said to be born with us, as our chief inheritance. In a certain sense all men are historians. Is not every memory written quite full with Annals, wherein joy and mourning, conquest and loss manifoldly alternate; and, with or without philosophy, the whole fortunes of one little inward Kingdom, and all its politics, foreign and domestic, stand ineffaceably recorded? Our very speech is curiously historical. Most men, you may observe, speak only to narrate; not in imparting what they have thought, which indeed were often a very small matter, but in exhibiting what they have undergone or seen, which is a quite unlimited one, do talkers dilate. Cut us off from Narrative, how would the stream of conversation, even among the wisest, languish into detached handfuls, and among the foolish utterly evaporate! Thus, as we do nothing but enact History, we say little but recite it; nay, rather, in that widest sense, our whole spiritual life is built thereon. For, strictly considered, what is all Knowledge too but recorded Experience, and a product of History; of which, therefore, Reasoning and Belief, no less than Action and Passion, are essential materials?

Under a limited, and the only practicable shape, History proper, that part of History which treats of remarkable action, has, in all modern as well as ancient times, ranked among the highest arts, and perhaps never stood higher than in these times of ours. For whereas, of old, the charm of History lay chiefly in gratifying our common appetite for the wonderful, for the unknown; and her office was but as that of a Minstrel and Story-teller, she has now farther become a School-mistress, and professes to instruct in gratifying. Whether, with the stateliness of that venerable character, she may not have taken up something of its austerity and frigidity; whether in the logical terseness of a Hume or Robertson, the graceful ease and gay pictorial heartiness of a Herodotus or Froissart may not be wanting, is not the question for us here. Enough that all learners, all inquiring minds of every order, are gathered round her footstool, and reverently pondering her lessons, as the true basis of Wisdom. Poetry, Divinity, Politics, Physics, have each their adherents and adversaries; each little guild supporting a defensive and offensive war for its own special domain; while the domain of History is as a Free Emporium, where all these belligerents peaceably meet and furnish themselves; and Sentimentalist and Utilitarian, Sceptic and Theologian, with one voice advise us: Examine History, for it is 'Philosophy teaching by Experience.'

Far be it from us to disparage such teaching, the very attempt at which must be precious. Neither shall we too rigidly inquire: How much it has hitherto profited? Whether most of what little practical wisdom men have, has come from study of professed History, or from other less boasted sources, whereby, as matters now stand, a Marlborough may become great in the world's business, with no History save what he derives from Shakspeare's Plays? Nay, whether in that same teaching by Experience, historical Philosophy has yet properly deciphered the first element of all science in this kind: What the aim and significance of that wondrous changeful Life it investigates and paints may be? Whence the course of man's destinies in this Earth originated, and whither they are tending? Or, indeed, if they have any course and tendency, are really guided forward by an unseen mysterious Wisdom, or only circle in blind mazes without recognisable guidance? Which questions, altogether fundamental, one might think, in any Philosophy of History, have, since the era when Monkish Annalists were wont to answer them by the long-ago extinguished light of their Missal and Breviary, been by most philosophical Historians only glanced at dubiously and from afar; by many, not so much as glanced at.

The truth is, two difficulties, never wholly surmountable, lie in the way. Before Philosophy can teach by Experience, the Philosophy has to be in readiness, the Experience must be gathered and intelligently recorded. Now, overlooking the former consideration, and with regard only to the latter, let any one who has examined the current of human affairs, and how intricate, perplexed, unfathomable, even when seen into with our own eyes, are their thousandfold blending movements, say whether the true representing of it is easy or impossible. Social Life is the aggregate of all the individual men's Lives who constitute society; History is the essence of innumerable Biographies. But if one Biography, nay, our own Biography, study and recapitulate it as we may, remains in so many points unintelligible to us; how much more must these million, the very facts of which, to say nothing of the purport of them, we know not, and cannot know!

Neither will it adequately avail us to assert that the general inward condition of Life is the same in all ages; and that only the remarkable deviations from the common endowment and common lot, and the more important variations which the outward figure of Life has from time to time undergone, deserve memory and record. The inward condition of Life, it may rather be affirmed, the conscious or half-conscious aim of mankind, so far as men are not mere digesting-machines, is the same in no two ages; neither are the more important outward variations easy to fix on, or always well capable of representation. Which was the greatest innovator, which was the more important personage in man's history, he who first led armies over the Alps, and gained the victories of Cannæ and Thrasymene; or the nameless boor who first hammered out for himself an iron spade? When the oak-tree is felled, the whole forest echoes with it; but a hundred acorns are planted silently by some unnoticed breeze. Battles and war-tumults, which for the time din every ear, and with joy or terror intoxicate every heart, pass away like tavern-brawls; and, except some few Marathons and Morgartens, are remembered by accident, not by desert. Laws themselves, political Constitutions, are not our Life, but only the house wherein our Life is led: nay, they are but the bare walls of the house: all whose essential furniture, the inventions and traditions, and daily habits that regulate and support our existence, are the work not of Dracos and Hampdens, but of Phœnician mariners, of Italian masons and Saxon metallurgists, of philosophers, alchymists, prophets, and all the long-forgotten train of artists and artisans; who from the first have been jointly teaching us how to think and how to act, how to rule over spiritual and over physical Nature. Well may we say that of our History the more important part is lost without recovery; and,—as thanksgivings were once wont to be offered 'for unrecognised mercies,'—look with reverence into the dark untenanted places of the Past, where, in formless oblivion, our chief benefactors, with all their sedulous endeavours, but not with the fruit of these, lie entombed.

So imperfect is that same Experience, by which Philosophy is to teach. Nay, even with regard to those occurrences which do stand recorded, which, at their origin have seemed worthy of record, and the summary of which constitutes what we now call History, is not our understanding of them altogether incomplete; is it even possible to represent them as they were? The old story of Sir Walter Raleigh's looking from his prison-window, on some street tumult, which afterwards three witnesses reported in three different ways, himself differing from them all, is still a true lesson for us. Consider how it is that historical documents and records originate; even honest records, where the reporters were unbiased by personal regard; a case which, were nothing more wanted, must ever be among the rarest. The real leading features of a historical Transaction, those movements that essentially characterise it, and alone deserve to be recorded, are nowise the foremost to be noted. At first, among the various witnesses, who are also parties interested, there is only vague wonder, and fear or hope, and the noise of Rumour's thousand tongues; till, after a season, the conflict of testimonies has subsided into some general issue; and then it is settled, by majority of votes, that such and such a 'Crossing of the Rubicon,' an 'Impeachment of Strafford,' a 'Convocation of the Notables,' are epochs in the world's history, cardinal points on which grand world-revolutions have hinged. Suppose, however, that the majority of votes was all wrong; that the real cardinal points lay far deeper: and had been passed over unnoticed, because no Seer, but only mere Onlookers, chanced to be there! Our clock strikes when there is a change from hour to hour; but no hammer in the Horologe of Time peals through the universe when there is a change from Era to Era. Men understand not what is among their hands: as calmness is the characteristic of strength, so the weightiest causes may be most silent. It is, in no case, the real historical Transaction, but only some more or less plausible scheme and theory of the Transaction, or the harmonised result of many such schemes, each varying from the other and all varying from truth, that we can ever hope to behold.

Nay, were our faculty of insight into passing things never

so complete, there is still a fatal discrepancy between our manner of observing these, and their manner of occurring. The most gifted man can observe, still more can record, only the *series* of his own impressions: his observation, therefore, to say nothing of its other imperfections, must be *successive*, while the things done were often *simultaneous*; the things done were not a series, but a group. It is not in acted, as it is in written History: actual events are nowise so simply related to each other as parent and offspring are; every single event is the offspring not of one, but of all other events, prior or contemporaneous, and will in its turn combine with all others to give birth to new: it is an ever-living, ever-working Chaos of Being, wherein shape after shape bodies itself forth from innumerable elements. And this Chaos, boundless as the habitation and duration of man, unfathomable as the soul and destiny of man, is what the historian will depict, and scientifically gauge, we may say, by threading it with single lines of a few ells in length! For as all Action is, by its nature, to be figured as extended in breadth and in depth, as well as in length; that is to say, is based on Passion and Mystery, if we investigate its origin; and spreads abroad on all hands, modifying and modified; as well as advances towards completion,—so all Narrative is, by its nature, of only one dimension; only travels forward towards one, or towards successive points: Narrative is *linear*, Action is *solid*. Alas for our 'chains,' or chainlets, of 'causes and effects,' which we so assiduously track through certain handbreadths of years and square miles, when the whole is a broad, deep Immensity, and each atom is 'chained' and complected with all! Truly, if History is Philosophy teaching by Experience, the writer fitted to compose History is hitherto an unknown man. The Experience itself would require All-knowledge to record it,—were the All-wisdom needful for such Philosophy as would interpret it, to be had for asking. Better were it that mere earthly Historians should lower such pretensions, more suitable for Omniscience than for human science; and aiming only at some picture of the things acted, which picture itself will at best be a poor approximation, leave the inscrutable purport of them an acknowledged secret; or at most, in reverent Faith, far different from that teaching of Philosophy, pause over the mysterious vestiges of Him, whose path is in the great deep of Time, whom History indeed reveals, but only all History, and in Eternity, will clearly reveal.

Such considerations truly were of small profit, did they, instead of teaching us vigilance and reverent humility in our inquiries into History, abate our esteem for them, or discourage us from unweariedly prosecuting them. Let us search more and more into the Past; let all men explore it, as the true fountain of knowledge; by whose light alone, consciously or unconsciously employed, can the Present and the Future be interpreted or guessed at. For though the whole meaning lies far beyond our ken; yet in that complex Manuscript, covered over with formless inextricably-entangled unknown characters,—nay, which is a *Palimpsest*, and had once prophetic writing, still dimly legible there,—some letters, some words, may be deciphered; and if no complete Philosophy, here and there an intelligible precept, available in practice, be gathered: well understanding, in the mean while, that it is only a little portion we have deciphered; that much still remains to be interpreted; that History is a real Prophetic Manuscript, and can be fully interpreted by no man.

But the Artist in History may be distinguished from the Artisan in History; for here, as in all other provinces, there are Artists and Artisans; men who labour mechanically in a department, without eye for the Whole, not feeling that there is a Whole; and men who inform and ennoble the humblest department with an Idea of the Whole, and habitually know that only in the Whole is the Partial to be truly discerned. The proceedings and the duties of these two, in regard to History, must be altogether different. Not, indeed, that each has not a real worth, in his several degree. The simple husbandman can till his field, and by knowledge he has gained of its soil, sow it with the fit grain, though the deep rocks and central fires are unknown to him: his little crop hangs under and over the firmament of stars, and sails through whole untracked celestial spaces, between Aries and Libra; nevertheless it ripens for him in due season, and he gathers it safe into his barn. As a husbandman he is blameless in disregarding those higher wonders; but as a thinker, and faithful inquirer into Nature, he were wrong. So likewise is it with the Historian, who examines some special aspect of History; and from this or that combination of circumstances, political, moral, economical, and the issues it has led to, infers that such and such properties belong to human society, and that the like circumstances will produce the like issue; which inference, if other trials confirm it, must be held true and practically valuable. He is wrong only, and an artisan, when he fancies that these properties, discovered or discoverable, exhaust the matter: and sees not, at every step, that it is inexhaustible.

However, that class of cause-and-effect speculators, with whom no wonder would remain wonderful, but all things in Heaven and Earth must be computed and 'accounted for'; and even the Unknown, the Infinite in man's Life, had under the words *enthusiasm*, *superstition*, *spirit of the age* and so forth, obtained, as it were, an algebraical symbol and given value,—have now wellnigh played their part in European culture; and may be considered, as in most countries, even in England itself where they linger the latest, verging towards extinction. He who reads the inscrutable Book of Nature as if it were a Merchant's Ledger, is justly suspected of having never seen that Book, but only some school Synopsis thereof; from which, if taken for the real Book, more error than insight is to be derived.

Doubtless also, it is with a growing feeling of the infinite nature of History, that in these times, the old principle, division of labour, has been so widely applied to it. The Political Historian, once almost the sole cultivator of History, has now found various associates, who strive to elucidate other phases of human Life; of which, as hinted above, the political conditions it is passed under are but one, and though the primary, perhaps not the most important, of the many outward arrangements. Of this Historian himself, moreover, in his own special department, new and higher things are beginning to be expected. From of old, it was too often to be reproachfully observed of him, that he dwelt with disproportionate fondness in Senate-houses, in Battle-fields, nay, even in Kings' Antechambers; forgetting, that far away from such scenes, the mighty tide of Thought and Action was still rolling on its wondrous course, in gloom and brightness; and in its thousand remote valleys, a whole world of Existence, with or without an earthly sun of Happiness to warm it, with or without a heavenly sun of Holiness to purify and sanctify it, was blossoming and fading, whether the 'famous victory' were won or lost. The time seems coming when much of this must be amended; and he who sees no world but that of courts and camps; and writes only how soldiers were drilled and shot, and how this ministerial conjuror out-conjured that other, and then guided, or at least held, something which he called the rudder of Government, but which was rather the spigot of Taxation, wherewith, in place of steering, he could tap, and the more cunningly the nearer the lees,—will pass for a more or less instructive Gazetteer, but will no longer be called a Historian.

However, the Political Historian, were his work performed with all conceivable perfection, can accomplish but a part, and still leaves room for numerous fellow-labourers. Foremost among these comes the Ecclesiastical Historian; endeavouring, with catholic or sectarian view, to trace the progress of the Church; of that portion of the social establishments, which respects our religious condition; as the other portion does our civil, or rather, in the long-run, our economical condition. Rightly conducted, this department were undoubtedly the more important of the two; inasmuch as it concerns us more to understand how man's moral well-being had been and might be promoted, than to understand in the like sort his physical well-being; which latter is ultimately the aim of all Political arrangements. For the physically happiest is simply the safest, the strongest; and, in all conditions of Government, Power (whether of wealth as in these days, or of arms and adherents as in old days) is the only outward emblem and purchase-money of Good. True Good, however, unless we reckon Pleasure synonymous with it, is said to be rarely, or rather never, offered for sale in the market where that coin passes current. So that, for man's true advantage, not the outward condition of his life, but the inward and spiritual, is of prime influence; not the form of Government he lives under, and the power he can accumulate there, but the Church he is a member of, and the degree of moral elevation he can acquire by means of its instruction. Church History, then, did it speak wisely, would have momentous secrets to teach us: nay, in its highest degree, it were a sort of continued Holy Writ; our Sacred Books being, indeed, only a History of the primeval Church, as it first arose in man's soul, and symbolically embodied itself in his external life. How far our actual Church Historians fall below such unattainable standards, nay, below quite attainable approximations thereto, we need not point out. Of the Ecclesiastical Historian we have to complain, as we did of his Political fellow-craftsman, that his inquiries turn rather on the outward mechanism, the mere hulls and superficial accidents of the object, than on the object itself: as if the Church lay in Bishops' Chapter-houses, and Ecumenic Council-halls, and Cardinals' Conclaves, and not far more in the hearts of Believing Men; in whose walk and conversation, as influenced thereby, its chief manifestations were to be looked for, and its progress or decline ascertained. The History of the Church is a History of the Invisible as well as of the Visible Church; which latter, if disjoined from the former, is but a vacant edifice; gilded, it may be, and overhung with old votive gifts, yet useless, nay, pestilentially unclean; to write whose history is less important than to forward its downfall.

Of a less ambitious character are the Histories that relate to special separate provinces of human Action; to Sciences, Practical Arts, Institutions and the like; matters which do not imply an epitome of man's whole interest and form of life; but wherein, though each is still connected with all, the spirit of each, at least its material results, may be in some degree evolved without so strict a reference to that of the others. Highest in dignity and difficulty, under this head, would be our histories of Philosophy, of man's opinions and theories respecting the nature of his Being, and relations to the Universe Visible and Invisible: which History, indeed, were it fitly treated, or fit for right treatment, would be a province of Church History; the logical or dogmatical province thereof; for Philosophy, in its true sense, is or should be the soul, of which Religion, Worship is the body; in the healthy state of things the Philosopher and Priest were one and the same. But Philosophy itself is far enough from wearing this character; neither have its Historians been men, generally speaking, that could in the smallest degree approximate it thereto. Scarcely since the rude era of the Magi and Druids has that same healthy identification of Priest and Philosopher had place in any country: but rather the worship of divine things, and the scientific investigation of divine things, have been in quite different hands, their relations not friendly but hostile. Neither have the Brückers and Bühles, to say nothing of the many unhappy Enfields who have treated of that latter department, been more than barren reporters, often unintelligent and unintelligible reporters, of the doctrine uttered; without force to discover how the doctrine originated, or what reference it bore to its time and country, to the spiritual position of mankind there and then. Nay, such a task did not perhaps lie before them as a thing to be attempted

Art also and Literature are intimately blended with Religion; as it were, outworks and abutments, by which that highest pinnacle in our inward world gradually connects itself with the general level, and becomes accessible therefrom. He who should write a proper History of Poetry, would depict for us the successive Revelations which man had obtained of the Spirit of Nature; under what aspects he had caught and endeavoured to body forth some glimpse of that unspeakable Beauty, which in its highest clearness is Religion, is the inspiration of a Prophet, yet in one or the other degree must inspire every true Singer, were his theme never so humble. We should see by what steps men had ascended to the Temple; how near they had approached; by what ill hap they had, for long periods, turned away from it, and grovelled on the plain with no music in the air, or blindly struggled towards other heights. That among all our Eichhorns and Wartons there is no such Historian, must be too clear to every one. Nevertheless let us not despair of far nearer approaches to that excellence. Above all, let us keep the Ideal of it ever in our eye; for thereby alone have we even a chance to reach it.

Our histories of Laws and Constitutions, wherein many a Montesquieu and Hallam has laboured with acceptance, are of a much simpler nature; yet deep enough if thoroughly investigated; and useful, when authentic, even with little depth. Then we have Histories of Medicine, of Mathematics, of Astronomy, Commerce, Chivalry, Monkery; and Goguets and Beckmanns have come forward with what might be the most bountiful contribution of all, a History of Inventions. Of all which sorts, and many more not here enumerated, not yet devised and put in practice, the merit and the proper scheme may, in our present limits, require no exposition.

In this manner, though, as above remarked, all Action is extended three ways, and the general sum of human Action is a whole Universe, with all limits of it unknown, does History strive by running path after path, through the Impassable, in manifold directions and intersections, to secure for us some oversight of the Whole; in which endeavour, if each Historian look well around him from his path, tracking it out with the *eye*, not, as is more common, with the *nose*, she may at last prove not altogether unsuccessful. Praying only that increased division of labour do not here, as elsewhere, aggravate our already strong Mechanical tendencies, so that in the manual dexterity for parts we lose all command over the whole, and the hope of any Philosophy of History be farther off than ever, —let us all wish her great and greater success.

FROM *Sartor Resartus*

Sartor Resartus was written at Craigenputtock between October 1830 and July 1831. Carlyle took the manuscript to London, but was unable to find any publisher prepared to take the risk of printing so odd and revolutionary a book. At last James Fraser published the book in serial form in *Fraser's Magazine*, where it appeared in volumes viii to x, from 1833 to 1834.

'I think I can practically prophesy that . . . it would be apt at least to *keep the eyes* of the Public on you', Carlyle wrote to Fraser: but in fact it was received with what the publisher called 'the most unqualified disapproval'. *Sartor Resartus* was not published in book form in this country until 1838, although an American edition appeared in 1836.

The first of the three books of *Sartor* is printed here.

FROM

Sartor Resartus

BOOK FIRST

CHAPTER I

PRELIMINARY

No Philosophy of Clothes yet, notwithstanding all our Science. Strangely forgotten that Man is by nature a *naked* animal. The English mind all-too practically absorbed for any such inquiry. Not so, deep-thinking Germany. Advantage of Speculation having free course. Editor receives from Professor Teufelsdröckh his new Work on Clothes.

CONSIDERING our present advanced state of culture, and how the Torch of Science has now been brandished and borne about, with more or less effect, for five thousand years and upwards; how, in these times especially, not only the Torch still burns, and perhaps more fiercely than ever, but innumerable Rushlights, and Sulphur-matches, kindled thereat, are also glancing in every direction, so that not the smallest cranny or doghole in Nature or Art can remain unilluminated,—it might strike the reflective mind with some surprise that hitherto little or nothing of a fundamental character, whether in the way of Philosophy or History, has been written on the subject of Clothes.

Our Theory of Gravitation is as good as perfect: Lagrange, it is well known, has proved that the Planetary System, on this scheme, will endure forever; Laplace, still more cunningly, even guesses that it could not have been made on any other scheme. Whereby, at least, our nautical Logbooks can be better kept; and water-transport of all kinds has grown more commodious. Of Geology and Geognosy we know enough: what with the labours of our Werners and Huttons, what with the ardent genius of their disciples, it has come about that now, to many a Royal Society, the Creation of a World is little more mysterious than the cooking of a dumpling; concerning which last, indeed, there have been minds to whom the question, *How the apples were got in*, presented difficulties. Why mention our disquisitions on the Social Contract, on the Standard of Taste, on the Migrations of the Herring? Then, have we not a Doctrine of Rent, a Theory of Value; Philosophies of Language, of History, of Pottery, of Apparitions, of Intoxicating Liquors? Man's whole life and environment have been laid open and elucidated; scarcely a fragment or fibre of his Soul, Body, and Possessions, but has been probed, dissected, distilled, desiccated, and scientifically decomposed: our spiritual Faculties, of which it appears there are not a few, have their Stewarts, Cousins, Royer Collards: every cellular, vascular, muscular Tissue glories in its Lawrences, Majendies, Bichâts.

How, then, comes it, may the reflective mind repeat, that the grand Tissue of all Tissues, the only real Tissue, should have been quite overlooked by Science,—the vestural Tissue, namely, of woollen or other cloth; which Man's Soul wears as its outmost wrappage and overall; wherein his whole other Tissues are included and screened, his whole Faculties work, his whole Self lives, moves, and has its being? For if, now and then, some straggling broken-winged thinker has cast an owl's-glance into this obscure region, the most have soared over it altogether heedless; regarding Clothes as a property, not an accident, as quite natural and spontaneous, like the leaves of trees, like the plumage of birds. In all speculations they have tacitly figured man as a *Clothed Animal*; whereas he is by nature a *Naked Animal*; and only in certain circumstances, by purpose and device, masks himself in Clothes. Shakespeare says, we are creatures that look before and after: the more surprising that we do not look round a little, and see what is passing under our very eyes.

But here, as in so many other cases, Germany, learned, indefatigable, deep-thinking Germany comes to our aid. It is, after all, a blessing that, in these revolutionary times, there should be one country where abstract Thought can still take shelter; that while the din and frenzy of Catholic Emancipations, and Rotten Boroughs, and Revolts of Paris, deafen every French and every English ear, the German can stand peaceful on his scientific watch-tower; and, to the raging, struggling multitude here and elsewhere, solemnly, from hour to hour, with preparatory blast of cowhorn, emit his *Höret ihr Herren und lasset's Euch sagen*; in other words, tell the Universe, which so often forgets that fact, what o'clock it really is. Not unfrequently the Germans have been blamed for an unprofitable diligence; as if they struck into devious courses, where nothing was to be had but the toil of a rough journey; as if, forsaking the gold-mines of finance and that political slaughter of fat oxen whereby a man himself grows fat, they were apt to run goose-hunting into regions of bilberries and crowberries, and be swallowed up at last in remote peat-bogs. Of that unwise science, which, as our Humorist expresses it,

> 'By geometric scale
> Doth take the size of pots of ale;'

still more, of that altogether misdirected industry, which is seen vigorously thrashing mere straw, there can nothing defensive be said. In so far as the Germans are chargeable with such, let them take the consequence. Nevertheless be it remarked, that even a Russian steppe has tumuli and gold ornaments; also many a scene that looks desert and rock-bound from the distance, will unfold itself, when visited, into rare valleys. Nay, in any case, would Criticism erect not only finger-posts and turnpikes, but spiked gates and impassable barriers, for the mind of man? It is written, 'Many shall run to and fro, and knowledge shall be increased.' Surely the plain rule is, Let each considerate person have his way, and see what it will lead to. For not this man and that man, but all men make up mankind, and their united tasks the task of mankind. How often have we seen some such adventurous, and perhaps much-censured wanderer light on some out-lying, neglected, yet vitally momentous province; the hidden treasures of which he first discovered, and kept proclaiming till the general eye and effort were directed thither, and the conquest was completed;—thereby, in these his seemingly so aimless rambles, planting new standards, founding new habitable colonies, in the immeasurable circumambient realm of Nothingness and Night! Wise man was he who counselled that Speculation should have free course, and look fearlessly towards all the thirty-two points of the compass, whithersoever and howsoever it listed.

Perhaps it is proof of the stunted condition in which pure Science, especially pure moral Science, languishes among us English; and how our mercantile greatness, and invaluable Constitution, impressing a political or other immediately practical tendency on all English culture and endeavour, cramps the free flight of Thought,—that this, not Philosophy of Clothes, but recognition even that we have no such Philosophy, stands here for the first time published in our language. What English intellect could have chosen such a topic, or by chance stumbled on it? But for that same unshackled, and even sequestered condition of the German Learned, which permits and induces them to fish in all manner of waters, with all manner of nets, it seems probable enough, this abstruse Inquiry might, in spite of the results it leads to, have continued dormant for indefinite periods. The Editor of these sheets, though otherwise boasting himself a man of confirmed speculative habits, and perhaps discursive enough, is free to confess, that never, till these last months, did the above very plain considerations, on our total want of a Philosophy of Clothes, occur to him; and then, by quite foreign suggestion. By the arrival, namely, of a new Book from Professor Teufelsdröckh of Weissnichtwo; treating expressly of this subject, and in a style which, whether understood or not, could not even by the blindest be overlooked. In the present Editor's way of thought, this remarkable Treatise, with its Doctrines, whether as judicially acceded to, or judicially denied, has not remained without effect.

'*Die Kleider, ihr Werden und Wirken* (Clothes, their Origin and Influence): *von Diog. Teufelsdröckh, J.U.D. etc. Stillschweigen und Cognie. Weissnichtwo*, 1831.

'Here,' says the *Weissnichtwo'sche Anzeiger*, 'comes a Volume of that extensive, close-printed, close-meditated sort, which, be it spoken with pride, is seen only in Germany, perhaps only in Weissnichtwo. Issuing from the hitherto irreproachable Firm of Stillschweigen and Company, with every external furtherance, it is of such internal quality as to set Neglect at defiance.' * * * * 'A work,' concludes the well-nigh enthusiastic Reviewer, 'interesting alike to the antiquary, the historian, and the philosophic thinker; a masterpiece of boldness, lynx-eyed acuteness, and rugged independent Germanism and Philanthropy (*derber Kerndeutschheit und Menschenliebe*); which will not, assuredly, pass current without opposition in high places; but must and will exalt the almost new name of Teufelsdröckh to the first ranks of Philosophy, in our German Temple of Honour.'

Mindful of old friendship, the distinguished Professor, in this the first blaze of his fame, which however does not dazzle him, sends hither a Presentation-copy of his Book; with compliments and encomiums which modesty forbids the present Editor to rehearse; yet without indicated wish or hope of any kind, except what may be implied in the concluding phrase: *Möchte es* (this remarkable Treatise) *auch im Brittischen Boden gedeihen*!

CHAPTER II

EDITORIAL DIFFICULTIES

How to make known Teufelsdröckh and his Book to English readers; especially *such* a book? Editor receives from the Hofrath Heuschrecke a letter promising Biographic Documents. Negotiations with Oliver Yorke. *Sartor Resartus* conceived. Editor's assurances and advice to his British reader.

If for a speculative man, 'whose seedfield,' in the sublime words of the Poet, 'is Time,' no conquest is important but that of new ideas, then might the arrival of Professor Teufelsdröckh's Book be marked with chalk in the Editor's calendar. It is indeed an 'extensive Volume,' of boundless, almost formless contents, a very Sea of Thought; neither calm nor clear, if you will; yet wherein the toughest pearl-diver may dive to his utmost depth, and return not only with sea-wreck but with true orients.

Directly on the first perusal, almost on the first deliberate inspection, it became apparent that here a quite new Branch of Philosophy, leading to as yet undescried ulterior results, was disclosed; farther, what seemed scarcely less interesting, a quite new human Individuality, an almost unexampled personal character, that, namely, of Professor Teufelsdröckh the Discloser. Of both which novelties, as far as might be possible, we resolved to master the significance. But as man is emphatically a proselytising creature, no sooner was such mastery even fairly attempted, than the new question arose: How might this acquired good be imparted to others, perhaps in equal need thereof: how could the philosophy of Clothes, and the Author of such Philosophy, be brought home, in any measure, to the business and bosoms of our own English Nation? For if new-got gold is said to burn the pockets till it be cast forth into circulation, much more may new truth.

Here, however, difficulties occurred. The first thought naturally was to publish Article after Article on this remarkable Volume, in such widely-circulating Critical Journals as the Editor might stand connected with, or by money or love procure access to. But, on the other hand, was it not clear that such matter as must here be revealed, and treated of, might endanger the circulation of any Journal extant? If, indeed, all party-divisions in the State, could have been abolished, Whig, Tory, and Radical, embracing in discrepant union; and all the Journals of the Nation could have been jumbled into one Journal, and the Philosophy of Clothes poured forth in incessant torrents therefrom, the attempt had seemed possible. But, alas, what vehicle of that sort have we, except *Fraser's Magazine*? A vehicle all strewed (figuratively speaking) with the maddest Waterloo-Crackers, exploding distractively and destructively, wheresoever the mystified passenger stands or sits; nay, in any case, understood to be, of late years, a vehicle full to overflowing, and inexorably shut! Besides, to state the Philosophy of Clothes without the Philosopher, the ideas of Teufelsdröckh without something of his personality, was it not to insure both of entire misapprehension? Now for Biography, had it been otherwise admissible, there were no adequate documents, no hope of obtaining such, but rather, owing to circumstances, a special despair. Thus did the Editor see himself, for the while, shut out from all public utterance of these extraordinary Doctrines, and constrained to revolve them, not without disquietude, in the dark depths of his own mind.

So had it lasted for some months; and now the Volume on Clothes, read and again read, was in several points becoming lucid and lucent; the personality of its Author more and more surprising, but, in spite of all that memory and conjecture could do, more and more enigmatic; whereby the old disquietude seemed fast settling into fixed discontent,—when altogether unexpectedly arrives a Letter from Herr Hofrath Heuschrecke, our Professor's chief friend and associate in Weissnichtwo, with whom we had not previously corresponded. The Hofrath, after much quite extraneous matter, began dilating largely on the 'agitation and attention' which the Philosophy of Clothes was exciting in its own German Republic of Letters; on the deep significance and tendency of his Friend's Volume; and then, at length, with great circumlocution, hinted at the practicability of conveying 'some knowledge of it, and of him, to England and through England to the distant West': a work on Professor Teufelsdröckh 'were undoubtedly welcome to the *Family*, the *National*, or any other of those patriotic *Libraries*, at present the glory of British Literature'; might work revolutions in Thought; and so forth; —in conclusion, intimating not obscurely, that should the present Editor feel disposed to undertake a Biography of Teufelsdröckh, he, Hofrath Heuschrecke, had it in his power to furnish the requisite Documents.

As in some chemical mixture, that has stood long evaporating, but would not crystallise, instantly when the wire or other fixed substance is introduced, crystallisation commences, and rapidly proceeds till the whole is finished, so was it with the Editor's mind and this offer of Heuschrecke's. Form rose out of void solution and discontinuity; like united itself with like in definite arrangement: and soon either in actual vision and possession, or in fixed reasonable hope, the image of the whole Enterprise had shaped itself, so to speak, into a solid mass. Cautiously yet courageously, through the twopenny post, application to the famed redoubtable OLIVER YORKE was now made: an interview, interviews with that singular man have taken place; with more of assurance on our side, with less of satire (at least of open satire) on his, than we anticipated;—for the rest, with such issue as is now visible. As to those same 'patriotic *Libraries*,' the Hofrath's counsel could only be viewed with silent amazement; but with his offer of Documents we joyfully and almost instantaneously closed. Thus, too, in the sure expectation of these, we already see our task begun; and this our *Sartor Resartus*, which is properly a 'Life and Opinions of Herr Teufelsdröckh,' hourly advancing.

Of our fitness for the Enterprise, to which we have such title and vocation, it were perhaps uninteresting to say more. Let the British reader study and enjoy, in simplicity of heart, what is here presented him, and with whatever metaphysical acumen and talent for meditation he is possessed of. Let him strive to keep a free, open sense; cleared from the mists of prejudice, above all from the paralysis of cant; and directed rather to the Book itself than to the Editor of the Book. Who or what such Editor may be, must remain conjectural, and even insignificant:[1] it is a voice publishing tidings of the Philosophy of Clothes; undoubtedly a Spirit addressing Spirits: whoso hath ears, let him hear.

On one other point the Editor thinks it needful to give warning: namely, that he is animated with a true though perhaps a feeble attachment to the Institutions of our An-

[1] With us even he still communicates in some sort of mask, or muffler; and, we have reason to think, under a feigned name!—O.Y.

cestors; and minded to defend these, according to ability, at all hazards; nay, it was partly with a view to such defence that he engaged in this undertaking. To stem, or if that be impossible, profitably to divert the current of Innovation, such a Volume as Teufelsdröckh's, if cunningly planted down, were no despicable pile, or floodgate, in the logical wear.

For the rest, be it nowise apprehended, that any personal connexion of ours with Teufelsdröckh, Heuschrecke, or this Philosophy of Clothes, can pervert our judgment, or sway us to extenuate or exaggerate. Powerless, we venture to promise, are those private Compliments themselves. Grateful they may well be; as generous illusions of friendship; as fair mementos of bygone unions, of those nights and suppers of the gods, when, lapped in the symphonies and harmonies of Philosophic Eloquence, though with baser accompaniments, the present Editor revelled in that feast of reason, never since vouchsafed him in so full measure! But what then? *Amicus Plato, magis amica veritas*; Teufelsdröckh is our friend, Truth is our divinity. In our historical and critical capacity, we hope we are strangers to all the world; have feud or favour with no one,—save indeed the Devil, with whom, as with the Prince of Lies and Darkness, we do at all times wage internecine war. This assurance, at an epoch when puffery and quackery have reached a height unexampled in the annals of mankind, and even English Editors, like Chinese Shopkeepers, must write on their door-lintels *No cheating here*,—we thought it good to premise.

CHAPTER III

REMINISCENCES

Teufelsdröckh at Weissnichtwo. Professor of Things in General at the University there: Outward aspect and character; memorable coffee-house utterances; domicile and watch-tower: Sights thence of City-Life by day and by night; with reflections thereon. Old 'Liza and her ways. Character of Hofrath Heuschrecke, and his relation to Teufelsdröckh.

To the Author's private circle the appearance of this singular Work on Clothes must have occasioned little less surprise than it has to the rest of the world. For ourselves, at least, few things have been more unexpected. Professor Teufelsdröckh, at the period of our acquaintance with him, seemed to lead a quite still and self-contained life: a man devoted to the higher Philosophies, indeed; yet more likely, if he published at all, to publish a refutation of Hegel and Bardili, both of whom, strangely enough, he included under a common ban; than to descend, as he has here done, into the angry noisy Forum, with an Argument that cannot but exasperate and divide. Not, that we can remember, was the Philosophy of Clothes once touched upon between us. If through the high, silent, meditative Transcendentalism of our Friend we detected any practical tendency whatever, it was at most Political, and towards a certain prospective, and for the present quite speculative, Radicalism; as indeed some correspondence, on his part, with Herr Oken of Jena was now and then suspected; though his special contributions to the *Isis* could never be more than surmised at. But, at all events, nothing Moral, still less anything Didactico-Religious, was looked for from him.

Well do we recollect the last words he spoke in our hearing; which indeed, with the Night they were uttered in, are to be forever remembered. Lifting his huge tumbler of *Gukguk*,[1] and for a moment lowering his tobacco-pipe, he stood up in full coffeehouse (it was *Zur Grünen Gans*, the largest in Weissnichtwo, where all the Virtuosity, and nearly all the Intellect of the place assembled of an evening); and there, with low, soul-stirring tone, and the look truly of an angel, though whether of a white or of a black one might be dubious, proposed this toast: *Die Sache der Armen in Gottes und Teufels Namen* (The Cause of the Poor, in Heaven's name and ——'s)! One full shout, breaking the leaden silence; then a gurgle of innumerable emptying bumpers, again followed by universal cheering, returned him loud acclaim. It was the finale of the night: resuming their pipes; in the highest enthusiasm, amid volumes of tobacco-smoke; triumphant, cloud-capt without and within, the assembly broke up, each to his thoughtful

[1] Gukguk is unhappily only an academical—beer.

pillow. *Bleibt doch ein echter Spass- und Galgen-vogel,* said several; meaning thereby that, one day, he would probably be hanged for his democratic sentiments. *Wo steckt doch der Schalk?* added they, looking round: but Teufelsdröckh had retired by private alleys, and the Compiler of these pages beheld him no more.

In such scenes has it been our lot to live with this Philosopher, such estimate to form of his purposes and powers. And yet, thou brave Teufelsdröckh, who could tell what lurked in thee? Under those thick locks of thine, so long and lank, overlapping roof-wise the gravest face we ever in this world saw, there dwelt a most busy brain. In thy eyes too, deep under their shaggy brows, and looking out so still and dreamy, have we not noticed gleams of an ethereal or else a diabolic fire, and half-fancied that their stillness was but the rest of infinite motion, the *sleep* of a spinning-top? Thy little figure, there as, in loose ill-brushed threadbare habiliments, thou sattest, amid litter and lumber, whole days, to 'think and smoke tobacco,' held in it a mighty heart. The secrets of man's Life were laid open to thee; thou sawest into the mystery of the Universe, farther than another; thou hadst *in petto* thy remarkable Volume of Clothes. Nay, was there not in that clear logically-founded Transcendentalism of thine; still more, in thy meek, silent, deep-seated Sansculottism, combined with a true princely Courtesy of inward nature, the visible rudiments of such speculation? But great men are too often unknown, or what is worse, misknown. Already, when we dreamed not of it, the warp of thy remarkable Volume lay on the loom; and silently, mysterious shuttles were putting-in the woof!

How the Hofrath Heuschrecke is to furnish biographical data, in this case, may be a curious question; the answer of which, however, is happily not our concern, but his. To us it appeared, after repeated trial, that in Weissnichtwo, from the archives or memories of the best-informed classes, no Biography of Teufelsdröckh was to be gathered; not so much as a false one. He was a stranger there, wafted thither by what is called the course of circumstances; concerning whose parentage, birthplace, prospects, or pursuits, curiosity had indeed made inquiries, but satisfied herself with the most indistinct replies. For himself, he was a man so still and altogether unparticipating, that to question him even afar off on such particulars was a thing of more than usual delicacy: besides, in his sly way, he had ever some quaint turn, not without its satirical edge, wherewith to divert such intrusions, and deter you from the like. Wits spoke of him secretly as if he were a kind of Melchizedek, without father or mother of any kind; sometimes, with reference to his great historic and statistic knowledge, and the vivid way he had of expressing himself like an eyewitness of distant transactions and scenes, they called him the *Ewige Jude*, Everlasting, or as we say, Wandering Jew.

To the most, indeed, he had become not so much a Man as a Thing; which Thing doubtless they were accustomed to see, and with satisfaction; but no more thought of accounting for than for the fabrication of their daily *Allgemeine Zeitung*, or the domestic habits of the Sun. Both were there and welcome; the world enjoyed what good was in them, and thought no more of the matter. The man Teufelsdröckh passed and repassed, in his little circle, as one of those originals and nondescripts, more frequent in German Universities than elsewhere; of whom, though you see them alive, and feel certain enough that they must have a History, no History seems to be discoverable; or only such as men give of mountain rocks and antediluvian ruins: That they have been created by unknown agencies, are in a state of gradual decay, and for the present reflect light and resist pressure; that is, are visible and tangible objects in this phantasm world, where so much other mystery is.

It was to be remarked that though, by title and diploma, *Professor der Allerley-Wissenschaft*, or as we should say in English, 'Professor of Things in General,' he had never delivered any Course; perhaps never been incited thereto by any public furtherance or requisition. To all appearance, the enlightened Government of Weissnichtwo, in founding their

New University, imagined they had done enough, if 'in times like ours,' as the half-official Program expressed it, 'when all things are, rapidly or slowly, resolving themselves into Chaos, a Professorship of this kind had been established; whereby, as occasion called, the task of bodying somewhat forth again from such Chaos might be, even slightly, facilitated.' That actual Lectures should be held, and Public Classes for the 'Science of Things in General,' they doubtless considered premature; on which ground too they had only established the Professorship, nowise endowed it; so that Teufelsdröckh, 'recommended by the highest Names,' had been promoted thereby to a Name merely.

Great, among the more enlightened classes, was the admiration of this new Professorship: how an enlightened Government had seen into the Want of the Age (*Zeitbedürfniss*); how at length, instead of Denial and Destruction, we were to have a science of Affirmation and Reconstruction; and Germany and Weissnichtwo were where they should be, in the vanguard of the world. Considerable also was the wonder at the new Professor, dropt opportunely enough into the nascent University; so able to lecture, should occasion call; so ready to hold his peace for indefinite periods, should an enlightened Government consider that occasion did not call. But such admiration and such wonder, being followed by no act to keep them living, could last only nine days; and, long before our visit to that scene, had quite died away. The more cunning heads thought it was all an expiring clutch at popularity, on the part of a Minister, whom domestic embarrassments, court intrigues, old age, and dropsy soon afterwards finally drove from the helm.

As for Teufelsdröckh, except by his nightly appearances at the *Grüne Gans*, Weissnichtwo saw little of him, felt little of him. Here, over his tumbler of Gukguk, he sat reading Journals; sometimes contemplatively looking into the clouds of his tobacco-pipe, without other visible employment: always, from his mild ways, an agreeable phenomenon there; more especially when he opened his lips for speech; on which occasions the whole Coffee-house would hush itself into silence, as if sure to hear something noteworthy. Nay, perhaps to hear a whole series and river of the most memorable utterances; such as, when once thawed, he would for hours indulge in, with fit audience: and the more memorable, as issuing from a head apparently not more interested in them, not more conscious of them, than is the sculptured stone head of some public fountain, which through its brass mouth-tube emits water to the worthy and the unworthy; careless whether it be for cooking victuals or quenching conflagrations; indeed, maintains the same earnest assiduous look, whether any water be flowing or not.

To the Editor of these sheets, as to a young enthusiastic Englishman, however unworthy, Teufelsdröckh opened himself perhaps more than to the most. Pity only that we could not then half guess his importance, and scrutinise him with due power of vision! We enjoyed, what not three men in Weissnichtwo could boast of, a certain degree of access to the Professor's private domicile. It was the attic floor of the highest house in the Wahngasse; and might truly be called the pinnacle of Weissnichtwo, for it rose sheer up above the contiguous roofs, themselves rising from elevated ground. Moreover, with its windows it looked towards all the four *Orte*, or as the Scotch say, and we ought to say, *Airts*: the sitting-room itself commanded three; another came to view in the *Schlafgemach* (bed-room) at the opposite end; to say nothing of the kitchen, which offered two, as it were, *duplicates*, and showing nothing new. So that it was in fact the speculum or watch-tower of Teufelsdröckh; wherefrom, sitting at ease, he might see the whole life-circulation of that considerable City; the streets and lanes of which, with all their doing and driving (*Thun und Treiben*), were for the most part visible there.

'I look down into all that wasp-nest or bee-hive,' have we heard him say, 'and witness their wax-laying and honey-making, and poison-brewing, and choking by sulphur. From the Palace esplanade, where music plays while Serene Highness is pleased to eat his victuals, down to the low lane, where in her door-sill the aged widow, knitting for a thin livelihood, sits to feel the afternoon sun, I see it all; for, except the Schlosskirche weathercock, no biped stands so high. Couriers arrive bestrapped and bebooted, bearing Joy and Sorrow bagged-up in pouches of leather; there, topladen, and with four swift horses, rolls-in the country Baron and his household; here, on timber-leg, the lamed Soldier hops painfully along, begging alms: a thousand carriages, and wains, and cars, come tumbling-in with Food, with young Rusticity, and other Raw Produce, inanimate or animate, and go tumbling out again with Produce manufactured. That living flood, pouring through these streets, of all qualities and ages, knowest thou whence it is coming, whither it is going? *Aus der Ewigkeit, zu der Ewigkeit hin*: From Eternity, onwards to Eternity! These are Apparitions: what else? Are they not Souls rendered visible: in Bodies, that took shape and will lose it, melting into air? Their solid Pavement is a Picture of the Sense; they walk on the bosom of Nothing, blank Time is behind them and before them. Or fanciest thou, the red and yellow Clothes-screen yonder, with spurs on its heels and feather in its crown, is but of Today, without a Yesterday or a Tomorrow; and had not rather its Ancestor alive when Hengst and Horsa overran thy Island? Friend, thou seest here a living link in that Tissue of History, which inweaves all Being: watch well, or it will be past thee, and seen no more.

'*Ach, mein Lieber!*' said he once, at midnight, when we had returned from the Coffee-house in rather earnest talk, 'it is a true sublimity to dwell here. These fringes of lamplight, struggling up through smoke and thousandfold exhalation, some fathoms into the ancient reign of Night, what thinks Boötes of them, as he leads his Hunting-dogs over the Zenith in their leash of sidereal fire? That stifled hum of Midnight, when Traffic has lain down to rest; and the chariot-wheels of Vanity, still rolling here and there through distant streets, are bearing her to Halls roofed-in, and lighted to the due pitch for her; and only Vice and Misery, to prowl or to moan like nightbirds, are abroad: that hum, I say, like the stertorous, unquiet slumber of sick Life, is heard in Heaven! Oh, under that hideous coverlet of vapours, and putrefactions, and unimaginable gases, what a Fermenting-vat lies simmering and hid! The joyful and the sorrowful are there; men are dying there, men are being born; men are praying,—on the other side of a brick partition, men are cursing; and around them all is the vast, void Night. The proud Grandee still lingers in his perfumed saloons, or reposes within damask curtains; Wretchedness cowers into truckle-beds, or shivers hunger-stricken into its lair of straw: in obscure cellars, *Rouge-et-Noir* languidly emits its voice-of-destiny to haggard hungry Villains; while Councillors of State sit plotting, and playing their high chess-game, whereof the pawns are Men. The Lover whispers his mistress that the coach is ready; and she, full of hope and fear, glides down, to fly with him over the borders: the Thief, still more silently, sets-to his picklocks and crowbars, or lurks in wait till the watchmen first snore in their boxes. Gay mansions, with supper-rooms, and dancing-rooms, are full of light and music and high-swelling hearts; but, in the Condemned Cells, the pulse of life beats tremulous and faint, and bloodshot eyes look-out through the darkness, which is around and within, for the light of a stern last morning. Six men are to be hanged on the morrow: comes no hammering from the *Rabenstein*?—their gallows must even now be o' building. Upwards of five-hundred-thousand two-legged animals without feathers lie round us, in horizontal positions; their heads all in nightcaps, and full of the foolishest dreams. Riot cries aloud, and staggers and swaggers in his rank dens of shame; and the Mother, with streaming hair, kneels over her pallid dying infant, whose cracked lips only her tears now moisten.—All these heaped and huddled together, with nothing but a little carpentry and masonry between them;—crammed in, like salted fish in their barrel;—or weltering, shall I say, like an Egyptian pitcher of tamed vipers, each struggling to get its *head above* the others: *such* work goes on under that smoke-counterpane!—But I, *mein Werther*, sit above it all; I am alone with the Stars.'

We looked in his face to see whether, in the utterance of such extraordinary Night-thoughts, no feeling might be traced there; but with the light we had, which indeed was only a single tallow-light, and far enough from the window, nothing save that old calmness and fixedness was visible.

These were the Professor's talking seasons: most commonly he spoke in mere monosyllables, or sat altogether silent and smoked; while the visitor had liberty either to say what he listed, receiving for answer an occasional grunt; or to look round for a space, and then take himself away. It was a strange apartment; full of books and tattered papers, and miscellaneous shreds of all conceivable substances, 'united in a common element of dust.' Books lay on tables, and below tables; here fluttered a sheet of manuscript, there a torn handkerchief, or nightcap hastily thrown aside; ink-bottles alternated with bread-crusts, coffee-pots, tobacco-boxes, Periodical Literature, and Blücher Boots. Old Lieschen (Lisekin, 'Liza), who was his bed-maker and stove-lighter, his washer and wringer, cook, errand-maid, and general lion's-provider, and for the rest a very orderly creature, had no sovereign authority in this last citadel of Teufelsdröckh; only some once in the month she half-forcibly made her way thither, with broom and duster, and (Teufelsdröckh hastily saving his manuscripts) effected a partial clearance, a jail-delivery of such lumber as was not Literary. These were her *Erdbeben* (earthquakes), which Teufelsdröckh dreaded worse than the pestilence; nevertheless, to such length he had been forced to comply. Glad would he have been to sit here philosophising forever, or till the litter, by accumulation, drove him out of doors: but Lieschen was his right-arm, and spoon, and necessary of life, and would not be flatly gainsayed. We can still remember the ancient woman; so silent that some thought her dumb; deaf also you would often have supposed her; for Teufelsdröckh, and Teufelsdröckh only, would she serve or give heed to; and with him she seemed to communicate chiefly by signs; if it were not rather by some secret divination that she guessed all his wants, and supplied them. Assiduous old dame! she scoured, and sorted, and swept, in her kitchen, with the least possible violence to the ear; yet all was tight and right there:

hot and black came the coffee ever at the due moment; and the speechless Lieschen herself looked out on you, from under her clean white coif with its lappets, through her clean withered face and wrinkles, with a look of helpful intelligence, almost of benevolence.

Few strangers, as above hinted, had admittance hither: the only one we ever saw there, ourselves excepted, was the Hofrath Heuschrecke, already known, by name and expectation, to the readers of these pages. To us, at that period, Herr Heuschrecke seemed one of those purse-mouthed, crane-necked, clean-brushed, pacific individuals, perhaps sufficiently distinguished in society by this fact, that, in dry weather or in wet, 'they never appear without their umbrella.' Had we not known with what 'little wisdom' the world is governed; and how, in Germany as elsewhere, the ninety-and-nine Public Men can for most part be but mute train-bearers to the hundredth, perhaps but stalking-horses and willing or unwilling dupes,—it might have seemed wonderful how Herr Heuschrecke should be named a *Rath*, or Councillor, and Counsellor, even in Weissnichtwo. What counsel to any man, or to any woman, could this particular Hofrath give; in whose loose, zigzag figure; in whose thin visage, as it went jerking to and fro, in minute incessant fluctuation,—you traced rather confusion worse confounded; at most, Timidity and physical Cold? Some indeed said withal, he was 'the very Spirit of Love embodied': blue earnest eyes, full of sadness and kindness; purse ever open, and so forth; the whole of which, we shall now hope, for many reasons, was not quite groundless. Nevertheless friend Teufelsdröckh's outline, who indeed handled the burin like few in these cases, was probably the best: *Er hat Gemüth und Geist, hat wenigstens gehabt, doch ohne Organ, ohne Schicksals-Gunst; ist gegenwärtig aber halb-zerrüttet, halb-erstarrt*, 'He has heart and talent, at least has had such, yet without fit mode of utterance, or favour of Fortune; and so is now half-cracked, half-congealed.'—What the Hofrath shall think of this when he sees it, readers may wonder: we, safe in the stronghold of Historical Fidelity, are careless.

The main point, doubtless, for us all, is his love of Teufelsdröckh, which indeed was also by far the most decisive feature of Heuschrecke himself. We are enabled to assert that he hung on the Professor with the fondness of a Boswell for his Johnson. And perhaps with the like return; for Teufelsdröckh treated his gaunt admirer with little outward regard, as some half-rational or altogether irrational friend, and at best loved him out of gratitude and by habit. On the other hand, it was curious to observe with what reverent kindness, and a sort of fatherly protection, our Hofrath, being the elder, richer, and as he fondly imagined far more practically influential of the two, looked and tended on his little Sage, whom he seemed to consider as a living oracle. Let but Teufelsdröckh open his mouth, Heuschrecke's also unpuckered itself into a free doorway, besides his being all eye and all ear, so that nothing might be lost: and then, at every pause in the harangue, he gurgled-out his pursy chuckle of a cough-laugh (for the machinery of laughter took some time to get in motion, and seemed crank and slack), or else his twanging nasal, *Bravo! Das glaub' ich*; in either case, by way of heartiest approval. In short, if Teufelsdröckh was Dalai-Lama, of which, except perhaps in his self-seclusion, and godlike indifference, there was no symptom, then might Heuschrecke pass for his chief Talapoin, to whom no dough-pill he could knead and publish was other than medicinal and sacred.

In such environment, social, domestic, physical, did Teufelsdröckh, at the time of our acquaintance, and most likely does he still, live and meditate. Here, perched-up in his high Wahngasse watch-tower, and often, in solitude, outwatching the Bear, it was that the indomitable Inquirer fought all his battles with Dulness and Darkness; here, in all probability, that he wrote this surprising Volume on *Clothes*. Additional particulars: of his age, which was of that standing middle sort you could only guess at; of his wide surtout; the colour of his trousers, fashion of his broad-brimmed steeple-hat, and so forth, we might report, but do not. The Wisest truly is, in these times, the Greatest; so that an enlightened curiosity, leaving Kings and suchlike to rest very much on their own basis, turns more and more to the Philosophic Class; nevertheless, what reader expects that, with all our writing and reporting, Teufelsdröckh could be brought home to him, till once the Documents arrive? His Life, Fortunes, and Bodily Presence, are as yet hidden from us, or matter only of faint conjecture. But, on the other hand, does not his Soul lie enclosed in this remarkable Volume, much more truly than Pedro Garcia's did in the buried Bag of Doubloons? To the soul of Diogenes Teufelsdröckh, to his opinions, namely, on the 'Origin and Influence of Clothes,' we for the present gladly return.

CHAPTER IV

CHARACTERISTICS

Teufelsdröckh and his Work on Clothes: Strange freedom of speech; transcendentalism; force of insight and expression; multifarious learning: Style poetic, uncouth: Comprehensiveness of his humour and moral feeling. How the Editor once saw him laugh. Different kinds of Laughter and their significance.

It were a piece of vain flattery to pretend that this Work on Clothes entirely contents us; that it is not, like all works of genius, like the very Sun, which, though the highest published creation, or work of genius, has nevertheless black spots and troubled nebulosities amid its effulgence,—a mixture of insight, inspiration, with dulness, double-vision, and even utter blindness.

Without committing ourselves to those enthusiastic praises and prophesyings of the *Weissnichtwo'sche Anzeiger*, we admitted that the Book had in a high degree excited us to self-activity, which is the best effect of any book; that it had even operated changes in our way of thought; nay, that it promised to prove, as it were, the opening of a new mine-shaft, wherein the whole world of Speculation might henceforth dig to unknown depths. More especially it may now be declared that

Professor Teufelsdröckh's acquirements, patience of research, philosophic and even poetic vigour, are here made indisputably manifest; and unhappily no less his prolixity and tortuosity and manifold ineptitude; that, on the whole, as in opening new mine-shafts is not unreasonable, there is much rubbish in his Book, though likewise specimens of almost invaluable ore. A paramount popularity in England we cannot promise him. Apart from the choice of such a topic as Clothes, too often the manner of treating it betokens in the Author a rusticity and academic seclusion, unblamable, indeed inevitable in a German, but fatal to his success with our public.

Of good society Teufelsdröckh appears to have seen little, or has mostly forgotten what he saw. He speaks-out with a strange plainness; calls many things by their mere dictionary names. To him the Upholsterer is no Pontiff, neither is any Drawing-room a Temple, were it never so begilt and overhung: 'a whole immensity of Brussels carpets, and pier-glasses, and or-molu,' as he himself expresses it, 'cannot hide from me that such Drawing-room is simply a section of Infinite Space, where so many God-created Souls do for the time meet together.' To Teufelsdröckh the highest Duchess is respectable, is venerable; but nowise for her pearl bracelets and Malines laces: in his eyes, the star of a Lord is little less and little more than the broad button of Birmingham spelter in a Clown's smock; 'each is an implement,' he says, 'in its kind; a tag for *hooking-together*; and, for the rest, was dug from the earth, and hammered on a stithy before smith's fingers.' Thus does the Professor look in men's faces with a strange impartiality, a strange scientific freedom; like a man unversed in the higher circles, like a man dropped thither from the Moon. Rightly considered, it is in this peculiarity, running through his whole system of thought, that all these short-comings, over-shootings, and multiform perversities, take rise: if indeed they have not a second source, also natural enough, in his Transcendental Philosophies, and humour of looking at all Matter and Material things as Spirit; whereby truly his case were but the more hopeless, the more lamentable.

To the Thinkers of this nation, however, of which class it is firmly believed there are individuals yet extant, we can safely recommend the Work: nay, who knows but among the fashionable ranks too, if it be true, as Teufelsdröckh maintains, that 'within the most starched cravat there passes a windpipe and weasand, and under the thickliest embroidered waistcoat beats a heart,'—the force of that rapt earnestness may be felt, and here and there an arrow of the soul pierce through? In our wild Seer, shaggy, unkempt, like a Baptist living on locusts and wild honey, there is an untutored energy, a silent, as it were unconscious, strength, which except in the higher walks of Literature, must be rare. Many a deep glance, and often with unspeakable precision, has he cast into mysterious Nature, and the still more mysterious Life of Man. Wonderful it is with what cutting words, now and then, he severs asunder the confusion; shears down, were it furlongs deep, into the true centre of the matter; and there not only hits the nail on the head, but with crushing force smites it home, and buries it.—On the other hand, let us be free to admit, he is the most unequal writer breathing. Often after some such feat, he will play truant for long pages, and go dawdling and dreaming, and mumbling and maundering the merest commonplaces, as if he were asleep with eyes open, which indeed he is.

Of his boundless Learning, and how all reading and literature in most known tongues, from *Sanchoniathon* to *Dr. Lingard*, from your Oriental *Shasters*, and *Talmuds*, and *Korans*, with Cassini's *Siamese Tables*, and Laplace's *Mécanique Céleste*, down to *Robinson Crusoe* and the *Belfast Town and Country Almanack*, are familiar to him,—we shall say nothing: for unexampled as it is with us, to the Germans such universality of study passes without wonder, as a thing commendable, indeed, but natural, indispensable, and there of course. A man that devotes his life to learning, shall he not be learned?

In respect of style our Author manifests the same genial capability, marred too often by the same rudeness, inequality, and apparent want of intercourse with the higher classes. Occasionally, as above hinted, we find consummate vigour, a true inspiration; his burning thoughts step forth in fit burning words, like so many full-formed Minervas, issuing amid flame and splendour from Jove's head; a rich, idiomatic diction, picturesque allusions, fiery poetic emphasis, or quaint tricksy turns; all the graces and terrors of a wild Imagination, wedded to the clearest Intellect, alternate in beautiful vicissitude. Were it not that sheer sleeping and soporific passages; circumlocutions, repetitions, touches even of pure doting jargon, so often intervene! On the whole, Professor Teufelsdröckh is not a cultivated writer. Of his sentences perhaps not more than nine-tenths stand straight on their legs; the remainder are in quite angular attitudes, buttressed-up by props (of parentheses and dashes), and ever with this or the other tagrag hanging from them; a few even sprawl-out helplessly on all sides, quite broken-backed and dismembered. Nevertheless, in almost his very worst moods, there lies in him a singular attraction. A wild tone pervades the whole utterance of the man, like its keynote and regulator; now screwing itself aloft as into the Song of Spirits, or else the shrill mockery of Fiends; now sinking in cadences, not without melodious heartiness, though sometimes abrupt enough, into the common pitch, when we hear it only as a monotonous hum; of which hum the true character is extremely difficult to fix. Up to this hour we have never fully satisfied ourselves whether it is a tone and hum of real Humour, which we reckon among the very highest qualities of genius, or some echo of mere Insanity and Inanity, which doubtless ranks below the very lowest.

Under a like difficulty, in spite even of our personal intercourse, do we still lie with regard to the Professor's moral feeling. Gleams of an ethereal love burst forth from him, soft wailings of infinite pity; he could clasp the whole Universe into his bosom, and keep it warm; it seems as if under that rude exterior there dwelt a very seraph. Then again he is so sly and still, so imperturbably saturnine; shows such indifference, malign coolness towards all that men strive after; and ever with some half-visible wrinkle of a bitter sardonic humour, if indeed it be not mere stolid callousness,—that you look on him almost with a shudder, as on some incarnate Mephistopheles, to whom this great terrestrial and celestial Round, after all, were but some huge foolish Whirligig, where kings and beggars, and angels and demons, and stars and street-sweepings, were chaotically whirled, in which only children could take interest. His look, as we mentioned, is probably the gravest ever seen: yet it is not of that cast-iron gravity frequent enough among our own Chancery suitors; but rather the gravity as of some silent, high-encircled mountain-pool, perhaps the crater of an extinct volcano; into whose black deeps you fear to gaze: those eyes, those lights that sparkle in it, may indeed be reflexes of the heavenly Stars, but perhaps also glances from the region of Nether Fire!

Certainly a most involved, self-secluded, altogether enigmatic nature, this of Teufelsdröckh! Here, however, we gladly recall to mind that once we saw him *laugh*; once only, perhaps it was the first and last time in his life; but then such a peal of laughter, enough to have awakened the Seven Sleepers! It was of Jean Paul's doing: some single billow in that vast World-Mahlstrom of Humour, with its heaven-kissing coruscations, which is now, alas, all congealed in the frost of death! The large-bodied Poet and the small, both large enough in soul, sat talking miscellaneously together, the present Editor being privileged to listen; and now Paul, in his serious way, was giving one of those inimitable 'Extra-harangues'; and, as it chanced, On the Proposal for a *Cast-metal King*: gradually a light kindled on our Professor's eyes and face, a beaming, mantling, loveliest light; through those murky features, a radiant, ever-young Apollo looked; and he burst forth like the neighing of all Tattersall's,—tears streaming down his cheeks, pipe held aloft, foot clutched into the air,—loud, long-continuing, uncontrollable; a laugh not of the face and diaphragm only, but of the whole man from head to heel. The present Editor, who laughed indeed, yet with measure, began to fear all was not right: however, Teufelsdröckh composed himself, and sank into his old stillness; on his inscrutable countenance there was, if anything, a slight look of shame; and Richter himself could not rouse him again. Readers who have any tincture of Psychology know how much is to be inferred from this; and that no man who has once heartily and wholly laughed can be altogether irreclaimably bad. How much lies in Laughter: the cipher-key, wherewith we decipher the whole man! Some men wear an everlasting barren simper; in the smile of others lies a cold glitter as of ice: the fewest are able to laugh, what can be called laughing, but only sniff and titter and snigger from the throat outwards; or at best, produce some whiffling husky cachinnation, as if they were laughing through wool: of none such comes good. The man who cannot laugh is not only fit for treasons, stratagems, and spoils; but his whole life is already a treason and a stratagem.

Considered as an Author, Herr Teufelsdröckh has one scarcely pardonable fault, doubtless his worst: an almost total want of arrangement. In this remarkable Volume, it is true, his adherence to the mere course of Time produces, through the Narrative portions, a certain show of outward method; but of true logical method and sequence there is too little. Apart from its multifarious sections and subdivisions, the Work naturally falls into two Parts; a Historical-Descriptive, and a Philosophical-Speculative: but falls, unhappily, by no firm line of demarcation; in that labyrinthic combination, each Part overlaps, and indents, and indeed runs quite through the other. Many sections are of a debatable rubric, or even quite nondescript and unnameable; whereby the Book not only loses in accessibility, but too often distresses us like some mad banquet, wherein all courses had been confounded, and fish and flesh, soup and solid, oyster-sauce, lettuces, Rhine-wine and French mustard, were hurled into one huge tureen or trough, and the hungry Public invited to help itself. To bring what order we can out of this Chaos shall be part of our endeavour.

CHAPTER V

THE WORLD IN CLOTHES

Futile cause-and-effect Philosophies. Teufelsdröckh's Orbis Vestitus. Clothes first invented for the sake of ornament. Picture of our progenitor, the Aboriginal Savage. Wonders of growth and progress in mankind's history. Man defined as a Tool-using Animal.

'As Montesquieu wrote a *Spirit of Laws*,' observes our Professor, 'so could I write a *Spirit of Clothes*; thus, with an *Esprit des Lois*, properly an *Esprit de Coutumes*, we should have an *Esprit de Costumes*. For neither in tailoring nor in legislating does man proceed by mere Accident, but the hand is ever guided on by mysterious operations of the mind. In all his Modes, and habilatory endeavours, an Architectural Idea will be found lurking; his Body and the Cloth are the site and materials whereon and whereby his beautified edifice, of a Person, is to be built. Whether he flow gracefully out in folded mantles, based on light sandals; tower-up in high headgear, from amid peaks, spangles and bell-girdles; swell-out in starched ruffs, buckram stuffings, and monstrous tuberosities; or girth himself into separate sections, and front the world an Agglomeration of four limbs,—will depend on the nature of such Architectural Idea: whether Grecian, Gothic, Later-Gothic, or altogether Modern, and Parisian or Anglo-Dandiacal. Again, what meaning lies in Colour! From the soberest drab to the high-flaming scarlet, spiritual idiosyncrasies unfold themselves in choice of Colour: if the Cut betoken Intellect and Talent, so does the Colour betoken Temper and Heart. In all which, among nations as among individuals, there is an incessant, indubitable, though infinitely complex working of Cause and Effect: every snip of the Scissors has been regulated and prescribed by ever-active Influences, which doubtless to Intelligences of a superior order are neither invisible nor illegible.

'For such superior Intelligences a Cause-and-Effect Philosophy of Clothes, as of Laws, were probably a comfortable winter-evening entertainment: nevertheless, for inferior Intelligences, like men, such Philosophies have always seemed to me uninstructive enough. Nay, what is your Montesquieu himself but a clever infant spelling Letters from a hieroglyphical prophetic Book, the lexicon of which lies in Eternity, in Heaven? —Let any Cause-and-Effect Philosopher explain, not why I wear such and such a Garment, obey such and such a Law; but even why *I* am *here*, to wear and obey anything!—Much, therefore, if not the whole, of that same *Spirit of Clothes* I shall suppress, as hypothetical, ineffectual, and even impertinent: naked Facts, and Deductions drawn therefrom in quite another than that omniscient style, are my humbler and proper province.'

Acting on which prudent restriction, Teufelsdröckh has nevertheless contrived to take-in a well-nigh boundless extent of field; at least, the boundaries too often lie quite beyond our horizon. Selection being indispensable, we shall here glance-over his First Part only in the most cursory manner.

This First Part is, no doubt, distinguished by omnivorous learning, and utmost patience and fairness: at the same time, in its results and delineations, it is much more likely to interest the Compilers of some *Library* of General, Entertaining, Useful, or even Useless Knowledge than the miscellaneous readers of these pages. Was it this Part of the Book which Heuschrecke had in view, when he recommended us to that joint-stock vehicle of publication, 'at present the glory of British Literature'? If so, the Library Editors are welcome to dig in it for their own behoof.

To the First Chapter, which turns on Paradise and Fig-leaves, and leads us into interminable disquisitions of a mythological, metaphorical, cabalistico-sartorial and quite antediluvian cast, we shall content ourselves with giving an unconcerned approval. Still less have we to do with 'Lilis, Adam's first wife, whom, according to the Talmudists, he had before Eve, and who bore him, in that wedlock, the whole progeny of aerial, aquatic, and terrestrial Devils,'—very needlessly, we think. On this portion of the Work, with its profound glances into the *Adam-Kadmon*, or Primeval Element, here strangely brought into relation with the *Nifl* and *Muspel* (Darkness and Light) of the antique North, it may be enough to say, that its correctness of deduction, and depth of Talmudic and Rabbinical lore have filled perhaps not the worst Hebraist in Britain with something like astonishment.

But, quitting this twilight region, Teufelsdröckh hastens from the Tower of Babel, to follow the dispersion of Mankind over the whole habitable and habilable globe. Walking by the light of Oriental, Pelasgic, Scandinavian, Egyptian, Otaheitean, Ancient and Modern researches of every conceivable kind, he strives to give us in compressed shape (as the Nürnbergers give an *Orbis Pictus*) an *Orbis Vestitus*; or view of the costumes of all mankind, in all countries, in all times. It is here that to the Antiquarian, to the Historian, we can triumphantly say: Fall to! Here is learning: an irregular Treasury, if you will; but inexhaustible as the Hoard of King Nibelung, which twelve wagons in twelve days, at the rate of three journeys a day, could not carry off. Sheepskin cloaks and wampum belts; phylacteries, stoles, albs; chlamydes, togas, Chinese silks, Afghaun shawls, trunk-hose, leather breeches, Celtic philibegs (though breeches, as the name *Gallia Braccata* indicates, are the more ancient), Hussar cloaks, Vandyke tippets, ruffs, fardingales, are brought vividly before us,—even the Kilmarnock nightcap is not forgotten. For most part, too, we must admit that the Learning, heterogeneous as it is, and tumbled-down quite pell-mell, is true concentrated and purified Learning, the drossy parts smelted out and thrown aside.

Philosophical reflections intervene, and sometimes touching pictures of human life. Of this sort the following has surprised us. The first purpose of Clothes, as our Professor imagines, was not warmth or decency, but ornament. 'Miserable indeed,' says he, 'was the condition of the Aboriginal Savage, glaring fiercely from under his fleece of hair, which with the beard reached down to his loins, and hung round him like a matted cloak; the rest of his body sheeted in its thick natural fell. He loitered in the sunny glades of the forest, living on wild-fruits; or, as the ancient Caledonian, squatted himself in morasses, lurking for his bestial or human prey; without implements, without arms, save the ball of heavy Flint, to which, that his sole possession and defence might not be lost, he had attached a long cord of plaited thongs; thereby recovering as well as hurling it with deadly unerring skill. Nevertheless, the pains of Hunger and Revenge once satisfied, his next care was not Comfort but Decoration (*Putz*). Warmth he found in the toils of the chase; or amid dried leaves, in his hollow tree, in his bark shed, or natural grotto: but for Decoration he must have Clothes. Nay, among wild people, we find tattooing and painting even prior to Clothes. The first spiritual want of a barbarous man is Decoration, as indeed we still see among the barbarous classes in civilised countries.

'Reader, the heaven-inspired melodious Singer; loftiest Serene Highness; nay thy own amber-locked, snow-and-rose-bloom Maiden, worthy to glide sylphlike almost on air, whom thou lovest, worshippest as a divine Presence, which, indeed, symbolically taken, she is,—has descended, like thyself, from that same hair-mantled, flint-hurling Aboriginal Anthropophagus! Out of the eater cometh forth meat; out of the strong cometh forth sweetness. What changes are wrought, not by Time, yet in Time! For not Mankind only, but all that Mankind does or beholds, is in continual growth, re-genesis and self-perfecting vitality. Cast forth thy Act, thy Word, into the ever-living, ever-working Universe: it is a seed-grain that cannot die; unnoticed today (says one), it will be found flourishing as a Banyan-grove (perhaps, alas, as a Hemlock-forest!) after a thousand years.

'He who first shortened the labour of Copyists by device of *Movable Types* was disbanding hired Armies, and cashiering most Kings and Senates, and creating a whole new Democratic world: he had invented the Art of Printing. The first ground handful of Nitre, Sulphur, and Charcoal drove Monk Schwartz's pestle through the ceiling: what will the last do?

Achieve the final undisputed prostration of Force under Thought, of Animal courage under Spiritual. A simple invention it was in the old-world Grazier,—sick of lugging his slow Ox about the country till he got it bartered for corn or oil,—to take a piece of Leather, and thereon scratch or stamp the mere Figure of an Ox (or *Pecus*); put it in his pocket, and call it *Pecunia*, Money. Yet hereby did Barter grow Sale, the Leather Money is now Golden and Paper, and all miracles have been out-miracled; for there are Rothschilds and English National Debts; and whoso has sixpence is sovereign (to the length of sixpence) over all men; commands cooks to feed him, philosophers to teach him, kings to mount guard over him,—to the length of sixpence.—Clothes too, which began in foolishest love of Ornament, what have they not become! Increased Security and pleasurable Heat soon followed: but what of these? Shame, divine Shame, (*Schaam*, Modesty), as yet a stranger to the Anthropophagous bosom, arose there mysteriously under Clothes; a mystic grove-encircled shrine for the Holy in man. Clothes gave us individuality, distinctions, social polity; Clothes have made Men of us; they are threatening to make Clothes-screens of us.

'But, on the whole,' continues our eloquent Professor, 'Man is a Tool-using Animal (*Handthierendes Thier*). Weak in himself, and of small stature, he stands on a basis, at most for the flattest-soled, of some half-square foot, insecurely enough; has to straddle out his legs, lest the very wind supplant him. Feeblest of bipeds! Three quintals are a crushing load for him; the steer of the meadow tosses him aloft, like a waste rag. Nevertheless he can use Tools, can devise Tools: with these the granite mountain melts into light dust before him; he kneads glowing iron, as if it were soft paste; seas are his smooth highway, winds and fire his unwearying steeds. Nowhere do you find him without Tools: without Tools he is nothing, with Tools he is all.'

Here may we not, for a moment, interrupt the stream of Oratory with a remark, that this Definition of the Tool-using Animal appears to us, of all that Animal-sort, considerably the precisest and best? Man is called a Laughing Animal: but do not the apes also laugh, or attempt to do it; and is the manliest man the greatest and oftenest laugher? Teufelsdröckh himself, as we said, laughed only once. Still less do we make of that other French Definition of the Cooking Animal; which, indeed, for rigorous scientific purposes, is as good as useless. Can a Tartar be said to cook, when he only readies his steak by riding on it? Again, what Cookery does the Greenlander use, beyond stowing-up his whale-blubber, as a marmot, in the like case, might do? Or how would Monsieur Ude prosper among those Orinocco Indians who, according to Humboldt, lodge in crow-nests, on the branches of trees; and, for half the year, have no victuals but pipe-clay, the whole country being under water? But, on the other hand, show us the human being, of any period or climate, without his Tools: those very Caledonians, as we saw, had their Flint-ball, and Thong to it, such as no brute has or can have.

'Man is a Tool-using Animal,' concludes Teufelsdröckh in his abrupt way; 'of which truth Clothes are but one example: and surely if we consider the interval between the first wooden Dibble fashioned by man, and those Liverpool Steam-carriages, or the British House of Commons, we shall note what progress he has made. He digs up certain black stones from the bosom of the earth, and says to them, *Transport me and this luggage at the rate of five-and-thirty miles an hour*; and they do it: he collects, apparently by lot, six-hundred and fifty-eight miscellaneous individuals, and says to them, *Make this nation toil for us, bleed for us, hunger and sorrow and sin for us*; and they do it.'

CHAPTER VI

APRONS

Divers Aprons in the world with divers uses. The Military and Police Establishment Society's working Apron. The Episcopal Apron with its corner tucked in. The Laystall. Journalists now our only Kings and Clergy.

ONE of the most unsatisfactory Sections in the whole Volume is that on *Aprons*. What though stout old Gao, the Persian Blacksmith, 'whose Apron, now indeed hidden under jewels, because raised in revolt which proved successful, is still the royal standard of that country'; what though John Knox's Daughter, 'who threatened Sovereign Majesty that she would catch her husband's head in her Apron, rather than he should lie and be a bishop'; what though the Landgravine Elizabeth, with many other Apron worthies,—figure here? An idle wire-drawing spirit, sometimes even a tone of levity, approaching to conventional satire, is too clearly discernible. What, for example, are we to make of such sentences as the following?

'Aprons are Defences; against injury to cleanliness, to safety, to modesty, sometimes to roguery. From the thin slip of notched silk (as it were, the emblem and beatified ghost of an Apron), which some highest-bred housewife, sitting at Nürnberg Workboxes and Toyboxes, has gracefully fastened on; to the thick-tanned hide, girt round him with thongs, wherein the Builder builds, and at evening sticks his trowel; or to those jingling sheet-iron Aprons, wherein your otherwise half-naked Vulcans hammer and smelt in their smelt-furnace,—is there not range enough in the fashion and uses of this Vestment? How much has been concealed, how much has been defended in Aprons! Nay, rightly considered, what is your whole Military and Police Establishment, charged at uncalculated millions, but a huge scarlet-coloured, iron-fastened Apron, wherein Society works (uneasily enough); guarding itself from some soil and stithy-sparks, in this Devil's-smithy (*Teufelsschmiede*) of a world? But of all Aprons the most puzzling to me hitherto has been the Episcopal or Cassock. Wherein consists the usefulness of this Apron? The Overseer (*Episcopus*) of Souls, I notice, has tucked in the corner of it, as if his day's work were done: what does he shadow forth thereby?' &c. &c.

Or again, has it often been the lot of our readers to read such stuff as we shall now quote?

'I consider those printed Paper Aprons, worn by the Parisian Cooks, as a new vent, though a slight one, for Typography; therefore as an encouragement to modern Literature, and deserving of approval; nor is it without satisfaction that I hear of a celebrated London Firm having in view to introduce the same fashion, with important extensions, in England.'—We who are on the spot hear of no such thing; and indeed have reason to be thankful that hitherto there are other vents for our Literature, exuberant as it is.—Teufelsdröckh continues: 'If such supply of printed Paper should rise so far as to choke-up the highways and public thoroughfares, new means must of necessity be had recourse to. In a world existing by Industry, we grudge to employ fire as a destroying element, and not as a creating one. However, Heaven is omnipotent, and will find us an outlet. In the mean while, is it not beautiful to see five-million quintals of Rags picked annually from the Laystall; and annually, after being macerated, hot-pressed, printed-on, and sold,—returned thither; filling so many hungry mouths by the way? Thus is the Laystall, especially with its Rags or Clothes-rubbish, the grand Electric Battery, and Fountain-of-motion, from which and to which the Social Activities (like vitreous and resinous Electricities) circulate, in larger or smaller circles, through the mighty billowy, stormtost Chaos of Life, which they keep alive!'—Such passages fill us, who love the man, and partly esteem him, with a very mixed feeling.

Farther down we meet with this: 'The Journalists are now the true Kings and Clergy: henceforth Historians, unless they are fools, must write not of Bourbon Dynasties, and Tudors and Hapsburgs; but of Stamped Broad-sheet Dynasties, and quite new successive Names, according as this or the other Able Editor, or Combination of Able Editors, gains the world's ear. Of the British Newspaper Press, perhaps the most important of all, and wonderful enough in its secret constitution and procedure, a valuable descriptive History already exists, in that language, under the title of *Satan's Invisible World Displayed*; which, however, by search in all the Weissnichtwo Libraries, I have not yet succeeded in procuring (*vermöchte nicht aufzutreiben*).'

Thus does the good Homer not only nod, but snore. Thus does Teufelsdröckh, wandering in regions where he had little business, confound the old authentic Presbyterian Witch-finder with a new, spurious, imaginary Historian of the *Brittische Journalistik*; and so stumble on perhaps the most egregious blunder in Modern Literature!

CHAPTER VII

MISCELLANEOUS-HISTORICAL

How Men and Fashions come and go. German Costume in the fifteenth century. By what strange chances do we live in History! The costume of Bolivar's Cavalry.

HAPPIER is our Professor, and more purely scientific and historic, when he reaches the Middle Ages in Europe, and down to the end of the Seventeenth Century; the true era of extravagance in Costume. It is here that the Antiquary and Student of Modes comes upon his richest harvest. Fantastic garbs, beggaring all fancy of a Teniers or a Callot, succeeded each other, like monster devouring monster in a Dream. The whole too in brief authentic strokes, and touched not seldom with that breath of genius which makes even old raiment live. Indeed, so learned, precise, graphical, and everyway interesting have we found these Chapters, that it may be thrown-out as a pertinent question for parties concerned, Whether or not a good English translation thereof might henceforth be profitably incorporated with Mr. Merrick's valuable Work *On Ancient Armour*? Take, by way of example, the following sketch; as authority for which Paulinus's *Zeitkürzende Lust* (ii. 678) is, with seeming confidence, referred to:

'Did we behold the German fashionable dress of the Fifteenth Century, we might smile; as perhaps those bygone Germans, were they to rise again, and see our haberdashery, would cross themselves, and invoke the Virgin. But happily no bygone German, or man, rises again; thus the Present is not needlessly trammelled with the Past; and only grows out of it, like a Tree, whose roots are not intertangled with its branches, but lie peaceably underground. Nay it is very mournful, yet not useless, to see and know, how the Greatest and Dearest, in a short while, would find his place quite filled-up here, and no room for him; the very Napoleon, the very Byron, in some seven years, has become obsolete, and were now a foreigner to his Europe. This is the law of Progress secured; and in Clothes, as in all other external things whatsoever, no fashion will continue.

'Of the military classes in those old times, whose buff-belts, complicated chains and gorgets, huge churn-boots, and other riding and fighting gear have been bepainted in modern Romance, till the whole has acquired somewhat of a sign-post character.—I shall here say nothing: the civil and pacific classes, less touched upon, are wonderful enough for us.

'Rich men, I find, have *Teusinke*' (a perhaps untranslateable article); 'also a silver girdle, whereat hang little bells; so that when a man walks, it is with continual jingling. Some few, of musical turn, have a whole chime of bells (*Glockenspiel*) fastened there; which, especially in sudden whirls, and the other accidents of walking, has a grateful effect. Observe too how fond they are of peaks, and Gothic-arch intersections. The male world wears peaked caps, an ell long, which hang bobbing over the side (*schief*): their shoes are peaked in front, also to the length of an ell, and laced on the side with tags; even the wooden shoes have their ell-long noses: some also clap bells on the peak. Further, according to my authority, the men have breeches without seat (*ohne Gesäss*): these they fasten peakwise to their shirts; and the long round doublet must overlap them.

'Rich maidens, again, flit abroad in gowns scolloped out behind and before, so that back and breast are almost bare. Wives of quality, on the other hand, have train-gowns four or five ells in length; which trains there are boys to carry. Brave Cleopatras, sailing in their silk-cloth Galley, with a Cupid for steersman! Consider their welts, a handbreadth thick, which waver round them by way of hem; the long flood of silver buttons, or rather silver shells, from throat to shoe, wherewith these same welt-gowns are buttoned. The maidens have bound silver snoods about their hair, with gold spangles, and pendent flames (*Flammen*), that is, sparkling hair-drops: but of their mother's headgear who shall speak? Neither in love of grace is comfort forgotten. In winter weather you behold the whole fair creation (that can afford it) in long mantles, with skirts wide below, and, for hem, not one but two sufficient hand-broad welts; all ending atop in a thick well-starched Ruff, some twenty inches broad: these are their Ruff-mantles (*Kragenmäntel*).

'As yet among the womankind hoop-petticoats are not; but the men have doublets of fustian, under which lie multiple ruffs of cloth, pasted together with batter (*mit Teig zusammengekleistert*), which create protuberance enough. Thus do the two sexes vie with each other in the art of Decoration; and as usual the stronger carries it.'

Our Professor, whether he have humour himself or not, manifests a certain feeling of the Ludicrous, a sly observance of it, which, could emotion of any kind be confidently predicated of so still a man, we might call a real love. None of those bell-girdles, bushel-breeches, cornuted shoes, or other the like phenomena, of which the History of Dress offers so many, escape him: more especially the mischances, or striking adventures, incident to the wearers of such, are noticed with due fidelity. Sir Walter Raleigh's fine mantle, which he spread in the mud under Queen Elizabeth's feet, appears to provoke little enthusiasm in him; he merely asks, Whether at that period the Maiden Queen 'was red-painted on the nose, and white-painted on the cheeks, as her tirewomen, when from spleen and wrinkles she would no longer look in any glass, were wont to serve her?' We can answer that Sir Walter knew well what he was doing, and had the Maiden Queen been stuffed parchment dyed in verdigris, would have done the same.

Thus too, treating of those enormous habiliments, that were not only slashed and galooned, but artificially swollen-out on the broader parts of the body, by introduction of Bran,—our Professor fails not to comment on that luckless Courtier, who having seated himself on a chair with some projecting nail on it, and therefrom rising, to pay his *devoir* on the entrance of Majesty, instantaneously emitted several pecks of dry wheat-dust: and stood there diminished to a spindle, his galoons and slashes dangling sorrowful and flabby round him. Whereupon the Professor publishes this reflection:

'By what strange chances do we live in History? Erostratus by a torch; Milo by a bullock; Henry Darnley, an unfledged booby and bustard, by his limbs; most Kings and Queens by being born under such and such a bed-tester; Boileau Despréaux (according to Helvetius) by the peck of a turkey; and this ill-starred individual by a rent in his breeches,—for no Memoirist of Kaiser Otto's Court omits him. Vain was the prayer of Themistocles for a talent of Forgetting: my Friends, yield cheerfully to Destiny, and read since it is written.'—Has Teufelsdröckh to be put in mind that, nearly related to the impossible talent of Forgetting, stands that talent of Silence, which even travelling Englishmen manifest?

'The simplest costume,' observes our Professor, 'which I anywhere find alluded to in History, is that used as regimental, by Bolivar's Cavalry, in the late Columbian wars. A square Blanket, twelve feet in diagonal, is provided (some were wont to cut-off the corners, and make it circular): in the centre a slit is effected eighteen inches long; through this the mother-naked Trooper introduces his head and neck; and so rides shielded from all weather, and in battle from many strokes (for he rolls it about his left arm); and not only dressed, but harnessed and draperied.'

With which picture of a State of Nature, affecting by its singularity, and Old-Roman contempt of the superfluous, we shall quit this part of our subject.

CHAPTER VIII

THE WORLD OUT OF CLOTHES

Teufelsdröckh's Theorem, 'Society founded upon Cloth'; his Method, Intuition quickened by Experience.—The mysterious question, Who am I? Philosophic systems all at fault: A deeper meditation has always taught, here and there an individual, that all visible things are appearances only; but also emblems and revelations of God. Teufelsdröckh first comes upon the question of Clothes: Baseness to which Clothing may bring us.

If in the Descriptive-Historical portion of this Volume, Teufelsdröckh, discussing merely the *Werden* (Origin and successive Improvement) of Clothes, has astonished many a reader, much more will he in the Speculative-Philosophical portion, which treats of their *Wirken*, or Influences. It is here that the present Editor first feels the pressure of his task; for here properly the higher and new Philosophy of Clothes commences: an untried, almost inconceivable region, or chaos; in venturing upon which, how difficult, yet how unspeakably important is it to know what course, of survey and conquest, is the true one; where the footing is firm substance and will bear us, where it is hollow, or mere cloud, and may engulf us! Teufelsdröckh undertakes no less than to expound the moral, political, even religious Influences of Clothes; he undertakes to make manifest, in its thousandfold bearings, this grand Proposition, that Man's earthly interests, 'are all hooked and buttoned together, and held up, by Clothes.' He says in so many words, 'Society is founded upon Cloth'; and again, 'Society sails through the Infinitude on Cloth, as on a Faust's Mantle, or rather like the Sheet of clean and unclean beasts in the Apostle's Dream; and without such Sheet or Mantle, would sink to endless depths, or mount to inane limboes, and in either case be no more.'

By what chains, or indeed infinitely complected tissues, of meditation this grand Theorem is here unfolded, and innumerable practical Corollaries are drawn therefrom, it were perhaps a mad ambition to attempt exhibiting. Our Professor's method is not, in any case, that of common school Logic, where the truths all stand in a row, each holding by the skirts of the other; but at best that of practical Reason, proceeding by large Intuition over whole systematic groups and kingdoms; whereby, we might say, a noble complexity, almost like that of Nature, reigns in his Philosophy, or spiritual Picture of Nature: a mighty maze, yet, as faith whispers, not without a plan. Nay we complained above, that a certain ignoble complexity, what we must call mere confusion, was also discernible. Often, also, we have to exclaim: Would to Heaven those same Biographical Documents were come! For it seems as if the demonstration lay much in the Author's individuality; as if it were not Argument that had taught him, but Experience. At present it is only in local glimpses, and by significant fragments, picked often at wide-enough intervals from the original Volume, and carefully collated, that we can hope to impart some outline or foreshadow of this Doctrine. Readers of any intelligence are once more invited to favour us with their most concentrated attention: let these, after intense consideration, and not till then, pronounce, Whether on the utmost verge of our actual horizon there is not a looming as of Land; a promise of new Fortunate Islands, perhaps whole undiscovered Americas, for such as have canvas to sail thither?—As exordium to the whole, stand here the following long citation:

'With men of a speculative turn,' writes Teufelsdröckh, there come seasons, meditative, sweet, yet awful hours, when in wonder and fear you ask yourself that unanswerable question: Who am *I*; the thing that can say "I" (*das Wesen das sich* Ich *nennt*)? The world, with its loud trafficking, retires into the distance; and, through the paper-hangings, and stone-walls, and thick-plied tissues of Commerce and Polity, and all the living and lifeless integuments (of Society and a Body), wherewith your Existence sits surrounded,—the sight reaches forth into the void Deep, and you are alone with the Universe, and silently commune with it, as one mysterious Presence with another.

'Who am I; what is this ME? A Voice, a Motion, an Appearance;—some embodied, visualised Idea in the Eternal Mind? *Cogito, ergo sum.* Alas, poor Cogitator, this takes us but a little way. Sure enough, I am; and lately was not: but Whence? How? Whereto? The answer lies around, written in all colours and motions, uttered in all tones of jubilee and wail, in thousand-figured, thousand-voiced, harmonious Nature: but where is the cunning eye and ear to whom that God-written Apocalypse will yield articulate meaning? We sit as in a boundless Phantasmagoria and Dream-grotto; boundless, for the faintest star, the remotest century, lies not even nearer the verge thereof: sounds and many-coloured visions flit round our sense; but Him, the Unslumbering, whose work both Dream and Dreamer are, we see not; except in rare half-waking moments, suspect not. Creation, says one, lies before us, like a glorious Rainbow; but the Sun that made it lies behind us, hidden from us. Then, in that strange Dream, how we clutch at shadows as if they were substances; and sleep deepest while fancying ourselves most awake! Which of your Philosophical Systems is other than a dream-theorem; a net quotient, confidently given out, where divisor and dividend are both unknown? What are all your national Wars, with their Moscow Retreats, and sanguinary hate-filled Revolutions, but the Somnambulism of uneasy Sleepers? This Dreaming, this Somnambulism is what we on Earth call Life; wherein the most indeed undoubtedly wander, as if they knew right hand from left; yet they only are wise who know that they know nothing.

'Pity that all Metaphysics had hitherto proved so inexpressibly unproductive! The secret of Man's Being is still like the Sphinx's secret: a riddle that he cannot rede; and for ignorance of which he suffers death, the worst death, a spiritual. What are your Axioms, and Categories, and Systems, and Aphorisms? Words, words. High Air-castles are cunningly built of Words, the Words well bedded also in good Logic-mortar; wherein, however, no Knowledge will come to lodge. *The whole is greater than the part*: how exceedingly true! *Nature abhors a vacuum*: how exceedingly false and calumnious! Again, *Nothing can act but where it is*: with all my heart; only, WHERE is it? Be not the slave of Words: is not the Distant, the Dead, while I love it, and long for it, and mourn for it, Here, in the genuine sense, as truly as the floor I stand on? But that same WHERE, with its brother WHEN, are from the first the master-colours of our Dream-grotto; say rather, the Canvas (the warp and woof thereof) whereon all our Dreams and Life-visions are painted. Nevertheless, has not a deeper meditation taught certain of every climate and age, that the WHERE and WHEN, so mysteriously inseparable from all our thoughts, are but superficial terrestrial adhesions to thought; that the Seer may discern them where they mount up out of the celestial EVERYWHERE and FOREVER: have not all nations conceived their God as Omnipresent and Eternal; as existing in a universal HERE, an everlasting Now? Think well, thou too wilt find that Space is but a mode of our human Sense, so likewise Time; there *is* no Space and no Time: WE are—we know not what;—light-sparkles floating in the æther of Diety!

'So that this so solid-seeming World, after all, were but an air-image, our ME the only reality: and Nature, with its thousandfold production and destruction, but the reflex of our own inward Force, the "phantasy of our Dream"; or what the Earth-Spirit in *Faust* names it, *the living visible Garment of God*:

' "In Being's floods, in Action's storm,
I walk and work, above, beneath,
Work and weave in endless motion!
Birth and Death,
An infinite ocean;
A seizing and giving
The fire of Living:
'Tis thus at the roaring Loom of Time I ply,
And weave for God the Garment thou seest Him by."

Of twenty millions that have read and spouted this thunder-speech of the *Erdgeist*, are there yet twenty units of us that have learned the meaning thereof?

'It was in some such mood, when wearied and fordone with these high speculations, that I first came upon the question of Clothes. Strange enough, it strikes me, is this same fact of there being Tailors and Tailored. The Horse I ride has his own whole fell: strip him of the girths and flaps and extraneous tags I have fastened round him, and the noble creature is his own sempster and weaver and spinner; nay his own bootmaker, jeweller, and man-milliner; he bounds free through the valleys, with a perennial rainproof court-suit on his body; wherein warmth and easiness of fit have reached perfection; nay, the graces also have been considered, and frills and fringes, with gay variety of colour, featly appended, and ever in the right place, are not wanting. While I—good Heaven!—have thatched myself over with the dead fleeces of sheep, the bark of vegetables, the entrails of worms, the hides of oxen or seals, the felt of furred beasts; and walk abroad a moving Rag-screen, overheaped with shreds and tatters raked from the Charnel-house of Nature, where they would have rotted, to rot on me more slowly! Day after day, I must thatch myself anew; day after day, this despicable thatch must lose some film of its thickness; some film of it, frayed away by tear and wear, must be brushed-off into the Ashpit, into the Laystall; till by degrees the whole has been brushed thither, and I, the dust-making, patent Rag-grinder, get new material to grind down. O subter-brutish! vile! most vile! For have not I too a compact all-enclosing Skin, whiter or dingier? Am I a botched mass of tailors' and cobblers' shreds, then; or a tightly-articulated, homogeneous little Figure, automatic, nay alive?

'Strange enough how creatures of the human-kind shut their eyes to plainest facts; and by the mere inertia of Oblivion and Stupidity, live at ease in the midst of Wonders and Terrors. But indeed man is, and was always, a blockhead and dullard; much readier to feel and digest, than to think and consider. Prejudice, which he pretends to hate, is his absolute lawgiver; mere use-and-wont everywhere leads him by the nose; thus let but a Rising of the Sun, let but a Creation of the World happen *twice*, and it ceases to be marvellous, to be noteworthy, or noticeable. Perhaps not once in a lifetime does it occur to your ordinary biped, of any country or generation, be he gold-mantled Prince, or russet-jerkined Peasant, that his Vestments and his Self are not one and indivisible; that *he* is naked, without vestments, till he buy or steal such, and by forethought sew and button them.

'For my own part, these considerations, of our Clothes-thatch, and how, reaching inwards even to our heart of hearts, it tailorises and demoralises us, fill me with a certain horror at myself and mankind; almost as one feels at those Dutch Cows, which, during the wet season, you see grazing deliberately with jackets and petticoats (of striped sacking), in the meadows of Gouda. Nevertheless there is something great in the moment when a man first strips himself of adventitious wrappages; and sees indeed that he is naked, and, as Swift has it, "a forked straddling animal with bandy legs"; yet also a Spirit, and unutterable Mystery of Mysteries.'

CHAPTER IX

ADAMITISM

The universal utility of Clothes, and their higher mystic virtue, illustrated. Conception of Mankind stripped naked; and immediate consequent dissolution of civilised Society.

Let no courteous reader take offence at the opinions broached in the conclusion of the last Chapter. The Editor himself, on first glancing over that singular passage, was inclined to exclaim: What, have we got not only a Sansculottist, but an enemy to Clothes in the abstract? A new Adamite, in this century, which flatters itself that it is the Nineteenth, and destructive both to Superstition and Enthusiasm?

Consider, thou foolish Teufelsdröckh, what benefits unspeakable all ages and sexes derive from Clothes. For example, when thou thyself, a watery, pulpy, slobbery freshman and new-comer in this Planet, sattest muling and puking in thy nurse's arms; sucking thy coral, and looking forth into the world in the blankest manner, what hadst thou been without thy blankets, and bibs, and other nameless hulls? A terror to thyself and mankind! Or hast thou forgotten the day when thou first receivedst breeches, and thy long clothes became short? The village where thou livedst was all apprised of the fact; and neighbour after neighbour kissed thy pudding-cheek, and gave thee, as handsel, silver or copper coins, on that the first gala-day of thy existence. Again, wert not thou, at one period of life, a Buck, or Blood, or Macaroni, or Incroyable, or Dandy, or by whatever name, according to year and place, such phenomenon is distinguished? In that one word lie included mysterious volumes. Nay, now when the reign of folly is over, or altered, and thy clothes are not for triumph but for defence, hast thou always worn them perforce, and as a consequence of Man's Fall; never rejoiced in them as in a warm movable House, a Body round thy Body, wherein that strange THEE of thine sat snug, defying all variations of Climate? Girt with thick double-milled kerseys; half-buried under shawls and broadbrims, and overalls and mud-boots, thy very fingers cased in doeskin and mittens, thou hast bestrode that 'Horse I ride'; and, though it were in wild winter, dashed through the world, glorying in it as if thou wert its lord. In vain did the sleet beat round thy temples; it lighted only on thy impenetrable, felted or woven, case of wool. In vain did the winds howl,—forests sounding and creaking, deep calling unto deep,—and the storms heap themselves together into one huge Arctic whirlpool: thou flewest through the middle thereof, striking fire from the highway; wild music hummed in thy ears, thou too wert as a 'sailor of the air'; the wreck of matter and the crash of worlds was thy element and propitiously wafting tide. Without Clothes, without bit or saddle, what hadst thou been; what had thy fleet quadruped been?—Nature is good, but she is not the best: here truly was the victory of Art over Nature. A thunderbolt indeed might have pierced thee; all short of this thou couldst defy.

Or, cries the courteous reader, has your Teufelsdröckh forgotten what he said lately about 'Aboriginal Savages,' and their 'condition miserable indeed'? Would he have all this unsaid; and us betake ourselves again to the 'matted cloak,' and go sheeted in a 'thick natural fell'?

Nowise, courteous reader! The Professor knows full well what he is saying; and both thou and we, in our haste, do him wrong. If Clothes, in these times, 'so tailorise and demoralise us,' have they no redeeming value; can they not be altered to serve better; must they of necessity be thrown to the dogs? The truth is, Teufelsdröckh, though a Sansculottist, is no Adamite; and much perhaps as he might wish to go forth before this degenerate age 'as a Sign,' would nowise wish to do it, as those old Adamites did, in a state of Nakedness. The ultility of Clothes is altogether apparent to him: nay perhaps he has an insight into their more recondite, and almost mystic qualities, what we might call the omnipotent virtue of Clothes, such as was never before vouchsafed to any man. For example:

'You see two individuals,' he writes, 'one dressed in fine Red, the other in coarse threadbare Blue: Red says to Blue, "Be hanged and anatomised"; Blue hears with a shudder, and (O wonder of wonders!) marches sorrowfully to the gallows; is there noosed-up, vibrates his hour, and the surgeons dissect him, and fit his bones into a skeleton for medical purposes. How is this; or what make ye of your *Nothing can act but where it is*? Red has no physical hold of Blue, no *clutch* of him, is nowise in *contact* with him: neither are those ministering Sheriffs and Lord-Lieutenants and Hangmen and Tipstaves so related to commanding Red, that he can tug them hither and thither; but each stands distinct within his own skin. Nevertheless, as it is spoken, so is it done: the articulated Word sets all hands in Action; and Rope and Improved-drop perform their work.

'Thinking reader, the reason seems to me twofold: First, that *Man is a Spirit,* and bound by invisible bonds to *All Men*; secondly, that *he wears Clothes,* which are the visible emblems of that fact. Has not your Red hanging-individual a horsehair wig, squirrel-skins, and a plush-gown; whereby all mortals know that he is a JUDGE?—Society, which the more I think of it astonishes me the more, is founded upon Cloth.

'Often in my atrabiliar moods, when I read of pompous ceremonials, Frankfort Coronations, Royal Drawing-rooms, Levees, Couchees; and how the ushers and macers and pursuivants are all in waiting; how Duke this is presented by Archduke that, and Colonel A by General B, and innumerable Bishops, Admirals, and miscellaneous Functionaries, are advancing gallantly to the Anointed Presence; and I strive, in my remote privacy, to form a clear picture of that solemnity,—on a sudden, as by some enchanter's wand, the—shall I speak it?—the Clothes fly-off the whole dramatic corps; and Dukes, Grandees, Bishops, Generals, Anointed Presence itself, every mother's son of them, stand straddling there, not a shirt on them; and I know not whether to laugh or weep. This physical or psychical infirmity, in which perhaps I am not singular, I have, after hesitation, thought right to publish, for the solace of those afflicted with the like.'

Would to Heaven, say we, thou hadst thought right to keep it secret! Who is there now that can read the five columns of Presentations in his Morning Newspaper without a shudder? Hypochondriac men, and all men are to a certain extent hypochondriac, should be more gently treated. With what readiness our fancy, in this shattered state of the nerves, follows out the consequences which Teufelsdröckh, with a devilish coolness, goes on to draw:

'What would Majesty do, could such an accident befall in reality; should the buttons all simultaneously start, and the solid wool evaporate, in very Deed, as here in Dream? *Ach Gott!* How each skulks into the nearest hiding-place; their high State Tragedy (*Haupt- und Staats-Action*) becomes a Pickle-herring-Farce to weep at, which is the worst kind of Farce; *the tables* (according to Horace), and with them, the whole fabric of Government, Legislation, Property, Police, and Civilised Society, *are dissolved*, in wails and howls.'

Lives the man that can figure a naked Duke of Windlestraw addressing a naked House of Lords? Imagination, choked as in mephitic air, recoils on itself, and will not forward with the picture. The Woolsack, the Ministerial, the Opposition Benches—*infandum! infandum!* And yet why is the thing impossible? Was not every soul, or rather every body, of these Guardians of our Liberties, naked, or nearly so, last night; 'a forked Radish with a head fantastically carved'? And why might he not, did our stern fate so order it, walk out to St. Stephen's, as well as into bed, in that no-fashion; and there, with other similar Radishes, hold a Bed of Justice? 'Solace of those afflicted with the like!' Unhappy Teufelsdröckh, had man ever such a 'physical or psychical infirmity' before? And now how many, perhaps, may thy unparalleled confession (which we, even to the sounder British world, and goaded-on by Critical and Biographical duty, grudge to reimpart) incurably infect therewith! Art thou the malignest of Sansculottists, or only the maddest?

'It will remain to be examined,' adds the inexorable Teufelsdröckh, 'in how far the Scarecrow, as a Clothed Person, is not also entitled to benefit of clergy, and English trial by jury: nay perhaps, considering his high function (for is not he too a Defender of Property, and Sovereign armed with the *terrors* of the Law?), to a certain royal Immunity and Inviolability; which, however, misers and the meaner class of persons are not always voluntarily disposed to grant him.' * * * * 'O my friends, we are (in Yorick Sterne's words) but as "turkeys driven, with a stick and red clout, to the market": or if some drivers, as they do in Norfolk, take a dried bladder and put peas in it, the rattle thereof terrifies the boldest!'

CHAPTER X

PURE REASON

A Naked World possible, nay actually exists, under the clothed one. Man, in the eye of Pure Reason, a visible God's Presence. The beginning of all wisdom, to look fixedly on Clothes till they become transparent. Wonder, the basis of Worship: Perennial in man. Modern Sciolists who cannot wonder: Teufelsdröckh's contempt for, and advice to them.

It must now be apparent enough that our Professor, as above hinted, is a speculative Radical, and of the very darkest tinge; acknowledging, for most part, in the solemnities and paraphernalia of civilised Life, which we make so much of, nothing but so many Cloth-rags, turkey-poles, and 'bladders with dried peas.' To linger among such speculations, longer than mere Science requires, a discerning public can have no wish. For our purposes the simple fact that such a *Naked World* is possible, nay actually exists (under the Clothed one), will be sufficient. Much, therefore, we omit about 'Kings wrestling naked on the green with Carmen,' and the Kings being thrown: 'dissect them with scalpels,' says Teufelsdröckh; 'the same viscera, tissues, livers, lights, and other life-tackle, are there: examine their spiritual mechanism; the same great Need, great Greed, and little Faculty; nay ten to one but the Carman, who understands draught-cattle, the rimming of wheels, something of the laws of unstable and stable equilibrium, with other branches of wagon-science, and has actually put forth his hand and operated on Nature, is the more cunningly gifted of the two. Whence, then, their so unspeakable difference? From Clothes.' Much also we shall omit about confusion of Ranks, and Joan and My Lady, and how it would be everywhere 'Hail fellow well met,' and Chaos were come again: all which to any one that has once fairly pictured-out the grand mother-idea, *Society in a state of Nakedness*, will spontaneously suggest itself. Should some sceptical individual still entertain doubts whether in a world without Clothes, the smallest Politeness, Polity, or even Police, could exist, let him turn to the original Volume, and view there the boundless Serbonian Bog of Sansculottism, stretching sour and pestilential: over which we have lightly flown; where not only whole armies but whole nations might sink! If indeed the following argument, in its brief riveting emphasis, be not of itself incontrovertible and final:

'Are we Opossums; have we natural Pouches, like the Kangaroo? Or how, without Clothes, could we possess the master-organ, soul's seat, and true pineal gland of the Body Social: I mean, a Purse?'

Nevertheless it is impossible to hate Professor Teufelsdröckh; at worst, one knows not whether to hate or to love him. For though, in looking at the fair tapestry of human Life, with its royal and even sacred figures, he dwells not on the obverse alone, but here chiefly on the reverse; and indeed turns out the rough seams, tatters, and manifold thrums of that unsightly wrong-side, with an almost diabolic patience and indifference, which must have sunk him in the estimation of most readers,—there is that within which unspeakably distinguishes him from all other past and present Sansculottists. The grand unparalleled peculiarity of Teufelsdröckh is, that with all this Descendentalism, he combines a Transcendentalism, no less superlative; whereby if on the one hand he degrade man below most animals, except those jacketed Gouda Cows, he, on the other, exalts him beyond the visible Heavens, almost to an equality with the Gods.

'To the eye of vulgar Logic,' says he, 'what is man? An omnivorous Biped that wears Breeches. To the eye of Pure Reason what is he? A Soul, a Spirit, and divine Apparition. Round his mysterious Me, there lies, under all those wool-rags, a Garment of Flesh (or of Senses), contextured in the Loom of Heaven; whereby he is revealed to his like, and dwells with them in Union and Division; and sees and fashions for himself a Universe, with azure Starry Spaces, and long Thousands of Years. Deep-hidden is he under that strange Garment; amid Sounds and Colours and Forms, as it were, swathed-in, and inextricably over-shrouded: yet it is sky-woven, and worthy of a God. Stands he not thereby in the centre of Immensities, in the conflux of Eternities? He feels; power has been given him to know, to believe; nay does not the spirit of Love, free in its celestial primeval brightness, even here, though but for moments, look through? Well said Saint Chrysostom, with his lips of gold, "the true SHEKINAH is Man": where else is the GOD's-PRESENCE manifested not to our eyes only, but to our hearts, as in our fellow-man?'

In such passages, unhappily too rare, the high Platonic Mysticism of our Author, which is perhaps the fundamental element of his nature, bursts forth, as it were, in full flood: and, through all the vapour and tarnish of what is often so perverse, so mean in his exterior and environment, we seem to look into a whole inward Sea of Light and Love;—though, alas, the grim coppery clouds soon roll together again, and hide it from view.

Such tendency to Mysticism is everywhere traceable in this man; and indeed, to attentive readers, must have been long ago apparent. Nothing that he sees but has more than a common meaning, but has two meanings: thus, if in the highest Imperial Sceptre and Charlemagne-Mantle, as well as in the poorest Ox-goad and Gipsy-Blanket, he finds Prose, Decay, Contemptibility; there is in each sort Poetry also, and a reverend Worth. For Matter, were it never so despicable, is Spirit, the manifestation of Spirit: were it never so honourable, can it be more? The thing Visible, nay the thing Imagined, the thing in any way conceived as Visible, what is it but a Garment, a Clothing of the higher, celestial Invisible, 'unimaginable, formless, dark with excess of bright'? Under which point of view the following passage, so strange in purport, so strange in phrase, seems characteristic enough:

'The beginning of all Wisdom is to look fixedly on Clothes, or even with armed eyesight, till they become *transparent.* "The Philosopher," says the wisest of this age, "must station himself in the middle": how true! The Philosopher is he to whom the Highest has descended, and the Lowest has mounted up; who is the equal and kindly brother of all.

'Shall we tremble before clothwebs and cobwebs, whether woven in Arkwright looms, or by the silent Arachnes that weave unrestingly in our imagination? Or, on the other hand, what is there that we cannot love; since all was created by God?

'Happy he who can look through the Clothes of a Man (the woollen, and fleshly, and official Bank-paper and State-paper Clothes) into the Man himself; and discern, it may be, in this or the other Dread Potentate, a more or less incompetent Digestive-apparatus; yet also an inscrutable venerable mystery, in the meanest Tinker that sees with eyes!'

For the rest, as is natural to a man of this kind, he deals much in the feeling of Wonder; insists on the necessity and high worth of universal Wonder; which he holds to be the only reasonable temper for the denizen of so singular a Planet as ours. 'Wonder,' says he, 'is the basis of Worship: the reign of wonder is perennial, indestructible in Man; only at certain stages (as the present), it is, for some short season, a reign *in partibus infidelium.*' That progress of Science, which is to destroy Wonder, and in its stead substitute Mensuration and Numeration, finds small favour with Teufelsdröckh, much as he otherwise venerates these two latter processes.

'Shall your Science,' exclaims he, 'proceed in the small chink-lighted, or even oil-lighted, underground workshop of Logic alone; and man's mind become an Arithmetical Mill, whereof Memory is the Hopper, and mere Tables of Sines and Tangents, Codification, and Treatises of what you call Political Economy, are the Meal? And what is that Science, which the scientific head alone, were it screwed off, and (like the Doctor's in the Arabian Tale) set in a basin to keep it alive, could prosecute without shadow of a heart,—but one other of the mechanical and menial handicrafts, for which the Scientific Head (having a Soul in it) is too noble an organ? I mean that Thought without Reverence is barren, perhaps poisonous; at best, dies like cookery with the day that called it forth; does not live, like sowing, in successive tilths and wider-spreading harvests, bringing food and plenteous increase to all Time.'

In such wise does Teufelsdröckh deal hits, harder or softer, according to ability; yet ever, as we would fain persuade ourselves, with charitable intent. Above all, that class of 'Logic-choppers, and treble-pipe Scoffers, and professed Enemies to Wonder; who, in these days, so numerously patrol as night-constables about the Mechanics' Institute of Science, and cackle like true Old-Roman geese and goslings round their Capitol, on any alarm, or on none; nay who often, as illuminated Sceptics, walk abroad into peaceable society, in full daylight, with rattle and lantern, and insist on guiding you and guarding you therewith, though the Sun is shining, and the street populous with mere justice-loving men:' that whole class is inexpressibly wearisome to him. Hear with what uncommon animation he perorates:

'The man who cannot wonder, who does not habitually wonder (and worship), were he President of innumerable Royal Societies, and carried the whole *Mécanique Céleste* and *Hegel's Philosophy*, and the epitome of all Laboratories and Observatories with their results, in his single head,—is but a Pair of Spectacles behind which there is no Eye. Let those who have Eyes look through him, then he may be useful.

'Thou wilt have no Mystery and Mysticism; wilt walk through thy world by the sunshine of what thou callest Truth, or even by the hand-lamp of what I call Attorney-Logic; and "explain" all, "account" for all, or believe nothing of it? Nay, thou wilt attempt laughter; whoso recognises the unfathomable, all-pervading domain of Mystery, which is everywhere under our feet and among our hands; to whom the Universe is an Oracle and Temple, as well as a Kitchen and Cattle-stall, —he shall be a delirious Mystic; to him thou, with sniffing charity, wilt protrusively proffer thy hand-lamp, and shriek, as one injured, when he kicks his foot through it?—*Armer Teufel!* Doth not thy cow calve, doth not thy bull gender? Thou thyself, wert thou not born, wilt thou not die? "Explain" me all this, or do one of two things: Retire into private places with thy foolish cackle; or, what were better, give it up, and weep, not that the reign of wonder is done, and God's world all disembellished and prosaic, but that thou hitherto art a Dilettante and sandblind Pedant.'

CHAPTER XI

PROSPECTIVE

Nature not an Aggregate, but a Whole. All visible things are emblems, Clothes; and exist for a time only. The grand scope of the Philosophy of Clothes.—Biographic Documents arrive. Letter from Heuschrecke on the importance of Biography. Heterogeneous character of the documents: Editor sorely perplexed; but desperately grapples with his work.

THE Philosophy of Clothes is now to all readers, as we predicted it would do, unfolding itself into new boundless expansions, of a cloudcapt, almost chimerical aspect, yet not without azure loomings in the far distance, and streaks as of an Elysian brightness; the highly questionable purport and promise of which it is becoming more and more important for us to ascertain. Is that a real Elysian brightness, cries many a timid wayfarer, or the reflex of Pandemonian lava? Is it of a truth leading us into beatific Asphodel meadows, or the yellow-burning marl of a Hell-on-Earth?

Our Professor, like other Mystics, whether delirious or inspired, gives an Editor enough to do. Ever higher and dizzier are the heights he leads us to; more piercing, all-comprehending, all-confounding are his views and glances. For example, this of Nature being not an Aggregate but a Whole:

'Well sang the Hebrew Psalmist: "If I take the wings of the morning and dwell in the uttermost parts of the universe, God is there." Thou thyself, O cultivated reader, who too probably art no Psalmist, but a Prosaist, knowing GOD only by tradition, knowest thou any corner of the world where at least FORCE is not? The drop which thou shakest from thy wet hand, rests not where it falls, but tomorrow thou findest it swept away; already on the wings of the Northwind, it is nearing the Tropic of Cancer. How came it to evaporate, and not lie motionless? Thinkest thou there is ought motionless; without Force, and utterly dead?

'As I rode through the Schwarzwald, I said to myself: That little fire which glows star-like across the dark-growing (*nachtende*) moor, where the sooty smith bends over his anvil, and thou hopest to replace thy lost horse-shoe,—is it a detached, separated speck, cut-off from the whole Universe; or indissolubly joined to the whole? Thou fool, that smithy-fire was (primarily) kindled at the Sun; is fed by air that circulates from before Noah's Deluge, from beyond the Dogstar; therein, with Iron Force, and Coal Force, and the far stranger Force of Man, are cunning affinities and battles and victories of Force brought about; it is a little ganglion, or nervous centre, in the great vital system of Immensity. Call it, if thou wilt, an unconscious Altar, kindled on the bosom of the All; whose iron sacrifice, whose iron smoke and influence reach quite through the All; whose dingy Priest, not by word, yet by brain and sinew, preaches forth the mystery of Force; nay preaches forth (exoterically enough) one little textlet from the Gospel of Freedom, the Gospel of Man's Force, commanding, and one day to be all-commanding.

'Detached, separated! I say there is no such separation: nothing hitherto was ever stranded, cast aside; but all, were it only a withered leaf, works together with all; is borne forward on the bottomless, shoreless flood of Action, and lives through perpetual metamorphoses. The withered leaf is not dead and lost, there are Forces in it and around it, though working in inverse order; else how could it *rot*? Despise not the rag from which man makes Paper, or the litter from which the earth makes Corn. Rightly viewed no meanest object is insignificant; all objects are as windows, through which the philosophic eye looks into Infinitude itself.'

Again, leaving that wondrous Schwarzwald Smithy-Altar, what vacant, high-sailing air-ships are these, and whither will they sail with us?

'All visible things are emblems; what thou seest is not there on its own account; strictly taken, is not there at all: Matter exists only spiritually, and to represent some Idea, and *body* it forth. Hence Clothes, as despicable as we think them, are so unspeakably significant. Clothes, from the King's mantle downwards, are emblematic, nor of want only, but of a manifold cunning Victory over Want. On the other hand, all Emblematic things are properly Clothes, thought-woven or hand-woven; must not the Imagination weave Garments, visible Bodies, wherein the else invisible creations and inspirations of our Reason are, like Spirits, revealed, and first become all-powerful; —the rather if, as we often see, the Hand too aid her, and (by wool Clothes or otherwise) reveal such even to the outward eye?

'Men are properly said to be clothed with Authority, clothed with Beauty, with Curses, and the like. Nay, if you consider it, what is Man himself, and his whole terrestrial Life, but an Emblem; a Clothing or visible Garment for that divine ME of his, cast hither, like a light-particle, down from Heaven? Thus is he said also to be clothed with a Body.

'Language is called the Garment of Thought: however, it should rather be, Language is the Flesh-Garment, the Body, of Thought. I said that Imagination wove this Flesh-Garment; and does not she? Metaphors are her stuff: examine Language; what, if you except some few primitive elements (of natural sound), what is it all but Metaphors, recognised as such, or no longer recognised; still fluid and florid, or now solid-grown and colourless? If those same primitive elements are the osseous fixtures in the Flesh-Garment, Language,—then are Metaphors its muscles and tissues and living integuments. An unmetaphorical style you shall in vain seek for: is not your very *Attention* a *Stretching-to*? The difference lies here: some styles are lean, adust, wiry, the muscle itself seems osseous; some are even quite pallid, hunger-bitten and dead-looking; while others again glow in the flush of health and vigorous self-growth, sometimes (as in my own case) not without an apoplectic tendency. Moreover, there are sham Metaphors, which overhanging that same Thought's-Body (best naked), and deceptively bedizening, or bolstering it out, may be called its false stuffings, superfluous show-cloaks (*Putz-Mäntel*), and tawdry woollen rags: whereof he that runs and reads may gather whole hampers,—and burn them.'

Than which paragraph on Metaphors did the reader ever chance to see a more surprisingly metaphorical? However, that is not our chief grievance; the Professor continues:

'Why multiply instances? It is written, the Heavens and the Earth shall fade away like a Vesture; which indeed they are: the Time-vesture of the Eternal. Whatsoever sensibly exists, whatsoever represents Spirit to Spirit, is properly a Clothing, a suit of Raiment, put on for a season, and to be laid off. Thus in this one pregnant subject of CLOTHES, rightly understood, is included all that men have thought, dreamed, done, and been: the whole External Universe and what it holds is but Clothing; and the essence of all Science lies in the PHILOSOPHY OF CLOTHES.'

Towards these dim infinitely-expanded regions, close-bordering on the impalpable Inane, it is not without apprehension, and perpetual difficulties, that the Editor sees himself journeying and struggling. Till lately a cheerful daystar of hope hung before him, in the expected Aid of Hofrath Heuschrecke; which daystar, however, melts now, not into the red of morning, but into a vague, gray half-light, uncertain whether dawn of day or dusk of utter darkness. For the last week, these so-called Biographical Documents are in his hand. By the kindness of a Scottish Hamburg Merchant, whose name, known to the whole mercantile world, he must not mention; but whose honourable courtesy, now and often before spontaneously manifested to him, a mere literary stranger, he cannot soon forget,—the bulky Weissnichtwo Packet, with all its Customhouse seals, foreign hieroglyphs, and miscellaneous tokens of Travel, arrived here in perfect safety, and free of cost. The reader shall now fancy with what hot haste it was broken up, with what breathless expectation glanced over; and, alas, with what unquiet disappointment it has, since then, been often thrown down, and again taken up.

Hofrath Heuschrecke, in a too long-winded Letter, full of compliments, Weissnichtwo politics, dinners, dining repartees, and other ephemeral trivialities, proceeds to remind us of what we knew well already: that however it may be with Metaphysics, and other abstract Science originating in the Head (*Verstand*) alone, no Life-Philosophy (*Lebensphilosophie*), such as this of Clothes pretends to be, which originates equally in the Character (*Gemüth*), and equally speaks thereto, can attain its significance till the Character itself is known and seen; 'till the Author's View of the World (*Weltansicht*), and how he actively and passively came by such view, are clear: in short till a Biography of him has been philosophico-poetically written, and philosophico-poetically read.' 'Nay,' adds he, 'were the speculative scientific Truth even known, you still, in this inquiring age, ask yourself, Whence came it, and Why, and How?—and rest not, till, if no better may be, Fancy have shaped-out an answer; and either in the authentic lineaments of Fact, or the forged ones of Fiction, a complete picture and Genetical History of the Man and his spiritual Endeavour lies before you. But why,' says the Hofrath, and indeed say we, 'do I dilate on the uses of our Teufelsdröckh's Biography? The great Herr Minister von Goethe has penetratingly remarked that "Man is properly the *only* object that interests man": thus I too have noted, that in Weissnichtwo our whole conversation is little or nothing else but Biography or Auto-Biography; ever humano-anecdotical (*menschlich-anekdotisch*). Biography is by nature the most universally profitable, universally pleasant of all things; especially Biography of distinguished individuals.

'By this time, *mein Verehrtester* (my Most Esteemed),' continues he, with an eloquence which, unless the words be purloined from Teufelsdröckh, or some trick of his, as we suspect, is well-nigh unaccountable, 'by this time you are fairly plunged (*vertieft*) in that mighty forest of Clothes-Philosophy; and looking round, as all readers do, with astonishment enough. Such portions and passages as you have already mastered, and brought to paper, could not but awaken a strange curiosity touching the mind they issued from; the perhaps unparalleled psychical mechanism, which manufactured such matter, and emitted it to the light of day. Had Teufelsdröckh also a father and mother; did he, at one time, wear drivel-bibs, and live on spoon-meat? Did he ever, in rapture and tears, clasp a friend's bosom to his; looks he also wistfully into the long burial-aisle of the Past, where only winds, and their low harsh moan, give inarticulate answer? Has he fought duels;—good Heaven! how did he comport himself when in Love? By what singular stair-steps, in short, and subterranean passages, and sloughs of Despair, and steep Pisgah hills, has he reached this wonderful prophetic Hebron (a true Old-Clothes Jewry) where he now dwells?

'To all these natural questions the voice of public History is as yet silent. Certain only that he has been, and is, a Pilgrim, and a Traveller from a far Country; more or less footsore and travel-soiled; has parted with road-companions; fallen among thieves, been poisoned by bad cookery, blistered with bugbites; nevertheless, at every stage (for they have let him pass), has had the Bill to discharge. But the whole particulars of his Route, his Weather-observations, the picturesque Sketches he took, though all regularly jotted down (in indelible sympathetic-ink by an invisible interior Penman), are these nowhere forthcoming? Perhaps quite lost: one other leaf of that mighty Volume (of human Memory) left to fly abroad, unprinted, unpublished, unbound up, as waste paper; and to rot, the sport of rainy winds?

'No, *verehrtester Herr Herausgeber*, in no wise! I here, by the unexampled favour you stand in with our Sage, send not a Biography only, but an Autobiography: at least the materials for such; wherefrom, if I misreckon not, your perspicacity will draw fullest insight: and so the whole Philosophy and Philosopher of Clothes will stand clear to the wondering eyes of England, nay thence, through America, through Hindostan, and the antipodal New Holland, finally conquer (*einnehmen*) great part of this terrestrial Planet!'

And now let the sympathising reader judge of our feeling when, in place of this same Autobiography with 'fullest insight,' we find—Six considerable PAPER-BAGS, carefully sealed and marked successively, in gilt China-ink, with the symbols of the Six southern Zodiacal Signs, beginning at Libra; in the inside of which sealed Bags lie miscellaneous masses of Sheets, and oftener Shreds and Snips, written in Professor Teufelsdröckh's scarce legible *cursiv-schrift*; and treating of all imaginable things under the Zodiac and above it, but of his own personal history only at rare intervals, and then in the most enigmatic manner.

Whole fascicles there are, wherein the Professor, or, as he here, speaking in the third person, calls himself, 'the Wanderer,' is not once named. Then again, amidst what seems to be a Metaphysico-theological Disquisition, 'Detached Thoughts on the Steam-engine,' or, 'The continued Possibility of Prophecy,' we shall meet with some quite private, not unimportant Biographical fact. On certain sheets stand Dreams, authentic or not, while the circumjacent waking Actions are omitted. Anecdotes, oftenest without date of place or time, fly loosely on separate slips, like Sibylline leaves. Interspersed also are long purely Autobiographical delineations; yet without connexion, without recognisable coherence; so unimportant, so superfluously minute, they almost remind us of 'P.P. Clerk of this Parish.' Thus does famine of intelligence alternate with waste. Selection, order, appears to be unknown to the Professor. In all Bags the same imbroglio; only perhaps in the Bag *Capricorn*, and those near it, the confusion a little worse confounded. Close by a rather eloquent Oration, 'On receiving the Doctor's-Hat,' lie wash-bills, marked *bezahlt* (settled). His Travels are indicated by the Street-Advertisements of the various cities he has visited; of which Street-Advertisements, in most living tongues, here is perhaps the completest collection extant.

So that if the Clothes-Volume itself was too like a Chaos, we have now instead of the solar Luminary that should still it, the airy Limbo which by intermixture will farther volatilise and discompose it! As we shall perhaps see it our duty ultimately to deposit these Six Paper-Bags in the British Museum, farther description, and all vituperation of them, may be spared. Biography or Autobiography of Teufelsdröckh there is, clearly enough, none to be gleaned here: at most some sketchy, shadowy fugitive likeness of him may, by unheard-of efforts, partly of intellect, partly of imagination, on the side of Editor and of Reader, rise up between them. Only as a gaseous-chaotic Appendix to that aqueous-chaotic Volume can the contents of the Six Bags hover round us, and portions thereof be incorporated with our delineation of it.

Daily and nightly does the Editor sit (with green spectacles) deciphering these unimaginable Documents from their perplexed *cursiv-schrift*; collating them with the almost equally unimaginable Volume, which stands in legible print. Over such a universal medley of high and low, of hot, cold, moist and dry, is he here struggling (by union of like with like, which is Method) to build a firm Bridge for British travellers. Never perhaps since our first Bridge-builders, Sin and Death, built that stupendous Arch from Hell-gate to the Earth, did any Pontifex, or Pontiff, undertake such a task as the present Editor. For in this Arch too, leading, as we humbly presume, far otherwards than that grand primeval one, the materials are to be fished-up from the weltering deep, and down from the simmering air, here one mass, there another, and cunningly cemented, while the elements boil beneath: nor is there any supernatural force to do it with; but simply the Diligence and feeble thinking Faculty of an English Editor, endeavouring to evolve printed Creation out of a German printed and written Chaos, wherein, as he shoots to and fro in it, gathering, clutching, piecing the Why to the far-distant Wherefore, his whole Faculty and Self are like to be swallowed up.

Patiently, under these incessant toils and agitations, does the Editor, dismissing all anger, see his otherwise robust health declining; some fraction of his allotted natural sleep nightly leaving him, and little but an inflamed nervous-system to be looked for. What is the use of health, or of life, if not to do some work therewith? And what work nobler than transplanting foreign Thought into the barren domestic soil; except indeed planting Thought of your own, which the fewest are privileged to do? Wild as it looks, this Philosophy of Clothes, can we ever reach its real meaning, promises to reveal new-coming Eras, the first dim rudiments and already-budding germs of a nobler Era, in Universal History. Is not such a prize worth some striving? Forward with us, courageous reader; be it towards failure, or towards success! The latter thou sharest with us; the former also is not all our own.

FROM The French Revolution

In his late life Carlyle said that he would not have known what to make of the world but for the French Revolution. The remark shows the spirit in which he approached the writing of history. Before writing of any historical event he tried to fit that event into an interpretation of all history and all literature as a kind of vast religious poem. This point of view should always be borne in mind when considering *The French Revolution*. In a sense it is true, as John Stuart Mill said, that the sub-title of the book should be not 'A History' but 'A Poem'.

The French Revolution was begun in 1834, although much reading for it had occupied Carlyle during ten years and more; the manuscript of the first volume was burned, through Mill's carelessness, in March 1835, and the difficulty of rewriting it was immensely increased by the fact that Carlyle had destroyed his notes; the book was finished on 12 January 1837. Carlyle read the last sentences to his wife, and then said to her: 'I know not whether this book is worth anything, nor what the world will do with it, or misdo, or entirely forbear to do (as is likeliest), but this I could tell the world: You have not had for a hundred years any book that came more direct and flamingly sincere from the heart of a living man.' *The French Revolution* was published by Fraser in June 1837; it was the first of Carlyle's works to bear his name on the title page.

The extracts chosen are one from the First Volume, covering the period from August to September 1789; and the account in the Third Volume of the fall of the Girondins.

FROM

The French Revolution

VOLUME ONE

BOOK SEVENTH

THE INSURRECTION OF WOMEN

CHAPTER I

PATROLLOTISM

No, Friends, this Revolution is not of the consolidating kind. Do not fires, fevers, sown seeds, chemical mixtures, men, events,—all embodiments of Force that work in this miraculous Complex of Forces named Universe,—go on *growing*, through their natural phases and developments each according to its kind; reach their height, reach their visible decline; finally sink under, vanishing, and what we call *die*? They all grow; there is nothing but what grows, and shoots forth into its special expansion,—once give it leave to spring. Observe too that each grows with a rapidity proportioned, in general, to the madness and unhealthiness there is in it; slow regular growth, though this also ends in death, is what we name health and sanity.

A Sansculottism, which has prostrated Bastilles, which has got pike and musket, and now goes burning Châteaus, passing resolutions and haranguing under roof and sky, may be said to have sprung; and, by law of Nature, must grow. To judge by the madness and diseasedness both of itself, and of the soil and element it is in, one might expect the rapidity and monstrosity would be extreme.

Many things, too, especially all diseased things, grow by

shoots and fits. The first grand fit and shooting-forth of Sansculottism was that of Paris conquering its King; for Bailly's figure of rhetoric was all-too sad a reality. The King is conquered; going at large on his parole; on condition, say, of absolutely good behaviour,—which, in these circumstances, will unhappily mean no behaviour whatever. A quite untenable position, that of Majesty put on its good behaviour! Alas, is it not natural that whatever lives try to keep itself living? Whereupon his Majesty's behaviour will soon become exceptionable; and so the Second grand Fit of Sansculottism, that of putting him in durance, cannot be distant.

Necker, in the National Assembly, is making moan, as usual, about his Deficit: Barriers and Customhouses burnt; the Tax-gatherer hunted, not hunting; his Majesty's Exchequer all but empty. The remedy is a Loan of thirty millions; then, on still more enticing terms, a Loan of eighty millions: neither of which Loans, unhappily, will the Stockjobbers venture to lend. The Stockjobber has no country, except his own black pool of *Agio*.

And yet, in those days, for men that have a country, what a glow of patriotism burns in many a heart; penetrating inwards to the very purse! So early as the 7th of August, a *Don Patriotique*, 'Patriotic Gift of jewels to a considerable extent,' has been solemnly made by certain Parisian women; and solemnly accepted with honourable mention. Whom forthwith all the world takes to imitating and emulating. Patriotic Gifts, always with some heroic eloquence, which the President must answer and the Assembly listen to, flow in from far and near: in such number that the honourable mention can only be performed in 'lists published at stated epochs.' Each gives what he can: the very cordwainers have behaved munificently; one landed proprietor gives a forest; fashionable society gives its shoe-buckles, takes cheerfully to shoeties. Unfortunate-females give what they 'have amassed in loving.'[1] The smell of all cash, as Vespasian thought, is good.

[1] *Histoire Parlementaire*, ii. 427.

Beautiful, and yet inadequate! The Clergy must be 'invited' to melt their superfluous Church-plate,—in the Royal Mint. Nay finally, a Patriotic Contribution, of the forcible sort, has to be determined on, though unwillingly: let the fourth part of your declared yearly revenue, for this once only, be paid down; so shall a National Assembly make the Constitution, undistracted at least by insolvency. Their own wages, as settled on the 17th of August, are but Eighteen Francs a day, each man; but the Public Service must have sinews, must have money. To *appease* the Deficit; not to '*combler*, or choke, the Deficit,' if you or mortal could! For withal, as Mirabeau was heard saying, 'it is the Deficit that saves us.'

Towards the end of August, our National Assembly in its constitutional labours has got so far as the question of *Veto*: shall Majesty have a Veto on the National Enactments; or not have a Veto? What speeches were spoken, within doors and without; clear, and also passionate logic; imprecations, comminations; gone happily, for most part, to Limbo! Through the cracked brain and uncracked lungs of Saint-Huruge, the Palais Royal rebellows with Veto. Journalism is busy, France rings with Veto. 'I never shall forget,' says Dumont, 'my going to Paris, one of those days, with Mirabeau; and the crowd of people we found waiting for his carriage about Le Jay the Bookseller's shop. They flung themselves before him; conjuring him, with tears in their eyes, not to suffer the *Veto Absolu*. They were in a frenzy: "Monsieur le Comte, you are the People's father, you must save us; you must defend us against those villains who are bringing back Despotism. If the King get this Veto, what is the use of National Assembly? We are slaves; all is done." '[1] Friends, *if* the sky fall, there will be catching of larks! Mirabeau, adds Dumont, was eminent on such occasions: he answered vaguely, with a Patrician imperturbability, and bound himself to nothing.

Deputations go to the Hôtel-de-Ville; anonymous Letters to Aristocrats in the National Assembly, threatening that

[1] *Souvenirs sur Mirabeau*, p. 156.

fifteen thousand, or sometimes that sixty thousand, 'will march to illuminate you.' The Paris Districts are astir; Petitions signing: Saint-Huruge sets forth from the Palais Royal with an escort of fifteen hundred individuals, to petition in person. Resolute, or seemingly so, is the tall shaggy Marquis, is the Café de Foy: but resolute also is Commandant-General-Lafayette. The streets are all beset by Patrols: Saint-Huruge is stopped at the *Barrière des Bons Hommes*; he may bellow like the bulls of Bashan, but absolutely must return. The brethren of the Palais Royal 'circulate all night,' and make motions, under the open canopy; all Coffeehouses being shut. Nevertheless Lafayette and the Townhall do prevail; Saint-Huruge is thrown into prison; *Veto Absolu* adjusts itself into *Suspensive Veto*, prohibition not for ever, but for a term of time; and this doom's-clamour will grow silent, as the others have done.

So far has Consolidation prospered, though with difficulty; repressing the Nether Sansculottic world; and the Constitution shall be made. With difficulty: amid jubilee and scarcity; Patriotic Gifts, Bakers'-queues; Abbé-Fauchet Harangues, with their *Amen* of platoon-musketry! Scipio-Americanus has deserved thanks from the National Assembly and France. They offer him stipends and emoluments to a handsome extent; all which stipends and emoluments he, covetous of far other blessedness than mere money, does, in his chivalrous way, without scruple, refuse.

To the Parisian common man, meanwhile, one thing remains inconceivable: that now when the Bastille is down, and French Liberty restored, grain should continue so dear. Our Rights of Man are voted, Feudalism and all Tyranny abolished; yet behold we stand *in queue*! Is it Aristocrat forestallers; a Court still bent on intrigues? Something is rotten somewhere.

And yet, alas, what to do? Lafayette, with his Patrols, prohibits everything, even complaint. Saint-Huruge and other heroes of the *Veto* lie in durance. People's-Friend Marat was seized; Printers of Patriotic Journals are fettered and forbidden; the very Hawkers cannot cry, till they get licence and leaden badges. Blue National Guards ruthlessly dissipate all groups; scour, with levelled bayonets, the Palais Royal itself. Pass, on your affairs, along the Rue Taranne, the Patrol, presenting his bayonet, cries, *To the left!* Turn into the Rue Saint-Bénoit, he cries, *To the right!* A judicious Patriot (like Camille Desmoulins, in this instance) is driven, for quietness' sake, to take the gutter.

O much-suffering People, our glorious Revolution is evaporating in tricolor ceremonies and complimentary harangues! Of which latter, as Loustalot acridly calculates, 'upwards of two thousand have been delivered within the last month at the Townhall alone.'[1] And our mouths, unfilled with bread, are to be shut, under penalties? The Caricaturist promulgates his emblematic Tablature: *Le Patrouillotisme chassant le Patriotisme*, Patriotism driven out by Patrollotism. Ruthless Patrols; long superfine harangues; and scanty ill-baked loaves, more like baked Bath bricks,—which produce an effect on the intestines! Where will this end? In consolidation?

CHAPTER II

O RICHARD, O MY KING

FOR, alas, neither is the Townhall itself without misgivings. The Nether Sansculottic world has been suppressed hitherto: but then the Upper Court-world! Symptoms there are that the Œil-de-Bœuf is rallying.

More than once in the Townhall Sanhedrim, often enough from those outspoken Bakers'-queues, has the wish uttered itself: O that our Restorer of French Liberty were here; that he could see with his own eyes, not with the false eyes of Queens and Cabals, and his really good heart be enlightened! For falsehood still environs him; intriguing Dukes de Guiche, with Bodyguards; scouts of Bouillé; a new flight of intriguers, now that the old is flown. What else means this advent of the

[1] *Révolutions de Paris Newspaper* (cited in *Histoire Parlementaire*, ii. 357).

Regiment de Flandre; entering Versailles, as we hear, on the 23d of September, with two pieces of cannon? Did not the Versailles National Guard do duty at the Château? Had they not Swiss; Hundred Swiss; *Gardes-du-Corps*, Bodyguards so-called? Nay, it would seem, the number of Bodyguards on duty has, by a manœuvre, been doubled: the new relieving Battalion of them arrived at its time; but the old relieved one does not *depart*!

Actually, there runs a whisper through the best-informed Upper-Circles, or a nod still more portentous than whispering, of his Majesty's flying to Metz; of a Bond (to stand by him therein), which has been signed by Noblesse and Clergy, to the incredible amount of thirty, or even of sixty thousand. Lafayette coldly whispers it, and coldly asseverates it, to Count d'Estaing at the Dinner-table; and D'Estaing, one of the bravest men, quakes to the core lest some lackey overhear it; and tumbles thoughtful, without sleep, all night.[1] Regiment de Flandre, as we said, is clearly arrived. His Majesty, they say, hesitates about sanctioning the Fourth of August; makes observations, of chilling tenor, on the very Rights of Man! Likewise, may not all persons, the Bakers'-queues themselves discern, on the streets of Paris, the most astonishing number of Officers on furlough, Crosses of St. Louis, and suchlike? Some reckon 'from a thousand to twelve hundred.' Officers of all uniforms; nay one uniform never before seen by eye: green faced with red! The tricolor cockade is not always visible: but what, in the name of Heaven, may these *black* cockades, which some wear, foreshadow?

Hunger whets everything, especially Suspicion and Indignation. Realities themselves, in this Paris, have grown unreal, preternatural. Phantasms once more stalk through the brain of hungry France. O ye laggards and dastards, cry shrill voices from the Queues, if ye had the hearts of men, ye would take your pikes and secondhand firelocks, and look into it; not leave your wives and daughters to be starved, murdered and worse!

[1] *Brouillon de Lettre de M. d'Estaing à la Reine* (in *Histoire Parlementaire*, iii. 24).

—Peace, women! The heart of man is bitter and heavy; Patriotism, driven out by Patrollotism, knows not what to resolve on.

The truth is, the Œil-de-Bœuf has rallied; to a certain unknown extent. A changed Œil-de-Bœuf; with Versailles National Guards, in their tricolor cockades, doing duty there; a Court all flaring with tricolor! Yet even to a tricolor Court men will rally. Ye loyal hearts, burnt-out Seigneurs, rally round your Queen! With wishes; which will produce hopes; which will produce attempts!

For indeed self-preservation being such a law of Nature, what can a rallied Court do, but attempt and endeavour, or call it *plot*,—with such wisdom and unwisdom as it has? They will fly, escorted, to Metz, where brave Bouillé commands; they will raise the Royal Standard: the Bond-signatures shall become armed men. Were not the King so languid! Their Bond, if at all signed, must be signed without his privity.—Unhappy King, *he* has but one resolution: not to have a civil war. For the rest, he still hunts, having ceased lockmaking; he still dozes, and digests; is clay in the hands of the potter. Ill will it fare with him, in a world where all is helping itself; where, as has been written, 'whosoever is not hammer must be stithy'; and 'the very hyssop on the wall grows there, in that chink, because the whole Universe could not prevent its growing!'

But as for the coming-up of this Regiment de Flandre, may it not be urged that there were Saint-Huruge Petitions, and continual meal-mobs? Undebauched Soldiers, be there plot, or only dim elements of a plot, are always good. Did not the Versailles Municipality (an old Monarchic one, not yet refounded into a Democratic) instantly second the proposal? Nay the very Versailles National Guard, wearied with continual duty at the Château, did not object; only Draper Lecointre, who is now Major Lecointre, shook his head.—Yes, Friends, surely it was natural this Regiment de Flandre should be sent for, since it could be got. It was natural that, a sight of military bandoleers, the heart of the rallied Œil-de-Bœuf should revive; and Maids of Honour, and gentlemen of honour, speak comfortable words to epauletted defenders and to one another. Natural also, and mere common civility, that the Bodyguards, a Regiment of Gentlemen, should invite their Flandre brethren to a Dinner of welcome!—Such invitation, in the last days of September, is given and accepted.

Dinners are defined as 'the *ultimate* act of communion'; men that can have communion in nothing else, can sympathetically eat together, can still rise into some glow of brotherhood over food and wine. The Dinner is fixed on, for Thursday the First of October; and ought to have a fine effect. Further, as such Dinner may be rather extensive, and even the Noncommissioned and the Common man be introduced, to see and to hear, could not his Majesty's Opera Apartment, which has lain quite silent ever since Kaiser Joseph was here, be obtained for the purpose?—The Hall of the Opera is granted; the Salon d'Hercule shall be drawing-room. Not only the Officers of Flandre, but of the Swiss, of the Hundred Swiss; nay of the Versailles National Guard, such of them as have any loyalty, shall feast: it will be a Repast like few.

And now suppose this Repast, the solid part of it, transacted; and the first bottle over. Suppose the customary loyal toasts drunk; the King's health, the Queen's with deafening vivats;—that of the Nation 'omitted,' or even 'rejected.' Suppose champagne flowing; with pot-valorous speech, with instrumental music; empty featherheads growing ever the noisier, in their own emptiness, in each others' noise. Her Majesty, who looks unusually sad tonight (his Majesty sitting dulled with the day's hunting), is told that the sight of it would cheer her. Behold! She enters there, issuing from her State-rooms, like the Moon from clouds, this fairest unhappy Queen of Hearts; royal Husband by her side, young Dauphin in her arms! She descends from the Boxes, amid splendour and acclaim; walks queenlike round the Tables; gracefully escorted, gracefully nodding; her looks full of sorrow, yet of gratitude and daring, with the hope of France on her mother-bosom! And now, the band striking up, *O Richard, O mon Roi, l'univers t'abandonne* (O Richard, O my King, the world is all forsaking thee), could man do other than rise to height of pity, of loyal valour? Could featherheaded young ensigns do other than, by white Bourbon Cockades, handed them from fair fingers; by waving of swords, drawn to pledge the Queen's health; by trampling of National Cockades; by scaling the Boxes, whence intrusive murmurs may come; by vociferation, tripudiation, sound, fury and distraction, within doors and without,—testify what tempest-tost state of vacuity they are in? Till champagne and tripudiation do their work; and all lie silent, horizontal; passively slumbering with meed-of-battle dreams!—

A natural Repast; in ordinary times, a harmless one: now fatal, as that of Thyestes; as that of Job's Sons, when a strong wind smote the four corners of their banquet-house! Poor ill-advised Marie-Antoinette; with a woman's vehemence, not with a sovereign's foresight! It was so natural, yet so unwise. Next day, in public speech of ceremony, her Majesty declares herself 'delighted with the Thursday.'

The heart of the Œil-de-Bœuf glows into hope; into daring, which is premature. Rallied Maids of Honour, waited on by Abbés, sew 'white cockades'; distribute them, with words, with glances, to epauletted youths; who, in return, may kiss, not without fervour, the fair sewing fingers. Captains of horse and foot go swashing with 'enormous white cockades'; nay one Versailles National Captain has mounted the like, so witching were the words and glances, and laid aside his tricolor! Well may Major Lecointre shake his head with a look of severity; and speak audible resentful words. But now a swashbuckler, with enormous white cockade, overhearing the Major, invites him insolently, once and then again elsewhere, to recant; and failing that, to duel. Which latter feat Major Lecointre declares that he will not perform, not at least by any known laws of fence; that he nevertheless will, according to mere law of Nature, by dirk and blade, 'exterminate' any 'vile gladiator' who may insult him or the Nation;—whereupon (for the Major is actually drawing his implement) 'they are parted,' and no weasands slit.[1]

CHAPTER III

BLACK COCKADES

But fancy what effect this Thyestes Repast, and trampling on the National Cockade, must have had in the *Salle des Menus*; in the famishing Bakers'-queues at Paris! Nay such Thyestes Repasts, it would seem, continue. Flandre has given its Counter-Dinner to the Swiss and Hundred Swiss; then on Saturday there has been another.

Yes, here with us is famine; but yonder at Versailles is food, enough and to spare! Patriotism stands in queue, shivering hunger-struck, insulted by Patrollotism; while bloodyminded Aristocrats, heated with excess of high living, trample on the National Cockade. Can the atrocity be true? Nay look: green uniforms faced with red; black cockades,—the colour of Night! are we to have military onfall; and death also by starvation? For, behold, the Corbeil Cornboat, which used to come twice a day, with its plaster-of-paris meal, now comes only once. And the Townhall is deaf; and the men are laggard and dastard!—At the Café de Foy, this Saturday evening, a new thing is seen, not the last of its kind: a woman engaged in public speaking. Her poor man, she says, was put to silence by his District; their Presidents and Officials would not let him speak. Wherefore she here, with her shrill tongue, will speak; denouncing, while her breath endures, the Corbeil Boat, the plaster-of-paris bread, sacrilegious Opera-dinners, green uniforms, Pirate Aristocrats, and those black cockades of theirs!—

Truly, it is time for the black cockades at least to vanish. Them Patrollotism itself will not protect. Nay sharp-tempered 'M. Tassin,' at the Tuileries parade on Sunday morning, forgets all National military rule; starts from the ranks,

[1] *Moniteur* (in *Histoire Parlementaire*, iii, 59); *Deux Amis*, iii. 128–141; Campan, ii. 70–85; etc. etc.

wrenches down one black cockade which is swashing ominous there, and tramples it fiercely into the soil of France. Patrollotism itself is not without suppressed fury. Also the Districts begin to stir; the voice of President Danton reverberates in the Cordeliers: People's-Friend Marat has flown to Versailles and back again;—swart bird, not of the halcyon kind.[1]

And so Patriot meets promenading Patriot, this Sunday; and sees his own grim care reflected on the face of another. Groups, in spite of Patrollotism, which is not so alert as usual, fluctuate deliberative; groups on the Bridges, on the Quais, at the patriotic Cafés. And ever as any black cockade may emerge, rises the many-voiced growl and bark: *À bas*, Down! All black cockades are ruthlessly plucked off: one individual picks his up again; kisses it, attempts to refix it; but a 'hundred canes start into the air,' and he desists. Still worse went it with another individual; doomed, by extempore *Plebiscitum*, to the Lanterne; saved, with difficulty, by some active *Corps-de-Garde*.—Lafayette sees signs of an effervescence; which he doubles his Patrols, doubles his diligence, to prevent. So passes Sunday the 4th of October 1789.

Sullen is the male heart, repressed by Patrollotism; vehement is the female, irrepressible. The public-speaking woman at the Palais Royal was not the only speaking one:—Men know not what the pantry is, when it grows empty; only house-mothers know. O women, wives of men that will only calculate and not act! Patrollotism is strong; but Death, by starvation and military onfall, is stronger. Patrollotism represses male Patriotism: but female Patriotism? Will Guards named National thrust their bayonets into the bosoms of women? Such thought, or rather such dim unshaped raw material of a thought, ferments universally under the female nightcap; and, by earliest daybreak, on slight hint, will explode.

[1] Camille's Newspaper, *Révolutions de Paris et de Brabant* (in *Histoire Parlementaire*, iii. 108).

CHAPTER IV

THE MENADS

If Voltaire once, in splenetic humour, asked his countrymen: 'But you, *Gualches*, what have you invented?' they can now answer: The Art of Insurrection. It was an art needed in these last singular times: an art for which the French nature, so full of vehemence, so free from depth, was perhaps of all others the fittest.

Accordingly, to what a height, one may well say of perfection, has this branch of human industry been carried by France, within the last half-century! Insurrection, which Lafayette thought might be 'the most sacred of duties,' ranks now, for the French people, among the duties which they can perform. Other mobs are dull masses; which roll onwards with a dull fierce heat, but emit no light-flashes of genius as they go. The French mob, again, is among the liveliest phenomena of our world. So rapid, audacious; so clear-sighted, inventive, prompt to seize the moment; instinct with life to its finger-ends! That talent, were there no other, of spontaneously standing in queue, distinguishes, as we said, the French People from all Peoples, ancient and modern.

Let the Reader confess too that, taking one thing with another, perhaps few terrestrial Appearances are better worth considering than mobs. Your mob is a genuine outburst of Nature; issuing from, or communicating with, the deepest deep of Nature. When so much goes grinning and grimacing as a lifeless Formality, and under the stiff buckram no heart can be felt beating, here once more, if nowhere else, is a Sincerity and Reality. Shudder at it; or even shriek over it, if thou must; nevertheless consider it. Such a Complex of human Forces and Individualities hurled forth, in their transcendental mood, to act and react, on circumstances and on one another; to work out what it is in them to work. The thing they will do is known to no man; least of all to themselves. It is the inflammablest immeasurable Firework, generating, consuming itself. With what phases, to what extent, with what results it will burn off, Philosophy and Perspicacity conjecture in vain.

'Man,' as has been written, 'is for ever interesting to man; nay properly there is nothing else interesting.' In which light also may we not discern why most Battles have become so wearisome? Battles, in these ages, are transacted by mechanism; with the slightest possible development of human individuality or spontaneity: men now even die, and kill one another, in an artificial manner. Battles ever since Homer's time, when they were Fighting Mobs, have mostly ceased to be worth looking at, worth reading of or remembering. How many wearisome bloody Battles does History strive to represent; or even, in a husky way, to sing:—and she would omit or carelessly slur-over this one Insurrection of Women?

A thought, or dim raw-material of a thought, was fermenting all night, universally in the female head, and might explode. In squalid garret, on Monday morning, Maternity awakes, to hear children weeping for bread. Maternity must forth to the streets, to the herb-markets and Bakers'-queues; meets there with hunger-stricken Maternity, sympathetic, exasperative. O we unhappy women! But, instead of Bakers'-queues, why not to Aristocrats' palaces, the root of the matter? *Allons!* Let us assemble. To the Hôtel-de-Ville; to Versailles; to the Lanterne!

In one of the Guardhouses of the Quartier-Saint-Eustache, 'a young woman' seizes a drum—for how shall National Guards give fire on women, on a young woman? The young woman seizes the drum; sets forth, beating it, 'uttering cries relative to the dearth of grains.' Descend, O mothers; descend, ye Judiths, to food and revenge!—All women gather and go; crowds storm all stairs, force out all women: the female Insurrectionary Force, according to Camille, resembles the English Naval one; there is a universal 'Press of women.' Robust Dames of the Halle, slim Mantua-makers, assiduous, risen with the dawn; ancient Virginity tripping to matins; the

Housemaid, with early broom; all must go. Rouse ye, O women; the laggard men will not act; they say, we ourselves may act!

And so, like snowbreak from the mountains, for every staircase is a melted brook, it storms; tumultuous, wild-shrilling, towards the Hôtel-de-Ville. Tumultuous; with or without drum-music: for the Faubourg Saint-Antoine also has tucked-up its gown; and with besom-staves, fire-irons, and even rusty pistols (void of ammunition), is flowing on. Sound of it flies, with a velocity of sound, to the utmost Barriers. By seven o'clock, on this raw October morning, fifth of the month, the Townhall will see wonders. Nay, as chance would have it, a male party are already there; clustering tumultuously round some National Patrol, and a Baker who has been seized with short weights. They are there; and have even lowered the rope of the Lanterne. So that the official persons have to smuggle forth the short-weighing Baker by back-doors, and even send 'to all the Districts' for more force.

Grand it was, says Camille, to see so many Judiths, from eight to ten thousand of them in all, rushing out to search into the root of the matter! Not unfrightful it must have been; ludicro-terrific, and most unmanageable. At such hour the overwatched Three Hundred are not yet stirring: none but some Clerks, a company of National Guards; and M. de Gouvion, the Major-general. Gouvion has fought in America for the cause of civil Liberty; a man of no inconsiderable heart, but deficient in head. He is, for the moment, in his back apartment; assuaging Usher Maillard, the Bastille-sergeant, who has come, as too many do, with 'representations.' The assuagement is still incomplete when our Judiths arrive.

The National Guards form on the outer stairs with levelled bayonets; the ten thousand Judiths press up, resistless; with obtestations, with outspread hands,—merely to speak to the Mayor. The rear forces them; nay, from male hands in the rear, stones already fly: the National Guard must do one of two things; sweep the Place de Grève with cannon, or else open to right and left. They open; the living deluge rushes in. Through all rooms and cabinets, upwards to the topmost belfry: ravenous; seeking arms, seeking Mayors, seeking justice;—while, again, the better-dressed speak kindly to the Clerks; point out the misery of these poor women; also their ailments, some even of an interesting sort.[1]

Poor M. de Gouvion is shiftless in this extremity;—a man shiftless, perturbed: who will one day commit suicide. How happy for him that Usher Maillard the shifty was there, at the moment, though making representations! Fly back, thou shifty Maillard: seek the Bastille Company; and O return fast with it; above all, with thy own shifty head. For, behold, the Judiths can find no Mayor or Municipal; scarcely, in the topmost belfry, can they find poor Abbé Lefèvre the Powder-distributor. Him, for want of a better, they suspend there: in the pale morning light; over the top of all Paris, which swims in one's failing eyes:—a horrible end? Nay the rope broke, as French ropes often did; or else an Amazon cut it. Abbé Lefèvre falls, some twenty feet, rattling among the leads; and lives long years after, though always with 'a *tremblement* in the limbs.'[2]

And now doors fly under hatchets; the Judiths have broken the Armory; have seized guns and cannons, three money-bags, paper-heaps; torches flare: in few minutes, our brave Hôtel-de-Ville, which dates from the Fourth Henry, will, with all that it holds, be in flames!

CHAPTER V

USHER MAILLARD

In flames, truly,—were it not that Usher Maillard, swift of foot, shifty of head, has returned!

Maillard, of his own motion,—for Gouvion or the rest would not even sanction him,—snatches a drum; descends the Porch-stairs, ran-tan, beating sharp, with loud rolls, his Rogues'-

[1] *Deux Amis*, iii. 141–166.
[2] Dusaulx, *Prise de la Bastille*, note, p. 281.

march: To Versailles! *Allons; à Versailles!* As men beat on kettle or warming-pan, when angry she-bees, or say, flying desperate wasps, are to be hived; and the desperate insects hear it, and cluster round it,—simply as round *a* guidance, where there was none: so now these Menads round shifty Maillard, Riding-Usher of the Châtelet. The axe pauses uplifted; Abbé Lefèvre is left half-hanged: from the belfry downwards all vomits itself. What a rub-a-dub is that? Stanislas Maillard, Bastille hero, will lead us to Versailles? Joy to thee, Maillard; blessed art thou above Riding-Ushers! Away, then, away!

The seized cannon are yoked with seized cart-horses; brown-locked Demoiselle Théroigne, with pike and helmet, sits there as gunneress, 'with haughty eye and serene fair countenance'; comparable, some think, to the *Maid* of Orléans, or even recalling 'the idea of Pallas Athene.'[1] Maillard (for his drum still rolls) is, by heaven-rending acclamation, admitted General. Maillard hastens the languid march. Maillard, beating rhythmic, with sharp ran-tan, all along the Quais, leads forward, with difficulty, his Menadic host. Such a host—marched not in silence! The bargeman pauses on the River; all wagoners and coach-drivers fly; men peer from windows,—not women, lest they be pressed. Sight of sights: Bacchantes, in these ultimate Formalised Ages! Bronze Henri looks on, from his Pont-Neuf; the Monarchic Louvre, Medicean Tuileries see a day like none heretofore seen.

And now Maillard has his Menads in the *Champs Elysées* (Fields *Tartarean* rather); and the Hôtel-de-Ville has suffered comparatively nothing. Broken doors; an Abbé Lefèvre, who shall never more distribute powder; three sacks of money, most part of which (for Sansculottism, though famishing, is not without honour) shall be returned:[2] this is all the damage. Great Maillard! A small nucleus of Order is round his drum; but his outskirts fluctuate like the mad Ocean: for Rascality male and female is flowing in on him, from the four winds: guidance there is none but in his single head and two drum-sticks.

[1] *Deux Amis*, iii. 157. [2] *Hist. Parl.* iii. 310.

O Maillard, when, since War first was, had General of Force such a task before him as thou this day? Walter the Penniless still touches the feeling heart: but then Walter had sanction; had space to turn in; and also his Crusaders were of the male sex. Thou, this day, disowned of Heaven and Earth, art General of Menads. Their inarticulate frenzy thou must, on the spur of the instant, render into articulate words, into actions that are not frantic. Fail in it, this way or that! Pragmatical Officiality, with its penalties and law-books, waits before thee; Menads storm behind. If such hewed off the melodious head of Orpheus, and hurled it into the Peneus waters, what may they not make of thee,—thee rhythmic merely, with no music but a sheep-skin drum!—Maillard did not fail. Remarkable Maillard, if fame were not an accident, and History a distillation of Rumour, how remarkable wert thou!

On the Elysian Fields there is pause and fluctuation; but, for Maillard, no return. He persuades his Menads, clamorous for arms and the Arsenal, that no arms are in the Arsenal; that an unarmed attitude, and petition to a National Assembly, will be the best: he hastily nominates or sanctions generalesses, captains of tens and fifties;—and so, in loosest-flowing order, to the rhythm of some 'eight drums' (having laid aside his own), with the Bastille Volunteers bringing up his rear, once more takes the road.

Chaillot, which will promptly yield baked loaves, is not plundered; nor are the Sèvres Potteries broken. The old arches of Sèvres Bridge echo under Menadic feet; Seine River gushes on with its perpetual murmur; and Paris flings after us the boom of tocsin and alarm-drum,—inaudible, for the present, amid shrill-sounding hosts, and the splash of rainy weather. To Meudon, to Saint-Cloud, on both hands, the report of them is gone abroad; and hearths, this evening, will have a topic. The press of women still continues, for it is the cause of all Eve's Daughters, mothers that are, or that ought to be. No carriage-lady, were it with never such hysterics, but must dismount, in the mud roads, in her silk shoes, and walk.[1] In this

[1] *Deux Amis*, iii. 159.

manner, amid wild October weather, they, a wild unwinged, stork-flight, through the astonished country wend their way. Travellers of all sorts they stop; especially travellers or couriers from Paris. Deputy Lechapelier, in his elegant vesture, from his elegant vehicle, looks forth amazed through this spectacles; apprehensive for life;—states eagerly that he is Patriot-Deputy Lechapelier, and even Old-President Lechapelier, who presided on the Night of Pentecost, and is original member of the Breton Club. Thereupon 'rises huge shout of *Vive Lechapelier*, and several armed persons spring up behind and before to escort him.'[1]

Nevertheless, news, despatches from Lafayette, or vague noise of rumour, have pierced through, by side roads. In the National Assembly, while all is busy discussing the order of the day; regretting that there should be Anti-National Repasts in Opera-halls; that his Majesty should still hesitate about accepting the Rights of Man, and hang conditions and peradventures on them,—Mirabeau steps up to the President, experienced Mounier as it chanced to be; and articulates, in bass undertone: '*Mounier, Paris marche sur nous* (Paris is marching on us).'—'May be (*Je n'en sais rien*)!'—'Believe it or disbelieve it, that is not my concern; but Paris, I say, is marching on us. Fall suddenly unwell; go over to the Château; tell them this. There is not a moment to lose.'—'Paris marching on us?' responds Mounier, with an atrabiliar accent: 'Well, so much the better! We shall the sooner be a Republic.' Mirabeau quits him, as one quits an experienced President getting blindfold into deep waters; and the order of the day continues as before.

Yes, Paris is marching on us; and more than the women of Paris! Scarcely was Maillard gone, when M. de Gouvion's message to all the Districts, and such tocsin and drumming of the *générale*, began to take effect. Armed National Guards from every District; especially the Grenadiers of the Centre, who are our old Gardes Françaises, arrive, in quick sequence,

[1] *Deux Amis*, ii. 177; *Dictionnaire des Hommes Marquans*, ii. 379.

on the Place de Grève. An 'immense people' is there; Saint-Antoine, with pike and rusty firelock, is all crowding thither, be it welcome or unwelcome. The Centre Grenadiers are received with cheering: 'It is not cheers that we want,' answer they gloomily; 'the Nation has been insulted; to arms, and come with us for orders!' Ha, sits the wind *so*? Patriotism and Patrollotism are now one!

The Three Hundred have assembled; 'all the Committees are in activity'; Lafayette is dictating despatches for Versailles, when a Deputation of the Centre Grenadiers introduces itself to him. The Deputation makes military obeisance; and thus speaks, not without a kind of thought in it: '*Mon Général*, we are deputed by the Six Companies of Grenadiers. We do not think you a traitor, but we think the Government betrays you; it is time that this end. We cannot turn our bayonets against women crying to us for bread. The people are miserable, the source of the mischief is at Versailles: we must go seek the King, and bring him to Paris. We must exterminate (*exterminer*) the *Regiment de Flandre* and the *Gardes-du-Corps*, who have dared to trample on the National Cockade. If the King be too weak to wear his crown, let him lay it down. You will crown his Son, you will name a Council of Regency: and all will go better.'[1] Reproachful astonishment paints itself on the face of Lafayette; speaks itself from his eloquent chivalrous lips: in vain. 'My General, we would shed the last drop of our blood for you; but the root of the mischief is at Versailles; we must go and bring the King to Paris; all the people wish it, *tout le peuple le veut*.'

My General descends to the outer staircase; and harangues: once more in vain. 'To Versailles! To Versailles!' Mayor Bailly, sent for through floods of Sansculottism, attempts academic oratory from his gilt state-coach; realises nothing but infinite hoarse cries of: 'Bread! To Versailles!'—and gladly shrinks within doors. Lafayette mounts the white charger; and again harangues, and reharangues: with eloquence, with firmness, indignant demonstration; with all things but persuasion. 'To

[1] *Deux Amis*, iii. 161.

Versailles! To Versailles!' So lasts it, hour after hour;—for the space of half a day.

The great Scipio-Americanus can do nothing; not so much as escape. '*Morbleu, mon Général,*' cry the Grenadiers serrying their ranks as the white charger makes a motion that way, 'you will not leave us, you will abide with us!' A perilous juncture: Mayor Bailly and the Municipals sit quaking within doors; my General is prisoner without: the Place de Grève, with its thirty thousand Regulars, its whole irregular Saint-Antoine and Saint-Marceau, is one minatory mass of clear or rusty steel; all hearts set, with a moody fixedness, on one object. Moody, fixed are all hearts: tranquil is no heart,—if it be not that of the white charger, who paws there, with arched neck, composedly champing his bit; as if no World, with its Dynasties and Eras, were now rushing down. The drizzly day bends westward; the cry is still: 'To Versailles!'

Nay now, borne from afar, come quite sinister cries; hoarse, reverberating in long-drawn hollow murmurs, with syllables too like those of '*Lanterne!*' Or else, irregular Sansculottism may be marching off, of itself, with pikes, nay with cannon. The inflexible Scipio does at length, by aide-de-camp, ask of the Municipals: Whether or not he may go? A Letter is handed out to him, over armed heads; sixty thousand faces flash fixedly on his, there is stillness and no bosom breathes, till he have read. By Heaven, he grows suddenly pale! Do the Municipals permit? 'Permit, and even order,'—since he can no other. Clangour of approval rends the welkin. To your ranks, then; let us march!

It is, as we compute, towards three in the afternoon. Indignant National Guards may dine for once from their haversack: dined or undined, they march with one heart. Paris flings-up her windows, 'claps hands,' as the Avengers, with their shrilling drums and shalms tramp by; she will then sit pensive, apprehensive, and pass rather a sleepless night.[1] On the white charger, Lafayette, in the slowest possible manner, going and coming, and eloquently haranguing among the ranks, rolls on-

[1] *Deux Amis*, iii. 165.

ward with his thirty thousand. Saint-Antoine, with pike and cannon, has preceded him; a mixed multitude, of all and of no arms, hovers on his flanks and skirts; the country once more pauses agape: *Paris marche sur nous.*

CHAPTER VI

TO VERSAILLES

For, indeed, about this same moment, Maillard has halted his draggled Menads on the last hill-top; and now Versailles, and the Château of Versailles, and far and wide the inheritance of Royalty opens to the wondering eye. From far on the right, over Marly and Saint-Germain-en-Laye; round towards Rambouillet, on the left: beautiful all; softly embosomed; as if in sadness, in the dim moist weather! And near before us is Versailles, New and Old; with that broad frondent *Avenue de Versailles* between,—stately-frondent, broad, three hundred feet as men reckon, with its four Rows of Elms; and then the *Château de Versailles*, ending in royal Parks and Pleasances, gleaming Lakelets, Arbours, Labyrinths, the *Ménagerie*, and Great and Little Trianon. High-towered dwellings, leafy pleasant places; where the gods of this lower world abide: whence, nevertheless, black Care cannot be excluded; whither Menadic Hunger is even now advancing, armed with pike-thyrsi!

Yes, yonder, Mesdames, where our straight frondent Avenue, joined, as you note, by Two frondent brother Avenues from this hand and from that, spreads out into Place Royal and Palace Forecourt,—yonder is the *Salle des Menus.* Yonder an august Assembly sits regenerating France. Forecourt, Grand Court, Court of Marble, Court narrowing into Court you may discern next, or fancy: on the extreme verge of which that glass-dome, visibly glittering like a star of hope, is the—Œil-de-Bœuf! Yonder, or nowhere in the world, is bread baked for us. But, O Mesdames, were not one thing good: That our cannons, with Demoiselle Théroigne and all show of war, be put to the rear? Submission beseems petitioners of a National Assembly; we are strangers in Versailles,—whence, too audibly, there comes even now a sound as of tocsin and *générale*! Also to put on, if possible, a cheerful countenance hiding our sorrows; and even to sing? Sorrow, pitied of the Heavens, is hateful, suspicious to the Earth.—So counsels shifty Maillard; haranguing his Menads, on the heights near Versailles.[1]

Cunning Maillard's dispositions are obeyed. The draggled Insurrectionists advance up the Avenue, 'in three columns,' among the four Elm-rows; 'singing *Henri Quatre*,' with what melody they can; and shouting *Vive le Roi*. Versailles, though the Elm-rows are dripping wet, crowds from both sides, with: '*Vivent nos Parisiennes*, Our Paris ones for ever!'

Prickers, scouts have been out towards Paris, as the rumour deepened: whereby his Majesty, gone to shoot in the Woods of Meudon, has been happily discovered, and got home; and the *générale* and tocsin set a-sounding. The Bodyguards are already drawn up in front of the Palace Grates; and look down the Avenue de Versailles; sulky, in wet buckskins.Flandre too is there, repentant of the Opera-Repast. Also Dragoons dismounted are there. Finally Major Lecointre, and what he can gather of the Versailles National Guard;—though it is to be observed, our Colonel, that same sleepless Count d'Estaing, giving neither order nor ammunition, has vanished most improperly; one supposes, into the Œil-de-Bœuf. Red-coated Swiss stand within the Grates, under arms. There likewise, in their inner room, 'all the Ministers,' Saint-Priest, Lamentation Pompignan and the rest, are assembled with M. Necker: they sit with him there; blank, expecting what the hour will bring.

President Mounier, though he answered Mirabeau with a *tant mieux*, and affected to slight the matter, had his own forebodings. Surely, for these four weary hours he has reclined not on roses! The order of the day is getting forward: a Deputation

[1] See *Hist. Parl.* iii. 70–117; *Deux Amis*, iii. 166–177, etc.

to his Majesty seems proper, that it might please him to grant 'Acceptance pure and simple' to those Constitution-Articles of ours; the 'mixed qualified Acceptance,' with its per-adventures, is satisfactory to neither gods nor men.

So much is clear. And yet there is more, which no man speaks, which all men now vaguely understand. Disquietude, absence of mind is on every face; Members whisper, uneasily come and go: the order of the day is evidently not the day's want. Till at length, from the outer gates, is heard a rustling and justling, shrill uproar and squabbling, muffled by walls; which testifies that the hour is come! Rushing and crushing one hears now; then enter Usher Maillard, with a Deputation of Fifteen muddy dripping Women,—having, by incredible industry, and aid of all the macers, persuaded the rest to wait out of doors. National Assembly shall now, therefore, look its august task directly in the face: regenerative Constitutionalism has an unregenerate Sansculottism bodily in front of it; crying, 'Bread! Bread!'

Shifty Maillard, translating frenzy into articulation; repressive with the one hand, expostulative with the other, does his best; and really, though not bred to public speaking, manages rather well:—In the present dreadful rarity of grains, a Deputation of Female Citizens has, as the august Assembly can discern, come out from Paris to petition. Plots of Aristocrats are too evident in the matter; for example, one miller has been bribed 'by a bank-note of 200 livres' not to grind,—name unknown to the Usher, but fact provable, at least indubitable. Further, it seems, the National Cockade has been trampled on; also there are Black Cockades, or were. All which things will not an august National Assembly, the hope of France, take into its wise immediate consideration?

And Menadic Hunger, irrepressible, crying 'Black Cockades,' crying 'Bread, Bread,' adds, after such fashion: Will it not?—Yes, Messieurs, if a Deputation to his Majesty, for the 'Acceptance pure and simple,' seemed proper,—how much more now, for 'the afflicting situation of Paris'; for the calming of this effervescence! President Mounier, with a speedy

Deputation, among whom we notice the respectable figure of Doctor Guillotin, gets himself forward on march. Vice-President shall continue the order of the day; Usher Maillard shall stay by him to repress the women. It is four o'clock, of the miserablest afternoon, when Mounier steps out.

O experienced Mounier, what an afternoon; the last of thy political existence! Better had it been to 'fall suddenly unwell,' while it was yet time. For, behold, the Esplanade, over all its spacious expanse, is covered with groups of squalid dripping Women; of lankhaired male Rascality, armed with axes, rusty pikes, old muskets, iron-shod clubs (*bâtons ferrés*, which end in knives or swordblades, a kind of extempore bill-hook);—looking nothing but hungry revolt. The rain pours: Gardes-du-Corps go caracoling through the groups 'amid hisses'; irritating and agitating what is but dispersed here to reunite there.

Innumerable squalid women beleaguer the President and Deputation; insist on going with him: has not his Majesty himself, looking from the window, sent out to ask, What we wanted? 'Bread, and speech with the King (*Du pain, et parler au Roi*),' that was the answer. Twelve women are clamorously added to the Deputation; and march with it, across the Esplanade; through dissipated groups, caracoling Bodyguards and the pouring rain.

President Mounier, unexpectedly augmented by Twelve women, copiously escorted by Hunger and Rascality, is himself mistaken for a group: himself and his Women are dispersed by caracolers; rally again with difficulty, among the mud.[1] Finally the Grates are opened; the Deputation gets access, with the Twelve women too in it; of which latter, Five shall even see the face of his Majesty. Let wet Menadism, in the best spirits it can, expect their return.

[1] Mounier, *Exposé Justificatif* (cited in *Deux Amis*, iii. 185).

CHAPTER VII

AT VERSAILLES

BUT already Pallas Athene (in the shape of Demoiselle Théroigne) is busy with Flandre and the dismounted Dragoons. She, and such women as are fittest, go through the ranks; speak with an earnest jocosity; clasp rough troopers to their patriot bosom, crush down spontoons and musketoons with soft arms: can a man, that were worthy of the name of man, attack famishing patriot women?

One reads that Théroigne had bags of money, which she distributed over Flandre:—furnished by whom? Alas, with money-bags one seldom sits on insurrectionary cannon. Calumnious Royalism! Théroigne had only the limited earnings of her profession of unfortunate-female; money she had not, but brown locks, the figure of a Heathen Goddess and an eloquent tongue and heart.

Meanwhile Saint-Antoine, in groups and troops, is continually arriving; wetted, sulky; with pikes and impromptu billhooks: driven thus far by popular fixed-idea. So many hirsute figures driven hither, in that manner: figures that have come to do they know not what; figures that have come to see it done! Distinguished among all figures, who is this, of gaunt stature, with leaden breastplate, though a small one;[1] bushy in red grizzled locks; nay with long tile-beard? It is Jourdan, unjust dealer in mules; a dealer no longer, but a Painter's Model, playing truant this day. From the necessities of Art comes his long tile-beard; whence his leaden breastplate (unless indeed he were some Hawker licensed by leaden badge) may have come, will perhaps remain for ever a Historical Problem. Another Saul among the people we discern: '*Père Adam*, Father Adam,' as the groups name him; to us better known as bull-voiced Marquis Saint-Huruge; hero of the

[1] See Weber, ii. 185–231.

Veto; a man that has had losses, and deserved them. The tall Marquis, emitted some days ago from limbo, looks peripatetically on this scene from under his umbrella, not without interest. All which persons and things, hurled together as we see; Pallas Athene, busy with Flandre; patriotic Versailles National Guards, short of ammunition, and deserted by D'Estaing their Colonel, and commanded by Lecointre their Major; then caracoling Bodyguards, sour, dispirited, with their buckskins wet; and finally this flowing sea of indignant Squalor,—may they not give rise to occurrences?

Behold, however, the Twelve She-deputies return from the Château. Without President Mounier, indeed; but radiant with joy, shouting '*Life to the King and his House.*' Apparently the news are good, Mesdames? News of the best! Five of us were admitted to the internal splendours, to the Royal Presence. This slim damsel, 'Louison Chabray, worker in sculpture, aged only seventeen,' as being of the best looks and address, her we appointed speaker. On whom, and indeed on all of us, his Majesty looked nothing but graciousness. Nay when Louison, addressing him, was like to faint, he took her in his royal arms, and said gallantly, 'It was well worth while (*Elle en valût bien la peine*).' Consider, O Women, what a King! His words were of comfort, and that only: there shall be provision sent to Paris, if provision is in the world; grains shall circulate free as air; millers shall grind, or do worse, while their millstones endure; and nothing be left wrong which a Restorer of French Liberty can right.

Good news these; but, to wet Menads, all-too incredible! There seems no proof, then? *Words* of comfort,—they are words only; which will feed nothing. O miserable People, betrayed by Aristocrats, who corrupt thy very messengers! In his royal arms, Mademoiselle Louison? In his arms? Thou shameless minx, worthy of a name—that shall be nameless! Yes, thy skin is soft: ours is rough with hardship; and well wetted, waiting here in the rain. No children hast thou hungry at home; only alabaster dolls, that weep not! The traitress!

To the Lanterne!—And so poor Louison Chabray, no asseveration or shrieks availing her, fair slim damsel, late in the arms of Royalty, has a garter round her neck, and furibund Amazons at each end; is about to perish so,—when two Bodyguards gallop up, indignantly dissipating; and rescue her. The miscredited Twelve hasten back to the Château, for an 'answer in writing.'

Nay, behold, a new flight of Menads, with 'M. Brunout Bastille Volunteer,' as impressed-commandant, at the head of it. These also will advance to the Grate of the Grand Court, and see what is toward. Human patience, in wet buckskins, has its limits. Bodyguard Lieutenant M. de Savonnières for one moment lets his temper, long provoked, long pent, give way. He not only dissipates these latter Menads; but caracoles and cuts, or indignantly flourishes, at M. Brunout, the impressed-commandant; and, finding great relief in it, even chases him; Brunout flying nimbly, though in a pirouette manner, and now with sword also drawn. At which sight of wrath and victory, two other Bodyguards (for wrath is contagious, and to pent Bodyguards is so solacing) do likewise give way; give chase, with brandished sabre, and in the air make horrid circles. So that poor Brunout has nothing for it but to retreat with accelerated nimbleness, through rank after rank; Parthian-like, fencing as he flies; above all, shouting lustily, '*On nous laisse assassiner*, They are getting us assassinated!'

Shameful! Three against one! Growls come from the Lecointrian ranks; bellowings,—lastly shots. Savonnières' arm is raised to strike: the bullet of a Lecointrian musket shatters it; the brandished sabre jingles down harmless. Brunout has escaped, this duel well ended: but the wild howl of war is everywhere beginning to pipe!

The Amazons recoil; Saint-Antoine has its cannon pointed (full of grapeshot); thrice applies the lit flambeau; which thrice refuses to catch,—the touchholes are so wetted; and voices cry: '*Arrêtez, il n'est pas temps encore*, Stop, it is not yet time!'[1] Messieurs of the Garde-du-Corps, ye had orders not to

[1] *Deux Amis*, ii. 192–201.

fire; nevertheless two of you limp dismounted, and one war-horse lies slain. Were it not well to draw back out of shot-range; finally to file off,—into the interior? If in so filing off, there did a musketoon or two discharge itself at these armed shopkeepers, hooting and crowing, could man wonder? Draggled are your white cockades of an enormous size; would to Heaven they were got exchanged for tricolor ones! Your buckskins are wet, your hearts heavy. Go, and return not!

The Bodyguards file off, as we hint; giving and receiving shots; drawing no life-blood; leaving boundless indignation. Some three times in the thickening dusk, a glimpse of them is seen, at this or the other Portal: saluted always with execrations, with the whew of lead. Let but a Bodyguard show face, he is hunted by Rascality;—for instance, poor 'M. de Moucheton of the Scotch Company,' owner of the slain war-horse; and has to be smuggled off by Versailles Captains. Or rusty firelocks belch after him, shivering asunder his—hat. In the end, by superior Order, the Bodyguards, all but the few on immediate duty, disappear; or as it were abscond; and march, under cloud of night, to Rambouillet.[1]

We remark also that the Versaillese have now got ammunition: all afternoon, the official Person could find none; till, in these so critical moments, a patriotic Sublieutenant set a pistol to his ear, and would thank him to find some,—which he thereupon succeeded in doing. Likewise that Flandre, disarmed by Pallas Athene, says openly, it will not fight with citizens; and for token of peace has exchanged cartridges with the Versaillese.

Sansculottism is now among mere friends; and can 'circulate freely'; indignant at Bodyguards;—complaining also considerably of hunger.

[1] Weber, ubi supra.

CHAPTER VIII

THE EQUAL DIET

But why lingers Mounier; returns not with his Deputation? It is six, it is seven o'clock; and still no Mounier, no Acceptance pure and simple.

And, behold, the dripping Menads, not now in deputation but in mass, have penetrated into the Assembly: to the shamefulest interruption of public speaking and order of the day. Neither Maillard nor Vice-President can restrain them, except within wide limits; not even, except for minutes, can the lion-voice of Mirabeau, though they applaud it: but ever and anon they break-in upon the regeneration of France with cries of: 'Bread; not so much discoursing! *Du pain; pas tant de longs discours!*'—So insensible were these poor creatures to bursts of parliamentary eloquence!

One learns also that the royal Carriages are getting yoked, as if for Metz. Carriages, royal or not, have verily showed themselves at the back Gates. They even produced, or quoted, a written order from our Versailles Municipality,—which is a Monarchic not a Democratic one. However, Versailles Patrols drove them in again; as the vigilant Lecointre had strictly charged them to do.

A busy man, truly, is Major Lecointre, in these hours. For Colonel d'Estaing loiters invisible in the Œil-de-Bœuf; invisible, or still more questionably *visible* for instants: then also a too loyal Municipality requires supervision: no order, civil or military, taken about any of these thousand things! Lecointre is at the Versailles Townhall: he is at the Grate of the Grand Court; communing with Swiss and Bodyguards. He is in the ranks of Flandre; he is here, he is there: studious to prevent bloodshed; to prevent the Royal Family from flying to Metz; the Menads from plundering Versailles.

At the fall of night, we behold him advance to those armed

groups of Saint-Antoine, hovering all-too grim near the Salle des Menus. They receive him in a half-circle; twelve speakers behind cannons with lighted torches in hand, the cannon-mouths *towards* Lecointre: a picture for Salvator! He asks, in temperate but courageous language: What they, by this their journey to Versailles, do specially want? The twelve speakers reply, in few words inclusive of much: 'Bread, and the end of these brabbles; *Du pain, et la fin des affaires.*' When the *affairs* will end, no Major Lecointre, nor no mortal, can say; but as to bread, he inquires, How many are you?—learns that they are six hundred, that a loaf each will suffice; and rides off to the Municipality to get six hundred loaves.

Which loaves, however, a Municipality of Monarchic temper will not give. It will give two tons of rice rather,—could you but know whether it should be boiled or raw. Nay when this too is accepted, the Municipals have disappeared;—ducked under, as the Six-and-twenty Long-gowned of Paris did; and, leaving not the smallest vestige of rice, in the boiled or raw state, they there vanish from History!

Rice comes not; one's hope of food is balked; even one's hope of vengeance: is not M. de Moucheton of the Scotch Company, as we said, deceitfully smuggled off? Failing all which, behold only M. de Moucheton's slain war-horse, lying on the Esplanade there! Saint-Antoine, balked, esurient, pounces on the slain war-horse; flays it; roasts it, with such fuel, of paling, gates, portable timber as can be come at, not without shouting; *and*, after the manner of ancient Greek Heroes, *they lifted their hands to the daintily readied repast*; such as it might be.[1] Other Rascality prowls discursive; seeking what it may devour. Flandre will retire to its barracks; Lecointre also with his Versaillese,—all but the vigilant Patrols, charged to be doubly vigilant.

So sink the shadows of night, blustering, rainy; and all paths grow dark. Strangest Night ever seen in these regions,—perhaps since the Bartholomew Night, when Versailles, as Bassompierre writes of it, was a *chétif château*. O for the Lyre

[1] Weber; *Deux Amis*, etc.

of some Orpheus, to constrain, with touch of melodious strings, these mad masses into Order! For here all seems fallen asunder, in wide-yawning dislocation. The highest, as in down-rushing of a World, is come in contact with the lowest: the Rascality of France beleaguering the Royalty of France; 'iron-shod batons' lifted round the diadem, not to guard it! With denunciations of bloodthirsty Anti-National Bodyguards, are heard dark growlings against a Queenly Name.

The Court sits tremulous, powerless; varies with the varying temper of the Esplanade, with the varying colour of the rumours from Paris. Thick-coming rumours; now of peace, now of war. Necker and all the Ministers consult; with a blank issue. The Œil-de-Bœuf is one tempest of whispers:—We will fly to Metz; we will not fly. The royal Carriages again attempt egress,—though for trial merely; they are again driven in by Lecointre's Patrols. In six hours nothing has been resolved on; not even the Acceptance pure and simple.

In six hours? Alas, he who, in such circumstances, cannot resolve in six minutes, may give up the enterprise: him Fate has already resolved for. And Menadism, meanwhile, and Sansculottism takes counsel with the National Assembly; grows more and more tumultuous there. Mounier returns not; Authority nowhere shows itself; the Authority of France lies, for the present, with Lecointre and Usher Maillard.—This then is the abomination of desolation; come suddenly, though long foreshadowed as inevitable! For, to the blind, all things are sudden. Misery which, through long ages, had no spokesman, no helper, will now be its own helper and speak for itself. The dialect, one of the rudest, is, what it could be, *this*.

At eight o'clock there returns to our Assembly not the Deputation; but Doctor Guillotin announcing that it will return; also that there is hope of the Acceptance pure and simple. He himself has brought a Royal Letter, authorising and commanding the freest 'circulation of grains.' Which Royal Letter Menadism with its whole heart applauds. Conformably to which the Assembly forthwith passes a Decree; also received with rapturous Menadic plaudits:—Only could not an august

Assembly contrive further to '*fix* the price of bread at eight sous the halfquartern; butchers'-meat at six sous the pound'; which seem fair rates? Such motion do 'a multitude of men and women,' irrepressible by Usher Maillard, now make; does an august Assembly hear made. Usher Maillard himself is not always perfectly measured in speech; but if rebuked, he can justly excuse himself by the peculiarity of the circumstances.[1]

But finally, this Decree well passed, and the disorder continuing; and Members melting away, and no President Mounier returning,—what can the Vice-President do but also melt away? The Assembly melts, under such pressure, into deliquium; or, as it is officially called, adjourns. Maillard is despatched to Paris, with the 'Decree concerning Grains' in his pocket; he and some women, in carriages belonging to the King. Thitherward slim Louison Chabray has already set forth, with that 'written answer' which the Twelve She-deputies returned in to seek. Slim sylph, she has set forth, through the black muddy country: she has much to tell, her poor nerves so flurried; and travels, as indeed today on this road all persons do, with extreme slowness. President Mounier has not come, nor the Acceptance pure and simple; though six hours with their events have come; though courier on courier reports that Lafayette is coming. Coming, with war or with peace? It is time that the Château also should determine on one thing or another; that the Château also should show itself alive, if it would continue living!

Victorious, joyful after such delay, Mounier does arrive at last, and the hard-earned Acceptance with him; which now, alas, is of small value. Fancy Mounier's surprise to find his Senate, whom he hoped to charm by the Acceptance pure and simple, all gone; and in its stead a Senate of Menads! For as Erasmus's Ape mimicked, say with wooden splint, Erasmus shaving, so do these Amazons hold, in mock majesty, some confused parody of National Assembly. They make motions; deliver speeches; pass enactments; productive at least of loud laughter. All galleries and benches are filled; a Strong

[1] *Moniteur* (in *Hist. Parl.* iii. 105).

Dame of the Market is in Mounier's Chair. Not without difficulty, Mounier, by aid of macers and persuasive speaking, makes his way to the Female-President; the Strong Dame, before abdicating, signifies that, for one thing, she and indeed her whole senate male and female (for what was one roasted war-horse among so many?) are suffering very considerably from hunger.

Experienced Mounier, in these circumstances, takes a twofold resolution: To reconvoke his Assembly Members by sound of drum; also to procure a supply of food. Swift messengers fly, to all bakers, cooks, pastrycooks, vintners, restorers; drums beat, accompanied with shrill vocal proclamation, through all streets. They come: the Assembly Members come; what is still better, the provisions come. On tray and barrow come these latter; loaves, wine, great store of sausages. The nourishing baskets circulate harmoniously along the benches; *nor*, according to the Father of Epics, *did any soul lack a fair share of victual* (δαῖτος ἐΐσης, *an equal diet*); highly desirable at the moment.[1]

Gradually some hundred or so of Assembly Members get edged in, Menadism making way a little, round Mounier's chair; listen to the Acceptance pure and simple; and begin, what is the order of the night, 'discussion of the Penal Code.' All benches are crowded; in the dusky galleries, duskier with unwashed heads, is a strange 'coruscation,'—of impromptu bill hooks.[2] It is exactly five months this day since these same galleries were filled with high-plumed jewelled Beauty, raining bright influences; and now? To such length have we got in regenerating France. Methinks the travail-throes are of the sharpest!—Menadism will not be restrained from occasional remarks; asks, 'What is the use of Penal Code? The thing we want is Bread.' Mirabeau turns round with lion-voiced rebuke; Menadism applauds him; but recommences.

Thus they, chewing tough sausages, discussing the Penal Code, make night hideous. What the issue will be? Lafayette

[1] *Deux Amis*, iii. 208.

[2] *Courrier de Provence* (Mirabeau's Newspaper), No. 50, p. 19.

with his thirty thousand must arrive first: him, who cannot now be distant, all men expect, as the messenger of Destiny.

CHAPTER IX

LAFAYETTE

TOWARDS midnight lights flare on the hill; Lafayette's lights! The roll of his drums comes up the Avenue de Versailles. With peace, or with war? Patience, friends! With neither. Lafayette is come, but not yet the catastrophe.

He has halted and harangued so often, on the march; spent nine hours on four leagues of road. At Montreuil, close on Versailles, the whole Host had to pause; and, with uplifted right hand, in the murk of Night, to these pouring skies, swear solemnly to respect the King's Dwelling; to be faithful to King and National Assembly. Rage is driven down out of sight, by the laggard march; the thirst of vengeance slaked in weariness and soaking clothes. Flandre is again drawn out under arms: but Flandre, grown so patriotic, now needs no 'exterminating.' The wayworn Battalions halt in the Avenue: they have, for the present, no wish so pressing as that of shelter and rest.

Anxious sits President Mounier; anxious the Château. There is a message coming from the Château, that M. Mounier would please to return thither with a fresh Deputation, swiftly; and so at least *unite* our two anxieties. Anxious Mounier does of himself send, meanwhile, to apprise the General that his Majesty has been so gracious as to grant us the Acceptance pure and simple. The General, with a small advance column, makes answer in passing; speaks vaguely some smooth words to the National President,—glances, only with the eye, at that so mixtiform National Assembly; then fares forward towards the Château. There are with him two Paris Municipals; they were chosen from the Three Hundred for that errand. He gets admittance through the locked and padlocked Grates, through sentries and ushers, to the Royal Halls.

The Court, male and female, crowds on his passage, to read their doom on his face; which exhibits, say Historians, a mixture 'of sorrow, of fervour and valour,' singular to behold.[1] The King, with Monsieur, with Ministers and Marshals, is waiting to receive him: He 'is come,' in his highflown chivalrous way, 'to offer his head for the safety of his Majesty's.' The two Municipals state the wish of Paris: four things, of quite pacific tenor. First, that the honour of guarding his sacred person be conferred on patriot National Guards;—say, the Centre Grenadiers, who as Gardes Françaises were wont to have that privilege. Second, that provisions be got, if possible. Third, that the Prisons, all crowded with political delinquents, may have judges sent them. Fourth, *that it would please his Majesty to come and live in Paris*. To all which four wishes, except the fourth, his Majesty answers readily, Yes; or indeed may almost say that he has already answered it. To the fourth he can answer only, Yes or No; would so gladly answer, Yes *and* No!—But, in any case, are not their dispositions, thank Heaven, so entirely pacific? There is time for deliberation. The brunt of the danger seems past!

Lafayette and D'Estaing settle the watches; Centre Grenadiers are to take the Guard-room they of old occupied as Gardes Françaises;—for indeed the Gardes-du-Corps, its late ill-advised occupants, are gone mostly to Rambouillet. That is the order of *this* night; sufficient for the night is the evil thereof. Whereupon Lafayette and the two Municipals, with highflown chivalry, take their leave.

So brief has the interview been, Mounier and his Deputation were not yet got up. So brief and satisfactory. A stone is rolled from every heart. The fair Palace Dames publicly declare that this Lafayette, detestable though he be, is their saviour for once. Even the ancient vinaigrous *Tantes* admit it; the King's Aunts, ancient *Graille* and Sisterhood, known to us of old. Queen Marie-Antoinette has been heard often say the like. She alone, among all women and all men, wore a face of

[1] *Mémoire de M. le Comte de Lally-Tollendal* (Janvier 1790), pp. 161–165.

courage, of lofty calmness and resolve, this day. She alone saw clearly what she *meant* to do; and Theresa's Daughter *dares* do what she means, were all France threatening her: abide where her children are, where her husband is.

Towards three in the morning all things are settled; the watches set, the Centre Grenadiers put into their old Guard-room, and harangued; the Swiss, and few remaining Body-guards harangued. The wayworn Paris Battalions, consigned to 'the hospitality of Versailles,' lie dormant in spare-beds, spare-barracks, coffeehouses, empty churches. A troop of them, on their way to the Church of Saint-Louis, awoke poor Weber, dreaming troublous, in the Rue Sartory. Weber has had his waistcoat-pocket full of balls all day; 'two hundred balls, and two *pears* of powder'! For waistcoats were waistcoats then, and had flaps down to mid-thigh. So many balls he has had all day; but no opportunity of using them: he turns over now, execrating disloyal bandits; swears a prayer or two, and straight to sleep again.

Finally the National Assembly is harangued; which thereupon, on motion of Mirabeau, discontinues the Penal Code, and dismisses for this night. Menadism, Sansculottism has cowered into guardhouses, barracks of Flandre, to the light of cheerful fire; failing that, to churches, officehouses, sentry-boxes, wheresoever wretchedness can find a lair. The troublous Day has brawled itself to rest: no lives yet lost but that of one war-horse. Insurrectionary Chaos lies slumbering round the Palace, like Ocean round a Diving-Bell,—no crevice yet disclosing itself.

Deep sleep has fallen promiscuously on the high and on the low; suspending most things, even wrath and famine. Darkness covers the Earth. But, far on the North-east, Paris flings-up her great yellow gleam; far into the wet black Night. For all is illuminated there, as in the old July Nights; the streets deserted, for alarm of war; the Municipals all wakeful; Patrols hailing, with their hoarse *Who-goes*. There, as we discover, our poor slim Louison Chabray, her poor nerves all fluttered, is arriving about this very hour. There Usher Maillard will arrive, about an hour hence, 'towards four in the morning.' They report, successively, to a wakeful Hôtel-de-Ville what comfort they can; which again, with early dawn, large comfortable Placards shall impart to all men.

Lafayette, in the Hôtel de Noailles, not far from the Château, having now finished haranguing, sits with his Officers consulting: at five o'clock the unanimous best counsel is, that a man so tost and toiled for twenty-four hours and more, fling himself on a bed, and seek some rest.

Thus, then, has ended the First Act of the Insurrection of Women. How it will turn on the morrow? The morrow, as always, is with the Fates! But his Majesty, one may hope, will consent to come honourably to Paris; at all events, he can visit Paris. Anti-National Bodyguards, here and elsewhere, must take the National Oath; make reparation to the Tricolor; Flandre will swear. There may be much swearing; much public speaking there will infallibly be: and so, with harangues and vows, may the matter in some handsome way wind itself up.

Or, alas, may it not be all otherwise, *un*handsome; the consent not honourable, but extorted, ignominious? Boundless Chaos of Insurrection presses slumbering round the Palace, like Ocean round a Diving-Bell; and may penetrate at any crevice. Let but that accumulated insurrectionary mass find entrance! Like the infinite inburst of water; or say rather, of inflammable, self-igniting fluid; for example, 'turpentine-and-phosphorus oil,'—fluid known to Spinola Santerre!

CHAPTER X

THE GRAND ENTRIES

THE dull dawn of a new morning, drizzly and chill, had but broken over Versailles, when it pleased Destiny that a Bodyguard should look out of window, on the right wing of the

Château, to see what prospect there was in Heaven and in Earth. Rascality male and female is prowling in view of him. His fasting stomach is, with good cause, sour; he perhaps cannot forbear a passing malison on them; least of all can he forbear answering such.

Ill words breed worse: till the worst word come; and then the ill deed. Did the maledicent Bodyguard, getting (as was too inevitable) better malediction than he gave, load his musketoon, and threaten to fire; nay actually fire? Were wise who wist! It stands asserted; to us not credibly. But be this as it may, menaced Rascality, in whinnying scorn, is shaking at all Grates: the fastening of one (some write, it was a chain merely) gives way; Rascality is in the Grand Court whinnying louder still.

The maledicent Bodyguard, more Bodyguards than he do now give fire; a man's arm is shattered. Lecointre will depose[1] that 'the Sieur Cardine, a National Guard without arms, was stabbed.' But see, sure enough, poor Jerôme l'Héritier, an unarmed National Guard he too, 'cabinet-maker, a saddler's son, of Paris,' with the down of youthhood still on his chin,—he reels death-stricken; rushes to the pavement, scattering it with his blood and brains!—Alleleu! Wilder than Irish wakes rises the howl; of pity, of infinite revenge. In few moments, the Grate of the inner and inmost Court, which they name Court of Marble, this too is forced, or surprised, and bursts open: the Court of Marble too is overflowed: up the Grand Staircase, up all stairs and entrances rushes the living Deluge! Deshuttes and Varigny, the two sentry Bodyguards, are trodden down, are massacred with a hundred pikes. Women snatch their cutlasses, or any weapon, and storm-in Menadic:—other women lift the corpse of shot Jerôme; lay it down on the Marble steps; there shall the livid face and smashed head, dumb for ever, *speak*.

Wo now to all Bodyguards, mercy is none for them! Miomandre de Sainte-Marie pleads with soft words, on the Grand Staircase, 'descending four steps':—to the roaring tornado. His

[1] *Déposition de Lecointre* (in *Hist. Parl.* iii. 111–115).

comrades snatch him up, by the skirts and belts; literally, from the jaws of Destruction; and slam-to their Door. This also will stand few instants; the panels shivering in, like potsherds. Barricading serves not: fly fast, ye Bodyguards: rabid Insurrection, like the Hellhound Chase, uproaring at your heels!

The terror-struck Bodyguards fly, bolting and barricading; it follows. Whitherward? Through hall on hall: wo, now! towards the Queen's Suite of Rooms, in the farthest room of which the Queen is now asleep. Five sentinels rush through that long Suite; they are in the Anteroom knocking loud: 'Save the Queen!' Trembling women fall at their feet with tears: are answered: 'Yes, we will die; save ye the Queen!'

Tremble not, women, but haste: for, lo, another voice shouts far through the outermost door, 'Save the Queen!' and the door is shut. It is brave Miomandre's voice that shouts this second warning. He has stormed across imminent death to do it; fronts imminent death, having done it. Brave Tardivet du Repaire, bent on the same desperate service, was borne down with pikes; his comrades hardly snatched him in again alive. Miomandre and Tardivet: let the names of these two Bodyguards, as the names of brave men should, live long.

Trembling Maids-of-Honour, one of whom from afar caught glimpse of Miomandre as well as heard him, hastily wrap the Queen; not in robes of state. She flies for her life, across the Œil-de-Bœuf; against the main door of which too Insurrection batters. She is in the King's Apartment, in the King's arms; she clasps her children amid a faithful few. The Imperial-hearted bursts into mother's tears: 'O my friends, save me and my children; *O mes amis, sauvez-moi et mes enfans!*' The battering of Insurrectionary axes clangs audible across the Œil-de-Bœuf. What an hour!

Yes, Friends; a hideous fearful hour; shameful alike to Governed and Governor; wherein Governed and Governor ignominiously testify that their relation is at an end. Rage, which had brewed itself in twenty thousand hearts for the last four-and-twenty hours, has taken *fire*: Jerôme's brained corpse lies there as live-coal. It is, as we said, the infinite Element bursting in; wild surging through all corridors and conduits.

Meanwhile the poor Bodyguards have got hunted mostly into the Œil-de-Bœuf. They may die there, at the King's threshold; they can do little to defend it. They are heaping *tabourets* (stools of honour), benches and all movables against the door; at which the axe of Insurrection thunders.—But did brave Miomandre perish, then, at the Queen's outer door? No, he was fractured, slashed, lacerated, left for dead; he has nevertheless crawled hither; and shall live, honoured of loyal France. Remark also, in flat contradiction to much which has been said and sung, that Insurrection did *not* burst that door he had defended; but hurried elsewhither, seeking new Bodyguards.[1]

Poor Bodyguards, with their Thyestes Opera-Repast! Well for them that Insurrection has only pikes and axes; no right sieging-tools! It shakes and thunders. Must they all perish miserably, and Royalty with them? Deshuttes and Varigny, massacred at the first inbreak, have been beheaded in the Marble Court; a sacrifice to Jerôme's *manes*: Jourdan with the tile-beard did that duty willingly; and asked, If there were no more? Another captive they are leading round the corpse, with howl-chantings: may not Jourdan again tuck-up his sleeves?

And louder and louder rages Insurrection within, plundering if it cannot kill; louder and louder it thunders at the Œil-de-Bœuf: what can now hinder its bursting-in?—On a sudden it ceases; the battering has ceased! Wild-rushing; the cries grow fainter; there is silence, or the tramp of regular steps; then a friendly knocking: 'We are the Centre Grenadiers, old Gardes Françaises: Open to us, Messieurs of the Garde-du-Corps; we have not forgotten how you saved us at Fontenoy!'[2] The door is opened; enter Captain Gondran and the Centre Grenadiers: there are military embracings; there is sudden deliverance from death into life.

[1] Campan, ii. 75–87.
[2] Toulongeon, i. 144.

Strange Sons of Adam! It was to 'exterminate' these Gardes-du-Corps that the Centre Grenadiers left home: and now they have rushed to save them from extermination. The memory of common peril, of old help, melts the rough heart; bosom is clasped to bosom, not in war. The King shows himself, one moment, through the door of his Apartment, with: 'Do not hurt my Guards!'—'*Soyons frères*, Let us be brothers!' cries Captain Gondran; and again dashes off, with levelled bayonets, to sweep the Palace clear.

Now too Lafayette, suddenly roused, not from sleep (for his eyes had not yet closed), arrives; with passionate popular eloquence, with prompt military word of command. National Guards, suddenly roused, by sound of trumpet and alarm-drum, are all arriving. The death-melly ceases: the first sky-lambent blaze of Insurrection is got damped down; it burns now, if unextinguished yet flameless, as charred coals do, and not inextinguishable. The King's Apartments are safe. Ministers, Officials, and even some loyal National Deputies are assembling round their Majesties. The consternation will, with sobs and confusion, settle down gradually, into plan and counsel, better or worse.

But glance now, for a moment, from the royal windows! A roaring sea of human heads, inundating both Courts; billowing against all passages: Menadic women; infuriated men, mad with revenge, with love of mischief, love of plunder! Rascality has slipped its muzzle; and now bays, three-throated, like the Dog of Erebus. Fourteen Bodyguards are wounded; two massacred, and as we saw, beheaded; Jourdan asking, 'Was it worth while to come so far for two?' Hapless Deshuttes and Varigny! Their fate surely was sad. Whirled down so suddenly to the abyss; as men are, suddenly, by the wide thunder of the Mountain Avalanche, awakened not by *them*, awakened far off by others! When the Château Clock last struck, they two were pacing languid, with poised musketoon; anxious mainly that the next hour would strike. It has struck; to them inaudible. Their trunks lie mangled: their heads parade, 'on pikes twelve feet long,' through the streets of Versailles; and shall, about noon, reach the Barriers of Paris,—a too ghastly contradiction to the large comfortable Placards that have been posted there!

The other captive Bodyguard is still circling the corpse of Jerôme, amid Indian war-whooping; bloody Tilebeard, with tucked sleeves, brandishing his bloody axe; when Gondran and the Grenadiers come in sight. 'Comrades, will you see a man massacred in cold blood?'—'Off, butchers!' answer they; and the poor Bodyguard is free. Busy runs Gondran, busy run Guards and Captains; scouring all corridors; dispersing Rascality and Robbery; sweeping the Palace clear. The mangled carnage is removed; Jerôme's body to the Townhall, for inquest: the fire of Insurrection gets damped, more and more, into measurable, manageable heat.

Transcendent things of all sorts, as in the general outburst of multitudinous Passion, are huddled together; the ludicrous, nay the ridiculous, with the horrible. Far over the billowy sea of heads, may be seen Rascality, caprioling on horses from the Royal Stud. The Spoilers these; for Patriotism is always infected so, with a proportion of mere thieves and scoundrels. Gondran snatched their prey from them in the Château; whereupon they hurried to the Stables, and took horse there. But the generous Diomedes' steeds, according to Weber, disdained such scoundrel-burden; and, flinging-up their royal heels, did soon project most of it, in parabolic curves, to a distance, amid peals of laughter; and were caught. Mounted National Guards secured the rest.

Now too is witnessed the touching last-flicker of Etiquette; which sinks not here, in the Cimmerian World-wreckage, without a sign; as the house-cricket might still chirp in the pealing of a Trump of Doom. 'Monsieur,' said some Master of Ceremonies (one hopes it might be De Brézé), as Lafayette, in these fearful moments, was rushing towards the inner Royal Apartments, '*Monsieur, le Roi vous accorde les grandes entrées*, Monsieur, the King grants you the Grand Entries,'—not finding it convenient to refuse them![1]

[1] Toulongeon, i. App. 120.

CHAPTER XI

FROM VERSAILLES

HOWEVER, the Paris National Guard, wholly under arms, has cleared the Palace, and even occupies the nearer external spaces; extruding miscellaneous Patriotism, for most part, into the Grand Court, or even into the Forecourt.

The Bodyguards, you can observe, have now of a verity 'hoisted the National Cockade': for they step forward to the windows or balconies, hat aloft in hand, on each hat a huge tricolor; and fling over their bandoleers in sign of surrender; and shout *Vive la Nation*. To which how can the generous heart respond but with, *Vive le Roi: vivent les Gardes-du-Corps*? His Majesty himself has appeared with Lafayette on the balcony, and again appears: *Vive le Roi* greets him from all throats; but also from some one throat is heard, '*Le Roi à Paris*, The King to Paris!'

Her Majesty too, on demand, shows herself, though there is peril in it: she steps out on the balcony, with her little boy and girl. 'No children, *Point d'enfans!*' cry the voices. She gently pushes back her children; and stands alone, her hands serenely crossed on her breast: 'Should I die,' she had said, 'I will do it.' Such serenity of heroism has its effect. Lafayette, with ready wit, in his highflown chivalrous way, takes that fair queenly hand, and, reverently kneeling, kisses it: thereupon the people do shout *Vive la Reine*. Nevertheless, poor Weber 'saw' (or even thought he saw; for hardly the third part of poor Weber's experiences, in such hysterical days, will stand scrutiny) 'one of these brigands level his musket at her Majesty,'—with or without intention to shoot; for another of the brigands 'angrily struck it down.'

So that all, and the Queen herself, nay the very Captain of the Bodyguards, have grown National! The very Captain of the Bodyguards steps out now with Lafayette. On the hat of the repentant man is an enormous tricolor; large as a soup-platter or sunflower; visible to the utmost Forecourt. He takes the National Oath with a loud voice, elevating his hat; at which sight all the army raise their bonnets on their bayonets, with shouts. Sweet is reconcilement to the heart of man. Lafayette has sworn Flandre; he swears the remaining Bodyguards, down in the Marble Court; the people clasp them in their arms:—O my brothers, why would ye force us to slay you? Behold, there is joy over you, as over returning prodigal sons!—The poor Bodyguards, now National and tricolor, exchange bonnets, exchange arms; there shall be peace and fraternity. And still '*Vive le Roi*'; and also '*Le Roi à Paris*,' not now from one throat, but from all throats as one, for it is the heart's wish of all mortals.

Yes, *The King to Paris*: what else? Ministers may consult, and National Deputies wag their heads: but there is now no other possibility. You have forced him to go willingly. 'At one o'clock!' Lafayette gives audible assurance to that purpose; and universal Insurrection, with immeasurable shout, and a discharge of all the fire-arms, clear and rusty, great and small, that it has, returns him acceptance. What a sound; heard for leagues: a doom-peal!—That sound too rolls away; into the Silence of Ages. And the Château of Versailles stands ever since vacant, hushed-still; its spacious Courts grassgrown, responsive to the hoe of the weeder. Times and generations roll on, in their confused Gulf-current; and buildings, like builders, have their destiny.

Till one o'clock, then, there will be three parties, National Assembly, National Rascality, National Royalty, all busy enough. Rascality rejoices; women trim themselves with tricolor. Nay motherly Paris has sent her Avengers sufficient 'cartloads of loaves'; which are shouted over, which are gratefully consumed. The Avengers, in return, are searching for grain-stores; loading them in fifty wagons; that so a National King, probable harbinger of all blessings, may be the evident bringer of plenty, for one.

And thus has Sansculottism made prisoner its King; *revok-*

ing his parole. The Monarchy has fallen; and not so much as honourably: no, ignominiously; with struggle, indeed, oft-repeated; but then with unwise struggle; wasting its strength in fits and paroxysms; at every new paroxysm foiled more pitifully than before. Thus Broglie's whiff of grapeshot, which might have been something, has dwindled to the pot-valour of an Opera Repast, and *O Richard, O mon Roi*. Which, again, we shall see dwindle to a Favras Conspiracy, a thing to be settled by the hanging of one Chevalier.

Poor Monarchy! But what save foulest defeat can await that man, who wills, and yet wills not? Apparently the King either has a right, assertible as such to the death, before God and man; or else he has no right. Apparently, the one or the other; could he but know which! May Heaven pity him! Were Louis wise, he would this day abdicate.—Is it not strange so few Kings abdicate; and none yet heard of has been known to commit suicide? Fritz the First, of Prussia, alone tried it; and they cut the rope.[1]

As for the National Assembly, which decrees this morning that it 'is inseparable from his Majesty,' and will follow him to Paris, there may one thing be noted: its extreme want of bodily health. After the Fourteenth of July there was a certain sickliness observable among honourable Members; so many demanding passports, on account of infirm health. But now, for these following days, there is a perfect murrain: President Mounier, Lally Tollendal, Clermont Tonnere, and all Constitutional Two-Chamber Royalists needing change of air; as most No-Chamber Royalists had formerly done.

For, in truth, it is the *second Emigration* this that has now come; most extensive among Commons Deputies, Noblesse, Clergy: so that 'to Switzerland alone there go sixty thousand.' They will return in the day of accounts! Yes, and have hot welcome.—But Emigration on Emigration is the peculiarity of France. One Emigration follows another; grounded on

[1] Calumnious rumour, current long since, in loose vehicles (*Edinburgh Review* on *Mémoires de Bastille*, for example), concerning Friedrich Wilhelm and his ways, then so mysterious and miraculous to many; —not the least truth in it! (*Note of* 1868.)

reasonable fear, unreasonable hope, largely also on childish pet. The highflyers have gone first, now the lower flyers; and ever the lower will go, down to the crawlers. Whereby, however, cannot our National Assembly so much the more commodiously make the Constitution; your Two-Chamber Anglomaniacs being all safe, distant on foreign shores? Abbé Maury is seized and sent back again: he, tough as tanned leather, with eloquent Captain Cazalès and some others, will stand it out for another year.

But here, meanwhile, the question arises: Was Philippe d'Orléans seen, this day, 'in the Bois de Boulogne, in grey surtout'; waiting under the wet sere foliage, what the day might bring forth? Alas, yes, the Eidolon of him was,—in Weber's and other such brains. The Châtelet shall make large inquisition into the matter, examining a hundred and seventy witnesses, and Deputy Chabroud publish his Report; but disclose nothing *further*.[1] What, then, has caused these two unparalleled October Days? For surely such dramatic exhibition never yet enacted itself without Dramatist and Machinist. Wooden Punch emerges not, with his domestic sorrows, into the light of day, unless the wire be pulled: how can human mobs? Was it not D'Orléans, then, and Laclos, Marquis Sillery, Mirabeau and the sons of confusion; hoping to drive the King to Metz, and gather the spoil? Nay was it not, quite contrariwise, the Œil-de-Bœuf, Bodyguard Colonel de Guiche, Minister Saint-Priest and high-flying Loyalists; hoping also to drive him to Metz, and try it by the sword of civil war? Good Marquis Toulongeon, the Historian and Deputy, feels constrained to admit that it was *both*.[2]

Alas, my Friends, credulous incredulity is a strange matter. But when a whole Nation is smitten with Suspicion, and sees a dramatic miracle in the very operation of the gastric juices, what help is there? Such Nation is already a mere hypochondriac bundle of diseases; as good as changed into glass; atrabiliar, decadent; and will suffer crises. Is not Suspicion

[1] *Rapport de Chabroud* (*Moniteur*, du 31 Decembre 1789).
[2] Toulongeon, i. 150.

itself the one thing to be suspected, as Montaigne feared only fear?

Now, however, the short hour has struck. His Majesty is in his carriage, with his Queen, sister Elizabeth and two royal children. Not for another hour can the infinite Procession get marshalled and under way. The weather is dim drizzling; the mind confused; the noise great.

Processional marches not a few our world has seen; Roman triumphs and ovations, Cabiric cymbal-beatings, Royal progresses, Irish funerals; but this of the French Monarchy marching to its bed remained to be seen. Miles long, and of breadth losing itself in vagueness, for all the neighbouring country crowds to see. Slow; stagnating along, like shoreless Lake, yet with a noise like Niagara, like Babel and Bedlam. A splashing and a tramping; a hurrahing, uproaring, musket-volleying;—the truest segment of Chaos seen in these latter Ages! Till slowly it disembogue itself, in the thickening dusk, into expectant Paris, through a double row of faces all the way from Passy to the Hôtel-de-Ville.

Consider this: Vanguard of National troops; with trains of artillery; of pikemen and pikewomen, mounted on cannons, on carts, hackney-coaches, or on foot;—tripudiating, in tricolor ribbons from head to heel; loaves stuck on the points of bayonets, green boughs stuck in gun-barrels.[1] Next, as main-march, 'fifty cart-loads of corn,' which have been lent, for peace, from the stores of Versailles. Behind which follow stragglers of the Garde-du-Corps; all humiliated, in Grenadier bonnets. Close on these comes the Royal Carriage; come Royal Carriages: for there are a Hundred National Deputies too, among whom sits Mirabeau,—his remarks not given. Then finally, pellmell, as rear-guard, Flandre, Swiss, Hundred Swiss, other Body-guards, Brigands, whosoever cannot get before. Between and among all which masses flows without limit Saint-Antoine and the Menadic Cohort. Menadic especially about the Royal Carriage; tripudiating there, covered with tricolor;

[1] Mercier, *Nouveau Paris*, iii. 21.

singing 'allusive songs'; pointing with one hand to the Royal Carriage, which the allusions hit, and pointing to the Provision-wagons with the other hand, and these words: 'Courage, Friends! We shall not want bread now; we are bringing you the Baker, the Bakeress and Baker's-boy (*le Boulanger, la Boulangère et le petit Mitron*).'[1]

The wet day draggles the tricolor, but the joy is unextinguishable. Is not all well now? '*Ah, Madame, notre bonne Reine*,' said some of these Strong-women some days hence, 'Ah, Madame, our good Queen, don't be a traitor any more (*ne soyez plus traître*), and we will all love you!' Poor Weber went splashing along, close by the Royal Carriage, with the tear in his eye: 'their Majesties did me the honour,' or I thought they did it, 'to testify, from time to time, by shrugging of the shoulders, by looks directed to Heaven, the emotions they felt.' Thus, like frail cockle, floats the royal Life-boat, helmless, on black deluges of Rascality.

Mercier, in his loose way, estimates the Procession and assistants at two hundred thousand. He says it was one boundless inarticulate Haha;—*transcendent* World-Laughter; comparable to the Saturnalia of the Ancients. Why not? Here too, as we said, is Human Nature once more human; shudder at it whoso is of shuddering humour; yet, behold, it is human. It has 'swallowed all formulas'; it tripudiates even so. For which reason they that collect Vases and Antiques, with figures of Dancing Bacchantes 'in wild and all-but impossible positions,' may look with some interest on it.

Thus, however, has the slow-moving Chaos, or modern Saturnalia of the Ancients, reached the Barrier; and must halt, to be harangued by Mayor Bailly. Thereafter it has to lumber along, between the double row of faces, in the transcendent heaven-lashing Haha; two hours longer, towards the Hôtel-de-Ville. Then again to be harangued there, by several persons; by Moreau de Saint-Méry among others; Moreau of the Three-thousand orders, now National Deputy for St. Domingo. To all

[1] Toulongeon, i. 134–161; *Deux Amis*, iii. c. 9; etc. etc.

which poor Louis, 'who seemed to experience a slight emotion' on entering this Townhall, can answer only that he 'comes with pleasure, with confidence among his people.' Mayor Bailly, in reporting it, forgets 'confidence': and the poor Queen says eagerly: 'Add, with confidence.'—'Messieurs,' rejoins Mayor Bailly, 'you are happier than if I had not forgotten.'

Finally, the King is shown on an upper balcony, by torch-light, with a huge tricolor in his hat: 'and all the people,' says Weber, 'grasped one another's hand';—thinking *now* surely the New Era was born. Hardly till eleven at night can Royalty get to its vacant, long-deserted Palace of the Tuileries; to lodge there, somewhat in strolling-player fashion. It is Tuesday the 6th of October 1789.

Poor Louis has Two other Paris Processions to make: one ludicrous-ignominious like this; the other not ludicrous nor ignominious, but serious, nay sublime.

VOLUME THREE

BOOK THIRD

THE GIRONDINS

CHAPTER I

CAUSE AND EFFECT

THIS huge Insurrectionary Movement, which we liken to a breaking-out of Tophet and the Abyss, has swept away Royalty, Aristocracy, and a King's life. The question is, What will it next do; how will it henceforth shape itself? Settle down into a reign of Law and Liberty; according as the habits, persuasions and endeavours of the educated, moneyed, respectable class prescribe? That is to say: the volcanic lava-flood, bursting up in the manner described, will explode and flow according to Girondin Formula and preëstablished rule of Philosophy? If so, for our Girondin friends it will be well.

Meanwhile were not the prophecy rather, that as no external force, Royal or other, now remains which could control this Movement, the Movement will follow a course of its own; probably a very original one? Further, that whatsoever man or men can best interpret the inward tendencies it has, and give them voice and activity, will obtain the lead of it? For the rest, that as a thing *without* order, a thing proceeding from beyond and beneath the region of order, it must work and welter, not as a Regularity but as a Chaos; destructive and self-destructive; always till something that *has* order arise, strong enough to bind it into subjection again? Which something, we may further conjecture, will not be a Formula, with philosophical propositions and forensic eloquence; but a Reality, probably with a sword in its hand!

As for the Girondin Formula, of a respectable Republic for the Middle Classes, all manner of Aristocracies being now sufficiently demolished, there seems little reason to expect that the business will stop there. *Liberty, Equality, Fraternity*, these are the words; enunciative and prophetic. Republic for the respectable washed Middle Classes, how can that be the fulfilment thereof? Hunger and nakedness, and nightmare oppression lying heavy on Twenty-five million hearts; this, not the wounded vanities or contradicted philosophies of philosophical Advocates, rich Shopkeepers, rural Noblesse, was the prime mover in the French Revolution; as the like will be in all such Revolutions, in all countries. Feudal Fleur-de-lys had become an insupportably bad marching-banner, and needed to be torn and trampled: but Moneybag of Mammon (for that, in these times, is what the respectable Republic for the Middle Classes will signify) is a still worse, while it lasts. Properly, indeed, it is the worst and basest of all banners and symbols of dominion among men; and indeed is possible only in a time of general Atheism, and Unbelief in anything save in brute Force and Sensualism; pride of birth, pride of office, any known kind of pride being a degree better than purse-pride. Freedom, Equality, Brotherhood: not in the Moneybag, but far elsewhere, will Sansculottism seek these things.

We say therefore that an Insurrectionary France, loose of control from without, destitute of supreme order from within, will form one of the most tumultuous Activities ever seen on this Earth; such as no Girondin Formula can regulate. An immeasurable force, made up of forces manifold, heterogeneous, compatible and incompatible. In plainer words, this France must needs split into Parties; each of which seeking to make itself good, contradiction, exasperation will arise; and Parties on Parties find that they cannot work together, cannot exist together.

As for the number of Parties there will, strictly counting, be as many Parties as there are opinions. According to which rule, in this National Convention itself, to say nothing of France generally, the number of Parties ought to be Seven-hundred and Forty-nine; for every unit entertains his opinion. But now, as every unit has at once an individual nature or necessity to follow his own road, and a gregarious nature or necessity to see himself travelling by the side of others,—what can there be but dissolutions, precipitations, endless turbulence of attracting and repelling; till once the master-element get evolved, and this wild alchemy arrange itself again?

To the length of Seven-hundred and Forty-nine Parties, however, no Nation was ever yet seen to go. Nor indeed much beyond the length of Two Parties; two at a time;—so invincible is man's tendency to unite, with all the invincible divisiveness he has! Two Parties, we say, are the usual number at one time: let these two fight it out, all minor shades of party rallying under the shade likest them; when the one has fought down the other, then it, in its turn, may divide, self-destructive; and so the process continue, as far as needful. This is the way of Revolutions, which spring up as the French one has done; when the so-called Bonds of Society snap asunder; and all Laws that are not Laws of Nature become naught and Formulas merely.

But, quitting these somewhat abstract considerations, let History note this concrete reality which the streets of Paris exhibit, on Monday the 25th of February 1793. Long before daylight that morning, these streets are noisy and angry. Petitioning enough there has been; a Convention often solicited. It was but yesterday there came a Deputation of Washerwomen with Petition; complaining that not so much as soap could be had; to say nothing of bread, and condiments of bread. The cry of women, round the Salle de Manége, was heard plaintive: '*Du pain et du savon*, Bread and soap.'[1]

And now from six o'clock, this Monday morning, one perceives the Bakers' Queues unusually expanded, angrily agitating themselves. Not the Baker alone, but two Section Commissioners to help him, manage with difficulty the daily distribution of loaves. Soft-spoken assiduous, in the early candle-light, are Baker and Commissioners: and yet the pale chill February sunrise discloses an unpromising scene. Indignant Female Patriots, partly supplied with bread, rush now to the shops,

[1] *Moniteur*, etc. (*Hist. Parl.* xxiv. 332–348).

declaring that they will have groceries. Groceries enough: sugar-barrels rolled forth into the street, Patriot Citoyennes weighing it out at a just rate of elevenpence a pound; likewise coffee-chests, soap-chests, nay cinnamon and cloves-chests, with *aquavitæ* and other forms of alcohol,—at a just rate, which some do not pay; the pale-faced Grocer silently wringing his hands! What help? The distributive Citoyennes are of violent speech and gesture, their long Eumenides-hair hanging out of curl; nay in their girdles pistols are seen sticking: some, it is even said, have *beards*,—male Patriots in petticoats and mob-cap. Thus, in the street of Lombards, in the street of Five-Diamonds, street of Pulleys, in most streets of Paris does it effervesce, the live-long day; no Municipality, no Mayor Pache, though he was War-Minister lately, sends military against it, or aught against it but persuasive-eloquence, till seven at night, or later.

On Monday gone five weeks, which was the twenty-first of January, we saw Paris, beheading its King, stand silent, like a petrified City of Enchantment: and now on this Monday it is so noisy, selling sugar! Cities, especially Cities in Revolution, are subject to these alternations; the secret courses of civic business and existence effervescing and efflorescing, in this manner, as a concrete Phenomenon to the eye. Of which Phenomenon, when secret existence becoming public effloresces on the street, the philosophical cause and effect is not so easy to find. What, for example, may be the accurate philosophical meaning, and meanings, of this sale of sugar? These things that have become visible in the street of Pulleys and over Paris, whence are they, we say; and whither?—

That Pitt has a hand in it, the gold of Pitt: so much, to all reasonable Patriot men, may seem clear. But then, through what agents of Pitt? Varlet, Apostle of Liberty, was discerned again of late, with his pike and red nightcap. Deputy Marat published in his Journal, this very day, complaining of the bitter scarcity, and sufferings of the people, till he seemed to get wroth: 'If your Rights of Man were anything but a piece of written paper, the plunder of a few shops, and a forestaller or two hung up at the door-lintels, would put an end to such things.'[1] Are not these, say the Girondins, pregnant indications? Pitt has bribed the Anarchists; Marat is the agent of Pitt: hence this sale of sugar. To the Mother Society, again, it is clear that the scarcity is factitious; is the work of Girondins, and suchlike; a set of men sold partly to Pitt; sold wholly to their own ambitions and hard-hearted pedantries; who will not fix the grain-prices, but prate pedantically of free-trade; wishing to starve Paris into violence, and embroil it with the Departments: *hence* this sale of sugar.

And, alas, if to these two notabilities, of a Phenomenon and such Theories of a Phenomenon, we add this third notability, That the French Nation has believed, for several years now, in the possibility, nay certainty and near advent, of a universal Millennium, or reign of Freedom, Equality, Fraternity, wherein man should be the brother of man, and sorrow and sin flee away? Not bread to eat, nor soap to wash with; and the reign of Perfect Felicity ready to arrive, due always since the Bastille fell! How did our hearts burn within us, at that Feast of Pikes, when brother flung himself on brother's bosom; and in sunny jubilee, Twenty-five millions burst forth into sound and cannon-smoke! Bright was our Hope then, as sunlight; red-angry is our Hope grown now, as consuming fire. But, O Heavens, what enchantment is it, or devilish legerdemain, of such effect, that Perfect Felicity, always within arm's length, could never be laid hold of, but only in her stead Controversy and Scarcity? This set of traitors after that set! Tremble, ye traitors; dread a People which calls itself patient, long-suffering; but which cannot always submit to have its pocket picked, in this way,—of a Millennium!

Yes, Reader, here is the miracle. Out of that putrescent rubbish of Scepticism, Sensualism, Sentimentalism, hollow Machiavelism, such a Faith has verily risen; flaming in the heart of a People. A whole People, awakening as it were to consciousness in deep misery, believes that it is within reach

[1] *Hist. Parl.* xxiv. 353–356.

of a Fraternal Heaven-on-Earth. With longing arms, it struggles to embrace the Unspeakable; cannot embrace it, owing to certain causes.—Seldom do we find that a whole People can be said to have any Faith at all; except in things which it can eat and handle. Whensoever it gets any Faith, its history becomes spirit-stirring, noteworthy. But since the time when steel Europe shook itself simultaneously at the word of Hermit Peter, and rushed towards the Sepulchre where God had lain, there was no universal impulse of Faith that one could note. Since Protestantism went silent, no Luther's voice, no Zisca's drum any longer proclaiming that God's Truth was *not* the Devil's Lie; and the Last of the Cameronians (Renwick was the name of him; honour to the name of the brave!) sank, shot, on the Castle-hill of Edinburgh, there was no partial impulse of Faith among Nations. Till now, behold, once more, this French Nation believes! Herein, we say, in that astonishing Faith of theirs, lies the miracle. It is a Faith undoubtedly of the more prodigious sort, even among Faiths; and will embody itself in prodigies. It is the soul of that world-prodigy named French Revolution; whereat the world still gazes and shudders.

But, for the rest, let no man ask History to explain by cause and effect how the business proceeded henceforth. This battle of Mountain and Gironde, and what follows, is the battle of Fanaticisms and Miracles; unsuitable for cause and effect. The sound of it, to the mind, is as a hubbub of voices in distraction; little of articulate is to be gathered by long listening and studying; only battle-tumult, shouts of triumph, shrieks of despair. The Mountain has left no Memoirs; the Girondins have left Memoirs, which are too often little other than long-drawn Interjections, of *Woe is me*, and *Cursed be ye*. So soon as History can philosophically delineate the conflagration of a kindled Fireship, she may try this other task. Here lay the bitumen-stratum, there the brimstone one; so ran the vein of gunpowder, of nitre, terebinth and foul grease: this, were she inquisitive enough, History might partly know. But how they acted and reacted below decks, one fire-stratum playing into the other, by its nature and the art of man, now when all hands ran raging, and the flames lashed high over shrouds and top-mast: this let not History attempt.

The Fireship is old France, the old French Form of Life; her crew a Generation of men. Wild are their cries and their ragings there, like spirits tormented in that flame. But, on the whole, are they not *gone*, O Reader? Their Fireship and they, frightening the world, have sailed away; its flames and its thunders quite away, into the Deep of Time. One thing therefore History will do: pity them all; for it went hard with them all. Not even the seagreen Incorruptible but shall have some pity, some human love, though it takes an effort. And now, so much once thoroughly attained, the rest will become easier. To the eye of equal brotherly pity, innumerable perversions dissipate themselves; exaggerations and execrations fall off, of their own accord. Standing wistfully on the safe shore, we will look, and see, what is of interest to us, what is adapted to us.

CHAPTER II

CULOTTIC AND SANSCULOTTIC

Gironde and Mountain are now in full quarrel; their mutual rage, says Toulongeon, is growing a 'pale' rage. Curious, lamentable: all these men have the word Republic on their lips; in the heart of every one of them is a passionate wish for something which he calls Republic: yet see their death-quarrel! So, however, are men made. Creatures who live in confusion; who, once thrown together, can readily fall into that confusion of confusions which quarrel is, simply because their confusions differ from one another; still more because they seem to differ! Men's words are a poor exponent of their thought; nay their thought itself is a poor exponent of the inward unnamed Mystery, wherefrom both thought and action have their birth. No man can explain himself, can get himself explained; men see not one another, but distorted phantasms which they call one another; which they hate and go to battle with: for all battle is well said to be *misunderstanding*.

But indeed that similitude of the Fireship; of our poor French brethren, so fiery themselves, working also in an *element* of fire, was not insignificant. Consider it well, there is a shade of the truth in it. For a man, once committed headlong to republican or any other Transcendentalism, and fighting and fanaticising amid a Nation of his like, becomes as it were enveloped in an ambient atmosphere of Transcendentalism and Delirium: his individual self is lost in something that is not himself, but foreign though inseparable from him. Strange to think of, the man's cloak still seems to hold the same man: and yet the man is not there, his volition is not there; nor the source of what he will do and devise; instead of the man and his volition there is a piece of Fanaticism and Fatalism incarnated in the shape of him. He, the hapless incarnated Fanaticism, goes his road; no man can help him, he himself least of all. It is a wonderful, tragical predicament;—such as human language, unused to deal with these things, being contrived for the uses of common life, struggles to shadow out in figures. The ambient element of material fire is not wilder than this of Fanaticism; nor, though visible to the eye, is it more real. Volition bursts forth involuntary-voluntary; rapt along; the movement of free human minds becomes a raging tornado of fatalism, blind as the winds; and Mountain and Gironde, when they recover themselves, are alike astounded to see *where* it has flung and dropt them. To such height of miracle can men work on men; the Conscious and the Unconscious blended inscrutably in this our inscrutable Life; endless Necessity environing Freewill!

The weapons of the Girondins are Political Philosophy, Respectability, and Eloquence. Eloquence, or call it rhetoric, really of a superior order; Vergniaud, for instance, turns a period as sweetly as any man of that generation. The weapons of the Mountain are those of mere Nature: Audacity and Impetuosity which may become Ferocity, as of men complete in their determination, in their conviction; nay of men, in some cases, who as Septemberers must either prevail or perish. The ground to be fought for is Popularity: further you may either seek Popularity with the friends of Freedom and Order, or with the friends of Freedom Simple; to seek it with both has unhappily become impossible. With the former sort, and generally with the Authorities of the Departments, and such as read Parliamentary Debates, and are of Respectability, and of a peace-loving moneyed nature, the Girondins carry it. With the extreme Patriot again, with the indigent Millions, especially with the Population of Paris who do not read so much as hear and see, the Girondins altogether lose it, and the Mountain carries it.

Egoism, nor meanness of mind, is not wanting on either side. Surely not on the Girondin side; where in fact the instinct of self-preservation, too prominently unfolded by circumstances, cuts almost a sorry figure; where also a certain finesse, to the length even of shuffling and shamming, now and then shows itself. They are men skilful in Advocate-fence. They have been called the Jesuits of the Revolution;[1] but that is too hard a name. It must be owned likewise that this rude blustering Mountain has a sense in it of what the Revolution means; which these eloquent Girondins are totally void of. Was the Revolution made, and fought for, against the world, these four weary years, that a Formula might be substantiated; that Society might become *methodic*, demonstrable by logic; and the old Noblesse with their pretensions vanish? Or ought it not withal to bring some glimmering of light and alleviation to the Twenty-five Millions, who sat in darkness, heavy-laden, till they rose with pikes in their hands? At least and lowest, one would think, it should bring them a proportion of bread to live on? There is in the Mountain here and there; in Marat People's-friend; in the incorruptible Seagreen himself, though otherwise so lean and formulary, a heartfelt knowledge of this latter fact;—without which knowledge all other knowledge here is naught, and the choicest forensic eloquence is as sounding brass and a tinkling cymbal. Most cold, on the other hand,

[1] Dumouriez, *Mémoires*, iii. 314.

most patronising, unsubstantial is the tone of the Girondins towards 'our poorer brethren';—those brethren whom one often hears of under the collective name of 'the masses,' as if they were not persons at all, but mounds of combustible explosive material, for blowing down Bastilles with! In very truth, a Revolutionist of this kind, is he not a Solecism? Disowned by Nature and Art; deserving only to be erased, and disappear! Surely, to our poorer brethren of Paris, all this Girondin patronage sounds deadening and killing: if finespoken and incontrovertible in logic, then all the falser, all the hatefuler in fact.

Nay doubtless, pleading for Popularity, here among our poorer brethren of Paris, the Girondin has a hard game to play. If he gain the ear of the Respectable at a distance, it is by insisting on September and suchlike; it is at the expense of this Paris where he dwells and perorates. Hard to perorate in such an auditory! Wherefore the question arises: Could not we get ourselves out of this Paris? Twice or oftener such an attempt is made. If not we ourselves, thinks Guadet, then at least our *Suppléans* might do it. For every Deputy has his *Suppléant*, or Substitute, who will take his place if need be: might not these assemble, say at Bourges, which is a quiet episcopal Town, in quiet Berri, forty good leagues off? In that case, what profit were it for the Paris Sansculottery to insult us; our *Suppléans* sitting quiet in Bourges, to whom we could run? Nay, even the Primary electoral Assemblies, thinks Guadet, might be reconvoked, and a New Convention got, with new orders from the Sovereign People; and right glad were Lyons, were Bordeaux, Rouen, Marseilles, as yet Provincial Towns, to welcome us in their turn, and become a sort of Capital Towns; and teach these Parisians reason.

Fond schemes; which all misgo! If decreed, in heat of eloquent logic, today, they are repealed, by clamour and passionate wider considerations, on the morrow.[1] Will you, O Girondins, parcel us into separate Republics, then; like the Swiss, like your Americans; so that there be no Metropolis or

[1] *Moniteur*, 1793, No. 140, etc.

indivisible French Nation any more? Your Departmental Guard seemed to point that way! Federal Republic? Federalist? Men and Knitting-women repeat *Fédéraliste*, with or without much Dictionary-meaning; but go on repeating it, as is usual in such cases, till the meaning of it becomes almost magical, fit to designate all mystery of Iniquity; and *Fédéraliste* has grown a word of Exorcism and *Apage-Satanas*. But furthermore, consider what 'poisoning of public opinion' in the Departments, by these Brissot, Gorsas, Caritat-Condorcet Newspapers! And then also what counter-poisoning, still feller in quality, by a *Père Duchesne* of Hébert, brutalest Newspaper yet published on Earth; by a *Rougiff* of Guffroy; by the 'incendiary leaves of Marat'! More than once, on complaint given and effervescence rising, it is decreed that a man cannot both be Legislator and Editor; that he shall choose between the one function and the other.[1] But this too, which indeed could help little, is revoked or eluded; remains a pious wish mainly.

Meanwhile, as the sad fruit of such strife, behold, O ye National Representatives, how, between the friends of Law and the friends of Freedom everywhere, mere heats and jealousies have arisen; fevering the whole Republic! Department, Provincial Town is set against Metropolis, Rich against Poor, Culottic against Sansculottic, man against man. From the Southern Cities come Addresses of an almost inculpatory character; for Paris has long suffered Newspaper calumny. Bordeaux demands a reign of Law and Respectability, meaning Girondism, with emphasis. With emphasis Marseilles demands the like. Nay, from Marseilles there come *two* Addresses: one Girondin; one Jacobin Sansculottic. Hot Rebecqui, sick of this Convention-work, has given place to his Substitute, and gone home; where also, with such jarrings, there is work to be sick of.

Lyons, a place of Capitalists and Aristocrats, is in still worse state; almost in revolt. Chalier the Jacobin Town-Councillor has got, too literally, to daggers-drawn with Nièvre-Chol the *Modératin* Mayor; one of your Moderate, perhaps Aristocrat,

[1] *Hist. Parl.* xxv. 25, etc.

Royalist or Federalist Mayors! Chalier, who pilgrimed to Paris 'to behold Marat and the Mountain,' has verily kindled himself at their sacred urn: for on the 6th of February last, History or Rumour has seen him haranguing his Lyons Jacobins in a quite transcendental manner, with a drawn dagger in his hand; recommending (they say) sheer September methods, patience being worn out; and that the Jacobin Brethren should, impromptu, work the Guillotine themselves! One sees him still, in Engravings: mounted on a table; foot advanced, body contorted; a bald, rude, slope-browed, infuriated visage of the canine-species, the eyes starting from their sockets; in his puissant right-hand the brandished dagger, or horse-pistol, as some give it; other dog-visages kindling under him:—a man not likely to end well! However, the Guillotine was *not* got together impromptu, that day, 'on the Pont Saint-Clair,' or elsewhere; but indeed continued lying rusty in its loft:[1] Nièvre-Chol with military went about, rumbling cannon, in the most confused manner; and the 'nine hundred prisoners' received no hurt. So distracted is Lyons grown, with its cannons rumbling. Convention Commissioners must be sent thither forthwith: if even they can appease it, and keep the Guillotine in its loft?

Consider finally if, on all these mad jarrings of the Southern Cities, and of France generally, a traitorous Crypto-Royalist class is not looking and watching; ready to strike in, at the right season! Neither is there bread; neither is there soap: see the Patriot women selling out sugar, at a just rate of twenty-two sous per pound! Citizen Representatives, it were verily well that your quarrels finished, and the reign of Perfect Felicity began.

CHAPTER III

GROWING SHRILL

On the whole, one cannot say that the Girondins are wanting to themselves, so far as good-will might go. They prick

[1] *Hist. Parl.* xxiv. 385–93; xxvi. 229, etc.

assiduously into the sore-places of the Mountain; from principle, and also from Jesuitism.

Besides September, of which there is now little to be made except effervescence, we discern two sore-places, where the Mountain often suffers: Marat, and Orléans Egalité. Squalid Marat, for his own sake and for the Mountain's, is assaulted ever and anon; held up to France, as a squalid blood-thirsty Portent, inciting to the pillage of shops; of whom let the Mountain have the credit! The Mountain murmurs, ill at ease: this 'Maximum of Patriotism,' how shall they either own him or disown him? As for Marat personally, he, with his fixed-idea, remains invulnerable to such things; nay the People's-friend is very evidently rising in importance, as his befriended People rises. No shrieks now, when he goes to speak; occasional applauses rather, furtherance which breeds confidence. The day when the Girondins proposed to 'decree him accused' (*décréter d'accusation*, as they phrase it) for that February Paragraph, of 'hanging up a Forestaller or two at the door-lintels,' Marat proposes to have *them* 'decreed insane'; and, descending the Tribune-steps, is heard to articulate these most unsenatorial ejaculations: '*Les cochons, les imbéciles*, Pigs, idiots!' Oftentimes he croaks harsh sarcasm, having really a rough rasping tongue, and a very deep fund of contempt for fine outsides; and once or twice, he even laughs, nay 'explodes into laughter, *rit aux éclats*,' at the gentilities and superfine airs of these Girondin 'men of statesmanship,' with their pedantries, plausibilities, pusillanimities: 'these two years,' says he, 'you have been whining about attacks, and plots, and danger from Paris; and you have not a scratch to show for yourselves.'[1]—Danton gruffly rebukes him, from time to time: a Maximum of Patriotism whom one can neither own nor disown!

But the second sore-place of the Mountain is this anomalous Monseigneur Equality Prince d'Orléans. Behold these men, says the Gironde; with a whilom Bourbon Prince among them: they are creatures of the D'Orléans Faction; they will have Philippe made King; one King no sooner guillotined than

[1] *Moniteur*, Séance du 20 Mai 1793.

another made in his stead! Girondins have moved, Buzot moved long ago, from principle and also from jesuitism, that the whole race of Bourbons should be marched forth from the soil of France; this Prince Egalité to bring up the rear. Motions which might produce some effect on the public;—which the Mountain, ill at ease, knows not what to do with.

And poor Orléans Egalité himself, for one begins to pity even him, what does he do with them? The disowned of all parties, the rejected and foolishly bedrifted hither and thither, to what corner of Nature can he now drift with advantage? Feasible hope remains not for him: unfeasible hope, in pallid doubtful glimmers, there may still come, bewildering, not cheering or illuminating,—from the Dumouriez quarter; and how if not the time-wasted Orléans Egalité, then perhaps the young unworn Chartres Egalité might rise to be a kind of King? Sheltered, if shelter it be, in the clefts of the Mountain, poor Egalité will wait: one refuge in Jacobinism, one in Dumouriez and Counter-Revolution, are there not two chances? However, the look of him, Dame Genlis says, is grown gloomy; sad to see. Sillery also, the Genlis's Husband, who hovers about the Mountain, not on it, is in a bad way. Dame Genlis is come to Raincy, out of England and Bury St. Edmunds, in these days; being summoned by Egalité, with her young charge, Mademoiselle Egalité,—that so Mademoiselle might not be counted among Emigrants and hardly dealt with. But it proves a ravelled business: Genlis and charge find that they must return to the Netherlands; must wait on the Frontiers, for a week or two; till Monseigneur, by Jacobin help, get it wound up. 'Next morning,' says Dame Genlis, 'Monseigneur, gloomier than ever, gave me his arm, to lead me to the carriage. I was greatly troubled; Mademoiselle burst into tears; her Father was pale and trembling. After I had got seated, he stood immovable at the carriage-door, with his eyes fixed on me; his mournful and painful look seemed to implore pity;—"*Adieu, Madame!*" said he. The altered sound of his voice completely overcame me; unable to utter a word, I held out my hand; he grasped it close; then turning, and advancing sharply towards the postillions, he gave them a sign, and we rolled away.'[1]

Nor are Peace-makers wanting; of whom likewise we mention two; one fast on the crown of the Mountain, the other not yet alighted anywhere: Danton and Barrère. Ingenious Barrère, Old-Constituent and Editor, from the slopes of the Pyrenees, is one of the usefulest men of this Convention, in his way. Truth may lie on both sides, on either side, or on neither side; my friends, ye must give and take: for the rest, success to the winning side! This is the motto of Barrère. Ingenious, almost genial; quick-sighted, supple, graceful; a man that will prosper. Scarcely Belial in the assembled Pandemonium was plausibler to ear and eye. An indispensable man: in the great *Art of Varnish* he may be said to seek his fellow. Has there an explosion arisen, as many do arise, a confusion, unsightliness, which no tongue can speak of, nor eye look on; give it to Barrère; Barrère shall be Committee-Reporter of it; you shall see it transmute itself into a regularity, into the very beauty and improvement that was needed. Without one such man, we say, how were this Convention bestead! Call him not, as exaggerative Mercier does, 'the greatest liar in France': nay it may be argued there is not truth enough in him to make a real lie of. Call him, with Burke, Anacreon of the Guillotine, and a man serviceable to this Convention.

The other Peace-maker whom we name is Danton. Peace, O peace with one another! cries Danton often enough: Are we not alone against the world; a little band of brothers? Broad Danton is loved by all the Mountain; but they think him too easy-tempered, deficient in suspicion: he has stood between Dumouriez and much censure, anxious not to exasperate our only General: in the shrill tumult Danton's strong voice reverberates, for union and pacification. Meetings there are; dinings with the Girondins: it is so pressingly essential that there be union. But the Girondins are haughty and respectable: this Titan Danton is not a man of Formulas, and there rests on him a shadow of September. 'Your Girondins have no

[1] Genlis, *Mémoires* (London, 1825), iv. 118.

confidence in me': this is the answer a conciliatory Meillan gets from him; to all the arguments and pleadings this conciliatory Meillan can bring, the repeated answer is, '*Ils n'ont point de confiance.*'[1]—The tumult will get ever shriller; rage is growing pale.

In fact, what a pang is it to the heart of a Girondin, this first withering probability that the despicable unphilosophic anarchic Mountain, after all, may triumph! Brutal Septemberers, a fifth-floor Tallien, 'a Robespierre without an idea in his head,' as Condorcet says, 'or a feeling in his heart': and yet we, the flower of France, cannot stand against them; behold, the sceptre departs from us; from us and goes to them! Eloquence, Philosophism, Respectability avail not: 'against Stupidity the very gods fight to no purpose,

'*Mit der Dummheit kämpfen Götter selbst vergebens!*'

Shrill are the plaints of Louvet; his thin existence all acidified into rage and preternatural insight of suspicion. Wroth is young Barbaroux; wroth and scornful. Silent, like a Queen with the aspic on her bosom, sits the wife of Roland; Roland's Accounts never yet got audited, his name become a byword. Such is the fortune of war, especially of revolution. The great gulf of Tophet and Tenth of August opened itself at the magic of your eloquent voice; and lo now, it will not close at your voice! It is a dangerous thing such magic. The Magician's Famulus got hold of the forbidden Book, and summoned a goblin: *Plaît-il,* What is your will? said the goblin. The Famulus, somewhat struck, bade him fetch water: the swift goblin fetched it, pail in each hand; but lo, would not cease fetching it! Desperate, the Famulus shrieks at him, smites at him, cuts him in two; lo, *two* goblin water-carriers ply; and the house will be swum away in Deucalion Deluges.

[1] *Mémoires de Meillan, Représentant du Peuple* (Paris, 1823), p. 51.

CHAPTER IV

FATHERLAND IN DANGER

Or rather we will say, this Senatorial war might have lasted long; and Party tugging and throttling with Party might have suppressed and smothered one another, in the ordinary bloodless Parliamentary way; on one condition: that France had been at least able to exist, all the while. But this Sovereign People has a digestive faculty, and cannot do without bread. Also we are at war, and must have victory; at war with Europe, with Fate and Famine: and behold, in the spring of the year, all victory deserts us.

Dumouriez had his outposts stretched as far as Aix-la-Chapelle, and the beautifulest plan for pouncing on Holland, by stratagem, flat-bottomed boats and rapid intrepidity; wherein too he had prospered so far; but unhappily could prosper no further. Aix-la-Chapelle is lost; Maestricht will not surrender to mere smoke and noise: the flat-bottomed boats have to launch themselves again, and return the way they came. Steady now, ye rapidly intrepid men; retreat with firmness, Parthian-like! Alas, were it General Miranda's fault; were it the War-minister's fault; or were it Dumouriez's own fault and that of Fortune: enough, there is nothing for it but retreat,—well if it be not even flight; for already terror-stricken cohorts and stragglers pour off, not waiting for order; flow disastrous, as many as ten thousand of them, without halt till they see France again.[1] Nay worse: Dumouriez himself is perhaps secretly turning traitor? Very sharp is the tone in which he writes to our Committees. Commissioners and Jacobin Pillagers have done such incalculable mischief; Hassenfratz sends neither cartridges nor clothing; shoes we have, deceptively 'soled with wood and pasteboard.' Nothing in short is right. Danton and Lacroix, when it was they that were Commissioners, would needs join Belgium to France;—of which Dumouriez might have made the prettiest little Duchy

[1] Dumouriez, iv. 16–73.

for his own secret behoof! With all these things the General is wroth; and writes to us in a sharp tone. Who knows what this hot little General is meditating? Dumouriez Duke of Belgium or Brabant; and say, Egalité the Younger King of France: there were an end for our Revolution!—Committee of Defence gazes, and shakes its head: who except Danton, defective in suspicion, could still struggle to be of hope?

And General Custine is rolling back from the Rhine Country; conquered Mentz will be reconquered, the Prussians gathering round to bombard it with shot and shell. Mentz may resist, Commissioner Merlin, the Thionviller, 'making sallies, at the head of the besieged';—resist to the death; but not longer than that. How sad a reverse for Mentz! Brave Forster, brave Lux planted Liberty-trees, amid *ça-ira*-ing music, in the snow-slush of last winter, there; and made Jacobin Societies; and got the Territory incorporated with France; they came hither to Paris, as Deputies or Delegates, and have their eighteen francs a-day: but see, before once the Liberty-tree is got rightly in leaf, Mentz is changing into an explosive crater; vomiting fire, bevomited with fire!

Neither of these men shall again see Mentz; they have come hither only to die. Forster has been round the Globe; he saw Cook perish under Owyhee clubs; but like this Paris he has yet seen or suffered nothing. Poverty escorts him: from home there can nothing come, except Job's-news; the eighteen daily francs, which we here as Deputy or Delegate with difficulty 'touch,' are in paper *assignats*, and sink fast in value. Poverty disappointment, inaction, obloquy; the brave heart slowly breaking! Such is Forster's lot. For the rest, Demoiselle Théroigne smiles on you in the Soirées; 'a beautiful brown-locked face,' of an exalted temper; and contrives to keep her carriage. Prussian Trenck, the poor subterranean Baron, jargons and jangles in an unmelodious manner. Thomas Paine's face is red-pustuled, 'but the eyes uncommonly bright.' Convention Deputies ask you to dinner: very courteous; and 'we all play at *plumpsack*.'[1] 'It is the Explosion and New-

[1] Forster's *Briefwechsel*, ii. 514, 460, 631.

creation of a World,' says Forster; 'and the actors in it, such small mean objects, buzzing round one like a handful of flies.'—

Likewise there is war with Spain. Spain will advance through the gorges of the Pyrenees; rustling with Bourbon banners, jingling with artillery and menace. And England has donned the red coat; and marches, with Royal Highness of York, —whom some once spake of inviting to be our King. Changed that humour now: and ever more changing; till no hatefuler thing walk this Earth than a denizen of that tyrannous Island; and Pitt be declared and decreed, with effervescence, '*L'ennemi du genre humain*, The enemy of mankind'; and, very singular to say, you make order that no Soldier of Liberty give quarter to an Englishman. Which order, however, the Soldier of Liberty does but partially obey. We will take no Prisoners then, say the Soldiers of Liberty; they shall all be 'Deserters' that we take.[1] It is a frantic order; and attended with inconvenience. For surely, if you give no quarter, the plain issue is that you will get none; and so the business become as broad as it was long.—Our 'recruitment of Three-hundred Thousand men,' which was the decreed force for this year, is like to have work enough laid to its hand.

So many enemies come wending on; penetrating through throats of mountains, steering over the salt sea; towards all points of our territory; rattling chains at us. Nay, worst of all: there is an enemy within our own territory itself. In the early days of March, the Nantes Postbags do not arrive; there arrive only instead of them Conjecture, Apprehension, bodeful wind of Rumour. The bodefulest proves true. Those fanatic Peoples of La Vendée will no longer keep under: their fire of insurrection, heretofore dissipated with difficulty, blazes out anew, after the King's Death, as a wide conflagration; not riot but civil war. Your Cathelineaus, your Stofflets, Charettes, are other men than was thought: behold how their Peasants, in mere russet and hodden, with their rude arms, rude array, with their fanatic Gaelic frenzy and wild-yelling battle-cry of

[1] See Dampmartin, *Evénemens*, ii. 213–230.

God and the King, dash at us like a dark whirlwind; and blow the best-disciplined Nationals we can get into panic and *sauve-qui-peut*! Field after field is theirs; one sees not where it will end. Commandant Santerre may be sent there; but with non-effect; he might as well have returned and brewed beer.

It has become peremptorily necessary that a National Convention cease arguing, and begin acting. Yield one party of you to the other, and do it swiftly. No theoretic outlook is here, but the close certainty of ruin; the very day that is passing over us must be provided for.

It was Friday the Eighth of March when this Job's-post from Dumouriez, thickly preceded and escorted by so many other Job's-posts, reached the National Convention. Blank enough are most faces. Little will it avail whether our Septemberers be punished or go unpunished; if Pitt and Cobourg are coming in, with one punishment for us all; nothing now between Paris itself and the Tyrants but a doubtful Dumouriez, and hosts in loose-flowing loud retreat!—Danton the Titan rises in this hour as always in the hour of need. Great is his voice, reverberating from the domes:—Citizen-Representatives, shall we not, in such crisis of Fate, lay aside discords? Reputation: O what is the reputation of this man or of that? '*Que mon nom soit flétri; que la France soit libre:* Let my name be blighted; Let France be free!' It is necessary now again that France rise, in swift vengeance, with her million right-hands, with her heart as of one man. Instantaneous recruitment in Paris; let every Section of Paris furnish its thousands; every Section of France! Ninety-six Commissioners of us, two for each Section of the Forty-eight, they must go forthwith, and tell Paris what the Country needs of her. Let Eighty more of us be sent, post-haste, over France; to spread the fire-cross, to call forth the might of men. Let the Eighty also be on the road, before this sitting rise. Let them go, and think what their errand is. Speedy Camp of Fifty-thousand between Paris and the North Frontier; for Paris will pour forth her volunteers! Shoulder to shoulder; one strong universal death-defiant rising and rushing; we shall hurl back these Sons of Night yet again; and France, in spite of the world, be free![1]—So sounds the Titan's voice: into all Section-houses; into all French hearts. Sections sit in Permanence, for recruitment, enrolment, that very night. Convention Commissioners, on swift wheels, are carrying the fire-cross from Town to Town, till all France blaze.

And so there is Flag of *Fatherland in Danger* waving from the Townhall, Black Flag from the top of Notre-Dame Cathedral; there is Proclamation, hot eloquence; Paris rushing out once again to strike its enemies down. That, in such circumstances, Paris was in no mild humour can be conjectured. Agitated streets; still more agitated round the Salle de Manége! Feuillans-Terrace crowds itself with angry Citizens, angrier Citizenesses; Varlet perambulates with portable chair: ejaculations of no measured kind, as to perfidious fine-spoken *Hommes d'état*, friends of Dumouriez, secret-friends of Pitt and Cobourg, burst from the hearts and lips of men. To fight the enemy? Yes, and even to 'freeze him with terror, *glacer d'effroi*': but first to have domestic Traitors punished! Who are they that, carping and quarrelling, in their jesuitic most *moderate* way, seek to shackle the Patriotic movement? That divide France against Paris, and poison public opinion in the Departments? That when we ask for bread, and a Maximum fixed-price, treat us with lectures on Free-trade in grains? Can the human stomach satisfy itself with lectures on Free-trade; and are we to fight the Austrians in a moderate manner, or in an immoderate? This Convention must be *purged*.

'Set up a swift Tribunal for Traitors, a Maximum for Grains': thus speak with energy the Patriot Volunteers, as they defile through the Convention Hall, just on the wing to the Frontiers;—perorating in that heroical Cambyses' vein of theirs: beshouted by the Galleries and Mountain; bemurmured by the Right-side and Plain. Nor are prodigies wanting: lo, while a Captain of the Section Poissonnière perorates with vehemence about Dumouriez, Maximum and Crypto-Royalist Traitors, and his troop beat chorus with him, waving their

[1] *Moniteur* (in *Hist. Parl.* xxv. 6).

Banner overhead, the eye of a Deputy discerns, in this same Banner, that the *cravates* or streamers of it have Royal fleurs-de-lys! The Section-Captain shrieks; his troop shriek, horror-struck, and 'trample the Banner under foot': seemingly the work of some Crypto-Royalist Plotter? Most probable:[1]—or perhaps at bottom, only the *old* Banner of the Section, manufactured prior to the Tenth of August, when such streamers were according to rule![2]

History, looking over the Girondin Memoirs, anxious to disentangle the truth of them from the hysterics, finds these days of March, especially this Sunday the Tenth of March, play a great part. Plots, plots; a plot for murdering the Girondin Deputies; Anarchists and Secret-Royalists plotting, in hellish concert, for that end! The far greater part of which is hysterics. What we do find indisputable is, that Louvet and certain Girondins were apprehensive they might be murdered on Saturday, and did not go to the evening sitting; but held council with one another, each inciting his fellow to do something resolute, and end these Anarchists: to which, however, Pétion, opening the window, and finding the night very wet, answered only, '*Ils ne feront rien,*' and 'composedly resumed his violin,' says Louvet;[3] thereby, with soft Lydian tweedledeeing, to wrap himself against eating cares. Also that Louvet felt especially liable to being killed; that several Girondins went abroad to seek beds: liable to being killed; but were not. Further that, in very truth, Journalist Deputy Gorsas, poisoner of the Departments, he and his Printer had their houses broken into (by a tumult of Patriots, among whom red-capped Varlet, American Fournier loom forth, in the darkness of the rain and riot); had their wives put in fear; their presses, types, and circumjacent equipments beaten to ruin; no Mayor interfering in time; Gorsas himself escaping, pistol in hand, 'along the coping of the back wall.' Further, that Sunday, the morrow, was not a workday; and the streets were more

[1] *Choix des Rapports*, xi. 277.
[2] *Hist. Parl.* xxv. 72.
[3] Louvet, *Mémoires*, p. 72.

agitated than ever: Is it a new September, then, that these Anarchists intend? Finally, that no September came;—and also that hysterics, not unnaturally, had reached almost their acme.[1]

Vergniaud denounces and deplores; in sweetly turned periods. Section Bonconseil, *Good-counsel* so-named, not Mauconseil or *Ill-counsel* as it once was,—does a far notabler thing: demands that Vergniaud, Brissot, Guadet, and other denunciatory, fine-spoken Girondins, to the number of Twenty-two, be put under arrest! Section Good-counsel, so named ever since the Tenth of August, is sharply rebuked, like a Section of Ill-counsel:[2] but its word is spoken, and will not fall to the ground.

In fact, one thing strikes us in these poor Girondins: their fatal shortness of vision; nay fatal poorness of character, for that is the root of it. They are as strangers to the People they would govern; to the thing they have come to work in. Formulas, Philosophies, Respectabilities, what has been written in Books, and admitted by the Cultivated Classes: *this* inadequate *Scheme* of Nature's working is all that Nature, let her work as she will, can reveal to these men. So they perorate and speculate; and call on the Friends of Law, when the question is not Law or No-Law, but Life or No-Life. Pedants of the Revolution, if not Jesuits of it! Their Formalism is great; great also is their Egoism. France rising to fight Austria has been raised only by plot of the Tenth of March, to kill Twenty-two of *them*! This Revolution Prodigy, unfolding itself into terrific stature and articulation, by its own laws and Nature's, not by the laws of Formula, has become unintelligible, incredible as an impossibility, the 'waste chaos of a Dream.' A Republic founded on what they call the Virtues; on what we call the Decencies and Respectabilities: this they will have, and nothing but this. Whatsoever other Republic Nature and Reality send, shall be considered as not sent; as a kind of Nightmare Vision, and thing non-extant; disowned by the Laws of Nature and of Formula. Alas, dim for the best eyes is this Reality; and as

[1] Meillan, pp. 23, 24; Louvet, pp. 71–80.
[2] *Moniteur* (Séance du 12 Mars), 15 Mars.

for these men, they will not look at it with eyes at all, but only through 'facetted spectacles' of Pedantry, wounded Vanity; which yield the most portentous fallacious spectrum. Carping and complaining for ever of Plots and Anarchy, they will do one thing; prove, to demonstration, that the Reality will not translate into their Formula; that they and their Formula are incompatible with the Reality: and, in its dark wrath, the Reality will extinguish it and them! What a man *kens* he *cans*. But the beginning of a man's doom is, that vision be withdrawn from him; that he sees not the reality, but a false spectrum of the reality; and following that, step darkly, with more or less velocity, downwards to the utter Dark; to Ruin, which is the great Sea of Darkness, whither all falsehoods, winding or direct, continually flow!

This Tenth of March we may mark as an epoch in the Girondin destinies; the rage so exasperated itself, the misconception so darkened itself. Many desert the sittings; many come to them armed.[1] An honourable Deputy, setting out after breakfast, must now, besides taking his Notes, see whether his Priming is in order.

Meanwhile with Dumouriez in Belgium it fares ever worse. Were it again General Miranda's fault, or some other's fault, there is no doubt whatever but the 'Battle of Nerwinden,' on the 18th of March, is lost; and our rapid retreat has become a far too rapid one. Victorious Cobourg, with his Austrian prickers, hangs like a dark cloud on the rear of us: Dumouriez never off horseback night or day; engagement every three hours; our whole discomfited Host rolling rapidly inwards, full of rage, suspicion, and *sauve-qui-peut*! And then Dumouriez himself, what his intents may be? Wicked seemingly and not charitable! His despatches to Committee openly denounce a factious Convention, for the woes it has brought on France and him. And his speeches—for the General has no reticence! The execution of the Tyrant this Dumouriez calls the Murder of the King. Danton and Lacroix, flying thither as Commis-

[1] Meillan, *Mémoires*, pp. 85, 24.

sioners once more, return very doubtful; even Danton now doubts.

Three Jacobin Missionaries, Proly, Dubuisson, Pereyra, have flown forth; sped by a wakeful Mother Society: they are struck dumb to hear the General speak. The Convention, according to this General, consists of three-hundred scoundrels and four-hundred imbeciles: France cannot do without a King. 'But we have executed our King.' 'And what is it to me,' hastily cries Dumouriez, a General of no reticence, 'whether the King's name be *Ludovicus* or *Jacobus*?' 'Or *Philippus*!' rejoins Proly;—and hastens to report progress. Over the Frontiers such hope is there.

CHAPTER V

SANSCULOTTISM ACCOUTRED

LET us look, however, at the grand internal Sansculottism and Revolution Prodigy, whether it stirs and waxes: there and not elsewhere may hope still be for France. The Revolution Prodigy, as Decree after Decree issues from the Mountain, like creative *fiats*, accordant with the nature of the Thing,—is shaping itself rapidly, in these days, into terrific stature and articulation, limb after limb. Last March 1792, we saw all France flowing in blind terror; shutting town-barriers, boiling pitch for Brigands: happier, this March, that it is a seeing terror; that a creative Mountain exists, which can say *fiat*! Recruitment proceeds with fierce celerity: nevertheless our Volunteers hesitate to set out, till Treason be punished at home; they do not fly to the frontiers; but only fly hither and thither, demanding and denouncing. The Mountain must speak new *fiat* and new *fiats*.

And does it not speak such? Take, as first example, those *Comités Révolutionnaires* for the arrestment of Persons Suspect. Revolutionary Committee, of Twelve chosen Patriots, sits in every Township of France; examining the Suspect, seeking arms, making domiciliary visits and arrestments;—caring, generally, that the Republic suffer no detriment. Chosen by universal suffrage, each in its Section, they are a kind of elixir of Jacobinism; some Forty-four Thousand of them awake and alive over France! In Paris and all Towns, every house-door must have the names of the inmates legibly printed on it, 'at a height not exceeding five feet from the ground'; every Citizen must produce his certificatory *Carte de Civisme*, signed by Section-President; every man be ready to give account of the faith that is in him. Persons Suspect had as well depart this soil of Liberty! And yet departure too is bad: all Emigrants are declared Traitors, their property become National; they are 'dead in Law,'—save, indeed, that for *our* behoof they shall 'live yet fifty years in Law,' and what heritages may fall to them in that time become National too! A mad vitality of Jacobinism, with Forty-four Thousand centres of activity, circulates through all fibres of France.

Very notable also is the *Tribunal Extraordinaire*:[1] decreed by the Mountain; some Girondins dissenting, for surely such a Court contradicts every formula;—other Girondins assenting, nay coöperating, for do not we all hate Traitors, O ye people of Paris?—Tribunal of the Seventeenth, in Autumn last, was swift; but this shall be swifter. Five Judges; a standing Jury, which is named from Paris and the Neighbourhood, that there be not delay in naming it: they are subject to no Appeal; to hardly any Law-forms, but must 'get themselves convinced' in all readiest ways; and for security are bound 'to vote audibly'; audibly, in the hearing of a Paris Public. This is the *Tribunal Extraordinaire*; which, in few months, getting into most lively action, shall be entitled *Tribunal Révolutionnaire*; as indeed it from the very first has entitled itself: with a Herman or a Dumas for Judge-President, with a Fouquier-Tinville for Attorney-General, and a Jury of such as Citizen Leroi, who has surnamed himself *Dix-Août*, 'Leroi *August-Tenth*,' it will become the wonder of the world. Herein has Sansculottism fashioned for itself a Sword of Sharpness: a

[1] *Moniteur*, No. 70 (du 11 Mars), No. 76, etc.

weapon magical; tempered in the Stygian hell-waters; to the edge of it all armour, and defence of strength or of cunning shall be soft; it shall mow down Lives and Brazen-gates; and the waving of it shed terror through the souls of men.

But speaking of an amorphous Sansculottism taking form, ought we not, above all things, to specify how the Amorphous gets itself a Head? Without metaphor, this Revolution Government continues hitherto in a very anarchic state. Executive Council of Ministers, Six in number, there is: but they, especially since Roland's retreat, have hardly known whether they were Ministers or not. Convention Committees sit supreme over them; but then each Committee as supreme as the others: Committee of Twenty-one, of Defence, of General Surety; simultaneous or successive, for specific purposes. The Convention alone is all-powerful,—especially if the Commune go with it; but is too numerous for an administrative body. Wherefore, in this perilous quick-whirling condition of the Republic, before the end of March we obtain our small *Comité de Salut Public*;[1] as it were, for miscellaneous accidental purposes requiring despatch;—as it proves, for a sort of universal supervision, and universal subjection. They are to report weekly, these new Committee-men; but to deliberate in secret. Their number is Nine, firm Patriots all, Danton one of them; renewable every month;—yet why not reëlect them if they turn out well? The flower of the matter is, that they are but nine; that they sit in secret. An insignificant-looking thing at first, this Committee, but with a principle of growth in it! Forwarded by fortune, by internal Jacobin energy, it will reduce all Committees and the Convention itself to mute obedience, the Six Ministers to Six assiduous Clerks; and work its will on the Earth and under Heaven for a season. A 'Committee of Public Salvation' whereat the world still shrieks and shudders.

If we call that Revolutionary Tribunal a Sword, which Sansculottism has provided for itself, then let us call the 'Law of the Maximum' a Provender-scrip, or Haversack, wherein,

[1] *Moniteur*, No. 83 (du 24 Mars 1793), Nos. 86, 98, 99, 100.

better or worse, some ration of bread may be found. It is true, Political Economy, Girondin free-trade, and all law of supply and demand, are hereby hurled topsyturvy: but what help? Patriotism must live; the 'cupidity of farmers' seems to have no bowels. Wherefore this Law of the Maximum, fixing the highest price of grains, is, with infinite effort, got passed;[1] and shall gradually extend itself into a Maximum for all manner of *comestibles* and commodities: with such scrambling and topsy-turvying as may be fancied! For now if, for example, the farmer will not sell? The farmer shall be forced to sell. An accurate Account of what grain he has shall be delivered in to the Constituted Authorities: let him see that he say not too much; for in that case, his rents, taxes and contributions will rise proportionally: let him see that he say not too little; for, on or before a set day, we shall suppose in April, *less* than one-third of this declared quantity must remain in his barns, more than two-thirds of it must have been thrashed and sold. One can denounce him, and raise penalties.

By such inextricable overturning of all Commercial relations will Sansculottism keep life in; since not otherwise. On the whole, as Camille Desmoulins says once, 'while the Sansculottes fight, the Monsieurs must pay.' So there come *Impôts Progressifs*, Ascending Taxes; which consume, with fast-increasing voracity, the 'superfluous-revenue' of men: beyond fifty-pounds a-year, you are not exempt; rising into the hundreds, you bleed freely; into the thousands and tens of thousands, you bleed gushing. Also there come Requisitions; there comes 'Forced-Loan of a Milliard,' some Fifty-Millions Sterling, which of course they that *have* must lend. Unexampled enough; it has grown to be no country for the Rich, this; but a country for the Poor! And then if one fly, what steads it? Dead in Law; nay kept alive fifty years yet, for *their* accursed behoof! In this manner therefore it goes; topsy-turvying, *ça-ira*-ing;—and withal there is endless sale of Emigrant National-Property, there is Cambon with endless cornucopia of Assignats. The Trade and Finance of Sanscu-

[1] *Moniteur* (du 20 Avril, etc. to 20 Mai, 1793).

lottism; and how, with Maximum and Bakers' queues, with Cupidity, Hunger, Denunciation, and Paper-money, it led its galvanic-life, and began and ended,—remains the most interesting of all Chapters in Political Economy: still to be written.

All which things, are they not clean against Formula? O Girondin Friends, it is not a Republic of the Virtues we are getting; but only a Republic of the Strengths, virtuous and other!

CHAPTER VI

THE TRAITOR

BUT Dumouriez, with his fugitive Host, with his King *Ludovicus* or King *Philippus*? There lies the crisis; there hangs the question: Revolution Prodigy, or Counter-Revolution?—One wide shriek covers that North-east region. Soldiers, full of rage, suspicion and terror, flock hither and thither; Dumouriez, the many-counselled, never off horseback, knows now no counsel that were not worse than none: the counsel, namely, of joining himself with Cobourg; marching to Paris, extinguishing Jacobinism, and, with some new King Ludovicus or King Philippus, restoring the Constitution of 1791![1]

Is wisdom quitting Dumouriez; the herald of Fortune quitting him? Principle, faith political or other, beyond a certain faith of mess-rooms, and honour of an officer, had him not to quit. At any rate his quarters in the Burgh of Saint-Amand; his head-quarters in the Village of Saint-Amand des Boues, a short way off,—have become a Bedlam. National Representatives, Jacobin Missionaries are riding and running; of the 'three Towns,' Lille, Valenciennes, or even Condé, which Dumouriez wanted to snatch for himself, not one can be snatched; your Captain is admitted, but the Town-gate is closed on him, and then alas the Prison-gate, and 'his men wander about the ramparts.' Couriers gallop breathless; men wait, or seem waiting, to assassinate, to be assassinated; Battalions nigh frantic

[1] Dumouriez, *Mémoires*, iv. c. 7–10.

with such suspicion and uncertainty, with *Vive-la-République* and *Sauve-qui-peut,* rush this way and that;—Ruin and Desperation in the shape of Cobourg lying entrenched close by.

Dame Genlis and her fair Princess d'Orléans find this Burgh of Saint-Amand no fit place for them; Dumouriez's protection is grown worse than none. Tough Genlis, one of the toughest women; a woman, as it were, with nine lives in her; whom nothing will beat: she packs her bandboxes; clear for flight in a private manner. Her beloved Princess she will—leave here, with the Prince Chartres Egalité her Brother. In the cold grey of the April morning, we find her accordingly established in her hired vehicle, on the street of Saint-Amand; postillions just cracking their whips to go,—when behold the young Princely Brother, struggling hitherward, hastily calling; bearing the Princess in his arms! Hastily he has clutched the poor young lady up, in her very night-gown, nothing saved of her goods except the watch from the pillow: with brotherly despair he flings her in, among the bandboxes, into Genlis's chaise, into Genlis's arms: Leave her not, in the name of Mercy and Heaven! A shrill scene, but a brief one:—the postillions crack and go. Ah, whither? Through by-roads and broken hill-passes; seeking their way with lanterns after nightfall; through perils, and Cobourg Austrians, and suspicious French Nationals: finally, into Switzerland; safe though nigh moneyless.[1] The brave young Egalité has a most wild Morrow to look for; but now only himself to carry through it.

For indeed over at that Village named *of the Mudbaths,* Saint-Amand des Boues, matters are still worse. About four o'clock on Tuesday afternoon, the 2d of April 1793, two Couriers come galloping as if for life; *Mon Général!* Four National Representatives, War-Minister at their head, are posting hitherward from Valenciennes; are close at hand,—with what intents one may guess! While the Couriers are yet speaking, War-Minister and National Representatives, old Camus the Archivist for chief speaker of them, arrive. Hardly

[1] Genlis, iv. 139.

has *Mon Général* had time to order out the Hussar Regiment de Berchigny; that it take rank and wait near by, in case of accident. And so, enter War-Minister Beurnonville, with an embrace of friendship, for he is an old friend; enter Archivist Camus and the other three following him.

They produce Papers, invite the General to the bar of the Convention: merely to give an explanation or two. The General finds it unsuitable, not to say impossible, and that 'the service will suffer.' Then comes reasoning; the voice of the old Archivist getting loud. Vain to reason loud with this Dumouriez; he answers mere angry irreverences. And so, amid plumed staff-officers, very gloomy-looking; in jeopardy and uncertainty, these poor National messengers debate and consult, retire and reënter, for the space of some two hours: without effect. Whereupon Archivist Camus, getting quite loud, proclaims, in the name of the National Convention, for he has the power to do it, That General Dumouriez is *arrested*: 'Will you obey the National mandate, General?'—'*Pas dans ce moment-ci*, Not at this particular moment,' answers the General also aloud; then glancing the other way, utters certain unknown vocables, in a mandatory manner; seemingly a German word-of-command.[1] Hussars clutch the Four National Representatives, and Beurnonville the War-Minister; pack them out of the apartment; out of the Village, over the lines to Cobourg, in two chaises that very night,—as hostages, prisoners; to lie long in Maestricht and Austrian strongholds![2] *Jacta est alea.*

This night Dumouriez prints his 'Proclamation'; this night and the morrow the Dumouriez Army, in such darkness visible, and rage of semi-desperation as there is, shall meditate what the General is doing, what they themselves will do in it. Judge whether this Wednesday was of halcyon nature, for any one! But on the Thursday morning, we discern Dumouriez with small escort, with Chartres Egalité and a few staff-officers, ambling along the Condé Highway: perhaps they are for

[1] Dumouriez, iv. 159, etc.
[2] Their Narrative, written by Camus (in Toulongeon, iii. app. 60–87).

Condé, and trying to persuade the Garrison there; at all events, they are for an interview with Cobourg, who waits in the woods by appointment, in that quarter. Nigh the Village of Doumet, three National Battalions, a set of men always full of Jacobinism, sweep past us; marching rather swiftly,—seemingly in mistake, by a way we had not ordered. The General dismounts, steps into a cottage, a little from the wayside; will give them right order in writing. Hark! what strange growling is heard; what barkings are heard, loud yells of '*Traitors*,' of '*Arrest*': the National Battalions have wheeled round, are emitting shot! Mount, Dumouriez, and spring for life! Dumouriez and Staff strike the spurs in, deep; vault over ditches, into the fields, which prove to be morasses; sprawl and plunge for life; bewhistled with curses and lead. Sunk to the middle, with or without horses, several servants killed, they escape out of shot-range, to General Mack the Austrian's quarters. Nay they return on the morrow, to Saint-Amand and faithful foreign Berchigny; but what boots it? The Artillery has all revolted, is jingling off to Valenciennes; all have revolted, are revolting; except only foreign Berchigny, to the extent of some poor fifteen hundred, none will follow Dumouriez against France and Indivisible Republic: Dumouriez's occupation's gone.[1]

Such an instinct of Frenchhood and Sansculottism dwells in these men: they will follow no Dumouriez nor Lafayette, nor any mortal on such errand. Shriek may be of *Sauve-qui-peut*, but will also be of *Vive-la-République*. New National Representatives arrive; new General Dampierre, soon killed in battle; new General Custine: the agitated Hosts draw back to some Camp of Famars; make head against Cobourg as they can.

And so Dumouriez is in the Austrian quarters; his drama ended, in this rather sorry manner. A most shifty, wiry man; one of Heaven's Swiss; that wanted only work. Fifty years of unnoticed toil and valour; one year of toil and valour, not unnoticed, but seen of all countries and centuries; then thirty other years again unnoticed, of Memoir-writing, English

[1] *Mémoires*, iv. 162–180.

Pension, scheming and projecting to no purpose: Adieu, thou Swiss of heaven, worthy to have been something else!

His Staff go different ways. Brave young Egalité reaches Switzerland and the Genlis Cottage; with a strong crabstick in his hand, a strong heart in his body: his Princedom is now reduced to that. Egalité the Father sat playing whist, in his Palais Egalité, at Paris, on the 6th day of this same month of April, when a catchpole entered: Citoyen Egalité is wanted at the Convention Committee![1] Examination, requiring Arrestment; finally requiring Imprisonment, transference to Marseilles and the Castle of If! Orléansdom has sunk in the black waters; Palais Egalité, which was Palais Royal, is like to become Palais National.

CHAPTER VII

IN FIGHT

Our Republic, by paper Decree, may be 'One and Indivisible'; but what profits it while these things are? Federalists in the Senate, renegadoes in the Army, traitors everywhere! France, all in desperate recruitment since the Tenth of March, does not fly to the frontier, but only flies hither and thither. This defection of contemptuous diplomatic Dumouriez falls heavy on the fine-spoken high-sniffing *Hommes d'état* whom he consorted with; forms a second epoch in their destinies.

Or perhaps more strictly we might say, the second Girondin epoch, though little noticed then, began on the day when, in reference to this defection, the Girondins broke with Danton. It was the first day of April; Dumouriez had not yet plunged across the morasses to Cobourg, but was evidently meaning to do it, and our Commissioners were off to arrest him; when what does the Girondin Lasource see good to do, but rise, and jesuitically question and insinuate at great length, whether a main accomplice of Dumouriez had not probably been—

[1] See Montgaillard, iv. 144.

Danton! Gironde grins sardonic assent; Mountain holds its breath. The figure of Danton, Levasseur says, while this speech went on, was noteworthy. He sat erect with a kind of internal convulsion struggling to keep itself motionless; his eye from time to time flashing wilder, his lip curling in Titanic scorn.[1] Lasource, in a fine-spoken attorney manner, proceeds: there is this probability to his mind, and there is that; probabilities which press painfully on him, which cast the Patriotism of Danton under a painful shade;—which painful shade, he, Lasource, will hope that Danton may find it not impossible to dispel.

'*Les Scélérats!*' cries Danton, starting up, with clenched right-hand, Lasource having done; and descends from the Mountain, like a lava-flood: his answer not unready. Lasource's probabilities fly like idle dust; but leave a result behind them. 'Ye were right, friends of the Mountain,' begins Danton, 'and I was wrong: there is no peace possible with these men. Let it be war, then! They will not save the Republic with us: it shall be saved without them; saved in spite of them.' Really a burst of rude Parliamentary eloquence this; which is still worth reading in the old *Moniteur*. With fire-words the exasperated rude Titan rives and smites these Girondins; at every hit the glad Mountain utters chorus; Marat, like a musical *bis*, repeating the last phrase.[2] Lasource's probabilities are gone; but Danton's pledge of battle remains lying.

A third epoch, or scene in the Girondin Drama, or rather it is but the completion of this second epoch, we reckon from the day when the patience of virtuous Pétion finally boiled over; and the Girondins, so to speak, took up this battle-pledge of Danton's, and decreed Marat accused. It was the eleventh of the same month of April, on some effervescence rising, such as often rose; and President had covered himself, mere Bedlam now ruling; and Mountain and Gironde were rushing on one another with clenched right-hands, and even with pistols in

[1] *Mémoires de Réné Levasseur* (Bruxelles, 1830), i. 164.
[2] Séance du 1 Avril 1793 (in *Hist. Parl.* xxv. 24–35).

them; when, behold, the Girondin Duperret drew a sword! Shriek of horror rose, instantly quenching all other effervescence, at sight of the clear murderous steel; whereupon Duperret returned it to the leather again;—confessing that he did indeed draw it, being instigated by a kind of sacred madness, '*sainte fureur*,' and pistols held at him; but that if he parricidally had chanced to scratch the outmost skin of National Representation with it, he too carried pistols, and would have blown his brains out on the spot.[1]

But now in such posture of affairs, virtuous Pétion rose, next morning, to lament these effervescences, this endless Anarchy invading the Legislative Sanctuary itself; and here, being growled at and howled at by the Mountain, his patience, long tried, did, as we say, boil over; and he spake vehemently, in high key, with foam on his lips; 'whence,' says Marat, 'I concluded he had got *la rage*,' the rabidity, or dog-madness. Rabidity smites others rabid: so there rises new foam-lipped demand to have Anarchists extinguished; and specially to have Marat put under Accusation. Send a representative to the Revolutionary Tribunal? Violate the inviolability of a Representative? Have a care, O Friends! This poor Marat has faults enough; but against Liberty or Equality, what fault? That he has loved and fought for it, not wisely but too well. In dungeons and cellars, in pinching poverty, under anathema of men; even so, in such fight, has he grown so dingy, bleared; even so has his head become a Stylites one! Him you will fling to your Sword of Sharpness; while Cobourg and Pitt advance on us, fire-spitting?

The Mountain is loud, the Gironde is loud and deaf; all lips are foamy. With 'Permanent-Session of twenty-four hours,' with vote by roll-call, and a deadlift effort, the Gironde carries it: Marat is ordered to the Revolutionary Tribunal, to answer for that February Paragraph of Forestallers at the door-lintel, with other offences; and, after a little hesitation, he obeys.[2]

[1] *Hist. Parl.* xv. 397.
[2] *Moniteur* (du 16 Avril 1793, et seqq.).

Thus is Danton's battle-pledge taken up; there is, as he said there would be, 'war without truce or treaty, *ni trève ni composition.*' Wherefore, close now with one another, Formula and Reality, in death-grips, and wrestle it out; both of you cannot live, but only one!

CHAPTER VIII

IN DEATH-GRIPS

It proves what strength, were it only of inertia, there is in established Formulas, what weakness in nascent Realities, and illustrates several things, that this death-wrestle should still have lasted some six weeks or more. National business, discussion of the Constitutional Act, for our Constitution should decidedly be got ready, proceeds along with it. We even change our Locality; we shift, on the Tenth of May, from the old Salle de Manége into our new Hall, in the Palace, once a King's but now the Republic's, of the Tuileries. Hope and ruth, flickering against despair and rage, still struggle in the minds of men.

It is a most dark confused death-wrestle, this of the six weeks. Formalist frenzy against Realist frenzy; Patriotism, Egoism, Pride, Anger, Vanity, Hope and Despair, all raised to the frenetic pitch: Frenzy meets Frenzy, like dark clashing whirlwinds; neither understands the other; the weaker, one day, will understand that *it* is verily swept down! Girondism is strong as established Formula and Respectability: do not as many as Seventy-two of the Departments, or say respectable Heads of Departments, declare for us? Calvados, which loves its Buzot, will even rise in revolt, so hint the Addresses; Marseilles, cradle of Patriotism, will rise; Bordeaux will rise, and the Gironde Department, as one man; in a word, who will *not* rise, were our *Représentation Nationale* to be insulted, or one hair of a Deputy's head harmed! The Mountain, again, is strong as Reality and Audacity. To the Reality of the

Mountain are not all furthersome things possible? A new Tenth of August, if needful; nay a new Second of September!—

But, on Wednesday afternoon, Twenty-fourth day of April, year 1793, what tumult as of fierce jubilee is this? It is Marat returning from the Revolutionary Tribunal! A week or more of death-peril: and now there is triumphant acquittal; Revolutionary Tribunal can find no accusation against this man. And so the eye of History beholds Patriotism, which had gloomed unutterable things all week, break into loud jubilee, embrace its Marat; lift him into a chair of triumph, bear him shoulder-high through the streets. Shoulder-high is the injured People's-friend, crowned with an oak-garland; amid the wavy sea of red night-caps, carmagnole jackets, grenadier bonnets and female mob-caps; far-sounding like a sea! The injured People's-friend has here reached his culminating point; he too strikes the stars with his sublime head.

But the Reader can judge with what face President Lasource, he of the 'painful probabilities,' who presides in this Convention Hall, might welcome such jubilee-tide, when it got thither, and the Decreed of Accusation floating on the top of it! A National Sapper, spokesman on the occasion, says, the People know their Friend, and love his life as their own; 'whosoever wants Marat's head must get the Sapper's first.'[1] Lasource answered with some vague painful mumblement,—which, says Levasseur, one could not help tittering at.[2] Patriot Sections, Volunteers not yet gone to the Frontiers, come demanding the 'purgation of traitors from your own bosom'; the expulsion, or even the trial and sentence, of a factious Twenty-two.

Nevertheless the Gironde has got its Commission of Twelve; a Commission specially appointed for investigating these troubles of the Legislative Sanctuary: let Sansculottism say what it will, Law shall triumph. Old-Constituent Rabaut Saint-Etienne presides over this Commission: 'it is the last

[1] Séance du 26 Avril, An 1er (in *Moniteur*, No. 116).
[2] Levasseur, *Mémoires*, i. c. 6.

plank whereon a wrecked Republic may perhaps still save herself.' Rabaut and they therefore sit, intent; examining witnesses; launching arrestments; looking out into a waste dim sea of troubles,—the womb of *Formula*, or perhaps her grave! Enter not that sea, O Reader! There are dim desolation and confusion; raging women and raging men. Sections come demanding Twenty-two; for the *number* first given by Section Bonconseil still holds, though the names should even vary. Other Sections, of the wealthier kind, come denouncing such demand; nay the same Section will demand today, and denounce the demand tomorrow, according as the wealthier sit, or the poorer. Wherefore, indeed, the Girondins decree that all Sections shall close 'at ten in the evening'; before the working people come: which Decree remains without effect. And nightly the Mother of Patriotism wails doleful; doleful, but her eye kindling! And Fournier l'Américain is busy, and the two banker Freys, and Varlet Apostle of Liberty; the bull-voice of Marquis St.-Huruge is heard. And shrill women vociferate from all Galleries, the Convention ones and downwards. Nay a 'Central Committee' of all the Forty-eight Sections looms forth huge and dubious; sitting dim in the *Archevêché*, sending Resolutions, receiving them: a Centre of the Sections; in dread deliberation as to a New Tenth of August!

One thing we will specify, to throw light on many: the aspect under which, seen through the eyes of these Girondin Twelve, or even seen through one's own eyes, the Patriotism of the softer sex presents itself. There are Female Patriots, whom the Girondins call Megæras, and count to the extent of eight thousand; with serpent-hair, all out of curl; who have changed the distaff for the dagger. They are of 'the Society called Brotherly,' *Fraternelle*, say *Sisterly*, which meets under the roof of the Jacobins. 'Two thousand daggers,' or *so*, have been ordered,—doubtless for them. They rush to Versailles, to raise more women; but the Versailles women will not rise.[1]

[1] Buzot, *Mémoires*, pp. 69, 84; Meillan, *Mémoires*, pp. 192, 195, 196. See *Commission des Douze* (in *Choix des Rapports*, xii. 69–131).

Nay behold, in National Garden of Tuileries,—Demoiselle Théroigne herself is become as a brown-locked Diana (were that possible) attacked by her own dogs, or she-dogs! The Demoiselle, keeping her carriage, is for Liberty indeed, as she has full well shown; but then for Liberty with Respectability: whereupon these serpent-haired Extreme She Patriots do now fasten on her, tatter her, shamefully fustigate her, in their shameful way; almost fling her into the Garden-ponds, had not help intervened. Help, alas, to small purpose. The poor Demoiselle's head and nervous-system, none of the soundest, is so tattered and fluttered that it will never recover; but flutter worse and worse, till it crack; and within year and day we hear of her in madhouse and strait-waistcoat, which proves permanent!—Such brown-locked Figure did flutter, and inarticulately jabber and gesticulate, little able to *speak* the obscure meaning it had, through some segment of the Eighteenth Century of Time. She disappears here from the Revolution and Public History for evermore.[1]

Another thing we will not again specify, yet again beseech the Reader to imagine: the reign of Fraternity and Perfection. Imagine, we say, O Reader, that the Millennium were struggling on the threshold, and yet not so much as groceries could be had,—owing to traitors. With what impetus would a man strike traitors, in that case! Ah, thou canst not imagine it; thou hast thy groceries safe in the shops, and little or no hope of a Millennium ever coming!—But indeed, as to the temper there was in men and women, does not this one fact say enough: the height Suspicion had risen to? Preternatural we often called it; seemingly in the language of exaggeration: but listen to the cold deposition of witnesses. Not a musical Patriot can blow himself a snatch of melody from the French Horn, sitting mildly pensive on the housetop, but Mercier will recognise it to be a signal which one Plotting Committee is making to another. Distraction has possessed Harmony herself; lurks in

[1] *Deux Amis*, vii. 77–80; Forster, i. 514; Moore, i. 70. She did not die till 1817; in the Salpêtrière, in the most abject state of insanity; see Esquirol, *Des Maladies Mentales* (Paris, 1838), i. 445–50.

the sound of *Marseillaise* and *Ça-ira.*[1] Louvet, who can see as deep into a millstone as the most, discerns that we shall be invited back to our old Hall of the Manége, by a Deputation; and then the Anarchists will massacre Twenty-two of us, as we walk over. It is Pitt and Cobourg; the gold of Pitt.—Poor Pitt! They little know what work he has with his own Friends of the People; getting them bespied, beheaded, their habeas-corpuses suspended, and his own Social Order and strong-boxes kept tight,—to fancy him raising mobs among his neighbours!

But the strangest fact connected with French or indeed with human Suspicion, is perhaps this of Camille Desmoulins. Camille's head, one of the clearest in France, has got itself so saturated through every fibre with Preternaturalism of Suspicion, that looking back on that Twelfth of July 1789, when the thousands rose round him, yelling responsive at his word in the Palais-Royal Garden, and took cockades, he finds it explicable only on this hypothesis, That they were all hired to do it, and set on by the Foreign and other Plotters. 'It was not for nothing,' says Camille with insight, 'that this multitude burst up round me when I spoke!' No, not for nothing. Behind, around, before, it is one huge Preternatural Puppet-play of Plots; Pitt pulling the wires.[2] Almost I conjecture that I, Camille myself, am a Plot, and wooden with wires.—The force of insight could no further go.

Be this as it will, History remarks that the Commission of Twelve, now clear enough as to the Plots; and luckily having 'got the threads of them all by the end,' as they say,—are launching Mandates of Arrest rapidly in these May days; and carrying matters with a high hand; resolute that the sea of troubles shall be restrained. What chief Patriot, Section-President even, is safe? They can arrest him; tear him from his warm bed, because he has made irregular Section Arrest-

[1] Mercier, *Nouveau Paris*, vi. 63.

[2] See *Histoire des Brissotins*, par Camille Desmoulins (a Pamphlet of Camille's, Paris, 1793).

ments! They arrest Varlet Apostle of Liberty. They arrest Procureur-Substitute Hébert, *Père Duchesne*; a Magistrate of the People, sitting in Townhall; who, with high solemnity of martyrdom, takes leave of his colleagues; prompt he, to obey the Law; and solemnly acquiescent, disappears into prison.

The swifter fly the Sections, energetically demanding him back; demanding not arrestment of Popular Magistrates, but of a traitorous Twenty-two. Section comes flying after Section;—defiling energetic, with their Cambyses-vein of oratory: nay the Commune itself comes, with Mayor Pache at its head; and with question not of Hébert and the Twenty-two alone, but with this ominous old question made new, 'Can you save the Republic, or must we do it?' To whom President Max Isnard makes fiery answer: If by fatal chance, in any of those tumults which since the Tenth of March are ever returning, Paris were to lift a sacrilegious finger against the National Representation, France would rise as one man, in never-imagined vengeance, and shortly 'the traveller would ask, on which side of the Seine Paris had stood'![1] Whereat the Mountain bellows only louder, and every Gallery; Patriot Paris boiling round.

And Girondin Valazé has nightly conclaves at his house; sends billets, 'Come punctually, and well armed, for there is to be business.' And Megæra women perambulate the streets, with flags, with lamentable *alleleu*.[2] And the Convention-doors are obstructed by roaring multitudes: fine-spoken *Hommes d'état* are hustled, maltreated, as they pass; Marat will apostrophise you, in such death-peril, and say, Thou too art of them. If Roland ask leave to quit Paris, there is order of the day. What help? Substitute Hébert, Apostle Varlet, must be given back; to be crowned with oak-garlands. The Commission of Twelve, in a Convention overwhelmed with roaring Sections, is broken; then on the morrow, in a Convention of rallied Girondins, is reinstated. Dim Chaos, or the sea of troubles, is struggling through all its elements; writhing and chafing towards some Creation.

[1] *Moniteur*, Séance du 25 Mai 1793.
[2] Meillan, *Mémoires*, p. 195; Buzot, pp. 69, 84.

CHAPTER IX

EXTINCT

ACCORDINGLY, on Friday the Thirty-first of May 1793, there comes forth into the summer sunlight one of the strangest scenes. Mayor Pache with Municipality arrives at the Tuileries Hall of Convention; sent for, Paris being in visible ferment; and gives the strangest news.

How, in the grey of this morning, while we sat Permanent in Townhall, watchful for the commonweal, there entered, precisely as on a Tenth of August, some Ninety-six extraneous persons; who declared themselves to be in a state of Insurrection; to be plenipotentiary Commissioners from the Forty-eight Sections, sections or members of the Sovereign People, all in a state of Insurrection; and further, that we, in the name of said Sovereign in Insurrection, were dismissed from office. How we thereupon laid off our sashes, and withdrew into the adjacent Saloon of Liberty. How, in a moment or two, we were called back; and reinstated; the Sovereign pleasing to think us still worthy of confidence. Whereby, having taken new oath of office, we on a sudden find ourselves Insurrectionary Magistrates, with extraneous Committee of Ninety-six sitting by us; and a Citoyen Henriot, one whom some accuse of Septemberism, is made Generalissimo of the National Guard; and, since six o'clock, the tocsins ring, and the drums beat:—Under which peculiar circumstances, what would an august National Convention please to direct us to do?[1]

Yes, there is the question! 'Break the Insurrectionary Authorities,' answer some with vehemence. Vergniaud at least will have 'the National Representatives all die at their post'; this is sworn to, with ready loud acclaim. But as to breaking the Insurrectionary Authorities,—alas, while we yet debate, what sound is that? Sound of the Alarm-Cannon on the Pont Neuf; which it is death by the Law to fire without order from us!

[1] *Débats de la Convention* (Paris, 1828), iv. 187–223; *Moniteur*, Nos. 152–4, An 1er.

It does boom off there nevertheless; sending a stound through all hearts. And the tocsins discourse stern music; and Henriot with his Armed Force has enveloped us! And Section succeeds Section, the livelong day; demanding with Cambyses-oratory, with the rattle of muskets, That traitors, Twenty-two or more, be punished; that the Commission of Twelve be irrecoverably broken. The heart of the Gironde dies within it; distant are the Seventy-two respectable Departments, this fiery Municipality is near! Barrère is for a middle course; granting something. The Commission of Twelve declares that, not waiting to be broken, it hereby breaks itself, and is no more. Fain would Reporter Rabaut speak his and its last words; but he is bellowed off. Too happy that the Twenty-two are still left unviolated!—Vergniaud, carrying the laws of refinement to a great length, moves, to the amazement of some, that 'the Sections of Paris have deserved well of their country.' Whereupon, at a late hour of the evening, the deserving Sections retire to their respective places of abode. Barrère shall report on it. With busy quill and brain he sits, secluded; for him no sleep tonight. Friday the last of May has ended in this manner.

The Sections have deserved well: but ought they not to deserve better? Faction and Girondism is struck down for the moment, and consents to be a nullity; but will it not, at another favourabler moment rise, still feller; and the Republic have to be saved in spite of it? So reasons Patriotism, still Permanent; so reasons the Figure of Marat, visible in the dim Section-world, on the morrow. To the conviction of men!—And so at eventide of Saturday, when Barrère had just got the thing all varnished by the labour of a night and day, and his Report was setting off in the evening mail-bags, tocsin peals out *again*. *Générale* is beating; armed men taking station in the Place Vendôme and elsewhere, for the night; supplied with provisions and liquor. There, under the summer stars, will they wait, this night, what is to be seen and to be done, Henriot and Townhall giving due signal.

The Convention, at sound of *générale*, hastens back to its

Hall; but to the number only of a Hundred; and does little business, puts off business till the morrow. The Girondins do not stir out thither, the Girondins are abroad seeking beds.—Poor Rabaut, on the morrow morning, returning to his post, with Louvet and some others, through streets all in ferment, wrings his hands, ejaculating, '*Illa suprema dies!*'[1] It has become Sunday the 2d day of June, year 1793, by the old style; by the new style, year One of Liberty, Equality, Fraternity. We have got to the last scene of all, that ends this history of the Girondin Senatorship.

It seems doubtful whether any terrestrial Convention had ever met in such circumstances as this National one now does. Tocsin is pealing; Barriers shut; all Paris is on the gaze, or under arms. As many as a Hundred Thousand under arms they count: National Force; and the Armed Volunteers, who should have flown to the Frontiers and La Vendée; but would not, treason being unpunished; and only flew hither and thither! So many, steady under arms, environ the National Tuileries and Garden. There are horse, foot, artillery, sappers with beards: the artillery one can see with their camp-furnaces in this National Garden, heating bullets red, and their match is lighted. Henriot in plumes rides, amid a plumed Staff: all posts and issues are safe; reserves lie out, as far as the Wood of Boulogne; the choicest Patriots nearest the scene. One other circumstance we will note: that a careful Municipality, liberal of camp-furnaces, has not forgotten provision-carts. No member of the Sovereign need now go home to dinner; but can keep rank—plentiful victual circulating unsought. Does not this People understand Insurrection? Ye, *not* uninventive, *Gualches*!—

Therefore let a National Representation, 'mandatories of the Sovereign,' take thought of it. Expulsion of your Twenty-two, and your Commission of Twelve: we stand here till it be done! Deputation after Deputation, in ever stronger language, comes with that message. Barrère proposes a middle course:—

[1] Louvet, *Mémoires*, p. 89.

Will not perhaps the inculpated Deputies consent to withdraw voluntarily; to make a generous demission and self-sacrifice for the sake of one's country? Isnard, repentant of that search on which river-bank Paris stood, declares himself ready to demit. Ready also is *Te-Deum* Fauchet; old Dusaulx of the Bastille, '*vieux radoteur*, old dotard,' as Marat calls him, is still readier. On the contrary, Lanjuinais, the Breton declares that there is one man who never will demit voluntarily; but will protest to the uttermost, while a voice is left him. And he accordingly goes on protesting; amid rage and clangour; Legendre crying at last: 'Lanjuinais, come down from the Tribune, or I will fling thee down, *ou je te jette en bas!*' For matters are come to extremity. Nay they do clutch hold of Lanjuinais, certain zealous Mountain-men; but cannot fling him down, for he 'cramps himself on the railing'; and 'his clothes get torn.' Brave Senator, worthy of pity! Neither will Barbaroux demit; he 'has sworn to die at his post, and will keep that oath.' Whereupon the Galleries all rise with explosion; brandishing weapons, some of them; and rush out, saying: '*Allons*, then; we must save our country!' Such a Session is this of Sunday the second of June.

Churches fill, over Christian Europe, and then empty themselves; but this Convention empties not, the while: a day of shrieking contention, of agony, humiliation, and tearing of coat-skirts; *illa suprema dies!* Round stand Henriot and his Hundred Thousand, copiously refreshed from tray and basket: nay he is 'distributing five francs a-piece,' we Girondins saw it with our eyes; five francs to keep them in heart! And distraction of armed riot encumbers our borders, jangles at our Bar; we are prisoners in our own Hall: Bishop Grégoire could not get out for a *besoin actuel* without four gendarmes to wait on him! What is the character of a National Representative become? And now the sunlight falls yellower on western windows, and the chimney-tops are flinging longer shadows; the refreshed Hundred Thousand, nor their shadows, stir not! What to resolve on? Motion rises, superfluous one would think, That the Convention go forth in a body; ascertain with its own eyes whether it is free or not. Lo, therefore, from the Eastern

Gate of the Tuileries, a distressed Convention issuing; handsome Hérault Séchelles at their head; he with hat on, in sign of public calamity, the rest bareheaded,—towards the Gate of the Carrousel; wondrous to see: towards Henriot and his plumed Staff. 'In the name of the National Convention, make way!' Not an inch of way does Henriot make: 'I receive no orders, till the Sovereign, yours and mine, have been obeyed.' The Convention presses on; Henriot prances back, with his Staff, some fifteen paces, 'To arms! Cannoneers, to your guns!' —flashes out his puissant sword, as the Staff all do, and the Hussars all do. Cannoneers brandish the lit match; Infantry present arms,—alas, in the level way, as if for firing! Hatted Hérault leads his distressed flock, through their pinfold of a Tuileries again; across the Garden, to the Gate on the opposite side. Here is Feuillans-Terrace, alas, there is our old Salle de Manége; but neither at this Gate of the Pont Tournant is there egress. Try the other; and the other: no egress! We wander disconsolate through armed ranks; who indeed salute with *Live the Republic*, but also with *Die the Gironde*. Other such sight, in the year One of Liberty, the westering sun never saw.

And now behold Marat meets us; for he lagged in this Suppliant Procession of ours: he has got some hundred elect Patriots at his heels; he orders us, in the Sovereign's name, to return to our place, and do as we are bidden and bound. The Convention returns. 'Does not the Convention,' says Couthon with a singular power of face, 'see that it is free,'—none but friends round it? The Convention, overflowing with friends and armed Sectioners, proceeds to vote as bidden. Many will not vote, but remain silent; some one or two protest, in words, the Mountain has a clear unanimity. Commission of Twelve, and the denounced Twenty-two, to whom we add Ex-Ministers Clavière and Lebrun: these, with some slight extempore alterations (this or that orator proposing, but Marat disposing), are voted to be under 'Arrestment in their own houses.' Brissot, Buzot, Vergniaud, Guadet, Louvet, Gensonné, Barbaroux, Lasource, Lanjuinais, Rabaut,—Thirty-two, by the tale; all that we have known as Girondins, and more than we have known. They, 'under the safeguard of the French People'; by and by, under the safeguard of two Gendarmes each, shall dwell peaceably in their own houses; as Non-Senators; till further order. Herewith ends *Séance* of Sunday the second of June 1793.

At ten o'clock, under mild stars, the Hundred Thousand, their work well finished, turn homewards. Already yesterday, Central Insurrection Committee had arrested Madame Roland; imprisoned her in the Abbaye. Roland has fled, no man knows whither.

Thus fell the Girondins, by Insurrection; and became extinct as a Party: not without a sigh from most Historians. The men were men of parts, of Philosophic culture, decent behaviour; not condemnable in that they were but Pedants, and had not better parts; not condemnable, but most unfortunate. They wanted a Republic of the Virtues, wherein themselves should be head; and they could only get a Republic of the Strengths, wherein others than they were head.

For the rest, Barrère shall make Report of it. The night concludes with a 'civic promenade by torchlight':[1] surely the true reign of Fraternity is now not far?

[1] Buzot, *Mémoires*, p. 310. See *Pièces Justificatives*, of Narratives, Commentaries, etc. in Buzot, Louvet, Meillan; *Documens Complémentaires*, in *Hist. Parl.* xxviii. 1–78.

BOOK FOURTH

TERROR

CHAPTER I

CHARLOTTE CORDAY

IN the leafy months of June and July, several French Departments germinate a set of rebellious *paper*-leaves, named Proclamations, Resolutions, Journals, or Diurnals, 'of the Union for Resistance to Oppression.' In particular, the Town of Caen, in Calvados, sees its paper-leaf of *Bulletin de Caen* suddenly bud, suddenly establish itself as Newspaper there; under the Editorship of Girondin National Representatives!

For among the proscribed Girondins are certain of a more desperate humour. Some, as Vergniaud, Valazé, Gensonné, 'arrested in their own houses,' will await with stoical resignation what the issue may be. Some, as Brissot, Rabaut, will take to flight, to concealment; which, as the Paris Barriers are opened again in a day or two, is not yet difficult. But others there are who will rush, with Buzot, to Calvados; or far over France, to Lyons, Toulon, Nantes and elsewhither, and then rendezvous at Caen: to awaken as with war-trumpet the respectable Departments; and strike down an anarchic Mountain Faction; at least not yield without a stroke at it. Of this latter temper we count some score or more, of the Arrested, and of the Not-yet-arrested: a Buzot, a Barbaroux, Louvet, Guadet, Pétion, who have escaped from Arrestment in their own homes; a Salles, a Pythagorean Valady, a Duchâtel, the Duchâtel that came in blanket and nightcap to vote for the life of Louis, who have escaped from danger and likelihood of Arrestment. These, to the number at one time of Twenty-seven, do accordingly lodge here, at the '*Intendance*, or Departmental Mansion,' of the town of Caen in Calvados; welcomed by Persons in Authority; welcomed and defrayed, having no money of their own. And the *Bulletin de Caen* comes forth, with the most animating paragraphs: How the Bordeaux Department, the Lyons Department, this Department after the other is declaring itself; sixty, or say sixty-nine, or seventy-two[1] respectable Departments either declaring, or ready to declare. Nay Marseilles, it seems, will march on Paris by itself, if need be. So has Marseilles Town said, That she will march. But on the other hand, that Montélimart Town has said, No thoroughfare; and means even to 'bury herself' under her own stone and mortar first,—of this be no mention in *Bulletin de Caen.*

Such animating paragraphs we read in this new Newspaper; and fervours and eloquent sarcasm: tirades against the Mountain, from the pen of Deputy Salles; which resemble, say friends, Pascal's *Provincials.* What is more to the purpose, these Girondins have got a General in chief, one Wimpfen, formerly under Dumouriez; also a secondary questionable General Puisaye, and others; and are doing their best to raise a force for war. National Volunteers, whosoever is of right heart: gather in, ye National Volunteers, friends of Liberty; from our Calvados Townships, from the Eure, from Brittany, from far and near: forward to Paris, and extinguish Anarchy! Thus at Caen, in the early July days, there is a drumming and parading, a perorating and consulting: Staff and Army; Council; Club of *Carabots,* Anti-jacobin friends of Freedom, to denounce atrocious Marat. With all which, and the editing of *Bulletins,* a National Representative has his hands full.

At Caen it is most animated; and, as one hopes, more or less animated in the 'Seventy-two Departments that adhere to us.' And in a France begirt with Cimmerian invading Coalitions, and torn with an internal La Vendée, *this* is the conclusion we have arrived at: To put down Anarchy by Civil War! *Durum et durum,* the Proverb says, *non faciunt murum.* La Vendée burns: Santerre can do nothing there; he may return home and brew beer. Cimmerian bombshells fly all along the North. That Siege of Mentz is become famed;—lovers of the Picturesque (as Goethe will testify), washed country-people of both sexes,

[1] Meillan, pp. 72, 73; Louvet, p. 129.

stroll thither on Sundays, to see the artillery work and counterwork; 'you only duck a little while the shot whizzes past.'[1] Condé is capitulating to the Austrians; Royal Highness of York, these several weeks, fiercely batters Valenciennes. For, alas, our fortified Camp of Famars was stormed; General Dampierre was killed; General Custine was blamed,—and indeed is now come to Paris to give 'explanations.'

Against all which the Mountain and atrocious Marat must even make head as they can. They, anarchic Convention as they are, publish Decrees, expostulatory, explanatory, yet not without severity; they ray-forth Commissioners, singly or in pairs, the olive-branch in one hand, yet the sword in the other. Commissioners come even to Caen; but without effect. Mathematical Romme, and Prieur named of the Côte d'Or, venturing thither, with their olive and sword, are packed into prison: there may Romme lie, under lock and key, 'for fifty days'; and meditate his New Calendar, if he please. Cimmeria, La Vendée, and Civil War! Never was Republic One and Indivisible at a lower ebb.—

Amid which dim ferment of Caen and the World, History specially notices one thing: in the lobby of the Mansion *de l'Intendance*, where busy Deputies are coming and going, a young Lady with an aged valet, taking grave graceful leave of Deputy Barbaroux.[2] She is of stately Norman figure; in her twenty-fifth year; of beautiful still countenance: her name is Charlotte Corday, heretofore styled D'Armans, while Nobility still was. Barbaroux has given her a Note to Deputy Duperret, —him who once drew his sword in the effervescence. Apparently she will to Paris on some errand? 'She was a Republican before the Revolution, and never wanted energy.' A completeness, a decision is in this fair female Figure: 'by energy she means the spirit that will prompt one to sacrifice himself for his country.' What if she, this fair young Charlotte, had emerged from her secluded stillness, suddenly like a Star; cruel-lovely, with half-angelic, half-dæmonic splendour; to

[1] *Belagerung von Mainz* (Goethe's *Werke*, xxx. 278–334).
[2] Meillan, p. 75; Louvet, p. 114.

gleam for a moment, and in a moment be extinguished: to be held in memory, so bright-complete was she, through long centuries!—Quitting Cimmerian Coalitions without, and the dim-simmering Twenty-five millions within, History will look fixedly at this one fair Apparition of a Charlotte Corday; will note whither Charlotte moves, how the little Life burns forth so radiant, then vanishes swallowed of the Night.

With Barbaroux's Note of Introduction, and slight stock of luggage, we see Charlotte on Tuesday the 9th of July seated in the Caen Diligence, with a place for Paris. None takes farewell of her, wishes her Good-journey: her Father will find a line left, signifying that she is gone to England, that he must pardon her, and forget her. The drowsy Diligence lumbers along; amid drowsy talk of Politics, and praise of the Mountain; in which she mingles not: all night, all day, and again all night. On Thursday, not long before noon, we are at the bridge of Neuilly; here is Paris with her thousand black domes, the goal and purpose of thy journey! Arrived at the Inn de la Providence in the Rue des Vieux Augustins, Charlotte demands a room; hastens to bed; sleeps all afternoon and night, till the morrow morning.

On the morrow morning, she delivers her Note to Duperret. It relates to certain Family Papers which are in the Minister of the Interior's hands; which a Nun at Caen, an old Convent-friend of Charlotte's, has need of; which Duperret shall assist her in getting: this then was Charlotte's errand to Paris? She has finished this, in the course of Friday;—yet says nothing of returning. She has seen and silently investigated several things. The Convention, in bodily reality, she has seen; what the Mountain is like. The living physiognomy of Marat she could not see; he is sick at present, and confined to home.

About eight on the Saturday morning, she purchases a large sheath-knife in the Palais Royal; then straightway, in the Place des Victoires, takes a hackney-coach: 'To the Rue de l'Ecole de Médecine, No. 44.' It is the residence of the Citoyen Marat!—The Citoyen Marat is ill, and cannot be seen; which seems to disappoint her much. Her business is with

Marat, then? Hapless beautiful Charlotte; hapless squalid Marat! From Caen in the utmost West, from Neuchâtel in the utmost East, they two are drawing nigh each other; they two have, very strangely, business together.—Charlotte, returning to her Inn, despatches a short Note to Marat; signifying that she is from Caen, the seat of rebellion; that she desires earnestly to see him, and 'will put it in his power to do France a great service.' No answer. Charlotte writes another Note, still more pressing; sets out with it by coach, about seven in the evening, herself. Tired day-labourers have again finished their Week; huge Paris is circling and simmering, manifold, according to its vague wont: this one fair Figure has decision in it; drives straight,—towards a purpose.

It is yellow July evening, we say, the thirteenth of the month; eve of the Bastille day,—when 'M. Marat,' four years ago, in the crowd of the Pont Neuf, shrewdly required of that Besenval Hussar-party, which has such friendly dispositions, 'to dismount, and give up their arms, then'; and became notable among Patriot men. Four years; what a road he has travelled;—and sits now, about half-past seven of the clock, stewing in slipper-bath; sore afflicted; ill of Revolution Fever,—of what other malady this History had rather not name. Excessively sick and worn, poor man: with precisely elevenpence-halfpenny of ready-money, in paper; with slipper-bath; strong three-footed stool for writing on, the while; and a squalid—Washerwoman, one may call her: that is his civic establishment in Medical-School Street; thither and not elsewhither has his road led him. Not to the reign of Brotherhood and Perfect Felicity; yet surely on the way towards that?—Hark, a rap again! A musical woman's voice, refusing to be rejected: it is the Citoyenne who would do France a service. Marat, recognising from within, cries, Admit her. Charlotte Corday is admitted.

Citoyen Marat, I am from Caen the seat of rebellion, and wished to speak with you.—Be seated, *mon enfant*. Now what are the Traitors doing at Caen? What Deputies are at Caen?—Charlotte names some Deputies. 'Their heads shall fall within a fortnight,' croaks the eager People's-friend, clutching his tablets to write: *Barbaroux*, *Pétion*, writes he with bare shrunk arm, turning aside in the bath; *Pétion*, and *Louvet*, and—Charlotte has drawn her knife from the sheath; plunges it, with one sure stroke, into the writer's heart. '*À moi, chère amie*, Help, dear!' no more could the Death-choked say or shriek. The helpful Washerwoman running in, there is no Friend of the People, or Friend of the Washerwoman left; but his life with a groan gushes out, indignant, to the shades below.[1]

And so Marat People's-friend is ended; the lone Stylites has got hurled down suddenly from his Pillar,—*whitherward* He that made him knows. Patriot Paris may sound triple and tenfold, in dole and wail; reëchoed by Patriot France; and the Convention, 'Chabot pale with terror, declaring that they are to be all assassinated,' may decree him Pantheon Honours, Public Funeral, Mirabeau's dust making way for him; and Jacobin Societies, in lamentable oratory, summing up his character, parallel him to One, whom they think it honour to call 'the good Sansculotte,'—whom we name not here;[2] also a Chapel may be made, for the urn that holds his Heart, in the Place du Carrousel; and new-born children be named Marat; and Lago-di-Como Hawkers bake mountains of stucco into unbeautiful Busts; and David paint his Picture, or Death-Scene; and such other Apotheosis take place as the human genius, in these circumstances, can devise: but Marat returns no more to the light of this Sun. One sole circumstance we have read with clear sympathy, in the old *Moniteur* Newspaper: how Marat's Brother comes from Neuchâtel to ask of the Convention, 'that the deceased Jean-Paul Marat's musket be given him.'[3] For Marat too had a brother and natural affections; and was wrapped once in swaddling-clothes, and slept safe in a cradle like the rest of us. Ye children of men!—A sister of his, they say, lives still to this day in Paris.

[1] *Moniteur*, Nos. 197, 198, 199; *Hist. Parl.* xxviii. 301–5; *Deux Amis*, 1. 368–374.

[2] See *Eloge funèbre de Jean-Paul Marat*, prononcé à Strasbourg (in Barbaroux, pp. 125–131); Mercier, etc.

[3] Séance du 16 Septembre 1793.

As for Charlotte Corday, her work is accomplished; the recompense of it is near and sure. The *chère amie*, and neighbours of the house, flying at her, she 'overturns some movables,' entrenches herself till the gendarmes arrive; then quietly surrenders; goes quietly to the Abbaye Prison: she alone quiet, all Paris sounding, in wonder, in rage or admiration, round her. Duperret is put in arrest, on account of her; his Papers sealed, —which may lead to consequences. Fauchet, in like manner, though Fauchet had not so much as heard of her. Charlotte, confronted with these two Deputies, praises the grave firmness of Duperret, censures the dejection of Fauchet.

On Wednesday morning, the thronged Palais de Justice and Revolutionary Tribunal can see her face; beautiful and calm: she dates it 'fourth day of the Preparation of Peace.' A strange murmur ran through the Hall, at sight of her; you could not say of what character.[1] Tinville has his indictments and tape-papers: the cutler of the Palais Royal will testify that he sold her the sheath-knife; 'All these details are needless,' interrupted Charlotte; 'it is I that killed Marat.' By whose instigation?—'By no one's.' What tempted you, then? His crimes. 'I killed one man,' added she, raising her voice extremely (*extrêmement*), as they went on with their questions, 'I killed one man to save a hundred thousand; a villain to save innocents; a savage wild-beast to give repose to my country. I was a Republican before the Revolution; I never wanted energy.' There is therefore nothing to be said. The public gazes astonished: the hasty limners sketch her features, Charlotte not disapproving: the men of law proceed with their formalities. The doom is Death as a murderess. To her Advocate she gives thanks; in gentle phrase, in high-flown classical spirit. To the Priest they send her she gives thanks; but needs not any shriving, any ghostly or other aid from him.

On this same evening therefore, about half-past seven o'clock, from the gate of the Conciergerie, to a City all on tiptoe, the fatal Cart issues; seated on it a fair young creature, sheeted in red smock of Murderess; so beautiful, serene, so full

[1] *Procès de Charlotte Corday*, etc. (*Hist. Parl.* xxviii. 311–338

of life; journeying towards death,—alone amid the World. Many take off their hats, saluting reverently; for what heart but must be touched?[1] Others growl and howl. Adam Lux, of Mentz, declares that she is greater than Brutus; that it were beautiful to die with her: the head of this young man seems turned. At the Place de la Révolution, the countenance of Charlotte wears the same still smile. The executioners proceed to bind her feet; she resists, thinking it meant as an insult; on a word of explanation, she submits with cheerful apology. As the last act, all being now ready, they take the neckerchief from her neck; a blush of maidenly shame overspreads that fair face and neck; the cheeks were still tinged with it when the executioner lifted the severed head, to show it to the people. 'It is most true,' says Forster, 'that he struck the cheek insultingly; for I saw it with my eyes: the Police imprisoned him for it.'[2]

In this manner have the Beautifulest and the Squalidest come in collision, and extinguished one another. Jean-Paul Marat and Marie-Anne Charlotte Corday both, suddenly, are no more. 'Day of the Preparation of Peace?' Alas, how were peace possible or preparable, while, for example, the hearts of lovely Maidens, in their convent-stillness, are dreaming not of Love-paradises and the light of Life, but of Codrus' sacrifices and Death well-earned? That Twenty-five million hearts have got to such temper, this *is* the Anarchy; the soul of it lies in this: whereof not peace can be the embodiment! The death of Marat, whetting old animosities tenfold, will be worse than any life. O ye hapless Two, mutually extinctive, the Beautiful and the Squalid, sleep ye well,—in the Mother's bosom that bore you both!

This is the History of Charlotte Corday; most definite, most complete; angelic-dæmonic: like a Star! Adam Lux goes home, half-delirious; to pour forth his Apotheosis of her, in paper and print; to propose that she have a statue with this inscription, *Greater than Brutus*. Friends represent his danger; Lux is reckless; thinks it were beautiful to die with her.

[1] *Deux Amis*, x. 374–384. [2] *Briefwechsel*, i. 508.

CHAPTER II

IN CIVIL WAR

But during these same hours, another guillotine is at work, on another: Charlotte, for the Girondins, dies at Paris today; Chalier, by the Girondins, dies at Lyons tomorrow.

From rumbling of cannon along the streets of that City, it has come to firing of them, to rabid fighting: Nièvre Chol and the Girondins triumph;—behind whom there is, as everywhere, a Royalist Faction waiting to strike in. Trouble enough at Lyons; and the dominant party carrying it with a high hand! For, indeed, the whole South is astir; incarcerating Jacobins; arming for Girondins: wherefore we have got a 'Congress of Lyons'; also a 'Revolutionary Tribunal of Lyons,' and Anarchists shall tremble. So Chalier was soon found guilty, of Jacobinism, of murderous Plot, 'address with drawn dagger on the sixth of February last'; and, on the morrow, he also travels his final road, along the streets of Lyons, 'by the side of an ecclesiastic, with whom he seems to speak earnestly,'—the axe now glittering nigh. He could weep, in old years, this man, and 'fall on his knees on the pavement,' blessing Heaven at sight of Federation Programs or the like; then he pilgrimed to Paris, to worship Marat and the Mountain: now Marat and he are both gone;—we said he could not end well. Jacobinism groans inwardly, at Lyons; but dare not outwardly. Chalier, when the Tribunal sentenced him, made answer: 'My death will cost this City dear.'

Montélimart Town is not buried under its ruins; yet Marseilles is actually marching, under order of a 'Lyons Congress'; is incarcerating Patriots; the very Royalists now showing face. Against which a General Cartaux fights, though in small force; and with him an Artillery Major, of the name of—Napoleon Buonaparte. This Napoleon, to prove that the Marseillese have no chance ultimately, not only fights but writes; publishes his *Supper of Beaucaire*, a Dialogue which has become curious.[1]

[1] See Hazlitt, ii. 529–41.

Unfortunate Cities, with their actions and their reactions! Violence to be paid with violence in geometrical ratio; Royalism and Anarchism both striking in; —the final net-amount of which geometrical series, what man shall sum?

The Bar of Iron has never yet floated in Marseilles Harbour; but the body of Rebecqui was found floating, self-drowned there. Hot Rebecqui, seeing how confusion deepened, and Respectability grew poisoned with Royalism, felt that there was no refuge for a Republican but death. Rebecqui disappeared: no one knew whither; till, one morning, they found the empty case or body of him risen to the top, tumbling on the salt waves;[1] and perceived that Rebecqui had withdrawn for ever.—Toulon likewise is incarcerating Patriots; sending delegates to Congress; intriguing, in case of necessity, with the Royalists and English. Montpellier, Bordeaux, Nantes: all France, that is not under the swoop of Austria and Cimmeria, seems rushing into madness and suicidal ruin. The Mountain labours; like a volcano in a burning volcanic Land. Convention Committees, of Surety, of Salvation, are busy night and day: Convention Commissioners whirl on all highways; bearing olive-branch and sword, or now perhaps sword only. Chaumette and Municipals come daily to the Tuileries demanding a Constitution: it is some weeks now since he resolved, in Townhall, that a Deputation 'should go every day,' and demand a Constitution, till one were got;[2] whereby suicidal France might rally and pacify itself; a thing inexpressibly desirable.

This then is the fruit your Antianarchic Girondins have got from that Levying of War in Calvados? This fruit, we may say; and no other whatsoever. For indeed, before either Charlotte's or Chalier's head had fallen, the Calvados War itself had, as it were, vanished, dreamlike, in a shriek! With 'seventy-two Departments' on our side, one might have hoped better things. But it turns out that Respectabilities, though they will vote, will not fight. Possession always is nine points in Law; but in

[1] Barbaroux, p. 29.
[2] *Deux Amis*, x. 345.

Lawsuits of *this* kind, one may say, it is ninety-and-nine points. Men do what they were wont to do; and have immense irresolution and inertia: they obey him who has the symbols that claim obedience. Consider what, in modern society, this one fact means: the Metropolis is with our enemies! Metropolis, *Mother-city*; rightly so named: all the rest are but as her children, her nurselings. Why, there is not a leathern Diligence, with its post-bags and luggage-boots, that lumbers out from her, but is as a huge life-pulse; she is the heart of all. Cut short that one leathern Diligence, how much is cut short!—General Wimpfen, looking practically into the matter, can see nothing for it but that one should fall back on Royalism; get into communication with Pitt! Dark innuendos he flings out, to that effect: whereat we Girondins start, horrorstruck. He produces as his Second in command a certain '*Ci-devant*,' one Comte Puisaye; entirely unknown to Louvet; greatly suspected by him.

Few wars, accordingly, were ever levied of a more insufficient character than this of Calvados. He that is curious in such things may read the details of it in the Memoirs of that same *Ci-devant* Puisaye, the much-enduring man and Royalist: How our Girondin National forces, marching off with plenty of wind-music, were drawn out about the old Château of Brécourt, in the wood-country near Vernon, to meet the Mountain National forces advancing from Paris. How on the fifteenth afternoon of July, they did meet;—and, as it were, shrieked mutually, and took mutually to flight, without loss. How Puisaye thereafter,—for the Mountain Nationals fled first, and we thought ourselves the victors,—was roused from his warm bed in the Castle of Brécourt; and had to gallop without boots; our Nationals, in the night-watches, having fallen unexpectedly into *sauve-qui-peut*:—and in brief the Calvados War had burnt priming; and the only question now was, Whitherward to vanish, in what hole to hide oneself![1]

The National Volunteers rush homewards, faster than they came. The Seventy-two Respectable Departments, says

[1] *Mémoires de Puisaye* (London, 1803), ii. 142–67.

Meillan, 'all turned round and forsook us, in the space of four-and-twenty hours.' Unhappy those who, as at Lyons for instance, have gone too far for turning! 'One morning,' we find placarded on our Intendance Mansion, the Decree of Convention which casts us *Hors la loi*, into Outlawry; placarded by our Caen Magistrates;—clear hint that we also are to vanish. Vanish indeed: but whitherward? Gorsas has friends in Rennes; he will hide there,—unhappily will not lie hid. Gaudet, Lanjuinais are on cross roads; making for Bordeaux. To Bordeaux! cries the general voice, of Valour alike and of Despair. Some flag of Respectability still floats there, or is thought to float.

Thitherward therefore; each as he can! Eleven of these ill-fated Deputies, among whom we may count as twelfth, Friend Riouffe the Man of Letters, do an original thing: Take the uniform of National Volunteers, and retreat southward with the Breton Battalion, as private soldiers of that corps. These brave Bretons had stood truer by us than any other. Nevertheless, at the end of a day or two, they also do now get dubious, self-divided; we must part from them; and, with some half-dozen as convoy or guide, retreat by ourselves,—a solitary marching detachment, through waste regions of the West.[1]

CHAPTER III

RETREAT OF THE ELEVEN

It is one of the notablest Retreats, this of the Eleven, that History presents: The handful of forlorn Legislators retreating there, continually, with shouldered firelock and well-filled cartridge-box, in the yellow autumn; long hundreds of miles between them and Bordeaux; the country all getting hostile, suspicious of the truth; simmering and buzzing on all sides, more and more. Louvet has preserved the Itinerary of it; a piece worth all the rest he ever wrote.

[1] Louvet, pp. 101–37; Meillan, pp. 81, 241–70.

O virtuous Pétion, with thy early-white head, O brave young Barbaroux, has it come to this? Weary ways, worn shoes, light purse;—encompassed with perils as with a sea! Revolutionary Committees are in every Township; of Jacobin temper; our friends all cowed, our cause the losing one. In the Borough of Moncontour, by ill chance, it is market-day: to the gaping public such transit of a solitary Marching Detachment is suspicious; we have need of energy, of promptitude and luck, to be allowed to march through. Hasten, ye weary pilgrims! The country is getting up; noise of you is bruited day after day, a solitary Twelve retreating in this mysterious manner: with every new day, a wider wave of inquisitive pursuing tumult is stirred up, till the whole West will be in motion. 'Cussy is tormented with gout, Buzot is too fat for marching.' Riouffe, blistered, bleeding, marches only on tiptoe; Barbaroux limps with sprained ankle, yet ever cheery, full of hope and valour. Light Louvet glances hare-eyed, not hare-hearted: only virtuous Pétion's serenity 'was but once seen ruffled.'[1] They lie in straw-lofts, in woody brakes; rudest paillasse on the floor of a secret friend is luxury. They are seized in the dead of night by Jacobin mayors and tap of drum; get off by firm countenance, rattle of muskets and ready wit.

Of Bordeaux, through fiery La Vendée and the long geographical spaces that remain, it were madness to think: well if you can get to Quimper on the sea-coast, and take shipping there. Faster, ever faster! Before the end of the march, so hot has the country grown, it is found advisable to march all night. They do it; under the still night-canopy they plod along;—and yet behold, Rumour has outplodded them. In the paltry Village of Carhaix (be its thatched huts and bottomless peat-bogs long notable to the Traveller), one is astonished to find light still glimmering: citizens are awake, with rushlights burning, in that nook of the terrestrial Planet; as we traverse swiftly the one poor street, a voice is heard saying, 'There they are, *Les voilà qui passent!*'[2] Swifter, ye doomed lame Twelve: speed ere

[1] Meillan, pp. 119–137.
[2] Louvet, pp. 138–164.

they can arm; gain the Woods of Quimper before day, and lie squatted there!

The doomed Twelve do it; though with difficulty, with loss of road, with peril and the mistakes of a night. In Quimper are Girondin friends, who perhaps will harbour the homeless, till a Bordeaux ship weigh. Wayworn, heartworn, in agony of suspense, till Quimper friendship get warning, they lie there, squatted under the thick wet boscage; suspicious of the face of man. Some pity to the brave; to the unhappy! Unhappiest of all Legislators, O when ye packed your luggage, some score or two-score months ago, and mounted this or the other leathern vehicle, to be Conscript Fathers of a regenerated France, and reap deathless laurels,—did you think your journey was to lead *hither*? The Quimper Samaritans find them squatted; lift them up to help and comfort; will hide them in sure places. Thence let them dissipate gradually; or there they can lie quiet, and write *Memoirs*, till a Bordeaux ship sail.

And thus, in Calvados, all is dissipated; Romme is out of prison, meditating his Calendar; ringleaders are locked in his room. At Caen the Corday family mourns in silence: Buzot's House is a heap of dust and demolition; and amid the rubbish sticks a Gallows, with this inscription, *Here dwelt the Traitor Buzot, who conspired against the Republic*. Buzot and the other vanished Deputies are *hors la loi*, as we saw; their lives free to take where they can be found. The worse fares it with the poor Arrested visible Deputies at Paris. 'Arrestment at home' threatens to become 'Confinement in the Luxembourg'; to end: *where?* For example, what pale-visaged thin man is this, journeying towards Switzerland as a Merchant of Neuchâtel, whom they arrest in the town of Moulins? To Revolutionary Committee he is suspect. To Revolutionary Committee, on probing the matter, he is evidently: Deputy Brissot! Back to thy Arrestment, poor Brissot; or indeed to strait confinement, —whither others are fated to follow. Rabaut has built himself a false-partition, in a friend's house; lives, in invisible darkness, between two walls. It will end, this same Arrestment business, in Prison, and the Revolutionary Tribunal.

Nor must we forget Duperret, and the seal put on his papers by reason of Charlotte. One Paper is there, fit to breed wo enough: A secret solemn Protest against that *suprema dies* of the Second of June! This Secret Protest our poor Duperret had drawn up, the same week, in all plainness of speech; waiting the time for publishing it: to which Secret Protest his signature, and that of other honourable Deputies not a few, stands legibly appended. And now, if the seals were once broken, the Mountain still victorious? Such Protesters, your Merciers, Bailleuls, Seventy-three by the tale, what yet remains of Respectable Girondism in the Convention, may tremble to think!—These are the fruits of levying civil war.

Also we find, that in these last days of July, the famed Siege of Mentz is *finished*: the Garrison to march out with honours of war; not to serve against the Coalition for a year. Lovers of the Picturesque, and Goethe standing on the Chaussée of Mentz, saw, with due interest, the Procession issuing forth, in all solemnity:

'Escorted by Prussian horse came first the French Garrison. Nothing could look stranger than this latter; a column of Marseillese, slight, swarthy, parti-coloured, in patched clothes, came tripping on;—as if King Edwin had opened the Dwarf Hill, and sent out his nimble Host of Dwarfs. Next followed regular troops; serious, sullen; not as if downcast or ashamed. But the remarkablest appearance, which struck every one, was that of the Chasers (*Chasseurs*) coming out mounted: they had advanced quite silent to where we stood, when their Band struck up the *Marseillaise*. This revolutionary *Te-Deum* has in itself something mournful and bodeful, however briskly played; but at present they gave it in altogether slow time, proportionate to the creeping step they rode at. It was piercing and fearful, and a most serious-looking thing, as these cavaliers, long, lean men, of a certain age, with mien suitable to the music, came pacing on: singly you might have likened them to Don Quixote; in mass, they were highly dignified.

'But now a single troop became notable: that of the Commissioners or *Représentans*. Merlin of Thionville, in hussar uniform, distinguishing himself by wild beard and look, had another person in similar costume on his left; the crowd shouted out, with rage, at sight of this latter, the name of a Jacobin Townsman and Clubbist; and shook itself to seize him. Merlin drew bridle; referred to his dignity as French Representative, to the vengeance that should follow any injury done; he would advise every one to compose himself, for this was not the *last time* they would see him here.'[1] Thus rode Merlin; threatening in defeat. But what now shall stem that tide of Prussians setting-in through the opened Northeast? Lucky if fortified Lines of Weissembourg, and impassabilities of Vosges Mountains confine it to French Alsace, keep it from submerging the very heart of the country!

Furthermore, precisely in the same days, Valenciennes Siege is finished, in the Northwest:—fallen, under the red hail of York! Condé fell some fortnight since. Cimmerian Coalition presses on. What seems very notable too, on all these captured French Towns there flies not the Royalist fleur-de-lys, in the name of a new Louis the Pretender; but the Austrian flag flies; as if Austria meant to keep them for herself! Perhaps General Custine, still in Paris, can give some explanation of the fall of these strong-places? Mother Society, from tribune and gallery, growls loud that he ought to do it;—remarks, however, in a splenetic manner that 'the *Monsieurs* of the Palais Royal' are calling Long-life to this General.

The Mother Society, purged now, by successive 'scrutinies or *épurations*,' from all taint of Girondism, has become a great Authority: what we can call shield-bearer or bottle-holder, nay call it fugleman, to the purged National Convention itself. The Jacobins Debates are reported in the *Moniteur*, like Parliamentary ones.

[1] *Belagerung von Mainz* (Goethe's *Works*, xxx. 315).

CHAPTER IV

O NATURE

BUT looking more specially into Paris City, what is this that History, on the 10th of August, Year One of Liberty, 'by old-style, year 1793,' discerns there? Praised be the Heavens, a new Feast of Pikes!

For Chaumette's 'Deputation every day' has worked out its result: a Constitution. It was one of the rapidest Constitutions ever put together; made, some say in eight days, by Hérault Séchelles and others; probably a workmanlike, road-worthy Constitution enough;—on which point, however, we are, for some reasons, little called to form a judgment. Workmanlike or not, the Forty-four Thousand Communes of France, by overwhelming majorities, did hasten to accept it; glad of any Constitution whatsoever. Nay Departmental Deputies have come, the venerablest Republicans of each Department, with solemn message of Acceptance; and now what remains but that our new Final Constitution be proclaimed, and sworn to, in Feast of Pikes? The Departmental Deputies, we say, are come some time ago; Chaumette very anxious about them, lest Girondin *Monsieurs*, Agio-jobbers, or were it even *Filles de joie* of a Girondin temper, corrupt their morals.[1] Tenth of August, immortal Anniversary, greater almost than Bastille July, is the Day.

Painter David has not been idle. Thanks to David and the French genius, there steps forth into the sunlight, this day, a Scenic Phantasmagory unexampled:—whereof History, so occupied with Real Phantasmagories, will say but little.

For one thing, History can notice with satisfaction, on the ruins of the Bastille, a *Statue of Nature*; gigantic, spouting water from her two *mamelles*. Not a Dream this; but a fact, palpable visible. There she spouts, great Nature; dim, before daybreak. But as the coming Sun ruddies the East, come

[1] *Deux Amis*, xi. 73.

countless Multitudes, regulated and unregulated; come Departmental Deputies, come Mother Society and Daughters; comes National Convention, led on by handsome Hérault; soft wind-music breathing note of expectation. Lo, as great Sol scatters his first fire-handful, tipping the hills and chimney-heads with gold, Hérault is at great Nature's feet (she is plaster-of-paris merely); Hérault lifts, in an iron saucer, water spouted from the sacred breasts; drinks of it, with an eloquent Pagan Prayer, beginning, 'O Nature!' and all the Departmental Deputies drink, each with what best suitable ejaculation or prophetic-utterance is in him;—amid breathings, which become blasts, of wind-music; and the roar of artillery and human throats: finishing well the first act of this solemnity.

Next are processionings along the Boulevards: Deputies or Officials bound together by long indivisible tricolor riband general 'members of the Sovereign' walking pell-mell, with pikes, with hammers, with the tools and emblems of their crafts; among which we notice a Plough, and ancient Baucis and Philemon seated on it, drawn by their children. Many-voiced harmony and dissonance filling the air. Through Triumphal Arches enough: at the basis of the first of which, we descry—whom thinkest thou?—the Heroines of the Insurrection of Women. Strong Dames of the Market, they sit there (Théroigne too ill to attend, one fears), with oak-branches, tricolor bedizenment; firm seated on their Cannons. To whom handsome Hérault, making pause of admiration, addresses soothing eloquence; whereupon they rise and fall into the march.

And now mark, in the Place de la Révolution, what other august Statue may this be; veiled in canvas,—which swiftly we shear off, by pulley and cord? The *Statue of Liberty*! She too is of plaster, hoping to become of metal; stands where a Tyrant Louis Quinze once stood. 'Three thousand birds' are let loose, into the whole world, with labels round their neck, *We are free; imitate us*. Holocaust of Royalist and *ci-devant* trumpery, such as one could still gather, is burnt; pontifical eloquence must be uttered, by handsome Hérault, and Pagan orisons offered up.

And then forward across the River; where is new enormous Statuary; enormous plaster Mountain; Hercules-*Peuple*, with uplifted all-conquering club; 'many-headed Dragon of Girondin Federalism rising from fetid marsh':—needing new eloquence from Hérault. To say nothing of Champ-de-Mars, and Fatherland's Altar there; with urn of slain Defenders, Carpenter's-level of the Law; and such exploding, gesticulating and perorating, that Hérault's lips must be growing white, and his tongue cleaving to the roof of his mouth.[1]

Towards six o'clock let the wearied President, let Paris Patriotism generally sit down to what repast, and social repasts, can be had; and with flowing tankard or light-mantling glass, usher in this New and Newest Era. In fact, is not Romme's New Calendar getting ready? On all house-tops flicker little tricolor Flags, their flagstaff a Pike and Liberty-Cap. On all house-walls,—for no Patriot not suspect will be behind another,—there stand printed these words: *Republic one and indivisible; Liberty, Equality, Fraternity, or Death.*

As to the New Calendar, we may say here rather than elsewhere that speculative men have long been struck with the inequalities and incongruities of the Old Calendar; that a New one has long been as good as determined on. Maréchal the Atheist, almost ten years ago, proposed a New Calendar, free at least from superstition: this the Paris Municipality would now adopt, in defect of a better; at all events, let us have either this of Maréchal's or a better,—the New Era being come. Petitions, more than once, have been sent to that effect; and indeed, for a year past, all Public Bodies, Journalists, and Patriots in general, have dated *First Year of the Republic.* It is a subject not without difficulties. But the Convention has taken it up; and Romme, as we say, has been meditating it; not Maréchal's New Calendar, but a better New one of Romme's and our own. Romme, aided by a Monge, a Lagrange and others, furnishes mathematics; Fabre d'Eglantine furnishes poetic nomenclature: and so, on the 5th of October 1793, after

[1] *Choix des Rapports*, xii. 432–42.

trouble enough, they bring forth this New Republican Calendar of theirs, in a complete state; and by Law get it put in action.

Four equal Seasons, Twelve equal Months of Thirty days each; this makes three hundred and sixty days; and five odd days remain to be disposed of. The five odd days we will make Festivals, and name the five *Sansculottides*, or Days without Breeches. Festival of Genius; Festival of Labour; of Actions; of Rewards; of Opinion: these are the five Sansculottides. Whereby the great Circle, or Year, is made complete: solely every fourth year, whilom called Leap-year, we introduce a sixth Sansculottide; and name it Festival of the Revolution. Now as to the day of commencement, which offers difficulties, is it not one of the luckiest coincidences that the Republic herself commenced on the 21st of September; close on the Autumnal Equinox? Autumnal Equinox, at midnight for the meridian of Paris, in the year whilom Christian 1792, from that moment shall the New Era reckon itself to begin. *Vendémiaire*, *Brumaire*, *Frimaire*; or as one might say, in mixed English, *Vintagearious*, *Fogarious*, *Frostarious*: these are our three Autumn months. *Nivose*, *Pluviose*, *Ventose*, or say, *Snowous*, *Rainous*, *Windous*, make our Winter season. *Germinal*, *Floréal*, *Prairial*, or *Buddal*, *Floweral*, *Meadowal*, are our Spring season. *Messidor*, *Thermidor*, *Fructidor*, that is to say (*dor* being Greek for *gift*), *Reapidor*, *Heatidor*, *Fruitidor*, are Republican Summer. These Twelve, in a singular manner, divide the Republican Year. Then as to minuter subdivisions, let us venture at once on a bold stroke: adopt your decimal subdivision; and instead of the world-old Week, or *Se'ennight*, make it a *Tennight*, or *Décade*;—not without results. There are three Decades, then, in each of the months, which is very regular; and the *Décadi*, or Tenth-day, shall always be the 'Day of Rest.' And the Christian Sabbath, in that case? Shall shift for itself!

This, in brief, is the New Calendar of Romme and the Convention; calculated for the meridian of Paris, and Gospel of Jean Jacques: not one of the least afflicting occurrences for the actual British reader of French History;—confusing the soul with *Messidors, Meadowals*; till at last, in self-defence, one is forced to construct some ground-scheme, or rule of Commutation from New-style to Old-style, and have it lying by him. Such ground-scheme, almost worn out in our service, but still legible and printable, we shall now in a Note, present to the reader. For the Romme Calendar, in so many Newspapers, Memoirs, Public Acts, has stamped itself deep into that section of Time: a New Era that lasts some Twelve years and odd is not to be despised.[1] Let the reader, therefore, with such ground-scheme, help himself, where needful, out of New-style into Old-style, called also 'slave-style, *stile-esclave*';—whereof we, in these pages, shall as much as possible use the latter only.

Thus with new Feast of Pikes, and New Era or New Calendar, did France accept her New Constitution: the most Democratic Constitution ever committed to paper. How it will work in practice? Patriot Deputations, from time to time,

[1] September 22d of 1792 is Vendémiaire 1st of Year One, and the new months are all of 30 days each; therefore:

To the number of the day in	ADD	We have the number of the day in	DAYS
Vendémiaire	21	September	30
Brumaire	21	October	31
Frimaire	20	November	30
Nivose	20	December	31
Pluviose	19	January	31
Ventose	18	February	28
Germinal	20	March	31
Floréal	19	April	30
Prairial	19	May	31
Messidor	18	June	30
Thermidor	18	July	31
Fructidor	17	August	31

There are 5 Sansculottides, and in leap-year a sixth, to be added at the end of Fructidor. Romme's first Leap-year is '*An* 4' (1795, not 1796), which is another troublesome circumstance, every fourth year, from 'September 23d' round to 'February 29' again.

The New Calendar ceased on the 1st of January 1806. See *Choix des Rapports*, xiii. 83–99; xix. 199.

solicit fruition of it; that it be set a-going. Always, however, this seems questionable; for the moment, unsuitable. Till, in some weeks, *Salut Public*, through the organ of Saint-Just, makes report, that, in the present alarming circumstances, the state of France is Revolutionary; that her 'Government must be Revolutionary till the Peace.' Solely as Paper, then, and as a Hope, must this poor new Constitution exist;—in which shape we may conceive it lying, even now, with an infinity of other things, in that Limbo near the Moon. Further than paper it never got, nor ever will get.

CHAPTER V

SWORD OF SHARPNESS

In fact, it is something quite other than paper theorems, it is iron and audacity that France now needs.

Is not La Vendée still blazing;—alas too literally; rogue Rossignol burning the very corn-mills? General Santerre could do nothing there; General Rossignol, in blind fury, often in liquor, can do less than nothing. Rebellion spreads, grows ever madder. Happily these lean Quixote-figures, whom we saw retreating out of Mentz, 'bound not to serve against the Coalition for a year,' have got to Paris. National Convention packs them into post-vehicles and conveyances; sends them swiftly, by post, into La Vendée. There valiantly struggling in obscure battle and skirmish, under rogue Rossignol, let them, unlaureled, save the Republic, and 'be cut down gradually to the last man.'[1]

Does not the Coalition, like a fire-tide, pour in; Prussia through the opened Northeast; Austria, England through the Northwest? General Houchard prospers no better there than General Custine did: let him look to it! Through the Eastern and the Western Pyrenees Spain has deployed itself; spreads, rustling with Bourbon banners, over the face of the South.

[1] *Deux Amis*, xi. 147; xiii. 160–92, etc.

Ashes and embers of confused Girondin civil war covered that region already. Marseilles is damped down, not quenched; to be quenched in blood. Toulon, terror-struck, too far gone for turning, has flung itself, ye righteous Powers, into the hands of the English! On Toulon Arsenal there flies a flag,—nay not even the Fleur-de-lys of a Louis Pretender; there flies that accursed St. George's Cross of the English and Admiral Hood! What remnant of sea-craft, arsenals, roperies, war-navy France had, has given itself to these enemies of human nature, '*ennemis du genre humain.*' Beleaguer it, bombard it, ye Commissioners Barras, Fréron, Robespierre Junior; thou General Cartaux, General Dugommier; above all, thou remarkable Artillery-Major, Napoleon Buonaparte! Hood is fortifying himself, victualling himself; means, apparently, to make a new Gibraltar of it.

But lo, in the Autumn night, late night, among the last of August, what sudden red sunblaze is this that has risen over Lyons City; with a noise to deafen the world? It is the Powder-tower of Lyons, nay the Arsenal with four Powder-towers, which has caught fire in the Bombardment; and sprung into the air, carrying 'a hundred and seventeen houses' after it. With a light, one fancies, as of the noon sun; with a roar second only to the Last Trumpet! All living sleepers far and wide it has awakened. What a sight was that, which the eye of History saw, in the sudden nocturnal sunblaze! The roofs of hapless Lyons, and all its domes and steeples made momentarily clear; Rhone and Saone streams flashing suddenly visible; and height and hollow, hamlet and smooth stubblefield, and all the region round;—heights, alas, all scarped and counter-scarped, into trenches, curtains, redoubts; blue Artillerymen, little Powder-devilkins, plying their hell-trade there through the *not* ambrosial night! Let the darkness cover it again; for it pains the eye. Of a truth, Chalier's death is costing the City dear. Convention Commissioners, Lyons Congresses have come and gone; and action there was and reaction; bad ever growing worse; till it has come to this; Commissioner Dubois-Crancé, 'with seventy-thousand men, and all the Artillery of several Provinces,' bombarding Lyons day and night.

Worse things still are in store. Famine is in Lyons, and ruin and fire. Desperate are the sallies of the besieged; brave Précy, their National Colonel and Commandant, doing what is in man: desperate but ineffectual. Provisions cut off; nothing entering our city but shot and shells! The Arsenal has roared aloft; the very Hospital will be battered down, and the sick buried alive. A black Flag hung on this latter noble Edifice, appealing to the pity of the besiegers; for though maddened, were they not still our brethren? In their blind wrath, they took it for a flag of defiance, and aimed thitherward the more. Bad is growing ever worse here: and how will the worse stop, till it have grown worst of all? Commissioner Dubois will listen to no pleading, to no speech, save this only, We surrender at discretion. Lyons contains in it subdued Jacobins; dominant Girondins; secret Royalists. And now, mere deaf madness and cannon-shot, enveloping them, will not the desperate Municipality fly, at last, into the arms of Royalism itself? Majesty of Sardinia was to bring help, but it failed. Emigrant d'Autichamp, in name of the Two Pretender Royal Highnesses, is coming through Switzerland with help; coming, not yet come; Précy hoists the Fleur-de-lys!

At sight of which all true Girondins sorrowfully fling down their arms:—Let our Tricolor brethren storm us, then, and slay us in their wrath; with *you* we conquer not. The famishing women and children are sent forth: deaf Dubois sends them back;—rains in mere fire and madness. Our 'redoubts of cotton-bags' are taken, retaken; Précy under his Fleur-de-lys is valiant as Despair. What will become of Lyons? It is a siege of seventy days.[1]

Or see, in these same weeks, far in the Western waters: breasting through the Bay of Biscay, a greasy dingy little Merchant-ship, with Scotch skipper; under hatches whereof sit, disconsolate,—the last forlorn nucleus of Girondism, the Deputies from Quimper! Several have dissipated themselves

[1] *Deux Amis*, xi. 80–143.

whithersoever they could. Poor Rioffe fell into the talons of Revolutionary Committee and Paris Prison. The rest sit here under hatches; reverend Pétion with his grey hair, angry Buzot, suspicious Louvet, brave young Barbaroux, and others. They have escaped from Quimper, in this sad craft; are now tacking and struggling; in danger from the waves, in danger from the English, in still worse danger from the French;—banished by Heaven and Earth to the greasy belly of this Scotch skipper's Merchant-vessel, unfruitful Atlantic raving round. They are for Bordeaux, if peradventure hope yet linger there. Enter not Bordeaux, O Friends! Bloody Convention Representatives, Tallien and suchlike, with their Edicts, with their Guillotine, have arrived there; Respectability is driven under ground; Jacobinism lords it on high. From that Réole landing-place, or *Beak of Ambès*, as it were, pale Death, waving his Revolutionary Sword of Sharpness, waves you elsewhither!

On one side or the other of that Bec d'Ambès, the Scotch Skipper with difficulty moors, a dexterous greasy man; with difficulty lands his Girondins;—who, after reconnoitering, must rapidly burrow in the Earth; and so, in subterranean ways, in friends' back-closets, in cellars, barn-lofts, in caves of Saint-Emilion and Libourne, stave-off cruel Death.[1] Unhappiest of all Senators!

CHAPTER VI

RISEN AGAINT TYRANTS

Against all which incalculable impediments, horrors and disasters, what can a Jacobin Convention oppose? The uncalculating Spirit of Jacobinism, and Sansculottic sansformulistic Frenzy! Our Enemies press-in on us, says Danton, but they shall not conquer us, 'we will burn France to ashes rather, *nous brûlerons la France*.'

Committees, of *Sûreté*, of *Salut*, have raised themselves '*à la*

[1] Louvet, pp. 180–199.

hauteur, to the height of circumstances.' Let all mortals raise themselves *à la hauteur*. Let the Forty-four thousand Sections and their Revolutionary Committees stir every fibre of the Republic; and every Frenchman feel that he is to do or die. They are the life-circulation of Jacobinism, these Sections and Committees: Danton, through the organ of Barrère and *Salut Public*, gets decreed, That there be in Paris, by law, two meetings of Section weekly; also that the Poorer Citizen be *paid* for attending, and have his day's-wages of Forty Sous.[1] This is the celebrated 'Law of the Forty Sous'; fiercely stimulant to Sansculottism, to the life-circulation of Jacobinism.

On the twenty-third of August, Committee of Public Salvation, as usual through Barrère, had promulgated, in words not unworthy of remembering, their Report, which is soon made into a Law, of *Levy in Mass*. 'All France, and whatsoever it contains of men or resources, is put under requisition,' says Barrère; really in Tyrtæan words, the best we know of his. 'The Republic is one vast besieged city.' Two-hundred and fifty Forges shall, in these days, be set up in the Luxembourg Garden, and round the outer wall of the Tuileries; to make gun-barrels; in sight of Earth and Heaven! From all hamlets, towards their Departmental Town; from all Departmental Towns, towards the appointed Camp and seat of war, the Sons of Freedom shall march; their banner is to bear: '*Le Peuple Français debout contre les Tyrans*, The French People risen against Tyrants. The young men shall go to the battle; it is their task to conquer: the married men shall forge arms, transport baggage and artillery; provide subsistence: the women shall work at soldier's clothes, make tents; serve in the hospitals: the children shall scrape old-linen into surgeon's-lint: the aged men shall have themselves carried into public places, and there, by their words, excite the courage of the young; preach hatred to Kings and unity to the Republic.'[2] Tyrtæan words; which tingle through all French hearts.

In this humour, then, since no other serves, will France rush

[1] *Moniteur*, Séance du 5 Septembre 1793.
[2] *Débats*, Séance du 23 Août 1793.

against its enemies. Headlong, reckoning no cost or consequence; heeding no law or rule but that supreme law, Salvation of the People! The weapons are, all the iron that is in France; the strength is, that of all the men, women, and children that are in France. There, in their two-hundred and fifty shed-smithies, in Garden of Luxembourg or Tuileries, let them forge gun-barrels, in sight of Heaven and Earth.

Nor with heroic daring against the Foreign foe, can black vengeance against the Domestic be wanting. Life-circulation of the Revolutionary Committees being quickened by that *Law of the Forty Sous*, Deputy Merlin,—not the Thionviller, whom we saw ride out of Mentz, but Merlin of Douai, named subsequently Merlin *Suspect*,—comes, about a week after, with his world-famous *Law of the Suspect*: ordering all Sections, by their Committees, instantly to arrest all Persons Suspect; and explaining withal who the Arrestable and Suspect specially are. 'Are suspect,' says he, 'all who by their actions, by their connexions, speakings, writings have'—in short become Suspect.[1] Nay Chaumette, illuminating the matter still further, in his Municipal Placards and Proclamations, will bring it about that you may almost recognise a Suspect on the streets, and clutch him there,—off to Committee and Prison. Watch well your words, watch well your looks: if Suspect of nothing else, you may grow, as came to be a saying, 'Suspect of being Suspect'! For are we not in a state of Revolution?

No frightfuler Law ever ruled in a Nation of men. All Prisons and Houses of Arrest in French land are getting crowded to the ridge-tile: Forty-four thousand Committees, like as many companies of reapers or gleaners, gleaning France, are gathering their harvest, and storing it in these Houses. Harvest of Aristocrat tares! Nay, lest the Forty-four thousand, each on its own harvest-field, prove insufficient, we are to have an ambulant 'Revolutionary Army': six-thousand strong, under right captains, this shall perambulate the country at large, and strike-in wherever it finds such harvest-work slack. So have

[1] *Moniteur*, Séance du 17 Septembre 1793.

Municipality and Mother Society petitioned; so has Convention decreed.[1] Let Aristocrats, Federalists, Monsieurs vanish, and all men tremble: 'the Soil of Liberty shall be purged,'—with a vengeance!

Neither hitherto has the Revolutionary Tribunal been keeping holiday. Blanchelande, for losing Saint-Domingo; 'Conspirators of Orléans,' for 'assassinating,' for assaulting the sacred Deputy Léonard-Bourdon; these with many Nameless, to whom life was sweet, have died. Daily the great Guillotine has its due. Like a black Spectre, daily at eventide glides the Death-tumbril through the variegated throng of things. The variegated street shudders at it, for the moment; next moment forgets it: The Aristocrats! They were guilty against the Republic; their death, were it only that their goods are confiscated, will be useful to the Republic; *Vive la République!*

In the last days of August fell a notabler head: General Custine's. Custine was accused of harshness, of unskilfulness, perfidiousness; accused of many things: found guilty, we may say, of one thing, unsuccessfulness. Hearing his unexpected Sentence, 'Custine fell down before the Crucifix,' silent for the space of two hours: he fared, with moist eyes and a look of prayer, towards the Place de la Révolution; glanced upwards at the clear suspended axe; then mounted swiftly aloft,[2] swiftly was struck away from the lists of the Living. He had fought in America; he was a proud, brave man; and his fortune led him *hither*.

On the 2d of this same month, at three in the morning, a vehicle rolled off, with closed blinds, from the Temple to the Conciergerie. Within it were two Municipals; and Marie-Antoinette, once Queen of France! There in that Conciergerie, in ignominious dreary cell, she, secluded from children, kindred, friend and hope, sits long weeks; expecting when the end will be.[3]

[1] *Ibid.* Séances du 5, 9, 11 Septembre.

[2] *Deux Amis*, xi. 148–188.

[3] See *Mémoires particuliers de la Captivité à la Tour du Temple* (by the Duchesse d'Angoulême, Paris, 21 Janvier 1817).

The Guillotine, we find, gets always a quicker motion, as other things are quickening. The Guillotine, by its speed of going, will give index of the general velocity of the Republic. The clanking of its huge axe, rising and falling there, in horrid systole-diastole, is portion of the whole enormous life-movement and pulsation of the Sansculottic System!—'Orléans Conspirators' and Assaulters had to die, in spite of much weeping and entreating; so sacred is the person of a Deputy. Yet the sacred can become desecrated: your very Deputy is not greater than the Guillotine. Poor Deputy Journalist Gorsas: we saw him hide at Rennes, when the Calvados War burnt priming. He stole, afterwards, in August, to Paris; lurked several weeks about the Palais *ci-devant* Royal; was seen there, one day; was clutched, identified, and without ceremony, being already 'out of the Law,' was sent to the Place de la Révolution. He died, recommending his wife and children to the pity of the Republic. It is the ninth day of October 1793. Gorsas is the first Deputy that dies on the scaffold; he will not be the last.

Ex-Mayor Bailly is in Prison; Ex-Procureur Manuel. Brissot and our poor Arrested Girondins have become Incarcerated Indicted Girondins; universal Jacobinism clamouring for their punishment. Duperret's Seals are *broken*! Those Seventy-three Secret Protesters, suddenly one day, are reported upon, are decreed accused; the Convention-doors being 'previously shut,' that none implicated might escape. They were marched, in a very rough manner, to Prison that evening. Happy those of them who chanced to be absent! Condorcet has vanished into darkness; perhaps, like Rabaut, sits between two walls, in the house of a friend.

CHAPTER VII

MARIE-ANTOINETTE

On Monday the Fourteenth of October 1793, a Cause is pending in the Palais de Justice, in the new Revolutionary Court, such as those old stone-walls never witnessed: the Trial of Marie-Antoinette. The once brightest of Queens, now tarnished, defaced, forsaken, stands here at Fouquier-Tinville's Judgment-bar; answering for her life. The Indictment was delivered her last night.[1] To such changes of human fortune what words are adequate? Silence alone is adequate.

There are few Printed things one meets with of such tragic, almost ghastly, significance as those bald Pages of the *Bulletin du Tribunal Révolutionnaire*, which bear title, *Trial of the Widow Capet*. Dim, dim, as if in disastrous eclipse; like the pale kingdoms of Dis! Plutonic Judges, Plutonic Tinville; encircled, nine times, with Styx and Lethe, with Fire-Phlegethon and Cocytus named of Lamentation! The very witnesses summoned are like Ghosts: exculpatory, inculpatory, they themselves are all hovering over death and doom; they are known, in our imagination, as the prey of the Guillotine. Tall *ci-devant* Count d'Estaing, anxious to show himself Patriot, cannot escape; nor Bailly, who, when asked If he knows the Accused, answers with a reverent inclination towards her, 'Ah, yes, I know Madame.' Ex-Patriots are here, sharply dealt with, as Procureur Manuel; Ex-Ministers, shorn of their splendour. We have cold Aristocratic impassivity, faithful to itself even in Tartarus; rabid stupidity, of Patriot Corporals, Patriot Washerwomen, who have much to say of Plots, Treasons, August Tenth, old Insurrection of Women. For all now has become a crime in her who has *lost*.

Marie-Antoinette, in this her utter abandonment, and hour of extreme need, is not wanting to herself, the imperial woman. Her look, they say, as that hideous Indictment was reading, continued calm; 'she was sometimes observed moving her fingers, as when one plays on the piano.' You discern, not without interest, across that dim Revolutionary Bulletin itself, how she bears herself queenlike. Her answers are prompt, clear, often of Laconic brevity; resolution, which has grown contemptuous without ceasing to be dignified, veils itself in calm words. 'You persist, then, in denial?'—'My plan is not denial:

[1] *Procès de la Reine* (*Deux Amis*, xi. 251–381).

it is the truth I have said, and I persist in that.' Scandalous Hébert has borne his testimony as to many things: as to one thing, concerning Marie-Antoinette and her little Son,—wherewith Human Speech had better not further be soiled. She has answered Hébert; a Juryman begs to observe that she has not answered as to *this*. 'I have not answered,' she exclaims with noble emotion, 'because Nature refuses to answer such a charge brought against a Mother. I appeal to all the Mothers that are here.' Robespierre, when he heard of it, broke out into something almost like swearing at the brutish blockheadism of this Hébert;[1] on whose foul head his foul lie has recoiled. At four o'clock on Wednesday morning, after two days and two nights of interrogating, jury-charging, and other darkening of counsel, the result comes out: sentence of Death. 'Have you anything to say?' The Accused shook her head, without speech. Night's candles are burning out; and with her too Time is finishing, and it will be Eternity and Day. This Hall of Tinville's is dark, ill-lighted except where she stands. Silently she withdraws from it, to die.

Two Processions, or Royal Progresses, three-and-twenty years apart, have often struck us with a strange feeling of contrast. The first is of a beautiful Archduchess and Dauphiness, quitting her Mother's City, at the age of Fifteen; towards hopes such as no other Daughter of Eve then had: 'On the morrow,' says Weber an eye-witness, 'the Dauphiness left Vienna. The whole city crowded out; at first with a sorrow which was silent. She appeared: you saw her sunk back into her carriage; her face bathed in tears; hiding her eyes now with her handkerchief, now with her hands; several times putting out her head to see yet again this Palace of her Fathers, whither she was to return no more. She motioned her regret, her gratitude to the good Nation, which was crowding here to bid her farewell. Then arose not only tears; but piercing cries, on all sides. Men and women alike abandoned themselves to such expression of their sorrow. It was an audible sound of wail, in

[1] Villate, *Causes secrètes de la Révolution de Thermidor* (Paris, 1825), p. 179.

the streets and avenues of Vienna. The last Courier that followed her disappeared, and the crowd melted away.'[1]

The young imperial Maiden of Fifteen has now become a worn discrowned Widow of Thirty-eight; grey before her time: this is the last Procession: 'Few minutes after the Trial ended, the drums were beating to arms in all Sections; at sunrise the armed force was on foot, cannons getting placed at the extremities of the Bridges, in the Squares, Crossways, all along from the Palais de Justice to the Place de la Révolution. By ten o'clock, numerous patrols were circulating in the Streets; thirty thousand foot and horse drawn up under arms. At eleven, Marie-Antoinette was brought out. She had on an undress of *piqué blanc*: she was led to the place of execution, in the same manner as an ordinary criminal; bound, on a Cart; accompanied by a Constitutional Priest in Lay dress; escorted by numerous detachments of infantry and cavalry. These, and the double row of troops all along her road, she appeared to regard with indifference. On her countenance there was visible neither abashment nor pride. To the cries of *Vive la République* and *Down with Tyranny*, which attended her all the way, she seemed to pay no heed. She spoke little to her Confessor. The tricolor Streamers on the housetops occupied her attention, in the Streets du Roule and Saint-Honoré; she also noticed the Inscriptions on the house-fronts. On reaching the Place de la Révolution, her looks turned towards the *Jardin National*, whilom Tuileries; her face at that moment gave signs of lively emotion. She mounted the Scaffold with courage enough; at a quarter past Twelve, her head fell; the Executioner showed it to the people, amid universal long-continued cries of *Vive la République*.'[2]

CHAPTER VIII

THE TWENTY-TWO

Whom next, O Tinville! The next are of a different colour: our poor Arrested Girondin Deputies. What of them could still

[1] Weber, i. 6. [2] *Deux Amis*, xi. 301.

be laid hold of; our Vergniaud, Brissot, Fauchet, Valazé, Gensonné; the once flower of French Patriotism, Twenty-two by the tale: *hither*, at Tinville's Bar, onward from 'safeguard of the French People,' from confinement in the Luxembourg, imprisonment in the Conciergerie, have they now, by the course of things, arrived. Fouquier-Tinville must give what account of them he can.

Undoubtedly this Trial of the Girondins is the greatest that Fouquier has yet had to do. Twenty-two, all chief Republicans, ranged in a line there; the most eloquent in France; Lawyers too; not without friends in the auditory. How will Tinville prove these men guilty of Royalism, Federalism, Conspiracy against the Republic? Vergniaud's eloquence awakes once more; 'draws tears,' they say. And Journalists report, and the Trial lengthens itself out day after day; 'threatens to become eternal,' murmur many. Jacobinism and Municipality rise to the aid of Fouquier. On the 28th of the month, Hébert and others come in deputation to inform a Patriot Convention that the Revolutionary Tribunal is quite 'shackled by Forms of Law'; that a Patriot Jury ought to have 'the power of cutting short, of *terminer les débats*, when they feel themselves convinced.' Which pregnant suggestion, of cutting short, passes itself, with all despatch, into a Decree.

Accordingly, at ten o'clock on the night of the 30th of October, the Twenty-two, summoned back once more, receive this information, That the Jury feeling themselves convinced have cut short, have brought in their verdict; that the Accused are found guilty, and the Sentence on one and all of them is, Death with confiscation of goods.

Loud natural clamour rises among the poor Girondins; tumult; which can only be repressed by the gendarmes. Valazé stabs himself; falls down dead on the spot. The rest, amid loud clamour and confusion, are driven back to their Conciergerie; Lasource exclaiming, 'I die on the day when the People have lost their reason; ye will die when they recover it.'[1]

[1] *Δημοσθένους εἰπόντος, 'Αποκτενοῦσί σὲ 'Αθηναῖοι, Φωκίων· "Αν μανῶσιν, εἶπε σὲ δ', ἐάν σωφρονῶσι.*—Plut. *Opp.* t. iv. p. 310, ed. Reiske, 1776.

No help! Yielding to violence, the Doomed uplift the Hymn of the Marseillese; return singing to their dungeon.

Riouffe, who was their Prison-mate in these last days, has lovingly recorded what death they made. To our notions, it is not an edifying death. Gay satirical *Pot-pourri* by Ducos; rhymed Scenes of Tragedy, wherein Barrère and Robespierre discourse with Satan; death's eve spent in 'singing' and 'sallies of gaiety,' with 'discourses on the happiness of peoples': these things, and the like of these, we have to accept for what they are worth. It is the manner in which the Girondins make *their* Last Supper. Valazé, with bloody breast, sleeps cold in death; hears not the singing. Vergniaud has his dose of poison; but it is not enough for his friends, it is enough only for himself; wherefore he flings it from him; presides at this Last Supper of the Girondins, with wild coruscations of eloquence, with song and mirth. Poor human Will struggles to assert itself; if not in this way, then in that.[1]

But on the morrow morning all Paris is out; such a crowd as no man had seen. The Death-carts, Valazé's cold corpse stretched among the yet living Twenty-one, roll along. Bare-headed, hands bound; in their shirt-sleeves, coat flung loosely round the neck: so fare the eloquent of France; bemurmured, beshouted. To the shouts of *Vive la République*, some of them keep answering with counter-shouts of *Vive la République*. Others, as Brissot, sit sunk in silence. At the foot of the scaffold they again strike up, with appropriate variations, the Hymn of the Marseillese. Such an act of music; conceive it well! The yet Living chant there; the chorus so rapidly wearing weak! Samson's axe is rapid; one head per minute, or little less. The chorus is wearing weak; the chorus is worn *out*;—farewell for evermore, ye Girondins. Te-Deum Fauchet has become silent; Valazé's dead head is lopped: the sickle of the Guillotine has reaped the Girondins all away. 'The eloquent, the young, the beautiful and brave!' exclaims Riouffe. O Death, what feast is toward in thy ghastly Halls!

[1] *Mémoires de Riouffe* (in *Mémoires sur les Prisons*, Paris, 1823), pp. 48 55.

Nor, alas, in the far Bordeaux region will Girondism fare better. In caves of Saint-Emilion, in loft and cellar, the weariest months roll on; apparel worn, purse empty; wintry November come; under Tallien and his Guillotine, all hope now gone. Danger drawing ever nigher, difficulty pressing ever straiter, they determine to separate. Not unpathetic the farewell; tall Barbaroux, cheeriest of brave men, stoops to clasp his Louvet: 'In what place soever thou findest my Mother,' cries he, 'try to be instead of a son to her: no resource of mine but I will share with thy Wife, should chance ever lead me where she is.'[1]

Louvet went with Guadet, with Salles and Valadi; Barbaroux with Buzot and Pétion. Valadi soon went southward, on a way of his own. The two friends and Louvet had a miserable day and night; the 14th of the November month, 1793. Sunk in wet, weariness, and hunger, they knock, on the morrow, for help, at a friend's country-house; the faint-hearted friend refuses to admit them. They stood therefore under trees, in the pouring rain. Flying desperate, Louvet thereupon will to Paris. He sets forth, there and then, splashing the mud on each side of him, with a fresh strength gathered from fury or frenzy. He passes villages, finding 'the sentry asleep in his box in the thick rain'; he is gone, before the man can call after him. He bilks Revolutionary Committees; rides in carriers' carts, covered carts and open; lies hidden in one, under knapsacks and cloaks of soldiers' wives on the Street of Orléans, while men search for him; has hairbreadth escapes that would fill three romances: finally he gets to Paris to his fair Helpmate; gets to Switzerland, and waits better days.

Poor Guadet and Salles were both taken, ere long; they died by the Guillotine in Bordeaux; drums beating to drown their voice. Valadi also is caught, and guillotined. Barbaroux and his two comrades weathered it longer, into the summer of 1794; but not long enough. One July morning, changing their hiding-place, as they have often to do, 'about a league from Saint-Emilion, they observe a great crowd of country-people':

[1] Louvet, p. 213.

doubtless Jacobins come to take them? Barbaroux draws a pistol, shoots himself dead. Alas, and it was not Jacobins; it was harmless villagers going to a village wake. Two days afterwards, Buzot and Pétion were found in a Cornfield, their bodies half-eaten by dogs.[1]

Such was the end of Girondism. They arose to regenerate France, these men; and have accomplished *this*. Alas, whatever quarrel we had with them, has not their cruel fate abolished it? Pity only survives. So many excellent souls of heroes sent down to Hades; they themselves given as a prey of dogs and all manner of birds! But, here too, the will of the Supreme Power was accomplished. As Vergniaud said: 'the Revolution, like Saturn, is devouring its own children.'

[1] *Recherches Historiques sur les Girondins* (in *Mémoires de Buzot*), p. 107.

FROM Chartism

'I have finished', Carlyle wrote in his Journal on 8 November 1839, 'a long review article, thick pamphlet or little volume, entitled *Chartism.*' The piece had been written for the Tory *Quarterly Review*: but its editor, J. G. Lockhart, did not dare to print what was, from a Tory point of view, dangerous stuff. *Chartism* was then shown to Mill, who was delighted with it, and wished to publish it as 'a kind of final shout' from his dying Radical *Westminster Review.* Carlyle, however, decided to publish 'this piece . . . about the poor, their rights and their wrongs', as a separate book. It appeared under James Fraser's imprint in December 1839.

Rather more than a third part of *Chartism* is printed here, namely Chapters I, III, V, VI, VII.

FROM

Chartism

'It never smokes but there is fire.'—*Old Proverb.*

CHAPTER I

CONDITION-OF-ENGLAND QUESTION

A FEELING very generally exists that the condition and disposition of the Working Classes is a rather ominous matter at present; that something ought to be said, something ought to be done, in regard to it. And surely, at an epoch of history when the 'National Petition' carts itself in wagons along the streets, and is presented 'bound with iron hoops, four men bearing it,' to a Reformed House of Commons; and Chartism numbered by the million and half, taking nothing by its iron-hooped Petition, breaks out into brickbats, cheap pikes, and even into sputterings of conflagration, such very general feeling cannot be considered unnatural! To us individually this matter appears, and has for many years appeared, to be the most ominous of all practical matters whatever; a matter in regard to which if something be not done, something will *do* itself one day, and in a fashion that will please nobody. The time is verily come for acting in it; how much more for consultation about acting in it, for speech and articulate inquiry about it!

We are aware that, according to the newspapers, Chartism is extinct; that a Reform Ministry has 'put down the chimera of Chartism' in the most felicitous effective manner. So say the newspapers;—and yet, alas, most readers of newspapers know withal that it is indeed the 'chimera' of Chartism, not the reality, which has been put down. The distracted incoherent embodiment of Chartism, whereby in late months it took shape and became visible, this has been put down; or rather has fallen down and gone asunder by gravitation and law of nature: but the living essence of Chartism has not been put down. Chartism means the bitter discontent grown fierce and mad, the wrong condition therefore or the wrong disposition, of the Working Classes of England. It is a new name for a thing which has had many names, which will yet have many. The matter of Chartism is weighty, deep-rooted, far-extending; did not begin yesterday; will by no means end this day or tomorrow. Reform Ministry, constabulary rural police, new levy of soldiers, grants of money to Birmingham; all this is well, or is not well; all this will put down only the embodiment or 'chimera' of Chartism. The essence continuing, new and ever new embodiments, chimeras madder or less mad, have to con tinue. The melancholy fact remains, that this thing known at present by the name of Chartism does exist; has existed; and, either 'put down,' into secret treason, with rusty pistols, vitriol-bottle and match-box, or openly brandishing pike and torch (one knows not in which case *more* fatal-looking), is like to exist till quite other methods have been tried with it. What means this bitter discontent of the Working Classes? Whence comes it, whither goes it? Above all, at what price, on what terms, will it probably consent to depart from us and die into rest? These are questions.

To say that it is mad, incendiary, nefarious, is no answer. To say all this, in never so many dialects, is saying little. 'Glasgow Thuggery,' 'Glasgow Thugs'; it is a witty nickname: the practice of 'Number 60' entering his dark room, to contract for and settle the price of blood with operative assassins. in a Christian city, once distinguished by its rigorous Christian ism, is doubtless a fact worthy of all horror: but what will horror do for it? What will execration; nay, at bottom, what will condemnation and banishment to Botany Bay do for it? Glasgow Thuggery, Chartist torch-meetings, Birmingham riots, Swing conflagrations, are so many symptoms on the surface; you abolish the symptom to no purpose, if the disease is left untouched. Boils on the surface are curable or incurable,—small matter which, while the virulent humour festers deep within; poisoning the sources of life; and certain enough to find for itself ever new boils and sore issues; ways of announcing that it continues there, that it would fain not continue there.

Delirious Chartism will not have raged entirely to no purpose, as indeed no earthly thing does so, if it have forced all thinking men of the community to think of this vital matter, too apt to be overlooked otherwise. Is the condition of the English working people wrong; so wrong that rational working men cannot, will not, and even should not rest quiet under it? A most grave case, complex beyond all others in the world; a case wherein Botany Bay, constabulary rural police, and suchlike, will avail but little. Or is the discontent itself mad, like the shape it took? Not the condition of the working people that is wrong; but their disposition, their own thoughts, beliefs and feelings that are wrong? This too were a most grave case, little less alarming, little less complex than the former one. In this case too, where constabulary police and mere rigour of coercion seems more at home, coercion will by no means do all, coercion by itself will not even do much. If there do exist general madness of discontent, then sanity and some measure of content must be brought about again,—not by constabulary police alone. When the thoughts of a people, in the great mass of it, have grown mad, the combined issue of that people's workings will be a madness, an incoherency and ruin! Sanity will have to be recovered for the general mass; coercion itself will otherwise cease to be able to coerce.

We have heard it asked, Why Parliament throws no light on this question of the Working Classes, and the condition or disposition they are in? Truly to a remote observer of Parliamentary procedure it seems surprising, especially in late Reformed times, to see what space this question occupies in the Debates of the Nation. Can any other business whatsoever be so pressing on legislators? A Reformed Parliament, one would think, should inquire into popular discontents *before* they get the length of pikes and torches! For what end at all are men, Honourable Members and Reformed Members, sent to St. Stephen's, with clamour and effort; kept talking, struggling, motioning and counter-motioning? The condition of the great body of people in a country is the condition of the country itself: this you would say is a truism in all times; a truism rather pressing to get recognised as a truth now, and be acted upon, in these times. Yet read Hansard's Debates, or the Morning Papers, if you have nothing to do! The old grand question, whether A is to be in office or B, with the innumerable subsidiary questions growing out of that, courting paragraphs and suffrages for a blessed solution of that: Canada question, Irish Appropriation question, West-India question, Queen's Bedchamber question; Game Laws, Usury Laws; African Blacks, Hill Coolies, Smithfield cattle, and Dog-carts, —all manner of questions and subjects, except simply this the alpha and omega of all! Surely Honourable Members ought to speak of the Condition-of-England question too. Radical Members, above all; friends of the people; chosen with effort, by the people, to interpret and articulate the dumb deep want of the people! To a remote observer they seem oblivious of their duty. Are they not there, by trade, mission, and express appointment of themselves and others, to speak for the good of the British Nation? Whatsoever great British interest can the least speak for itself, for that beyond all they are called to speak. They are either speakers for that great dumb toiling class which cannot speak, or they are nothing that one can well specify.

Alas, the remote observer knows not the nature of Parliaments: how Parliaments, extant there for the British Nation's sake, find that they are extant withal for their own sake; how Parliaments travel so naturally in their deep-rutted routine, commonplace worn into ruts axle-deep, from which only strength, insight and courageous generous exertion can lift any Parliament or vehicle; how in Parliaments, Reformed or Unreformed, there may chance to be a strong man, an original, clear-sighted, great-hearted, patient and valiant man, or to be none such;—how, on the whole, Parliaments, lumbering along in their deep ruts of commonplace, find, as so many of us otherwise do, that the ruts *are* axle-deep, and the travelling very toilsome of itself, and for the day the evil thereof sufficient! What Parliaments ought to have done in this business, what they will, can or cannot yet do, and where the limits of their faculty and culpability may lie, in regard to it, were a long investigation; into which we need not enter at this moment. What they have done is unhappily plain enough. Hitherto, on this most national of questions, the Collective Wisdom of the Nation has availed us as good as nothing whatever.

And yet, as we say, it is a question which cannot be left to the Collective Folly of the Nation! In or out of Parliament, darkness, neglect, hallucination must contrive to cease in regard to it; true insight into it must be had. How inexpressibly useful were true insight into it; a genuine understanding by the upper classes of society what it is that the under classes intrinsically mean; a clear interpretation of the thought which at heart torments these wild inarticulate souls, struggling there, with inarticulate uproar, like dumb creatures in pain, unable to speak what is in them! Something they do mean; some true thing withal, in the centre of their confused hearts, —for they are hearts created by Heaven too: to the Heaven it is clear what thing; to us not clear. Would that it were! Perfect clearness on it were equivalent to remedy of it. For, as is well said, all battle is misunderstanding; did the parties know one another, the battle would cease. No man at bottom means injustice; it is always for some obscure distorted image of a right that he contends: an obscure image diffracted, exaggerated, in the wonderfulest way, by natural dimness and selfishness; getting tenfold more diffracted by exasperation of contest, till at length it become all but irrecognisable; yet still the image of a right. Could a man own to himself that the thing he fought for was wrong, contrary to fairness and the law of reason, he would own also that it thereby stood condemned and hopeless; he could fight for it no longer. Nay, independently of right, could the contending parties get but accurately to discern one another's might and strength to contend, the one would peaceably yield to the other and to Necessity; the contest in this case too were over. No African expedition now, as in the days of Herodotus, is fitted out *against the South-wind.* One expedition was satisfactory in that department. The South-wind Simoon continues blowing occasionally, hateful as ever, maddening as ever; but one expedition was enough. Do we not all submit to Death? The highest sentence of the law, sentence of death, is passed on all of us by the fact of birth; yet we live patiently under it, patiently undergo it when the hour comes. Clear undeniable right, clear undeniable might: either of these once ascertained puts an end to battle. All battle is a confused experiment to ascertain one and both of these.

What are the rights, what are the mights of the discontented Working Classes in England at this epoch? He were an Œdipus, and deliverer from sad social pestilence, who could resolve us fully! For we may say beforehand, The struggle that divides the upper and lower in society over Europe, and more painfully and notably in England than elsewhere, this too is a struggle which will end and adjust itself as all other struggles do and have done, by making the right clear and the might clear; not otherwise than by that. Meantime, the questions, Why are the Working Classes discontented; what is their condition, economical, moral, in their houses and their hearts, as it is in reality and as they figure it to themselves to be; what do they complain of; what ought they, and ought they not to complain of?—these are measurable questions; on some of these any common mortal, did he but turn his eyes to them, might throw some light. Certain researches and considerations of ours on the matter, since no one else will undertake it, are now to be made public. The researches have yielded us little, almost nothing; but the considerations are of old date, and press to have utterance. We are not without hope that our general notion of the business, if we can get it uttered at all, will meet some assent from many candid men.

CHAPTER III

NEW POOR-LAW

To read the Reports of the Poor-Law Commissioners, if one had faith enough, would be a pleasure to the friend of humanity. One sole recipe seems to have been needful for the woes of England: 'refusal of out-door relief.' England lay in sick discontent, writhing powerless on its fever-bed, dark, nigh desperate, in wastefulness, want, improvidence, and eating care, till like Hyperion down the eastern steeps, the Poor-Law Commissioners arose, and said, Let there be work-houses, and bread of affliction and water of affliction there! It was a simple invention; as all truly great inventions are. And see, in any quarter, instantly as the walls of the workhouse arise, misery and necessity fly away, out of sight,—out of being, as is fondly hoped, and dissolve into the inane; industry, frugality, fertility, rise of wages, peace on earth and goodwill towards men do,—in the Poor-Law Commissioners' Reports,—infallibly, rapidly or not so rapidly, to the joy of all parties, supervene. It was a consummation devoutly to be wished. We have looked over these four annual Poor-Law Reports with a variety of reflections; with no thought that our Poor-Law Commissioners are the inhuman men their enemies accuse them of being; with a feeling of thankfulness rather that there do exist men of that structure too; with a persuasion deeper and deeper that Nature, who makes nothing to no purpose, has not made either them or their Poor-Law Amendment Act in vain. We hope to prove that they and it were an indispensable element, harsh but salutary, in the progress of things.

That this Poor-law Amendment Act meanwhile should be, as we sometimes hear it named, the 'chief glory' of a Reform Cabinet, betokens, one would imagine, rather a scarcity of glory there. To say to the poor, Ye shall eat the bread of affliction and drink the water of affliction, and be very miserable while here, required not so much a stretch of heroic faculty in any sense, as due toughness of bowels. If paupers are made miserable, paupers will needs decline in multitude. It is a secret known to all rat-catchers: stop up the granary-crevices, afflict with continual mewing, alarm, and going-off of traps, your 'chargeable labourers' disappear, and cease from the establishment. A still briefer method is that of arsenic; perhaps even a milder, where otherwise permissible. Rats and paupers can be abolished; the human faculty was from of old adequate to grind them down, slowly or at once, and needed no ghost or Reform Ministry to teach it. Furthermore when one hears of 'all the labour of the country being absorbed into employment' by this new system of affliction, when labour complaining of want can find no audience, one cannot but pause. That misery and unemployed labour should 'disappear' in that case is natural enough; should go out of sight,—but out of existence? What we do know is, that 'the rates are diminished,' as they cannot well help being; that no statistic tables as yet report much increase of deaths by starvation: this we do know, and not very conclusively anything more than this. If this be absorption of all the labour of the country, then all the labour of the country is absorbed.

To believe practically that the poor and luckless are here only as a nuisance to be abraded and abated, and in some permissible manner made away with, and swept out of sight, is not an amiable faith. That the arrangements of good and ill success in this perplexed scramble of a world, which a blind goddess was always thought to preside over, are in fact the work of a seeing goddess or god, and require only not to be meddled with: what stretch of heroic faculty or inspiration of genius was needed to teach one that? To button your pockets and stand still, is no complex recipe. *Laissez faire, laissez passer!* Whatever goes on, ought it not to go on; 'the widow picking nettles for her children's dinner; and the perfumed seigneur delicately lounging in the Œil-de-Bœuf, who has an alchemy whereby he will extract from her the third nettle, and name it rent and law'? What is written and enacted, has it not black-on-white to show for itself? Justice is justice; but all attorney's parchment is of the nature of Targum or sacred-parchment. In brief, ours is a world requiring only to be well let alone. Scramble along, thou insane scramble of a world, with thy pope's tiaras, king's mantles and beggar's gabardines, chivalry-ribbons and plebeian gallows-ropes, where a Paul shall die on the gibbet and a Nero sit fiddling as imperial Cæsar; *thou* art all right, and shalt scramble even so; and whoever in the press is trodden down, has only to lie there and be trampled broad:—Such at bottom seems to be the chief social principle, if principle it have, which the Poor-Law Amendment Act has the merit of courageously asserting, in opposition to many things. A chief social principle which this present writer, for one, will by no manner of means believe in, but pronounce at all fit times to be false, heretical and damnable, if ever aught was!

And yet, as we said, Nature makes nothing in vain; not even a Poor-Law Amendment Act. For withal we are far from joining in the outcry raised against these poor Poor-Law Commissioners, as if they were tigers in men's shape; as if their Amendment Act were a mere monstrosity and horror, deserving instant abrogation. They are not tigers; they are men filled with an idea of a theory: their Amendment Act, heretical and damnable as a whole truth, is orthodox and laudable as a *half*-truth; and was imperatively required to be put in practice. To create men filled with a theory, that refusal of out-door relief was the one thing needful: Nature had no readier way of getting out-door relief refused. In fact, if we look at the old Poor-Law, in its assertion of the opposite social principle, that Fortune's awards are *not* those of Justice, we shall find it to have become still more unsupportable, demanding, if England was not destined for speedy anarchy, to be done away with.

Any law, however well meant as a law, which has become a bounty on unthrift, idleness, bastardy and beer-drinking, must be put an end to. In all ways it needs, especially in these times, to be proclaimed aloud that for the idle man there is no place in this England of ours. He that will not work, and save according to his means, let him go elsewhither; let him know that for *him* the Law has made no soft provision, but a hard and stern one; that by the Law of Nature, which the Law of England would vainly contend against in the long-run, *he* is doomed either to quit these habits, or miserably be extruded from this Earth, which is made on principles different from these. He that will not work according to his faculty, let him perish according to his necessity: there is no law juster than that. Would to Heaven one could preach it abroad into the hearts of all sons and daughters of Adam, for it is a law applicable to all; and bring it to bear, with practical obligation strict as the Poor-Law Bastille, on all! We had then, in good truth, a 'perfect constitution of society'; and 'God's fair Earth and Task-garden, where whosoever is not working must be begging or stealing,' were then actually what always, through so many changes and struggles, it is endeavouring to become.

That this law of 'No work no recompense' should first of all be enforced on the *manual* worker, and brought stringently home to him and his numerous class, while so many other classes and persons still go loose from it, was natural to the case. Let it be enforced there, and rigidly made good. It behoves to be enforced everywhere, and rigidly made good;—alas, not by such simple methods as 'refusal of out-door relief,' but by far other and costlier ones; which too, however, a bountiful Providence is not unfurnished with, nor, in these latter generations (if we will understand their convulsions and confusions), sparing to apply. Work is the mission of man in this Earth. A day is ever struggling forward, a day will arrive in some approximate degree, when he who has no work to do, by whatever name he may be named, will not find it good to show himself in our quarter of the Solar System; but may go and look out elsewhere, If there be any *Idle* Planet discoverable?—Let the honest working man rejoice that such law, the first of Nature, has been made good on him; and hope that, by and by, all else will be made good. It is the beginning of all. We define the harsh New Poor-Law to *be* withal a 'protection of the thrifty labourer against the thriftless and dissolute'; a thing inexpressibly important; a *half*-result, detestable, if you will, when looked upon as the whole result; yet without which the whole result is forever unattainable. Let wastefulness, idleness, drunkenness, improvidence take the fate which God has appointed them; that their opposites may also have a chance for *their* fate. Let the Poor-Law Administrators be considered as useful labourers whom Nature has furnished with a whole theory of the universe, that they might accomplish an indispensable fractional practice there, and prosper in it in spite of much contradiction.

We will praise the New Poor-Law, farther, as the probable preliminary of *some* general charge to be taken of the lowest classes by the higher. Any general charge whatsoever, rather than a conflict of charges, varying from parish to parish; the emblem of darkness, of unreadable confusion. Supervisal by the central government, in what spirit soever executed, is supervisal from a centre. By degrees the object will become clearer, as it is at once made thereby universally conspicuous. By degrees true vision of it will become attainable, will be universally attained; whatsoever order regarding it is just and wise, as grounded on the truth of it, will then be capable of being taken. Let us welcome the New Poor-Law as the harsh beginning of much, the harsh ending of much! Most harsh and barren lies the new ploughers' fallow-field, the crude subsoil all turned up, which never saw the sun; which as yet grows no herb; which has 'out-door relief' for no one. Yet patience: innumerable weeds and corruptions lie sagely turned down and extinguished under it; this same crude subsoil is the first step of all true husbandry; by Heaven's blessing and the skyey influences, fruits that are good and blessed will yet come of it.

For, in truth, the claim of the poor labourer is something quite other than that 'Statute of the Forty-third of Elizabeth' will ever fulfil for him. Not to be supported by roundsmen systems, by never so liberal parish doles, or lodged in free and easy workhouses when distress overtakes him; not for this, however in words he may clamour for it; not for this, but for something far different does the heart of him struggle. It is 'for justice' that he struggles; for 'just wages,'—not in money alone! An ever-toiling inferior, he would fain (though as yet he knows it not) find for himself a superior that should lovingly and wisely govern: is not that too the 'just wages' of his service done? It is for a manlike place and relation, in this world where he sees himself a man, that he struggles. At bottom, may we not say, it is even for this, That guidance and government, which he cannot give himself, which in our so complex world he can no longer do without, might be afforded him? The thing he struggles for is one which no Forty-third of Elizabeth is in any condition to furnish him, to put him on the road towards getting. Let him quit the Forty-third of Elizabeth altogether; and rejoice that the Poor-Law Amendment Act has, even by harsh methods and against his own will, forced him away from it. That was a broken reed to lean on, if there ever was one; and did but run into his lamed right-hand. Let him cast it far from him, that broken reed, and look to quite the opposite point of the heavens for help. His unlamed right-hand, with the cunning industry that lies in it, is not this defined to be 'the sceptre of our Planet'? He that can work is a born king of something; is in communion with Nature, is master of a thing or things, is a priest and king of Nature so far. He that can work at nothing is but a usurping king, be his trappings what they may; he is the born slave of all things. Let a man honour his craftmanship, his *can-do*; and know that his rights of man have no concern at all with the Forty-third of Elizabeth.

CHAPTER V

RIGHTS AND MIGHTS

It is not what a man outwardly has or wants that constitutes the happiness or misery of him. Nakedness, hunger, distress of all kinds, death itself have been cheerfully suffered, when the heart was right. It is the feeling of *injustice* that is insupportable to all men. The brutalest black African cannot bear that he should be used unjustly. No man can bear it, or ought to bear it. A deeper law than any parchment-law whatsoever, a law written direct by the hand of God in the inmost being of man, incessantly protests against it. What is injustice? Another name for *dis*order, for unveracity, unreality; a thing which veracious created Nature, even because it is not Chaos and a waste-whirling baseless Phantasm, rejects and disowns. It is not the outward pain of injustice; that, were it even the flaying of the back with knotted scourges, the severing of the head with guillotines, is comparatively a small matter. The real smart is the soul's pain and stigma, the hurt inflicted on the moral self. The rudest clown must draw himself up into attitude of battle, and resistance to the death, if such be offered him. He cannot live under it; his own soul aloud, and all the Universe with silent continual beckonings, says, It cannot be. He must revenge himself; *revancher* himself, make himself good again,—that so *meum* may be mine, *tuum* thine, and each party standing clear on his own basis, order be restored. There is something infinitely respectable in this, and we may say universally respected; it is the common stamp of manhood vindicating itself in all of us, the basis of whatever is worthy in all of us, and through superficial diversities, the same in all.

As *dis*order, insane by the nature of it, is the hatefulest of things to man, who lives by sanity and order, so injustice is the worst evil, some call it the only evil, in this world. All men submit to toil, to disappointment, to unhappiness; it is their lot here; but in all hearts, inextinguishable by sceptic logic, by sorrow, perversion or despair itself, there is a small still voice intimating that it is not the final lot; that wild, waste, incoherent as it looks, a God presides over it; that it is not an injustice, but a justice. Force itself, the hopelessness of resist ance, has doubtless a composing effect;—against inanimate *Simooms*, and much other infliction of the like sort, we have found it suffice to produce complete composure. Yet one would say, a permanent Injustice even from an Infinite Power would prove unendurable by men. If men had lost belief in a God, their only resource against a blind No-God, of Necessity and Mechanism, that held them like a hideous World-Steamengine, like a hideous Phalaris' Bull, imprisoned in its own iron belly, would be, with or without hope,—*revolt*. They could, as Novalis says, by a 'simultaneous universal act of suicide,' *depart* out of the World-Steamengine; and end, if not in victory, yet in invincibility, and unsubduable protest that such World-Steamengine was a failure and a stupidity.

Conquest, indeed, is a fact often witnessed; conquest, which seems mere wrong and force, everywhere asserts itself as a right among men. Yet if we examine, we shall find that, in this world, no conquest could ever become permanent, which did not withal show itself beneficial to the conquered as well as to conquerors. Mithridates King of Pontus, come now to extremity, 'appealed to the patriotism of his people'; but, says the history, 'he had squeezed them, and fleeced and plundered them for long years'; his requisitions, flying irregular, devastative, like the whirlwind, were less supportable than Roman strictness and method, regular though never so rigorous: he therefore appealed to their patriotism in vain. The Romans conquered Mithridates. The Romans, having conquered the world, held it conquered, *because* they could best govern the world; the mass of men found it nowise pressing to revolt; their fancy might be afflicted more or less, but in their solid interests they were better off than before.

So too in this England long ago, the old Saxon Nobles, disunited among themselves, and in power too nearly equal, could not have governed the country well; Harold being slain, their last chance of governing it, except in anarchy and civil war, was over: a new class of strong Norman Nobles, entering with a strong man, with a succession of strong men at the head of them, and not disunited, but united by many ties, by their very community of language and interest, had there been no other, *were* in a condition to govern it; and did govern it, we can believe, in some rather tolerable manner, or they would not have continued there. They acted, little conscious of such function on their part, as an immense volunteer Police Force, stationed everywhere, united, disciplined, feudally regimented, ready for action; strong Teutonic men; who, on the whole, proved effective men, and drilled this wild Teutonic people into unity and peaceable coöperation better than others could have done! How *can-do*, if we will well interpret it, unites itself with *shall-do* among mortals; how strength acts ever as the right-arm of justice; how might and right, so frightfully discrepant at first, are ever in the long-run one and the same,—is a cheering consideration, which always in the black tempestuous vortices of this world's history, will shine out on us, like an everlasting polar star.

Of conquest we may say that it never yet went by brute force and compulsion; conquest of that kind does not endure. Conquest, along with power of compulsion, an essential universally in human society, must bring benefit along with it, or men, of the ordinary strength of men, will fling it out. The strong man, what is he if we will consider? The wise man; the man with the gift of method, of faithfulness and valour, all of which are of the basis of wisdom; who has insight into what is what, into what will follow out of what, the eye to see and the hand to do; who is *fit* to administer, to direct, and guidingly command: he is the strong man. His muscles and bones are no stronger than ours; but his soul is stronger, his soul is wiser, clearer,—is better and nobler, for that is, has been and ever will be, the root of all clearness worthy of such a name. Beautiful it is, and a gleam from the same eternal pole-star visible amid the destinies of men, that all talent, all intellect is in the first place moral;—what a world were this otherwise! But it is the heart always that sees, before the head *can* see: let us know that; and know therefore that the Good alone is deathless and victorious, that Hope is sure and steadfast, in all phases of this 'Place of Hope.'—Shiftiness, quirk, attorney-cunning is a kind of thing that fancies itself, and is often fancied, to be talent; but it is luckily mistaken in that. Succeed truly it does, what is called succeeding; and even must in general succeed, if the dispensers of success be of due stupidity: men of due stupidity will needs say to it, "*Thou* art wisdom, rule thou!" Whereupon it rules. But Nature answers, "No, this ruling of thine is not according to *my* laws; thy wisdom was not wise enough!

Dost thou take me too for a Quackery? For a Conventionality and Attorneyism? This chaff that thou sowest into my bosom, though it pass at the poll-booth and elsewhere for seed-corn, *I* will not grow wheat out of it, for it is chaff!"

But to return. Injustice, infidelity to truth and fact and Nature's order, being properly the one evil under the sun, and the feeling of injustice the one intolerable pain under the sun, our grand question as to the condition of these working men would be: Is it just? And first of all, What belief have they themselves formed about the justice of it? The words they promulgate are notable by way of answer; their actions are still more notable. Chartism with its pikes, Swing with his tinder-box, speak a most loud though inarticulate language. Glasgow Thuggery speaks aloud too, in a language we may call infernal. What kind of 'wild-justice' must it be in the hearts of these men that prompts them, with cold deliberation, in conclave assembled, to doom their brother workman, as the deserter of his order and his order's cause, to die as a traitor and deserter; and have him executed, since not by any public judge and hangman, then by a private one;—like your old Chivalry *Fehmgericht*, and Secret-Tribunal, suddenly in this strange guise become new; suddenly rising once more on the astonished eye, dressed now not in mail-shirts but in fustian jackets, meeting not in Westphalian forests but in the paved Gallowgate of Glasgow! Not loyal loving obedience to those placed over them, but a far other temper, must animate these men! It is frightful enough. Such temper must be widespread, virulent among the many, when even in its worst acme it can take such a form in a few. But indeeed decay of loyalty in all senses, disobedience, decay of religious faith, has long been noticeable and lamentable in this largest class, as in other smaller ones. Revolt, sullen revengeful humour of revolt against the upper classes, decreasing respect for what their temporal superiors command, decreasing faith for what their spiritual superiors teach, is more and more the universal spirit of the lower classes. Such spirit may be blamed, may be vindicated; but all men must recognise it as extant there, all may know that it is mournful, that unless altered it will be fatal. Of lower classes so related to upper, happy nations are not made! To whatever other griefs the lower classes labour under, this bitterest and sorest grief now superadds itself: the unendurable conviction that they are unfairly dealt with, that their lot in this world is not founded on right, not even on necessity and might, and is neither what it should be, nor what it shall be.

Or why do we ask of Chartism, Glasgow Trades-unions, and suchlike? Has not broad Europe heard the question put, and answered, on the great scale; has not a FRENCH REVOLUTION been? Since the year 1789, there is now half a century complete; and a French Revolution not yet complete! Whosoever will look at that enormous Phenomenon may find many meanings in it, but this meaning as the ground of all: That it was a revolt of the oppressed lower classes against the oppressing or neglecting upper classes: not a French revolt only; no, a European one; full of stern monition to all countries of Europe. These Chartisms, Radicalisms, Reform Bill, Tithe Bill, and infinite other discrepancy, and acrid argument and jargon that there is yet to be, are *our* French Revolution: God grant that we, with our better methods, may be able to transact it by argument alone!

The French Revolution, now that we have sufficiently execrated its horrors and crimes, is found to have had withal a great meaning in it. As indeed, what great thing ever happened in this world, a world understood always to be made and governed by a Providence and Wisdom, not by an Unwisdom, without meaning somewhat? It was a tolerably audible voice of proclamation, and universal *oyez*! to all people, this of three-and-twenty years' close fighting, sieging, conflagrating, with a million or two of men shot dead: the world ought to know by this time that it was verily meant in earnest, that same Phenomenon, and had its own reasons for appearing there! Which accordingly the world begins now to do. The French Revolution is seen, or begins everywhere to be seen, 'as the crowning phenomenon of our Modern Time'; 'the inevitable stern end of much; the fearful, but also wonderful, indispensable and sternly beneficent beginning of much.' He who would understand the struggling convulsive unrest of European society, in any and every country, at this day, may read it in broad glaring lines there, in that the most convulsive phenomenon of the last thousand years. Europe lay pining, obstructed, moribund; quack-ridden, hag-ridden,—is there a hag, or spectre of the Pit, so baleful, hideous as your accredited quack, were he never so close-shaven, mild-spoken, plausible to himself and others? Quack-ridden: in that one word lies all misery whatsoever. Speciosity in all departments usurps the place of reality, thrusts reality away; instead of performance, there is appearance of performance. The quack is a Falsehood Incarnate; and speaks, and makes and does mere falsehoods, which Nature with her veracity has to disown. As chief priest, as chief governor, he stands there, intrusted with much. The husbandman of 'Time's Seedfield'; he is the world's hired sower, hired and solemnly appointed to sow the kind true earth with wheat this year, that next year all men may have bread. He, miserable mortal, deceiving and self-deceiving, sows it, as we said, not with corn but with chaff; the world nothing doubting, harrows it in, pays him his wages, dismisses him with blessing, and—next year there has no corn sprung. Nature has disowned the chaff, declined growing chaff, and behold now there is no bread! It becomes necessary, in such case, to do several things; not soft things some of them, but hard.

Nay, we will add that the very circumstance of quacks in unusual quantity getting domination, indicates that the heart of the world is *already* wrong. The imposter is false; but neither are his dupes altogether true: is not his first grand dupe the falsest of all,—himself namely? Sincere men, of never so limited intellect, have an instinct for discriminating sincerity. The cunningest Mephistopheles cannot deceive a simple Margaret of honest heart; 'it stands written on his brow.' Masses of people capable of being led away by quacks are themselves of partially untrue spirit. Alas, in such times it grows to be the universal belief, sole accredited knowingness and the contrary of it accounted puerile enthusiasm, this sorrowfulest *dis*belief that there is properly speaking any truth in the world; that the world was, has been or ever can be guided, except by simulation, dissimulation, and the sufficiently dextrous practice of pretence. The faith of men is dead: in what has guineas in its pocket, beefeaters riding behind it, and cannons trundling before it, they can believe; in what has none of these things they cannot believe. Sense for the true and false is lost; there is properly no longer any true or false. It is the heyday of Imposture; of Semblance recognising itself, and getting itself recognised, for Substance. Gaping multitudes listen; unlistening multitudes see not but that it is all right, and in the order of Nature. Earnest men, one of a million, shut their lips; suppressing thoughts, which there are no words to utter. To them it is too visible that spiritual life has departed; that material life, in whatsoever figure of it, cannot long remain behind. To them it seems as if our Europe of the Eighteenth Century, long hag-ridden, vexed with foul enchanters, to the length now of gorgeous Domdaniel *Parcs-aux-cerfs* and 'Peasants living on meal-husks and boiled grass,' had verily sunk down to die and dissolve; and were now, with its French Philosophisms, Hume Scepticisms, Diderot Atheisms, maundering in the final deliration; writhing, with its Seven-years Silesian robber-wars, in the final agony. Glory to God, our Europe was not to die but to live! Our Europe rose like a frenzied giant; shook all that poisonous magician trumpery to right and left, trampling it stormfully under foot; and declared aloud that there was strength in him, not for life only, but for new and infinitely wider life. Antæus-like the giant had struck his foot once more upon Reality and the Earth; there only, if in this Universe at all, lay strength and healing for him. Heaven knows, it was not a gentle process; no wonder that it was a fearful process, this same 'Phœnix fire-consummation!' But the alternative was it or death; the merciful Heavens, merciful in their severity, sent us it rather.

And so the 'rights of man' were to be written down on paper; and experimentally wrought upon towards elaboration, in huge battle and wrestle, element conflicting with element, from side to side of this earth, for three-and-twenty years. Rights of man, wrongs of man? It is a question which has swallowed whole nations and generations; a question—on which we will not enter here. Far be it from us! Logic has small business with this question at present; logic has no plummet that will sound it at any time. But indeed the rights of man, as has been not unaptly remarked, are little worth ascertaining in comparison to the *mights* of man,—to what portion of his rights he has any chance of being able to make good! The accurate final rights of man lie in the far deeps of the Ideal, where 'the Ideal weds itself to the Possible,' as the Philosophers say. The ascertainable temporary rights of man vary not a little, according to place and time. They are known to depend much on what a man's convictions of them are. The Highland wife, with her husband at the foot of the gallows. patted him on the shoulder (if there be historical truth in Joseph Miller), and said amid her tears: 'Go up, Donald, my man; the Laird bids ye.' To her it seemed the rights of lairds were great, the rights of men small; and she acquiesced. Deputy Lapoule, in the *Salle des Menus* at Versailles, on the 4th of August 1789, demanded (he did actually 'demand,' and by unanimous vote obtain) that the 'obsolete law' authorising a Seigneur, on his return from the chase or other needful fatigue, to slaughter not above two of his vassals, and refresh his feet in their warm blood and bowels, should be 'abrogated.' From such obsolete law, or mad tradition and phantasm of an obsolete law, down to any corn-law, game-law, rotten-borough law, or other law or practice clamoured of in this time of ours, the distance travelled over is great!

What are the rights of men? All men are justified in demanding and searching for their rights; moreover, justified or not, they will do it: by Chartisms, Radicalisms, French Revolutions, or whatsoever methods they have. Rights surely are right: on the other hand, this other saying is most true, 'Use every man according to his *rights*, and who shall escape whipping?' These two things, we say, are both true; and both are essential to make up the whole truth. All good men know always and feel, each for himself, that the one is not less true than the other; and act accordingly. The contradiction is of the surface only; as in opposite sides of the same fact: universal in this *dualism* of a life we have. Between these two extremes, Society and all human things must fluctuatingly adjust themselves the best they can.

And yet that there is verily a 'rights of man' let no mortal doubt. An ideal of right does dwell in all men, in all arrangements, pactions and procedures of men: it is to this ideal of right, more and more developing itself as it is more and more approximated to, that human Society forever tends and struggles. We say also that any given thing either *is* unjust or else just; however obscure the arguings and strugglings on it be, the thing in itself there as it lies, infallibly enough, *is* the one or the other. To which let us add only this, the first, last article of faith, the alpha and omega of all faith among men, That nothing which is unjust can hope to continue in this world. A faith true in all times, more or less forgotten in most, but altogether frightfully brought to remembrance again in ours! Lyons fusilladings, Nantes noyadings, reigns of terror, and such other universal battle-thunder and explosion; these, if we will understand them, were but a new irrefragable preaching abroad of that. It would appear that Speciosities which are not Realities cannot any longer inhabit this world. It would appear that the unjust thing has no friend in the Heaven, and a majority against it on the Earth; nay, that *it* has at bottom all men for its enemies; that it may take shelter in this fallacy and then in that, but will be hunted from fallacy to fallacy till it find no fallacy to shelter-in any more, but must march and go elsewhither;—that, in a word, it ought to prepare incessantly for decent departure, before *in*decent departure, ignominious drumming out, nay, savage smiting out and burning out, overtake it!

Alas, was that such new tidings? Is it not from of old indubitable, that Untruth, Injustice which is but acted untruth, has no power to continue in this true Universe of ours? The tidings was world-old, or older, as old as the Fall of Lucifer, and yet in that epoch unhappily it was new tidings, unexpected, incredible; and there had to be such earthquakes and shakings of the nations before it could be listened to, and laid to heart even slightly! Let us lay it to heart, let us know it well, that new shakings be not needed. Known and laid to heart it must everywhere be, before peace can pretend to come. This seems to us the secret of our convulsed era; this which is so easily written, which is and has been and will be so hard to bring to pass. All true men, high and low, each in his sphere, are consciously or unconsciously bringing it to pass; all false and half-true men are fruitlessly spending themselves to hinder it from coming to pass.

CHAPTER VI

LAISSEZ-FAIRE

From all which enormous events, with truths old and new embodied in them, what innumerable practical inferences are to be drawn! Events are written lessons, glaring in huge hieroglyphic picture-writing, that all may read and know them: the terror and horror they inspire is but the note of preparation for the truth they are to teach; a mere waste of terror if that be not learned. Inferences enough; most didactic, practically applicable in all departments of English things! One inference, but one inclusive of all, shall content us here; this namely: That *Laissez-faire* has as good as done its part in a great many provinces; that in the province of the Working Classes, *Laissez-faire* having passed its New Poor-Law, has reached the suicidal point, and now, as *felo-de-se,* lies dying there, in torchlight meetings and suchlike; that, in brief, a government of the under classes by the upper on a principle of *Let-alone* is no longer possible in England in these days. This is the one inference inclusive of all. For there can be no acting or doing of any kind, till it be recognised that there is a thing to be done; the thing once recognised, doing in a thousand shapes becomes possible. The Working Classes cannot any longer go on without government; without being *actually* guided and governed; England cannot subsist in peace till, by some means or other, some guidance and government for them is found.

For, alas, on us too the rude truth has come home. Wrapt pages and speciosities all worn off, the haggard naked fact speaks to us: Are these millions taught? Are these millions guided? We have a Church, the venerable embodiment of an idea which may well call itself divine; which our fathers for long ages, feeling it to be divine, have been embodying as we see: it is a Church well furnished with equipments and appurtenances; educated in universities; rich in money; set on high places that it may be conspicuous to all, honoured of all. We have an Aristocracy of landed wealth and commercial wealth, in whose hands lies the law-making and the law-administering; an Aristocracy rich, powerful, long secure in its place; an Aristocracy with more faculty put free into its hands than was ever before, in any country or time, put into the hands of any class of men. This Church answers: Yes, the people are taught. This Aristocracy, astonishment in every feature, answers: Yes, surely the people are guided! Do we not pass what Acts of Parliament are needful; as many as thirty-nine for the shooting of the partridges alone? Are there not treadmills, gibbets; even hospitals, poor-rates, New Poor-Law? So answers Church; so answers Aristocracy, astonishment in every feature.

Fact, in the mean while, takes his lucifer-box, sets fire to wheat-stacks; sheds an all-too dismal light on several things. Fact searches for his third-rate potato, not in the meekest humour, six-and-thirty weeks each year; and does not find it. Fact passionately joins Messiah Thom of Canterbury, and has himself shot for a new fifth-monarchy brought in by Bedlam. Fact holds his fustian-jacket *Fehmgericht* in Glasgow City. Fact carts his Petition over London streets, begging that you would simply have the goodness to grant him universal suffrage and 'the five points,' by way of remedy. These are not symptoms of teaching and guiding.

Nay, at bottom, is it not a singular thing this of *Laissez-*

faire, from the first origin of it? As good as an *abdication* on the part of governors; an admission that they are henceforth incompetent to govern, that they are not there to govern at all, but to do—one knows not what! The universal demand of *Laissez-faire* by a people from its governors or upper classes, is a soft-sounding demand; but it is only one step removed from the fatalist. '*Laissez-faire*,' exclaims a sardonic German writer, 'What is this universal cry for *Laissez-faire*? Does it mean that human affairs require no guidance; that wisdom and forethought cannot guide them better than folly and accident? Alas, does it not mean: "*Such* guidance is worse than none! Leave us alone of *your* guidance; eat your wages, and sleep!" ' And now if guidance have grown indispensable, and the sleep continue, what becomes of the sleep and its wages?—In those entirely surprising circumstances to which the Eighteenth Century had brought us, in the time of Adam Smith, *Laissez-faire* was a reasonable cry;—as indeed, in all circumstances, for a wise governor there will be meaning in the principle of it. To wise governors you will cry: 'See what you will, and will not, let alone.' To unwise governors, to hungry Greeks throttling down hungry Greeks on the floor of a St. Stephen's, you will cry: 'Let *all* things alone: for Heaven's sake meddle ye with nothing!'

How *Laissez-faire* may adjust itself in other provinces we say not: but we do venture to say, and ask whether events everywhere, in world-history and parish-history, in all manner of dialects are not saying it, That in regard to the lower orders of society, and their governance and guidance, the principle of *Laissez-faire* has terminated, and is no longer applicable at all, in this Europe of ours, still less in this England of ours. Not misgovernment, nor yet no-government; only government will now serve. What is the meaning of the 'five points,' if we will understand them? What are all popular commotions and maddest bellowings, from Peterloo to the Place-de-Grève itself? Bellowings, *in*articulate cries as of a dumb creature in rage and pain; to the ear of wisdom they are inarticulate prayers: 'Guide me, govern me! I am mad and miserable, and cannot guide myself!' Surely of all 'rights of man,' this right of the ignorant man to be guided by the wiser, to be, gently or forcibly, held in the true course by him, is the indisputablest. Nature herself ordains it from the first; Society struggles towards perfection by enforcing and accomplishing it more and more. If Freedom have any meaning, it means enjoyment of this right, wherein all other rights are enjoyed. It is a sacred right and duty, on both sides; and the summary of all social duties whatsoever between the two. Why does the one toil with his hands, if the other be not to toil, still more unweariedly, with heart and head? The brawny craftsman finds it no child's-play to mould his unpliant rugged masses; neither is guidance of men a dilettantism: what it becomes when treated as a dilettantism, we may see! The wild horse bounds homeless through the wilderness, is not led to stall and manger; but neither does he toil for you, but for himself only.

Democracy, we are well aware, what is called 'self-government' of the multitude by the multitude, is in words the thing everywhere passionately clamoured for at present. Democracy makes rapid progress in these latter times, and ever more rapid, in a perilous accelerative ratio; towards democracy, and that only, the progress of things is everywhere tending as to the final goal and winning-post. So think, so clamour the multitudes everywhere. And yet all men may see, whose sight is good for much, that in democracy can lie no finality; that with the completest winning of democracy there is nothing yet won,—except emptiness, and the free chance to win! Democracy is, by the nature of it, a self-cancelling business; and gives in the long-run a net result of *zero*. Where no government is wanted, save that of the parish-constable, as in America with its boundless soil, every man being able to find work and recompense for himself, democracy may subsist; not elsewhere, except briefly, as a swift transition towards something other and farther. Democracy never yet, that we heard of, was able to accomplish much work, beyond that same cancelling of itself. Rome and Athens are themes for the schools; unexceptionable for that purpose. In Rome and Athens, as elsewhere, if we look practically, we shall find that it was not by loud voting and debating of many, but by wise insight and ordering of a few that the work was done. So is it ever, so will it ever be.

The French Convention was a Parliament elected 'by the five points,' with ballot-boxes, universal suffrages, and what not, as perfectly as Parliament can hope to be in this world; and had indeed a pretty spell of work to do, and did it. The French Convention had to cease from being a free Parliament, and become more arbitrary than any Sultan Bajazet, before it could so much as subsist. It had to purge out its argumentative Girondins, elect its supreme Committee of *Salut*, guillotine into silence and extinction all that gainsaid it, and rule and work literally by the sternest despotism ever seen in Europe, before it could rule at all. Napoleon was not president of a republic; Cromwell tried hard to rule in that way, but found that he could not. These, 'the armed soldiers of democracy,' had to chain democracy under their feet, and become despots over it, before they could work out the earnest obscure purpose of democracy itself!

Democracy, take it where you will in our Europe, is found but as a regulated method of rebellion and abrogation; it abrogates the old arrangement of things; and leaves, as we say, *zero* and vacuity for the institution of a new arrangement. It is the consummation of No-government and *Laissez-faire.* It may be natural for our Europe at present; but cannot be the ultimatum of it. Not towards the impossibility, 'self-government' of a multitude by a multitude; but towards some possibility, government by the wisest, does bewildered Europe struggle. The blessedest possibility: not misgovernment, not *Laissez-faire*, but veritable government! Cannot one discern too, across all democratic turbulence, clattering of ballot-boxes and infinite sorrowful jangle, needful or not, that this at bottom is the wish and prayer of all human hearts, everywhere and at all times: 'Give me a leader; a true leader, not a false sham-leader; a true leader, that he may guide me on the true way, that I may be loyal to him, that I may swear fealty to him and follow him, and feel that it is well with me!' The relation of the taught to their teacher, of the loyal subject to his guiding king, is, under one shape or another, the vital element of human Society; indispensable to it, perennial in it; without which, as a body reft of its soul, it falls down into death, and with horrid noisome dissolution passes away and disappears.

But verily in these times, with their new stern Evangel, that Speciosities which are not Realities can no longer be, all Aristocracies, Priesthoods, Persons in Authority, are called upon to consider. What is an Aristocracy? A corporation of the Best, of the Bravest. To this joyfully, with heart-loyalty, do men pay the half of their substance, to equip and decorate their Best, to lodge them in palaces, set them high over all. For it is of the nature of men, in every time, to honour and love their Best; to know no limits in honouring them. Whatsoever Aristocracy *is* still a corporation of the Best, is safe from all peril, and the land it rules is a safe and blessed land. Whatsoever Aristocracy does not even attempt to be that, but only to wear the clothes of that, is not safe; neither is the land it rules in safe! For this now is our sad lot, that we must find a *real* Aristocracy, that an apparent Aristocracy, how plausible soever, has become inadequate for us. One way or other, the world will absolutely need to be governed; if not by this class of men, then by that. One can predict, without gift of prophecy, that the era of routine is nearly ended. Wisdom and faculty alone, faithful, valiant, ever-zealous, not pleasant but painful, continual effort will suffice. Cost what it may, by one means or another, the toiling multitudes of this perplexed, overcrowded Europe must and will find governors. '*Laissez-faire,* Leave them to do?' The thing they will *do,* if so left, is too frightful to think of! It has been *done* once, in sight of the whole earth, in these generations: can it need to be done a second time?

For a Priesthood, in like manner, whatsoever its titles, possessions, professions, there is but one question: Does it teach and spiritually guide this people, yea or no? If yea, then is all well. But if no, then let it strive earnestly to alter, for as yet there is nothing well! Nothing, we say: and indeed is not this that we call spiritual guidance properly the soul of the whole, the life and eyesight of the whole? The world asks of its Church in these times, more passionately than of any other Institution any question, 'Canst thou teach us or not?'—A Priesthood in France, when the world asked, 'What canst thou do for us?' answered only, aloud and ever louder, 'Are we not of God? Invested with all power?'—till at length France cut short this controversy too, in what frightful way we know. To all men who believed in the Church, to all men who believed in God and the soul of man, there was no issue of the French Revolution half so sorrowful as that. France cast out its benighted blind Priesthood into destruction; yet with what a loss to France also! A solution of continuity, what we may well call such; and this where continuity is so momentous: the New, whatever it may be, cannot now *grow* out of the Old, but is severed sheer asunder from the Old,—how much lies wasted in that gap! That one whole generation of thinkers should be without a religion to believe, or even to contradict; that Christianity, in thinking France, should as it were fade away so long into a remote extraneous tradition, was one of the saddest facts connected with the future of that country. Look at such Political and Moral Philosophies, St.-Simonisms, Robert-Macairisms, and the 'Literature of Desperation'! Kingship was perhaps but a cheap waste, compared with this of the Priestship; under which France still, all but unconsciously, labours; and may long labour, remediless the while. Let others consider it, and take warning by it! France is a pregnant example in all ways. Aristocracies that do not govern, Priesthoods that do not teach; the misery of that, and the misery of altering that,—are written in Belshazzar fire-letters on the history of France.

Or does the British reader, safe in the assurance that 'England is not France,' call all this unpleasant doctrine of ours ideology, perfectibility, and a vacant dream? Does the British reader, resting on the faith that what has been these two generations was from the beginning, and will be to the end, assert to himself that things are already as they can be, as they must be; that on the whole, no Upper Classes did ever 'govern' the Lower, in this sense of governing? Believe it not, O British reader! Man is man everywhere; dislikes to have 'sensible species' and 'ghosts of defunct bodies' foisted on him, in England even as in France.

How much the Upper Classes did actually, in any the most perfect Feudal time, return to the Under by way of recompense, in government, guidance, protection, we will not undertake to specify here. In Charity-Balls, Soup-Kitchens, in Quarter-Sessions, Prison-Discipline and Treadmills, we can well believe the old Feudal Aristocracy not to have surpassed the new. Yet we do say that the old Aristocracy were the governors of the Lower Classes, the guides of the Lower Classes; and even, at bottom, that they existed as an Aristocracy because they were found adequate for that. Not by Charity-Balls and Soup-Kitchens; not so; far otherwise! But it was their happiness that, in struggling for their own objects, they *had* to govern the Lower Classes, even in this sense of governing. For, in one word, *Cash Payment* had not then grown to be the universal sole nexus of man to man; it was something other than money that the high then expected from the low, and could not live without getting from the low. Not as buyer and seller alone, of land or what else it might be, but in many senses still as soldier and captain, as clansman and head, as loyal subject and guiding king, was the low related to the high. With the supreme triumph of Cash, a changed time has entered; there must a changed Aristocracy enter. We invite the British reader to meditate earnestly on these things.

Another thing, which the British reader often reads and hears in this time, is worth his meditating for a moment: That Society 'exists for the protection of property.' To which it is added, that the poor man also has property, namely, his 'labour,' and the fifteen-pence or three-and-sixpence a-day he can get for that. True enough, O friends, 'for protecting *property*'; most true: and indeed, if you will once sufficiently enforce that Eighth Commandment, the whole 'rights of man' are well cared for; I know no better definition of the rights of man. *Thou shalt not steal, thou shalt not be stolen from:* what a Society were that; Plato's Republic, More's Utopia mere emblems of it! Give every man what is his, the accurate price of what he has done and been, no man shall any more complain, neither shall the earth suffer any more. For the protection of property, in very truth, and for that alone!

And now what is thy property? That parchment title-deed, that purse thou buttonest in thy breeches-pocket? Is that thy valuable property? Unhappy brother, most poor insolvent brother, I without parchment at all, with purse oftenest in the flaccid state, imponderous, which will not fling against the wind, have quite other property than that! I have the miraculous breath of Life in me, breathed into my nostrils by Almighty God. I have affections, thoughts, a god-given *capability* to be and do; rights, therefore,—the right for instance to thy love if I love thee, to thy guidance if I obey thee: the strangest rights, whereof in church-pulpits one still hears something, though almost unintelligible now; rights stretching high into Immensity, far into Eternity! Fifteen-pence a-day; three-and-sixpence a-day; eight hundred pounds and odd a-day, dost thou call that my property? I value that little; little all I could purchase with that. For truly, as is said, what matters it? In torn boots, in soft-hung carriages-and-four, a man gets always to his journey's end. Socrates walked barefoot, or in wooden shoes, and yet arrived happily. They never asked him, *What* shoes or conveyance? never, What wages hadst thou? but simply, What work didst thou?—Property, O brother? 'Of my very body I have but a life-rent.' As for this flaccid purse of mine, 'tis something, nothing; has been the slave of pick-pockets, cutthroats, Jew-brokers, gold-dust robbers; 'twas his, 'tis mine;—'tis thine, if thou care much to steal it. But my soul, breathed into me by God, my *Me* and what capability is there; that is mine, and I will resist the stealing of it. I call that mine and not thine; I will keep that, and do what work I can with it: God has given it me, the Devil shall not take it away! Alas, my friends, Society exists and has existed for a great many purposes, not so easy to specify!

Society, it is understood, does not in any age prevent a man from being what he *can be*. A sooty African *can* become a Toussaint L'Ouverture, a murderous Three-fingered Jack, let the yellow West Indies say to it what they will. A Scottish Poet, 'proud of his name and country,' *can* apply fervently to 'Gentlemen of the Caledonian Hunt,' and become a gauger of beer-barrels, and tragical immortal broken-hearted Singer; the stifled echo of his melody audible through long centuries, one other note in 'that sacred *Miserere*' that rises up to Heaven, out of all times and lands. What I *can be* thou decidedly wilt not hinder me from being. Nay, even for being what I *could be*, I have the strangest claims on thee,—not convenient to adjust at present! Protection of breeches-pocket property? O reader, to what shifts is poor Society reduced, struggling to give still some account of herself, in epochs when Cash Payment has become the sole nexus of man to man! On the whole, we will advise Society not to talk at all about what she exists for; but rather with her whole industry to exist, to try how she can keep existing! That is her best plan. She may depend upon it, if she ever, by cruel chance, did come to exist only for protection of breeches-pocket property, she would lose very soon the gift of protecting even that, and find her career in our lower world on the point of terminating!—

For the rest, that in the most perfect Feudal Ages, the Ideal of Aristocracy nowhere lived in vacant serene purity as an Ideal, but always as a poor imperfect Actual, little heeding or not knowing at all that an Ideal lay in it,—this too we will cheerfully admit. Imperfection, it is known, cleaves to human things; far is the Ideal departed from, in most times; very far! And yet so long as an Ideal (any soul of Truth) does, in never so confused a manner, exist and work within the Actual, it is a tolerable business. Not so, when the Ideal has entirely departed, and the Actual owns to itself that it has no Idea, no soul of Truth any longer: at that degree of imperfection human things cannot continue living; they are obliged to alter or expire, when they attain to that. Blotches and diseases exist on the skin and deeper, the heart continuing whole; but it is another matter when the heart itself becomes diseased; when there is no heart, but a monstrous gangrene pretending to exist there as heart!

On the whole, O reader, thou wilt find everywhere that things which have had an existence among men have first of all had to have a truth and worth in them, and were not semblances but realities. Nothing not a reality ever yet got men to pay bed and board to it for long. Look at Mahometanism itself! Dalai-Lamaism, even Dalai-Lamaism, one rejoices to discover, may be worth its victuals in this world; not a quackery but a sincerity; not a nothing but a something! The mistake of those who believe that fraud, force, injustice, whatsoever untrue thing, howsoever cloaked and decorated, was ever or can ever be the principle of man's relations to man, is great and the greatest. It is the error of the infidel; in whom the truth as yet is *not*. It is an error pregnant with mere errors and miseries; an error fatal, lamentable, to be abandoned by all men.

CHAPTER VII

NOT LAISSEZ-FAIRE

How an Aristocracy, in these present times and circumstances, could, if never so well disposed, set about governing the Under Class? What they should do; endeavour or attempt to do? That is even the question of questions:—the question which *they* have to solve; which it is our utmost function at present to tell them, lies there for solving, and must and will be solved.

Insoluble we cannot fancy it. One select class Society has furnished with wealth, intelligence, leisure, means outward and inward for governing; another huge class, furnished by Society with none of those things, declares that it must be governed: Negative stands fronting Positive; if Negative and Positive *cannot* unite,—it will be worse for both! Let the faculty and earnest constant effort of England combine round this matter; let it once be recognised as a vital matter. Innumerable things our Upper Classes and Law-givers might 'do'; but the preliminary of all things, we must repeat, is to know that a thing must needs be done. We lead them here to the shore of a boundless continent; ask them, Whether they do not with their own eyes see it, see strange symptoms of it, lying huge, dark, unexplored, inevitable; full of hope, but also full of difficulty, savagery, almost of despair? Let them enter; they must enter; Time and Necessity have brought them hither; where they are is no continuing! Let them enter; the first step once taken, the next will have become clearer, all future steps will become possible. It is a great problem for all of us; but for themselves, we may say, more than for any. On them chiefly, as the expected solvers of it, will the failure of a solution first fall. One way or other there must and will be a solution.

True, these matters lie far, very far indeed, from the 'usual habits of Parliament,' in late times; from the routine course of any Legislative or Administrative body of men that exists among us. Too true! And that is even the thing we complain of: had the mischief been looked into as it gradually rose, it would not have attained this magnitude. That self-cancelling Donothingism and *Laissez-faire* should have got so ingrained into our Practice, is the source of all these miseries. It is too true that Parliament, for the matter of near a century now, has been able to undertake the adjustment of almost one thing alone, of itself and its own interests; leaving other interests to rub along very much as they could and would. True, this was the practice of the whole Eighteenth Century; and struggles still to prolong itself into the Nineteenth,—which, however, is no longer the time for it!

Those Eighteenth-century Parliaments, one may hope, will become a curious object one day. Are not these same '*Memoirs*' of Horace Walpole, to an unparliamentary eye, already a curious object? One of the clearest-sighted men of the Eighteenth Century writes down his Parliamentary observation of it there; a determined despiser and merciless dissector of cant; a liberal withal, one who will go all lengths, for the 'glorious revolution,' and resist Tory principles to the death: he writes, with an indignant elegiac feeling, how Mr. This, who had voted so and then voted so, and was the son of this and the brother of that, and had such claims to the fat appointment, was nevertheless scandalously postponed to Mr. That;—whereupon are not the affairs of this nation in a bad way? How hungry Greek meets hungry Greek on the floor of St. Stephen's, and wrestles him and throttles him till he has to cry, Hold! the office is thine!—of this does Horace write.—One must say, the destinies of nations do not always rest entirely on Parliament. One must say, it is a wonderful affair that science of 'government,' as practised in the Eighteenth Century of the Christian era, and still struggling to practise itself. One must say, it was a lucky century that could get it so practised: a century which had inherited richly from its predecessors; and also which did, not unnaturally, bequeath to its successors a French Revolution, general overturn, and reign of terror;—intimating, in most audible thunder, conflagration, guillotinement, cannonading and universal war and earthquake, that such century with its practices had *ended.*

Ended;—for decidedly that course of procedure will no longer serve. Parliament will absolutely, with whatever effort, have to lift itself out of those deep ruts of donothing routine; and learn to say, on all sides, something more edifying than *Laissez-faire.* If Parliament cannot learn it, what is to become of Parliament? The toiling millions of England ask of their English Parliament foremost of all, Canst thou govern us or not? Parliament with its privileges is strong; but Necessity and the Laws of Nature are stronger than it. If Parliament cannot do this thing, Parliament we prophesy will do some other thing and things which, in the strangest and not the happiest way, will forward its being done,—not much to the advantage of Parliament probably! Done, one way or other, the thing must be. In these complicated times, with Cash Payment as the sole nexus between man and man, the toiling

Classes of mankind declare, in their confused but most emphatic way, to the Untoiling, that they will be governed; that they must,—under penalty of Chartisms, Thuggeries, Rick-burnings, and even blacker things than those. Vain also is it to think that the misery of one class, of the great universal under class, can be isolated, and kept apart and peculiar, down in that class. By infallible contagion, evident enough to reflection, evident even to Political Economy that will reflect, the misery of the lowest spreads upwards and upwards till it reaches the very highest; till all has grown miserable, palpably false and wrong; and poor drudges hungering 'on meal-husks and boiled grass' do, by circuitous but sure methods, bring kings' heads to the block!

Cash payment the sole nexus; and there are so many things which cash will not pay! Cash is a great miracle; yet it has not all power in Heaven, nor even on Earth. 'Supply and demand' we will honour also; and yet how many 'demands' are there, entirely indispensable, which have to go elsewhere than to the shops, and produce quite other than cash, before they can get their supply! On the whole, what astonishing payments does cash make in this world! Of your Samuel Johnson, furnished with 'fourpence-halfpenny a-day,' and solid lodging at nights on the paved streets, as his payment, we do not speak;—not in the way of complaint: it is a world-old business for the like of him, that same arrangement or a worse; perhaps the man, for his own uses, had need even of that, and of no better. Nay, is not Society, busy with its Talfourd Copyright Bill and the like, struggling to do something effectual for that man;—enacting with all industry that his own creation be accounted his own manufacture, and continue unstolen, on his own market-stand, for so long as sixty years? Perhaps Society is right there; for discrepancies on that side too may become excessive. All men are not patient docile Johnsons; some of them are half-mad inflammable Rousseaus. Such, in peculiar times, you may drive too far. Society in France, for example, was not destitute of cash: Society contrived to pay Philippe d'Orléans not yet Egalité three hundred thousand a-year and odd, for driving cabriolets through the streets of Paris and other work done; but in cash, encouragement, arrangement, recompense or recognition of any kind, it had nothing to give this same half-mad Rousseau for his work done; whose brain in consequence, *too* 'much enforced' for a weak brain, uttered hasty sparks, *Contrat Social* and the like, which proved not so quenchable again! In regard to that species of men too, who knows whether *Laissez-faire* itself (which is Serjeant Talfourd's Copyright Bill continued to eternity instead of sixty years) will not turn out insufficient, and have to cease, one day?—

Alas, in regard to so very many things, *Laissez-faire* ought partly to endeavour to cease! But in regard to poor Sans-potato peasants, Trades-Union craftsmen, Chartist cotton-spinners, the time has come when it must either cease or a worse thing straightway begin,—a thing of tinder-boxes, vitriol-bottles, secondhand pistols, a visibly insupportable thing in the eyes of all.

FROM

On Heroes, Hero-Worship and the Heroic in History

On Heroes, Hero-Worship and the Heroic in History, generally known as *Heroes and Hero-Worship*, was originally a series of six lectures delivered by Carlyle in May 1840. The audience included Lady Byron, Mrs. Gaskell, Edward FitzGerald and the actor Macready. 'The beautiful people listened with boundless tolerance,' Carlyle wrote to Emerson. 'I meant to tell them, among other things, that man was still alive, Nature not dead or like to die; that all true men continued true to this hour. . . . Not so much as Oliver Cromwell would I allow to have been a quack.' The lectures were printed in book form 'with emendations and additions' in 1841.

The lecture reproduced here is the last of the series, and was delivered on 22 May 1840.

FROM

On Heroes, Hero-Worship and the Heroic in History

LECTURE VI

THE HERO AS KING. CROMWELL, NAPOLEON: MODERN REVOLUTIONISM

We come now to the last form of Heroism; that which we call Kingship. The Commander over Men; he to whose will our wills are to be subordinated, and loyally surrender themselves, and find their welfare in doing so, may be reckoned the most important of Great Men. He is practically the summary for us of *all* the various figures of Heroism; Priest, Teacher, whatsoever of earthly or of spiritual dignity we can fancy to reside in a man, embodies itself here, to *command* over us, to furnish us with constant practical teaching, to tell us for the day and hour what we are to *do*. He is called *Rex*, Regulator, *Roi*: our own name is still better; King, *Könning*, which means *Can*-ning, Able-man.

Numerous considerations, pointing towards deep, questionable, and indeed unfathomable regions, present themselves here: on the most of which we must resolutely for the present forbear to speak at all. As Burke said that perhaps fair *Trial by Jury* was the soul of Government, and that all legislation, administration, parliamentary debating, and the rest of it, went on, in 'order to bring twelve impartial men into a jury-box';—so, by much stronger reason, may I say here, that the finding of your *Ableman* and getting him invested with the *symbols of ability*, with dignity, worship (*worth*-ship), royalty, kinghood, or whatever we call it, so that *he* may actually have room to guide according to his faculty of doing it,—is the business, well or ill accomplished, of all social procedure whatsoever in this world! Hustings-speeches, Parliamentary motions, Reform Bills, French Revolutions, all mean at heart this; or else nothing. Find in any country the Ablest Man that exists there; raise *him* to the supreme place, and loyally reverence him: you have a perfect government for that country; no ballot-box, parliamentary eloquence, voting, constitution-building, or other machinery whatsoever can improve it a whit. It is in the perfect state; an ideal country. The Ablest Man; he means also the truest-hearted, justest, the Noblest Man: what he *tells us to do* must be precisely the wisest, fittest, that we could anywhere or anyhow learn;—the thing which it will in all ways behove us, with right loyal thankfulness, and nothing doubting, to do! Our *doing* and life were then, so far as government could regulate it, well regulated; that were the ideal of constitutions.

Alas, we know very well that Ideals can never be completely embodied in practice. Ideals must ever lie a very great way off; and we will right thankfully content ourselves with any not intolerable approximation thereto! Let no man, as Schiller says, too querulously 'measure by a scale of perfection the meagre product of reality' in this poor world of ours. We will esteem him no wise man; we will esteem him a sickly, discontented, foolish man. And yet, on the other hand, it is never to be forgotten that Ideals do exist; that if they be not approximated to at all, the whole matter goes to wreck! Infallibly. No bricklayer builds a wall *perfectly* perpendicular, mathematically this is not possible; a certain degree of perpendicularity suffices him; and he, like a good bricklayer, who must have done with his job, leaves it so. And yet if he sway *too much* from the perpendicular; above all, if he throw plummet and level quite away from him, and pile brick on brick heedless, just as it comes to hand—! Such bricklayer, I think, is in a bad way. *He* has forgotten himself: but the Law of Gravitation does not forget to act on him; he and his wall rush-down into confused welter of ruin!—

This is the history of all rebellions, French Revolutions, social explosions in ancient or modern times. You have put the too *Un*able Man at the head of affairs! The too ignoble, unvaliant, fatuous man. You have forgotten that there is any rule, or natural necessity whatever, of putting the Able Man there. Brick must lie on brick as it may and can. Unable Simulacrum of Ability, *quack*, in a word, must adjust himself with quack, in all manner of administration of human things;—which accordingly lie unadministered, fermenting into unmeasured masses of failure, of indigent misery: in the outward, and in the inward or spiritual, miserable millions stretch-out the hand for their due supply, and it is not there. The 'law of gravitation' acts; Nature's laws do none of them forget to act. The miserable millions burst-forth into Sansculottism, or some other sort of madness: bricks and bricklayer lie as a fatal chaos!—

Much sorry stuff written some hundred years ago or more, about the 'Divine right of Kings,' moulders unread now in the Public Libraries of this country. Far be it from us to disturb the calm process by which it is disappearing harmlessly from the earth, in those repositories! At the same time, not to let the immense rubbish go without leaving us, as it ought, some soul of it behind—I will say that it did mean something; something true, which it is important for us and all men to keep in mind. To assert that in whatever man you chose to lay hold of (by this or the other plan of clutching at him); and clapt a round piece of metal on the head of, and called King,—there straightway came to reside a divine virtue, so that *he* became a kind of god, and a Divinity inspired him with faculty and right to rule over you to all lengths: this,—what can we do with this but leave it to rot silently in the Public Libraries? But I will say withal, and that is what these Divine-right men meant, That in Kings, and in all human Authorities, and relations that men god-created can form among each other, there is verily either a Divine Right or else a Diabolic Wrong; one or the other of these two! For it is false altogether, what the last Sceptical Century taught us, that this world is a steam-engine. There is a God in this world; and a God's-sanction, or else the violation of such, does look-out from all ruling and obedience, from all moral acts of men. There is no act more moral between men than that of rule and obedience. Woe to him that claims obedience when it is not due; woe to him that refuses it when it is! God's law is in that, I say, however the Parchment-laws may run: there is a Divine Right or else a Diabolic Wrong at the heart of every claim that one man makes upon another.

It can do none of us harm to reflect on this: in all the relations of life it will concern us; in Loyalty and Royalty, the highest of these. I esteem the modern error, That all goes by self-interest and the checking and balancing of greedy knaveries, and that, in short, there is nothing divine whatever in the association of men, a still more despicable error, natural as it is to an unbelieving century, than that of a 'divine right' in people *called* Kings. I say, Find me the true *Könning*, King, or Able-man, and he *has* a divine right over me. That we knew in some tolerable measure how to find him, and that all men were ready to acknowledge his divine right when found: this is precisely the healing which a sick world is everywhere, in these ages, seeking after! The true King, as guide of the practical, has ever something of the Pontiff in him,—guide of the spiritual, from which all practice has its rise. This too is a true saying, That the *King* is head of the *Church*.—But we will leave the Polemic stuff of a dead century to lie quiet on its book-shelves.

Certainly it is a fearful business, that of having your Able-man to *seek*, and not knowing in what manner to proceed about it! That is the world's sad predicament in these times of ours. They are times of revolution, and have long been. The bricklayer with his bricks, no longer heedful of plummet or the law of gravitation, have toppled, tumbled, and it all welters as we see! But the beginning of it was not the French Revolution;

that is rather the *end*, we can hope. It were truer to say, the *beginning* was three centuries further back: in the Reformation of Luther. That the thing which still called itself Christian Church had become a Falsehood, and brazenly went about pretending to pardon men's sins for metallic coined money, and to do much else which in the everlasting truth of Nature it did *not* now do: here lay the vital malady. The inward being wrong, all outward went ever more and more wrong. Belief died away; all was Doubt, Disbelief. The builder *cast away* his plummet; said to himself, 'What is gravitation? Brick lies on brick there!' Alas, does it not still sound strange to many of us, the assertion that there *is* a God's-truth in the business of god-created men; that all is not a kind of grimace, an 'expediency,' diplomacy, one knows not what!—

From that first necessary assertion of Luther's, 'You, self-styled *Papa*, you are no Father in God at all; you are—a Chimera, whom I know not how to name in polite language!' —from that onwards to the shout which rose round Camille Desmoulins in the Palais-Royal, '*Aux armes!*' when the people had burst-up against *all* manner of Chimeras,—I find a natural historical sequence. That shout too, so frightful, half-infernal, was a great matter. Once more the voice of awakened nations; —starting confusedly, as out of nightmare, as out of death-sleep, into some dim feeling that Life was real; that God's-world was not an expediency and diplomacy! Infernal;—yes, since they would not have it otherwise. Infernal, since not celestial or terrestrial! Hollowness, insincerity *has* to cease; sincerity of some sort has to begin. Cost what it may, reigns of terror, horrors of French Revolution or what else, we have to return to truth. Here is a Truth, as I said: a Truth clad in hell-fire, since they would not but have it so!—

A common theory among considerable parties of men in England and elsewhere used to be, that the French Nation had, in those days, as it were gone *mad*; that the French Revolution was a general act of insanity, a temporary conversion of France and large sections of the world into a kind of Bedlam. The Event had risen and raged; but was a madness and nonentity,—gone now happily into the region of Dreams and the Picturesque!—To such comfortable philosophers, the Three Days of July 1830 must have been a surprising phenomenon. Here is the French Nation risen again, in musketry and death-struggle, out shooting and being shot, to make that same mad French Revolution good! The sons and grandsons of those men, it would seem, persist in the enterprise: they do not disown it; they will have it made good; will have themselves shot, if it be not made good! To philosophers who had made-up their life-system on that 'madness' quietus, no phenomenon could be more alarming. Poor Niebuhr, they say, the Prussian Professor and Historian, fell broken-hearted in consequence; sickened, if we can believe it, and died of the Three Days! It was surely not a very heroic death;—little better than Racine's, dying because Louis Fourteenth looked sternly on him once. The world had stood some considerable shocks, in its time; might have been expected to survive the Three Days too, and be found turning on its axis after even them! The Three Days told all mortals that the old French Revolution, mad as it might look, was not a transitory ebullition of Bedlam, but a genuine product of this Earth where we all live; that it was verily a Fact, and that the world in general would do well everywhere to regard it as such.

Truly, without the French Revolution, one would not know what to make of an age like this at all. We will hail the French Revolution, as shipwrecked mariners might the sternest rock, in a world otherwise all of baseless sea and waves. A true Apocalypse, though a terrible one, to this false withered artificial time; testifying once more that Nature is *preter*-natural; if not divine, then diabolic; that Semblance is not Reality; that it has to become Reality, or the world will take-fire under it,—burn *it* into what it is, namely Nothing! Plausibility has ended; empty Routine has ended; much has ended. This, as with a Trump of Doom, has been proclaimed to all men. They are the wisest who will learn it soonest. Long confused generations before it be learned; peace impossible till it be! The earnest man, surrounded, as ever, with a world of inconsistencies, can wait patiently, patiently strive to do *his* work, in the midst of that. Sentence of Death is written down in Heaven against all that; sentence of Death is now proclaimed on the Earth against it; this he with his eyes may see. And surely, I should say, considering the other side of the matter, what enormous difficulties lie there, and how fast, fearfully fast, in all countries, the inexorable demand for solution of them is pressing on,—he may easily find other work to do than labouring in the Sansculottic province at this time of day!

To me, in these circumstances, that of 'Hero-worship' becomes a fact inexpressibly precious; the most solacing fact one sees in the world at present. There is an everlasting hope in it for the management of the world. Had all traditions, arrangements, creeds, societies that men ever instituted, sunk away, this would remain. The certainty of Heroes being sent us; our faculty, our necessity, to reverence Heroes when sent: it shines like a polestar through smoke-clouds, dust-clouds, and all manner of down-rushing and conflagration.

Hero-worship would have sounded very strange to those workers and fighters in the French Revolution. Not reverence for Great Men; not any hope or belief, or even wish, that Great Men could again appear in the world! Nature, turned into a 'Machine,' was as if effete now; could not any longer produce Great Men:—I can tell her, she may give-up the trade altogether, then; we cannot do without Great Men!— But neither have I any quarrel with that of 'Liberty and Equality'; with the faith that, wise great men being impossible, a level immensity of foolish small men would suffice. It was a natural faith then and there. 'Liberty and Equality; no Authority needed any longer. Hero-worship, reverence for *such* Authorities, has proved false, is itself a falsehood; no more of it! We have had such *forgeries*, we will now trust nothing. So many base plated coins passing in the market, the belief has now become common that no gold any longer exists,—and even that we can do very well without gold!' I find this, among other things, in that universal cry of Liberty and Equality; and find it very natural, as matters then stood.

And yet surely it is but the *transition* from false to true. Considered as the whole truth, it is false altogether;—the product of entire sceptical blindness, as yet only *struggling* to see. Hero-worship exists for ever, and everywhere: not Loyalty alone; it extends from divine adoration down to the lowest practical regions of life. 'Bending before men,' if it is not to be a mere empty grimace, better dispensed with than practised, is Hero-worship,—a recognition that there does dwell in that presence of our brother something divine; that every created man, as Novalis said, is a 'revelation in the Flesh.' They were Poets too, that devised all those graceful courtesies which make life noble! Courtesy is not a falsehood or grimace; it need not be such. And Loyalty, religious Worship itself, are still possible; nay still inevitable.

May we not say, moreover, while so many of our late Heroes have worked rather as revolutionary men, that nevertheless every Great Man, every genuine man, is by the nature of him a son of Order, not of Disorder? It is a tragical position for a true man to work in revolutions. He seems an anarchist; and indeed a painful element of anarchy does encumber him at every step,—him to whose whole soul anarchy is hostile, hateful. His mission is Order; every man's is. He is here to make what was disorderly, chaotic, into a thing ruled, regular. He is the missionary of Order. Is not all work of man in this world a *making of Order*? The carpenter finds rough trees; shapes them, constrains them into square fitness, into purpose and use. We are all born enemies of Disorder: it is tragical for us all to be concerned in image-breaking and down-pulling; for the Great Man, *more* a man than we, it is doubly tragical.

Thus too all human things, maddest French Sansculottisms, do and must work towards Order. I say, there is not a *man* in them, raging in the thickest of the madness, but is impelled withal, at all moments, towards Order. His very life means that; Disorder is dissolution, death. No chaos but it seeks a *centre* to revolve round. While man is man, some Cromwell or Napoleon is the necessary finish of a Sansculottism.—Curious:

in those days when Hero-worship was the most incredible thing to every one, how it does come-out nevertheless, and assert itself practically, in a way which all have to credit. Divine *right*, take it on the great scale, is found to mean divine *might* withal! While old false Formulas are getting trampled everywhere into destruction, new genuine Substances unexpectedly unfold themselves indestructible. In rebellious ages, when Kingship itself seems dead and abolished, Cromwell, Napoleon step-forth again as Kings. The history of these men is what we have now to look at, as our last phasis of Heroism. The old ages are brought back to us; the manner in which Kings were made, and Kingship itself first took rise, is again exhibited in the history of these Two.

We have had many civil-wars in England; wars of Red and White Roses, wars of Simon de Montfort; wars enough, which are not very memorable. But that war of the Puritans has a significance which belongs to no one of the others. Trusting to your candour, which will suggest on the other side what I have not room to say, I will call it a section once more of that great universal war which alone makes-up the true History of the World,—the war of Belief against Unbelief! The struggle of men intent on the real essence of things, against men intent on the semblances and forms of things. The Puritans, to many, seem mere savage Iconoclasts, fierce destroyers of Forms; but it were more just to call them haters of *untrue* Forms. I hope we know how to respect Laud and his King as well as them. Poor Laud seems to me to have been weak and ill-starred, not dishonest; an unfortunate Pedant rather than anything worse. His 'Dreams' and superstitions, at which they laugh so, have an affectionate, lovable kind of character. He is like a College-Tutor, whose whole world is forms, College-rules; whose notion is that these are the life and safety of the world. He is placed suddenly, with that unalterable luckless notion of his, at the head not of a College but of a Nation, to regulate the most complex deep-reaching interests of men. He thinks they ought to go by the old decent regulations; nay that their salvation will lie in extending and improving these. Like a weak man, he drives with spasmodic vehemence towards his purpose; cramps himself to it, heeding no voice of prudence, no cry of pity: He will have his College-rules obeyed by his Collegians; that first; and till that, nothing. He is an ill-starred Pedant, as I said. He would have it the world was a College of that kind, and the world *was not* that. Alas, was not his doom stern enough? Whatever wrongs he did, were they not all frightfully avenged on him?

It is meritorious to insist on forms; Religion and all else naturally clothes itself in forms. Everywhere the *formed* world is the only habitable one. The naked formlessness of Puritanism is not the thing I praise in the Puritans; it is the thing I pity,—praising only the spirit which had rendered that inevitable! All substances clothe themselves in forms: but there are suitable true forms, and then there are untrue, unsuitable. As the briefest definition, one might say, Forms which *grow* round a substance, if we rightly understand that, will correspond to the real nature and purport of it, will be true, good; forms which are consciously *put* round a substance, bad. I invite you to reflect on this. It distinguishes true from false in Ceremonial Form, earnest solemnity from empty pageant, in all human things.

There must be a veracity, a natural spontaneity in forms. In the commonest meeting of men, a person making, what we call, 'set speeches,' is not he an offence? In the mere drawing-room, whatsoever courtesies you see to be grimaces, prompted by no spontaneous reality within, are a thing you wish to get away from. But suppose now it were some matter of vital concernment, some transcendent matter (as Divine Worship is), about which your whole soul, struck dumb with its excess of feeling, knew not how to *form* itself into utterance at all, and preferred formless silence to any utterance there possible,—what should we say of a man coming forward to represent or utter it for you in the way of upholsterer-mummery? Such a man,—let him depart swiftly, if he love himself! You have lost your only son; are mute, struck down, without even tears: an importunate man importunately offers to celebrate Funeral Games for him in the manner of the Greeks! Such mummery is not only not to be accepted,—it is hateful, unendurable. It is what the old Prophets called 'Idolatry,' worshipping of hollow *shows*; what all earnest men do and will reject. We can partly understand what those poor Puritans meant. Laud dedicating that St. Catherine Creed's Church, in the manner we have it described; with his multiplied ceremonial bowings, gesticulations, exclamations: surely it is rather the rigorous formal *Pedant*, intent on his 'College-rules,' than the earnest Prophet, intent on the essence of the matter!

Puritanism found *such* forms insupportable; trampled on such forms;—we have to excuse it for saying, No form at all rather than such! It stood preaching in its bare pulpit, with nothing but the Bible in its hand. Nay, a man preaching from his earnest *soul* into the earnest *souls* of men: is not this virtually the essence of all Churches whatsoever? The nakedest, savagest reality, I say, is preferable to any semblance, however dignified. Besides, it will clothe itself with *due* semblance by and by, if it be real. No fear of that; actually no fear at all. Given the living *man*, there will be found *clothes* for him; he will find himself clothes. But the suit-of-clothes pretending that *it* is both clothes and man—!—We cannot 'fight the French' by three-hundred-thousand red uniforms; there must be *men* in the inside of them! Semblance, I assert, must actually *not* divorce itself from Reality. If Semblance do,—why then there must be men found to rebel against Semblance, for it has become a lie! These two Antagonisms at war here, in the case of Laud and the Puritans, are as old nearly as the world. They went to fierce battle over England in that age; and fought-out their confused controversy to a certain length, with many results for all of us.

In the age which directly followed that of the Puritans, their cause or themselves were little likely to have justice done them. Charles Second and his Rochesters were not the kind of men you would set to judge what the worth or meaning of such men might have been. That there could be any faith or truth in the life of a man, was what these poor Rochesters, and the age they ushered-in, had forgotten. Puritanism was hung on gibbets,—like the bones of the leading Puritans. Its work nevertheless went on accomplishing itself. All true work of a man, hang the author of it on what gibbet you like, must and will accomplish itself. We have our *Habeas-Corpus*, our free Representation of the People; acknowledgment, wide as the world, that all men are, or else must, shall, and will become, what we call *free* men;—men with their life grounded on reality and justice, not on tradition, which has become unjust and a chimera! This in part, and much besides this, was the work of the Puritans.

And indeed, as these things became gradually manifest, the character of the Puritans began to clear itself. Their memories were, one after another, taken *down* from the gibbet; nay a certain portion of them are now, in these days, as good as canonised. Eliot, Hampden, Pym, nay Ludlow, Hutchinson, Vane himself, are admitted to be a kind of Heroes; political Conscript Fathers, to whom in no small degree we owe what makes us a free England: it would not be safe for anybody to designate these men as wicked now. Few Puritans of note but find their apologists somewhere, and have a certain reverence paid them by earnest men. One Puritan, I think, and almost he alone, our poor Cromwell, seems to hang yet on the gibbet, and find no hearty apologist anywhere. Him neither saint nor sinner will acquit of great wickedness. A man of ability, infinite talent, courage, and so forth: but he betrayed the Cause. Selfish ambition, dishonesty, duplicity; a fierce, coarse, hypocritical *Tartufe*; turning all that noble Struggle for constitutional Liberty into a sorry farce played for his own benefit: this and worse is the character they give of Cromwell. And then there come contrasts with Washington and others; above all, with these noble Pyms and Hampdens, whose noble work he stole for himself, and ruined into a futility and deformity.

This view of Cromwell seems to me the not unnatural product of a century like the Eighteenth. As we said of the Valet, so of the Sceptic: He does not know a Hero when he sees him!

The Valet expected purple mantles, gilt sceptres, body-guards and flourishes of trumpets: the Sceptic of the Eighteenth century looks for regulated respectable Formulas, 'Principles,' or what else he may call them; a style of speech and conduct which has got to seem 'respectable,' which can plead for itself in a handsome articulate manner, and gain the suffrages of an enlightened sceptical Eighteenth century! It is, at bottom, the same thing that both the Valet and he expect: the garnitures of some *acknowledged* royalty, which *then* they will acknowledge! The King coming to them in the rugged *un*formulistic state shall be no King.

For my own share, far be it from me to say or insinuate a word of disparagement against such characters as Hampden, Eliot, Pym; whom I believe to have been right worthy and useful men. I have read diligently what books and documents about them I could come at;—with the honestest wish to admire, to love and worship them like Heroes; but I am sorrry to say, if the real truth must be told, with very indifferent success! At bottom, I found that it would not do. They are very noble men, these; step along in their stately way, with their measured euphemisms, philosophies, parliamentary eloquences, Ship-moneys, *Monarchies of Man*; a most constitutional, unblamable, dignified set of men. But the heart remains cold before them; the fancy alone endeavours to get-up some worship of them. What man's heart does, in reality, break-forth into any fire of brotherly love for these men? They are become dreadfully dull men! One breaks-down often enough in the constitutional eloquence of the admirable Pym, with his 'seventhly and lastly.' You find that it may be the admirablest thing in the world, but that it is heavy,—heavy as lead, barren as brick-clay; that, in a word, for you there is little or nothing now surviving there! One leaves all these Nobilities standing in their niches of honour: the rugged outcast Cromwell, he is the man of them all in whom one still finds human stuff. The great savage *Baresark*: he could write no euphemistic *Monarchy of Man*; did not speak, did not work with glib regularity; had no straight story to tell for himself anywhere. But he stood bare, not cased in euphemistic coat-of-mail; he grappled like a giant, face to face, heart to heart, with the naked truth of things! That, after all, is the sort of man for one. I plead guilty to valuing such a man beyond all other sorts of men. Smooth-shaven Respectabilities not a few one finds, that are not good for much. Small thanks to a man for keeping his hands clean, who would not touch the work but with gloves on!

Neither, on the whole, does this constitutional tolerance of the Eighteenth century for the other happier Puritans seem to be a very great matter. One might say, it is but a piece of Formulism and Scepticism, like the rest. They tell us, It was a sorrowful thing to consider that the foundation of our English Liberties should have been laid by 'Superstition.' These Puritans came forward with Calvinistic incredible Creeds, Anti-Laudisms, Westminster Confessions; demanding, chiefly of all, that they should have liberty to *worship* in their own way. Liberty to *tax* themselves: that was the thing they should have demanded! It was Superstition, Fanaticism, disgraceful ignorance of Constitutional Philosophy to insist on the other thing!—Liberty to *tax* oneself? Not to pay-out money from your pocket except on reason shown? No century, I think, but a rather barren one would have fixed on that as the first right of man! I should say, on the contrary, A just man will generally have better cause than *money* in what shape soever, before deciding to revolt against his Government. Ours is a most confused world; in which a good man will be thankful to see any kind of Government maintain itself in a not insupportable manner: and here in England, to this hour, if he is not ready to pay a great many taxes which *he* can see very small reason in, it will not go well with him, I think! He must try some other climate than this. Taxgatherer? Money? He will say: 'Take my money, since you *can*, and it is so desirable to you; take it,—and take yourself away with it; and leave me alone to my work here. *I* am still here; can still work, after all the money you have taken from me!' But if they come to him, and say, 'Acknowledge a Lie; pretend to say you are worshipping God, when you are not doing it: believe not the thing that *you* find true, but the thing that I find, or pretend to find true!' He will answer: 'No; by God's help, no! You may take my purse; but I cannot have my moral Self annihilated. The purse is any Highwayman's who might meet me with a loaded pistol: but the Self is mine and God my Maker's; it is not yours; and I will resist you to the death, and revolt against you, and, on the whole, front all manner of extremities, accusations and confusions, in defence of that!'—

Really, it seems to me the one reason which could justify revolting, this of the Puritans. It has been the soul of all just revolts among men. Not *Hunger* alone produced even the French Revolution; no, but the feeling of the insupportable all-pervading *Falsehood* which had now embodied itself in Hunger, in universal material Scarcity and Nonentity, and thereby become *indisputably* false in the eyes of all! We will leave the Eighteenth century with its 'liberty to tax itself.' We will not astonish ourselves that the meaning of such men as the Puritans remained dim to it. To men who believe in no reality at all, how shall a *real* human soul, the intensest of all realities, as it were the voice of this world's Maker still speaking to *us*,—be intelligible? What it cannot reduce into constitutional doctrines relative to 'taxing,' or other the like material interest, gross, palpable to the sense, such a century will needs reject as an amorphous heap of rubbish. Hampdens, Pyms, and Ship-money will be the theme of much constitutional eloquence, striving to be fervid;—which will glitter, if not as fire does, then as *ice* does: and the irreducible Cromwell will remain a chaotic mass of 'madness,' 'hypocrisy,' and much else.

From of old, I will confess, this theory of Cromwell's falsity has been incredible to me. Nay I cannot believe the like, of any Great Man whatever. Multitudes of Great Men figure in History as false selfish men; but if we will consider it, they are but *figures* for us, unintelligible shadows; we do not see into them as men that could have existed at all. A superficial unbelieving generation only, with no eye but for the surfaces and semblances of things, could form such notions of Great Men. Can a great soul be possible without a *conscience* in it, the essence of all *real* souls, great or small?—No, we cannot figure Cromwell as a Falsity and Fatuity; the longer I study him and his career, I believe this the less. Why should we? There is no evidence of it. Is it not strange that, after all the mountains of calumny this man has been subject to, after being represented as the very prince of liars, who never, or hardly ever, spoke truth, but always some cunning counterfeit of truth, there should not yet have been one falsehood brought clearly home to him? A prince of liars, and no lie spoken by him. Not one that I could yet get sight of. It is like Pococke asking Grotius, Where is your *proof* of Mahomet's Pigeon? No proof!—Let us leave all these calumnious chimeras, as chimeras ought to be left. They are not portraits of the man; they are distracted phantasms of him, the joint product of hatred and darkness.

Looking at the man's life with our own eyes, it seems to me, a very different hypothesis suggests itself. What little we know of his earlier obscure years, distorted as it has come down to us, does it not all betoken an earnest, affectionate, sincere kind of man? His nervous melancholic temperament indicates rather a seriousness *too* deep for him. Of those stories of 'Spectres'; of the white Spectre in broad daylight, predicting that he should be King of England, we are not bound to believe much;—probably no more than of the other black Spectre, or Devil in person, to whom the Officer *saw* him sell himself before Worcester Fight! But the mournful, over-sensitive, hypochondriac humour of Oliver, in his young years, is otherwise indisputably known. The Huntingdon Physician told Sir Philip Warwick himself, He had often been sent for at midnight; Mr. Cromwell was full of hypochondria, thought himself near dying, and 'had fancies about the Town-cross.' These things are significant. Such an excitable deep-feeling nature, in that rugged stubborn strength of his, is not the symptom of falsehood; it is the symptom and promise of quite other than falsehood!

The young Oliver is sent to study Law; falls, or is said to have fallen, for a little period, into some of the dissipations of youth; but if so, speedily repents, abandons all this: not much above twenty, he is married, settled as an altogether grave and quiet man. 'He pays-back what money he had won at gambling,' says the story;—he does not think any gain of that kind could be really *his*. It is very interesting, very natural, this 'conversion,' as they well name it; this awakening of a great true soul from the worldly slough, to see into the awful *truth* of things;—to see that Time and its shows all rested on Eternity, and this poor Earth of ours was the threshold either of Heaven or of Hell! Oliver's life at St. Ives and Ely, as a sober industrious Farmer, is it not altogether as that of a true and devout man? He has renounced the world and its ways; *its* prizes are not the thing that can enrich him. He tills the earth; he reads his Bible; daily assembles his servants round him to worship God. He comforts persecuted ministers, is fond of preachers; nay can himself preach,—exhorts his neighbours to be wise, to redeem the time. In all this what 'hypocrisy,' 'ambition,' 'cant,' or other falsity? The man's hopes, I do believe, were fixed on the other Higher World; his aim to get well *thither*, by walking well through his humble course in *this* world. He courts no notice: what could notice here do for him? 'Ever in his great Taskmaster's eye.'

It is striking, too, how he comes-out once into public view; he, since no other is willing to come: in resistance to a public grievance. I mean, in that matter of the Bedford Fens. No one else will go to law with Authority; therefore he will. That matter once settled, he returns back into obscurity, to his Bible and his Plough. 'Gain influence?' His influence is the most legitimate; derived from personal knowledge of him, as a just, religious, reasonable, and determined man. In this way he has lived till past forty; old age is now in view of him, and the earnest portal of Death and Eternity; it was at this point that he suddenly became 'ambitious'! I do not interpret his Parliamentary mission in that way!

His successes in Parliament, his successes through the war,

are honest successes of a brave man; who has more resolution in the heart of him, more light in the head of him than other men. His prayers to God; his spoken thanks to the God of Victory, who had preserved him safe, and carried him forward so far, through the furious clash of a world all set in conflict, through desperate-looking envelopments at Dunbar; through the death-hail of so many battles; mercy after mercy; to the 'crowning mercy' of Worcester Fight: all this is good and genuine for a deep-hearted Calvinistic Cromwell. Only to vain unbelieving Cavaliers, worshipping not God but their own 'lovelocks,' frivolities, and formalities, living quite apart from contemplations of God, living *without* God in the world, need it seem hypocritical.

Nor will his participation in the King's death involve him in condemnation with us. It is a stern business killing of a King! But if you once go to war with him, it lies *there*; this and all else lies there. Once at war, you have made wager of battle with him: it is he to die, or else you. Reconciliation is problematic; may be possible, or, far more likely, is impossible. It is now pretty generally admitted that the Parliament, having vanquished Charles First, had no way of making any tenable arrangement with him. The large Presbyterian party, apprehensive now of the Independents, were most anxious to do so; anxious indeed as for their own existence; but it could not be. The unhappy Charles, in those final Hampton-Court negotiations, shows himself as a man fatally incapable of being dealt with. A man who, once for all, could not and would not *understand*:—whose thought did not in any measure represent to him the real fact of the matter; nay worse, whose *word* did not at all represent his thought. We may say this of him without cruelty, with deep pity rather: but it is true and undeniable. Forsaken there of all but the *name* of Kingship, he still, finding himself treated with outward respect as a King, fancied that he might play-off party against party, and smuggle himself into his old power by deceiving both. Alas, they both *discovered* that he was deceiving them. A man whose *word* will not inform you at all what he means or will do, is not a man you can bargain with. You must get out of that man's way, or put him out of yours! The Presbyterians, in their despair, were still for believing Charles, though found false, unbelievable again and again. Not so Cromwell: 'For all our fighting,' says he, 'we are to have a little bit of paper?' No!—

In fact, everywhere we have to note the decisive practical *eye* of this man; how he drives towards the practical and practicable; has a genuine insight into what *is* fact. Such an intellect, I maintain, does not belong to a false man: the false man sees false shows, plausibilities, expediencies: the true man is needed to discern even practical truth. Cromwell's advice about the Parliament's Army, early in the contest, How they were to dismiss their city-tapsters, flimsy riotous persons, and choose substantial yeomen, whose heart was in the work, to be soldiers for them: this is advice by a man who *saw*. Fact answers, if you see into Fact! Cromwell's *Ironsides* were the embodiment of this insight of his; men fearing God; and without any other fear. No more conclusively genuine set of fighters ever trod the soil of England, or of any other land.

Neither will we blame greatly that word of Cromwell's to them; which was so blamed: 'If the King should meet me in battle, I would kill the King.' Why not? These words were spoken to men who stood as before a Higher than Kings. They had set more than their own lives on the cast. The Parliament may call it, in official language, a fighting '*for* the King'; but we, for our share, cannot understand that. To us it is no dilettante work, no sleek officiality; it is sheer rough death and earnest. They have brought it to the calling-forth of *War*; horrid internecine fight, man grappling with man in fire-eyed rage,—the *infernal* element in man called forth, to try it by that! *Do* that therefore; since that is the thing to be done.—The successes of Cromwell seem to me a very natural thing! Since he was not shot in battle, they were an inevitable thing. That such a man, with the eye to see, with the heart to dare, should advance, from post to post, from victory to victory, till the Huntingdon Farmer became, by whatever name you might call him, the acknowledged Strongest Man in England, virtually the King of England, requires no magic to explain it!—

Truly it is a sad thing for a people, as for a man, to fall into Scepticism, into dilettantism, insincerity; not to know a Sincerity when they see it. For this world, and for all worlds, what curse is so fatal? The heart lying dead, the eye cannot see. What intellect remains is merely the *vulpine* intellect. That a true *King* be sent them is of small use; they do not know him when sent. They say scornfully, Is this your King? The Hero wastes his heroic faculty in bootless contradiction from the unworthy; and can accomplish little. For himself he does accomplish a heroic life, which is much, which is all; but for the world he accomplishes comparatively nothing. The wild rude Sincerity, direct from Nature, is not glib in answering from the witness-box: in your small-debt *pie-powder* court, he is scouted as a counterfeit. The vulpine intellect 'detects' him. For being a man worth any thousand men, the response your Knox, your Cromwell gets, is an argument for two centuries whether he was a man at all. God's greatest gift to this Earth is sneeringly flung away. The miraculous talisman is a paltry plated coin, not fit to pass in the shops as a common guinea.

Lamentable this! I say, this must be remedied. Till this be remedied in some measure, there is nothing remedied. 'Detect quacks?' Yes do, for Heaven's sake; but know withal the men that are to be trusted! Till we know that, what is all our knowledge; how shall we even so much as 'detect'? For the vulpine sharpness, which considers itself to be knowledge, and 'detects' in that fashion, is far mistaken. Dupes indeed are many: but, of all *dupes*, there is none so fatally situated as he who lives in undue terror of being duped. The world does exist; the world has truth in it, or it would not exist! First recognise what is true, we shall *then* discern what is false; and properly never till then.

'Know the men that are to be trusted': alas, this is yet, in these days, very far from us. The sincere alone can recognise sincerity. Not a Hero only is needed, but a world fit for him; a world not of *Valets*;—the Hero comes almost in vain to it otherwise! Yes, it is far from us: but it must come; thank God, it is visibly coming. Till it do come, what have we? Ballot-boxes, suffrages, French Revolutions:—if we are as Valets, and do not know the Hero when we see him, what good are all these? A heroic Cromwell comes; and for a hundred-and-fifty years he cannot have a vote from us. Why, the insincere, unbelieving world is the *natural property* of the Quack, and of the Father of quacks and quackeries! Misery, confusion, unveracity are alone possible there. By ballot-boxes we alter the *figure* of our Quack; but the substance of him continues. The Valet-World *has* to be governed by the Sham-Hero, by the King merely *dressed* in King-gear. It is his; he is its! In brief, one of two things: We shall either learn to know a Hero, a true Governor and Captain, somewhat better, when we see him; or else go on to be for ever governed by the Unheroic;—had we ballot-boxes clattering at every street-corner, there were no remedy in these.

Poor Cromwell,—great Cromwell! The inarticulate Prophet; Prophet who could not *speak*. Rude, confused, struggling to utter himself, with his savage depth, with his wild sincerity; and he looked so strange, among the elegant Euphemisms, dainty little Falklands, didactic Chillingworths, diplomatic Clarendons! Consider him. An outer hull of chaotic confusion, visions of the Devil, nervous dreams, almost semi-madness; and yet such a clear determinate man's-energy working in the heart of that. A kind of chaotic man. The ray as of pure star-light and fire, working in such an element of boundless hypochondria, *un*formed black of darkness! And yet withal this hypochondria, what was it but the very greatness of the man? The depth and tenderness of his wild affections: the quantity of *sympathy* he had with things,—the quantity of insight he would yet get into the heart of things, the mastery he would yet get over things: this was his hypochondria. The man's misery, as man's misery always does, came of his greatness. Samuel Johnson too is that kind of man. Sorrow-stricken, half-distracted; the wild element of mournful *black* enveloping him,—wide as the world. It is the character of a prophetic man; a man with his whole soul *seeing*, and struggling to see.

On this ground, too, I explain to myself Cromwell's reputed confusion of speech. To himself the internal meaning was sun-clear; but the material with which he was to clothe it in utterance was not there. He had *lived* silent; a great unnamed sea of Thought round him all his days; and in his way of life little call to attempt *naming* or uttering that. With his sharp power of vision, resolute power of action, I doubt not he could have learned to write Books withal, and speak fluently enough;—he did harder things than writing of Books. This kind of man is precisely he who is fit for doing manfully all things you will set him on doing. Intellect is not speaking and logicising; it is seeing and ascertaining. Virtue, *Vir-tus*, manhood, *hero*-hood, is not fair-spoken immaculate regularity; it is first of all, what the Germans well name it, *Tugend* (*Taugend*, *dow*-ing or *Dough*-tiness), Courage and the Faculty to *do*. This basis of the matter Cromwell had in him.

One understands moreover how, though he could not speak in Parliament, he might *preach*, rhapsodic preaching; above all, how he might be great in extempore prayer. These are the free outpouring utterances of what is in the heart: method is not required in them; warmth, depth, sincerity are all that is required. Cromwell's habit of prayer is a notable feature of him. All his great enterprises were commenced with prayer. In dark inextricable-looking difficulties, his Officers and he used to assemble, and pray alternately, for hours, for days, till some definite resolution rose among them, some 'door of hope,' as they would name it, disclosed itself. Consider that. In tears, in fervent prayers, and cries to the great God, to have pity on them, to make His light shine before them. They, armed Soldiers of Christ, as they felt themselves to be; a little band of Christian Brothers, who had drawn the sword against a great black devouring world not Christian, but Mammonish, Devilish,—they cried to God in their straits, in their extreme need, not to forsake the Cause that was His. The light which now rose upon them,—how could a human soul, by any means at all, get better light? Was not the purpose so formed like to be precisely the best, wisest, the one to be followed without hesitation any more? To them it was as the shining of Heaven's own Splendour in the waste-howling darkness; the Pillar of Fire by night, that was to guide them on their desolate perilous way. *Was* it not such? Can a man's soul to this hour, get guidance by any other method than intrinsically by that same,—devout prostration of the earnest struggling soul before the Highest, the Giver of all Light; be such *prayer* a spoken, articulate, or be it a voiceless, inarticulate one? There is no other method. 'Hypocrisy?' One begins to be weary of all that. They who call it so, have no right to speak on such matters. They never formed a purpose, what one can call a purpose. They went about balancing expediencies, plausibilities; gathering votes, advices; they never were alone with the *truth* of a thing at all.—Cromwell's prayers were likely to be 'eloquent,' and much more than that. His was the heart of a man who *could* pray.

But indeed his actual Speeches, I apprehend, were not nearly so ineloquent, incondite, as they look. We find he was, what all speakers aim to be, an impressive speaker, even in Parliament; one who, from the first, had weight. With that rude passionate voice of his, he was always understood to *mean* something, and men wished to know what. He disregarded eloquence, nay despised and disliked it; spoke always without premeditation of the words he was to use. The Reporters, too, in those days seem to have been singularly candid; and to have given the Printer precisely what they found on their own note-paper. And withal, what a strange proof is it of Cromwell's being the premeditative ever-calculating hypocrite, acting a play before the world, That to the last he took no more charge of his Speeches! How came he not to study his words a little, before flinging them out to the public? If the words were true words, they could be left to shift for themselves.

But with regard to Cromwell's 'lying,' we will make one remark. This, I suppose, or something like this, to have been the nature of it. All parties found themselves deceived in him; each party understood him to be meaning *this*, heard him even say so, and behold he turns-out to have been meaning *that*! He was, cry they, the chief of liars. But now, intrinsically, is not all this the inevitable fortune, not of a false man in such times, but simply of a superior man? Such a man must have *reticences* in him. If he walk wearing his heart upon his sleeve for daws to peck at, his journey will not extend far! There is no use for any man's taking-up his abode in a house built of glass. A man always is to be himself the judge how much of his mind he will show to other men; even to those he would have work along with him. There are impertinent inquiries made: your rule is, to leave the inquirer *un*informed on that matter; not, if you can help it, *mis*informed, but precisely as dark as he was! This, could one hit the right phrase of response, is what the wise and faithful man would aim to answer in such a case.

Cromwell, no doubt of it, spoke often in the dialect of small subaltern parties; uttered to them a *part* of his mind. Each little party thought him all its own. Hence their rage, one and all, to find him not of their party, but of his own party! Was it his blame? At all seasons of his history he must have felt, among such people, how, if he explained to them the deeper insight he had, they must either have shuddered aghast at it, or believing it, their own little compact hypothesis must have gone wholly to wreck. They could not now have worked in his province any more; nay perhaps they could not now have worked in their own province. It is the inevitable position of a great man among small men. Small men, most active, useful, are to be seen everywhere, whose whole activity depends on some conviction which to you is palpably a limited one; imperfect, what we call an *error*. But would it be a kindness always, is it a duty always or often, to disturb them in that? Many a man, doing loud work in the world, stands only on some thin traditionality, conventionality; to him indubitable, to you incredible: break that beneath him, he sinks to endless depths! 'I might have my hand full of truth,' said Fontenelle, 'and open only my little finger.'

And if this be the fact even in matters of doctrine, how much more in all departments of practice! He that cannot withal *keep his mind to himself* cannot practise any considerable thing whatever. And we call it 'dissimulation,' all this? What would you think of calling the general of an army a dissembler because he did not tell every corporal and private soldier, who pleased to put the question, what his thoughts were about everything?—Cromwell, I should rather say, managed all this in a manner we must admire for its perfection. An endless vortex of such questioning 'corporals' rolled confusedly round him through his whole course; whom he did answer. It must have been as a great true-seeing man that he managed this too. Not one proved falsehood, as I said; not one! Of what man that ever wound himself through such a coil of things will you say so much?—

But in fact there are two errors, widely prevalent, which pervert to the very basis our judgments formed about such men as Cromwell; about their 'ambition,' 'falsity,' and suchlike. The first is what I might call substituting the *goal* of their career for the course and starting-point of it. The vulgar Historian of a Cromwell fancies that he had determined on being Protector of England, at the time when he was ploughing the marsh lands of Cambridgeshire. His career lay all mapped-out: a program of the whole drama; which he then step by step dramatically unfolded, with all manner of cunning, deceptive dramaturgy, as he went on,—the hollow, scheming Ὑποκριτής, or Play-actor, that he was! This is a radical perversion; all but universal in such cases. And think for an instant how different the fact is! How much does one of *us* foresee of his own life? Short way ahead of us it is all dim; an *un*wound skein of possibilities, of apprehensions, attemptabilities, vague-looming hopes. This Cromwell had *not* his life lying all in that fashion of Program, which he needed then, with that unfathomable cunning of his, only to enact dramatically, scene after scene! Not so. We see it so; but to him it was in no measure so. What absurdities would fall-away of themselves, were this one undeniable fact kept honestly in view by History! Historians indeed will tell you that they do keep it in view;—but look whether such is practically the fact! Vulgar History, as in this Cromwell's case, omits it altogether; even the best kinds of History only remember it now and then. To remember it duly with rigorous perfection, as in the fact it *stood*, requires indeed a rare faculty; rare, nay impossible. A very Shakspeare for faculty; or more than Shakspeare; who could *enact* a brother man's biography, see with the brother man's eyes at all points of his course what things *he* saw; in short, *know* his course and him, as few 'Historians' are like to do. Half or more of all the thick-plied perversions which distort our image of Cromwell, will disappear, if we honestly so much as try to represent them so; in sequence, as they *were*; not in the lump, as they are thrown-down before us.

But a second error, which I think the generality commit, refers to this same 'ambition' itself. We exaggerate the ambition of Great Men; we mistake what the nature of it is. Great Men are not ambitious in that sense; he is a small poor man that is ambitious so. Examine the man who lives in misery because he does not shine above other men; who goes about producing himself, pruriently anxious about his gifts and claims; struggling to force everybody, as it were begging everybody for God's sake, to acknowledge him a great man, and set him over the heads of men! Such a creature is among the wretchedest sights seen under this sun. A *great* man? A poor morbid prurient empty man; fitter for the ward of a hospital, than for a throne among men. I advise you to keep-out of his way. He cannot walk on quiet paths; unless you will look at him, wonder at him, write paragraphs about him, he cannot live. It is the *emptiness* of the man, not his greatness. Because there is nothing in himself, he hungers and thirsts that you would find something in him. In good truth, I believe no great man, not so much as a genuine man who had health and real substance in him of whatever magnitude, was ever much tormented in this way.

Your Cromwell, what good could it do him to be 'noticed' by noisy crowds of people? God his Maker already noticed him. He, Cromwell, was already there; no notice would make *him* other than he already was. Till his hair was grown grey; and Life from the downhill slope was all seen to be limited, not infinite but finite, and all a measurable matter *how* it went,—he had been content to plough the ground, and read his Bible. He in his old days could not support it any longer, without selling himself to Falsehood, that he might ride in gilt carriages to Whitehall, and have clerks with bundles of papers haunting him, 'Decide this, decide that,' which in utmost sorrow of heart no man can perfectly decide! What could gilt carriages do for this man? From of old, was there not in his life a weight of meaning, a terror and a splendour as of Heaven itself? His existence there as man set him beyond the need of gilding. Death, Judgment, and Eternity: these already lay as the background of whatsoever he thought or did. All his life lay begirt as in a sea of nameless Thoughts, which no speech of a mortal could name. God's Word, as the Puritan prophets of that time had read it: this was great, and all else was little to him. To call such a man 'ambitious,' to figure him as the prurient windbag described above, seems to me the poorest solecism. Such a man will say: 'Keep your gilt carriages and huzzaing mobs, keep your red-tape clerks, your influentialities, your important businesses. Leave me alone, leave me alone; there is *too much of life* in me already!' Old Samuel Johnson, the greatest soul in England in his day, was not ambitious. 'Corsica Boswell' flaunted at public shows with printed ribbons round his hat; but the great old Samuel stayed at home. The world-wide soul wrapt-up in its thoughts, in its sorrows;—what could paradings, and ribbons in the hat, do for it?

Ah yes, I will say again: The great *silent* men! Looking round on the noisy inanity of the world, words with little meaning, actions with little worth, one loves to reflect on the great Empire of *Silence*. The noble silent men, scattered here and there, each in his department; silently thinking, silently working; whom no Morning Newspaper makes mention of! They are the salt of the Earth. A country that has none or few of these is in a bad way. Like a forest which had no *roots*; which had all turned into leaves and boughs;—which must soon wither and be no forest. Woe for us if we had nothing but what we can *show*, or speak. Silence, the great Empire of Silence: higher than the stars; deeper than the Kingdoms of Death! It alone is great; all else is small.—I hope we English will long maintain our *grand talent pour le silence*. Let others that cannot do without standing on barrel-heads, to spout, and be seen of all the market-place, cultivate speech exclusively,—become a most green forest without roots! Solomon says, There is a time to speak; but also a time to keep silence. Of some great silent Samuel, not urged to writing, as old Samuel Johnson says he was, by *want of money*, and nothing other, one might ask, 'Why do not you too get up and speak; promulgate your system, found your sect?' 'Truly,' he will answer, 'I am *continent* of my thought hitherto; happily I have yet had the ability to keep it in me, no compulsion strong enough to speak it. My "system" is not for promulgation first of all; it is for serving myself to live by. That is the great purpose of it to me. And then the "honour"? Alas, yes;—but as Cato said of the statue: So many statues in that Forum of yours, may it not be better if they ask, Where is Cato's statue?'— —

But now, by way of counterpoise to this of Silence, let me say that there are two kinds of ambition; one wholly blamable, the other laudable and inevitable. Nature has provided that the great silent Samuel shall not be silent too long. The selfish wish to shine over others, let it be accounted altogether poor and miserable. 'Seekest thou great things? seek them not': this is most true. And yet, I say, there is an irrepressible tendency in every man to develop himself according to the magnitude which Nature has made him of; to speak-out, to act-out, what Nature has laid in him. This is proper, fit, inevitable; nay it is a duty, and even the summary of duties for a man. The meaning of life here on earth might be defined as consisting in this: To unfold your *self*, to work what thing you have the faculty for. It is a necessity for the human being, the first law of our existence. Coleridge beautifully remarks that the infant learns to *speak* by this necessity it feels.—We will say therefore: To decide about ambition, whether it is bad or not, you have two things to take into view. Not the coveting of the place alone, but the fitness of the man for the place withal: that is the question. Perhaps the place was *his*; perhaps he had a natural right, and even obligation, to seek the place! Mirabeau's ambition to be Prime Minister, how shall we blame it, if he were 'the only man in France that could have done any good there'? Hopefuler perhaps had he not so clearly *felt* how much good he could do! But a poor Necker, who could do no good, and had even felt that he could do none, yet sitting broken-hearted because they had flung him out, and he was now quit of it, well might Gibbon mourn over him.—Nature, I say, has provided amply that the silent great man shall strive to speak withal; *too* amply, rather!

Fancy, for example, you had revealed to the brave old Samuel Johnson, in his shrouded-up existence, that it was possible for him to do priceless divine work for his country and the whole world. That the perfect Heavenly Law might be made Law on this Earth; that the prayer he prayed daily, 'Thy kingdom come,' was at length to be fulfilled! If you had convinced his judgment of this; that it was possible, practicable; that he the mournful silent Samuel was called to take a part in it! Would not the whole soul of the man have flamed-up into a divine clearness, into noble utterance and determination to act; casting all sorrows and misgivings under his feet, counting all affliction and contradiction small,—the whole dark element of his existence blazing into articulate radiance of light and lightning? It were a true ambition this! And think now how it actually was with Cromwell. From of old, the sufferings of God's Church, true zealous Preachers of the truth flung into dungeons, whipt, set on pillories, their ears cropt-off, God's Gospel-cause trodden under foot of the unworthy: all this had lain heavy on his soul. Long years he had looked upon it, in silence, in prayer; seeing no remedy on Earth; trusting well that a remedy in Heaven's goodness would come,—that such a course was false, unjust, and could not last for ever. And now behold the dawn of it; after twelve years silent waiting, all England stirs itself; there is to be once more a Parliament, the Right will get a voice for itself: inexpressible well-grounded hope has come again into the Earth. Was not such a Parliament worth being a member of? Cromwell threw down his ploughs, and hastened thither.

He spoke there,—rugged bursts of earnestness, of a self-seen truth, where we get a glimpse of them. He worked there; he fought and strove, like a strong true giant of a man, through cannon-tumult and all else,—on and on, till the Cause *triumphed*, its once so formidable enemies all swept from before it, and the down of hope had become clear light of victory and certainty. That *he* stood there as the strongest soul of England, the undisputed Hero of all England,—what of this? It was possible that the Law of Christ's Gospel could now establish itself in the world! The Theocracy which John Knox in his pulpit might dream of as a 'devout imagination,' this practical man, experienced in the whole chaos of most rough practice, dared to consider as capable of being *realised*. Those that were highest in Christ's Church, the devoutest wisest men, were to rule the land: in some considerable degree, it might be so and should be so. Was it not *true*, God's truth? And if *true*, was it not then the very thing to do? The strongest practical intellect in England dared to answer, Yes! This I call a noble true purpose; is it not, in its own dialect, the noblest that could enter into the heart of Statesman or man? For a Knox to take it up was something; but for a Cromwell, with his great sound sense and experience of what our world *was*,—History, I think, shows it only this once in such a degree. I account it the culminating point of Protestantism; the most heroic phasis that 'Faith in the Bible' was appointed to exhibit here below. Fancy it: that it were made manifest to one of us, how we could make the Right supremely victorious over Wrong, and all that we had longed and prayed for, as the highest good to England and all lands, an attainable fact!

Well, I must say, the *vulpine* intellect, with its knowingness, its alertness, and expertness in 'detecting hypocrites,' seems to me a rather sorry business. We have had but one such Statesman in England; one man, that I can get sight of, who ever had in the heart of him any such purpose at all. One man, in the course of fifteen-hundred years; and this was his welcome. He had adherents by the hundred or the ten; opponents by the million. Had England rallied all round him,—why, then, England might have been a *Christian* land! As it is, vulpine knowingness sits yet at its hopeless problem, 'Given a world of Knaves, to educe an Honesty from their united action';—how cumbrous a problem, you may see in Chancery Law-Courts, and some other places! Till at length, by Heaven's just anger, but also by Heaven's great grace, the matter begins to stagnate; and this problem is becoming to all men a *palpably* hopeless one.—

But with regard to Cromwell and his purposes: Hume, and a multitude following him, come upon me here with an admission that Cromwell *was* sincere at first; a sincere 'Fanatic' at first, but gradually became a 'Hypocrite' as things opened round him. This of the Fanatic-Hypocrite is Hume's theory of it; extensively applied since,—to Mahomet and many others. Think of it seriously, you will find something in it; not much, not all, very far from all. Sincere hero hearts do not sink in this miserable manner. The Sun flings-forth impurities, gets balefully incrusted with spots; but it does not quench itself, and become no Sun at all, but a mass of Darkness! I will venture to say that such never befell a great deep Cromwell; I think, never. Nature's own lion-hearted Son; Antæus-like, his strength is got by *touching the Earth*, his Mother; lift him up from the Earth, lift him up into Hypocrisy, Inanity, his strength is gone. We will not assert that Cromwell was an immaculate man; that he fell into no faults, no insincerities among the rest. He was no dilettante professor of 'perfections,' 'immaculate conducts.' He was a rugged Orson, rending his rough way through actual true *work*,—doubtless with many a *fall* therein. Insincerities, faults, very many faults daily and hourly: it was too well known to him; known to God and him! The Sun was dimmed many a time; but the Sun had not himself grown a Dimness. Cromwell's last words, as he lay waiting for death, are those of a Christian heroic man. Broken prayers to God, that He would judge him and this Cause, He since man could not, in justice yet in pity. They are most touching words. He breathed-out his wild great soul, its toils and sins all ended now, into the presence of his Maker, in this manner.

I, for one, will not call the man a Hypocrite! Hypocrite, mummer, the life of him a mere theatricality; empty barren quack, hungry for the shouts of mobs? The man had made obscurity do very well for him till his head was grey; and now he *was*, there as he stood recognised unblamed, the virtual King of England. Cannot a man do without King's Coaches and Cloaks? Is it such a blessedness to have clerks for ever pestering you with bundles of papers in red tape? A simple Diocletian prefers planting of cabbages; a George Washington, no very immeasurable man, does the like. One would say, it is what any genuine man could do; and would do. The instant his real work were out in the matter of Kingship,—away with it!

Let us remark, meanwhile, how indispensable everywhere a *King* is, in all movements of men. It is strikingly shown, in this very War, what becomes of men when they cannot find a Chief Man, and their enemies can. The Scotch Nation was all but unanimous in Puritanism; zealous and of one mind about it, as in this English end of the Island was always far from being the case. But there was no great Cromwell among them; poor tremulous, hesitating, diplomatic Argyles and suchlike; none of them had a heart true enough for the truth, or durst commit himself to the truth. They had no leader; and the scattered Cavalier party in that country had one: Montrose, the noblest of all the Cavaliers; an accomplished, gallant-hearted, splendid man; what one may call the Hero-Cavalier. Well, look at it; on the one hand subjects without a King; on the other a King without subjects! The subjects without King can do nothing; the subjectless King can do something. This Montrose, with a handful of Irish or Highland savages, few of them so much as guns in their hands, dashes at the drilled Puritan armies like a wild whirlwind; sweeps them, time after time, some five times over, from the field before them. He was at one period, for a short while, master of all Scotland. One man; but he was a man: a million zealous men, but *without* the one; they against him were powerless! Perhaps of all the persons in that Puritan struggle, from first to last, the single indispensable one was verily Cromwell. To see and dare, and decide; to be a fixed pillar in the welter of uncertainty;—a King among them, whether they called him so or not.

Precisely here, however, lies the rub for Cromwell. His other proceedings have all found advocates, and stand generally justified; but this dismissal of the Rump Parliament and assumption of the Protectorship, is what no one can pardon him. He had fairly grown to be King in England; Chief Man of the victorious party in England: but it seems he could not do without the King's Cloak, and sold himself to perdition in order to get it. Let us see a little how this was.

England, Scotland, Ireland, all lying now subdued at the feet of the Puritan Parliament, the practical question arose, What was to be done with it? How will you govern these Nations, which Providence in a wondrous way has given-up to your disposal? Clearly those hundred surviving members of the Long Parliament, who sit there as supreme authority, cannot continue for ever to sit. What *is* to be done?—It was a question which theoretical constitution-builders may find easy to answer; but to Cromwell, looking there into the real practical facts of it, there could be none more complicated. He asked of the Parliament, What it was they would decide upon? It was for the Parliament to say. Yet the Soldiers too, however contrary to Formula, they who had purchased this victory with their blood, it seemed to them that they also should have something to say in it! We will not 'For all our fighting have nothing but a little piece of paper.' We understand that the Law of God's Gospel, to which He through us has given the victory, shall establish itself, or try to establish itself, in this land!

For three years, Cromwell says, this question had been

sounded in the ears of the Parliament. They could make no answer; nothing but talk, talk. Perhaps it lies in the nature of parliamentary bodies; perhaps no Parliament could in such case make any answer but even that of talk, talk! Nevertheless the question must and shall be answered. You sixty men there, becoming fast odious, even despicable, to the whole nation, whom the nation already calls Rump Parliament, *you* cannot continue to sit there: who or what then is to follow? 'Free Parliament,' right of Election, Constitutional Formulas of one sort or the other,—the thing is a hungry Fact coming on us, which we must answer or be devoured by it! And who are you that prate of Constitutional Formulas, rights of Parliament? You have had to kill your King, to make Pride's Purges, to expel and banish by the law of the stronger whosoever would not let your Cause prosper: there are but fifty or three-score of you left there, debating in these days. Tell us what we shall do; not in the way of Formula, but of practicable Fact!

How they did finally answer, remains obscure to this day. The diligent Godwin himself admits that he cannot make it out. The likeliest is, that this poor Parliament still would not, and indeed could not dissolve and disperse; that when it came to the point of actually dispersing, they again, for the tenth or twentieth time, adjourned it,—and Cromwell's patience failed him. But we will take the favourablest hypothesis ever started for the Parliament; the favourablest, though I believe it is not the true one, but too favourable.

According to this version: At the uttermost crisis, when Cromwell and his Officers were met on the one hand, and the fifty or sixty Rump Members on the other, it was suddenly told Cromwell that the Rump in its despair *was* answering in a very singular way; that in their splenetic envious despair, to keep-out the Army at least, these men were hurrying through the House a kind of Reform Bill,—Parliament to be chosen by the whole of England; equable electoral division into districts; free suffrage, and the rest of it! A very questionable, or indeed for *them* an unquestionable thing. Reform Bill, free suffrage of Englishmen? Why, the Royalists themselves, silenced indeed but not exterminated, perhaps out*number* us; the great numerical majority of England was always indifferent to our Cause, merely looked at it and submitted to it. It is in weight and force, not by counting of heads, that we are the majority! And now with your Formulas and Reform Bills, the whole matter, sorely won by our swords, shall again launch itself to sea; become a mere hope, and likelihood, *small* even as a likeli hood? And it is not a likelihood; it is a certainty, which we have won, by God's strength and our own right hands, and do now hold *here*. Cromwell walked down to these refractory Members; interrupted them in that rapid speed of their Reform Bill;—ordered them to begone, and talk there no more.—Can we not forgive him? Can we not understand him? John Milton, who looked on it all near at hand, could applaud him. The Reality had swept the Formulas away before it. I fancy, most men who were realities in England might see into the necessity of that.

The strong daring man, therefore, has set all manner of Formulas and logical superficialities against him; has dared appeal to the genuine Fact of this England, Whether it will support him or not? It is curious to see how he struggles to govern in some constitutional way; find some Parliament to support him; but cannot. His first Parliament, the one they call Barebones's Parliament, is, so to speak, a *Convocation of the Notables*. From all quarters of England the leading Ministers and chief Puritan Officials nominate the men most distinguished by religious reputation, influence, and attachment to the true Cause: these are assembled to shape-out a plan. They sanctioned what was past; shaped as they could what was to come. They were scornfully called *Barebones's Parliament*: the man's name, is seems, was not *Barebones*, but Barbone,—a good enough man. Nor was it a jest, their work; it was a most serious reality,—a trial on the part of these Puritan Notables how far the Law of Christ could become the Law of this England. There were men of sense among them, men of some quality; men of deep piety I suppose the most of them were. They failed, it seems, and broke-down, endeavouring to reform the

Court of Chancery! They dissolved themselves, as incompetent; delivered-up their power again into the hands of the Lord General Cromwell, to do with it what he liked and could.

What *will* he do with it? The Lord General Cromwell, 'Commander-in-chief of all the Forces raised and to be raised'; he hereby sees himself, at this unexampled juncture, as it were the one available Authority left in England, nothing between England and utter Anarchy but him alone. Such is the undeniable Fact of his position and England's, there and then. What will he do with it? After deliberation, he decides that he will *accept* it; will formally, with public solemnity, say and vow before God and men, 'Yes, the Fact is so, and I will do the best I can with it!' Protectorship, Instrument of Government,—these are the external forms of the thing; worked out and sanctioned as they could in the circumstances be, by the Judges, by the leading Official people, 'Council of Officers and Persons of interest in the Nation': and as for the thing itself, undeniably enough, at the pass matters had now come to, there *was* no alternative but Anarchy or that. Puritan England might accept it or not; but Puritan England was, in real truth, saved from suicide thereby!—I believe the Puritan People did, in an inarticulate, grumbling, yet on the whole grateful and real way, accept this anomalous act of Oliver's; at least, he and they together made it good, and always better to the last. But in their Parliamentary *articulate* way, they had their difficulties, and never knew fully what to say to it!—

Oliver's second Parliament, properly his *first* regular Parliament, chosen by the rule laid-down in the Instrument of Government, did assemble, and worked;—but got, before long, into bottomless questions as to the Protector's *right*, as to 'usurpation,' and so forth; and had at the earliest legal day to be dismissed. Cromwell's concluding Speech to these men is a remarkable one. So likewise to his third Parliament, in similar rebuke for their pedantries and obstinacies. Most rude, chaotic, all these Speeches are; but most earnest-looking. You would say, it was a sincere helpless man; not used to *speak* the great inorganic thought of him, but to act it rather!

A helplessness of utterance, in such bursting fulness of meaning. He talks much about 'births of Providence': All these changes, so many victories and events, were not forethoughts, and theatrical contrivances of men, of *me* or of men; it is blind blasphemers that will persist in calling them so! He insists with a heavy sulphurous wrathful emphasis on this. As he well might. As if a Cromwell in that dark huge game he had been playing, the world wholly thrown into chaos round him, had *foreseen* it all, and played it all off like a precontrived puppet-show by wood and wire! These things were foreseen by no man, he says; no man could tell what a day would bring forth: they were 'births of Providence,' God's finger guided us on, and we came at last to clear height of victory, God's Cause triumphant in these Nations; and you as a Parliament could assemble together, and say in what manner all this could be *organised*, reduced into rational feasibility among the affairs of men. You were to help with your wise counsel in doing that. 'You have had such an opportunity as no Parliament in England ever had.' Christ's Law, the Right and True, was to be in some measure made the Law of this land. In place of that, you have got into your idle pedantries, constitutionalities, bottomless cavillings and questionings about written laws for *my* coming here;—and would send the whole matter in Chaos again, because I have no Notary's parchment, but only God's voice from the battle-whirlwind, for being President among you! That opportunity is gone; and we know not when it will return. You have had your constitutional Logic; and Mammon's Law, not Christ's Law, rules yet in this land. 'God be judge between you and me!' These are his final words to them: Take you your constitution-formulas in your hand; and I my *in*formal struggles, purposes, realities and acts; and 'God be judge between you and me!'—

We said above what shapeless, involved chaotic things the printed Speeches of Cromwell are. *Wilfully* ambiguous, unintelligible, say the most: a hypocrite shrouding himself in confused Jesuitic jargon! To me they do not seem so. I will say rather, they afforded the first glimpses I could ever get into the reality of this Cromwell, nay into the possibility of him. Try to believe that he means something, search lovingly what that may be: you will find a real *speech* lying imprisoned in these broken rude tortuous utterances; a meaning in the great heart of this inarticulate man! You will, for the first time, begin to see that he was a man; not an enigmatic chimera, unintelligible to you, incredible to you. The Histories and Biographies written of this Cromwell, written in shallow sceptical generations that could not know or conceive of a deep believing man, are far more *obscure* than Cromwell's Speeches. You look through them only into the infinite vague of Black and the Inane. 'Heats and jealousies,' says Lord Clarendon himself: 'heats and jealousies,' mere crabbed whims, theories and crotchets; these induced slow sober quiet Englishmen to lay down their ploughs and work; and fly into red fury of confused war against the best-conditioned of Kings! *Try* if you can find that true. Scepticism writing about Belief may have great gifts; but it is really *ultra vires* there. It is Blindness laying-down the Laws of Optics.—

Cromwell's third Parliament split on the same rock as his second. Ever the constitutional Formula: How came *you* there? Show us some Notary parchment! Blind pedants:—'Why, surely the same power which makes you a Parliament, that, and something more, made me a Protector!' If my Protectorship is nothing, what in the name of wonder is your Parliamenteership, a reflex and creation of that?—

Parliaments having failed, there remained nothing but the way of Despotism. Military Dictators, each with his district, to *coerce* the Royalist and other gainsayers, to govern them, if not by act of Parliament, then by the sword. Formula shall *not* carry it, while the Reality is here! I will go on, protecting oppressed Protestants abroad, appointing just judges, wise managers, at home, cherishing true Gospel ministers; doing the best I can to make England a Christian England, greater than old Rome, the Queen of Protestant Christianity; I, since you will not help me; I while God leaves me life!—Why did he not give it up; retire into obscurity again, since the Law would not acknowledge him? cry several. That is where they mistake. For him there was no giving of it up! Prime Ministers have governed countries, Pitt, Pombal, Choiseul; and their word was a law while it held: but this Prime Minister was one that *could not get resigned*. Let him once resign, Charles Stuart and the Cavaliers waited to kill him; to kill the Cause *and* him. Once embarked, there is no retreat, no return. This Prime Minister could *retire* no-whither except into his tomb.

One is sorry for Cromwell in his old days. His complaint is incessant of the heavy burden Providence has laid on him. Heavy; which he must bear till death. Old Colonel Hutchinson, as his wife relates it, Hutchinson, his old battle-mate, coming to see him on some indispensable business, much against his will,—Cromwell 'follows him to the door,' in a most fraternal, domestic, conciliatory style; begs that he would be reconciled to him, his old brother in arms; says how much it grieves him to be misunderstood, deserted by true fellow-soldiers, dear to him from of old: the rigorous Hutchinson, cased in his Republican formula, sullenly goes his way.—And the man's head now white; his strong arm growing weary with its long work! I think always too of his poor Mother, now very old, living in that Palace of his; a right brave woman; as indeed they lived all an honest God-fearing Household there: if she heard a shot go-off, she thought it was her son killed. He had to come to her at least once a day, that she might see with her own eyes that he was yet living. The poor old Mother!——What had this man gained; what had he gained? He had a life of sore strife and toil, to his last day. Fame, ambition, place in History? His dead body was hung in chains; his 'place in History,'—place in History forsooth!—has been a place of ignominy, accusation, blackness, and disgrace; and here, this day, who knows if it is not rash in me to be among the first that ever ventured to pronounce him not a knave and liar, but a genuinely honest man! Peace to him. Did he not, in spite of all, accomplish much for us? *We* walk smoothly over his great rough heroic life; step-over his body sunk in the ditch there. We need not *spurn* it, as we step on it!—Let the Hero rest. It was not to *men's* judgment that he appealed; nor have men judged him very well.

Precisely a century and a year after this of Puritanism had got itself hushed-up into decent composure, and its results made smooth, in 1688, there broke-out a far deeper explosion, much more difficult to hush-up, known to all mortals, and like to be long known, by the name of French Revolution. It is properly the third and final act of Protestantism; the explosive confused return of mankind to Reality and Fact, now that they were perishing of Semblance and Sham. We call our English Puritanism the second act: 'Well then, the Bible is true; let us go by the Bible!' 'In Church,' said Luther; 'In Church and State,' said Cromwell, 'let us go by what actually *is* God's Truth.' Men have to return to reality; they cannot live on semblance. The French Revolution, or third act, we may well call the final one; for lower than that savage *Sansculottism* men cannot go. They stand there on the nakedest haggard Fact, undeniable in all seasons and circumstances; and may and must begin again confidently to build-up from that. The French explosion, like the English one, got its King,—who had no Notary parchment to show for himself. We have still to glance for a moment at Napoleon, our second modern King.

Napoleon does by no means seem to me so great a man as Cromwell. His enormous victories which reached over all Europe, while Cromwell abode mainly in our little England, are but as the high *stilts* on which the man is seen standing; the stature of the man is not altered thereby. I find in him no such *sincerity* as in Cromwell; only a far inferior sort. No silent walking, through long years, with the Awful Unnamable of this Universe; 'walking with God,' as he called it; and faith and strength in that alone: *latent* thought and valour, content to lie latent, then burst out as in blaze of Heaven's lightning! Napoleon lived in an age when God was no longer believed; the meaning of all Silence, Latency, was thought to be Nonentity: he had to begin not out of the Puritan Bible, but out of poor Sceptical *Encyclopédies*. This was the length the man carried it, Meritorious to get so far. His compact, prompt, everyway articulate character is in itself perhaps small, compared with our great chaotic *in*articulate Cromwell's. Instead of '*dumb* Prophet struggling to speak,' we have a portentous mixture of the Quack withal! Hume's notion of the Fanatic-Hypocrite, with such truth as it has, will apply much better to Napoleon that it did to Cromwell, to Mahomet, or the like,—where indeed taken strictly it has hardly any truth at all. An element of blamable ambition shows itself, from the first, in this man; gets the victory over him at last, and involves him and his work in ruin.

'False as a bulletin' became a proverb in Napoleon's time. He makes what excuse he could for it: that it was necessary to mislead the enemy, to keep-up his own men's courage, and so forth. On the whole, there are no excuses. A man in no case has liberty to tell lies. It had been, in the long-run, *better* for Napoleon too if he had not told any. In fact, if a man have any purpose reaching beyond the hour and day, meant to be found extant *next* day, what good can it ever be to promulgate lies? The lies are found-out; ruinous penalty is exacted for them. No man will believe the liar next time even when he speaks truth, when it is of the last importance that he be believed. The old cry of wolf!—A Lie is *no*-thing; you cannot of nothing make something; you make *nothing* at last, and lose your labour into the bargain.

Yet Napoleon *had* a sincerity: we are to distinguish between what is superficial and what is fundamental in insincerity. Across these outer manœuverings and quackeries of his, which were many and most blamable, let us discern withal that the man had a certain instinctive ineradicable feeling for reality; and did base himself upon fact, so long as he had any basis. He has an instinct of Nature better than his culture was. His *savans*, Bourrienne tells us, in that voyage to Egypt, were one evening busily occupied arguing that there could be no God. They had proved it, to their satisfaction, by all manner of logic. Napoleon looking up into the stars, answers, 'Very ingenious, Messieurs: but *who made* all that?' The Atheistic logic runs-off from him like water; the great Fact stares him in the face: 'Who made all that?' So too in Practice: he, as every man that can be great, or have victory in this world, sees, through all entanglements, the practical heart of the matter; drives straight towards that. When the steward of his Tuileries Palace was exhibiting the new upholstery, with praises, and demonstration how glorious it was, and how cheap withal, Napoleon, making little answer, asked for a pair of scissors, clipt one of the gold tassels from a window-curtain, put it in his pocket, and walked on. Some days afterwards, he produced it at the right moment, to the horror of his upholstery functionary; it was not gold but tinsel! In Saint Helena, it is notable how he still, to his last days, insists on the practical, the real. 'Why talk and complain; above all, why quarrel with one another? There is no *result* in it; it comes to nothing that one can *do*. Say nothing, if one can do nothing!' He speaks often so, to his poor discontented followers; he is like a piece of silent strength in the middle of their morbid querulousness there.

And accordingly was there not what we can call a *faith* in him, genuine so far as it went? That this new enormous Democracy asserting itself here in the French Revolution is an insuppressible Fact, which the whole world, with its old forces and institutions, cannot put down; this was a true insight of his, and took his conscience and enthusiasm along with it,— a *faith*. And did he not interpret the dim purport of it well? '*La carrière ouverte aux talens,* The implements to him who can handle them': this actually is the truth, and even the whole truth; it includes whatever the French Revolution, or any Revolution, could mean. Napoleon, in his first period, was a true Democrat. And yet by the nature of him, fostered too by his military trade, he knew that Democracy, if it were a true thing at all, could not be an anarchy: the man had a heart-hatred for anarchy. On that Twentieth of June (1792), Bourrienne and he sat in a coffee-house, as the mob rolled by: Napoleon expresses the deepest contempt for persons in authority that they do not restrain this rabble. On the Tenth of August he wonders why there is no man to command these poor Swiss; they would conquer if there were. Such a faith in

Democracy, yet hatred of anarchy, it is that carries Napoleon through all his great work. Through his brilliant Italian Campaigns, onwards to the Peace of Leoben, one would say, his inspiration is: 'Triumph to the French Revolution; assertion of it against these Austrian Simulacra that pretend to call it a Simulacrum!' Withal, however, he feels, and has a right to feel, how necessary a strong Authority is; how the Revolution cannot prosper or last without such. To bridle-in that great devouring, self-devouring French Revolution; to *tame* it, so that its intrinsic purpose can be made good, that it may become *organic*, and be able to live among other organisms and *formed* things, not as a wasting destruction alone: is not this still what he partly aimed at, as the true purport of his life; nay what he actually managed to do? Through Wagrams, Austerlitzes; triumph after triumph,—he triumphed so far. There was an eye to see in this man, a soul to dare and do. He rose naturally to be the King. All men saw that he *was* such. The common soldiers used to say on the march: 'These babbling *Avocats*, up at Paris; all talk and no work! What wonder it runs all wrong? We shall have to go and put our *Petit Caporal* there!' They went, and put him there; they and France at large. Chief-consulship, Emperorship, victory over Europe;—till the poor Lieutenant of *La Fère*, not unnaturally, might seem to himself the greatest of all men that had been in the world for some ages.

But at this point, I think, the fatal charlatan-element got the upper hand. He apostatised from his old faith in Facts, took to believing in Semblances; strove to connect himself with Austrian Dynasties, Popedoms, with the old false Feudalities which he once saw clearly to be false;—considered that *he* would found 'his Dynasty' and so forth; that the enormous French Revolution meant only that! The man was 'given-up to strong delusion, that he should believe a lie'; a fearful but most sure thing. He did not know true from false now when he looked at them,—the fearfulest penalty a man pays for yielding to untruth of heart. *Self* and false ambition had now become his god: *self*-deception once yielded to, *all* other deceptions follow naturally more and more. What a paltry patchwork of theatrical paper-mantles, tinsel and mummery, had this man wrapt his own great reality in, thinking to make it more real thereby! His hollow Pope's-*Concordat*, pretending to be a re-establishment of Catholicism, felt by himself to be the method of extirpating it, '*la vaccine de la religion*'; his ceremonial Coronations, consecrations by the old Italian Chimera in Notre-Dame,—'wanting nothing to complete the pomp of it,' as Augereau said, 'nothing but the half-million of men who had died to put an end to all that'! Cromwell's Inauguration was by the Sword and Bible; what we must call a genuinely *true* one. Sword and Bible were borne before him, without any chimera: were not these the *real* emblems of Puritanism; its true decoration and insignia? It had used them both in a very real manner, and pretended to stand by them now! But this, poor Napoleon mistook: he believed too much in the *Dupe-ability* of men; saw no fact deeper in man than Hunger and this! He was mistaken. Like a man that should build upon cloud; his house and he fall down in confused wreck, and depart out of the world.

Alas, in all of us this charlatan-element exists; and *might* be developed, were the temptation strong enough. 'Lead us not into temptation!' But it is fatal, I say, that it *be* developed. The thing into which it enters as a cognisable ingredient is doomed to be altogether transitory; and, however huge it may *look*, is in itself small. Napoleon's working, accordingly, what was it with all the noise it made? A flash as of gunpowder wide-spread; a blazing-up as of dry heath. For an hour the whole Universe seems wrapt in smoke and flame; but only for an hour. It goes out: the Universe with its old mountains and streams, its stars above and kind soil beneath, is still there.

The Duke of Weimar told his friends always, To be of courage; this Napoleonism was *unjust*, a falsehood, and could not last. It is true doctrine. The heavier this Napoleon trampled on the world, holding it tyrannously down, the fiercer would the world's recoil against him be, one day. Injustice pays itself with frightful compound-interest. I am not sure but he had better have lost his best park of artillery, or had his best regiment drowned in the sea, than shot that poor German Bookseller, Palm! It was a palpable tyrannous murderous injustice, which no man, let him paint an inch thick, could make-out to be other. It burnt deep into the hearts of men, it and the like of it; suppressed fire flashed in the eyes of men, as they thought of it,—waiting their day! Which day *came*: Germany rose round him.—What Napoleon *did* will in the long-run amount to what he did *justly*; what Nature with her laws will sanction. To what of reality was in him; to that and nothing more. The rest was all smoke and waste. *La carrière ouverte aux talens*: that great true Message, which has yet to articulate and fulfil itself everywhere, he left in a most inarticulate state. He was a great *ébauche*, a rude-draught never completed; as indeed what great man is other? Left in *too* rude a state, alas!

His notions of the world, as he expresses them there at St. Helena, are almost tragical to consider. He seems to feel the most unaffected surprise that it has all gone so; that he is flung-out on the rock here, and the World is still moving on its axis. France is great, and all-great; and at bottom, he is France. England itself, he says, is by Nature only an appendage of France; 'another Isle of Oleron to France.' So it was *by Nature*, by Napoleon-Nature; and yet look how in fact—HERE AM I! He cannot understand it: inconceivable that the reality has not corresponded to his program of it; that France was not all-great, that he was not France. 'Strong delusion,' that he should believe the thing to be which *is* not! The compact, clear-seeing, decisive Italian nature of him, strong, genuine, which he once had, has enveloped itself, half-dissolved itself, in a turbid atmosphere of French fanfaronade. The world was not disposed to be trodden-down underfoot; to be bound into masses, and built together, as *he* liked, for a pedestal to France and him: the world had quite other purposes in view! Napoleon's astonishment is extreme. But alas, what help now? He had gone that way of his; and Nature also had gone her way. Having once parted with Reality, he tumbles helpless in

Vacuity; no rescue for him. He had to sink there, mournfully as man seldom did; and break his great heart, and die,—this poor Napoleon: a great implement too soon wasted, till it was useless: our last Great Man!

Our last, in a double sense. For here finally these wide roamings of ours through so many times and places, in search and study of Heroes, are to terminate. I am sorry for it: there was pleasure for me in this business, if also much pain. It is a great subject, and a most grave and wide one, this which, not to be too grave about it, I have named *Hero-worship*. It enters deeply, as I think, into the secret of Mankind's ways and vitalest interests in this world, and is well worth explaining at present. With six months, instead of six days, we might have done better. I promised to break-ground on it; I know not whether I have even managed to do that. I have had to tear it up in the rudest manner in order to get into it at all. Often enough, with these abrupt utterances thrown-out isolated, unexplained, has your tolerance been put to the trial. Tolerance, patient candour, all-hoping favour and kindness, which I will not speak of at present. The accomplished and distinguished, the beautiful, the wise, something of what is best in England, have listened patiently to my rude words. With many feelings, I heartily thank you all; and say, Good be with you all!

FROM Past and Present

Past and Present was conceived on a visit paid by the Carlyles in September 1842 to some friends in Suffolk. On the way there Carlyle saw with indignation the workhouse of St. Ives in Huntingdonshire, where able-bodied men sat idle; and while in Suffolk he paid several visits to Bury St. Edmunds, and looked at the ruins of the abbey.

Past and Present was written between November 1842 and March 1843, and was published in April 1843. The book is written in three parts. Part One outlines the situation of Britain (taking as starting point that view of St. Ives workhouse); Part Two recreates the monastic life of the twelfth century, through the chronicle of a monk of St. Edmundsbury named Jocelin of Brakelond; in Part Three Carlyle draws contemporary morals from Jocelin's chronicle.

The extracts printed here are from the second part of the book.

FROM

Past and Present

CHAPTER VI

MONK SAMSON

WITHIN doors, down at the hill-foot, in our Convent here, we are a peculiar people,—hardly conceivable in the Arkwright Corn-Laws ages, of mere Spinning-Mills and Joe-Mantons! There is yet no Methodism among us, and we speak much of Secularities: no Methodism; our Religion is not yet a horrible restless Doubt, still less a far horribler composed Cant; but a great heaven-high Unquestionability, encompassing, interpenetrating the whole of Life. Imperfect as we may be, we are here, with our litanies, shaven crowns, vows of poverty, to testify incessantly and indisputably to every heart, That this Earthly Life and *its* riches and possessions, and good and evil hap, are not intrinsically a reality at all, but *are* a shadow of realities eternal, infinite; that this Time-world, as an air-image, fearfully *emblematic*, plays and flickers in the grand still mirror of Eternity; and man's little Life has Duties that are great, that are alone great, and go up to Heaven and down to Hell. This, with our poor litanies, we testify, and struggle to testify.

Which, testified or not, remembered by all men or forgotten by all men, does verily remain the fact, even in Arkwright Joe-Manton ages! But it is incalculable, when litanies have grown obsolete; when *fodercorns*, *avragiums*, and all human dues and reciprocities have been fully changed into one great due of *cash payment*; and man's duty to man reduces itself to handing him certain metal coins, or covenanted money-wages, and then shoving him out of doors; and man's duty to God becomes a cant, a doubt, a dim inanity, a 'pleasure of virtue' or suchlike;

and the thing a man does infinitely fear (the real *Hell* of a man) is, 'that he do not make money and advance himself,'—I say, it is incalculable what a change has introduced itself everywhere into human affairs! How human affairs shall now circulate everywhere not healthy life-blood in them, but, as it were, a detestable copperas banker's ink; and all is grown acrid, divisive, threatening dissolution; and the huge tumultuous Life of Society is galvanic, devil-ridden, too truly possessed by a devil! For, in short, Mammon *is* not a god at all; but a devil, and even a very despicable devil. Follow the Devil faithfully, you are sure enough to *go* to the Devil: whither else can you go?—In such situations, men look back with a kind of mournful recognition even on poor limited Monk-figures, with their poor litanies; and reflect, with Ben Jonson, that soul is indispensable, some degree of soul, even to save you the expense of salt!—

For the rest, it must be owned, we Monks of St. Edmundsbury are but a limited class of creatures, and seem to have a somewhat dull life of it. Much given to idle gossip; having indeed no other work, when our chanting is over. Listless gossip, for most part, and mitigated slander; the fruit of idleness, not of spleen. We are dull, insipid men, many of us; easy-minded; whom prayer and digestion of food will avail for a life. We have to receive all strangers in our Convent, and lodge them gratis; such and such sorts go by rule to the Lord Abbot and his special revenues; such and such to us and our poor Cellarer, however straitened. Jews themselves send their wives and little ones hither in war-time, into our *Pitanceria*; where they abide safe, with due *pittances*,—for a consideration. We have the fairest chances for collecting news. Some of us have a turn for reading Books; for meditation, silence; at times we even write Books. Some of us can preach, in English-Saxon, in Norman-French, and even in Monk-Latin; others cannot in any language or jargon, being stupid.

Failing all else, what gossip about one another! This is a perennial resource. How one hooded head applies itself to the ear of another, and whispers—*tacenda*. Willelmus Sacrista, for instance, what does he nightly, over in that Sacristy of his? Frequent bibations, '*frequentes bibationes et quædam tacenda,*' —eheu! We have '*tempora minutionis,*' stated seasons of blood-letting, when we are all let blood together; and then there is a general free-conference, a sanhedrim of clatter. Notwithstanding our vow of poverty, we can by rule amass to the extent of 'two shillings'; but it is to be given to our necessitous kindred, or in charity. Poor Monks! Thus too a certain Canterbury Monk was in the habit of 'slipping, *clanculo*, from his sleeve,' five shillings into the hand of his mother, when she came to see him, at the divine offices, every two months. Once, slipping the money clandestinely, just in the act of taking leave, he slipt it not into her hand, but on the floor, and another had it; whereupon the poor Monk, coming to know it, looked mere despair for some days; till Lanfranc the noble Archbishop, questioning his secret from him, nobly made the sum *seven* shillings,[1] and said, Never mind!

One Monk, of a taciturn nature, distinguishes himself among these babbling ones: the name of him Samson; he that answered Jocelin, '*Fili mi*, a burnt child shuns the fire.' They call him 'Norfolk *Barrator*,' or litigious person; for indeed, being of grave taciturn ways, he is not universally a favourite; he has been in trouble more than once. The reader is desired to mark this Monk. A personable man of seven-and-forty; stout-made, stands erect as a pillar; with bushy eyebrows, the eyes of him beaming into you in a really strange way; the face massive, grave, with 'a very eminent nose'; his head almost bald, its auburn remnants of hair, and the copious ruddy beard, getting slightly streaked with gray. This is Brother Samson; a man worth looking at.

He is from Norfolk, as the nickname indicates; from Tottington in Norfolk, as we guess; the son of poor parents there. He has told me Jocelin, for I loved him much, That once in his ninth year he had an alarming dream;—as indeed we are all somewhat given to dreaming here. Little Samson, lying uneasily in his crib at Tottington, dreamed that he saw the Arch

[1] *Eadmeri Hist.*, p. 8.

Enemy in person, just alighted in front of some grand building, with outspread bat-wings, and stretching forth detestable clawed hands to grip him, little Samson, and fly-off with him: whereupon the little dreamer shrieked desperate to St. Edmund for help, shrieked and again shrieked; and St. Edmund, a reverend heavenly figure, did come,—and indeed poor little Samson's mother, awakened by his shrieking, did come; and the Devil and the Dream both fled away fruitless. On the morrow, his mother, pondering such an awful dream, thought it were good to take him over to St. Edmund's own Shrine, and pray with him there. See, said little Samson at sight of the Abbey-Gate; see, mother, this is the building I dreamed of! His poor mother dedicated him to St. Edmund,—left him there with prayers and tears: what better could she do? The exposition of the dream, Brother Samson used to say, was this: *Diabolus* with outspread bat-wings shadowed forth the pleasures of this world, *voluptates hujus sæculi*, which were about to snatch and fly away with me, had not St. Edmund flung his arms round me, that is to say, made me a monk of his. A monk, accordingly, Brother Samson is; and here to this day where his mother left him. A learned man, of devout grave nature; has studied at Paris, has taught in the Town Schools here, and done much else; can preach in three languages, and, like Dr. Caius, 'has had losses' in his time. A thoughtful, firm-standing man; much loved by some, not loved by all; his clear eyes flashing into you, in an almost inconvenient way!

Abbot Hugo, as we said, had his own difficulties with him; Abbot Hugo had him in prison once, to teach him what authority was, and how to dread the fire in future. For Brother Samson, in the time of the Antipopes, had been sent to Rome on business; and, returning successful, was too late,—the business had all misgone in the interim! As tours to Rome are still frequent with us English, perhaps the reader will not grudge to look at the method of travelling thither in those remote ages. We happily have, in small compass, a personal narrative of it. Through the clear eyes and memory of Brother

Samson one peeps direct into the very bosom of that Twelfth Century, and finds it rather curious. The actual *Papa*, Father, or universal President of Christendom, as yet not grown chimerical, sat there; think of that only! Brother Samson went to Rome as to the real Light-fountain of this lower world; we now—!—But let us hear Brother Samson, as to his mode of travelling:

'You know what trouble I had for that Church of Woolpit; how I was despatched to Rome in the time of the Schism between Pope Alexander and Octavian; and passed through Italy at that season, when all clergy carrying letters for our Lord Pope Alexander were laid hold of, and some were clapt in prison, some hanged; and some, with nose and lips cut off, were sent forward to our Lord the Pope, for the disgrace and confusion of him (*in dedecus et confusionem ejus*). I, however, pretended to be Scotch, and putting on the garb of a Scotchman, and taking the gesture of one, walked along; and when anybody mocked at me, I would brandish my staff in the manner of that weapon they call *gaveloc*,[1] uttering comminatory words after the way of the Scotch. To those that met and questioned me who I was, I made no answer but: *Ride, ride Rome; turne Cantwereberei*.[2] Thus did I, to conceal myself and my errand, and get safer to Rome under the guise of a Scotchman.

'Having at last obtained a Letter from our Lord the Pope according to my wishes, I turned homewards again. I had to pass through a certain strong town on my road; and lo, the soldiers thereof surrounded me, seizing me, and saying: "This vagabond (*iste solivagus*), who pretends to be Scotch, is either a spy, or has Letters from the false Pope Alexander." And whilst they examined every stitch and rag of me, my leggings (*caligas*), breeches, and even the old shoes that I carried over my shoulder in the way of the Scotch,—I put my hand into the leather scrip I wore, wherein our Lord the Pope's Letter

[1] Javelin, missile pike. *Gaveloc* is still the Scotch name for *crowbar*.

[2] Does this mean, 'Rome forever; Canterbury *not*' (which claims an unjust Supremacy over us)! Mr. Rokewood is silent. Dryasdust would perhaps explain it,—in the course of a week or two of talking; did one dare to question him!

lay, close by a little jug (*ciffus*) I had for drinking out of; and the Lord God so pleasing, and St. Edmund, I got out both the Letter and the jug together; in such a way that, extending my arm aloft, I held the Letter hidden between jug and hand: they saw the jug, but the Letter they saw not. And thus I escaped out of their hands in the name of the Lord. Whatever money I had, they took from me; wherefore I had to beg from door to door, without any payment (*sine omni expensa*) till I came to England again. But hearing that the Woolpit Church was already given to Geoffry Ridell, my soul was struck with sorrow because I had laboured in vain. Coming home, therefore, I sat me down secretly under the Shrine of St. Edmund, fearing lest our Lord Abbot should seize and imprison me, though I had done no mischief; nor was there a monk who durst speak to me, nor a laic who durst bring me food except by stealth.'[1]

Such resting and welcoming found Brother Samson, with his worn soles, and strong heart! He sits silent, revolving many thoughts, at the foot of St. Edmund's Shrine. In the wide Earth, if it be not Saint Edmund, what friend or refuge has he? Our Lord Abbot, hearing of him, sent the proper officer to lead him down to prison, and clap 'foot-gyves on him' there. Another poor official furtively brought him a cup of wine; bade him 'be comforted in the Lord.' Samson utters no complaint; obeys in silence. 'Our Lord Abbot, taking counsel of it, banished me to Acre, and there I had to stay long.'

Our Lord Abbot next tried Samson with promotions; made him Subsacristan, made him Librarian, which he liked best of all, being passionately fond of Books: Samson, with many thoughts in him, again obeyed in silence; discharged his offices to perfection, but never thanked our Lord Abbot,—seemed rather as if looking into him, with those clear eyes of his. Whereupon Abbot Hugo said, *Se nunquam vidisse*, He had never seen such a man; whom no severity would break to complain, and no kindness soften into smiles or thanks:—a questionable kind of man!

[1] *Jocelini Chronica*, p. 36.

In this way, not without troubles, but still in an erect clear-standing manner, has Brother Samson reached his forty-seventh year; and his ruddy beard is getting slightly grizzled. He is endeavouring, in these days, to have various broken things thatched in; nay perhaps to have the Choir itself completed, for he can bear nothing ruinous. He has gathered 'heaps of lime and sand'; has masons, slaters working, he and *Warinus monachus noster*, who are joint keepers of the Shrine; paying out the money duly,—furnished by charitable burghers of St. Edmundsbury, they say. Charitable burghers of St. Edmundsbury? To me Jocelin it seems rather, Samson, and Warinus whom he leads, have privily hoarded the oblations at the Shrine itself, in these late years of indolent dilapidation, while Abbot Hugo sat wrapt inaccessible; and are struggling, in this prudent way, to have the rain kept out![1]—Under what conditions, sometimes, has Wisdom to struggle with Folly; get Folly persuaded to so much as thatch out the rain from itself! For, indeed, if the Infant govern the Nurse, what dextrous practice on the Nurse's part will not be necessary!

It is a new regret to us that, in these circumstances, our Lord the King's Custodiars, interfering, prohibited all building or thatching from whatever source; and no Choir shall be completed, and Rain and Time, for the present, shall have their way. Willelmus Sacrista, he of 'the frequent bibations and some things not to be spoken of'; he, with his red nose, I am of opinion, had made complaint to the Custodiars; wishing to do Samson an ill turn:—Samson his *Sub*-sacristan, with those clear eyes, could not be a prime favourite of his. Samson again obeys in silence.

CHAPTER VII

THE CANVASSING

Now, however, come great news to St. Edmundsbury: That there is to be an Abbot elected; that our interlunar

[1] *Jocelini Chronica*, p. 7.

obscuration is to cease; St. Edmund's Convent no more to be a doleful widow, but joyous and once again a bride! Often in our widowed state had we prayed to the Lord and St. Edmund, singing weekly a matter of 'one-and-twenty penitential Psalms, on our knees in the Choir,' that a fit Pastor might be vouchsafed us. And, says Jocelin, had some known what Abbot we were to get, they had not been so devout, I believe! —Bozzy Jocelin opens to mankind the floodgates of authentic Convent gossip; we listen, as in a Dionysius' Ear, to the inanest hubbub, like the voices at Virgil's Horn-Gate of Dreams. Even gossip, seven centuries off, has significance. List, list, how like men are to one another in all centuries:

'*Dixit quidam de quodam*, A certain person said of a certain person, "He, that *Frater*, is a good monk, *probabilis persona*; knows much of the order and customs of the church; and, though not so perfect a philosopher as some others, would make a very good Abbot. Old Abbot Ording, still famed among us, knew little of letters. Besides, as we read in Fables, it is better to choose a log for king, than a serpent never so wise, that will venomously hiss and bite his subjects."— "Impossible!" answered the other: "How can such a man make a sermon in the Chapter, or to the people on festival-days, when he is without letters? How can he have the skill to bind and to loose, he who does not understand the Scriptures? How—"?'

And then 'another said of another, *alius de alio*, "That *Frater* is a *homo literatus*, eloquent, sagacious; vigorous in discipline; loves the Convent much, has suffered much for its sake." To which a third party answers, "From all your great clerks, good Lord deliver us! From Norfolk barrators and surly persons, That it would please thee to preserve us, We beseech thee to hear us, good Lord."! Then another *quidam* said of another *quodam*, "That *Frater* is a good manager (*husebondus*)"; but was swiftly answered, "God forbid that a man who can neither read nor chant, nor celebrate the divine offices, an unjust person withal, and grinder of the faces of the poor, should ever be Abbot"!' One man, it appears, is nice in his victuals.

Another is indeed wise, but apt to slight inferiors; hardly at the pains to answer, if they argue with him too foolishly. And so each *aliquis* concerning his *aliquo*,—through whole pages of electioneering babble. 'For,' says Jocelin, 'So many men, as many minds.' Our Monks 'at time of blood-letting, *tempore minutionis*,' holding their sanhedrim of babble, would talk in this manner: Brother Samson, I remarked, never said anything; sat silent, sometimes smiling; but he took good note of what others said, and would bring it up, on occasion, twenty years after. As for me Jocelin, I was of opinion that 'some skill in Dialectics, to distinguish true from false,' would be good in an Abbot. I spake, as a rash Novice in those days, some conscientious words of a certain benefactor of mine; 'and behold, one of those sons of Belial' ran and reported them to him, so that he never after looked at me with the same face again! Poor Bozzy!—

Such is the buzz and frothy simmering ferment of the general mind and no-mind; struggling to 'make itself up,' as the phrase is, or ascertain what *it* does really want: no easy matter, in most cases. St. Edmundsbury, in that Candlemas season of the year 1182, is a busily fermenting place. The very clothmakers sit meditative at their looms; asking, Who shall be Abbot? The *sochemanni* speak of it, driving their ox-team afield; the old women with their spindles: and none yet knows what the days will bring forth.

The Prior, however, as our interim chief, must proceed to work; get ready 'Twelve Monks,' and set off with them to his Majesty at Waltham, there shall the election be made. An election, whether managed directly by ballot-box on public hustings, or indirectly by force of public opinion, or were it even by open alehouses, landlords' coercion, popular club-law, or whatever electoral methods, is always an interesting phenomenon. A mountain tumbling in great travail, throwing up dustclouds and absurd noises, is visibly there; uncertain yet what mouse or monster it will give birth to.

Besides, it is a most important social act; nay, at bottom,

the one important social act. Given the men a People choose, the People itself, in its exact worth and worthlessness, is given. A heroic people chooses heroes, and is happy; a valet or flunky people chooses sham-heroes, what are called quacks, thinking them heroes, and is not happy. The grand summary of a man's spiritual condition, what brings out all his hero-hood and insight, or all his flunkyhood and horn-eyed dimness, is this question put to him, What man dost thou honour? Which is thy ideal of a man; or nearest that? So too of a People: for a People too, every People, *speaks* its choice,—were it only by silently obeying, and not revolting,—in the course of a century or so. Nor are electoral methods, Reform Bills and suchlike, unimportant. A People's electoral methods are, in the long-run, the express image of its electoral *talent*; tending and gravitating perpetually, irresistibly, to a conformity with that: and are, at all stages, very significant of the People. Judicious readers, of these times, are not disinclined to see how Monks elect their Abbot in the Twelfth Century: how the St. Edmundsbury mountain manages its midwifery; and what mouse or man the outcome is.

CHAPTER VIII

THE ELECTION

ACCORDINGLY our Prior assembles us in Chapter; and, we adjuring him before God to do justly, nominates, not by our selection, yet with our assent, Twelve Monks, moderately satisfactory. Of whom are Hugo Third-Prior, Brother Dennis a venerable man, Walter the *Medicus*, Samson *Subsacrista*, and other esteemed characters,—though Willelmus *Sacrista*, of the red nose, too is one. These shall proceed straightway to Waltham; and there elect the Abbot as they may and can. Monks are sworn to obedience; must not speak too loud, under penalty of foot-gyves, limbo, and bread-and-water: yet monks too would know what it is they are obeying. The St. Edmundsbury Community has no hustings, ballot-box, indeed no open voting: yet by various vague manipulations, pulse-feelings, we struggle to ascertain what its virtual aim is, and succeed better or worse.

This question, however, rises; alas, a quite preliminary question: Will the *Dominus Rex* allow us to choose freely? It is to be hoped! Well, if so, we agree to choose one of our own Convent. If not, if the *Dominus Rex* will force a stranger on us, we decide on demurring, the Prior and his Twelve shall demur: we can appeal, plead, remonstrate; appeal even to the Pope, but trust it will not be necessary. Then there is this other question, raised by Brother Samson: What if the Thirteen should not themselves be able to agree? Brother Samson *Subsacrista*, one remarks, is ready oftenest with some question, some suggestion, that has wisdom in it. Though a servant of servants, and saying little, his words all tell, having sense in them; it seems by his light mainly that we steer ourselves in this great dimness.

What if the Thirteen should not themselves be able to agree? Speak, Samson, and advise.—Could not, hints Samson, Six of our venerablest elders be chosen by us, a kind of electoral committee, here and now: of these, 'with their hand on the Gospels, with their eye on the *Sacrosancta*,' we take oath that they will do faithfully; let these, in secret and as before God, agree on Three whom they reckon fittest; write their names in a Paper, and deliver the same sealed, forthwith, to the Thirteen: one of those Three the Thirteen shall fix on, if permitted. If not permitted, that is to say, if the *Dominus Rex* force us to demur,—the paper shall be brought back unopened, and publicly burned, that no man's secret bring him into trouble.

So Samson advises, so we act; wisely, in this and in other crises of the business. Our electoral committee, its eye on the Sacrosancta, is soon named, soon sworn; and we, striking-up the Fifth Psalm, '*Verba mea*,

'Give ear unto my words, O Lord,
My meditation weigh,'

march out chanting, and leave the Six to their work in the Chapter here. Their work, before long, they announce as finished: they, with their eye on the Sacrosancta, imprecating the Lord to weigh and witness their meditation, have fixed on Three Names, and written them in this Sealed Paper. Let Samson Subsacrista, general servant of the party, take charge of it. On the morrow morning, our Prior and his Twelve will be ready to get under way.

This, then, is the ballot-box and electoral winnowing-machine they have at St. Edmundsbury: a mind fixed on the Thrice Holy, an appeal to God on high to witness their meditation: by far the best, and indeed the only good electoral winnowing-machine,—if men have souls in them. Totally worthless, it is true, and even hideous and poisonous, if men have no souls. But without soul, alas, what winnowing-machine in human elections can be of avail? We cannot get along without soul; we stick fast, the mournfulest spectacle; and salt itself will not save us!

On the morrow morning, accordingly, our Thirteen set forth; or rather our Prior and Eleven; for Samson, as general servant of the party, has to linger, settling many things. At length he too gets upon the road; and, 'carrying the sealed Paper in a leather pouch hung round his neck; and *froccum bajulans in ulnis*' (thanks to thee, Bozzy Jocelin), 'his frockskirts looped over his elbow,' showing substantial stern-works, tramps stoutly along. Away across the Heath, not yet of Newmarket and horse-jockeying; across your Fleam-dike and Devil's-dike, no longer useful as a Mercian East-Anglian boundary or bulwark: continually towards Waltham, and the Bishop of Winchester's House there, for his Majesty is in that. Brother Samson, as purse-bearer, has the reckoning always, when there is one, to pay; 'delays are numerous,' progress none of the swiftest.

But, in the solitude of the Convent, Destiny thus big and in her birthtime, what gossiping, what babbling, what dreaming of dreams! The secret of the Three our electoral elders alone know: some Abbot we shall have to govern us; but which Abbot, oh, which! One Monk discerns in a vision of the night-watches, that we shall get an Abbot of our own body, without needing to demur: a prophet appeared to him clad all in white, and said 'Ye shall have one of yours, and he will rage among you like a wolf, *sæviet ut lupus*.' Verily!—then which of ours? Another Monk now dreams: he has seen clearly which; a certain Figure taller by head and shoulders than the other two, dressed in alb and *pallium*, and with the attitude of one about to fight;—which tall Figure a wise Editor would rather not name at this stage of the business! Enough that the vision is true: that Saint Edmund himself, pale and awful, seemed to rise from his Shrine, with naked feet, and say audibly, 'He *ille*, shall veil my feet'; which part of the vision also proves true. Such guessing, visioning, dim perscrutation of the momentous future: the very clothmakers, old women, all townsfolk speak of it,' and more than once it is reported in St. Edmundsbury, This one is elected; and then, This one, and That other.' Who knows?

But now, sure enough, at Waltham, 'on the second Sunday of Quadragesima,' which Dryasdust declares to mean the 22d day of February, year 1182, Thirteen St. Edmundsbury Monks are, at last, seen processioning towards the Winchester Manorhouse; and, in some high Presence-chamber and Hall of State, get access to Henry II. in all his glory. What a Hall,—not imaginary in the least, but entirely real and indisputable, though so extremely dim to us; sunk in the deep distances of Night! The Winchester Manorhouse has fled bodily, like a Dream of the old Night; not Dryasdust himself can show a wreck of it. House and people, royal and episcopal, lords and varlets, where are they? Why *there*, I say, Seven Centuries off; sunk *so* far in the Night, there they *are*; peep through the blankets of the old Night, and thou wilt see! King Henry himself is visibly there; a vivid, noble-looking man, with grizzled beard, in glittering uncertain costume; with earls round him, and bishops, and dignitaries, in the like. The Hall is large, and has for one thing an altar near it,—chapel and altar adjoining it; but what gilt seats, carved tables, carpeting of rush-cloth, what arras-hangings, and huge fire of logs:—alas, it has Human Life in it; and is not that the grand miracle, in what hangings or costume soever?—

The *Dominus Rex*, benignantly receiving our Thirteen with their obeisance, and graciously declaring that he will strive to act for God's honour and the Church's good, commands, 'by the Bishop of Winchester and Geoffrey the Chancellor,'—*Galfridus Cancellarius*, Henry's and the Fair Rosamond's authentic Son present here!—commands, 'That they, the said Thirteen, do now withdraw, and fix upon Three from their own Monastery.' A work soon done; the Three hanging ready round Samson's neck, in that leather pouch of his. Breaking the seal, we find the names,—what think *ye* of it, ye higher dignitaries, thou indolent Prior, thou Willelmus *Sacrista* with the red bottle-nose?—the names, in this order: of Samson *Subsacrista*, of Roger the distressed Cellarer, of Hugo *Tertius-Prior*.

The higher dignitaries, all omitted here, 'flush suddenly red in the face'; but have nothing to say. One curious fact and question certainly is, How Hugo Third-Prior, who was of the electoral committee, came to nominate *himself* as one of the Three? A curious fact, which Hugo Third-Prior has never yet entirely explained, that I know of!—However, we return, and report to the King our Three names; merely altering the order; putting Samson last, as lowest of all. The King, at recitation of our Three, asks us: 'Who are they? Were they born in my domain? Totally unknown to me! You must nominate three others.' Whereupon Willelmus Sacrista says, 'Our Prior must be named, *quia caput nostrum est*, being already our head.' And the Prior responds, 'Willelmus Sacrista is a fit man, *bonus vir est*,'—for all his red nose. Tickle me, Toby, and I'll tickle thee! Venerable Dennis too is named; none in his conscience can say nay. There are now Six on our List. 'Well,' said the King, 'they have done it swiftly, they! *Deus est cum eis*.' The Monks withdraw again; and Majesty revolves, for a little, with his *Pares* and *Episcopi*, Lords or '*Law-wards*' and Soul-Overseers, the thoughts of the royal breast. The Monks wait silent in an outer room.

In short while, they are next ordered, To add yet another three; but not from their own Convent; from other Convents, 'for the honour of my kingdom.' Here,—what is to be done here? We will demur, if need be! We do name three, however, for the nonce: the Prior of St. Faith's, a good Monk of St. Neot's, a good Monk of St. Alban's; good men all; all made abbots and dignitaries since, at this hour. There are now Nine upon our List. What the thoughts of the Dominus Rex may be farther? The Dominus Rex, thanking graciously, sends out word that we shall now strike off three. The three strangers are instantly struck off. Willelmus Sacrista adds, that he will of his own accord decline,—a touch of grace and respect for the *Sacrosancta*, even in Willelmus! The King then orders us to strike off a couple more; then yet one more: Hugo Third-Prior goes, and Roger *Cellerarius*, and venerable Monk Dennis;—and now there remain on our List two only, Samson Subsacrista and the Prior.

Which of these two? It were hard to say,—by Monks who may get themselves foot-gyved and thrown into limbo for speaking! We humbly request that the Bishop of Winchester and Geoffrey the Chancellor may again enter, and help us to decide. 'Which do you want?' asks the Bishop. Venerable Dennis made a speech, 'commending the persons of the Prior and Samson; but always in the corner of his discourse, *in angulo sui sermonis*, brought Samson in.' 'I see!' said the Bishop: 'We are to understand that your Prior is somewhat remiss; that you want to have him you call Samson for Abbot.' 'Either of them is good,' said venerable Dennis, almost trembling; 'but we would have the better, if it pleased God.' 'Which of the two *do* you want?' inquires the Bishop pointedly. 'Samson!' answered Dennis; 'Samson!' echoed all of the rest that durst speak or echo anything: and Samson is reported to the King accordingly. His Majesty, advising of it for a moment, orders that Samson be brought in with the other Twelve.

The King's Majesty, looking at us somewhat sternly, then says: 'You present to me Samson; I do not know him: had it been your Prior, whom I do know, I should have accepted him: however, I will now do as you wish. But have a care of yourselves. By the true eyes of God, *per veros oculos Dei*, if you manage badly, I will be upon you!' Samson, therefore, steps forward, kisses the King's feet; but swiftly rises erect again, swiftly turns towards the altar, uplifting with the other Twelve, in clear tenor-note, the Fifty-first Psalm, '*Miserere mei Deus*,

> 'After thy loving-kindness, Lord,
> Have mercy upon *me*';

with firm voice, firm step and head, no change in his countenance whatever. 'By God's eyes,' said the King, 'that one, I think, will govern the Abbey well.' By the same oath (charged to your Majesty's account), I too am precisely of that opinion! It is some while since I fell in with a likelier man anywhere than this new Abbot Samson. Long life to him, and may the Lord *have* mercy on him as Abbot!

Thus, then, have the St. Edmundsbury Monks, without express ballot-box or other good winnowing-machine, contrived to accomplish the most important social feat a body of men can do, to winnow-out the man that is to govern them: and truly one sees not that, by any winnowing-machine whatever, they could have done it better. O ye kind Heavens, there is in every Nation and Community a *fittest*, a wisest, bravest, best; whom could we find and make King over us, all were in very truth well;—the best that God and Nature had permitted *us* to make it! By what art discover him? Will the Heavens in their pity teach us no art; for our need of him is great!

Ballot-boxes, Reform Bills, winnowing-machines: all these are good, or are not so good;—alas, brethren, how *can* these, I say, be other than inadequate, be other than failures, melancholy to behold? Dim all souls of men to the divine, the high and awful meaning of Human Worth and Truth, we shall never, by all the machinery in Birmingham, discover the True and Worthy. It is written, 'if we are ourselves valets, there shall exist no hero for us; we shall not know the hero when we see him';—we shall take the quack for a hero; and cry, audibly through all ballot-boxes and machinery whatsoever, Thou art he; be thou King over us!

What boots it? Seek only deceitful Speciosity, money with gilt-carriages, 'fame' with newspaper-paragraphs, whatever name it bear, you will find only deceitful Speciosity; god-like Reality will be forever far from you. The Quack shall be legitimate inevitable King of you; no earthly machinery able to exclude the Quack. Ye shall be born thralls of the Quack, and suffer under him, till your hearts are near broken, and no French Revolution or Manchester Insurrection, or partial or universal volcanic combustions and explosions, never so many, can do more than 'change the *figure* of your Quack'; the essence of him remaining, for a time and times.—'How long, O Prophet?' say some, with a rather melancholy sneer. Alas, ye *un*prophetic, ever till this come about: Till deep misery, if nothing softer will, have driven you out of your Speciosities *into* your Sincerities; and you find that there either is a God-like in the world, or else ye are an unintelligible madness; that there is a God, as well as a Mammon and a Devil, and a Genius of Luxuries and canting Dilettantisms and Vain Shows! How long that will be, compute for yourselves. My unhappy brothers!—

CHAPTER IX

ABBOT SAMSON

So, then, the bells of St. Edmundsbury clang out one and all, and in church and chapel the organs go: Convent and Town, and all the west side of Suffolk, are in gala; knights, viscounts, weavers, spinners, the entire population, male and female, young and old, the very sockmen with their chubby infants,—out to have a holiday, and see the Lord Abbot arrive! And there is 'stripping barefoot' of the Lord Abbot at the Gate, and solemn leading of him in to the High Altar and Shrine; with sudden 'silence of all the bells and organs,' as we kneel in deep prayer there; and again with outburst of all the bells and organs, and loud *Te Deum* from the general human windpipe; and speeches by the leading viscount, and giving of the kiss of brotherhood; the whole wound-up with popular games, and dinner within doors of more than a thousand strong, *plus quam mille comedentibus in gaudio magno.*

In such manner is the selfsame Samson once again returning to us, welcomed on *this* occasion. He that went away with his frock-skirts looped over his arm, comes back riding high; suddenly made one of the dignitaries of this world. Reflective readers will admit that here was a trial for a man. Yesterday a poor mendicant, allowed to possess not above two shillings of money, and without authority to bid a dog run for him,—this man today finds himself a *Dominus Abbas*, mitred Peer of Parliament, Lord of manorhouses, farms, manors, and wide lands; a man with 'Fifty Knights under him,' and dependent, swiftly obedient multitudes of men. It is a change greater than Napoleon's; so sudden withal. As if one of the Chandos day-drudges had, on awakening some morning, found that *he* overnight was become Duke! Let Samson with his clear-beaming eyes see into that, and discern it if he can. We shall now get the measure of him by a new scale of inches, considerably more rigorous than the former was. For if a noble soul is rendered tenfold beautifuler by victory and prosperity, springing now radiant as into his own due element and sun-throne; an ignoble one is rendered tenfold and hundredfold uglier, pitifuler. Whatsoever vices, whatsoever weaknesses were in the man, the parvenu will show us them enlarged, as in the solar microscope, into frightful distortion. Nay, how many mere seminal principles of vice, hitherto all wholesomely kept latent, may we now see unfolded, as in the solar hothouse, into growth, into huge universally-conspicuous luxuriance and development!

But is not this, at any rate, a singular aspect of what political and social capabilities, nay, let us say, what depth and opulence of true social vitality, lay in those old barbarous ages, That the fit Governor could be met with under such disguises, could be recognised and laid hold of under such? Here he is discovered with a maximum of two shillings in his pocket, and a leather scrip round his neck; trudging along the highway, his frock-skirts looped over his arm. They think this is he nevertheless, the true Governor; and he proves to be so. Brethren, have we no need of discovering true Governors, but will sham ones forever do for us? These were absurd superstitious blockheads of Monks; and we are enlightened Ten-pound Franchisers, without taxes on knowledge! Where, I say, are our superior, are our similar or at all comparable discoveries? We also have eyes, or ought to have; we have hustings, telescopes; we have lights, link-lights and rush-lights of an enlightened free Press, burning and dancing everywhere, as in a universal torch-dance; singeing your whiskers as you traverse the public thoroughfares in town and country. Great souls, true Governors, go about under all manner of disguises now as then. Such telescopes, such enlightenment,—and such discovery! How comes it, I say; how comes it? Is it not lamentable; is it not even, in some sense, amazing?

Alas, the defect, as we must often urge and again urge, is less a defect of telescopes than of some eyesight. Those superstitious blockheads of the Twelfth Century had no telescopes, but they had still an eye; not ballot-boxes; only reverence for Worth, abhorrence of Unworth. It is the way with all barbarians. Thus Mr. Sale informs me, the old Arab Tribes would gather in liveliest *gaudeamus*, and sing, and kindle bonfires, and wreathe crowns of honour, and solemnly thank the gods that, in their Tribe too, a Poet had shown himself. As indeed they well might; for what usefuler, I say not nobler and heavenlier thing could the gods, doing their very kindest, send to any Tribe or Nation, in any time or circumstances? I declare to thee, my afflicted quack-ridden brother, in spite of thy astonishment, it is very lamentable! We English find a Poet, as brave a man as has been made for a hundred years or so anywhere under the Sun; and do we kindle bonfires, or thank the gods? Not at all. We, taking due counsel of it, set the man to gauge ale-barrels in the Burgh of Dumfries; and pique our selves on our 'patronage of genius.'

Genius, Poet: do we know what these words mean? An inspired Soul once more vouchsafed us, direct from Nature's own great fire-heart, to see the Truth, and speak it, and do it; Nature's own sacred voice heard once more athwart the dreary boundless element of hearsaying and canting, of twaddle and poltroonery, in which the bewildered Earth, nigh perishing, has *lost its way*. Hear once more, ye bewildered benighted mortals; listen once again to a voice from the inner Light-sea and Flame-sea, Nature's and Truth's own heart; know the Fact of your Existence what it is, put away the Cant of it which it is *not*; and knowing, do, and let it be well with you!—

George the Third is Defender of something we call 'the Faith' in those years; George the Third is head charioteer of the destinies of England, to guide them through the gulf of French Revolutions, American Independences; and Robert Burns is Gauger of ale in Dumfries. It is an Iliad in a nutshell. The physiognomy of a world now verging towards dissolution, reduced now to spasms and death-throes, lies pictured in that one fact,—which astonishes nobody, except at me for being astonished at it. The fruit of long ages of confirmed Valethood, entirely confirmed as into a Law of Nature; cloth-worship and quack-worship: entirely *confirmed* Valethood,—which will have to *un*confirm itself again; God knows, with difficulty enough!—

Abbot Samson had found a Convent all in dilapidation; rain beating through it, material rain and metaphorical, from all quarters of the compass. Willelmus Sacrista sits drinking nightly, and doing mere *tacenda*. Our larders are reduced to leanness, Jew harpies and unclean creatures our purveyors; in our basket is no bread. Old women with their distaffs rush out on a distressed Cellarer in shrill Chartism. 'You cannot stir abroad but Jews and Christians pounce upon you with unsettled bonds'; debts boundless seemingly as the National

Debt of England. For four years our new Lord Abbot never went abroad but Jew creditors and Christian, and all manner of creditors, were about him; driving him to very despair. Our Prior is remiss; our Cellarers, officials are remiss; our monks are remiss: what man is not remiss? Front this, Samson, thou alone art there to front it; it is thy task to front and fight this, and to die or kill it. May the Lord have mercy on thee!

To our antiquarian interest in poor Jocelin and his Convent, where the whole aspect of existence, the whole dialect, of thought, of speech, of activity, is so obsolete, strange, long-vanished, there now superadds itself a mild glow of human interest for Abbot Samson; a real pleasure, as at sight of man's work, especially of governing, which is man's highest work, done *well*. Abbot Samson had no experience in governing; had served no apprenticeship to the trade of governing,—alas, only the hardest apprenticeship to that of obeying. He had never in any court given *vadium* or *plegium*, says Jocelin; hardly ever seen a court, when he was set to preside in one. But it is astonishing, continues Jocelin, how soon he learned the ways of business; and, in all sorts of affairs, became expert beyond others. Of the many persons offering him their service, 'he retained one Knight skilled in taking *vadia* and *plegia*'; and within the year was himself well skilled. Nay, by and by, the Pope appoints him Justiciary in certain causes; the King one of his new Circuit Judges: official Osbert is heard saying, 'That Abbot is one of your shrewd ones, *disputator est*; if he go on as he begins, he will cut out every lawyer of us!'[1]

Why not? What is to hinder this Samson from governing? There is in him what far transcends all apprenticeships; in the man himself there exists a model of governing, something to govern by! There exists in him a heart-abhorrence of whatever is incoherent, pusillanimous, unveracious, that is to say, chaotic, *un*governed; of the Devil, not of God. A man of this kind cannot help governing! He has the living ideal of a governor in him; and the incessant necessity of struggling to unfold the same out of him. Not the Devil or Chaos, for any

[1] *Jocelini Chronica*, p. 25.

wages, will he serve; no, this man is the born servant of Another than them. Alas, how little avail all apprenticeships, when there is in your governor himself what we may well call *nothing* to govern by: nothing;—a general gray twilight, looming with shapes of expediencies, parliamentary traditions, division-lists, election-funds, leading-articles; this, with what of vulpine alertness and adroitness soever, is not much!

But indeed what say we, apprenticeship? Had not this Samson served, in his way, a right good apprenticeship to governing; namely, the harshest slave-apprenticeship to obeying! Walk this world with no friend in it but God and St. Edmund, you will either fall into the ditch, or learn a good many things. To learn obeying is the fundamental art of governing. How much would many a Serene Highness have learned, had he travelled through the world with water-jug and empty wallet, *sine omni expensa*; and, at his victorious return, sat down not to newspaper-paragraphs and city-illuminations, but at the foot of St. Edmund's Shrine to shackles and bread-and-water! He that cannot be servant of many, will never be master, true guide and deliverer of many;—that is the meaning of true mastership. Had not the Monk-life extraordinary 'political capabilities' in it; if not imitable by us, yet enviable? Heavens, had a Duke of Logwood, now rolling sumptuously to his place in the Collective Wisdom, but himself happened to plough daily, at one time, on seven-and-sixpence a week, with no out-door relief,—what a light, unquenchable by logic and statistic and arithmetic, would it have thrown on several things for him!

In all cases, therefore, we will agree with the judicious Mrs. Glass: 'First catch your hare!' First, get your man; all is got: he can learn to do all things, from making boots, to decreeing judgments, governing communities; and will do them like a man. Catch your no-man,—alas, have you not caught the terriblest Tartar in the world! Perhaps all the terribler, the quieter and gentler he looks. For the mischief that one blockhead, that every blockhead does, in a world so feracious, teeming with endless results as ours, no ciphering will sum up.

The quack bootmaker is considerable; as corn-cutters can testify, and desperate men reduced to buckskin and list-shoes. But the quack priest, quack high-priest, the quack king! Why do not all just citizens rush, half-frantic, to stop him, as they would a conflagration? Surely a just citizen *is* admonished by God and his own Soul, by all silent and articulate voices of this Universe, to do what in *him* lies towards relief of this poor blockhead-quack, and of a world that groans under him. Run swiftly; relieve him,—were it even by extinguishing him! For all things have grown so old, tinder-dry, combustible; and he is more ruinous than conflagration. Sweep him *down*, at least; keep him strictly within the hearth; he will then cease to be conflagration; he will then become useful, more or less, as culinary fire. Fire is the best of servants; but what a master! This poor blockhead too is born for uses; why, elevating him to mastership, will you make a conflagration, a parish-curse or world-curse of him?

CHAPTER X

GOVERNMENT

How Abbot Samson, giving his new subjects seriatim the kiss of fatherhood in the St. Edmundsbury chapterhouse, proceeded with cautious energy to set about reforming their disjointed distracted way of life; how he managed with his Fifty rough *Milites* (Feudal Knights), with his lazy Farmers, remiss refractory Monks, with Pope's Legates, Viscounts, Bishops, Kings; how on all sides he laid about him like a man, and putting consequence on premiss, and everywhere the saddle on the right horse, struggled incessantly to educe organic method out of lazily fermenting wreck,—the careful reader will discern, not without true interest, in these pages of Jocelin Boswell. In most antiquarian quaint costume, not of garments alone, but of thought, word, action, outlook and position, the substantial figure of a man with eminent nose, bushy brows and clear-flashing eyes, his russet beard growing daily grayer, is visible, engaged in true governing of men. It is beautiful how the chrysalis governing-soul, shaking off its dusty slough and prison, starts forth winged, a true royal soul! Our new Abbot has a right honest unconscious feeling, without insolence as without fear or flutter, of what he is and what others are. A courage to quell the proudest, an honest pity to encourage the humblest. Withal there is a noble reticence in this Lord Abbot: much vain unreason he hears; lays up without response. He is not there to expect reason and nobleness of others; he is there to give them of his own reason and nobleness. Is he not their servant, as we said, who can suffer from them, and for them; bear the burden their poor spindle-limbs totter and stagger under; and, in virtue of *being* their servant, govern them, lead them out of weakness into strength, out of defeat into victory!

One of the first Herculean Labours Abbot Samson undertook, or the very first, was to institute a strenuous review and radical reform of his economics. It is the first labour of every governing man, from *Paterfamilias* to *Dominus Rex*. To get the rain thatched out from you is the preliminary of whatever farther, in the way of speculation or of action, you may mean to do. Old Abbot Hugo's budget, as we saw, had become empty, filled with deficit and wind. To see his account-books clear, be delivered from those ravening flights of Jew and Christian creditors, pouncing on him like obscene harpies wherever he showed face, was a necessity for Abbot Samson.

On the morrow after his instalment he brings in a load of money-bonds, all duly stamped, sealed with this or the other Convent seal: frightful, unmanageable, a bottomless confusion of Convent finance. There they are;—but there at least they all are; all that shall be of them. Our Lord Abbot demands that all the official seals in use among us be now produced and delivered to him. Three-and-thirty seals turn up; are straightway broken, and shall seal no more: the Abbot only, and those duly authorised by him shall seal any bond. There are but two ways of paying debt: increase of industry in raising income, increase of thrift in laying it out. With iron energy, in slow but steady undeviating perseverance, Abbot Samson sets to work in both directions. His troubles are manifold: cunning *milites*, unjust bailiffs, lazy sockmen, he an inexperienced Abbot; relaxed lazy monks, not disinclined to mutiny in mass: but continued vigilance, rigorous method, what we call 'the eye of the master,' work wonders. The clear-beaming eyesight of Abbot Samson, steadfast, severe, all-penetrating,—it is like *Fiat lux* in that inorganic waste whirlpool; penetrates gradually to all nooks, and of the chaos makes a *kosmos* or ordered world!

He arranges everywhere, struggles unweariedly to arrange, and place on some intelligible footing, the 'affairs and dues, *res ac redditus*,' of his dominion. The Lakenheath eels cease to breed squabbles between human beings; the penny of *reap-silver* to explode into the streets the Female Chartism of St. Edmundsbury. These and innumerable greater things. Wheresoever Disorder may stand or lie, let it have a care; here is the man that has declared war with it, that never will make peace with it. Man is the Missionary of Order; he is the servant not of the Devil and Chaos, but of God and the Universe! Let all sluggards, and cowards, remiss, false-spoken, unjust, and otherwise diabolic persons have a care: this is a dangerous man for them. He has a mild grave face; a thoughtful sternness, a sorrowful pity: but there is a terrible flash of anger in him too; lazy monks often have to murmur, '*Sævit ut lupus*, He rages like a wolf; was not our Dream true!' 'To repress and hold-in such sudden anger he was continually careful,' and succeeded well: —right, Samson; that it may become in thee as noble central heat, fruitful, strong, beneficent; not blaze out, or the seldomest possible blaze out, as wasteful volcanoism to scorch and consume!

'We must first creep, and gradually learn to walk,' had Abbot Samson said of himself, at starting. In four years he has become a great walker; striding prosperously along; driving much before him. In less than four years, says Jocelin, the Convent Debts were all liquidated: the harpy Jews not only settled with, but banished, bag and baggage, out of the *Bannaleuca* (Liberties, *Banlieue*) of St. Edmundsbury,—so has the King's Majesty been persuaded to permit. Farewell to *you*, at any rate; let us, in no extremity, apply again to you! Armed men march them over the borders, dismiss them under stern penalties,—sentence of excommunication on all that shall again harbour them here: there were many dry eyes at their departure.

New life enters everywhere, springs up beneficent, the Incubus of Debt once rolled away. Samson hastes not; but neither does he pause to rest. This of the Finance is a lifelong business with him;—Jocelin's anecdotes are filled to weariness with it. As indeed to Jocelin it was of very primary interest.

But we have to record also, with a lively satisfaction, that spiritual rubbish is as little tolerated in Samson's Monastery as material. With due rigour, Willelmus Sacrista, and his bibations and *tacenda* are, at the earliest opportunity, softly yet irrevocably put an end to. The bibations, namely, had to end; even the building where they used to be carried on was razed from the soil of St. Edmundsbury, and 'on its place grow rows of beans': Willelmus himself, deposed from the Sacristy and all offices, retires into obscurity, into absolute taciturnity unbroken thenceforth to this hour. Whether the poor Willelmus did not still, by secret channels, occasionally get some slight wetting of vinous or alcoholic liquor,—now grown, in a manner, indispensable to the poor man? Jocelin hints not; one knows not how to hope, what to hope! But if he did, it was in silence and darkness; with an ever-present feeling that teetotalism was his only true course. Drunken dissolute Monks are a class of persons who had better keep out of Abbot Samson's way. *Sævit ut lupus*; was not the Dream true! murmured many a Monk. Nay Ranulf de Glanvill, Justiciary in Chief, took umbrage at him, seeing these strict ways; and watched farther with suspicion: but discerned gradually that there was nothing wrong, that there was much the opposite of wrong.

FROM

Oliver Cromwell's Letters and Speeches

Oliver Cromwell's Letters and Speeches began as an article written for Mill's *Westminster Review* in 1840, which expanded in Carlyle's mind to a biography of Cromwell, then to a history of the Civil War and the early years of the Commonwealth, and then was reduced to something like an autobiography, told through Cromwell's letters and speeches with Carlylean annotations and elucidations. *Cromwell*, one of the most painfully worked upon of Carlyle's books, was completed in 1844, and published in 1845.

Cromwell shows one of Carlyle's greatest virtues as a historian: his determination to dig down to verifiable fact, in a time when standards of scholarship did not approach the exactness of the present day. By printing the texts of Cromwell's letters, and interweaving his own comments, Carlyle destroyed permanently the contemporary idea of the Protector as one who 'lived a hypocrite and died a traitor,' replacing it by his own vision of Cromwell as one of the heroes of history.

The extracts chosen describe the Battle of Naseby, and the destruction of the Levellers' movement.

FROM

Oliver Cromwell's Letters and Speeches

LETTERS XXV–XXVII

PRINCE RUPERT had withdrawn without fighting; was now at Worcester with a considerable force, meditating new infall. For which end, we hear, he has sent 2,000 men across the country to his Majesty at Oxford, to convoy 'his Majesty's person and the Artillery' over to Worcester to him,—both of which objects are like to be useful there. The Committee of Both Kingdoms order the said Convoy to be attacked.

'The charge of this service they recommended particularly to General Cromwell, who, looking on himself now as discharged of military employment by the New Ordinance, which was to take effect within few days, and to have no longer opportunity to serve his country in that way,—was, the night before, come to Windsor, from his service in the West, to kiss the General's hand and take leave of him: when, in the morning ere he was come forth of his chamber, those commands, than which he thought of nothing less in all the world, came to him from the Committee of Both Kingdoms.'[1]

'The night before' must mean, to all appearance, the 22d of April. How Cromwell instantly took horse; plunged into

[1] Sprigge's *Anglia Rediviva* (London, 1647), p. 10. Sprigge was one of Fairfax's Chaplains; his Book, a rather ornate work, gives florid but authentic and sufficient account of this New-Model Army in all its features and operations, by which 'England' had 'come alive again.' A little sparing in dates; but correct where they are given. None of the old Books is better worth reprinting.—For some glimmer of notice concerning Joshua Sprigge himself, see Wood *in voce*,—and disbelieve altogether that 'Nat. Fiennes' had anything to do with this Book.

Oxfordshire, and on the 24th, at Islip Bridge, attacked and routed this said Convoy; and the same day, 'merely by dragoons' and fierce countenance, took Bletchington House, for which poor Colonel Windebank was shot, so angry were they: all this is known from Clarendon, or more authentically from Rushworth;[1] and here now is Cromwell's own account of it.

LETTER XXV

'COMMITTEE of Both Kingdoms,' first set up in February gone a year, when the Scotch Army came to help, has been the Executive in the War-department ever since; a great but now a rapidly declining authority. Sits at Derby House: Four Scotch; Twenty-one English, of whom Six a quorum. Johnston of Warriston is the notablest Scotchman; among the leading English are Philip Lord Wharton and the Younger Vane.[2]

'Watlington' is in the Southeast nook of Oxfordshire; a day's march from Windsor. 'Major-General Browne' commands at Abingdon; a City Wood-merchant once; a zealous soldier, of Presbyterian principles at present. The rendezvous at Watlington took place on Wednesday night; the 25th of April is Friday.

TO THE RIGHT HONOURABLE THE COMMITTEE OF BOTH KINGDOMS, AT DERBY HOUSE: THESE

Bletchington, 25th April 1645.

My Lords and Gentlemen,—According to your Lordships' appointment, I have attended your Service in these parts; and have not had so fit an opportunity to give you an account as now.

So soon as I received your commands, I appointed a rendezvous at Watlington. The body being come up, I marched to Wheatley

[1] vi. 23–24.

[2] List, and light as to its appointment, in *Commons Journals* (7th Feb. 1643-4), iii. 391; Baillie, ii. 141 et sæpius. Its Papers and Correspondence, a curious set of records, lie in very tolerable order in the State-Paper Office.

Bridge, having sent before to Major-General Browne for intelligence; and it being market-day at Oxford, from whence I likewise hoped, by some of the market-people, to gain notice where the Enemy was.

Towards night I received certain notice by Major-General Browne, that the Carriages were not stirred, that Prince Maurice was not here; and by some Oxford scholars, that there were Four Carriages and Wagons ready in one place, and in another Five; all, as I conceived, fit for a march.[1]

I received notice also that the Earl of Northampton's Regiment was quartered at Islip; wherefore in the evening I marched that way, hoping to have surprised them; but, by the mistake and failing of the forlorn-hope, they had an alarm there, and to all their quarters, and so escaped me; by means whereof they had time to draw all together.

I kept my body all night at Islip: and, in the morning, a party of the Earl of Northampton's Regiment, the Lord Wilmot's, and the Queen's, came to make an infall upon me. Sir Thomas Fairfax's Regiment[2] *was the first that took the field; the rest drew out with all possible speed. That which is the General's Troop charged a whole squadron of the Enemy, and presently broke it. Our other Troops coming seasonably on, the rest of the Enemy were presently put into confusion; so that we had the chase of them three or four miles; wherein we killed many, and took near Two-hundred prisoners, and about Four-hundred horse.*

Many of them escaped towards Oxford and Woodstock; divers were drowned; and others got into a strong House in Bletchington, belonging to Sir Thomas Cogan; wherein Colonel Windebank kept a garrison with near Two-hundred men. Whom I presently summoned; and after a long Treaty he went out, about twelve at night, with these Terms here enclosed; leaving us between Two and Three-hundred muskets, besides horse-arms, and other ammunition, and about Threescore-and-eleven horses more.

This was the mercy of God; and nothing is more due than a real

[1] 'march,' out towards Worcester.

[2] 'which was once mine,' he might have added, but modestly does not; only alluding to it from afar, in the next sentence.

acknowledgment. And though I have had greater mercies, yet none clearer: because, in the first 'place,' God brought them to our hands when we looked not for them; and delivered them out of our hands when we laid a reasonable design to surprise them, and which we carefully endeavoured. His mercy appears in this also, That I did much doubt the storming of the House, it being strong and well manned, and I having few dragoons, and this being not my business;—and yet we got it.

I hope you will pardon me if I say, God is not enough owned. We look too much to men and visible helps: this hath much hindered our success. But I hope God will direct all to acknowledge Him alone in all 'things.' Your most humble servant,

OLIVER CROMWELL.[1]

Poor Windebank was shot by sudden Court-martial, so enraged were they at Oxford,—for Cromwell had not even foot-soldiers, still less a battering gun. It was his poor young Wife, they said, she and other 'ladies on a visit there,' that had confused poor Windebank: he set his back to the wall of Merton College, and received his death-volley with a soldier's stoicism.[2] The Son of Secretary Windebank, who fled beyond seas long since.

LETTER XXVI

How Cromwell, sending off his new guns and stores to Abingdon, now shot across westward to 'Radcot Bridge' or 'Bampton-in-the-Bush'; and on the 26th gained a new victory there; and on the whole made a rather brilliant sally of it:—this too is known from Clarendon, or more authentically from Rushworth; but only the concluding unsuccessful part of this, the fruitless Summons to Farringdon, has left any trace in autograph.

[1] Pamphlet, in *Parliamentary History*, xiii. 459: read in the House, Monday 28th April (*Commons Journals*, iv. 124).—Letter to Fairfax on the same subject, Appendix, No. 7.

[2] Heath's *Chronicle*, p. 122.

TO THE GOVERNOR OF THE GARRISON IN FARRINGDON

29th April 1645.

Sir,—I summon you to deliver into my hands the House wherein you are, and your Ammunition, with all things else there; together with your persons, to be disposed of as the Parliament shall appoint. Which if you refuse to do, you are to expect the utmost extremity of war. I rest, your servant, *OLIVER CROMWELL.*[1]

This Governor, 'Roger Burgess,' is not to be terrified with fierce countenance and mere dragoons; he refuses. Cromwell condenses himself about Farringdon Town, 'sends for infantry' (but, we fear, gets none), and again summons:

LETTER XXVII

TO THE SAME; SAME DATE

Sir,—I understand by forty or fifty poor men whom you forced into your House, that you have many there whom you cannot arm, and who are not serviceable to you.

If these men should perish by your means, it were great inhumanity surely. Honour and honesty require this, That though you be prodigal of your own lives, yet not to be so of theirs. If God give you into my hands, I will not spare a man of you, if you put me to a storm. *OLIVER CROMWELL.*[2]

Roger Burgess, still unawed, refuses; Cromwell waits for infantry from Abingdon 'till 3 next morning,' then storms; loses fourteen men, with a captain taken prisoner;—and draws away, leaving Burgess to crow over him. The Army, which rose from Windsor yesterday, gets to Reading this day, and he must hasten thither.[3]

Yesterday, Wednesday, Monthly-fast day, all Preachers, by Ordinance of Parliament, were praying for 'God's merciful assistance to this New Army now on march, and His blessing

[1] Rushworth, vi. 26.
[2] Rushworth, vi. 26.
[3] For Bampton, etc. see Appendix, No. 7.

upon their endeavours.'[1] Consider it; actually 'praying'! It was a capability old London and its Preachers and Populations had; to us the incrediblest.

LETTER XXVIII

By Letter Twenty-eighth it will be seen that Lieutenant-General Cromwell has never yet resumed his Parliamentary duty. In fact, he is in the Associated Counties, raising force; 'for protection of the Isle of Ely,' and other purposes. To Fairfax and his Officers, to the Parliament, to the Committee of Both Kingdoms, to all persons, it is clear that Cromwell cannot be dispensed with. Fairfax and the Officers petition Parliament[2] that he may be appointed their Lieutenant-General, Commander-in-Chief of the Horse. There is a clear necessity in it. Parliament, the Commons somewhat more readily than the Lords, continue, by instalments of 'forty days,' of 'three months,' his services in the Army; and at length grow to regard him as a constant element there. A few others got similar leave of absence, similar dispensation from the Self-denying Ordinance. Sprigge's words, cited above, are no doubt veracious; yet there is trace of evidence[3] that Cromwell's continuance in the Army had, even by the framers of the Self-denying Ordinance, been considered a thing possible, a thing desirable. As it well might! To Cromwell himself there was no overpowering felicity in getting out to be shot at, except where wanted; he very probably, as Sprigge intimates, did let the matter in silence take its own course.

'TO THE RIGHT HONOURABLE SIR THOMAS FAIRFAX, GENERAL OF THE PARLIAMENT'S ARMY: THESE'

Huntingdon, 4th June 1645.

Sir,—I most humbly beseech you to pardon my long silence. I am conscious of the fault, considering the great obligations lying upon

[1] Rushworth, vi. 25.
[2] Their Letter (Newspapers, 9th–16th June), in *Cromwelliana*, p. 18.
[3] Godwin's *History of the Commonwealth* (London, 1824), i. 405.

me. But since my coming into these parts, I have been busied to secure that part of the Isle of Ely where I conceived most danger to be.

Truly I found it in a very ill posture: and it is yet but weak; without works, ammunition or men considerable,—and of money least: and then, I hope, you will easily conceive of the defence: and God has preserved us all this while to a miracle. The party under Vermuyden waits the King's Army, and is about Deeping; has a command to join with Sir John Gell, if he commands him. So 'too' the Nottingham Horse. I shall be bold to present you with intelligence as it comes to me.

I am bold to present this as my humble suit: That you would be pleased to make Captain Rawlins, this Bearer, a Captain of Horse. He has been so before; was nominated to the Model; is a most honest man. Colonel Sidney leaving his regiment, if it please you to bestow his *Troop on him, I am confident he will serve you faithfully. So, by God's assistance, will your most humble servant,*

OLIVER CROMWELL.[1]

The 'Vermuyden' mentioned here, who became Colonel Vermuyden, is supposed to be a son of the Dutch Engineer who drained the Fens. 'Colonel Sidney' is the celebrated Algernon; he was nominated in the 'Model,' but is 'leaving his regiment'; having been appointed Governor of Chichester.[2] Captain Rawlins does obtain a Company of Horse; under 'Colonel Sir Robert Pye.'[3]—Colonel Montague, afterwards Earl of Sandwich, has a Foot-Regiment here. Hugh Peters is 'Chaplain to the Train.'

BY EXPRESS

FAIRFAX, with his New-Model Army, has been beleaguering Oxford for some time past; but in a loose way, and making small progress hitherto. The King, not much apprehensive about Oxford, is in the Midland Counties; has just stormed

[1] Rushworth, vi. (London, 1701), p. 37.
[2] *Commons Journals*, iv. 136 (9th May 1645).
[3] Army-List, in Sprigge (p. 330).

Leicester ('last night of May,' says Clarendon,[1] a terrible night, and still more terrible 'daybreak' and day following it), which perhaps may itself relieve Oxford. His Majesty is since at halt, or in loose oscillating movement, 'hunting' on the hills, 'driving large herds of cattle before him,'—nobody, not even himself, yet knows whitherward. Whitherward? This is naturally a very agitating question for the neighbouring populations; but most of all intensely agitating for the Eastern Association,—though Cromwell, in that Huntingdon Letter, occupied with Ely and other Garrisons, seems to take it rather quietly. But two days later, we have trace of him at Cambridge, and of huge alarm round him there. Here is an old Piece of Paper still surviving; still emblematic of old dead days and their extinct agitations, when once we get to decipher it! They are the Cambridge Committee that write; 'the Army about Oxford,' we have seen, is Fairfax's.

'TO THE DEPUTY-LIEUTENANTS OF SUFFOLK: THESE'

Cambridge, 6th June 1645.

Gentlemen,—The cloud of the Enemy's Army hanging still upon the borders, and drawing towards Harborough, make some supposals that they aim at the Association. In regard whereof, we having information that the Army about Oxford was not yesterday advanced, albeit it was ordered so to do, we thought meet to give you intelligence thereof;—and therewith earnestly to propound to your consideration, That you will have in readiness what Horse and Foot may be had, that so a proportion may be drawn forth for this service, such as may be expedient.

And because we conceive that the exigence may require Horse and Dragoons, we desire That all your Horse and Dragoons may hasten to Newmarket; where they will receive orders for farther advance, according as the motion of the Enemy and of our Army shall require. And To allow both the several Troops of Dragoons and Horse one week's pay, to be laid down by the owner; which shall be repaid out of the public money out of the County; the pay of each Trooper being

[1] ii. 857.

14 *shillings per week, and of a Dragoon* 10s. 6d. *per week. Your servants,*

H. MILDMAY,	*W. SPRING,*
W. HEVENINGHAM,	*MAURICE BARROW,*
TI. MIDLTON (sic),	*NATHANIEL BACON,*
	FRANCIS RUSSELL,
	OLIVER CROMWELL,
	HUM. WALCOT,
	ISAAK PULLER,
	ED - - - [illegible.]

'*P.S.*' *The Place of Rendezvous for the Horse and Dragoons is to be at Newmarket; and for the Foot Bury.* —*Since the writing hereof, we received certain intelligence that the Enemy's Body, with* 60 *carriages, was upon his march towards the Association,* 3 *miles on this side Harborough, last night at* 4 *of the clock.*[1]

The Original, a hasty, blotted Paper, with the Signatures in two unequal columns (as imitated here), and with the Postscript crammed hurriedly into the corner, and written from another inkbottle as is still apparent,—represents to us an agitated scene in the old Committee-rooms at Cambridge that Friday. In *Rushworth* (see vi. 36–8), of the same date, and signed by the same parties, with some absentees (Oliver among them, probably now gone on other business) and more new arrivals,—is a Letter to Fairfax himself, urging him to speed over, and help them in their peril. They say, 'We had formerly written to the Counties to raise their Horse and Dragoons, and have now written,' as above for one instance, 'to quicken them.'—The Suffolk and other Horse, old Ironsides not hindmost, did muster; and in about a week hence there came other news from 'this side Harborough last night'!

LETTER XXIX

NASEBY

THE old Hamlet of Naseby stands yet, on its old hill-top, very much as it did in Saxon days, on the Northwestern

[1] Original, long stationary at Ipswich, is now (Jan. 1849) the property of John Wodderspoon, Esq., Mercury Office, Norwich.

border of Northamptonshire; some seven or eight miles from Market-Harborough in Leicestershire; nearly on a line, and nearly midway, between that Town and Daventry. A peaceable old Hamlet, of some eight-hundred souls; clay cottages for labourers, but neatly thatched and swept; smith's shop, saddler's shop, beer-shop, all in order; forming a kind of square, which leads off Southwards into two long streets: the old Church, with its graves, stands in the centre, the truncated spire finishing itself with a strange old Ball, held up by rods; a 'hollow copper Ball, which came from Boulogne in Henry the Eighth's time,'—which has, like Hudibras's breeches, 'been at the Siege of Bullen.' The ground is upland, moorland, though now growing corn; was not enclosed till the last generation, and is still somewhat bare of wood. It stands nearly in the heart of England: gentle Dulness, taking a turn at etymology, sometimes derives it from *Navel*; 'Navesby, quasi *Navels*by, from being' etc.: Avon Well, the distinct source of Shakspeare's Avon, is on the Western slope of the high grounds; Nen and Welland, streams leading towards Cromwell's Fen-country, begin to gather themselves from boggy places on the Eastern side. The grounds, as we say, lie high; and are still, in their new subdivisions, known by the name of 'Hills,' 'Rutput Hill,' 'Mill Hill,' 'Dust Hill,' and the like, precisely as in Rushworth's time: but they are not properly hills at all; they are broad blunt clayey masses, swelling towards and from each other, like indolent waves of a sea, sometimes of miles in extent.

It was on this high moor-ground, in the centre of England, that King Charles, on the 14th of June 1645, fought his last battle; dashed fiercely against the New-Model Army, which he had despised till then; and saw himself shivered utterly to ruin thereby. 'Prince Rupert, on the King's right wing, charged *up* the hill, and carried all before him'; but Lieutenant-General Cromwell charged downhill on the other wing, likewise carrying all before him,—and did *not* gallop off the field to plunder, he, Cromwell, ordered thither by the Parliament, had arrived from the Association two days before, 'amid shouts from the whole Army': he had the ordering of the Horse this morning. Prince Rupert, on returning from his plunder, finds the King's Infantry a ruin; prepares to charge again with the rallied Cavalry; but the Cavalry too, when it came to the point, 'broke all asunder,'—never to reassemble more. The chase went through Harborough; where the King had already been that morning, when in an evil hour he turned back, to revenge some 'surprise of an outpost at Naseby the night before,' and give the Roundheads battle.

Ample details of this Battle, and of the movements prior and posterior to it, are to be found in Sprigge, or copied with some abridgment into Rushworth; who has also copied a strange old Plan of the Battle; half plan, half picture, which the Sale-Catalogues are very chary of, in the case of Sprigge. By assiduous attention, aided by this Plan, as the old names yet stick to the localities, the Narrative can still be, and has lately been, pretty accurately verified, and the Figure of the old Battle dimly brought back again.[1] The reader shall imagine it, for the present.—On the crown of Naseby Height stands a modern Battle-monument; but, by an unlucky oversight, it is above a mile to the east of where the Battle really was. There are likewise two modern Books about Naseby and its Battle; both of them without value.

The Parliamentary Army stood ranged on the Height still partly called 'Mill Hill,' as in Rushworth's time, a mile and half from Naseby; the King's Army, on a parallel 'Hill,' its back to Harborough;—with the wide table of upland now named *Broad Moor* between them; where indeed the main brunt of the action still clearly enough shows itself to have been. There are hollow spots, of a rank vegetation, scattered over that Broad Moor; which are understood to have once been burial *mounds*;—some of which, one to my knowledge, have been (with more or less of sacrilege) verified as such. A friend of mine has in his cabinet two ancient grinder-teeth, dug lately from that ground,—and waits for an opportunity to rebury them there. Sound effectual grinders, one of them very

[1] Appendix, No. 8.

large; which ate their breakfast on the fourteenth morning of June two hundred years ago, and except to be clenched once in grim battle, had never work to do more in this world!—'A stack of dead bodies, perhaps about 100, had been buried in this Trench; piled as in a wall, a man's length thick: the skeletons lay in courses, the heads of one course to the heels of the next; one figure, by the strange position of the bones, gave us the hideous notion of its having been thrown in *before* death! We did not proceed far:—perhaps some half-dozen skeletons. The bones were treated with all piety; watched rigorously, over Sunday, till they could be covered in again.'[1] Sweet friends, for Jesus' sake forbear!—

At this Battle Mr. John Rushworth, our Historical Rushworth, had unexpectedly, for some instants, sight of a very famous person. Mr. John is Secretary to Fairfax; and they have placed him today among the Baggage-wagons, near Naseby Hamlet, above a mile from the fighting, where he waits in an anxious manner. It is known how Prince Rupert broke our left wing, while Cromwell was breaking their left. 'A Gentleman of Public Employment in the late Service near Naseby' writes next day, 'Harborough, 15th June, 2 in the morning,' a rough graphic Letter in the Newspapers,[2] wherein is this sentence:

* * 'A party of theirs, that broke through the left wing of horse, came quite behind the rear to our Train; the Leader of them, being a person somewhat in habit like the General, in a red montero, as the General had. He came as a friend; our commander of the guard of the Train went with his hat in his hand, and asked him, How the day went? thinking it had been the General: the Cavalier, who we since heard was Rupert, asked him and the rest, If they would have quarter? They cried No; gave fire, and instantly beat them off. It was a happy deliverance,'—without doubt.

There were taken here a good few 'ladies of quality in

[1] MS. *penes me.*

[2] King's Pamphlets, small 4to, no. 212, § 26, p. 2: the punctual contemporaneous Collector has named him with his pen: 'Mr. Rushworth's Letter, being the Secretary to his Excellency.'

carriages';—and above a hundred Irish ladies not of quality, tattery camp-followers 'with long skean-knives about a foot in length,' which they well knew how to use; upon whom I fear the Ordinance against Papists pressed hard this day.[1] The King's Carriage was also taken, with a Cabinet and many Royal Autographs in it, which when printed made a sad impression against his Majesty,—gave, in fact, a most melancholy view of the veracity of his Majesty, 'On the word of a King.'[2] All was lost!—

Here is Cromwell's Letter, written from Harborough, or 'Haverbrowe' as he calls it, that same night; after the hot Battle and hot chase were over. The original, printed long since in Rushworth, still lies in the British Museum,—with 'a strong steady signature,' which one could look at with interest. 'The Letter consists of two leaves; much worn, and now supported by pasting; red seal much defaced; is addressed on the second leaf:'

FOR THE HONOURABLE WILLIAM LENTHALL, SPEAKER OF THE COMMONS HOUSE OF PARLIAMENT: THESE

Harborough, 14th June 1645.

Sir,—Being commanded by you to this service, I think myself bound to acquaint you with the good hand of God towards you and us.

We marched yesterday after the King, who went before us from Daventry to Harborough; and quartered about six miles from him. This day we marched towards him. He drew-out to meet us; both Armies engaged. We, after three-hours fight very doubtful, at last routed his Army; killed and took about 5,000,—very many officers, but of what quality we yet know not. We took also about 200 car riages, all he had; and all his guns, being 12 in number, whereof two were demi-cannon, two demi-culverins, and I think the rest sackers. We pursued the Enemy from three miles short of Har-

[1] Whitlocke.

[2] *The King's Cabinet opened; or Letters taken in the Cabinet at Naseby Field* (London, 1645):—reprinted in *Harleian Miscellany* (London, 1810), v. 514.

borough to nine beyond, even to the sight of Leicester, whither the King fled.

Sir, this is none other but the hand of God; and to Him alone belongs the glory, wherein none are to share with Him. The General served you with all faithfulness and honour: and the best commendation I can give him is, That I daresay he attributes all to God, and would rather perish than assume to himself. Which is an honest and a thriving way:—and yet as much for bravery may be given to him, in this action, as to a man. Honest men served you faithfully in this action. Sir, they are trusty; I beseech you, in the name of God, not to discourage them. I wish this action may beget thankfulness and humility in all that are concerned in it. He that ventures his life for the liberty of his country, I wish he trust God for the liberty of his conscience, and you for the liberty he fights for. In this he rests, who is your most humble servant, *OLIVER CROMWELL.*[1]

John Bunyan, I believe, is this night in Leicester,—not yet writing his *Pilgrim's Progress* on Paper, but acting it on the face of the Earth, with a brown matchlock on his shoulder. Or rather, *without* the matchlock just at present; Leicester and he having been taken the other day. 'Harborough Church' is getting 'filled with prisoners' while Oliver writes,—and an immense contemporaneous tumult every where going on!

The 'honest men who served you faithfully' on this occasion are the considerable portion of the Army who have not yet succeeded in bringing themselves to take the Covenant. Whom the Presbyterian Party, rigorous for their own formula, call 'Schismatics,' 'Sectaries,' 'Anabaptists,' and other hard names; whom Cromwell, here and elsewhere, earnestly pleads for. To Cromwell, perhaps as much as to another, order was lovely, and disorder hateful; but he discerned better than some others what order and disorder really were. The forest-trees are not in 'order' because they are all clipt into the same shape of Dutch-dragons, and forced to die or grow in that way; but because in each of them there is the same genuine unity of life, from the inmost pith to the outmost leaf, and they do

[1] Harl. MSS. no. 7502, art. 5, p. 7; Rushworth, vi. 45.

grow according to that!—Cromwell naturally became the head of this Schismatic Party, intent to grow not as Dutch-dragons, but as real trees; a Party which naturally increased with the increasing earnestness of events and of men.—

The King stayed but a few hours in Leicester; he had taken Leicester, as we saw, some days before, and now it was to be re-taken from him some days after:—he stayed but a few hours here; rode on, that same night, to Ashby-de-la-Zouch, which he reached 'at daybreak,'—poor wearied King!—then again swiftly Westward, to Wales, to Ragland Castle, to this place and that; in the hope of raising some force, and coming to fight again; which, however, he could never do.[1] Some ten months more of roaming, and he, 'disguised as a groom,' will be riding with Parson Hudson towards the Scots at Newark.

The New-Model Army marched into the Southwest; very soon 'relieved Colonel Robert Blake' (Admiral Blake), and many others;—marched to ever new exploits and victories, which excite the pious admiration of Joshua Sprigge; and very soon swept all its enemies from the field, and brought this War to a close.[2]

The following Letters exhibit part of Cromwell's share in that business, and may be read with little commentary.

LETTER XXX

THE CLUBMEN

THE victorious Army, driving all before it in the Southwest, where alone the King had still any considerable fighting force, found itself opposed by a very unexpected enemy, famed in

[1] *Iter Carolinum*; being a succinct Relation of the necessitated Marches, Retreats and Sufferings of his Majesty Charles the First, from 10th January 1641 till the time of his Death, 1648: Collected by a daily Attendant upon his Sacred Majesty during all the said time. London, 1660.—It is reprinted in *Somers Tracts* (v. 263), but, as usual there, without any editing except a nominal one, though it somewhat needed more.

[2] A Journal of every day's March of the Army under his Excellency Sir Thomas Fairfax (in Sprigge, p. 331).

the old Pamphlets by the name of *Clubmen*. The design was at bottom Royalist; but the country-people in those regions had been worked upon by the Royalist Gentry and Clergy, on the somewhat plausible ground of taking up arms to defend themselves against the plunder and harassment of *both* Armies. The great mass of them were Neutrals; there even appeared by and by various transient bodies of 'Clubmen' on the Parliament side, whom Fairfax entertained occasionally to assist him in pioneering and other such services. They were called Clubmen, not, as M. Villemain supposes,[1] because they united in *Clubs*, but because they were armed with rough country weapons, mere bludgeons if no other could be had. Sufficient understanding of them may be gained from the following Letter of Cromwell, prefaced by some Excerpts.

From Rushworth: 'Thursday July 3d, Fairfax marched from Blandford to Dorchester, 12 miles; a very hot day. Where Colonel Sidenham, Governor of Weymouth, gave him information of the condition of those parts; and of the great danger from the Club-risers;' a set of men 'who would not suffer either contribution or victuals to be carried to the Parliament's garrisons. And the same night Mr. Hollis of Dorsetshire, the chief leader of the Clubmen, with some others of their principal men, came to Fairfax: and Mr. Hollis owned himself to be one of their leaders; affirming that it was fit the people should show their grievances and their strength. Fairfax treated them civilly, and promised they should have an answer the next morning. For they were so strong at that time, that it was held a point of prudence to be fair in demeanour towards them for a while; for if he should engage with General Goring and be put to the worst, these Clubmen would knock them on the head as they should fly for safety. —That which they desired from him was a safe-conduct for certain persons to go to the King and Parliament with Peti-

[1] Our French friends ought to be informed that M. Villemain's Book on Cromwell is, unluckily, a rather ignorant and shallow one.—Of M. Guizot, on the the other hand, we are to say that his Two Volumes, so far as they go, are the fruit of real ability and solid studies applied to those Transactions.

tions:'[1] which Fairfax in a very mild but resolute manner *refused.*

From Sprigge,[2] copied also into Rushworth with some inaccuracies: 'On Monday August 4th, Lieutenant-General Cromwell, having intelligence of some of their places of rendezvous for their several divisions, went forth' from Sherborne 'with a party of Horse to meet these Clubmen; being well satisfied of the danger of their design. As he was marching towards Shaftesbury with the party, they discovered some colours upon the top of a high Hill, full of wood and almost inaccessible. A Lieutenant with a small party was sent to them to know their meaning, and to acquaint them that the Lieutenant-General of the Army was there; whereupon Mr. Newman, one of their leaders, thought fit to come down, and told us, The intent was to desire to know why the gentlemen were taken at Shaftesbury on Saturday? The Lieutenant-General returned him this answer: That he held himself not bound to give him or them an account; what was done was by Authority; and they that did it were not responsible to them that had none: but not to leave them wholly unsatisfied, he told him, Those persons so met had been the occasion and stirrers of many tumultuous and unlawful meetings; for which they were to be tried by law; which trial ought not by them to be questioned or interrupted. Mr. Newman desired to go up to return the answer; the Lieutenant-General with a small party went with him; and had some conference with the people; to this purpose: That whereas they pretended to meet there to save their goods, they took a very ill course for that: to leave their houses was the way to *lose* their goods; and it was offered them, That justice should be done upon any who offered them violence: and as for the gentlemen taken at Shaftesbury, it was only to answer some things they were accused of, which they had done contrary to law and the peace of the Kingdom.—Herewith they seeming to be well satisfied, promised to return to their houses; and accordingly did so.

'These being thus quietly sent home, the Lieutenant-

[1] Rushworth, vi. 52. [2] Pp. 78–79.

General advanced farther, to a meeting of a greater number, of about 4000, who betook themselves to Hambledon Hill, near Shrawton. At the bottom of the Hill ours met a man with a musket, and asked, Whither he was going? he said, To the Club Army; ours asked, What he meant to do? he asked, What they had to do with that? Being required to lay-down his arms, he said He would first lose his life; but was not so good as his word, for though he cocked and presented his musket, he was prevented, disarmed, and wounded, but not'—Here, however, is Cromwell's own Narrative:

TO THE RIGHT HONOURABLE SIR THOMAS FAIRFAX, COMMANDER-IN-CHIEF OF THE PARLIAMENT'S FORCES, 'AT SHERBORNE: THESE'

'Shaftesbury,' 4th August 1645.

Sir,—I marched this morning towards Shaftesbury. In my way I found a party of Clubmen gathered together, about two miles on this side of the Town, towards you; and one Mr. Newman in the head of them,—who was one of those who did attend you at Dorchester, with Mr. Hollis. I sent to them to know the cause of their meeting: Mr. Newman came to me; and told me, That the Clubmen in Dorset and Wilts, to the number of ten-thousand, were to meet about their men who were taken away at Shaftesbury, and that their intendment was to secure themselves from plundering. To the first I told them, That although no account was due to them, yet I knew the men were taken by your authority, to be tried judicially for raising a Third Party in the Kingdom; and if they should be found guilty, they must suffer according to the nature of their offence; if innocent, I assured them you would acquit them. Upon this they said, If they have deserved punishment, they would not have anything to do with them; and so were quieted as to that point. For the other 'point,' I assured them, That it was your great care, not to suffer them in the least to be plundered, and that they should defend themselves from violence, and bring to your Army such as did them any wrong, where they should be punished with all severity: upon this, very quietly and peaceably they marched away to their houses, being very well satisfied and contented.

We marched on to Shaftesbury, where we heard a great body of them was drawn together about Hambledon Hill;—where indeed near two-thousand were gathered. I sent 'up' a forlorn-hope of about fifty Horse; who coming very civilly to them, they fired upon them; and ours desiring some of them to come to me, were refused with disdain. They were drawn into one of the old Camps,[1] *upon a very high Hill: I sent one Mr. Lee*[2] *to them, To certify the peaceableness of my intentions, and To desire them to peaceableness, and to submit to the Parliament. They refused, and fired at us. I sent him a second time, To let them know, that if they would lay-down their arms, no wrong should be done them. They still (through the animation of their leaders, and especially two vile Ministers) refused; I commanded your Captain-Lieutenant to draw-up to them, to be in readiness to charge; and if upon his falling on, they would lay-down arms, to accept them and spare them. When we came near, they refused his offer, and let-fly at him; killed about two of his men, and at least four horses. The passage not being for above three a-breast, kept us out: whereupon Major Desborow wheeled about; got in the rear of them, beat them from the work, and did some small execution upon them;—I believe killed not twelve of them but cut very many, 'and put them all to flight.' We have taken about 300; many of which are poor silly creatures, whom if you please to let me send home, they promise to be very dutiful for time to come, and 'will be hanged before they come out again.'*

The ringleaders which we have, I intend to bring to you. They had taken divers of the Parliament soldiers prisoners, besides Colonel Fiennes his men; and used them most barbarously; bragging, They hoped to see my Lord Hopton, and that he is to command them. They expected from Wilts great store; and gave out they meant to raise the siege at Sherborne, when 'once' they were all met. We have gotten great store of their arms, and they carried few or none home. We quarter about ten miles off, and purpose to draw our quarters near to you tomorrow. Your most humble servant,

OLIVER CROMWELL.[3]

[1] Roman Camps (Gough's *Camden*, i. 52).

[2] 'One Mr. Lee,who, upon the approach of ours, had come from them, (Sprigge, p. 79).

[3] Newspapers (*Cromwelliana*, p. 20).

'On Tuesday at night, August 5th, the Lieutenant-General' Cromwell 'with his party returned to Sherborne,' where the General and the rest were very busy besieging the inexpugnable Sir Lewis Dives.

'This work,' which the Lieutenant-General had now been upon, continues Sprigge, 'though unhappy, was very necessary.'[1] No messenger could be sent out but he was picked-up by these Clubmen; these once dispersed, 'a man might ride very quietly from Sherborne to Salisbury.' The inexpugnable Sir Lewis Dives (a thrasonical person known to the readers of Evelyn), after due battering, was now soon stormed: whereupon, by Letters found on him, it became apparent how deeply Royalist this scheme of Clubmen had been; 'Commissions for raising regiments of Clubmen'; the design to be extended over England at large, 'yea into the Associated Counties.' However, it has now come to nothing; and the Army turns Northward to the Siege of Bristol, where Prince Rupert is doing all he can to entrench himself.

THE LEVELLERS

WHILE Miss Dorothy Mayor is choosing her wedding-dresses, and Richard Cromwell is looking forward to a life of Arcadian felicity now near at hand, there has turned up for Richard's Father and other parties interested, on the public side of things, a matter of very different complexion, requiring to be instantly dealt with in the interim. The matter of the class called Levellers; concerning which we must now say a few words.

In 1647, as we saw, there were Army Adjutators; and among some of them wild notions afloat, as to the swift attainability of Perfect Freedom civil and religious, and a practical Millenium on this Earth; notions which required, in the Rendezvous at Corkbush-field, 'Rendezvous of Ware' as they oftenest call it, to be very resolutely trodden out.

[1] Sprigge, p. 81.

Eleven chief mutineers were ordered from the ranks in that Rendezvous; were condemned by swift Court-Martial to die; and Trooper Arnald, one of them, was accordingly shot there and then; which extinguished the mutiny for that time. War since, and Justice on Delinquents, England made a Free Commonwealth, and suchlike, have kept the Army busy: but a deep republican leaven, working all along among these men, breaks now again into very formidable development. As the following brief glimpses and excerpts may satisfy an attentive reader who will spread them out, to the due expansion, in his mind. Take first this glimpse into the civil province; and discern, with amazement, a whole submarine world of Calvinistic Sansculottism, Five-point Charter and the Rights of Man, threatening to emerge almost two centuries before its time!

'The Council of State,' says Whitlocke,[1] just while Mr. Barton is boggling about the Hursley Marriage-settlements, 'has intelligence of certain *Levellers* appearing at St. Margaret's Hill, near Cobham in Surrey, and at St. George's Hill,' in the same quarter: 'that they were digging the ground, and sowing it with roots and beans. One Everard, once of the Army, who terms himself a Prophet, is the chief of them': one Winstanley is another chief. 'They were Thirty men, and said that they should be shortly Four-thousand. They invited all to come in and help them; and promised them meat, drink, and clothes. They threaten to pull down park pales, and to lay all open; and threaten the neighbours that they will shortly make them all come up to the hills and work.' These infatuated persons, beginning a new era in this headlong manner on the chalk hills of Surrey, are laid hold of by certain Justices, 'by the country people,' and also by 'two troops of horse'; and complain loudly of such treatment; appealing to all men whether it be fair.[2] This is the account they give of themselves when brought before the General some days afterwards:

[1] 17th April 1649, p. 384.

[2] King's Pamphlets, small 4to. no. 427, § 6 (Declaration of the bloody and unchristian Acting of William Star, etc. in opposition to those that dig upon George-Hill in Surrey); *ib.* no. 418, § 5, etc.

'*April 20th*, 1649. Everard and Winstanley, the chief of those that digged at St. George's Hill in Surrey, came to the General and made a large declaration, to justify their proceedings. Everard said, He was of the race of the Jews,' as most men, called Saxon and other, properly are; 'That all the Liberties of the People were lost by the coming in of William the Conqueror; and that, ever since, the People of God had lived under tyranny and oppression worse than that of our Forefathers under the Egyptians. But now the time of deliverance was at hand; and God would bring His People out of this slavery, and restore them to their freedom in enjoying the fruits and benefits of the Earth. And that there had lately appeared to him, Everard, a vision; which bade him, Arise and dig and plough the Earth, and receive the fruits thereof. That their intent is to restore the Creation to its former condition. That as God had promised to make the barren land fruitful, so now what they did, was to restore the ancient Community of enjoying the Fruits of the Earth, and to distribute the benefit thereof to the poor and needy, and to feed the hungry and clothe the naked. That they intend not to meddle with any man's property, nor to break down any pales or enclosures,' in spite of reports to the contrary; 'but only to meddle with what is common and untilled, and to make it fruitful for the use of man. That the time will suddenly be, when all men shall willingly come in and give up their lands and estates, and submit to this Community of Goods.'

These are the principles of Everard, Winstanley, and the poor Brotherhood, seemingly Saxon, but properly of the race of the Jews, who were found dibbling beans on St. George's Hill, under the clear April skies in 1649, and hastily bringing in a new era in that manner. 'And for all such as will come in and work with them, they shall have meat, drink, and clothes, which is all that is necessary to the life of man: and as for money, there is not any need of it; nor of clothes more than to cover nakedness.' For the rest, 'That they will not defend themselves by arms, but will submit unto authority, and wait till the promised opportunity be offered, which they conceive to be at hand. And that as their forefathers lived in tents, so it would be suitable to their condition now to live in the same.

'While they were before the General, they stood with their hats on; and being demanded the reason thereof, they said, Because he was but their fellow-creature. Being asked the meaning of that phrase, Give honour to whom honour is due,—they said, Your mouths shall be stopped that ask such a question.'[1]

Dull Bulstrode hath 'set down this the more largely because it was the beginning of the appearance' of an extensive levelling doctrine, much to be 'avoided' by judicious persons, seeing it is 'a weak persuasion.' The germ of Quakerism and much else is curiously visible here. But let us look now at the military phasis of the matter; where 'a weak persuasion' mounted on cavalry horses, with sabres and fire-arms in its hand, may become a very perilous one.

Friday 20th April 1649. The Lieutenant-General has consented to go to Ireland; the City also will lend money; and now this Friday the Council of the Army meets at Whitehall to decide what regiments shall go on that service. 'After a solemn seeking of God by prayer,' they agree that it shall be by lot: tickets are put into a hat, a child draws them: the regiments, fourteen of foot and fourteen of horse, are decided on in this manner. 'The officers on whom the lot fell, in all the twenty-eight regiments, expressed much cheerfulness at the decision.' The officers did:—but the common men are by no means all of that humour. The common men, blown upon by Lilburn and his five small Beagles, have notions about England's *new* Chains, about the Hunting of Foxes from Triploe Heath, and in fact ideas concerning the capability that lies in man and in a free Commonwealth, which are of the most alarming description.

Thursday 26th April. This night, at the Bull in Bishopsgate, there has an alarming mutiny broken out in a troop of Whalley's regiment there. Whalley's men are not allotted for Ireland: but they refuse to quit London, as they are ordered; they want this and that first: they seize their colours from the

[1] Whitlocke, p. 384.

Cornet, who is lodged at the Bull there:—the General and the Lieutenant-General have to hasten thither; quell them, pack them forth on their march; seizing fifteen of them first, to be tried by Court-Martial. Tried by instant Court-Martial, five of them are found guilty, doomed to die, but pardoned; and one of them, Trooper Lockyer, is doomed and not pardoned. Trooper Lockyer is shot, in Paul's Churchyard, on the morrow. A very brave young man, they say; though but three-and-twenty, 'he has served seven years in these Wars,' ever since the Wars began. 'Religious' too, 'of excellent parts and much beloved';—but with hot notions as to human Freedom, and the rate at which the millenniums are attainable, poor Lockyer! He falls shot in Paul's Churchyard on Friday, amid the tears of men and women. Paul's Cathedral, we remark, is now a Horse-guard; horses stamp in the Canons' stalls there: and Paul's Cross itself, as smacking of Popery where in fact Alablaster once preached flat Popery, is swept altogether away, and its leaden roof melted into bullets, or mixed with tin for culinary pewter. Lockyer's corpse is watched and wept over, not without prayer, in the eastern regions of the City, till a new week come; and on Monday, this is what we see advancing westward by way of funeral to him.

'About one hundred went before the Corpse, five or six in a file; the Corpse was then brought, with six trumpets sounding a soldier's knell; then the Trooper's Horse came, clothed all over in mourning, and led by a footman. The Corpse was adorned with bundles of Rosemary, one half stained in blood; and the Sword of the deceased along with them. Some thousands followed in rank and file: all had seagreen-and-black Ribbon tied on their hats and to their breasts: and the women brought up the rear. At the new Churchyard in Westminster, some thousands more of the better sort met them, who thought not fit to march through the City. Many looked upon this funeral as an affront to the Parliament and Army; others called these people 'Levellers'; but they took no notice of any one's sayings.'[1]

[1] Whitlocke, p. 385.

That was the end of Trooper Lockyer: six trumpets wailing stern music through London streets; Rosemaries and Sword half-dipt in blood; funeral of many thousands in seagreen Ribbons and black:—testimony of a weak persuasion now looking somewhat perilous. Lieutenant-Colonel Lilburn and his five small Beagles, now in a kind of loose arrest under the Lieutenant of the Tower, make haste to profit by the general emotion; publish on the 1st of May[1] *their* 'Agreement of the People,'—their Bentham-Sieyes Constitution; Annual very exquisite Parliament, and other Lilburn apparatus; whereby the Perfection of Human Nature will with a maximum of rapidity be secured, and a millennium straightway arrive, sings the Lilburn Oracle.

May 9th. Richard Cromwell is safe wedded; Richard's Father is reviewing troops in Hyde Park, 'seagreen colours in some of their hats.' The Lieutenant-General speaks earnestly to them. Has not the Parliament been diligent, doing its best? It has punished Delinquents; it has voted, in these very days, resolutions for dissolving itself and assembling future Parliaments.[2] It has protected trade; got a good Navy afloat. You soldiers, there is exact payment provided for you. Martial Law? Death, or other punishment, of Mutineers? Well! Whoever cannot stand Martial Law is not fit to be a soldier: *his* best plan will be to lay-down his arms; he shall have his ticket, and get his arrears as we others do,—we that still mean to fight against the enemies of England and this Cause.[3]—One trooper showed signs of insolence; the Lieutenant-General suppressed him by rigour and by clemency; the seagreen ribbons were torn from such hats as had them. The humour of the men is not the most perfect. This Review was on Wednesday: Lilburn and his five small Beagles are, on Saturday, committed close Prisoners to the Tower, each rigorously to a cell of his own.

It is high time. For now the flame has caught the ranks of

[1] Whitlocke's date, p. 385.

[2] 15th April 1649, *Commons Journals*.

[3] Newspapers (in *Cromwelliana*, p. 56).

the Army itself, in Oxfordshire, in Gloucestershire, at Salisbury where head-quarters are; and rapidly there is, on all hands, a dangerous conflagration blazing out. In Oxfordshire, one Captain Thompson, not known to us before, has burst from his quarters at Banbury, with a party of Two-hundred, in these same days; has sent forth his *England's Standard Advanced*;[1] insisting passionately on the *New Chains* we are fettered with; indignantly demanding swift perfection of Human Freedom, justice on the murderers of Lockyer and Arnald;—threatening that if a hair of Lilburn and the five small Beagles be hurt, he will avenge it 'seventy-and-seven fold.' This Thompson's Party, swiftly attacked by his Colonel, is broken within the week; he himself escapes with a few, and still roves up and down. To join whom, or to communicate with Gloucestershire where help lies, there has, in the interim, open mutiny, 'above a Thousand strong,' with subalterns, with a Cornet Thompson, brother of the Captain, but without any leader of mark, broken out at Salisbury: the General and Lieutenant-General, with what force can be raised, are hastening thitherward in all speed. Now were the time for Lieutenant-Colonel Lilburn; now or never might noisy John do some considerable injury to the Cause he has at heart: but he sits, in these critical hours, fast within stone walls!

Monday 14th May. All Sunday the General and Lieutenant-General marched in full speed, by Alton, by Andover, towards Salisbury; the mutineers, hearing of them, start northward for Buckinghamshire, then for Berkshire; the General and Lieutenant-General turning also northward after them in hot chase. The mutineers arrive at Wantage; make for Oxfordshire by Newbridge; find the Bridge already seized; cross higher up by swimming; get to Burford, very weary, and 'turn out their horses to grass';—Fairfax and Cromwell still following in hot speed, 'a march of near fifty miles' that Monday. What boots it? there is no leader, noisy John is sitting fast within stone walls! The mutineers lie asleeep in Burford, their

[1] Given in Walker's *History of Independency*, part ii. 168; dated 6th May.

horses out at grass; the Lieutenant-General, having rested at a safe distance since dark, bursts into Burford as the clocks are striking midnight. He has beset some hundreds of the mutineers, 'who could only fire some shots out of windows';—has dissipated the mutiny, trodden down the Levelling Principle out of English affairs once more. Here is the last scene of the business; the rigorous Court-Martial having now sat; the decimated doomed Mutineers being placed on the leads of the Church to see:

Thursday 17*th May*. 'This day in Burford Churchyard, Cornet Thomson, brother to Thompson the chief leader, was brought to the place of execution; and expressed himself to this purpose: That it was just what did befall him; that God did not own the ways he went; that he had offended the General: he desired the prayers of the people; and told the soldiers who were appointed to shoot him, that when he held out his hands, they should do their duty. And accordingly he was immediately, after the sign given, shot to death. Next after him was a Corporal, brought to the same place of execution; where, looking upon his fellow-mutineers, he set his back against the wall; and bade them who were appointed to shoot, 'Shoot!' and died desperately. The third, being also a Corporal, was brought to the same place; and without the least acknowledgment of error, or show of fear, he pulled off his doublet, standing a pretty distance from the wall; and bade the soldiers do their duty; looking them in the face till they gave fire, not showing the least kind of terror or fearfulness of spirit,'—So die the Leveller Corporals; strong they, after their sort, for the Liberties of England; resolute to the very death. Misguided Corporals! But History, which has wept for a misguided Charles Stuart, and blubbered, in the most copious helpless manner, near two centuries now, whole floods of brine, enough to salt the Herring-fishery,—will not refuse these poor Corporals also her tributary sigh. With Arnald of the Rendezvous at Ware, with Lockyer of the Bull in Bishopsgate, and other misguided martyrs to the Liberties of England then and since, may they sleep well!

Cornet Dean, who now came forward as the next to be shot, 'expressed penitence'; got pardon from the General: and there was no more shooting. Lieutenant-General Cromwell went into the Church, called down the Decimated of the Mutineers; rebuked, admonished; said, The General in his mercy had forgiven them. Misguided men, would you ruin this Cause, which marvellous Providences have so confirmed to us to be the Cause of God? Go, repent; and rebel no more, lest a worse thing befall you! 'They wept,' says the old Newspaper; they retired to the Devizes for a time; were then restored to their regiments, and marched cheerfully for Ireland. —Captain Thompson, the Cornet's brother, the first of all the Mutineers, he too, a few days afterwards, was fallen-in with in Northamptonshire, still mutinous: his men took quarter; he himself 'fled to a wood'; fired and fenced there, and again desperately fired, declaring he would never yield alive;—whereupon 'a Corporal with seven bullets in his carbine' ended Captain Thompson too; and this formidable conflagration, to the last glimmer of it, was extinct.

Sansculottism, as we said above, has to lie submerged for almost two centuries yet. Levelling, in the practical civil or military provinces of English things, is forbidden to be. In the spiritual provinces it cannot be forbidden; for there it everywhere already is. It ceases dibbling beans on St. George's Hill near Cobham; ceases galloping in mutiny across the Isis to Burford;—takes into Quakerisms, and kingdoms which are not of this world. My poor friend Dryasdust lamentably tears his hair over the 'intolerance' of that old Time to Quakerism and suchlike. If Dryasdust had seen the dibbling on St. George's Hill, the threatened fall of 'park pales,' and the gallop to Burford, he would reflect that Conviction in an earnest age means, not lengthy Spouting in Exeter-Hall, but rapid silent Practice on the face of the Earth; and would perhaps leave his poor hair alone.

On Thursday night, 17th of the month, the General, Lieutenant-General, and chief Officers arrive at Oxford; lodge in All-Souls College; head-quarters are to be there for some days.

Solemnly welcomed by the reformed University; bedinnered, bespeeched; made Doctors, Masters, Bachelors, or what was suitable to their ranks, and to the faculties of this reformed University. Of which high doings, degrees and convocation-dinners, and eloquence by Proctor Zanchy, we say nothing,—being in haste for Ireland. This small benefit we have from the business: Anthony Wood, in his crabbed but authentic way, has given us biographical sketches of all these Graduates; biographies very lean, very perverse, but better than are commonly going then, and in the fatal scarcity not quite without value.[1]

Neither do we speak of the thanking in the House of Commons; or of the general Day of Thanksgiving for London, which is Thursday the 7th June (the day for England at large being Thursday 21st),[2]—and of the illustrious Dinner which the City gave the Parliament and Officers, and all the Dignitaries of England, when Sermon was done. It was at Grocers' Hall, this City dinner; really illustrious. Dull Bulstrode, Keeper, or one of the Keepers, of the Commonwealth Great Seal, was there,—Keeper of that lump of dignified metal, found since all rusty in the wall at Hursley: and my Lord of Pembroke, an Earl and Member of the Council of State, 'speaking very loud,' as his manner was, insisted that illustrious Bulstrode should take place above him. I have given place to Bishop Williams when he was Keeper; and the Commonwealth Great Seal is as good as any King's ever was;—illustrious Bulstrode, take place above me: so![3] 'On almost every dish was enamelled a bandrol with the word *Welcome*. No music but that of drum and trumpet'; no balderdash, or almost none, of speech without meaning; 'no drinking of healths or other

[1] Wood's *Athenæ*, iv. (*Fasti*, ii. 127–155): the Graduates of Saturday 19th May 1649, are, *Fairfax*, p. 148; *Cromwell*, p. 152; Colonels *Scrope*, Grosvenor, *Sir Hardress Waller*, *Ingoldsby*, *Harrison*, *Goff*, *Okey*; Adjutant-General Sedascue, Scoutmaster Rowe: and of Monday 21st, Lieutenant-Colonel *Cobbet*, p. 140; John Rushworth, Cornet *Joyce*, p. 138:—of whom those marked here in Italics have biographies worth looking at for an instant.

[2] *Commons Journals*, 26th May 1649.

[3] Whitlocke, p. 391.

incivility';—drinking of healths; a kind of invocation or prayer, addressed surely not to God, in that humour; probably therefore to the Devil, or to the Heathen gods; which is offensive to the well-constituted mind. Four-hundred pounds were given to the Poor of London, that they also might dine.[1]—

And now for Bristol and the Campaign in Ireland.

[1] Newspapers (in *Cromwelliana*, pp. 59, 60).

FROM Latter-Day Pamphlets

The *Latter-day Pamphlets* were published separately month by month, between 1 February and 1 August, 1850. They first appeared in book form also during that year. The pamphlets attempt a more specific analysis of Britain's social disorders than Carlyle had made before, and they express his dislike of orthodox Victorian Radicalism and rationalism in savage, and at times hysterical, terms. The first of the pamphlets, and one of the mildest of them, 'The Present Time,' is printed here in its entirety.

FROM

Latter-Day Pamphlets

NO. I

THE PRESENT TIME

[1st February 1850]

The Present Time, youngest-born of Eternity, child and heir of all the Past Times with their good and evil, and parent of all the Future, is ever a 'New Era' to the thinking man; and comes with new questions and significance, however commonplace it look; to know *it*, and what it bids us do, is ever the sum of knowledge for all of us. This new Day, sent us out of Heaven, this also has its heavenly omens;—amid the bustling trivialities and loud empty noises, its silent monitions, which, if we cannot read and obey, it will not be well with us! No;—nor is there any sin more fearfully avenged on men and Nations than that same, which indeed includes and presupposes all manner of sins: the sin which our old pious fathers called 'judicial blindness';—which we, with our light habits, may still call misinterpretation of the Time that now is; disloyalty to its real meanings and monitions, stupid disregard of these, stupid adherence active or passive to the counterfeits and mere current semblances of these. This is true of all times and days.

But in the days that are now passing-over us, even fools are arrested to ask the meaning of them; few of the generations of men have seen more impressive days. Days of endless calamity, disruption, dislocation, confusion worse confounded: if they are not days of endless hope too, then they are days of utter despair. For it is not a small hope that will suffice, the ruin being clearly, either in action or in prospect, universal. There must be a new world, if there is to be any world at all! That human things in our Europe can ever return to the old sorry routine, and proceed with any steadiness or continuance there; this small hope is not now a tenable one. These days of universal death must be days of universal newbirth, if the ruin is not to be total and final! It is a Time to make the dullest man consider; and ask himself, Whence *he* came? Whither he is bound?—A veritable 'New Era,' to the foolish as well as to the wise.

Not long ago, the world saw, with thoughtless joy which might have been very thoughtful joy, a real miracle not heretofore considered possible or conceivable in the world,—a Reforming Pope. A simple pious creature, a good country-priest, invested unexpectedly with the tiara, takes up the New Testament, declares that this henceforth shall be his rule of governing. No more finessse, chicanery, hypocrisy, or false or foul dealing of any kind: God's truth shall be spoken, God's justice shall be done, on the throne called of St. Peter: an honest Pope, Papa, or Father of Christendom, shall preside there. And such a throne of St. Peter; and such a Christendom, for an honest Papa to preside in! The European populations everywhere hailed the omen; with shouting and rejoicing, leading-articles and tar-barrels; thinking people listened with astonishment,—not with sorrow if they were faithful and wise; with awe rather as at the heralding of death, and with a joy as of victory beyond death! Something pious, grand and as if awful in that joy, revealing once more the Presence of a Divine Justice in this world. For, to such men it was very clear how this poor devoted Pope would prosper, with his New Testament in his hand. An alarming business, that of governing in the throne of St. Peter by the rule of veracity! By the rule of veracity, the so-called throne of St. Peter was openly declared, above three-hundred years ago, to be a falsity, a huge mistake, a pestilent dead carcass, which this Sun was weary of. More than three hundred years ago, the throne of St. Peter received peremptory judicial notice to quit; authentic order, registered in Heaven's chancery and since legible in the hearts of all brave men, to take itself away,—to begone, and let us have no more to do with *it* and its delusions and impious deliriums;—and it has been sitting every day since, it may depend upon it, at its own peril withal, and will have to pay exact damages yet for every day it has so sat. Law of veracity? What this Popedom had to do by the law of veracity, was to give-up its own foul galvanic life, an offence to gods and men; honestly to die, and get itself buried!

Far from this was the thing the poor Pope undertook in regard to it;—and yet, on the whole, it was essentially this too. 'Reforming Pope?' said one of our acquaintance, often in those weeks, 'Was there ever such a miracle? About to break-up that hugh imposthume too, by "curing" it? Turgot and Necker were nothing to this. God is great; and when a scandal is to end, brings some devoted man to take charge of it in hope, not in despair!'—But cannot he reform? asked many simple persons; —to whom our friend in grim banter would reply: 'Reform a Popedom,—hardly. A wretched old kettle, ruined from top to bottom, and consisting mainly now of foul *grime* and *rust*: stop the holes of it, as your antecessors have been doing, with temporary putty, it may hang-together yet a while; begin to hammer at it, solder at it, to what you call mend and rectify it,—it will fall to sherds, as sure as rust is rust; go all into nameless dissolution,—and the fat in the fire will be a thing worth looking at, poor Pope!'— —So accordingly it has proved. The poor Pope, amid felicitations and tar-barrels of various kinds, went on joyfully for a season: but he had awakened, he as no other man could do, the sleeping elements; mothers of the whirlwinds, conflagrations, earthquakes. Questions not very soluble at present, were even sages and heroes set to solve them, began everywhere with new emphasis to be asked. Questions which all official men wished, and almost hoped, to postpone till Doomsday. Doomsday itself *had* come; that was the terrible truth!—

For, sure enough, if once the law of veracity be acknowledged as the rule for human things, there will not anywhere be want of work for the reformer; in very few places do human things adhere quite closely to that law! Here was the Papa of Christendom proclaiming that such was actually the case;—whereupon all over Christendom such results as we have seen. The Sicilians, I think, were the first notable body that set-about applying this new strange rule sanctioned by the general Father; they said to themselves, We do not by the law of veracity belong to Naples and these Neapolitan Officials; we will, by favour of Heaven and the Pope, be free of these. Fighting ensued; insurrection, fiercely maintained in the Sicilian Cities; with much bloodshed, much tumult and loud noise, vociferation extending through all newspapers and countries. The effect of this, carried abroad by newspapers and rumour, was great in all places; greatest perhaps in Paris, which for sixty years past has been the City of Insurrections. The French People had plumed themselves on being, whatever else they were not, at least the chosen 'soldiers of liberty,' who took the lead of all creatures in that pursuit, at least; and had become, as their orators, editors and litterateurs diligently taught them, a People whose bayonets were sacred, a kind of Messiah People, saving a blind world in its own despite, and earning for themselves a terrestrial and even celestial glory very considerable indeed. And here were the wretched down-trodden populations of Sicily risen to rival them, and threatening to take the trade out of their hand.

No doubt of it, this hearing continually of the very Pope's glory as a Reformer, of the very Sicilians fighting divinely for liberty behind barricades,—must have bitterly aggravated the feeling of every Frenchman, as he looked around him, at home, on a Louis-Philippism which had became the scorn of all the world. '*Ichabod*; is the glory departing from us? Under the sun is nothing baser, by all accounts and evidences, than the system of repression and corruption, of shameless dishonesty and unbelief in anything but human baseness, that we now live under. The Italians, the very Pope, have become apostles of liberty, and France is— —what is France!'—We know what France suddenly became in the end of February next; and by a clear enough genealogy, we can trace a considerable share in that event to the good simple Pope with the New Testament in his hand. An outbreak, or at least a radical change and even inversion of affairs hardly to be achieved without an outbreak, everybody felt was inevitable in France: but it had been universally expected that France would as usual take the initiative in that matter; and had there been no reforming Pope, no insurrectionary Sicily, France had certainly not broken-out then and so, but only afterwards and otherwise. The French explosion, not anticipated by the cunningest men there on the spot scrutinising it, burst-up unlimited, complete, defying computation or control.

Close following which, as if by sympathetic subterranean electricities, all Europe exploded, boundless, uncontrollable; and we had the year 1848, one of the most singular, disastrous, amazing, and, on the whole, humiliating years the European world ever saw. Not since the irruption of the Northern Barbarians has there been the like. Everywhere immeasurable Democracy rose monstrous, loud, blatant, inarticulate as the voice of Chaos. Everywhere the Official holy-of-holies was scandalously laid bare to dogs and the profane:—Enter, all the world, see what kind of Official holy it is. Kings everywhere, and reigning persons, stared in sudden horror, the voice of the whole world bellowing in their ear, 'Begone, ye imbecile hypocrites, histrios not heroes! Off with you, off!'—and, what was peculiar and notable in this year for the first time, the Kings all made haste to go, as if exclaiming, 'We *are* poor histrios, we sure enough;—did you want heroes? Don't kill us; we couldn't help it!' Not one of them turned round, and stood upon his Kingship, as upon a right he could afford to die for, or to risk his skin upon; by no manner of means. That, I say, is the alarming peculiarity at present. Democracy, on this new occasion, finds all Kings *conscious* that they are but Playactors. The miserable mortals, enacting their High Life Below Stairs, with faith only that this Universe may perhaps be all a phantasm and hypocrisis,—the truculent

Constable of the Destinies suddenly enters: 'Scandalous Phantasms, what do *you* here? Are "solemnly constituted Impostors" the proper Kings of men? Did you think the Life of Man was a grimacing dance of apes? To be led always by the squeak of your paltry fiddle? Ye miserable, this Universe is not an upholstery Puppet-play, but a terrible God's Fact; and you, I think,—had not you better begone!' They fled precipitately, some of them with what we may call an exquisite ignominy,—in terror of the treadmill or worse. And everywhere the people, or the populace, take their own government upon themselves; and open 'kinglessness,' what we call *anarchy*,—how happy if it be anarchy *plus* a street-constable! —is everywhere the order of the day. Such was the history, from Baltic to Mediterranean, in Italy, France, Prussia, Austria, from end to end of Europe, in those March days of 1848. Since the destruction of the old Roman Empire by inroad of the Northern Barbarians, I have known nothing similar.

And so, then, there remained no King in Europe; no King except the Public Haranguer, haranguing on barrel-head, in leading-article; or getting himself aggregated into a National Parliament to harangue. And for about four months all France, and to a great degree all Europe, rough-ridden by every species of delirium, except happily the murderous for most part, was a weltering mob, presided over by M. de Lamartine at the Hôtel-de-Ville; a most eloquent fair-spoken literary gentleman, whom thoughtless persons took for a prophet, priest and heaven-sent evangelist, and whom a wise Yankee-friend of mine discerned to be properly 'the first stump-orator in the world, standing too on the highest stump,—for the time.' A sorrowful spectacle to men of reflection, during the time he lasted, that poor M. de Lamartine; with nothing in him but melodious wind and *soft sowder*, which he and others took for something divine and not diabolic! Sad enough: the eloquent latest impersonation of Chaos-come-again; able to talk for itself, and declare persuasively that *it* is Cosmos! However, you have but to wait a little, in such cases; all balloons do and must give-up their gas in the pressure of things, and are collapsed in a sufficiently wretched manner before long.

And so in City after City, street-barricades are piled, and truculent, more or less murderous insurrection begins; populace after populace rises, King after King capitulates or absconds; and from end to end of Europe Democracy has blazed-up explosive, much higher, more irresistible and less resisted than ever before; testifying too sadly on what a bottomless volcano, or universal powder-mine of most inflammable mutinous chaotic elements, separated from us by a thin earth-rind, Society with all its arrangements and acquirements everywhere, in the present epoch, rests! The kind of persons who excite or give signal to such revolutions,—students, young men of letters, advocates, editors, hot inexperienced enthusiasts, or fierce and justly bankrupt desperadoes, acting everywhere on the discontent of the millions and blowing it into flame,—might give rise to reflections as to the character of our epoch. Never till now did young men, and almost children, take such a command in human affairs. A changed time since the word *Senior* (Seigneur, or *Elder*) was first devised to signify 'lord,' or superior;—as in all languages of men we find it to have been! Not an honourable document this either, as to the spiritual condition of our epoch. In times when men love wisdom, the old man will ever be venerable, and be venerated, and reckoned noble: in times that love something else than wisdom, and indeed have little or no wisdom, and see little or none to love, the old man will cease to be venerated;—and looking more closely, also, you will find that in fact he has ceased to be venerable, and has begun to be contemptible; a foolish *boy* still, a boy without the graces, generosities, and opulent strength of young boys. In these days, what of *lordship* or leadership is still to be done, the youth must do it, not the mature or aged man; the mature man, hardened into sceptical egoism, knows no monition but that of his own frigid cautions, avarices, mean timidities; and can lead nowhither towards an object that even seems noble. But to return.

This mad state of matters will of course before long allay itself, as it has everywhere begun to do; the ordinary necessities of men's daily existence cannot comport with it, and these, whatever else is cast aside, will have their way. Some remounting,—very temporary remounting,—of the old machine, under new colours and altered forms, will probably ensue soon in most countries: the old histrionic Kings will be admitted back under conditions, under 'Constitutions,' with national Parliaments, or the like fashionable adjuncts; and everywhere the old daily life will try to begin again. But there is now no hope that such arrangements can be permanent; that they can be other than poor temporary makeshifts, which, if they try to fancy and make themselves permanent, will be displaced by new explosions, recurring more speedily than last time. In such baleful oscillation, afloat as amid raging bottomless eddies and conflicting sea-currents, not steadfast as on fixed foundations, must European Society continue swaying, now disastrously tumbling, then painfully readjusting itself, at ever shorter intervals,—till once the *new* rock-basis does come to light, and the weltering deluges of mutiny, and of need to mutiny, abate again!

For universal *Democracy*, whatever we may think of it, has declared itself as an inevitable fact of the days in which we live; and he who has any chance to instruct, or lead, in his days, must begin by admitting that: new street-barricades, and new anarchies, still more scandalous if still less sanguinary, must return and again return, till governing persons everywhere know and admit that. Democracy, it may be said everywhere, is here:—for sixty years now, ever since the grand or *First* French Revolution, that fact has been terribly announced to all the world; in message after message, some of them very terrible indeed; and now at last all the world ought really to believe it. That the world does believe it; that even Kings now as good as believe it, and know, or with just terror surmise, that they are but temporary phantasm Playactors, and that Democracy is the grand, alarming, imminent and indisputable Reality: this, among the scandalous phases we witnessed in the last two years, is a phasis full of hope: a sign that we are advancing closer and closer to the very Problem itself, which it will behove us to solve or die;—that all fighting and campaigning and coalitioning in regard to the *existence* of the Problem, is hopeless and superfluous henceforth. The gods have appointed it *so*; no Pitt, nor body of Pitts or mortal creatures can appoint it otherwise. Democracy, sure enough, is here: one knows not how long it will keep hidden underground even in Russia;—and here in England, though we object to it resolutely in the form of street-barricades and insurrectionary pikes, and decidedly will not open doors to it on those terms, the tramp of its million feet is on all streets and thoroughfares, the sound of its bewildered thousandfold voice is in all writings and speakings, in all thinkings and modes and activities of men: the soul that does not now, with hope or terror, discern *it*, is not the one we address on this occasion.

What *is* Democracy; this huge inevitable Product of the Destinies, which is everywhere the portion of our Europe in these latter days? There lies the question for us. Whence comes it, this universal big black Democracy; whither tends it; what is the meaning of it? A meaning it must have, or it would not be here. If we can find the right meaning of it, we may, wisely submitting or wisely resisting and controlling, still hope to live in the midst of it; if we cannot find the right meaning, if we find only the wrong or no meaning in it, to live will not be possible!—The whole social wisdom of the Present Time is summoned, in the name of the Giver of Wisdom, to make clear to itself, and lay deeply to heart with an eye to strenuous valiant practice and effort, what the meaning of this universal revolt of the European Populations, which calls itself Democracy, and decides to continue permanent, may be.

Certainly it is a drama full of action, event fast following event; in which curiosity finds endless scope, and there are interests at stake, enough to rivet the attention of all men, simple and wise. Whereat the idle multitude lift-up their voices, gratulating, celebrating sky-high; in rhyme and prose announcement, more than plentiful, that *now* the New Era, and long-expected Year One of Perfect Human Felicity has come. Glorious and immortal people, sublime French citizens, heroic barricades; triumph of civil and religious liberty—O Heaven! one of the inevitablest private miseries, to an earnest man in such circumstances, is this multitudinous efflux of oratory and psalmody, from the universal foolish human throat; drowning for the moment all reflection whatsoever, except the sorrowful one that you are fallen in an evil, heavy-laden, long-eared age, and must resignedly bear your part in the same. The front wall of your wretched old crazy dwelling, long denounced by you to no purpose, having at last fairly folded itself over, and fallen prostrate into the street, the floors, as may happen, will still hang-on by the mere beam-ends, and coherency of old carpentry, though in a sloping direction, and depend there till certain poor rusty nails and wormeaten dovetailings give way:—but is it cheering, in such circumstances, that the whole household burst-forth into celebrating the new joys of light and ventilation, liberty and picturesqueness of position, and thank God that now they have got a house to their mind? My dear household, cease singing and psalmodying; lay aside your fiddles, take out your work-implements, if you have any; for I can say with confidence the laws of gravitation are still active, and rusty nails, wormeaten dovetailings, and secret coherency of old carpentry, are not the best basis for a household!—In the lanes of Irish cities, I have heard say, the wretched people are sometimes found living, and perilously boiling their potatoes, on such swing-floors and inclined planes hanging-on by the joist-ends; but I did not hear that they sang very much in celebration of such lodging. No, they slid gently about, sat near the back wall, and perilously boiled their potatoes, in silence for most part!—

High shouts of exultation, in every dialect, by every vehicle of speech and writing, rise from far and near over this last avatar of Democracy in 1848: and yet, to wise minds, the first aspect it presents seems rather to be one of boundless misery and sorrow. What can be more miserable than this universal hunting-out of the high dignitaries, solemn functionaries, and potent, grave and reverend signiors of the world; this stormful rising-up of the inarticulate dumb masses everywhere, against those who pretended to be speaking for them and guiding them? These guides, then, were mere blind men only pretending to see? These rulers were not ruling at all; they had merely got-on the attributes and clothes of rulers, and were surreptitiously drawing the wages, while the work remained undone? The Kings were Sham-Kings, playacting as at Drury Lane;—and what were the people withal that took them for real?

It is probably the hugest disclosure of *falsity* in human things that was ever at one time made. These reverend Dignitaries that sat amid their far-shining symbols and long-sounding long-admitted professions, were mere Imposters, then? Not a true thing they were doing, but a false thing. The story they told men was a cunningly-devised fable; the gospels they preached to them were *not* an account of man's real position in this world, but an incoherent fabrication, of dead ghosts and unborn shadows, of traditions, cants, indolences, cowardices,—a falsity of falsities, which at last *ceases* to stick together. Wilfully and against their will, these high units of mankind were cheats, then; and the low millions who believed in them were dupes,—a kind of *inverse* cheats, too, or they would not have believed in them so long. A universal *Bankruptcy of Imposture*; that may be the brief definition of it. Imposture everywhere declared once more to be contrary to Nature; nobody will change its word into an act any farther:—fallen insolvent; unable to keep its head up by these false pretences, or make its pot boil any more for the present! A more scandalous phenomenon, wide as Europe, never afflicted the face of the sun. Bankruptcy everywhere; foul ignominy, and the abomination of desolation, in all high places: odious to look upon, as the carnage of a battle-field on the morrow morning;—a massacre not of the innocents; we cannot call it a massacre of the innocents; but a universal tumbling of Impostors and of Impostures into the street!—

Such a spectacle, can we call it joyful? There is a joy in it, to the wise man too; yes, but a joy full of awe, and as it were sadder than any sorrow,—like the vision of immortality, unattainable except through death and the grave! And yet who would not, in his heart of hearts, feel piously thankful that Imposture has fallen bankrupt? By all means let it fall bankrupt; in the name of God let it do so, with whatever misery to itself and to all of us. Imposture, be it known then,—known it must and shall be,—is hateful, unendurable to God and man. Let it understand this everywhere; and swiftly make ready for departure, wherever it yet lingers; and let it learn never to return, if possible! The eternal voices, very audibly again, are speaking to proclaim this message, from side to side of the world. Not a very cheering message, but a very indispensable one.

Alas, it is sad enough that Anarchy is here; that we are not permitted to regret its being here,—for who that had, for this divine Universe, an eye which was human at all, could wish that Shams of any kind, especially that Sham-Kings should continue? No: at all costs, it is to be prayed by all men that Shams may *cease*. Good Heavens, to what depths have we got, when this to many a man seems strange! Yet strange to many a man it does seem; and to many a solid Englishman, wholesomely digesting his pudding among what are called the cultivated classes, it seems strange exceedingly; a mad ignorant notion, quite heterodox, and big with mere ruin. He has been used to decent forms long since fallen empty of meaning, to plausible modes, solemnities grown ceremonial,—what you in your iconoclast humour call shams,—all his life long; never heard that there was any harm in them, that there was any getting-on without them. Did not cotton spin itself, beef grow, and groceries and spiceries come in from the East and the West, quite comfortably by the side of shams? Kings reigned, what they were pleased to call reigning; lawyers pleaded, bishops preached, and honourable members perorated; and to crown the whole, as if it were all real and no sham there, did not scrip continue saleable, and the banker pay in bullion, or paper with a metallic basis? 'The greatest sham, I have always thought, is he that would destroy shams.'

Even so. To such depth have *I*, the poor knowing person of this epoch, got;—almost below the level of lowest humanity, and down towards the state of apehood and oxhood! For never till in quite recent generations was such a scandalous blasphemy quietly set forth among the sons of Adam; never before did the creature called man believe generally in his heart that lies were the rule in this Earth; that in deliberate long-established lying could there be help or salvation for him, could there be at length other than hindrance and destruction for him. O Heavyside, my solid friend, this is the sorrow of sorrows: what on earth can become of us till this accursed enchantment, the general summary and consecration of delusions, be cast forth from the heart and life of one and all! Cast forth it will be; it must, or we are tending at all moments,—whitherward I do not like to name. Alas, and the casting of it out, to what heights and what depths will it lead us, in the sad universe mostly of lies and shams and hollow phantasms (grown very ghastly now), in which, as in a safe home, we have lived this century or two! To heights and depths of social and individual *divorce* from delusions,—of 'reform' in right sacred earnest, of indispensable amendment, and stern sorrowful abrogation and order to depart,—such as cannot well be spoken at present; as dare scarcely be thought at present; which nevertheless are very inevitable, and perhaps rather imminent several of them! Truly we have a heavy task of work before us; and there is a pressing call that we should seriously begin upon it, before it tumble into an inextricable mass, in which there will be no working, but only suffering and hopelessly perishing!—

Or perhaps Democracy, which we announce as now come, will itself manage it? Democracy, once modelled into suffrages, furnished with ballot-boxes and suchlike, will itself accomplish the salutary universal change from Delusive to Real, and make a new blessed world of us by and by?—To the great mass of men, I am aware, the matter presents itself quite on this hopeful side. Democracy they consider to *be* a kind of 'Government.' The old model, formed long since, and brought to perfection in England now two hundred years ago, has proclaimed itself to all Nations as the new healing for every woe: 'Set-up a Parliament,' the Nations everywhere say, when the old King is detected to be a Sham-King, and hunted out or not; 'set-up a Parliament; let us have suffrages, universal suffrages; and all either at once or by due degrees will be right, and a real Millenium come!' Such is their way of construing the matter.

Such, alas, is by no means my way of construing the matter; if it were, I should have had the happiness of remaining silent, and been without call to speak here. It is because the contrary of all this is deeply manifest to me, and appears to be forgotten by multitudes of my contemporaries, that I have had to undertake addressing a word to them. The contrary of all this;—and the farther I look into the roots of all this, the more hateful, ruinous and dismal does the state of mind all this could have originated in appear to me. To examine this recipe of a Parliament, how fit it is for governing Nations, nay, how fit it may now be, in these new times, for governing England itself where we are used to it so long: this, too, is an alarming inquiry, to which all thinking men, and good citizens of their country, who have an ear for the small still voices and eternal intimations, across the temporary clamours and loud blaring proclamations, are now solemnly invited. Invited by the rigorous fact itself; which will one day, and that perhaps soon, demand practical decision or redecision of it from us,—with enormous penalty if we decide it wrong! I think we shall all have to consider this question, one day; better perhaps now than later, when the leisure may be less. If a Parliament, with suffrages and universal or any conceivable kind of suffrages, *is* the method, then certainly let us set about discovering the kind of suffrages, and rest no moment till we have got them. But it is possible a Parliament may not be the method! Possible the inveterate notions of the English People may have settled it as the method, and the Everlasting Laws of Nature may have settled it as not the method! Not the whole method; nor the method at all, if taken as the whole? If a Parliament with never such suffrages is *not* the method settled by this latter authority, then it will urgently behove us to become aware of that fact, and to quit such method;—we may depend upon it, however unanimous *we* be, every step taken in that direction will, by the Eternal Law of things, be a step *from* improvement, not towards it.

Not towards it, I say, if so! Unanimity of voting,—that will do nothing for us if *so*. Your ship cannot double Cape Horn by its excellent plans of voting. The ship may vote this and that, above decks and below, in the most harmonious exquisitely constitutional manner: the ship, to get round Cape Horn, will find a set of conditions already voted for, and fixed with adamantine rigour by the ancient Elemental Powers, who are entirely careless how you vote. If you can, by voting or without voting, ascertain these conditions, and valiantly conform to them, you will get round the Cape: if you cannot,—the ruffian Winds will blow you ever back again; the inexorable Icebergs, dumb privy-councillors from Chaos, will nudge you with most chaotic 'admonition'; you will be flung half-frozen on the Patagonian cliffs, or admonished into shivers by your iceberg councillors, and sent sheer down to Davy Jones, and will never get round Cape Horn at all! Unanimity on board ship;—yes, indeed, the ship's crew may be very unanimous, which doubtless, for the time being, will be very comfortable to the ship's crew, and to their Phantasm Captain if they have one: but if the tack they unanimously steer upon is guiding them into the belly of the Abyss, it will not profit them much! —Ships accordingly do not use the ballot-box at all; and they reject the Phantasm species of Captains: one wishes much some other Entities,—since all entities lie under the same rigorous set of laws,—could be brought to show as much wisdom, and sense at least of self-preservation, the *first* command of Nature. Phantasm Captains with unanimous votings:

this is considered to be all the law and all the prophets, at present.

If a man could shake-out of his mind the universal noise of political doctors in this generation and in the last generation or two, and consider the matter face to face, with his own sincere intelligence looking at it, I venture to say he would find this a very extraordinary method of navigating, whether in the Straits of Magellan or the undiscovered Sea of Time. To prosper in this world, to gain felicity, victory and improvement, either for a man or a nation, there is but one thing requisite, That the man or nation can discern what the true regulations of the Universe are in regard to him and his pursuit, and can faithfully and steadfastly follow these. These will lead him to victory; whoever it may be that sets him in the way of these,—were it Russian Autocrat, Chartist Parliament, Grand Lama, Force of Public Opinion, Archbishop of Canterbury, M'Croudy the Seraphic Doctor with his Last-evangel of Political Economy,—sets him in the sure way to please the Author of this Universe, and is his friend of friends. And again, whoever does the contrary is, for a like reason, his enemy of enemies. This may be taken as fixed.

And now by what method ascertain the monition of the gods in regard to our affairs? How decipher, with best fidelity, the eternal regulation of the Universe; and read, from amid such confused embroilments of human clamour and folly, what the real Divine Message to us is? A divine message, or eternal regulation of the Universe, there verily is, in regard to every conceivable procedure and affair of man: faithfully following this, said procedure or affair will prosper, and have the whole Universe to second it, and carry it, across the fluctuating contradictions, towards a victorious goal; not following this, mistaking this, disregarding this, destruction and wreck are certain for every affair. How find it? All the world answers me, 'Count heads; ask Universal Suffrage, by the ballot-boxes, and that will tell.' Universal Suffrage, ballot-boxes, count of heads? Well,—I perceive we have got into strange spiritual latitudes indeed. Within the last half century or so, either the Universe or else the heads of men must have altered very much. Half a century ago, and down from Father Adam's time till then, the Universe, wherever I could hear tell of it, was wont to be of somewhat abstruse nature; by no means carrying its secret written on its face, legible to every passer-by; on the contrary, obstinately hiding its secret from all foolish, slavish, wicked, insincere persons, and partially disclosing it to the wise and noble-minded alone, whose number was not the majority in my time!

Or perhaps the chief end of man being now, in these improved epochs, to make money and spend it, his interests in the Universe have become amazingly simplified of late; capable of being voted-on with effect by almost anybody? 'To buy in the cheapest market, and sell in the dearest': truly if that is the summary of his social duties, and the final divine-message he has to follow, we may trust him extensively to vote upon that. But if it is *not*, and never was, or can be? If the Universe will not carry on its divine bosom any commonwealth of mortals that have no higher aim,—being still 'a Temple and Hall of Doom,' not a mere Weaving-shop and Cattle-pen? If the unfathomable Universe has decided to *reject* Human Beavers pretending to be Men; and will abolish, pretty rapidly perhaps, in hideous mud-deluges, their 'markets' and them, unless they think of it?—In that case it were better to think of it: and the Democracies and Universal Suffrages, I can observe, will require to modify themselves a good deal!

Historically speaking, I believe there was no Nation that could subsist upon Democracy. Of ancient Republics, and *Demoi* and *Populi*, we have heard much; but it is now pretty well admitted to be nothing to our purpose;—a universal-suffrage republic, or a general-suffrage one, or any but a most-limited-suffrage one, never came to light, or dreamed of doing so, in ancient times. When the mass of the population were slaves, and the voters intrinsically a kind of *kings*, or men born to rule others; when the voters were *real* 'aristocrats' and manageable dependents of such,—then doubtless voting, and confused jumbling of talk and intrigue, might, without immediate destruction, or the need of a Cavaignac to intervene with cannon and sweep the streets clear of it, go on; and beautiful development of manhood might be possible beside it, for a season. Beside it; or even, if you will, by means of it, and in virtue of it, though that is by no means so certain as is often supposed. Alas, no: the reflective constitutional mind has misgivings as to the origin of old Greek and Roman nobleness; and indeed knows not how this or any other human nobleness could well be 'originated,' or brought to pass, by voting or without voting, in this world, except by the grace of God very mainly;—and remembers, with a sigh, that of the Seven Sages themselves no fewer than three were bits of Despotic Kings, *Τύραννοι*, 'Tyrants' so-called (such being greatly wanted there); and that the other four were very far from Red Republicans, if of any political faith whatever! We may quit the Ancient Classical concern, and leave it to College-clubs and speculative debating-societies, in these late days.

Of the various French Republics that have been tried, or that are still on trial,—of these also it is not needful to say any word. But there is one modern instance of Democracy nearly perfect, the Republic of the United States, which has actually subsisted for threescore years or more, with immense success as is affirmed; to which many still appeal, as to a sign of hope for all nations, and 'Model Republic.' Is not America an instance in point? Why should not all Nations subsist and flourish on Democracy, as America does?

Of America it would ill beseem any Englishman, and me perhaps as little as another, to speak unkindly, to speak *unpatriotically*, if any of us even felt so. Sure enough, America is a great, and in many respects a blessed and hopeful phenomenon. Sure enough, these hardy millions of Anglo-saxon men prove themselves worthy of their genealogy; and, with the axe and plough and hammer, if not yet with any much finer kind of implements, are triumphantly clearing-out wide spaces, seedfields for the sustenance and refuge of mankind, arenas for the future history of the world; doing, in their day and generation, a creditable and cheering feat under the sun. But as to a

Model Republic, or a model anything, the wise among themselves know too well that there is nothing to be said. Nay, the title hitherto to be a Commonwealth or Nation at all, among the ἔθνη of the world, is, strictly considered, still a thing they are but striving for, and indeed have not yet done much towards attaining. Their Constitution, such as it may be, was made here, not there; went over with them from the Old-Puritan English workshop ready-made. Deduct what they carried with them from England ready-made,—their common English Language, and that same Constitution, or rather elixir of constitutions, their inveterate and now, as it were, inborn reverence for the Constable's Staff; two quite immense attainments, which England had to spend much blood, and valiant sweat of brow and brain, for centuries long, in achieving;—and what new elements of polity or nationhood, what noble new phasis of human arrangement, or social device worthy of Prometheus or of Epimetheus, yet comes to light in America? Cotton-crops and Indian-corn and dollars come to light; and half a world of untilled land, where populations that respect the constable can live, for the present *without* Government: this comes to light; and the profound sorrow of all nobler hearts, here uttering itself as silent patient unspeakable ennui, there coming out as vague elegiac wailings, that there is still next to nothing more. 'Anarchy *plus* a street-constable': that also is anarchic to me, and other than quite lovely!

I foresee, too, that, long before the waste lands are full, the very street-constable, on these poor terms, will have become impossible: without the waste lands, as here in our Europe, I do not see how he could continue possible many weeks. Cease to brag to me of America, and its model institutions and constitutions. To men in their sleep there is nothing granted in this world: nothing, or as good as nothing, to men that sit idly *caucusing* and ballot-boxing on the graves of their heroic ancestors, saying, 'It is well, it is well!' Corn and bacon are granted: not a very sublime boon, on such conditions; a boon moreover which, on such conditions, cannot last! No: America too will have to strain its energies, in quite other fashion than this; to crack its sinews, and all-but break its heart, as the rest of us have had to do, in thousandfold wrestle with the Pythons and mud-demons, before it can become a habitation for the gods. America's battle is yet to fight; and we, sorrowful though nothing doubting, will wish her strength for it. New Spiritual Pythons, plenty of them; enormous Megatherions, as ugly as were ever born of mud, loom huge and hideous out of the twilight Future on America; and she will have her own agony, and her own victory, but on other terms than she is yet quite aware of. Hitherto she but ploughs and hammers, in a very successful manner; hitherto, in spite of her 'roast-goose with apple-sauce,' she is not much. 'Roast-goose with apple-sauce for the poorest working-man': well, surely that is something,—thanks to your respect for the street-constable, and to your continents of fertile waste land;—but that, even if it could continue, is by no means enough; that is not even an instalment towards what will be required of you. My friend, brag not yet of our American cousins! Their quantity of cotton, dollars, industry and resources, I believe to be almost unspeakable; but I can by no means worship the like of these. What great human soul, what great thought, what great noble thing that one could worship, or loyally admire, has yet been produced there? None: the American cousins have yet done none of these things. 'What they have done?' growls Smelfungus, tired of the subject: 'They have doubled their population every twenty years. They have begotten, with a rapidity beyond recorded example, Eighteen Millions of the greatest *bores* ever seen in this world before,—that hitherto is their feat in History!'—And so we leave them, for the present; and cannot predict the success of Democracy, on this side of the Atlantic, from their example.

Alas, on this side of the Atlantic and on that, Democracy, we apprehend, is forever impossible! So much, with certainty of loud astonished contradiction from all manner of men at present, but with sure appeal to the Law of Nature and the ever-abiding Fact, may be suggested and asserted once more. The Universe itself is a Monarchy and Hierarchy; large liberty of 'voting' there, all manner of choice, utmost freewill, but with conditions inexorable and immeasurable annexed to every exercise of the same. A most free commonwealth of 'voters'; but with Eternal Justice to preside over it, Eternal Justice enforced by Almighty Power! This is the model of 'constitutions'; this: nor in any Nation where there has not yet (in some supportable and withal some constantly-increasing degree) been confided to the *Noblest,* with his select series of *Nobler,* the divine everlasting duty of directing and controlling the Ignoble, has the 'Kingdom of God,' which we all pray for, 'come,' nor can 'His will' even *tend* to be 'done on Earth as it is in Heaven' till then. My Christian friends, and indeed my Sham-Christian and Anti-Christian, and all manner of men, are invited to reflect on this. They will find it to be the truth of the case. The Noble in the high place, the Ignoble in the low; that is, in all times and in all countries, the Almighty Maker's Law.

To raise the Sham-Noblest, and solemnly consecrate *him* by whatever method, new-devised, or slavishly adhered to from old wont, this, little as we may regard it, is, in all times and countries, a practical blasphemy, and Nature will in no wise forget it. Alas, there lies the origin, the fatal necessity, of modern Democracy everywhere. It is the Noblest, not the Sham-Noblest; it is God-Almighty's Noble, not the Court-Tailor's Noble, nor the Able-Editor's Noble, that must in some approximate degree, be raised to the supreme place; he and not a counterfeit,—under penalties! Penalties deep as death, and at length terrible as hell-on-earth, my constitutional friend!—Will the ballot-box raise the Noblest to the chief place; does any sane man deliberately believe such a thing? That nevertheless is the indispensable result, attain it how we may: if that is attained, all is attained; if not that, nothing. He that cannot believe the ballot-box to be attaining it, will be comparatively indifferent to the ballot-box. Excellent for keeping the ship's crew at peace under their Phantasm Captain; but unserviceable, under such, for getting round Cape Horn. Alas, that there should be human beings requiring to have these things argued of, at this late time of day!

I say, it is the everlasting privilege of the foolish to be governed by the wise; to be guided in the right path by those who know it better than they. This is the first 'right of man'; compared with which all other rights are as nothing,—mere superfluities, corollaries which will follow of their own accord out of this; if they be not contradictions to this, and less than nothing! To the wise it is not a privilege; far other indeed. Doubtless, as bringing preservation to their country, it implies preservation of themselves withal; but intrinsically it is the harshest duty a wise man, if he be indeed wise, has laid to his hand. A duty which he would fain enough shirk; which accordingly, in these sad times of doubt and cowardly sloth, he has long everywhere been endeavouring to reduce to its minimum, and has in fact in most cases nearly escaped altogether. It is an ungoverned world; a world which we flatter ourselves will henceforth need no governing. On the dust of our heroic ancestors we too sit ballot-boxing, saying to one another, It is well, it is well! By inheritance of their noble struggles, we have been permitted to sit slothful so long. By noble toil, not by shallow laughter and vain talk, they made this English Existence from a savage forest into an arable inhabitable field for us; and we, idly dreaming it would grow spontaneous crops forever,—find it now in a too questionable state; peremptorily requiring real labour and agriculture again. Real 'agriculture' is not pleasant; much pleasanter to reap and winnow (with ballot-box or otherwise) than to plough!

Who would govern that can get along without governing? He that is fittest for it, is of all men the unwillingest unless constrained. By multifarious devices we have been endeavouring to dispense with governing; and by very superficial speculations, of *laissez-faire*, supply-and-demand, etc. etc. to persuade ourselves that it is best so. The Real Captain, unless it be some Captain of mechanical Industry hired by Mammon, where is he in these days? Most likely, in silence, in sad isolation somewhere, in remote obscurity; trying, if, in an evil ungoverned time, he cannot at least govern himself. The Real Captain undiscoverable; the Phantasm Captain everywhere very conspicuous:—it is thought Phantasm Captains, aided by ballot-boxes, are the true method, after all. They are much the pleasantest for the time being! And so no *Dux* or Duke of any sort, in any province of our affairs, now *leads*: the Duke's Bailiff *leads*, what little leading is required for getting-in the rents; and the Duke merely rides in the state-coach. It is everywhere so: and now at last we see a world all rushing towards strange consummations, because it is and has long been so!

I do not suppose any reader of mine, or many persons in England at all, have much faith in Fraternity, Equality and the Revolutionary Milleniums preached by the French Prophets in this age: but there are many movements here too which tend inevitably in the like direction; and good men, who would stand aghast at Red Republic and its adjuncts, seem to me travelling at full speed towards that or a similar goal! Certainly the notion everywhere prevails among us too, and preaches itself abroad in every dialect, uncontradicted anywhere so far as I can hear, That the grand panacea for social woes is what we call 'enfranchisement,' 'emancipation'; or, translated into practical language, the cutting asunder of human relations, wherever they are found grievous, as is like to be pretty universally the case at the rate we have been going for some generations past. Let us all be 'free' of one another; we shall then be happy. Free, without bond or connection except that of cash payment; fair day's wages for the fair day's work; bargained for by voluntary contract, and law of supply-and-demand: this is thought to be the true solution of all difficulties and injustices that have occurred between man and man.

To rectify the relation that exists between two men, is there no method, then, but that of ending it? The old relation has become unsuitable, obsolete, perhaps unjust; it imperatively requires to be amended; and the remedy is, Abolish it, let there henceforth be no relation at all. From the 'Sacrament of Marriage' downwards, human beings used to be manifoldly related, one to another, and each to all; and there was no relation among human beings, just or unjust, that had not its grievances and difficulties, its necessities on both sides to bear and forbear. But henceforth, be it known, we have changed all that, by favour of Heaven: 'the voluntary principle' has come-up, which will itself do the business for us; and now let a new Sacrament, that of *Divorce*, which we call emancipation, and spout-of on our platforms, be universally the order of the day! —Have men considered whither all this is tending, and what it certainly enough betokens? Cut every human relation which has anywhere grown uneasy sheer asunder; reduce whatsoever was compulsory to voluntary, whatsoever was permanent among us to the condition of nomadic:—in other words, loosen by assiduous wedges in every joint, the whole fabric of social existence, stone from stone; till at last, all now being loose enough, it can, as we already see in most countries, be overset by sudden outburst of revolutionary rage; and, lying as mere mountains of anarchic rubbish, solicit you to sing Fraternity etc. over it, and to rejoice in the new remarkable era of human progress we have arrived at.

Certainly Emancipation proceeds with rapid strides among us, this good while; and has got to such a length as might give rise to reflections in men of a serious turn. West-Indian Blacks are emancipated, and it appears refuse to work: Irish Whites have long been entirely emancipated; and nobody asks them to work, or on condition of finding them potatoes (which, of course, is indispensable), permits them to work.—Among speculative persons, a question has sometimes risen: In the progress of Emancipation, are we to look for a time when all the Horses also are to be emancipated, and brought to the supply-and-demand principle? Horses too have 'motives'; are acted-on by hunger, fear, hope, love of oats, terror of platted leather; nay, they have vanity, ambition, emulation, thankfulness, vindictiveness; some rude outline of all our human spiritualities,—a rude resemblance to us in mind and intelligence, even as they have in bodily frame. The Horse, poor dumb four-footed fellow, he too has his private feelings, his affections, gratitudes; and deserves good usage; no human master, without crime, shall treat him unjustly either, or recklessly lay-on the whip where it is not needed:—I am sure if I could make him 'happy,' I should be willing to grant a small vote (in addition to the late twenty millions) for that object!

Him too you occasionally tyrannise over; and with bad result to yourselves, among others; using the leather in a tyrannous unnecessary manner; withholding, or scantily furnishing, the oats and ventilated stabling that are due. Rugged horse-subduers, one fears they are a little tyrannous at times. 'Am I not a horse, and *half*-brother?'—To remedy which, so far as remediable, fancy—the horses all 'emancipated'; restored to their primeval right of property in the grass of this Globe: turned-out to graze in an independent supply-and-demand manner! So long as grass lasts, I dare say they are very happy, or think themselves so. And Farmer Hodge sallying forth, on a dry spring morning, with a sieve of oats in his hand, and agony of eager expectation in his heart, is he happy? Help me to plough this day, Black Dobbin: oats in full measure if thou wilt. 'Hlunh, No—thank!' snorts Black Dobbin; he prefers glorious liberty and the grass. Bay Darby, wilt not thou perhaps? 'Hlunh!' Gray Joan, then, my beautiful broad-bottomed mare,—O Heaven, she too answers Hlunh! Not a quadruped of them will plough a stroke for me. Corn-crops are *ended* in this world!—For the sake, if not of Hodge, then of Hodge's horses, one prays this benevolent practice might now cease, and a new and better one try to begin. Small kindness to Hodge's horses to emancipate them! The fate of all emancipated horses is, sooner or later, inevitable. To have in this habitable Earth no grass to eat,—in Black Jamaica gradually none, as in White Connemara already none;—to roam aimless, wasting the seed-fields of the world; and be hunted home to Chaos, by the due watch-dogs and due hell-dogs, with such horrors of forsaken wretchedness as were never seen before! These things are not sport; they are terribly true, in this country at this hour.

Between our Black West Indies and our White Ireland, between these two extremes of lazy refusal to work, and of famishing inability to find any work, what a world have we made of it, with our fierce Mammon-worships, and our benevolent philanderings, and idle godless nonsenses of one kind and another! Supply-and-demand, Leave-it-alone, Voluntary Principle, Time will mend it:—till British industrial existence seems fast becoming one huge poison-swamp of reeking pestilence physical and moral; a hideous *living* Golgotha of souls and bodies buried alive; such a Curtius' gulf, communicating with the Nether Deeps, as the Sun never saw till now. These scenes, which the *Morning Chronicle* is bringing home to all minds of men,—thanks to it for a service such as Newspapers have seldom done,—ought to excite unspeakable reflections in every mind. Thirty-thousand outcast Needlewomen working themselves swiftly to death; three-million Paupers rotting in forced idleness, *helping* said Needlewomen to die: these are but items in the sad ledger of despair.

Thirty-thousand wretched women, sunk in that putrefying well of abominations; they have oozed-in upon London, from the universal Stygian quagmire of British industrial life; are accumulated in the *well* of the concern, to that extent. British charity is smitten to the heart, at the laying-bare of such a scene; passionately undertakes, by enormous subscription of money, or by other enormous effort, to redress that individual horror; as I and all men hope it may. But, alas, what next? This general well and cesspool once baled clean out today, will begin before night to fill itself anew. The universal Stygian quagmire is still there; opulent in women ready to be ruined, and in men ready. Towards the same sad cesspool will these waste currents of human ruin ooze and gravitate as heretofore; except in draining the universal quagmire itself there is no remedy. 'And for that, what is the method?' cry many in an angry manner. To whom, for the present, I answer only, 'Not "emancipation," it would seem, my friends; not the cutting-loose of human ties, something far the reverse of that!'

Many things have been written about shirtmaking; but here

perhaps is the saddest thing of all, not written anywhere till now, that I know of. Shirts by the thirty-thousand are made at twopence-halfpenny each;—and in the mean while no needlewoman, distressed or other, can be procured in London by any housewife to give, for fair wages, fair help in sewing. Ask any thrifty house-mother, high or low, and she will answer. In high houses and in low, there is the same answer: no *real* needlewoman, 'distressed' or other, has been found attainable in any of the houses I frequent. Imaginary needle-women, who demand considerable wages, and have a deepish appetite for beer and viands, I hear of everywhere; but their sewing proves too often a distracted puckering and botching; not sewing, only the fallacious hope of it, a fond imagination of the mind. Good sempstresses are to be hired in every village; and in London, with its famishing thirty-thousand, not at all, or hardly.—Is not No-government beautiful in human business? To such length has the Leave-alone principle carried it, by way of organising labour, in this affair of shirtmaking. Let us hope the Leave-alone principle has now got its apotheosis; and taken wing towards higher regions than ours, to deal henceforth with a class of affairs more appropriate for it!

Reader, did you ever hear of 'Constituted Anarchy'? Anarchy; the choking, sweltering, deadly and killing rule of No-rule; the consecration of cupidity, and braying folly, and dim stupidity and baseness, in most of the affairs of men? Slopshirts attainable three-halfpence cheaper, by the ruin of living bodies and immortal souls? Solemn Bishops and high Dignitaries, *our* divine 'Pillars of Fire by night,' debating meanwhile, with their largest wigs and gravest look, upon something they call 'prevenient grace'? Alas, our noble men of genius, Heaven's *real* messengers to us, they also rendered nearly futile by the wasteful time;—preappointed they everywhere, and assiduously trained by all their pedagogues and monitors, to 'rise in Parliament,' to compose orations, write books, or in short speak *words*, for the approval of reviewers; instead of doing real kingly *work* to be approved of by the gods! Our 'Government,' a highly 'responsible' one; responsible to no God that I can hear of, but to the twenty-seven million *gods* of the shilling gallery. A Government tumbling and drifting on the whirlpools and mud-deluges, floating atop in a conspicuous manner, no-whither,—like the carcass of a drowned ass. Authentic *Chaos* come up into this sunny Cosmos again; and all men singing *Gloria in excelsis* to it. In spirituals and temporals, in field and workshop, from Manchester to Dorsetshire, from Lambeth Palace to the Lanes of Whitechapel, wherever men meet and toil and traffic together,—Anarchy, Anarchy; and only the street-constable (though with ever-increasing difficulty) still maintaining himself in the middle of it; that so, for one thing, this blessed exchange of slop-shirts for the souls of women may transact itself in a peaceable manner!—I, for my part, do profess myself in eternal opposition to this, and discern well that universal Ruin has us in the wind, unless we can get out of this. My friend Crabbe, in a late number of his *Intermittent Radiator*, pertinently enough exclaims:

'When shall we have done with all this of British Liberty, Voluntary Principle, Dangers of Centralisation, and the like? It is really getting too bad. For British Liberty, it seems, the people cannot be taught to read. British Liberty, shuddering to interfere with the rights of capital, takes six or eight millions of money annually to feed the idle labourer whom it dare not employ. For British Liberty we live over poisonous cesspools, gully-drains, and detestable abominations; and omnipotent London cannot sweep the dirt out of itself. British Liberty produces—what? Floods of Hansard Debates every year, and apparently little else at present. If these are the results of British Liberty, I, for one, move we should lay it on the shelf a little, and look-out for something other and farther. We have achieved British Liberty hundreds of years ago; and are fast growing, on the strength of it, one of the most absurd populations the Sun, among his great Museum of Absurdities, looks down upon at present.'

Curious enough: the model of the world just now is England and her Constitution; all Nations striving towards it: poor France swimming these last sixty years in seas of horrid dissolution and confusion, resolute to attain this blessedness of free voting, or to die in chase of it. Prussia too, solid Germany itself, has all broken out into crackling of musketry, loud pamphleteering and Frankfort parliamenting and palavering; Germany too will scale the sacred mountains, how steep soever, and, by talisman of ballot-box, inhabit a political Elysium henceforth. All the Nations have that one hope. Very notable, and rather sad to the humane onlooker. For it is sadly conjectured, all the Nations labour somewhat under a mistake as to England, and the causes of her freedom and her prosperous cotton-spinning; and have much misread the nature of her Parliament, and the effect of ballot-boxes and universal-suffrages there.

What if it were because the English Parliament was from the first, and is only just now ceasing to be, a Council of actual Rulers, real Governing Persons (called Peers, Mitred Abbots, Lords, Knights of the Shire, or howsoever called), actually *ruling* each his section of the country,—and possessing (it must be said) in the lump, or when assembled as a Council, uncommon patience, devoutness, probity, discretion and good fortune,—that the said Parliament ever came to be good for much? In that case it will not be easy to 'imitate' the English Parliament; and the ballot-box and suffrage will be the mere bow of Robin Hood, which it is given to very few to bend, or shoot with to any perfection. And if the Peers become mere big Capitalists, Railway Directors, gigantic Hucksters, Kings of Scrip, *without* lordly quality, or other virtue except cash; and the Mitred Abbots change to mere Able-Editors, masters of Parliamentary Eloquence, Doctors of Political Economy, and suchlike; and all *have* to be elected by a universal-suffrage ballot-box,—I do not see how the English Parliament itself will long continue sea-worthy! Nay, I find England in her own big dumb heart, wherever you come upon her in a silent meditative hour, begins to have dreadful misgivings about it.

The model of the world, then, is at once unattainable by

the world, and not much worth attaining? England, as I read the omens, is now called a second time to 'show the Nations how to live'; for by her Parliament, as chief governing entity, I fear she is not long for this world! Poor England must herself again, in these new strange times, the old methods being quite worn out, 'learn how to live.' That now is the terrible problem for England, as for all the Nations; and she alone of all, not *yet* sunk into open Anarchy, but left with time for repentance and amendment; she, wealthiest of all in material resource, in spiritual energy, in ancient loyalty to law, and in the qualities that yield such loyalty,—she perhaps alone of all may be able, with huge travail, and the strain of all her faculties, to accomplish some solution. She will have to try it, she has now to try it; she must accomplish it, or perish from her place in the world!

England, as I persuade myself, still contains in it many *kings*; possesses, as Old Rome did, many men not needing 'election' to command, but eternally elected for it by the Maker Himself. England's one hope is in these, just now. They are among the silent, I believe; mostly far away from platforms and public palaverings; not speaking forth the image of their nobleness in transitory words, but imprinting it, each on his own little section of the world, in silent facts, in modest valiant actions, that will endure forevermore. They must sit silent no longer. They are summoned to assert themselves; to act forth, and articulately vindicate, in the teeth of howling multitudes, of a world too justly *maddened* into all manner of delirious clamours, what of wisdom they derive from God. England, and the Eternal Voices, summon them; poor England never so needed them as now. Up, be doing everywhere: the hour of crisis has verily come! In all sections of English life, the god-made *king* is needed; is pressingly demanded in most; in some, cannot longer, without peril as of conflagration, be dispensed with. He, wheresoever he finds himself, can say, 'Here too am I wanted; here is the kingdom I have to subjugate, and introduce God's Laws into,—God's Laws, instead of Mammon's and M'Croudy's and the Old Anarch's! Here is my work, here or nowhere.'— —Are there many such, who will answer to the call, in England? It turns on that, whether England, rapidly crumbling in these very years and months, shall go down to the Abyss as her neighbours have all done, or survive to new grander destinies *without* solution of continuity! Probably the chief question of the world at present.

The true 'commander' and king; he who knows for himself the divine Appointments of this Universe, the Eternal Laws ordained by God the Maker, in conforming to which lies victory and felicity, in departing from which lies, and forever must lie, sorrow and defeat, for each and all of the Posterity of Adam in every time and every place; he who has sworn fealty to these, and dare alone against the world assert these, and dare not with the whole world at his back deflect from these;—he, I know too well, is a rare man. Difficult to discover; not quite discoverable, I apprehend, by manœuvring of ballot-boxes, and riddling of the popular clamour according to the most approved methods. He is not sold at any shop I know of, —though sometimes, as at the sign of the Ballot-box, he is advertised for sale. Difficult indeed to discover: and not very much assisted, or encouraged in late times, to discover *himself*; —which, I think, might be a kind of help? Encouraged rather, and commanded in all ways, if he be wise, to *hide* himself, and give place to the windy Counterfeit of himself; such as the universal-suffrages can recognise, such as loves the most sweet voices of the universal-suffrages!—O Peter, what becomes of such a People; what can become?

Did you never hear, with the mind's ear as well, that fateful Hebrew Prophecy, I think the fatefulest of all, which sounds daily through the streets, 'Ou' clo'! Ou' clo'!'—A certain People, once upon a time, clamorously voted by overwhelming majority, 'Not *he*; Barabbas, not he! *Him*, and what he is, and what he deserves, we know well enough: a reviler of the Chief Priests and sacred Chancery wigs; a seditious Heretic, physical-force Chartist, and enemy of his country and mankind: To the gallows and the cross with him! Barabbas is our man; Barabbas, we are for Barabbas!' They got Barabbas:

—have you well considered what a fund of purblind obduracy, of opaque *flunkyism* grown truculent and transcendent; what an eye for the phylacteries, and want of eye for the eternal noblenesses; sordid loyalty to the prosperous Semblances, and high-treason against the Supreme Fact, such a vote betokens in these natures? For it was the consummation of a long series of such; they and their fathers had long kept voting so. A singular People; who could both produce such divine men, and then could so stone and crucify them; a People terrible from the beginning!—Well, they got Barabbas; and they got, of course, such guidance as Barabbas and the like of him could give them; and, of course, they stumbled ever downwards and devilwards, in their truculent stiffnecked way; and—and, at this hour, after eighteen centuries of sad fortune, they prophetically sing 'Ou' clo'!' in all the cities of the world. Might the world, at this late hour, but take note of them, and understand their song a little!

Yes, there are some things the universal-suffrage can decide, —and about these it will be exceedingly useful to consult the universal-suffrage: but in regard to most things of importance, and in regard to the choice of men especially, there is (astonishing as it may seem) next to no capability on the part of universal-suffrage.—I request all candid persons, who have never so little originality of mind, and every man has a little, to consider this. If true, it involves such a change in our now-fashionable modes of procedure as fills me with astonishment and alarm. *If* popular suffrage is not the way of ascertaining what the Laws of the Universe are, and who it is that will best guide us in the way of these,—then woe is to us if we do not take another method. Delolme on the British Constitution will not save us; deaf will the Parcæ be to votes of the House, to leading-articles, constitutional philosophies. The other method —alas, it involves a stopping short, or vital change of direction, in the glorious career which all Europe, with shouts heaven-high, is now galloping along: and that, happen when it may, will, to many of us, be probably a rather surprising business!

One thing I do know, and can again assert with great confidence, supported by the whole Universe, and by some Two-hundred generations of men, who have left us some record of themselves there, That the few Wise will have, by one method or another, to take command of the innumerable Foolish; that they must be got to take it;—and that, in fact, since Wisdom, which means also Valour and heroic Nobleness, is alone strong in this world, and one wise man is stronger than all men unwise, they can be got. That they must take it; and having taken, must keep it, and do their God's-Message in it, and defend the same, at their life's peril, against all men and devils. This I do clearly believe to be the backbone of all Future Society, as it has been of all Past; and that without it, there is no Society possible in the world. And what a business *this* will be, before it end in some degree of victory again, and whether the time for shouts of triumph and tremendous cheers upon it is yet come, or not yet by a great way, I perceive too well! A business to make us all very serious indeed. A business not to be accomplished but by noble manhood, and devout all-daring, all-enduring loyalty to Heaven, such as fatally *sleeps* at present,—such as is not *dead* at present either, unless the gods have doomed this world of theirs to die! A business which long centuries of faithful travail and heroic agony, on the part of all the noble that are born to us, will not end; and which to us, of this 'tremendous cheering' century, it were blessedness very great to see successfully begun. Begun, tried by all manner of methods, if there is one wise Statesman or man left among us, it verily must be;—begun, successfully or unsuccessfully, we do hope to see it!

In all European countries, especially in England, one class of Captains and commanders of men, recognisable as the beginning of a new real and not imaginary 'Aristocracy,' has already in some measure developed itself: the Captains of Industry;—happily the class who above all, or at least first of all, are wanted in this time. In the doing of material work, we have already men among us that can command bodies of men. And surely, on the other hand, there is no lack of men needing to be commanded: the sad class of brother-men whom we had to describe as 'Hodge's emancipated horses,' reduced to roving famine,—this too has in all countries developed itself; and, in fatal geometrical progression, is ever more developing itself, with a rapidity which alarms every one. On this ground, if not on all manner of other grounds, it may be truly said, the 'Organisation of Labour' (*not* organisable by the mad methods tried hitherto) is the universal vital Problem of the world.

To bring these hordes of outcast captainless soldiers under due captaincy? This is really the question of questions; on the answer to which turns, among other things, the fate of all Governments, constitutional and other,—the possibility of their continuing to exist, or the impossibility. Captainless, uncommanded, these wretched outcast 'soldiers,' since they cannot starve, must needs become banditti, street-barricaders,—destroyers of every Government that *cannot* put them under captains, and send them upon enterprises, and in short render life human to them. Our English plan of Poor Laws, which we once piqued ourselves upon as sovereign, is evidently fast breaking down. Ireland, now admitted into the Idle Workhouse, is rapidly bursting it in pieces. That never was a 'human' destiny for any honest son of Adam; nowhere but in England could it have lasted at all; and now, with Ireland sharer in it, and the fulness of time come, it is as good as ended. Alas, yes. Here in Connemara, your crazy Ship of the State, otherwise dreadfully rotten in many of its timbers I believe, has sprung a leak: spite of all hands at the pump, the water is rising; the Ship, I perceive, will founder, if you cannot stop this leak!

To bring these Captainless under due captaincy? The anxious thoughts of all men that do think are turned upon that question; and their efforts, though as yet blindly and to no purpose, under the multifarious impediments and obscurations, all point thitherward. Isolated men, and their vague efforts, cannot do it. Government everywhere is called upon,—in England as loudly as elsewhere,—to give the initiative. A new strange task of these new epochs; which no Government, never so 'constitutional,' can escape from undertaking. For it is vitally necessary to the existence of Society itself; it must be undertaken, and succeeded in too, or worse will follow,—and, as we already see in Irish Connaught and some other places, will follow soon. To whatever thing still calls itself by the name of Government, were it never so constitutional and impeded by official impossibilities, all men will naturally look for help, and direction what to do, in this extremity. If help or direction is not given; if the thing called Government merely drift and tumble to and fro, no-whither, on the popular vortexes, like some carcass of a drowned ass, constitutionally put 'at the top of affairs,—popular indignation will infallibly accumulate upon it; one day, the popular lightning, descending forked and horrible from the black air, will annihilate said supreme carcass, and smite *it* home to its native ooze again!—Your Lordship, this is too true, though irreverently spoken: indeed one knows not how to speak of it; and to me it is infinitely sad and miserable, spoken or not!—Unless perhaps the Voluntary Principle will still help us through? Perhaps this Irish leak, in such a rotten distressed condition of the Ship, with all the crew so anxious about it, will be kind enough to stop of itself?—

Dismiss that hope, your Lordship! Let all real and imaginary Governors of England, at the pass we have arrived at, dismiss forever that fallacious fatal solace to their do-nothingism: of itself, too, clearly, the leak will never stop; by human skill and energy it must be stopped, or there is nothing but the sea-bottom for us all! A Chief Governor of England really ought to recognise his situation; to discern that, doing nothing, and merely drifting to and fro, in however constitutional a manner, he is a squanderer of precious moments, moments that perhaps are priceless; a truly alarming Chief Governor. Surely, to a Chief Governor of England, worthy of that high name,—surely to him, as to every living man, in every conceivable situation short of the Kingdom of the Dead,—there is *something* possible; some plan of action other than that of standing mildly, with crossed arms, till he and we—sink? Complex as his situation is, he, of all Governors now extant among these distracted Nations, has, as I compute, by far the greatest possibilities. The Captains, actual or potential, are there, and the million Captainless: and such resources for bringing them together as no other has. To these outcast soldiers of his, unregimented roving banditti for the present, or unworking workhouse prisoners who are almost uglier than banditti; to these flood of Irish Beggars, Able-bodied Paupers, and nomadic Lackalls, now stagnating or roaming everywhere, drowning the face of the world (too truly) into an untenantable swamp and Stygian quagmire, has the Chief Governor of this country no word whatever to say? Nothing but 'Rate in aid,' 'Time will mend it,' 'Necessary business of the Session'; and 'After me the Deluge'? A Chief Governor that can front his Irish difficulty, and steadily contemplate the horoscope of Irish and British Pauperism, and whitherward it is leading him and us, in this humour, must be a—What shall we call such a Chief Governor? Alas, in spite of old use and wont,—little other than a tolerated Solecism, growing daily more intolerable! He decidedly ought to have some word to say on this matter,—to be incessantly occupied in getting something which he could practically say!—Perhaps to the following, or a much finer effect?

Speech of the British Prime-Minister to the floods of Irish and other Beggars, the able-bodied Lackalls, nomadic or stationary, and the general assembly, outdoor and indoor, of the Pauper Populations of these Realms

'Vagrant Lackalls, foolish most of you, criminal many of you, miserable all; the sight of you fills me with astonishment and despair. What to do with you I know not; long have I been meditating, and is hard to tell. Here are some three millions of you, as I count: so many of you fallen sheer over into the abysses of open Beggary; and, fearful to think, every new unit that falls is *loading* so much more the chain that drags the others over. On the edge of the precipice hang uncounted millions; increasing, I am told, at the rate of 1200 a-day. They hang there on the giddy edge, poor souls, cramping themselves down, holding-on with all their strength; but falling, falling one after another; and the chain is getting *heavy*, so that ever more fall; and who at last will stand? What to do with you? The question, What to do with you? especially since the potato died, is like to break my heart!

'One thing, after much meditating, I have at last discovered, and now know for some time back: That you cannot be left to roam abroad in this unguided manner, stumbling over the precipices, and loading ever heavier the fatal *chain* upon those who might be able to stand; that this of locking you up in temporary Idle Workhouses, when you stumble, and subsisting you on Indian meal, till you can sally forth again on fresh roamings, and fresh stumblings, and ultimate descent to the devil;—that this is *not* the plan; and that it never was, or could out of England have been supposed to be, much as I have prided myself upon it!

'Vagrant Lackalls, I at last perceive, all this that has been sung and spoken, for a long while, about enfranchisement, emancipation, freedom, suffrage, civil and religious liberty over the world, is little other than sad temporary jargon, brought upon us by a stern necessity,—but now ordered by a sterner to take itself away again a little. Sad temporary jargon, I say: made-up of sense and nonsense,—sense in small quantities, and nonsense in very large;—and, if taken for the whole or permanent truth of human things, it is no better than fatal infinite nonsense eternally *untrue*. All men, I think, will soon have to quit this, to consider this as a thing pretty well achieved; and to look-out towards another thing much more needing achievement at the time that now is.

'All men will have to quit it, I believe. But to you, my indigent friends, the time for quitting it has palpably arrived! To talk of glorious self-government, of suffrages and hustings, and the fight of freedom and suchlike, is a vain thing in your case. By all human definitions and conceptions of the said fight of freedom, you for your part have lost it, and can fight no more. Glorious self-government is a glory not for you,—not for Hodge's emancipated horses, nor you. No; I say, No. You, for your part, have tried it, and *failed*. Left to walk your own road, the will-o'-wisps beguiled you, your short sight could not descry the pitfalls; the deadly tumult and press has whirled you hither and thither, regardless of your struggles and your shrieks; and here at last you lie; fallen flat into the ditch, drowning there and dying, unless the others that are still standing please to pick you up. The others that still stand have their own difficulties, I can tell you!—But you, by imperfect energy and redundant appetite, by doing too little work and drinking too much beer, you (I bid you observe) have proved that you cannot do it! You lie there plainly in the ditch. And I am to pick you up again, on these mad terms; help you ever again, as with our best heart's-blood, to do what, once for all, the gods have made impossible? To load the fatal *chain* with your perpetual staggerings and sprawlings; and ever again load it, till we all lie sprawling? My indigent, incompetent friends, I will not! Know that, whoever may be "sons of freedom," you for your part are not and cannot be such. Not "free" you, I think, whoever may be free. You palpably are fallen captive,—*caitiff*, as they once named it:—you do, silently, but eloquently, demand, in the name of mercy itself, that some genuine command be taken of you.

'Yes, my indigent incompetent friends; some genuine practical command. Such,—if I rightly interpret those mad Chartisms, Repeal Agitations, Red Republics, and other delirious inarticulate howlings and bellowings which all the populations of the world now utter, evidently cries of pain on their and your part,—is the demand which you, Captives, make of all men that are not Captive, but are still Free. Free men,—alas, had you ever any notion who the free men were, who the not-free, the incapable of freedom! The free men, if you could have understood it, they are the wise men; the patient, self-denying, valiant; the Nobles of the World; who can discern the Law of this Universe, what it is, and piously *obey* it; these, in late sad times, having cast you loose, you are fallen captive to greedy sons of profit-and-loss; to bad and ever to worse; and at length to Beer and the Devil. Algiers, Brazil or Dahomey hold nothing in them so authentically *slave* as you are, my indigent incompetent friends!

'Good Heavens, and I have to raise some eight or nine millions annually, six for England itself, and to wreck the morals of my working population beyond all money's worth, to keep the life from going out of *you*: a small service to you, as I many times bitterly repeat! Alas, yes; before high Heaven I must declare it such. I think the old Spartans, who would have killed you instead, had shown more "humanity," more of manhood, than I thus do! More humanity, I say, more of *man*-hood, and of sense for what the dignity of man demands imperatively of you and of me and of us all. We call it charity, beneficence, and other fine names, this brutish Workhouse Scheme of ours; and it is but sluggish heartlessness, and insincerity, and cowardly lowness of soul. Not "humanity" or manhood, I think; perhaps *ape*hood rather,—paltry imitancy, from the teeth outward, of what our heart never felt nor *our* understanding ever saw; dim indolent adherence to extraneous hearsays and extinct traditions; traditions now really about extinct; not living now to almost any of us, and still haunting with their spectralities and gibbering *ghosts* (in a truly baleful manner) almost all of us! Making this our struggling "Twelfth Hour of the Night" inexpressibly hideous!—

'But as for you, my indigent incompetent friends, I have to repeat with sorrow, but with perfect clearness, what is plainly undeniable, and is even clamorous to get itself admitted, that you are of the nature of *slaves*,—or if you prefer the word, of *nomadic, and now even vagrant and vagabond, servants that can find no master on those terms*; which seems to me a much uglier word. Emancipation? You have been "emancipated" with a vengeance! Foolish souls, I say the whole world cannot emancipate you. Fealty to ignorant Unruliness, to gluttonous sluggish Improvidence, to the Beerpot and the Devil, who is there that can emancipate a man in that predicament? Not a whole Reform Bill, a whole French

Revolution executed for his behoof alone: nothing but God the Maker can emancipate him, by making him anew.

'To forward which glorious consummation, will it not be well, O indigent friends, that you, fallen flat there, shall henceforth learn to take advice of others as to the methods of standing? Plainly I let you know, and all the world and the worlds know, that I for my part mean it so. Not as glorious unfortunate sons of freedom, but as recognised captives, as unfortunate fallen brothers requiring that I should command you, and if need were, control and compel you, can there henceforth be a relation between us. Ask me not for Indian meal; you shall be compelled to earn it first; know that on other terms I will not give you any. Before Heaven and Earth, and God the Maker of us all, I declare it is a scandal to see *such* a life kept in you, by the sweat and heart's-blood of your brothers; and that, if we cannot mend it, death were preferable! Go to, we must get out of this unutterable coil of nonsenses, constitutional, philanthropical, etc., in which (surely without mutual hatred, if with less of "love" than is supposed) we are all strangling one another! Your want of wants, I say, is that you be *commanded* in this world, not being able to command yourselves. Know therefore that it shall be so with you. Nomadism, I give you notice, has ended; needful permanency, soldier-like obedience, and the opportunity and the necessity of hard steady labour for your living, have begun. Know that the Idle Workhouse is shut against you henceforth; you cannot enter there at will, nor leave at will;—you shall enter a quite other Refuge, under conditions strict as soldiering, and not leave till I have done with you. He that prefers the glorious, (or perhaps even the rebellious *in*glorious) "career of freedom," let him prove that he can travel there, and be the master of himself; and right good speed to him. He who has proved that he cannot travel there or be the master of himself,—let him, in the name of all the gods, become a servant, and accept the just rules of servitude!

'Arise, enlist in my Irish, my Scotch and English "Regiments of the New Era,"—which I have been concocting, day and night, during these three Grouse-seasons (taking earnest incessant counsel, with all manner of Industrial Notabilities and men of insight, on the matter), and have now brought to a kind of preparation for incipiency, thank Heaven! Enlist there, ye poor wandering banditti; obey, work, suffer, abstain, as all of us have had to do: so shall you be useful in God's creation, so shall you be helped to gain a manful living for yourselves; not otherwise than so. Industrial Regiments'—[*Here numerous persons, with big wigs many of them, and austere aspect, whom I take to be Professors of the Dismal Science, start up in an agitated vehement manner: but the Premier resolutely beckons them down again*]—'Regiments not to fight the French or others, who are peaceable enough towards us; but to fight the Bogs and Wildernesses at home and abroad, and to chain the Devils of the Pit which are walking too openly among us.

'Work, for you? Work, surely, is not quite undiscoverable in an Earth so wide as ours, if we will take the right methods for it! Indigent friends, we will adopt this new relation (which is *old* as the world); this will lead us towards such. Rigorous conditions, not to be violated on either side, lie in this relation; conditions planted there by God Himself; which woe will betide us if we do not discover, gradually more and more discover, and conform to! Industrial Colonels, Workmasters, Taskmasters, Life-commanders, equitable as Rhadamanthus and inflexible as he: such, I perceive, you do need; and such, you being once put under law as soldiers are, will be discoverable for you. I perceive, with boundless alarm, that I shall have to set about discovering such,—I, since I am at the top of affairs, with all men looking to me. Alas, it is my new task in this New Era; and God knows, I too, little other than a red-tape Talking-machine, and unhappy Bag of Parliamentary Eloquence hitherto, am far behind with it! But street-barricades rise everywhere: the hour of Fate has come. In Connemara there has sprung a leak, since the potato died; Connaught, if it were not for Treasury-grants and rates-in-aid, would have to recur to Cannibalism even now, and Human Society would cease to pretend that it existed there. Done this thing must be. Alas, I perceive that if I cannot do it, then surely I shall die, and perhaps shall not have Christian burial! But I already raise near upon Ten Millions for feeding you in idleness, my nomadic friends; work, under due regulations, I really might try to get of'—[*Here arises indescribable uproar, no longer repressible, from all manner of Economists, Emancipationists, Constitutionalists, and miscellaneous Professors of the Dismal Science, pretty numerously scattered about; and cries of 'Private Enterprise,' 'Rights of Capital,' 'Voluntary Principle,' 'Doctrines of the British Constitution,' swollen by the general assenting hum of all the world, quite drown the Chief Minister for a while. He, with invincible resolution, persists; obtains hearing again:*]

'Respectable Professors of the Dismal Science, soft you a little. Alas, I know what you would say. For my sins, I have read much in those inimitable volumes of yours,—really I should think, some barrowfuls of them in my time,—and, in these last forty years of theory and practice, have pretty well seized what of Divine Message you were sent with to me. Perhaps as small a message, give me leave to say, as ever there was such a noise made about before. Trust me, I have not forgotten it, shall never forget it. Those Laws of the Shop-till are indisputable to me; and practically useful in certain departments of the Universe, as the multiplication-table itself. Once I even tried to sail through the Immensities with them, and to front the big coming Eternities with them; but I found it would not do. As the Supreme Rule of Statesmanship, or Government of Men,—since this Universe is not wholly a Shop,—no. You rejoice in my improved tariffs, free-trade movements and the like, on every hand; for which be thankful, and even sing litanies if you choose. But here at last, in the Idle-Workhouse movement,—unexampled yet on Earth or in the waters under the Earth,—I am fairly brought to a stand; and have had to make reflections, of the most alarming, and indeed awful, and as it were religious nature! Professors of the Dismal Science, I perceive that the length of your tether is now pretty well run; and that I must request you to talk a little lower in future. By the side of the shop-till,—see, your small "Law of God" is hung up, along with the multiplication-table itself. But beyond and above the shop-till, allow me to say, you shall as good as hold your peace. Respectable Professors, I perceive it is not now the Gigantic Hucksters, but it is the Immortal Gods, yes, they, in their terror and their beauty, in their wrath and their beneficence, that are coming into play in the affairs of this world! Soft you a little. Do not you interrupt me, but try to understand and help me!—

'Work, was I saying? My indigent unguided friends, I should think some work might be discoverable for you. Enlist, stand drill; become, from a nomadic Banditti of Idleness, Soldiers of Industry! I will lead you to the Irish Bogs, to the vacant desolations of Connaught now falling into Cannibalism, to mistilled Connaught, to ditto Munster, Leinster, Ulster, I will lead you: to the English fox-covers, furze-grown Commons, New Forests, Salisbury Plains: likewise to the Scotch Hill-sides, and bare rushy slopes, which as yet feed only sheep,—moist uplands, thousands of square miles in extent, which are destined yet to grow green crops, and fresh butter and milk and beef without limit (wherein no "Foreigner can compete with us"), were the Glasgow sewers once opened on them, and you with your Colonels carried thither. In the Three Kingdoms, or in the Forty Colonies, depend upon it, you shall be led to your work!

'To each of you I will then say: Here is work for you; strike into it with manlike, soldierlike obedience and heartiness, according to the methods here prescribed,—wages follow for you without difficulty; all manner of just remuneration, and at length emancipation itself follows. Refuse to strike into it; shirk the heavy labour, disobey the rules,—I will admonish and endeavour to incite you; if in vain, I will flog you; if still in vain, I will at last shoot you,—and make God's Earth, and the forlorn-hope in God's Battle, free of you. Understand it, I advise you! The Organisation of Labour'— —[*Left speaking*, says our reporter.]

'Left speaking': alas, that he should have to 'speak' so much! There are things that should be done, not spoken; that till the doing of them is begun, cannot well be spoken. He may have to 'speak' seven years yet, before a spade be struck into the Bog of Allen; and then perhaps it will be too late!—

You perceive, my friends, we have actually got into the 'New Era' there has been such propheysing of: here we all are, arrived at last;—and it is by no means the land flowing with milk and honey we were led to expect! Very much the reverse. A terrible *new* country this: no neighbours in it yet, that I can see, but irrational flabby monsters (philanthropic and other) of the giant species; hyænas, laughing hyænas, predatory wolves; probably *devils*, blue (or perhaps blue-and-yellow) devils, as St. Guthlac found in Croyland long ago. A huge untrodden haggard country, the 'chaotic battle-field of Frost and Fire'; a country of savage glaciers, granite mountains, of foul jungles, unhewed forests, quaking bogs;—which we shall have our own ados to make arable and habitable, I think! We must stick by it, however;—of all enterprises the impossiblest is that of getting out of *it*, and shifting into another. To work, then, one and all; hands to work!

FROM The Life of John Sterling

The Life of John Sterling was quickly and easily written in the early months of 1851, and was published in that year. Two chapters from it are printed here; the picture of Coleridge on Highgate Hill (a formal view which may be compared with the informal one printed on page 712 in Carlyle's letter written many years before to his brother Doctor John); and the tender and generous assessment of Sterling himself in the last chapter.

FROM

The Life of John Sterling

COLERIDGE

Coleridge sat on the brow of Highgate Hill, in those years, looking down on London and its smoke-tumult, like a sage escaped from the inanity of life's battle; attracting towards him the thoughts of innumerable brave souls still engaged there. His express contributions to poetry, philosophy, or any specific province of human literature or enlightenment, had been small and sadly intermittent; but he had, especially among young inquiring men, a higher than literary, a kind of prophetic or magician character. He was thought to hold, he alone in England, the key of German and other Transcendentalisms; knew the sublime secret of believing by 'the reason' what 'the understanding' had been obliged to fling out as incredible; and could still, after Hume and Voltaire had done their best and worst with him, profess himself an orthodox Christian, and say and print to the Church of England, with its singular old rubrics and surplices at Allhallowtide, *Esto perpetua.* A sublime man; who, alone in those dark days, had saved his crown of spiritual manhood; escaping from the black materialisms, and revolutionary deluges, with 'God, Freedom, Immortality' still his: a king of men. The practical intellects of the world did not much heed him, or carelessly reckoned him a metaphysical dreamer: but to the rising spirits of the young generation he had this dusky sublime character; and sat there as a kind of *Magus*, girt in mystery and enigma; his Dodona oak-grove (Mr. Gilman's house at Highgate) whispering strange things, uncertain whether oracles or jargon.

The Gilmans did not encourage much company, or excitation of any sort, round their sage; nevertheless access to him, if a youth did reverently wish it, was not difficult. He would stroll about the pleasant garden with you, sit in the pleasant rooms of the place,—perhaps take you to his own peculiar room, high up, with a rearward view, which was the chief view of all. A really charming outlook, in fine weather. Close at hand, wide sweep of flowery leafy gardens, their few houses mostly hidden, the very chimney-pots veiled under blossomy umbrage, flowed gloriously down hill, gloriously issuing in wide-tufted undulating plain-country, rich in all charms of field and town. Waving blooming country of the brightest green; dotted all over with handsome villas, handsome groves; crossed by roads and human traffic, here inaudible or heard only as a musical hum: and behind all swam, under olive-tinted haze, the illimitable limitary ocean of London, with its domes and steeples definite in the sun, big Paul's and the many memories attached to it hanging high over all. Nowhere, of its kind, could you see a grander prospect on a bright summer day, with the set of the air going southward,—southward, and so draping with the city-smoke not *you* but the city. Here for hours would Coleridge talk, concerning all conceivable or inconceivable things; and liked nothing better than to have an intelligent, or failing that, even a silent and patient human listener. He distinguished himself to all that ever heard him as at least the most surprising talker extant in this world,—and to some small minority, by no means to all, as the most excellent.

The good man, he was now getting old, towards sixty perhaps; and gave you the idea of a life that had been full of sufferings; a life heavy-laden, half-vanquished, still swimming painfully in seas of manifold physical and other bewilderment. Brow and head were round, and of massive weight, but the face was flabby and irresolute. The deep eyes, of a light hazel, were as full of sorrow as of inspiration; confused pain looked mildly from them, as in a kind of mild astonishment. The whole figure and air, good and amiable otherwise, might be called flabby and irresolute; expressive of weakness under possibility of strength. He hung loosely on his limbs, with knees bent, and stooping attitude; in walking, he rather shuffled than decisively stept; and a lady once remarked, he never could fix which side of the garden walk would suit him best, but continually shifted, in corkscrew fashion, and kept trying both. A heavy-laden, high-aspiring and surely much-suffering man. His voice, naturally soft and good, had contracted itself into a plaintive snuffle and sing-song; he spoke as if preaching,—you would have said, preaching earnestly and also hopelessly the weightiest things. I still recollect his 'object' and 'subject,' terms of continual recurrence in the Kantean province; and how he sang and snuffled them into 'om-m-mject' and 'sum-m-mject,' with a kind of solemn shake or quaver, as he rolled along. No talk, in his century or in any other, could be more surprising.

Sterling, who assiduously attended him, with profound reverence, and was often with him by himself, for a good many months, gives a record of their first colloquy.[1] Their colloquies were numerous, and he had taken note of many; but they are all gone to the fire, except this first, which Mr. Hare has printed,—unluckily without date. It contains a number of ingenious, true and half-true observations, and is of course a faithful epitome of the things said; but it gives small idea of Coleridge's way of talking;—this one feature is perhaps the most recognisable, 'Our interview lasted for three hours, during which he talked two hours and three quarters.' Nothing could be more copious than his talk; and furthermore it was always, virtually or literally, of the nature of a monologue; suffering no interruption, however reverent; hastily putting aside all foreign additions, annotations, or most ingenuous desires for elucidation, as well-meant superfluities which would never do. Besides, it was talk not flowing anywhither like a river, but spreading everywhither in inextricable currents and regurgitations like a lake or sea; terribly deficient in definite goal or aim, nay often in logical intelligibility; *what* you were to believe or do, on any earthly or heavenly thing, obstinately

[1] *Biography*, by Hare, pp. xvi–xxvi.

refusing to appear from it. So that, most times, you felt logically lost; swamped near to drowning in this tide of ingenious vocables, spreading out boundless as if to submerge the world.

To sit as a passive bucket and be pumped into, whether you consent or not, can in the long-run be exhilarating to no creature; how eloquent soever the flood of utterance that is descending. But if it be withal a confused unintelligible flood of utterance, threatening to submerge all known landmarks of thought, and drown the world and you!—I have heard Coleridge talk, with eager musical energy, two stricken hours, his face radiant and moist, and communicate no meaning whatsoever to any individual of his hearers,—certain of whom, I for one, still kept eagerly listening in hope; the most had long before given up, and formed (if the room were large enough) secondary humming groups of their own. He began anywhere: you put some question to him, made some suggestive observation: instead of answering this, or decidedly setting out towards answer of it, he would accumulate formidable apparatus, logical swim-bladders, transcendental life-preservers and other precautionary and vehiculatory gear, for setting out; perhaps did at last get under way,—but was swiftly solicited, turned aside by the glance of some radiant new game on this hand or that, into new courses; and ever into new; and before long into all the Universe, where it was uncertain what game you would catch, or whether any.

His talk, alas, was distinguished, like himself, by irresolution: it disliked to be troubled with conditions, abstinences, definite fulfilments;—loved to wander at its own sweet will, and make its auditor and his claims and humble wishes a mere passive bucket for itself! He had knowledge about many things and topics, much curious reading; but generally all topics led him, after a pass or two, into the high seas of theosophic philosophy, the hazy infinitude of Kantean transcendentalism, with its 'sum-m-mjects' and 'om-m-mjects.' Sad enough; for with such indolent impatience of the claims and ignorances of others, he had not the least talent for explaining this or anything unknown to them; and you swam and fluttered in the mistiest wide unintelligible deluge of things, for most part in a rather profitless uncomfortable manner.

Glorious islets, too, I have seen rise out of the haze; but they were few, and soon swallowed in the general element again. Balmy sunny islets, islets of the blest and the intelligible:—on which occasions those secondary humming groups would all cease humming, and hang breathless upon the eloquent words; till once your islet got wrapt in the mist again, and they could recommence humming. Eloquent artistically expressive words you always had; piercing radiances of a most subtle insight came at intervals; tones of noble pious sympathy, recognisable as pious though strangely coloured, were never wanting long; but in general you could not call this aimless, cloudcapt, cloud-based, lawlessly meandering human discourse of reason by the name of 'excellent talk,' but only of 'surprising'; and were reminded bitterly of Hazlitt's account of it: 'Excellent talker, very,—if you let him start from no premises and come to no conclusion.' Coleridge was not without what talkers call wit, and there were touches of prickly sarcasm in him, contemptuous enough of the world and its idols and popular dignitaries; he had traits even of poetic humour: but in general he seemed deficient in laughter; or indeed in sympathy for concrete human things either on the sunny or on the stormy side. One right peal of concrete laughter at some convicted flesh-and-blood absurdity, one burst of noble indignation at some injustice or depravity, rubbing elbows with us on this solid Earth, how strange would it have been in that Kantean haze-world, and how infinitely cheering amid its vacant air-castles and dim-melting ghosts and shadows! None such ever came. His life had been an abstract thinking and dreaming, idealistic, passed amid the ghosts of defunct bodies and of unborn ones. The moaning singsong of that theosophico-metaphysical monotony left on you, at last, a very dreary feeling.

In close colloquy, flowing within narrower banks, I suppose he was more definite and apprehensible; Sterling in aftertimes did not complain of his unintelligibility, or imputed it only to the abstruse high nature of the topics handled. Let us hope so, let us try to believe so! There is no doubt but Coleridge could speak plain words on things plain: his observations and responses on the trivial matters that occurred were as simple as the commonest man's, or were even distinguished by superior simplicity as well as pertinency. 'Ah, your tea is too cold, Mr. Coleridge!' mourned the good Mrs. Gilman once, in her kind, reverential and yet protective manner, handing him a very tolerable though belated cup.—'It's better than I deserve!' snuffled he, in a low hoarse murmur, partly courteous, chiefly pious, the tone of which still abides with me: 'It's better than I deserve!'

But indeed, to the young ardent mind, instinct with pious nobleness, yet driven to the grim deserts of Radicalism for a faith, his speculations had a charm much more than literary, a charm almost religious and prophetic. The constant gist of his discourse was lamentation over the sunk condition of the world; which he recognised to be given-up to Atheism and Materialism, full of mere sordid misbeliefs, mispursuits and misresults. All Science had become mechanical; the science not of men, but of a kind of human beavers. Churches themselves had died away into a godless mechanical condition; and stood there as mere Cases of Articles, mere Forms of Churches; like the dried carcasses of once-swift camels, which you find left withering in the thirst of the universal desert,—ghastly portents for the present, beneficent ships of the desert no more. Men's souls were blinded, hebetated; and sunk under the influence of Atheism and Materialism, and Hume and Voltaire: the world for the present was as an extinct world, deserted of God, and incapable of welldoing till it changed its heart and spirit. This, expressed I think with less of indignation and with more of long-drawn querulousness, was always recognisable as the ground-tone:—in which truly a pious young heart, driven into Radicalism and the opposition party, could not but recognise a too sorrowful truth; and ask of the Oracle, with all earnestness, What remedy, then?

The remedy, though Coleridge himself professed to see it

as in sunbeams, could not, except by processes unspeakably difficult, be described to you at all. On the whole, those dead Churches, this dead English Church especially, must be brought to life again. Why not? It was not dead; the soul of it, in this parched-up body, was tragically asleep only. Atheistic Philosophy was true on its side, and Hume and Voltaire could on their own ground speak irrefragably for themselves against any Church: but lift the Church and them into a higher sphere of argument, *they* died into inanition, the Church revivified itself into pristine florid vigour,—became once more a living ship of the desert, and invincibly bore you over stock and stone. But how, but how! By attending to the 'reason' of man, said Coleridge, and duly chaining-up the 'understanding' of man: the *Vernunft* (Reason) and *Verstand* (Understanding) of the Germans, it all turned upon these, if you could well understand them,—which you couldn't. For the rest, Mr. Coleridge had on the anvil various Books, especially was about to write one grand Book *On the Logos*, which would help to bridge the chasm for us. So much appeared, however: Churches, though proved false (as you had imagined), were still true (as you were to imagine): here was an Artist who could burn you up an old Church, root and branch; and then as the Alchymists professed to do with organic substances in general, distil you an 'Astral Spirit' from the ashes, which was the very image of the old burnt article, its airdrawn counterpart,—this you still had, or might get, and draw uses from, if you could. Wait till the Book on the Logos were done;—alas, till your own terrene eyes, blind with conceit and the dust of logic, were purged, subtilised and spiritualised into the sharpness of vision requisite for discerning such an 'om-m-mject.'—The ingenuous young English head, of those days, stood strangely puzzled by such revelations; uncertain whether it were getting inspired, or getting infatuated into flat imbecility; and strange effulgence, of new day or else of deeper meteoric night, coloured the horizon of the future for it.

Let me not be unjust to this memorable man. Surely there was here, in his pious, ever-labouring, subtle mind, a precious truth, or prefigurement of truth; and yet a fatal delusion withal. Prefigurement that, in spite of beaver sciences and temporary spiritual hebetude and cecity, man and his Universe were eternally divine; and that no past nobleness, or revelation of the divine, could or would ever be lost to him. Most true, surely, and worthy of all acceptance. Good also to do what you can with old Churches and practical Symbols of the Noble: nay, quit not the burnt ruins of them while you find there is still gold to be dug there. But, on the whole, do not think you can, by logical alchymy, distil astral spirits from them; or if you could, that said astral spirits, or defunct logical phantasms, could serve you in anything. What the light of your mind, which is the direct inspiration of the Almighty, pronounces incredible,—that, in God's name, leave uncredited; at your peril do not try believing that. No subtlest hocus-pocus of 'reason' *versus* 'understanding' will avail for that feat;—and it is terribly perilous to try it in these provinces!

The truth is, I now see, Coleridge's talk and speculation was the emblem of himself: in it, as in him, a ray of heavenly inspiration struggled, in a tragically ineffectual degree, with the weakness of flesh and blood. He says once, he 'had skirted the howling deserts of Infidelity'; this was evident enough: but he had not had the courage, in defiance of pain and terror, to press resolutely across said deserts to the new firm lands of Faith beyond; he preferred to create logical fatamorganas for himself on this hither side, and laboriously solace himself with these.

To the man himself Nature had given, in high measure, the seeds of a noble endowment; and to unfold it had been forbidden him. A subtle lynx-eyed intellect, tremulous pious sensibility to all good and all beautiful; truly a ray of empyrean light;—but imbedded in such weak laxity of character, in such indolences and esuriences as had made strange work with it. Once more, the tragic story of a high endowment with an insufficient will. An eye to discern the divineness of the Heaven's splendours and lightnings, the insatiable wish to revel in their godlike radiances and brilliances; but no heart to front the scathing terrors of them, which is the first condition of your conquering an abiding place there. The courage necessary for him, above all things, had been denied this man. His life, with such ray of the empyrean in it, was great and terrible to him; and he had not valiantly grappled with it, he had fled from it; sought refuge in vague day-dreams, hollow compromises, in opium, in theosophic metaphysics. Harsh pain, danger, necessity, slavish harnessed toil, were of all things abhorrent to him. And so the empyrean element, lying smothered under the terrene, and yet inextinguishable there, made sad writhings. For pain, danger, difficulty, steady slaving toil, and other highly disagreeable behests of destiny, shall in no wise be shirked by any brightest mortal that will approve himself loyal to his mission in this world; nay, precisely the higher he is, the deeper will be the disagreeableness, and the detestability to flesh and blood, of the tasks laid on him; and the heavier too, and more tragic, his penalties, if he neglect them.

For the old Eternal Powers do live forever; nor do their laws know any change, however we in our poor wigs and church-tippets may attempt to read their laws. To *steal* into Heaven,—by the modern method, of sticking ostrich-like your head into fallacies on Earth, equally as by ancient and by all conceivable methods,—is forever forbidden. High-treason is the name of that attempt; and it continues to be punished as such. Strange enough: here once more was a kind of Heaven-scaling Ixion; and to him, as to the old one, the just gods were very stern! The ever-revolving, never-advancing Wheel (of a kind) was his, through life; and from his Cloud-Juno did not he too procreate strange Centaurs, spectral Puseyisms, monstrous illusory Hybrids, and ecclesiastical Chimeras,—which now roam the earth in a very lamentable manner!

CONCLUSION

STERLING was of rather slim but well-boned wiry figure, perhaps an inch or two from six feet in height; of blonde complexion, without colour, yet not pale or sickly; dark-blonde hair, copious enough, which he usually wore short. The general aspect of him indicated freedom, perfect spontaneity, with a certain careless natural grace. In his apparel you could notice, he affected dim colours, easy shapes; cleanly always, yet even in this not fastidious or conspicuous: he sat or stood, oftenest, in loose sloping postures; walked with long strides, body carelessly bent, head flung eagerly forward, right hand perhaps grasping a cane, and rather by the middle to swing it, than by the end to use it otherwise. An attitude of frank, cheerful impetuosity, of hopeful speed and alacrity; which indeed his physiognomy, on all sides of it, offered as the chief expression. Alacrity, velocity, joyous ardour, dwelt in the eyes too, which were of brownish gray, full of bright kindly life, rapid and frank rather than deep or strong. A smile, half of kindly impatience, half of real mirth, often sat on his face. The head was long; high over the vertex; in the brow, of fair breadth, but not high for such a man.

In the voice, which was of good tenor sort, rapid and strikingly distinct, powerful too, and except in some of the higher notes harmonious, there was a clear-ringing *metallic* tone,—which I often thought was wonderfully physiognomic. A certain splendour, beautiful, but not the deepest or the softest, which I could call a splendour as of burnished metal,—fiery valour of heart, swift decisive insight and utterance, then a turn for brilliant elegance, also for ostentation, rashness, etc. etc.,—in short, a flash as of clear-glancing sharp-cutting steel, lay in the whole nature of the man, in his heart and in his intellect, marking alike the excellence and the limits of them both. His laugh, which on light occasions was ready and frequent, had in it no great depth of gaiety, or sense for the ludicrous in men or things; you might call it rather a good smile become vocal than a deep real laugh: with his whole man I never saw him laugh. A clear sense of the humorous he had, as of most other things; but in himself little or no true humour;—nor did he attempt that side of things. To call him deficient in sympathy would seem strange, him whose radiances and resonances went thrilling over all the world, and kept him in brotherly contact with all: but I may say his sympathies dwelt rather with the high and sublime than with the low or ludicrous; and were, in any field, rather light, wide and lively, than deep, abiding or great.

There is no Portrait of him which tolerably resembles. The miniature Medallion, of which Mr. Hare has given us an Engraving, offers us, with no great truth in physical details, one, and not the best, superficial expression of his face, as if that with vacuity had been what the face contained; and even that Mr. Hare's engraver has disfigured into the nearly or the utterly irrecognisable. Two Pencil-sketches, which no artist could approve of, hasty sketches done in some social hour, one by his friend Spedding, one by Baynim the Novelist, whom he slightly knew and had been kind to, tell a much truer story so far as they go: of these his Brother has engravings; but these also I must suppress as inadequate for strangers.

Nor in the way of Spiritual Portraiture does there, after so much writing and excerpting, anything of importance remain for me to say. John Sterling and his Life in this world were—such as has been already said. In purity of character, in the so-called moralities, in all manner of proprieties of conduct, so as tea-tables and other human tribunals rule them, he might be defined as perfect, according to the world's pattern: in these outward tangible respects the world's criticism of him must have been praise and that only. An honourable man, and good citizen; discharging, with unblamable correctness, all functions and duties laid on him by the customs (*mores*) of the society he lived in,—with correctness and something more. In all these particulars, a man perfectly *moral*, or of approved virtue according to the rules.

Nay in the far more essential tacit virtues, which are not marked on stone tables, or so apt to be insisted on by human creatures over tea or elsewhere,—in clear and perfect fidelity to Truth wherever found, in childlike and soldierlike, pious and valiant loyalty to the Highest, and what of good and evil that might send him,—he excelled among good men. The joys and the sorrows of his lot he took with true simplicity and acquiescence. Like a true son, not like a miserable mutinous rebel, he comported himself in this Universe. Extremity of distress, —and surely his fervid temper had enough of contradiction in this world,—could not tempt him into impatience at any time. By no chance did you ever hear from him a whisper of those mean repinings, miserable arraignings and questionings of the Eternal Power, such as weak souls even well disposed will sometimes give way to in the pressure of their despair; to the like of this he never yielded, or showed the least tendency to yield;—which surely was well on his part. For the Eternal Power, I still remark, will not answer the like of this, but silently and terribly accounts it impious, blasphemous and damnable, and now as heretofore will visit it as such. Not a rebel but a son, I said; willing to suffer when Heaven said, Thou shalt;—and withal, what is perhaps rarer in such a combination, willing to rejoice also, and right cheerily taking the good that was sent, whensoever or in whatever form it came.

A pious soul we may justly call him; devoutly submissive to the will of the Supreme in all things: the highest and sole essential form which Religion can assume in man, and without which all forms of religion are a mockery and a delusion in man. Doubtless, in so clear and filial a heart there must have dwelt the perennial feeling of silent worship; which silent feeling, as we have seen, he was eager enough to express by all good ways of utterance; zealously adopting such appointed forms and creeds as the Dignitaries of the World had fixed upon and solemnly named recommendable; prostrating his heart in such Church, by such accredited rituals and seemingly fit or half-fit methods, as his poor time and country had to offer him,—not rejecting the said methods till they stood convicted of palpable *un*fitness, and then doing it right gently withal, rather letting them drop as pitiably dead for him, than angrily hurling them out of doors as needing to be killed. By few Englishmen of his epoch had the thing called Church of England been more loyally appealed to as a spiritual mother.

And yet, as I said before, it may be questioned whether piety, what we call devotion or worship, was the principle deepest in him. In spite of his Coleridge discipleship, and his once headlong operations following thereon, I used to judge that his piety was prompt and pure rather than great or intense; that, on the whole, religious devotion was not the deepest element of him. His reverence was ardent and just, ever ready for the thing or man that deserved revering, or seemed to deserve it: but he was of too joyful, light and hoping a nature to go to the depths of that feeling, much more to dwell perennially in it. He had no fear in his composition; terror and awe did not blend with his respect of anything. In no scene or epoch could he have been a Church Saint, a fanatic enthusiast, or have worn-out his life in passive martyrdom, sitting patient in his grim coal-mine, looking at the 'three ells' of Heaven high overhead there. In sorrow he would not dwell; all sorrow he swiftly subdued, and shook away from him. How could you have made an Indian Fakeer of the Greek Apollo, 'whose bright eye lends brightness, and never yet saw a shadow'?—I should say, not religious reverence, rather artistic admiration was the essential character of him: a fact connected with all other facts in the physiognomy of his life and self, and giving a tragic enough character to much of the history he had among us.

Poor Sterling, he was by nature appointed for a Poet, then—a Poet after his sort, or recogniser and delineator of the Beautiful; and not for a Priest at all? Striving towards the sunny heights, out of such a level and through such an element as ours in these days is, he had strange aberrations appointed him, and painful wanderings amid the miserable gas-lights, bog-fires, dancing meteors and putrid phosphorescences which form the guidance of a young human soul at present! Not till after trying all manner of sublimely illuminated places, and finding that the basis of them was putridity, artificial gas and quaking bog, did he, when his strength was all done, discover his true sacred hill, and passionately climb thither while life was fast ebbing!—A tragic history, as all histories are; yet a gallant, brave and noble one, as not many are. It is what, to a radiant son of the Muses, and bright messenger of the harmonious Wisdoms, this poor world,—if he himself have not strength enough, and *inertia* enough, and amid his harmonious eloquences silence enough,—has provided at present. Many a high-striving, too-hasty soul, seeking guidance towards eternal excellence from the official Black-artists, and successful Professors of political, ecclesiastical, philosophical, commercial, general and particular Legerdemain, will recognise his own history in this image of a fellow-pilgrim's.

Over-haste was Sterling's continual fault; over-haste, and want of the due strength,—alas, mere want of the due *inertia* chiefly; which is so common a gift for most part; and proves so inexorably needful withal! But he was good and generous and true; joyful where there was joy, patient and silent where endurance was required of him; shook innumerable sorrows, and thick-crowding forms of pain, gallantly away from him; fared frankly forward, and with scrupulous care to tread on no one's toes. True, above all, one may call him; a man of perfect veracity in thought, word and deed. Integrity towards all men,—nay, integrity had ripened with him into chivalrous generosity; there was no guile or baseness anywhere found in him. Transparent as crystal; he could not hide anything sinister, if such there had been to hide. A more perfectly transparent soul I have never known. It was beautiful, to read all those interior movements; the little shades of affections, ostentations; transient spurts of anger, which never grew to the length of settled spleen: all so naïve, so childlike, the very faults grew beautiful to you.

And so he played his part among us, and has now ended it: in this first half of the Nineteenth Century, such was the shape of human destinies the world and he made out between them.

He sleeps now, in the little burying-ground of Bonchurch; bright, ever-young in the memory of others that must grow old; and was honourably released from his toils before the hottest of the day.

All that remains, in palpable shape, of John Sterling's activities in this world are those Two poor Volumes; scattered fragments gathered from the general waste of forgotten ephemera by the piety of a friend: an inconsiderable memorial; not pretending to have achieved greatness; only disclosing mournfully, to the more observant, that a promise of greatness was there. Like other such lives, like all lives, this is a tragedy; high hopes, noble efforts; under thickening difficulties and impediments, ever-new nobleness of valiant effort;—and the result death, with conquests by no means corresponding. A life which cannot challenge the world's attention; yet which does modestly solicit it, and perhaps on clear study will be found to reward it.

On good evidence let the world understand that here was a remarkable soul born into it; who, more than others, sensible to its influences, took intensely into him such tint and shape of feature as the world had to offer there and then; fashioning himself eagerly by whatsoever of noble presented itself; participating ardently in the world's battle, and suffering deeply in its bewilderments;—whose Life-pilgrimage accordingly is an emblem, unusually significant, of the world's own during those years of his. A man of infinite susceptivity; who caught everywhere, more than others, the colour of the element he lived in, the infection of all that was or appeared honourable, beautiful and manful in the tendencies of his Time;—whose history therefore is, beyond others, emblematic of that of his Time.

In Sterling's Writings and Actions, were they capable of being well read, we consider that there is for all true hearts, and especially for young noble seekers, and strivers towards what is highest, a mirror in which some shadow of themselves and of their immeasurably complex arena will profitably present itself. Here also is one encompassed and struggling even as they now are. This man also had said to himself, not in mere Catechism-words, but with all his instincts, and the question thrilled in every nerve of him, and pulsed in every drop of his blood: 'What is the chief end of man? Behold, I too would live and work as beseems a denizen of this Universe, a child of the Highest God. By what means is a noble life still possible for me here? Ye Heavens and thou Earth, oh, how?'—The history of this long-continued prayer and endeavour, lasting in various figures for near forty years, may now and for some time coming have something to say to men!

Nay, what of men or of the world? Here, visible to myself, for some while, was a brilliant human presence, distinguishable, honourable and lovable amid the dim common populations; among the million little beautiful, once more a beautiful human soul: whom I, among others, recognised and lovingly walked with, while the years and the hours were. Sitting now by his tomb in thoughtful mood, the new times bring a new duty for me. 'Why write the Life of Sterling?' I imagine I had a commission higher than the world's, the dictate of Nature herself, to do what is now done. *Sic prosit.*

FROM

History of Friedrich II of Prussia, Called Frederick the Great

The History of Friedrich II of Prussia, called Frederick the Great is by far the longest and the most painfully-conceived of all Carlyle's works. The book was thirteen years in the writing: and its author experienced many fluctuations of feeling about its worth, and about the quality of Frederick as hero. Such doubts were not shared by contemporary critics. The History was greeted with almost unqualified praise, from the issue of the first two volumes in September 1858, through the publication of volume three in May 1862, volume four in February 1864, and the last two volumes in March 1865.

The book does not conform to modern ideas of the form in which history should be written, or the way in which historical sources should be treated: it is, nevertheless, much more readable than those who have never read a word of it are inclined to believe. There are many magnificent accounts of battles: Rossbach might be replaced by Mollwitz or Dettingen or Leuthen, or a dozen others. In its caricatural quality, through which the French army is referred to throughout as the 'Dauphiness,' this chapter on Rossbach is typical of much else in the book.

FROM

History of Friedrich II of Prussia

CHAPTER VIII

BATTLE OF ROSSBACH

FRIEDRICH left Leipzig Sunday October 30th; encamped, that night, on the famous Field of Lützen; with the vanguard, he (as usual, and Mayer with him, who did some brisk smiting-home of what French there were); Keith and Duke Ferdinand following, with main body and rear.

Movements on the Soubise-Hilburghausen part are all retrograde again;—can Dauphiness Bellona do nothing, then, except shuttle forwards and then backwards according to Friedrich's absence or presence? The Soubise-Hildburghausen Army does immediately withdraw on this occasion, as on the former; and makes for the safe side of the Saale again, rapidly retreating before Friedrich, who is not above one to two of them,—more like one to three, now that Broglio's Detachment is come to hand. Broglio got to Merseburg October 26th,—guess 15,000 strong;—considerably out of repair, and glad to have done with such a march, and be within reach of Soubise. This is the Second Son of our old Blusterous Friend; a man who came to some mark, and to a great deal of trouble, in this War; and ended, readers know how, at the Siege of the Bastille thirty-two years afterwards!

So soon as rested, Broglio, by order, moves leftwards to Halle, to guard Saale Bridge there; Soubise himself edging after him to Merseburg, on a similar errand; and leaving Hildburghausen to take charge of Weissenfels and the Third Saale Bridge. That is Dauphiness's posture while Friedrich encamps at Lützen:—let impatient human nature fix these three places for itself, and hasten to the catastrophe of wretched Dauphiness. Soubise, it ought to be remembered, is not in the highest spirits; but his Officers in over-high, 'Doing this *petit Marquis de Brandebourg* the honour to have a kind of War with him (*de lui faire une espèce de guerre*),' as they term it. Being puffed-up with general vanity, and the newspaper rumour about Haddick's feat,—which, like the gloves it got, is going all to left-hand in this way. Hildburghausen and the others overrule Soubise; and indeed there is no remedy; 'Provision almost out;—how retreat to our magazines and our fastnesses, with Friedrich once across Saale, and sticking to the skirts of us?' Here, from eye-witnesses where possible, are the successive steps of Dauphiness towards her doom, which is famous in the world ever since.

'Monday 31st October 1757,' as the Town-Syndic of Weissenfels records, 'about eight in the morning,[1] the King of Prussia, with his whole Army' (or what seemed to us the whole, though it was but a half; Keith with the other half being within reach to northward, marching Merseburg way), 'came before this Town.' Has been here before; as Keith has, as Soubise and others have: a town much agitated lately by transit of troops. It was from the eastern, or high landward side, where the so-called Castle is, that Friedrich came: Castle built originally on some 'White Crag (*Weisse Fels*,' not now conspicuous), from which the town and whilom Duchy take name.

'We have often heard of Weissenfels, while the poor old drunken Duke lived, who used to be a Suitor of Wilhelmina's, liable to hard usage; and have marched through it, with the Salzburgers, in peaceable times. A solid pleasant-enough little place (6,000 souls or so); lies leant against high ground (White Crags, or whatever it once was) on the eastern or right bank of the Saale; a Town in part flat, in part very steep; the streets of it, or main street and secondaries, running off level enough from the River and Bridge; rising by slow degrees, but at last rapidly against the high ground or cliffs, just mentioned; a stiff acclivity

[1] Müller, *Schlacht bei Rossbach* ('a Centenary Piece,' Berlin, 1857,—containing several curious extracts), p. 44; *Helden-Geschichte*, iv. 643, 651–668.

of streets, till crowned by the so-called Castle, the "Augustus Burg" in those days, the "Friedrich-Wilhelm Barrack" in ours. It was on this crown of the cliffs that his Prussian Majesty appeared.

'Saale is of good breadth here; has done perhaps two hundred miles, since he started, in the Fichtelgebirge (*Pine Mountains*), on his long course Elbe-ward; received, only ten miles ago, his last big branch, the wide-wandering Unstrut, coming-in with much drainage from the northern parts:—in breadth, Saale may be compared to Thames, to Tay or Beauly; his depth not fordable, though nothing like so deep as Thames's; main cargo visible is rafts of timber: banks green, definite, scant of wood: river of rather dark complexion, mainly noiseless, but of useful pleasant qualities otherwise.'

From this Castle or landward side come Friedrich and his Prussians, on Monday morning about eight. 'The garrison, some 4,000 Reichs folk and a French Battalion or two, shut the Gates, and assembled in the Market-place,'—a big square, close at the foot of the Heights; 'on the other hand, from the top of the Heights' (*Klammerk* the particular spot), 'the Prussians cannonaded Town and Gates; to speedy bursting-open of the same; and rushed in over the walls of the Castle-court, and by other openings into the Town: so that the garrison above-said had to quit, and roll with all speed across the Saale Bridge, and set the same on fire behind them.' This was their remedy for all the Three Bridges, when attacked; but it succeeded nowhere so well as here.

'The fire was of extreme rapidity; prepared beforehand': Bridge all of dry wood coated with pitch;—'fire reinforced too, in view of such event, by all the suet, lard and oleaginous matter the Garrison could find in Weissenfels; some hundredweights of tallow-dips, for one item, going up on this occasion.' Bridge, 'worth 100,000 thalers,' is instantly ablaze: some 400 finding the Bridge so flamy, and the Prussians at their skirts, were obliged to surrender;—Feldmarschall Hildburghausen, sleeping about two miles off, gets himelf awakened in this unpleasant manner. Flying garrison halt on the other side of the River, where the rest of their army is; plant cannon there against quenching of the Bridge; and so keep firing, answered by the Prussians, with much noise and no great mischief, till 3 P.M., when the Bridge is quite gone (Tollkeeper's Lodge and all), and the enterprise of crossing there had plainly become impossible.

Friedrich quickly, about a mile farther down the River, has picked-out another crossing-place, in the interim, and founded some new adequate plank or raft bridge there; which, by diligence all night, will be crossable tomorrow. So that, except for amusing the enemy, the cannonading may cease at Weissenfels. A certain Duc de Crillon, in command at this Weissenfels Bridge-burning and cannonade, has a chivalrous Anecdote (amounting nearly to zero when well examined) about saving or sparing Friedrich's life on this interesting occasion: How, being now on the safe side of the River, he Crillon with his staff taking some refection of breakfast after the furious flurry there had been; there came to him one of his Artillery Captains, stationed in an Island in the River, asking, 'Shall I shoot the King of Prussia, Monseigneur? He is down reconnoitering his end of the Bridge: sha'n't I, then?' To whom Crillon gives a glass of wine and smilingly magnanimous answer to a negative effect.[1] Concerning which, one has to remark, Not only, *first*, that the Artillery Captain's power of seeing Friedrich (which is itself uncertain) would indeed mean the power of aiming at him, but differs immensely from that of hitting him with shot; so that this 'Shall I kill the King?' was mainly thrasonic wind from Captain Bertin. But *secondly*, that there is no 'Island' in the River thereabouts, for Captain Bertin to fire from! So that probably the whole story is wind or little more: dreamlike, or at best some idle thrasonic-theoretic question, on the part of Bertin; proper answer thereto (consisting mainly of a glass of wine) from Monseigneur:—all which, on retrospection, Monseigneur feels, or would fain feel, to have been not theoretic-thrasonic but practical, and of a rather godlike nature. Zero mainly, as we said; Friedrich thanks you for zero, Monseigneur.

'The Prussians were billeted in the Town that night,' says our Syndic; 'and in many a house there came to be twenty

[1] '*Mémoires militaires de Louis, etc., Duc de Crillon* (Paris, 1791), p. 166';—as cited by Preuss, ii. 88.

men, and even thirty and above it, lodged. All was quiet through the night; the French and the Reichs folk were drawn back upon the higher grounds, about Burgwerben and on to Tagwerben; and we saw their watchfires burning.' Friedrich's Bridge meanwhile, unmolested by the enemy, is getting ready.

Keith, looking across to Merseburg on the morrow morning (Tuesday Nov. 1st), whither he had marched direct with the other Half of the Army, finds Merseburg Bridge destroyed, or broken; and Soubise with batteries on the farther side, intending to dispute the passage. Keith despatches Duke Ferdinand to Halle, another twelve miles down, who finds Halle Bridge destroyed in like manner, and Broglio intending to dispute; which, however, on second thoughts, neither of them did. Friedrich's new Bridge at Herren-Mühle (*Lordship's Mill*) is of course an important point to them; Friedrich's passage now past dispute! 'Let us fall back,' say they, 'and rank ourselves a little; we are 50 or 60,000 strong; ill-off for provisions; but well able to retreat; and have permission to fight on this side of the River.'

The combined Army, 'Dauphiness,' or whatever we are to call it, does on Wednesday morning (November 2d) gather-in its cannon and outskirts, and give-up the Saale question; retire landwards to the higher grounds some miles; and dilligently get itself united, and into order of battle better or worse, near the Village of Mücheln (which means Kirk *Michael*, and is still written '*Sanct Michel*' by some on this occasion). There Dauphiness takes post, leaning on the heights, not in a very scientific way; leaving Keith and Ferdinand to rebuild their Bridges unmolested, and all Prussians to come across at discretion. Which they have diligently done (2d–3d November), by their respective Bridges; and on Thursday afternoon are all across, encamped at Bedra, in close neighbourhood to Mücheln; which Friedrich has been out reconnoitering, and finds that he can attack next morning very early.

Next morning, accordingly, 'by 2 o'clock, with a bright moon shining,' Friedrich is on horseback, his Army following.

But on examining by moonlight, the enemy had shifted their position; turned on their axis, more or less, into new wood-patches, new batteries and bogs; which has greatly mended their affair. No good attacking them so, thinks Friedrich; and returns to his Camp; slightly cannonaded, one wing of him, from some battery of the enemy; and immoderately crowded-over by them: 'Dare not, you see! Tried, and was defeated!' cry their newspapers and they,—for one day. Friedrich lodges again in Bedra this night, others say in Rossbach; shifts his own Camp a little; left wing of it now at Rossbach (*Horse-Brook*, or *Beck*, soon to be a world-famous Hamlet): the effects of hunger on the Dauphiness, so far from her supplies, will, he calculates, be stronger than on him, and will bring her to better terms shortly. Dauphiness needs bread; one may have fine clipping at the skirts of her, if she try retreat. That Dauphiness would play the prank she did next morning, Friedrich had not ventured to calculate.

Catastrophe of Dauphiness (Saturday 5th November 1757)

Meandering Saale is on one of his big turns, as he passes Weissenfels; turning, pretty rapidly here, from south-eastward, which he was a dozen miles ago, round to north-eastward again or northward altogether. which he gets to be at Merseburg, a dozen farther down. Right across from Weissenfels, lapped in this crook of the Saale, or washed by it on south side and on east, rises, with extreme laziness, a dull circular lump of country, six or eight miles in diameter; with Rossbach and half-a-dozen other scraggy sleepy Hamlets scattered on it;—which, till the morning of Saturday 5th November 1757, had not been notable to any visitor. The topmost point or points, for there are two (not discoverable except by tradition and guess), the country people do call Hills *Janus-Hügel*, *Pölzen-Hügel*,—Hill sensible to wagon-horses, in those bad loose tracks of sandy mud, but unimpressive on the Tourist, who has to admit that there seldom was so flat a Hill. Rising, let us guess, forty yards in the three or four miles it has had. Might be called a perceptibly potbellied plain, with more propriety; flat country, slightly puffed-up;—in shape not steeper than the mould of an immense tea-saucer would be. Tea-saucer 6 miles in diameter, 100 feet in depth, and of irregular contour, which indeed will sufficiently represent it. to the reader's mind.

Saale, at four or five miles distance, bounds this scraggy lump on the east and on the south. Westward and northward, springing about Mücheln on each hand, and setting off to right and to left Saale-ward, are what we take to be two brooks; at least are two hollows: and behind these, the country rises higher; undulating still on lazy terms, but now painted azure by the distance, not unpleasant to behold, with its litter all lapped out of sight, and its poor brooks tinkling forward (as we judge) into the Saale, Merseburg way, or reverse-wise into the Unstrut, the last big branch of Saale. Southward from our Janus Height, eight or nine miles off, may be seen some vestige of Freiburg; steeple or gilt weathercock faintly visible, on the Unstrut yonder;—which I take to be Soubise's bread-basket at present. And farther off, and opposite the *mouth* of the Unstrut, well across the Saale, lies another nameable Town (visible in clear weather, as a smoke-cloud at certain hours, about meal-time, when the kettles are on boil), the Town of Naumburg,—one of several German Naumburgs,—the Naumburg of Gustaf Adolf; where his slain body lay, on the night of Lützen Battle, with his poor Queen and others weeping over it. Naumburg is on the other side of Saale, not of importance to Soubise in such posture.

This is the circular block, or lump of country, on the north or north-west side of which Friedrich now lies, and which will become, he little thinks how memorable on the morrow. Over the heights, immediately eastward of Friedrich, there is a kind of hollow, or scooped-out place; shallow valley of some extent, which deserves notice against tomorrow: but in general the ground is lazily spherical, and without noticeable hollows or valleys when fairly away from the River. A dull blunt lump of country; made of sand and mud,—may have been grassy once, with broom on it, in the pastoral times; is now under poor plough-husbandry, arable or scratchable in all parts, and looks rather miserable in winter-time. No vestige of hedge on it, of shrub or bush; one tree, ugly but big, which may have been alive in Friedrich's time, stands not far from Rossbach Hamlet; one, and no more, discoverable in these areas.

Various Hamlets lie sprinkled about: very sleepy, rusty, irregular little places; huts and cattle-stalls huddled down, as if shaken from a bag; much straw, thick thatch and crumbly mud-brick; but looking warm and peaceable, for the Four-footed and the Twofooted; which latter, if you speak to them, are solid reasonable people, with energetic German eyes and hearts, though so ill-lodged. These Hamlets, needing shelter and spring-water, stand generally in some slight hollow, if well up the Height, as Rossbach is; sometimes, if near the bottom, they are nestled in a sudden dell or gash,—work of the primeval rains, accumulating from above, and ploughing-out their way. The rains, we can see, have been busy; but there is seldom the least stream visible, bottom being too sandy and porous. On the western slope, there is in our time a kind of coal, or coal-dust, dug up; in the way of quarrying, not of mining; and one or two big chasms of this sort are confusedly busy: the natives mix this valuable coal-dust with water, mould it into bricks, and so use as fuel: one of the features of these hamlets is the strange black bricks, standing on edge about the cottage-doors, to drip, and dry in the sun. For this or for other reasons, the westward slope appears to be the best; and has a major share of hamlets on it: Rossbach is high up, and looks over upon Mücheln, and its dim belfry and appurtenances, which lie safe across the hollow, perhaps two miles off,—safe from Friedrich, if there were eatables and lodging to be had in such a place. Friedrich's left wing is in Rossbach. Bedra where Friedrich's right wing is; Branderode where the Soubise right is; then Gröst, Schevenroda, Zeuchfeld, Pettstädt, Lunstädt,—especially Reichartswerben, where Soubise's right will come to be: these the reader may take note of in his Map. Several of them lie in ashes just then; plundered, re-plundered, and at last set fire to; so busy have Soubise's hungry people been, of late, in the Country they came to 'deliver.' The Freiburg road, the Naumburg road, both towards Merseburg, cross this Height; straight like the string, Saale by Weissenfels being the bow.

The *Herrenhaus* (Squire's Mansion) still stands in Rossbach, with the littery Hamlet at its flank: a high, pavilion-roofed, and though dilapidated, pretentious kind of House; some kind of court round it, some kind of hedge or screen of brushwood and brickwall: terribly in need of the besom, it and its environment throughout. King, I suppose, did lodge there overnight: certain it is the Squire was absent; and the Squire's Man, three days afterwards, reported to him as follows: * * * 'Saturday the 5th, about 8 A.M., his Majesty mounted to the roof of the Herrenhaus here, some tiles having been removed' (for that end, or by accident, is not said), 'and saw how the French and Reichs Army were getting in movement,' —wriggling out of their Camp leftwards, evidently aiming towards Gröst. 'In about an hour, near half their Army was through Gröst, and had turned southward, rather south-eastward from Gröst, out in the Rossbach and Almsdorf region, and proceeding still towards Pettstädt,'—towards Schevenroda more precisely, not towards Pettstädt yet. 'His Majesty looked always through the perspective: and to me was the grace done to be ever at his side, and to name for him the roads the French and Reichs Army was marching.'[1]

The King had heard of this phenomenon hours before, and had sent out hussars and scouts upon it; but now sees it with his eyes:—'Going for Freiburg, and their bread-cupboard,' thinks the King; who does not as yet make much of the movement; but will watch it well, and calculates to have a stroke at the rear end of it, in due season. With which view, the cavalry, Seidlitz and Mayer, are ordered to saddle; foot regiments, and all else, to be in readiness. This French-Reichs Dauphiness is not rapid in her field-exercise; and has a great deal of wriggling and unwinding before she can fairly pick herself out, and get

[1] Müller, p. 50; Rödenbeck, p. 326.

forward towards Schevenroda on the Freiburg road. In three or in two parallel columns, artillery between them, horse ahead, horse arear; haggling alone there;—making for their bread-baskets, thinks the King. A body of French, horse chiefly, under St. Germain, come out, in the Schortau-Almsdorf part, with some salvoing and prancing, as if intending to attack about Rossbach, where our left wing is: but his Majesty sees it to be a pretence merely; and St. Germain, motionless, and doing nothing but cannonade a little, seems to agree that it is so. Dauphiness continues her slow movements; King, in this Squire's Mansion of Rossbach, sits down to dinner, dinner with Officers at the usual hour of noon,—little dreaming what the Dauphiness has in her head.

Truth is, the Dauphiness is in exultant spirits, this morning; intending great things against a certain 'little Marquis of Brandenburg,' to whom one does so much honour. Generals looking down yesterday on the King of Prussia's Camp, able to count every man in it (and half the men being invisible, owing to bends of the ground), counted him to 10,000 or so; and had said, 'Pshaw, are not we above 50,000; let us end it! Take him on his left. Round yonder, till we get upon his left, and even upon his rear withal, St. Germain coöperating on the other side of him: on left, on rear, on front, at the same moment, is not that a sure game?' A very ticklish game, answers surly sagacious Lloyd: 'No general will permit himself to be taken in flank with his eyes open; and the King of Prussia is the unlikeliest you could try it with!'

Trying it meanwhile they are; marching along by the low grounds here, intending to sweep gradually leftwards towards Janus-Hill quarter; there to sweep home upon him, coil him up, left and rear and front, in their boa-constrictor folds, and end his trifle of an Army and him. 'Why not, if we do our duty at all, annihilate his trifle of an Army; take himself prisoner, and so end it?' Report says, Soubise had really, in some moment of enthusiasm lately, warned the Versailles populations to expect such a thing; and that the Duchess of Orleans forgetful of poor King Louis's presence, had in *her* enthusiasm, exclaimed: '*Tant mieux*, I shall at last see a King, then!' But perhaps it is a mere French epigram, such as the winds often generate there, and put down for fact.—Friedrich's retreat to Weissenfels is cut-off for Friedrich: an Austrian party has been at the Herren-Mühle Bridge this morning, has torn it up and pitched it into the river; planks far on to Merseburg by this time. and, in fact, unless Friedrich be nimble—But that he usually is.

Friedrich's dinner had gone on with deliberation for about two hours, Friedrich's intentions not yet known to any, but everybody, great and small, waiting eagerly for them, like greyhounds on the slip,—when Adjutant Gaudi, who had been on the Housetop the while, rushes into the Dining-room faster than he ought, and, with some tremor in his voice and eyes, reports hastily: 'At Schevenroda, at Pettstädt yonder! Enemy has turned left. Clearly for the left.'—'Well, and if he do? No flurry needed, Captain!' answered Friedrich,—(*not* in these precise words; but rebuking Gaudi, with a look not of laughter wholly, and with a certain question, as to the state of Gaudi's stomachic part, which is still known in traditionary circles, but is not mentionable here);—and went, with due gravity, himself to the roof, with his Officers. 'To the left, sure enough; meaning to attack us there': the thing Freidrich had despaired of is voluntarily coming, then;—and it is a thing of stern qualities withal; a wager of life, with glorious possibilities behind.

Friedrich earnestly surveys the phenomenon for some minutes; in some minutes, Friedrich sees his way through it, at least into it, and how he will do it. Off, eastward; march! Swift are his orders; almost still swifter the fulfilment of them. Prussian Army is a nimble article in comparison with Dauphiness! In half an hour's time, all is packed and to the road and, except Mayer and certain Free-Corps or Light-Horse, to amuse St. Germain and his Almsdorf people, there is not a Prussian visible in these localities to French eyes. 'At half-past two,' says the Squire's Man,—or let us take him a sentence earlier, to lose nothing of such a Document: 'At noon his

Majesty took dinner; sat till about two o'clock; then again went to the roof; and perceived that the Enemy's Army at Pettstädt were turning about the little Wood there north-eastward, as if for Lunstädt' (into the Lunstädt road);—'such cannonading too,' from those Almsdorf people, 'that the balls flew over our heads,'—or I tremulously thought so. At half-past two, the word was given, March! And good speed they made about it, in this Herrenhaus, and out of doors too, striking their tents, and cording-up and trimly shouldering everything with incredible brevity,' as if machinery were doing it; 'and at three, on the Prussian part, all was packed and out into the court for being carried off; and, in fact, the Prussian Army was on march at three.' Seidlitz, with all his Horse, vanishing round the corner of the Height; speeding along, invisible on his northern slope there, straight for the Janus-Pölzen Hill part; the Infantry followed, double-quick;—well knowing, each, what he has got to do.

But at this interesting point, the Editors,—small thanks to them, authentic but thrice-stupid mortals,—cut short our Eye-witness, not so much as telling us his name, some of them not even his date or whereabouts; and so the curtain tumbles down (as if its string had been cut, or suddenly eaten by unwise animals), and we are left to grey hubbub, and our own resources at secondhand. Except only that a French Officer,—one of those cannonading from Almsdorf, no doubt,—declares that 'it was like a change of scene in the Opera (*décoration d'Opéra*),[1] so very rapid; and that 'they all rolled-off eastward at quick time.' At extremely quick time;—and soon, in the slight hollow behind Janus Hügel, vanished from sight of these Almsdorf French, and of the Soubise-Hildburghausen Army in general. Which latter is agreeably surprised at the phenomenon; and draws a highly flattering conclusion from it. 'Gone, then; off at double-quick for Merseburg; aha!' think the Soubise-Hildburghausen people: 'Double-quick you too, my

[1] Letter in *Müller*, p. 60. In *Westphalen* (ii. 128–133) is a much superior French Letter, intercepted somewhere, and fallen to Duke Ferdinand; well worth reading, on Rossbach and the previous Affairs.

pretty men, lest they do whisk away, and we never get a stroke at them!'—

Seidlitz meanwhile, with his cavalry (thirty-eight squadrons, about 4,000 horse), is rapidly doing the order he has had. Seidlitz at a sharp military trot, and the infantry at double-quick to keep-up near him, which they cannot quite do, are, as we have said, making right across for the Pölzen-Hill and Janus-Hill quarter; their route the string, French route the bow; and are invisible to the French, owing to the heights between. Seidlitz, when he gets to the proper point eastward, will wheel about, front to southward, and be our left wing; infantry, as centre and right, will appear in like manner; and —we shall see!

The exultant Dauphiness, or Soubise-Hildburghausen Army (let us call it, for brevity's sake, Dauphiness or French, which it mainly was), on that rapid disappearance of the Prussians, never doubted but the Prussians were off on flight for Merseburg, to get across by the Bridge there. Whereat Dauphiness, doubly exultant, mended her own pace, cavalry at a sharp trot, infantry double-quick, but unable to keep up,—for the purpose of capturing or intercepting the runaway Prussians. Speed, my friends,—if you would do a stroke upon Friedrich, and show the Versailles people a King at last! Thus they, hurrying on, in two parallel columns,—infantry, long floods of it, coming double-quick but somewhat fallen behind; cavalry 7,000 or so, as vanguard,—faster and faster; sweeping forward on their southern side of the Janus-and-Pölzen slope, and now rather climbing the same.

Seidlitz has his hussar pickets on the top, to keep him informed as to their motions, and how far they are got. Seidlitz, invisible on the south slope of the Pölzen Hügel, finds about half-past three P.M. that he is now fairly ahead of Dauphiness; Seidlitz halts, wheels, comes to the top, 'Got the flank of them, sure enough!'—and without waiting signal or farther orders, every instant being precious, rapidly forms himself; and plunges down on these poor people. 'Compact as a wall, and with an incredible velocity (*d'une vitesse incroyable*),' says one of them. Figure the astonishment of Dauphiness; of poor Broglio, who commands the horse here. Taken in flank, instead of taking other people; intercepted, not in the least needing to intercept! Has no time to form, though he tried what he could. Only the two Austrian regiments got completely formed; the rest very incompletely; and Seidlitz, in the blaze of rapid steel, is in upon them. The two Austrian regiments, and two French that are named, made what debate was feasible;—courage nowise wanting, in such sad want of captaincy; nay, Soubise in person galloped into it, if that could have helped. But from the first, the matter was hopeless; Seidlitz slashing it at such a rate, and plunging through it and again through it, thrice, some say four times: so that, in the space of half an hour, this luckless cavalry was all tumbling off the ground; plunging down-hill, in full flight, across his own infantry or whatever obstacle, Seidlitz on the hips of it; and galloping madly over the horizon, towards Freiburg as it proved; and was not again heard of that day.

In about half an hour that bit of work was over; and Seidlitz, with his ranks trimmed again, had drawn himself southward a little, into the Hollow of Tageswerben, there to wait impending phenomena. For Friedrich with the Infantry is now emerging over Janus Hill, in a highly thunderous manner,—eighteen pieces of artillery going, and 'four big guns taken from the walls of Leipzig'; and there will be events anon. It is said, Hildburghausen, at the first glimpse of Friedrich over the hill-top, whispered to Soubise, 'We are lost, Royal Highness!'—'Courage!' Soubise would answer; and both, let us hope, did their utmost in this extremely bad predicament they had got into.

Friedrich's artillery goes at a murderous rate; had come in view, over the hill-top, before Seidlitz ended,—'nothing but the muzzles of it visible' (and the fire-torrents from it) to us poor French below. Friedrich's lines; or rather his one line, mere tip of his left wing,—only seven battalions in it, five of them under Keith from the second or reserve line; whole centre and right wing standing 'refused' in oblique rank, invisible, *behind* the Hill,—Friedrich's line, we say, the artillery to its right, shoots-out in mysterious Prussian rhythm, in echelons, in potences, obliquely down the Janus-Hill side; straight, rigid, regular as iron clockwork; and strides towards us, silent, with the lightning sleeping in it:—Friedrich has got the flank of Dauphiness, and means to keep it. Once and again and a third time, poor Soubise, with his poor regiments much in an imbroglio, here heaped on one another, there with wide gaps, halt being so sudden,—attempts to recover the flank, and pushes-out this regiment and the other, rightward, to be even with Friedrich. But sees with despair that it cannot be; that Friedrich with his echelons, potences and mysterious Prussian resources, pulls himself out like the pieces of a prospect-glass, piece after piece, hopelessly fast and seemingly no end to them; and that the flank is lost, and that—Unhappy Generals of Dauphiness, what a phenomenon for them! A terrible Friedrich, not fled to Merseburg at all; but mounted there on the Janus Hill, as on his saddle-horse, with face quite the other way;—and for holster-pistol, has plucked out twenty-two cannon. Clad verily in fire; Chimæra-like, *riding* the Janus Hill, in that manner; left leg (or wing) of him spurning us into the abysses, right one ready to help at discretion!

Hildburghausen, I will hope, does his utmost; Soubise, Broglio, for certain do. The French line is in front, next the Prussians: poor Generals of Dauphiness are panting to retrieve themselves. But with regiments jammed in this astonishing way, and got collectively into the lion's throat, what can be done? Steady, rigid as iron clockwork, the Prussian line strides forward; at forty-paces distance delivers its first shock of lightning, bursts into platoon fire; and so continues, steady at the rate of five shots a minute,—hard to endure by poor masses all in a coil. 'The artillery tore-down whole ranks of us,' says the Würtemberg Dragoon;[1] 'the Prussian musketry did terrible execution.'

Things began to waver very soon, French reeling back from the Prussian fire, Reichs troops rocking very uneasy, torn by

[1] His Letter in *Müller*, p. 83.

such artillery; when, to crown the matter, Seidlitz, seeing all things rock to the due extent, bursts out of Tageswerben Hollow, terribly compact and furious, upon the rear of them. Which sets all things into inextricable tumble; and the Battle is become a rout and a riding into ruin, no Battle ever more. Lasted twenty-five minutes, this second act of it, or till half-past four: after which, the curtains rapidly descending (Night's curtain, were there no other) cover the remainder; the only stage-direction, *Exeunt Omnes*. Which for a 50 or 60,000, ridden-over by Seidlitz Horse, was not quite an easy matter! They left, of killed and wounded, near 3,000; of prisoners, 5,000 (Generals among them 8, Officers 300): in sum, about 8,000; not to mention cannon, 67 or 72; with standards, flags, kettledrums and meaner baggages *ad libitum* in a manner. The Prussian loss was, 165 killed, 376 wounded;—between a sixteenth and a fifteenth part of theirs: in number the Prussians had been little more than one to three; 22,000 of all arms,—not above half of whom ever came into the fire; Seidlitz and seven battalions doing all the fighting that was needed. St. Germain tried to cover the retreat; but 'got broken,' he says,—Mayer bursting-in on him,—and soon went to slush like the others.

Seldom, almost never, not even at Crecy or Poictiers, was any Army better beaten. And truly, we must say, seldom did any better deserve it, so far as the Chief Parties went. Yes, Messieurs, this is the *petit Marquis de Brandebourg*; you will know this one, when you meet him again! The flight, the French part of it, was towards Freiburg Bridge; in full gallop, long after the chase had ceased; crossing of the Unstrut there, hoarse, many-voiced, all night; burning of the Bridge; found burnt, when Friedrich arrived next morning. He had encamped at Obschütz, short way from the field itself. French Army, Reichs Army, all was gone to staves, to utter chaotic wreck. Hildburghausen went by Naumburg; crossed the Saale there; bent homewards through the Weimar Country; one wild flood of ruin, swift as it could go; at Erfurt 'only one regiment was in rank, and marched through with drums beating.' His Army, which had been disgustingly unhappy from the first, and was now fallen fluid on these mad terms, flowed all away in different rills, each by the course straightest home; and Hildburghausen arriving at Bamberg, with hardly the ghost or mutilated skeleton of an Army, flung down his truncheon,—'A murrain on your Reichs Armies and regimental chaoses!'—and went indignantly home. Reichs Army had to begin at the beginning again; and did not reappear on the scene till late next Year, under a new Commander, and with slightly improved conditions.

Dauphiness Proper was in no better case; and would have flowed home in like manner, had not home been so far, and the way unknown. Twelve thousand of them rushed straggling through the Eichsfeld; plundering and harrying, like Cossacks or Calmucks: 'Army blown asunder, over a circle of forty-miles radius,' writes St. Germain: 'had the Enemy pursued us, after I got broken' (burst-in upon by Mayer and his Free-Corps people), 'we had been annihilated. Never did Army behave worse; the first cannon-salvo decided our rout and our shame.'[1]

In two-days time (November 7th), the French had got to Langensalza, fifty-five miles from the Battlefield of Rossbach; plundering, running, *sacre-dieu*-ing; a wild deluge of molten wreck, filling the Eichsfeld with its waste noises, making night hideous and day too;—in the villages Placards were stuck-up, appointing Nordhausen and Heiligenstadt for rallying-place.[2]

Soubise rode, with few attendants, all night towards Nordhausen,—eighty miles off, foot of the Brocken Country, where the Richelieu resources are;—Soubise with few attendants, face set towards the Brocken; himself, it is like, in a somewhat hag-ridden condition.

'The joy of poor Teutschland at large,' says one of my Notes, 'and how all Germans, Prussian and Anti-Prussian alike, flung-up their caps, with unanimous *Lebe-hoch*, at the news of Rossbach, has often been remarked; and indeed is still almost touching to see. The perhaps bravest Nation in the world, though the least braggart, very certainly *ein tapferes Volk* (as their Goethe calls them); so long insulted, snubbed and trampled-on, by a luckier, not a braver:—has not your exultant

[1] St. Germain to Verney: different Excerpts of Letters in the two weeks after Rossbach and before (given in Preuss, ii. 97).

[2] Müller, p. 73.

Dauphiness got a beautiful little dose administered her; and is gone off in foul shrieks, and pangs of the interior,—let no man ask whitherward! "*Si un Allemand peut avoir de l'esprit* (Can a German possibly have sharpness of wits)?" Well, yes, it would seem: here is one German graduate who understands his medicine-chest, and the quality of patients!—Dauphiness got no pity anywhere; plenty of epigrams, and mostly nothing but laughter even in Paris itself. Napoleon long after, who much admires Friedrich, finds that this Victory of Rossbach was inevitable; "but what fills me with astonishment and shame," adds he, "is that it was gained by six battalions and thirty squadrons" (seven properly, and thirty-eight) "over such a multitude!"[1]—It is well known, Napoleon, after Jena, as if Jena had not been enough for him, tore-down the first Monument of Rossbach, some poor ashlar Pyramid or Pillar, raised by the neighbourhood, with nothing more afflictive inscribed on it than a date; and sent it off in carts for Paris (where no stone of it ever arrived, the Thüringen carmen slinking-off, and leaving it scattered in different places over the face of Thüringen in general); so that they had the trouble of a new one lately.'[2]

From Friedrich the 'Army of the Circles,' that is, Dauphiness and Company,—called *Hoopers* or 'Coopers' (*Tonneliers*), with a desperate attempt at wit by pun,—get their Adieu in words withal. This is the famed *Congé de l'Armée des Cercles et des Tonneliers*; a short metrical Piece; called by Editors the most profane, most indecent, most etc.; and printed with asterisk veils drawn over the worst passages. Who shall dare, searching and rummaging for insight into Friedrich, and complaining that there is none, to lift any portion of the veil; and say, 'See—Faugh!' The cynicism, truly, but also the irrepressible honest exultation, has a kind of epic completeness, and fulness of sincerity; and, at bottom, the thing is nothing like so wicked as careless commentators have given out. Dare to look a little:

'*Adieu, grands écraseurs de rois*,' so it starts: 'Adieu, grand crushers of Kings; arrogant windbags, Turpin, Broglio, Soubise,—Hildburghausen with the grey beard, foolish still as when your beard was black in the Turk-War time:—brisk journey to you all!' That is the first stanza; unexceptionable, had we room. The second stanza is,—with the veils partially lifted; with probably '*Moïse*' put into the first blank, and into the third something of or belonging to '*César*,'—

> '*Je vous ai vu comme . . .*
> *Dans des ronces en certain lieu*
> *Eut l'honneur de voir . . .*
> *Ou comme au gré de sa luxure*
> *Le bon Nicomède à l'écart*
> *Aiguillonnait sa flamme impure*
> *Des . . . . .*

[1] Montholon, *Mémoires etc. de Napoléon* (Napoleon's *Précis des Guerres de Frédéric II*, vii. 210).

[2] Rödenbeck, *Beyträge*, i. 299; *ib*. p. 385, Lithograph of the poor extinct Monument itself.

Enough to say, the Author, with a wild burst of spiritual enthusiasm, sings the charms of the rearward part of certain men; and what a royal ecstatic felicity there sometimes is in indisputable survey of the same. He rises to the heights of Anti-Biblical profanity, quoting Moses on the Hill of Vision; sinks to the bottomless of human or ultra-human depravity, quoting King Nicomedes's experiences on Cæsar (happily known only to the learned); and, in brief, recognises that there is, on occasion, considerable beauty in that quarter of the human figure, when it turns on you opportunely. A most cynical, profane affair: yet, we must say by way of parenthesis, one which gives no countenance to Voltaire's atrocities of rumour about Friedrich himself in this matter; the reverse rather, if well read; being altogether theoretic, scientific; sings with gusto the glow of beauty you find in that unexpected quarter, —while *kicking* it deservedly and with enthusiasm. 'To see the'—what shall we call it: seat of honour, in fact, 'of your enemy'; has it not an undeniable charm? 'I own to you in confidence, O Soubise and Company, this fine laurel I have got, and was so in need of, is nothing more or other than the sight of your'—*four asterisks.* 'Oblige me, whenever clandestine Fate brings us together, by showing me that'—always that, if you would give me pleasure when we meet. 'And oh,' next stanza says, 'to think what our glory is founded on,'—on view of that unmentionable object, I declare to you!—And through other stanzas, getting smutty enough (though in theory only), which we need not prosecute farther.[1] A certain heartiness and epic greatness of cynicism, life's nakedness grown almost as if innocent again; an immense suppressed insuppressible Haha, on the part of this King. Strange *Te-Deum* indeed. Coming from the very heart, truly, as few of them do; but not, in other points, recommendable at all!—Here, of the night before, is something better:

To Wilhelmina

'Near Weissenfels' (Obschütz, in fact; does not yet know what the Battle will be *called*), '5th November 1757.

'At last, my dear Sister, I can announce you a bit of good news. You are doubtless aware that the Coopers with their circles had a mind to take Leipzig. I ran up, and drove them beyond Saale. The Duc de Richelieu sent them a reinforcement of twenty battalions and fourteen squadrons' (say 15,000 horse and foot); 'they then called themselves 63,000 strong. Yesterday I went to reconnoitre them; could not attack them in the post they held. This had rendered them rash. Today they came out with the intention of attacking me; but I took the start of them (*les ai prévenu*). It was a Battle *en douceur* (soft to one's wish). Thanks to God I have not a hundred men killed; the only General ill wounded is Meinecke. My brother Henri and General Seidlitz have slight hurts' (gunshots, not so slight, that of Seidlitz) 'in the arm. We

[1] *Œuvres de Frédéric*, xii. 70–73 (*written* at Freiburg, 6th November, when his Majesty got thither, and found the Bridge burnt).

have all the Enemy's cannon, all the' * * 'I am in full march to drive them over the Unstrut' (already driven, your Majesty; bridge burning).

'You, my dear Sister, my good, my divine and affectionate Sister' (faithful to the bone, in good truth, poor Wilhelmina), 'who deign to interest yourself in the fate of a Brother who adores you, deign also to share in my joy. The instant I have time, I will tell you more. I embrace you with my whole heart. Adieu. F.'[1]

Ulterior Fate of Dauphiness; flies over the Rhine in bad Fashion: Dauphiness's Ways with the Saxon Populations in her Deliverance-Work.

Friedrich had no more fighting with the French. November 9th, at Merseburg, in all stillness, Duke Ferdinand got his Britannic Commission, his full Powers, from Friedrich and the parties interested; in all stillness made his arrangements, as if for Magdeburg and his Governorship there,—Friedrich hastening off for Silesia the while. Duke Ferdinand did stay six days in Magdeburg, inspecting or pretending to inspect; very pleasant with his Sister and the Royalties that are now there; but at midnight of day sixth shot-off silently on wider errand. And, in sum, on Thursday 24th November 1757, appeared in Stade, on horseback at morning parade there; intimating, to what joy of the poor Brunswick Grenadiers and others, That he was come to take command; that Kloster-Zeven is abolished; that we are not an 'Observation Army,' rotting here in the parish pound, any longer, but an 'Allied Army' (such now our title), intending to strike for ourselves, and get out of pound straightway!—

'*Thursday 24th November—Tuesday 29th.* Duke Ferdinand did accordingly pick-up the reins of this distracted Affair; and, in a way wonderful to see, shot sanity into every fibre of it; and kept it sane and road-worthy for the Five Years coming. With a silent velocity, an energy, an imperturbable steadfastness and clear insight into cause and effect; which were creditable to the school he came from; and were a very joyful sight to Pitt and others concerned. So that from next Tuesday, "November 29th, before daylight," when Ferdinand's batteries began playing upon Harburg (French Fortress nearest to Stade), the reign of the French ceased in those Countries; and an astonished Richelieu and his French, lying scattered over all the West of Germany, in

[1] *Œuvres de Frédéric*, xxvii, 1. 310.

readiness for nothing but plunder, had to fall more or less distracted in their turn; and do a number of astonishing things. To try this and that, of futile, more or less frantic nature; be driven from post after post; be driven across the Aller first of all;—Richelieu to go home thereupon, and be succeeded by one still more incompetent.

'*December 13th*, a fortnight after Ferdinand's appearance, Richelieu had got to the safe side of the Aller (burning of Zelle Bridge and Zelle Town there, his last act in Germany); Ferdinand's quarters now wide enough; and vigorous speed of preparation going on for farther chase, were the weather mended. *February 17th* (1758), Ferdinand was on foot again; Prince de Clermont, the still more incompetent successor of Richelieu, gazing wide-eyed upon him, but doing nothing else: and for the next six weeks there was seen a once triumphant Richelieu-d'Estrées French Army, much in rags, much in disorder, in terror, and here and there almost in despair,—winging their way; like clouds of draggled poultry caught by a mastiff in the corn. Across Weser, across Ems, finally across the Rhine itself, every feather of them,—their long-drawn cackle, of a shrieky type, filling all Nature in those months; the mastiff steadily following.[1] To the astonishment of Pitt and mankind. Can this be the same Army that Royal Highness led to the Sea and the Parish Pound? The same identically, wasted to about two-thirds by Royal Highness; not a drum in it changed otherwise, only One Man different, —and he is the important one!

'Pitt, when the news of Rossbach came, awakening the bonfires and steeple-bells of England to such a pitch, had resolved on an emphatic measure: that of sending English Troops to reinforce our Allied Army, and its new General;—such an Ally as that Rossbach one being rare in the eyes of Pitt. "Postpone the meeting of Parliament, yet a few days, your Majesty," said Pitt, "till I get the estimates ready!"[2] To which Majesty assented, and all England with him: "England's own Cause," thinks Pitt, with confidence: "our way of conquering America,—and, in the circumstances, our one way!" English did land, accordingly; first instalment of them, a 12,000 (in August next), increased gradually to 20,000; with no end of furnishings to them and everybody; with results again satisfactory to Pitt; and very famous in the England that then was, dim as they are now grown.'

The effect of all which was, that Pitt, with his Ferdinands and reinforcements, found work for the French ever onwards from Rossbach; French also turning as if exclusively upon

---

[1] Mauvillon, i. 252–284 ('9th November 1757—1st April 1758'); Westphalen, i. 316–503 (abundantly explicit, authentic and even entertaining,—with the ample Correspondences, *ib.* ii. 147–350); Schaper, *Vie militaire du Maréchal Prince Ferdinand* (2 tomes, 8vo, Magdebourg, 1796, 1799), i. 7–100 (a careful Book; of an official exactitude, like Westphalen's,—and appears to be left incomplete like his).

[2] Thackeray, i, 310.

perfidious Albion: and the thing became, in Teutschland, as elsewhere, a duel of life and death between these natural enemies, —Teutschland the centre of it,—Teutschland and the accessible French Sea-Towns,—but the circumference of it going round from Manilla and Madras to Havanna and Quebec again. Wide-spread furious duel; prize, America and life. By land and sea; handsomely done by Pitt on both elements. Land part, we say, was always mainly in Germany, under Ferdinand,— In Hessen and the Westphalian Countries, as far west as Minden, as far east as Frankfurt-on-Mayn, generally well north of Rhine, well south of Elbe: that was, for five years coming, the cockpit or place of deadly fence between France and England. Friedrich's arena lies eastward of that, occasionally playing into it a little, and played into by it, and always in lively sympathy and consultation with it: but, except the French subsidisings, diplomatisings and great diligence against him in foreign Courts, Friedrich is, in practical respects, free of the French; and ever after Rossbach, Ferdinand and the English keep them in full work,—growing yearly too full. A heavy business for England and Ferdinand; which is happily kept extraneous to Friedrich thenceforth; to him and us; which is not on the stage of his affairs and ours, but is to be conceived always as vigorously proceeding alongside of it, close beyond the scenes, and liable at any time to make entry on him again:—of which we shall have to notice the louder occurrences and cardinal phases, but, for the future, nothing more.

Soubise, who had crept into the skirts of the Richelieu Army in Hanover or Hessen Country, had of course to take wing in that general flight before the mastiff. Soubise did not cross the Rhine with it; Soubise made off eastward;[1]—found new roost in Hanau-Frankfurt Country; and had thoughts of joining the Austrians in Bohemia next Campaign; but got new order,—such the pinches of a winged Clermont with a mastiff Ferdinand at his poor draggled tail;— and came back to the Ferdinand scene, to help there; and never saw Friedrich again. Both Broglio and he had a good deal of fighting (mostly beat-

[1] Westphalen, i. 501 ('end of March 1758').

ing) from Ferdinand; and a great deal of trouble and sorrow in the course of this War; but after Rossbach it is not Friedrich or we, it is Ferdinand and the Destinies that have to do with them. Poor Soubise, except that he was the creature of Generalissima Pompadour, which had something radically absurd in it, did not deserve all the laughter he got: a man of some chivalry, some qualities. As for Broglio, I remember always, not without human emotion, the two extreme points of his career as a soldier: Rossbach and the Fall of the Bastille. He was towards forty, when Friedrich bestrode the Janus Hill in that fiery manner; he was turned of seventy when, from the pavements of Paris, the Chimæra of Democracy rose on him, in fire of a still more horrible description.

Dauphiness-Bellona, in her special and in her widest sense, has made exit, then. Gone, like clouds of draggled poultry home across the Rhine. She was the most marauding Army lately seen, also the most gasconading, and had the least capacity for fighting: three worse qualities no army could have. How she fought, we have seen sufficiently. Before taking leave of her forever, readers, as she is a paragon in her kind, would perhaps take a glance or two at her marauding qualities,—by a good opportunity that offers. Plotho—at Regensburg, that a supreme Reichs Diet may know what a 'deliverance of Saxony' this has been, submits one day the following irrefragable Documents, 'which have happened,' not without good industry of my own, 'to fall into my' (Plotho's) 'hands.' They are Documents partly of epistolary, partly of a Petitionary form, presented to Polish Majesty, out of that Saxon Country; and have an *affidavit* quality about them, one and all.

1°. *Big Dauphiness* (that is, D'Estrées) *in the Wesel Countries, at an early Stage,—while still endeavouring what she could to behave well, having* 1,000 *marauders and the like* (A private Letter)

'*County Mark, 20th June* 1757. The French troops are going on here in a way to utterly ruin us. Schmidt, their President of Justice, whom they set-up in Cleve, has got orders to change all the Magistracies of the

Country' (Protestant by nature), 'so as that half the members shall be Catholic. Bielefeld was openly plundered by the French for three hours long. You cannot by possibility represent to yourself what the actual state of misery in these Countries is. A *scheffel* of rye costs three thalers sixteen groschen' (who knows how many times its natural price!). 'And now we are to be forced to eat the spoiled meal those French troops brought with them; which is gone to such a state no animal would have it. This poisoned meal we are to buy from them, ready money, at the price they fix; and that famine may induce us, they are about to stop the mills, and forcibly take away what little bread-corn we have left. God have pity on us, and deliver us soon! Next week we are to have a transit of 6,000 Pfalzers' (Kur-Pfalz, foolish idle fellow, and Kur-Baiern too, are both in subsidy of France, as usual; 6,000 Pfalzers just due here); 'these, I suppose, will sweep us clean bare."[1]

Wesel Fortress, Gate of the Rhine, could not be defended by Friedrich: and the Hanover Incapables, and England still all in St. Vitus, would not hear of undertaking it; left it wide-open for the French; never could recover it, or get the Rhine-Gate barred again, during the whole War. One hopes they repented;—but perhaps it was only Pitt and Duke Ferdinand that did so, instead! The Wesel Countries were at once occupied by the French; 'a conquest of her Imperial Majesty's'; continued to be administered in Imperial Majesty's name,—and are thriving as above.

2°. *Dauphiness Proper* (that is, Soubise) *in Thüringen, at a late Stage*

'*Letter from Freiburg, shortly after Rossbach.*—It was on the 23d October, a Sunday, that we of Freiburg had our first billeting of French; a body of cavalry from different regiments' (going to take Leipzig, take Torgau, what not): 'and from that day Freiburg never emptied of French, who kept marching through it in extraordinary quantities. The marching lasted fourteen days, namely, till the 6th November' (day *after* Rossbach; when they burnt our poor Bridge, and marched for the last time); 'and often the billeting was so heavy, that in a single house there were forty or fifty men. Who at all times had to be lodged and dieted gratis; nay, many householders, over and above the ordinary meal, were obliged to give them money too; and many poor people, who can scarcely get their own bit of bread, had to run and bring at once their sixteen or eighteen groschen' (pence) 'worth of wine, not to speak of coffee and sugar. And a great increase of the mischief it was always, that the soldiers and common people did not understand one another's language.'—Heavy billeting; but what was that? * * 'Vast, nearly impossible, quantities of forage and provision,' were wrung from us, as from all the other Towns and Villages about, 'under continual threatening to burn and rase us from the earth. Often did our French Colonel threaten, "He would have the cannon opened on Freiburg

[1] *Helden-Geschichte*, iv. 399.

straightway." Nay, had it stood by foraging, we might have reckoned ourselves lucky. But our straits increased day by day; and sheer plundering became more and more excessive.

'The robbing and torturing of travellers, the plundering and burning of Saxon villages'—'Almost all the Towns and Villages hereabouts are so plundered out, that many a one now has nothing but what he carries on his body. Plundering was universal: and no sooner was one party away, than another came, and still another; and often the same house was three or four times plundered. Branderode, a Village two leagues from this' (stands on the Field of Rossbach, if we look), 'is so ruined out, that nobody almost has anything left: Chief-Inspector Baron von Bose's Schloss there, with its splendid appointments, they ruined utterly; took all money, victuals, valuables, furniture, clothes, linen and beds, all they could carry; what could not be carried away, they cut, hewed and smashed to pieces; broke the wine-casks; and even tore-up the documents and letters they found lying in the place. Branderode Dorf was twice set fire to by them; and was, at last, with Zeuchfeld, which is an Amtsdorf,—after both has been plundered,—reduced to ashes. The Churches of Branderode and Zeuchfeld, with several other Churches, were plundered; the altars broken, the altar-cloths and other vestures cut to pieces, and the sacred vessels and cups carried away,—except' (for we have a notarial exactness, and will exaggerate nothing) 'that in the case of Branderode they sent the cup back. Of the pollution of the altars, and of the blasphemous songs these people sang in the churches, one cannot think without horror.

'And it was merely our pretended Allies and Protectors that have desecrated our divine service, utterly wasted our Country, reduced the inhabitants to want and desperation, and, in short, have so behaved that you would not know this region again. Truly these troops have realised for us most of the infamies we heard reported of the Cossacks, and their ravagings in Preussen lately.

'It is one of their smallest doings that they robbed a Saxon Clergyman' (name and circumstances can be given if required), 'three times over, on the public Highway; shot at him, tied him to a horse's tail and dragged him along with them; so that he is now lying ill, in danger of his life. On the whole, it is our beloved Pastors, Clergymen most of all, that have been plundered of everything they had.

'Balgart and Zschieplitz, both Villages half a league from this, have likewise been heavily plundered; they have even left the Parson nothing but what he wore on his back. Gröst,' another Rossbach place, 'which belongs to the Kammerjunker Heldorf, has likewise' * * *Ohe, satis!* —'All this happened between the 23d and 31st October; consequently before the Battle.' * * 'In many Villages you see the trees and fields sprinkled with feathers from the beds that have been slit-up.

'In several Villages belonging to the Royal Electoral Privy Councillor von Brühl' (who is properly the fountain of all this and of much other misery to us, if we knew it!), 'the plundering likewise had begun; and a quantity of about a hundred swine' (so ho!) 'had been cut in pieces: but in the midst of their work, the Allies heard that these were

Brühl estates, and ceased their havoc of them. These accordingly are the only lands in all this region whose fate has been tolerable.

'The appellation, every moment renewed, of "Heretic!" was the courteous address from these people to our fellow-Christians; "heretic dogs (*ketzerische Hunde*)" was a *Prädicat* always in their mouth.

'In Weischütz,' a mile or two from us, up the Unstrut, 'a French Colonel who wanted to ride out upon the works, made the there Pastor, Magister Schren, stoop down by way of horse-block, and mounted into the saddle from his back.' (Messieurs, you will kindle the wrath of mankind some day, and get a terrible plucking, with those high ways of yours!)

'Churches are all smashed; obscene songs were sung, in form of litany, from the pulpits and altars; what was done with the communion-vessels, when they were not worth stealing,'—is hideous to the religious sense, and shall not be mentioned in human speech.

3°. *The Broglio Reinforcement coming across to join Soubise, and perform at Rossbach* (Humble Petition from the Magistrates of Sangerhausen, To the King of Poland's Majesty):

Sangerhausen, 23d October 1757.—'Scarcely had we, with profound submission (*allerunterthänigst*), under date of the 13th current, represented to your Royal Majesty and Electoral Translucency how heavily we were pressed-down by the forage-requisitions and transits of troops, and the consequent expenditure in food, drinking, in oats and hay, which no one pays,—when directly thereafter, on the 14th of October, a new French party, of the Fischer Corps,'—Fischer is a mighty Hussar, scarcely inferior to Turpin; and stands in astonishing authority with Richelieu, and an Army whose object is plunder,[1]—'new party of the Fischer Corps, of some sixty men and horse, arrived in the Town; demanded meat, drink, oats and hay, and all things necessary; which they received from us;—and not only paid not one farthing for all this, but furthermore some of them, instead of thanks to their Landlord, Rossold, forcibly broke-up his press, drank his brandy, and carried-off a *Toute* (gather-all) with money in it. From a Tanner, Lindauer by name, they bargained for a buck-skin; and having taken, would not pay it. In the *Rathskeller* (Town Public-house) they drank much wine, and gave nothing for it: nay, on marching off,—because no mounted guide (*reitender Bote*) was at hand, and though they had before expressly said none such would be needed,—they rushed about like distracted persons (*wie rasende Leute*) in the market-place and in the streets; beat the people, tumbled them about, and lugged them along, in a violent manner; using abusive language to a frightful extent, and threatening every misfortune.

'Hardly were we rid of this confusion and astonishment, when, on October 21st, a whole swarm of horses, men, women, children and

---

[1] Ferdinand's Correspondents, *sæpius* (*Westphalen*, i. 40–127), etc etc.

wagons, which likewise all belonged to the Fischer Corps, and were commanded by First-Lieutenant Schmidt, came into our Town. This troop consisted of 80 men, part infantry, part cavalry; with some 80 work-horses, 10 baggage-wagons, and about 100 persons, women, sick people and the like. They stayed the whole night here; made meat, drink, corn, hay and whatever they needed be brought them; and went off next day without paying anything.

'Our Inns were now almost quite exhausted of forage in corn or hay; and we knew not how we were to pay what had been spent,—when the thirty French Light Cavalry, of whom we, with profound submission, on the 13th *hujus* gave your Royal Majesty and Electoral Translucency account, renewed their visit upon us; came, under the command of Rittmeister de Mocu, on the 22d of October' (while the baggage-wagons, work-horses, women, sick, and so forth, were hardly gone), 'towards evening, into the Town; consumed in meat and drink, oats and hay, and the like, what they could lay hold of; and next morning early marched away, paying, as their custom is, nothing.

'Not enough that,—besides the great forage contribution (*Lieferung*), which we already, with profound submission, notified to your Royal Majesty and Electoral Translucency as having been laid upon us; and that, by order of the Duc de Broglio, a new requisition is now laid on us, and he have had to engage for sixty-four more sacks of wheat, and thirty-two of rye (as is noted under head A, in the enclosed copy),—there has farther come on us, on the part of the Reichs Army, from Kreis-Commissarius Heldorf' (whose Schloss of Gröst, we perceive, they have since burnt, by way of thanks to him),[1] the simultaneous Order for instant delivery of Forage (as under head B, here enclosed)! Thus are we, at the appointed places, all at once to furnish such quantities, more than we can raise; and know not when or where we shall either for what has been already furnished, or for what is still to be, receive one penny of money: nay, over and above, we are to sustain the many marchings of troops, and provide to the same what meat, drink, oats, hay and so on, they require, without the least return of payment!

'So unendurable, and, taken all together, so hard (*sic*) begins the conduct of these troops, that profess being come as friends and helpers, to appear to us. And Heaven alone knows how long, under a continuance of such things, the subjects (whom the Hailstorm of last year had at any rate impoverished) shall be able to support the same. We would, were a reasonable delivery of forage laid upon us even at a low price, and the board and billet of the marching troops paid to us in part, lay-out our whole strength in helping to bear the burdens of the Father-land; but if such things go on, which will soon leave us only bare life and empty huts, we can look forward to nothing but our ruin and destruction. But, as it is not your Royal Majesty's and Electoral Translucency's most gracious will that we, your Most Supreme Self's most faithful subjects, should entirely perish, therefore we repeat our former most submissive prayer once again with hot (*sic*) sorrow of mind to Highest-the-Same; and sob most submissively for that help which

[1] Suprà, No. 2.

your Most Supreme Self, through most gracious mediation with the Duc de Richelieu, with the Reichs Army or wherever else, might perhaps most graciously procure for us. Who, in deepest longing thitherwards, with the most deepest devotion, remain—'[1] (*Names*, unfortunately, not given).

How many Saxons and Germans generally,—alas, how many men universally,—cry towards celestial luminaries of the governing kind with the most deepest devotion, in their extreme need, under their unsufferable injuries; and are truly like dogs in the backyard barking at the Moon. The Moon won't come down to them, and be eaten as green cheese; the Moon can't!—

4°. *Dauphiness after Rossbach.* 'Excise-Inspector Neitsche, at Bebra, near Weissenfels' (Bebra is well ahead from Freiburg and the burnt Bridge, and a good twenty-five miles west of Weissenfels), 'writes To the King of Poland's Majesty, *9th November* 1757:

'May it please your Royal Majesty and Electoral Translucency, out of your highest grace, to take knowledge, from the accompanying Registers *sub signo Martis*' (sign unknown to readers here), 'of the things which, in the name of this Township of Bebra, the Bürgermeister Johann Adam, with the Raths and others concerned, have laid before the Excise-Inspection here. As follows:

'It will be already well known to the Excise-Inspection that on the 7th of November (*a.c.*) of the current year' (day before yesterday, in fact!), 'the French Army so handled this place as to have not only taken from the inhabitants, by open force, all bread and articles of food, but likewise all clothes, beds, linens (*Wäsche*), and other portable goods; that it has broken, split to pieces, and emptied out, all chests, boxes, presses, drawers; has shot dead, in the backyards and on the thatch-roofs, all manner of feathered-stock, as hens, geese, pigeons; also carried forth with it all swine, cow, sheep and horse cattle; laid violent hands on the inhabitants, clapped guns, swords, pistols to their breast, and threatened to kill them unless they showed and brought out whatever goods they had; or else has hunted them wholly out of their houses, shooting at them, cutting, sticking and at last driving them away, thereby to have the freer room to rob and plunder: flung-out hay and other harvest-stock from the barns into the mud and dung, and had it trampled to ruin under the horses' feet; nay, in fact, has dealt with this place in so unpermitted a way as even to the most hard-hearted man must seem compassionable.'— —Poor fellows: *cetera desunt*; but that is enough! What can a Polish Majesty and Electoral Translucency do? Here too is a sorrowful howling to the Moon.[2]

** 'For a hundred miles round', writes St. Germain, 'the Country is

---

[1] *Helden-Geschichte*, iv. 688–691.

[2] *Helden-Geschichte*, iv. 692.

plundered and harried as if fire from Heaven had fallen on it; scarcely have our plunderers and marauders left the houses standing.'—'I lead a band of robbers, of assassins, fit for breaking on the wheel; they would turn tail at the first gunshot, and are always ready to mutiny. If the Government (*la Cour*,' with its Pompadour presiding, very unlikely for such an enterprise!) 'cannot lay the knife to the root of all this, we may give-up the notion of War.'[1] * *

Such a pitch have French Armies sunk to. When was there seen such a Bellona as Dauphiness before? Nay, in fact, she is the same devil-serving Army that Maréchal de Saxe commanded with such triumph,—Maréchal de Saxe in better luck for opponents; Army then in a younger stage of its development. Foaming then as sweet must, as new wine, in the hands of a skilful vintner, poisonous but brisk; not run, as now, to the vinegar state, intolerable to all mortals. She can now announce from her camp-theatres the reverse of the Roucoux program, 'Tomorrow, Messieurs, you are going to fight; our Manager foresees'—you will be beaten; and we cannot say what or where the next Piece will be! Impious, licentious, high-flaring efflorescence of all the Vices is not to be redeemed by the one Quasi-Virtue of readiness to be shot;—sweet of that kind, and sour of this, are the same substance, if you only wait. How kind was the Devil to his Saxe; and flew away with him in rosepink, while it was still time!

CHAPTER IX

FRIEDRICH MARCHES FOR SILESIA

THE fame of Friedrich is high enough again in the Gazetteer world; all people, and the French themselves, laughing at their grandiloquent Dauphiness-Bellona, and writing epigrams on Soubise. But Friedrich's difficulties are still enormous. One enemy coming with open mouth, you plunge-in upon, and ruin, on this hand; and it only gives you room to attempt upon another bigger one on that. Soubise he has finished hand-

[1] St. Germain, after Rossbach and before (in Preuss, *ubi suprà*).

somely, for this season; but now he must try conclusions with Prince Karl. Quick, towards Silesia, after this glorious Victory which the Gazetteers are celebrating.

The news out of Silesia are ominously doubtful, bad at the best. Duke Bevern, once Winterfeld was gone, had, as we observed, felt himself free to act; unchecked, but also unsupported, by counsel of the due heroism; and had acted unwisely. Made direct for Silesia, namely, where are meal-magazines and strong places. Prince Karl, they say, was also unwise; took no thought beforehand, or he might have gained marches, disputed rivers, Bober, Queiss, with Bevern, and as good as hindered him from ever getting to Silesia. So say critics, Retzow and others; perhaps looking too fixedly on one side of the question. Certain it is, Bevern marched in peace to Silesia; found it by no means the better place it had promised to be.

Prince Karl,—Daun there as second, but Karl now the dominant hand,—was on the heels of Bevern, march after march. Prince Karl cut athwart him by one cunning march, in Liegnitz Country; barring him from Schweidnitz, the chief stronghold of Silesia, and to appearance from Breslau, the chief city, too. Bevern, who did not want for soldiership, when reduced to his shifts, now made a beautiful manœuvre, say the critics; struck-out leftwards, namely, and crossed the Oder, as if making for Glogau, quite beyond Prince Karl's sphere of possibility,—but turned to right, not to left, when across, and got in upon Breslau from the other or east side of the River. Cunning manœuvre, if you will, and followed by cunning manœuvres: but the result is, Prince Karl has got Schweidnitz to rear, stands between Breslau and it; can besiege Schweidnitz when he likes, and no relief to it possible that will not cost a battle. A battle, thinks Friedrich, is what Bevern ought to have tried at first; a well-fought battle might have settled everything, and there was no other good likelihood in such an expedition: but now, by detaching reinforcements to this garrison and that, he has weakened himself beyond right power of fighting.[1] Schweidnitz is liable to siege; Breslau, with its poor

[1] *Œuvres de Frédéric*, iv. 141, 159.

walls and multitudinous population, can stand no siege worth mentioning; the Silesian strong places, not to speak of meal-magazines, are like to go a bad road. Quite dominant, this Prince Karl; placarding and proclaiming in all places, according to the new 'Imperial Patent,'[1] That Silesia is her Imperial Majesty's again! Which seems to be fast becoming the fact;—unless contradicted better. Quick!

Bevern has now, October 1st, no manœuvre left but to draw out of Breslau; post himself on the southern side of it, in a safe angle there, marshy Lohe in front, broad Oder to rear, Breslau at his right-hand with bread; and there intrenching himself by the best methods, wait slowly, in a sitting posture, events which are extensively on the gallop at present. One fancies, Had Winterfeld been still there! It is as brave an Army, 30,000 or more, as ever wore steel. Surely something could have been done with it;—something better than sit watching the events on full gallop all round! Bevern was a loyal, considerably skilful and valiant man; in the Battle of Lobositz, and elsewhere, we have seen him brave as a lion; but perhaps in the other kind of bravery wanted here, he—Well, his case was horribly difficult; full of intricacy. And he sat, no doubt in a very wretched state, consulting the oracles, with events (which are themselves oracular) going at such a pace.

Schweidnitz was besieged October 26th. Nadasti, with 20,000, was set to do it; Prince Karl, with 60,000, ready to protect him; Prince Bevern asking the oracles:—what a bit of news for Friedrich; breaking suddenly the effulgency of Rossbach with a bar of ominous black! Friedrich, still in the thick of pure Saxon business, makes instant arrangement for Silesia as well: Prince Henri, with such and such corps, to maintain the Saale, and guard Saxony; Marshal Keith, with such and such, to step-over into Bohemia, and raise contributions at least, and tread on the tail of the big Silesian snake: all this Friedrich settles within a week; takes certain corps of his own,

[1] In *Helden-Geschichte* (iv. 832, 833), Copy of it: 'Absolved from all prior Treaties by Prussian Majesty's attack on us, We' etc. etc. ('21st Sept. 1757').

effective about 13,000; and on November 13th marches from Leipzig. Round by Torgau, by Mühlberg, Grossenhayn; by Bautzen, Weissenberg, across the Queiss, across the Bober; and so, with long marches, strides continually forward, all hearts willing, and all limbs, though in this sad winter weather, towards relief of Schweidnitz.

At Grossenhayn, fifth day of the march, Friedrich learns that Schweidnitz is gone. November 12th–14th, Schweidnitz went by capitulation; contrary to everybody's hope or fear; certainly a very short defence for such a fortress. Fault of the Commandant, was everybody's first thought. Not probably the best of Commandants, said others gradually; but his garrison had Saxons in it;—one day '180 of them in a lump threw-down their arms, in the trenches, and went over to the Enemy.' Owing to whatsoever, the place is gone. Such towers, such curtains, star-ramparts; such an opulence of cannons, stores, munitions, a 30,000*l.* of hard cash, one item. All is gone, after a fortnight's siege. What a piece of news, as heard by Friedrich, coming at his utmost towards the scene itself! As seen by Bevern, too, in his questioning mood, it was an event of very oracular nature.

On Monday 14th Schweidnitz fell; Karl, with Nadasti reunited to him, was now 80,000 odd; and lost no time. On Tuesday next, *November 22d*, 1757, 'at three in the morning,' long hours before daybreak, Karl, with his 60,000, all learnedly arranged, comes rolling over upon hapless Bevern: with no end of cannonading and storm of war: *Battle of Breslau*, they call it; ruinous to Bevern. Of which we shall attempt no description: except to say, that Karl had five bridges on the Lohe, came across the Lohe by five Bridges; and that Bevern stood to his arms, steady as the rocks, to prevent his getting over, and to entertain him when over; that there were five principal attacks, renewed and re-renewed as long as needful, with torrents of shot, of death and tumult; over six or eight miles of country, for the space of fifteen hours. Battle comparable only to Malplaquet, said the Austrians; such a hurricane of artillery, strongly-entrenched enemy and loud doomsday of war. Did not end till nine at night; Austrians victorious, more or less, in four of their attacks or separate enterprises; that is to say, masters of the Lohe, and of the outmost Prussian villages and posts in front of the Prussian centre and right wing; victorious in that northern part;—but plainly unvictorious in the south-east or Prussian left wing,—farthest off from Breslau, and under Ziethen's command,—where they were driven across the Lohe again, and lost prisoners and cannons, or a cannon.[1]

Some of Bevern's people, grounding on this latter circumstance, and that they still held the Battlefield, or most part of it, wrote themselves victorious;—though in a dim brief manner, as if conscious of the contrary. Which indeed was the fact. At the council of war, which he summoned that evening, there were proposals of night-attack, and other fierce measures; but Bevern, rejecting the plan for a night-attack on the Austrian camp as too dubious, did, in the dark hours, through the silent streets of Breslau, withdraw himself across the Oder, instead; leaving 80 cannon, and 8,000 killed and wounded; an evidently beaten man and Army. And indeed did straightway disappear personally altogether, as no longer equal to events. Rode out, namely, to reconnoitre in the grey of his second sad morning, on this new Bank of the Oder; saw little except grey mist; but rode into a Croat outpost, only one poor groom attending him; and was there made prisoner:—intentionally, thought mankind; intentionally, thinks Friedrich, who was very angry with the poor man.[2]

The poor man was carried to Vienna, if readers care to know; but being a near Cousin there (second-cousin, no less, to the late Empress-Mother), was by the high now-reigning Empress-Queen received in a charmingly gracious manner, and sent home again without ransom. 'To Stettin!' beckoned Friedrich sternly from the distance, and would not see him at all: 'To Stettin, I say, your official post in time of peace! Com-

[1] In Seyfarth, Three Accounts; *Beylagen*, ii. 198, 221, 234 et seq.

[2] Preuss, ii. 102. More exact in Kutzen, *Der Tag von Leuthen* (Breslau, 1857,—an excellent exact little Compilation, from manifold sources well studied), pp. 166–169, date '24th November.'

mand me the invalid Garrison there; you are fit for nothing better!'—I will add one other thing, which unhappily will seem strange to readers: that there came no whisper of complaint from Bevern; mere silence, and loyal industry with his poor means, from Bevern; and that he proved heroically useful in Stettin two years hence, against the Swedes, against the Russians in the Siege-of-Colberg time; and gained Friedrich's favour again, with other good results. Which I observe was a common method with Prussian Generals and soldiers, when, unjustly or justly, they fell into trouble of this kind; and a much better one than that of complaining in the Newspapers, and demanding Commissions of Inquiry, presided over by Chaos and the Fourth-Estate, now is.

Bevern being with the Croats, the Prussian Army falls to General Kyau, as next in rank; who (directly in the teeth of fierce orders that are speeding hither for Bevern and him) marches away, leaving Breslau to its fate; and making towards Glogau, as the one sure point in this wreck of things. And Prince Karl, that same day, goes upon Breslau; which is in no case to resist and be bombarded: so that poor old General Lestwitz, the Prussian Commandant,—always thought to be a valiant old gentleman, but who had been wounded in the late Action, and was blamably discouraged,—took the terms offered, and surrendered without firing a gun. Garrison and he to march out, in 'Free Withdrawal'; these are the terms: Garrison was 4,000 and odd, mostly Silesian recruits; but there marched hardly 500 out with poor Lestwitz; the Silesian recruits,—persuaded by conceivable methods, that they were to be prisoners of war, and that, in short, Austria was now come to be King again, and might make inquiry into men's conduct, —found it safer to take service with Austria, to vanish into holes in Breslau or where they could; and, for instance, one regiment (or battalion, let us hide the name of it), on marching through the Gate, consisted only of nine chief officers and four men.[1]

[1] Müller, *Schlacht bei Leuthen* (Berlin, 1857,—professedly a mere abridgment and shadow of *Kutzen*: unindexed like it), p. 12 (with name and particulars).

There were lost 98 pieces of cannon; endless magazines and stores of war. A Breslau scandalously gone;—a Breslau preaching day after next (27th, which was Sunday), in certain of its churches, especially Cardinal Schaffgotsch in the Dom Insel doing it, Thanksgiving Sermons, as per order, with unction real or official, 'That our ancient sovereigns are restored to us': which Sermons,—except in the Schaffgotsch case, Prince Karl and the high Catholic world all there in gala,—were 'sparsely attended,' say my authors. The Austrians are at the top of their pride; and consider full surely that Silesia is theirs, though Friedrich were here twice over. 'What is Friedrich? We beat him at Kolin. His Prussians at Zittau, at Moys, at Breslau in the new Malplaquet, were we beaten by them? Hnh!'—and snort (in the Austrian messrooms), and snap their fingers at Friedrich and his coming.

It was at Görlitz (scene of poor Winterfeld's death) that Friedrich, 'on November 23d, the tenth day of his march,' first got rumour of the Breslau Malplaquet: 'endless cannonading heard thereabouts all yesterday!' said rumour from the east,—more and more steadily, as Friedrich hastened forward;—and that it was 'a victory for Bevern.' Till, at Naumburg on the Queiss, he gets the actual tidings: Bevern gone to the Croats, Breslau going, Kyau marching vague; and what kind of victory it was.

Ever from Grossenhayn onwards there had been message on message, more and more rigorous, precise and indignant, 'Do this, do that; your Dilection shall answer it with your head!'—not one message of which reached his Dilection, till Dilection and Fate (such the gallop of events) had done the contrary: and now Dilection and his head have made a finish of it. 'No,' answers Friedrich to himself; 'not till we are all finished!'—and pushes-on, he too, like a kind of Fate. 'What does or can he mean, then? say the Austrians, with scornful astonishment, and think his head must be turning: 'Will he beat us out of Silesia with his Potsdam Guard-Parade, then?' '*Potsdamsche Wacht-Parade*':—so they denominate his small Army; and are very mirthful in their messrooms. 'I will attack them, if they stood on the Zobtenberg, if they stood on the steeples of Breslau!' said Friedrich; and tramped diligently forward. Day after day, as the real tidings arrive, his outlook in Silesia is becoming darker and darker: a sternly dark march this altogether. Prince Karl has thrown a garrison into Liegnitz on Friedrich's road; Prince Karl lies encamped with Breslau at his back; has above 80,000 when fully gathered; and reigns supreme in those parts. Darker march there seldom was: all black save a light that burns in one heart, refusing to be quenched till death.

Friedrich sends orders that Kyau shall be put in arrest; that Ziethen shall be general of the Bevern wreck, shall bring it round by Glogau, and rendezvous with Friedrich at a place and day,—Parchwitz, 2d of December coming;—and be steady, my old Ziethen. Friedrich brushes past the Liegnitz Garrison, leaves Liegnitz and it a trifle to the right; arrives at Parchwitz November 28th; and there rests, or at least his weary troops do, till Ziethen come up; the King not very restful, with so many things to prearrange; a life or death crisis now nigh. Well, it is but death; and death has been fronted before now! We who are after the event, on the safe sunny side of it, can form small image of the horrors and the inward dubieties to him who is passing through it;—and how Hope is needed to shine heroically eternal in some hearts. Fire of Hope, that does not issue in mere blazings, mad audacities and chaotic despair, but advances with its eyes open, measuredly, counting its steps, to the wrestling-place,—this is a godlike thing; much available to mankind in all the battles they have; battles of steel, or of whatever sort.

Friedrich, at Parchwitz, assembled his Captains, and spoke to them; it was the night after Ziethen came in, night of December 3d, 1757; and Ziethen, no doubt, was there: for it is an authentic meeting, this at Parchwitz, and the words were taken down.

Friedrich's Speech to his Generals (Parchwitz, 3d December 1757)[1]

'It is not unknown to you, *meine Herren*, what disasters have befallen here, while we were busy with the French and Reichs Army. Schweidnitz is gone; Duke of Bevern beaten; Breslau gone, and all our war-stores there; good part of Silesia gone: and, in fact, my embarrassments would be at the insuperable pitch, had not I boundless trust in you, and your qualities, which have been so often manifested, as soldiers and sons of your Country. Hardly one among you but has distinguished himself by some nobly memorable action: all these services to the State and me I know well, and will never forget.

'I flatter myself, therefore, that in this case too nothing will be wanting which the State has a right to expect of your valour. The hour is at hand. I should think I had done nothing, if I left the Austrians in possession of Silesia. Let me apprise you, then: I intend, in spite of the Rules of Art, to attack Prince Karl's Army, which is nearly thrice our strength, wherever I find it. The question is not of his numbers, or the strength of his position: all this, by courage, by the skill of our methods, we will try to make good. This step I must risk, or everything is lost. We must beat the enemy, or perish all of us before his batteries. So I read the case; so I will act in it.

'Make this my determination known to all Officers of the Army; prepare the men for what work is now to ensue, and say that I hold myself entitled to demand exact fulfilment of orders. For you, when I reflect that you are Prussians, can I think that you will act unworthily? But if there should be one or another who dreads to share all dangers with me, he,'—continued his Majesty, with an interrogative look, and then pausing for answer,—'can have his Discharge this evening, and shall not suffer the least reproach from me.'—Modest strong bass murmur; meaning 'No, by the Eternal!' if you looked into the eyes and faces of the group. Never will Retzow

[1] From *Retzow*, i. 240–242 (slightly abridged).

Junior forget that scene, and how effulgently eloquent the veteran physiognomies were.

'Hah, I knew it,' said the King, with his most radiant smile, 'none of you would desert me! I depend on your help, then; and on victory as sure.'—The speech winds-up with a specific passage: 'The Cavalry regiment that does not on the instant, on order given, dash full plunge into the enemy, I will, directly after the Battle, unhorse, and make it a Garrison regiment. The Infantry battalion which, meet with what it may, shows the least sign of hesitating, loses its colours and its sabres, and I cut the trimmings from its uniform! Now good-night, Gentlemen: shortly we have either beaten the Enemy, or we never see one another again.'

An excellent temper in this Army; a rough vein of heroism in it, steady to the death;—and plenty of hope in it too, hope in Vater Fritz. 'Never mind,' the soldiers used to say, in John Duke of Marlborough's time, 'Corporal John will get us through it!'—That same evening Friedrich rode into the Camp, where the regiments he had were now all gathered, out of their cantonments, to march on the morrow. First regiment he came upon was the Life-Guard Cuirassiers: the men, in their accustomed way, gave him good-evening, which he cheerily returned. Some of the more veteran sort asked, ruggedly confidential, as well as loyal: 'What is thy news, then, so late?' 'Good news, children (*Kinder*): tomorrow you will beat the Austrians tightly!' 'That we will, by—!' answered they.—'But think only where they stand yonder, and how they have entrenched themselves?' said Friedrich. 'And if they had the Devil in front and all round them, we will knock them out; only thou lead us on!'—'Well, I will see what you can do: now lay you down, and sleep sound; and good sleep to you!' 'Good-night, Fritz!' answer all;[1] as Fritz ambles on to the next regiment, to which, as to every one, he will have some word.

Was it the famous Pommern regiment, this that he next spoke to,—who answered Loudon's summons to them once (as shall be noticed by and by) in a way ineffable, though unfor-

[1] Müller, p. 21 (from *Kaltenborn*, of whom *infrà*); Preuss, etc., etc.

gettable? Manteufel of Foot; yes, no other![1] They have their own opinion of their capacities against an enemy, and do not want for a good conceit of themselves. 'Well, children, how think you it will be tomorrow? They are twice as strong as we.' 'Never thou mind that; there are no Pommerners among them; thou knowest what the Pommerners can do!'—*Friedrich*: 'Yea, truly, that do I; otherwise I durst not risk the battle. Now good sleep to you! tomorrow, then, we shall either have beaten the Enemy or else be all dead.' 'Yea,' answered the whole regiment; 'dead, or else the Enemy beaten': and so went to deep sleep, preface to a deeper for many of them,—as beseems brave men. In this world it much beseems the brave man, uncertain about so many things, to be certain of himself for one thing.

These snatches of Camp Dialogue, much more the Speech preserved to us by Retzow Junior, appear to be true; though as to the dates, the circumstances, there has been debating.[2] Other Anecdotes, dubious or more, still float about in quantity; —of which let us give only one; that of the Deserter (which has merit as a myth). 'What made thee desert, then?' 'Hm, alas, your Majesty, we were got so down in the world, and had such a time of it!'—'Well, try it one day more; and if we cannot mend matters, thou and I will both desert.'

A learned Doctor, one of the most recent on these matters, is astonished why the Histories of Friedrich should be such dreary reading, and Friedrich himself so prosaic, barren an object; and lays the blame upon the Age, insensible to real greatness; led away by claptrap Napoleonisms, regardless of expense. Upon which Smelfungus takes him up, with a twitch:

'To my sad mind, Herr Doctor, it seems ascribable rather to the Dryasdust of these Ages, especially to the Prussian Dryasdust, sitting comfortable in his Academies, waving sublimely his long ears as he tramples human Heroisms into unintelligible pipeclay and dreary continents of sand and cinders, with the Doctors all applauding.

'Had the sacred Poet or man of real Human Genius, been at his work, for the thousand years last past, instead of idly fiddling far away from

---

[1] Archenholtz, ii. 61; and Kutzen, p. 35.

[2] Kutzen, pp. 175–181.

his work,—which surely is definable as being very mainly, That of *interpreting* human Heroisms; of painfully extricating, and extorting from the circumambient chaos of muddy babble, rumour and mendacity, some not inconceivable human and divine Image of them, more and more clear, complete and credible for mankind (poor mankind dumbly looking up to him for guidance, as to what it shall think of God and of Men in this Scene of Things),—I calculate, we should by this time have had a different Friedrich of it; O Heavens, a different world of it, in so many respects!

'My esteemed Herr Doctor, it is too painful a subject. Godlike fabulous Achilles, and the old Greek Kings of men, one perceives, after study, to be dim enough Grazier Sovereigns, "living among infinite dung," till their sacred Poet extricated them. And our *un*-sacred all-desecrating Dryasdust,—Herr Doctor, I must say, it fills me with despair! Authentic human Heroisms, not fabulous a whit, but true to the bone, and by all appearance very much nobler than those of godlike Achilles and pious Æneas ever could have been,—left in this manner, trodden under foot of man and beast; man and beast alike insensible that there is anything but common mud under foot, and grateful to anybody that will assure them there is nothing. Oh Doctor, oh Doctor! And the results of it—You need not go exclusively "to France" to look at them. They are too visible in the so-called "Social Hierarchies," and sublime gilt Doggeries, sacred and secular, of all modern Countries! Let us be silent, my friend.'—

'Prussian Dryasdust,' he says elsewhere, 'does make a terrible job of it; especially when he attempts to weep through his pipeclay, or rise with his long ears into the moral sublime. As to the German People, I find that they dimly have not wanted sensibility to Friedrich; that their multitudes of Anecdotes, still circulating among them in print and *vivâ voce*, are proof of this. Thereby they have at least made a *Myth* of Friedrich's History, and given some rhythmus, life and cheerful human substantiality to his work and him. Accept these Anecdotes as the Epic *they* could not write of him, but were longing to hear from somebody who could. Who has not yet appeared among mankind, nor will for some time. Alas, my friend, on piercing through the bewildering nimbus of babble, malignity, mendacity, which veils sevenfold the Face of Friedrich from us, and getting to see some glimpses of the Face itself, one is sorrowfully struck dumb once more. What a suicidal set of creatures; commanding as with one voice, That there shall be no Heroism more among them; that all shall be Doggery and Commonplace henceforth. "*Ach, mein lieber Sulzer*, you don't know that damned brood!"— —Well, well. "Solomon's Temple," the Moslem say, "had to be built under the chirping of ten thousand Sparrows." Ten thousand of them; committee of the whole house, unanimously of the opposite view;—and could not quite hinder it. That too is something!'—

More to our immediate purpose is this other thing: That the Austrians have been in Council of War; and, on deliberation, have decided to come out of their defences; to quit their strong Camp, which lies so eligibly, ahead of Breslau and arear of Lissa and of Schweidnitz Water yonder; to cross Schweidnitz Water, leave Lissa behind them; and meet this offensively aggressive Friedrich in pitched fight. Several had voted, No, why stir?—Daun especially, and others with emphasis. 'No need of fighting at all,' said Daun: 'we can defend Schweidnitz Water; ruin him before he ever get across.' 'Defend? Be assaulted by an Army like his?' urges Lucchesi, the other Chief General: 'It is totally unworthy of us! We have gained the game; all the honours ours; let us have done with it. Give him battle, since he fortunately wishes it; we finish him, and gloriously finish the War too!' So argued Lucchesi, with vivacity, persistency,—to his own ill luck, but evidently with approval from Prince Karl. Everybody sees, this is the way to Prince Karl's favour at present. 'Have not I reconquered Silesia?' thinks Prince Karl to himself; and beams applause on the high course, not the low prudent one.[1] In a word, the Austrians decide on stepping out to meet Friedrich in open battle: it was the first time they ever did so; and it was likewise the last.

Sunday December 4th, at four in the morning, Friedrich has marched from Parchwitz, straight towards the Austrian Camp;[2] he hears, one can fancy with what pleasure, that the Austrians are advancing towards him, and will not need to be forced in their strong position. His march is in four columns, Friedrich in the vanguard; quarters to be Neumarkt, a little Town about fourteen miles off. Within some miles of Neumarkt, early in the afternoon, he learns that there are a thousand Croats in the place, the Austrian Bakery at work there, and engineer people marking-out an Austrian Camp. 'On the Height beyond Neumarkt, that will be?' thinks Friedrich; for he knows this ground, having often done reviews here; to Breslau all the way on both hands, not a rood of it but is familiar to him. Which was a singular advantage, say the critics; and a point the Austrian Council of War should have taken more thought of

[1] Kutzen, pp. 45–48.

[2] Müller, p. 26.

Friedrich, before entering Neumarkt, sends a regiment to ride quietly round it on both sides, and to seize that Height he knows of. Height once seized, or ready for seizing, he bursts the barrier of Neumarkt; dashes-in upon the thousand Croats; flings-out the Croats in extreme hurry, musketry and sabre acting on them; they find their Height beset, their retreat cut-off, and that they must vanish. Of the 1,000 Croats, '569 were taken prisoners, and 120 slain,' in this unexpected sweeping-out of Neumarkt. Better still, in Neumarkt is found the Austrian Bakery, set-up and in full work;—delivers you 80,000 bread-rations hot-and-hot, which little expected to go such a road. On the Height, the Austrian stakes and engineer-tools were found sticking in the ground; so hasty had the flight been.

How Prince Karl came to expose his Bakery, his staff of life so far ahead of him? Prince Karl, it is clear, was a little puffed-up with high thoughts at this time. The capture of Schweidnitz, the late 'Malplaquet' (poorish Anti-Bevern Malplaquet), capture of Breslau, and the low and lost condition of Friedrich's Silesian affairs, had more or less turned everybody's head,—everybody's except Feldmarschall Daun's alone:—and witty mess-tables, we already said, were in the daily habit of mocking at Friedrich's march towards them with aggressive views, and called his insignificant little Army the 'Potsdam-Guard-Parade.'[1] That was the common triumphant humour; naturally shared-in by Prince Karl; the ready way to flatter him being to sing in that tune. Nobody otherwise can explain, and nobody in anywise can justify, Prince Karl's ignorance of Friedrich's advance, his almost voluntary losing of his staff-of-life in that manner.

Prince Karl's soldiers have each (in the cold form) three-days provision in their haversacks: they have come across the Weistritz River (more commonly called Schweidnitz Water), which was also the height of contemptuous imprudence; and lie encamped, this night,—in long line, not ill-chosen (once the River *is* behind),—perpendicular to Friedrich's march, some

[1] Cogniazzo, ii. 417–422.

ten miles ahead of him. Since crossing, they had learned with surprise, How their Bakery and Croats had been snapt-up; that Friedrich was not at a distance, but near;—and that arrangements could not be made too soon! Their position intersects the Great Road at right angles, as we hint; and has villages, swamps, woody knolls; especially, on each wing, good defences. Their right wing leans on Nypern and its impassable peatbogs, a Village two or three miles north from the Great Road; their centre is close behind another Village called Leuthen, about as far south from it: length of their bivouac is about five miles; which will become six or so, had Nadasti once taken post, who is to form the left wing, and go down as far as Sagschütz, southward of Leuthen. Seven battalions are in this Village of Leuthen, eight in Nypern, all the Villages secured; woods, scraggy abatis, redoubts, not forgotten: their cannon are numerous, though of light calibre. Friedrich has at least 71 heavy pieces; and 10 of them are formidably heavy,—brought from the walls of Glogau, with terrible labour to Ziethen; but with excellent effect, on this occasion and henceforth. They got the name of 'Boomers, Bellowers (*Die Brummer*),' those Ten. Friedrich was in great straits about artillery; and Retzow Senior recommended this hauling-up of the Ten Bellowers, which became celebrated in the years coming. And now we are on the Battle-ground, and must look into the Battle itself, if we can.

FROM Reminiscences

Carlyle's *Reminiscences* were published in 1881, within a few weeks of his death, under the editorship of his friend and executor, the historian James Anthony Froude. They contained a memoir of his father James Carlyle, written within a few days of his death in 1832; a memoir of his wife Jane Welsh Carlyle, written between May and July 1866 (Jane Carlyle died in April of that year); two lengthy pieces on his friends Edward Irving and Francis, Lord Jeffrey, written a little later; and notes on Wordsworth and Southey.

According to Froude, Carlyle had agreed that these memoirs should be published after his death: on the other hand, at the time of writing the memoir of Jane he said that 'I solemnly forbid them,' (his friends) 'each and all, to *publish* this Bit of Writing *as it stands here.*' Published, nevertheless, it was: and the furious arguments that followed are of little interest today. There can be no doubt that the reminiscences, and in particular the memoir of Jane, are among Carlyle's most astonishing feats as a writer. Rambling, hesitant, full of halts and self-apostrophising ejaculations, these writings are extraordinarily moving in their raw and hot sincerity; correction, whether by the hand of Carlyle or another, would have taken half the life out of them. They provide, also, the clearest evidence of that photographic memory for people, things and places that played a large part in his power as a writer. Working without notes or references, writing of things that had happened and people he had known forty and more years ago, he recalled incidents and phrases exactly as he and Jane had described them in letters of the time. There are errors, of course: what is remarkable is that they are so few.

The text of the memoirs of James Carlyle and Jane Welsh Carlyle which has been used here is that of the edition of 1887, in which the American scholar Charles Eliot Norton corrected many minor textual errors made by Froude. The footnotes to the memoir of James Carlyle are Norton's; those to the memoir of Jane Welsh Carlyle are some of them Norton's, and some my own. Many of Norton's footnotes seemed to me otiose; perhaps some of mine are, too. I have eliminated the square brackets which Norton used to indicate Carlyle's private reflections or self-admonition, but have retained those used to indicate a missing word. I have cut out the attack on Froude with which Norton's text opens, beginning with the notes made by Mrs. Carlyle's friend Geraldine Jewsbury, which prompted Carlyle to take up his pen. I have also transferred a short passage which Norton placed after 'all words are idle' on page 695, back to the body of Geraldine Jewsbury's narrative, where it seemed less obtrusive.

FROM

Reminiscences

JAMES CARLYLE

On Tuesday, January the 24th, 1832, I received tidings that my dear and worthy Father had departed out of this world. He was called away, by a death apparently of the mildest, on Sunday morning about six. He had taken what was thought a bad cold on the Monday preceding; but rose every day, and was sometimes out of doors. Occasionally he was insensible (as Pain usually soon made him of late years); but when spoken to recollected himself. He was up and at the Kitchen fire (at Scotsbrig)[1] on the Saturday evening about six: 'but was evidently growing fast worse in breathing.' 'About ten o'clock he fell into a sort of stupor,' writes my sister Jane, 'still breathing higher and with greater difficulty: he spoke little to any of us, seemingly unconscious of what he did; came over the bedside, and offered up a prayer to Heaven in such accents as it is impossible to forget. He departed almost without a struggle,' adds she, 'this morning at half-past six.' My mother adds, in her own hand: 'It is God that has done it; be still, my dear children—Your affectionate Mother—God support us all.' The funeral is to be on Friday: the present date is *Wednesday night.*

This stroke, altogether unexpected at the time, but which I have been long anticipating in general, falls heavy on me, as such needs must; yet not so as to stun me or unman me. Natural tears have come to my relief: I can look at my dear Father, and that section of the Past which he has made alive

[1] A farmhouse in the parish of Middlebie, about two miles and a half from Ecclefechan. The Carlyles removed to it in May 1826, and James Carlyle, the youngest son, continued tenant of the farm until 1880

for me, in a certain sacred sanctified light; and give way to what thoughts rise in me without feeling that they are weak and useless. The time till the Funeral was past, I instantly determined on passing with my Wife only, and all others were excluded. I have written to my Mother and to John;[1] have walked far and much (chiefly in the Regent's Park), and considered about many things; if so were I might accomplish this problem: To see clearly what my present calamity *means*; what I have lost, and what lesson my loss was to teach me.

As for the Departed, we ought to say that he was taken home 'like a shock of corn fully ripe:' he 'had finished the work that was given him to do,' and finished it (very greatly more than the most) as became a man; he was summoned too before he had ceased to be interesting, to be lovable (he was to the last the pleasantest man I had to speak with in Scotland); for many years too he had the End ever in his eye, and was studying to make all preparation for what in his strong way he called often 'that last, that awful change.' Ever at every new parting of late years I have noticed him wring my hand with a tenderer pressure; as if he felt that one other of our few meetings Here was over. Mercifully also has he been spared me, till I am abler to bear his loss; till (by manifold struggles) I too, as he did, feel my feet on the Everlasting Rock, and through Time with its Death can in some degree see into Eternity with its Life. So that I have repeated, not with unwet eyes, let me hope likewise, not with unsoftened heart, these old and forever true words: 'Blessed are the Dead that die in the Lord. They do rest from their labours, and their works follow them.' Yes their works follow them: the Force that had been lent my Father he honourably expended in manful welldoing: a portion of this Planet bears beneficent traces of his strong Hand and strong Head; nothing that he undertook to do but he did it faithfully and like a true man. I shall look on the Houses he built with a certain proud interest: they stand firm and sound to the heart, all over his little district: no one that comes after him will ever say, Here was the finger of a hollow Eye-servant.

[1] Dr. Carlyle, then absent in Rome.

They are little texts, for me, of the Gospel of man's Free-will. Nor will his Deeds and Sayings, in any case, be found unworthy, not false and barren, but genuine and fit. Nay am not I also the humble James Carlyle's work? I owe him much more than existence; I owe him a noble inspiring example (now that I can read it in that rustic character); it was he *exclusively* that determined on *educating* me, that from his small hard-earned funds, sent me to School and College; and made me whatever I am or may become. Let me not mourn for my Father; let me do worthily of him: so shall he still live, even Here, in me; and his worth plant itself honourably forth into new generations.

I purpose now, while the impression is more pure and clear within me, to mark down the main things I can recollect of my Father: to myself, if I live to after years, it may be instructive and interesting, as the Past grows ever holier the farther we leave it. My mind is calm enough to do it deliberately; and to do it truly the thought of that pale earnest face which even now lies stiffened into Death in that bed at Scotsbrig, with the infinite All of Worlds looking down on it,—will *certainly* impel me. Neither, should these lines survive myself and be seen by others, can the sight of them do harm to anyone. It is good to know how a true spirit will vindicate itself into truth and freedom, through what obstructions soever; how the 'acorn cast carelessly into the wilderness' will make room for itself, and grow to be an oak. This is one of the cases belonging to that class 'the Lives of remarkable men;' in which, it has been said, 'paper and ink should least of all be spared.' I call a man remarkable, who becomes a true Workman in this vineyard of the Highest: be his work that of Palace-building and Kingdom-founding, or only of delving and ditching, to me it is no matter, or *next to* none: *all* human work is transitory, small, in itself contemptible; only the worker thereof and the spirit that dwelt in him is significant. I proceed without order, or almost any forethought; anxious only to save what I have left, and mark it as it lies in me.

In several respects, I consider my Father as one of the most interesting men I have known. He was a man of perhaps *the* very largest natural endowment of any it has been my lot to converse with: none of us will ever forget that bold glowing style of his, flowing free from the untutored Soul; full of metaphors (though he knew not what a metaphor was), with all manner of potent words (which he appropriated and applied with a *surprising* accuracy, you often could not guess whence); brief, energetic; and which I should say conveyed the most perfect picture, definite, clear not in ambitious *colours* but in full *white* sunlight, of all the dialects I have ever listened to. Nothing did I ever hear him undertake to render visible, which did not become almost ocularly so. Never shall we again hear such speech as that was: the whole district knew of it; and laughed joyfully over it, not knowing how otherwise to express the feeling it gave them. Emphatic I have heard him beyond all men. In anger he had no need of oaths; his words were like sharp arrows that smote into the very heart. The fault was that he exaggerated (which tendency I also inherit); yet only in description and for the sake chiefly of *humorous* effect: he was a man of rigid, even scrupulous veracity; I have often heard him turn back, when he thought his strong words were misleading, and correct them into mensurative accuracy. *Ach, und dies alles ist hin!*

I call him a natural man; singularly free from all manner of affectation: he was among the last of the true men, which Scotland (on the old system) produced, or can produce; a man healthy in body and in mind; fearing God, and diligently working in God's Earth with contentment hope and unwearied resolution. *He* was never visited with Doubt; the old Theorem of the Universe was sufficient for him, and he worked well in it, and in all senses *successfully* and wisely as few now can do; so quick is the motion of Transition becoming: the new generation almost to a man must make 'their Belly their God,' and alas even find *that* an empty one. Thus curiously enough, and blessedly, *he* stood a true man on the verge of the Old; while his son stands here lovingly surveying him on the verge of the New, and sees the possibility of also being true there. God make the possibility, blessed possibility, into a reality!

A virtue he had which I should learn to imitate. *He never spoke of what was disagreeable and past.* I have often wondered and admired at this. The thing that he had nothing to *do* with, he did nothing with. This was a *healthy* mind. In like manner, I have seen him always when we young ones (half roguishly, and provokingly without doubt) were perhaps repeating sayings of his, sit as if he did not hear us at all: never once did I know him utter a word (only once that I remember of give a look) in such a case.

[*Thursday morning.*] Another virtue, the example of which has passed strongly into me, was his settled placid indifference to the clamours or the murmurs of Public Opinion. For the judgment of those that had no right or power to judge him, he seemed simply to care nothing at all. He very rarely *spoke* of despising such things, he contented himself with altogether disregarding them. Hollow babble it was; for him a thing as Fichte said 'that did not exist,' *das gar nicht existirte.* There was something truly great in this; the very perfection of it hid from you the extent of the attainment.

Or rather let me call it a new phasis of the *health* which in mind as in body was conspicuous in him. Like a healthy man, he wanted *only* to get along with his Task; whatsoever could not forward him in this (and how could Public Opinion and much else of the like sort do it?) was of no moment to him, was not there for him.

This great maxim of Philosophy he had gathered by the teaching of nature alone: That man was created to work, not to speculate, or feel, or dream. Accordingly he set his whole heart thitherwards: he did work wisely and unweariedly (*ohne Hast aber ohne Rast*), and perhaps *performed* more (with the tools he had) than any man I now know. It should have made me sadder than it did to hear the young ones sometimes complaining of his slow punctuality and thoroughness: he would leave nothing till it was *done.* Alas! the age of Substance and Solidity is gone (for the time); that of Show and hollow Superficiality (in all senses) is in full course—

And yet he was a man of open sense; wonderfully so. I could

have entertained him for days talking of *any* matter interesting to man. He delighted to hear of *all* things that were worth talking of; the mode of living men had, the mode of working, their opinions, virtues, whole spiritual and temporal environment. It is some two years ago (in summer) since I entertained him highly (he was hoeing turnips and perhaps I helped him) with an account of the character and manner of existence of Francis Jeffrey. Another evening he enjoyed (probably it was on that very visit) with the heartiest relish my description of the people (I think) of Turkey. The Chinese had astonished him much: in some Magazine (from Little's of Cressfield) he had got a sketch of *Macartney's Embassy*, the memory of which never left him. Adam Smith's *Wealth of Nations*, greatly as it lay out of his course, he had also fallen in with; and admired, and understood and remembered,—so far as he had any business with it.—I once wrote him about my being in Smithfield Market (seven years ago); of my seeing St. Paul's: both things interested him heartily, and dwelt with him. I had hoped to tell him much, much of what I saw in this second visit; and that many a long cheerful talk would have given us both some sunny hours: but *es konnte nimmer seyn!*—Patience! Hope!

At the same time he had the most entire and open contempt for all idle tattle, what he called 'clatter.' *Any* talk that had meaning in it he could listen to: what had *no* meaning in it, above all, what seemed false, he absolutely could and would not hear; but abruptly turned aside from it, or if that might not suit, with the besom of destruction swept it far away from him. Long may we remember his 'I don't believe thee;' his tongue-paralysing, cold, indifferent 'Hah!'—I should say of him, as I did of our Sister[1] whom we lost, that he seldom or never spoke except actually to convey an idea. Measured by quantity of words, he was a talker of fully average copiousness; by extent of meaning communicated, he was the most copious I have listened to. How, in few sentences, he would sketch you off an entire Biography, an entire Object or Transaction: keen, clear,

[1] Margaret, born 20th September 1803, died 22d June 1830.

rugged, genuine, completely rounded in! His words came direct from the heart, by the inspiration of the moment: 'It is no idle tale,' said he to some laughing rustics, while stating in his strong way some complaint against them; and their laughter died into silence. Dear good Father! There looked *honesty* through those clear earnest eyes; a sincerity that compelled belief and regard. 'Moffat!' said he one day to an incorrigible reaper, 'thou has every feature of a bad shearer: high, and rough, and little on't. Thou maun *alter* thy figure or slant the bog'—pointing to the man's road homewards.—

He was irascible, choleric, and we all dreaded his wrath. Yet passion never mastered him, or maddened him; it rather inspired him with new vehemence of insight, and more piercing emphasis of wisdom. It must have been a bold man that did not quail before that face, when glowing with indignation, grounded (for so it ever was) on the sense of right, and in resistance of wrong. More than once has he lifted up his strong voice in Tax Courts and the like before 'the Gentlemen' (what he knew of Highest among men), and rending asunder official sophistries, thundered even into their deaf ears the indignant sentence of natural justice, to the conviction of all.—Oh why did we laugh at these things while we loved them! There is a tragic greatness and sacredness in them now.

I can call my Father a brave man (*ein Tapferer*). Man's face he did not fear; God he always feared: his Reverence, I think, was considerably mixed with Fear. Yet not slavish Fear; rather Awe, as of unutterable Depths of Silence, through which flickered a trembling Hope. How he used to speak of Death (especially in late years) or rather to be silent, and *look* of it! There was no feeling in him here that he cared to hide: he trembled at the really terrible; the mock-terrible he cared nought for.—That last act of his Life; when in the last agony, with the thick ghastly vapours of Death rising round him to choke him, he burst through and called with a man's voice on the great God to have mercy on him: that was like the epitome and concluding summary of his whole Life. God gave him strength to wrestle with the King of Terrors, and as it were even then to prevail. All his strength came from God, and ever sought new nourishment there. God be thanked for it.

Let me not mourn that my Father's Force is all spent, that his Valour wars no longer. Has it not gained the victory? Let me imitate him rather; let his courageous heart beat anew in me, that when oppression and opposition unjustly threaten, I too may rise with his spirit to front them and subdue them.

On the whole, ought I not to rejoice that God was pleased to give me such a Father; that from earliest years, I had the example of a real Man (of God's own making) continually before me? Let me learn of *him*; let me 'write my Books as he built his Houses, and walk as blamelessly through this shadow-world'—(if God so will), to rejoin him at last. Amen!—Alas! such is the *mis*-education of these days, it is only among what are called the *un*educated classes (those educated by experience) that you can look for *a man*. Even among these, such a sight is growing daily rarer. My father, in several respects, has not, that I can think of, left his fellow. *Ultimus Romanorum!* Perhaps among Scottish Peasants what Samuel Johnson was among English Authors. I have a sacred pride in my Peasant Father, and would not exchange him even now for any King known to me. Gold, and the guinea-stamp; the Man, and the Clothes of the Man! Let me thank God for that greatest of blessings, and strive to live worthily of it.—

Though from the heart and practically even more than in words an independent man, he was by no means an insubordinate one. His bearing towards his Superiors I consider noteworthy, of a piece with himself. I think, in early life, when working at Springkell for a Sir W. Maxwell (the grandfather of the present Baronet), he had got an early respect impressed upon him for the character as well as station of a Gentleman. I have heard him often describe the grave wisdom and dignified deportment of that Maxwell, as of a true 'ruler of the people;' it used to remind me of the Gentlemen in Goethe. Sir William, like those he ruled over and benignantly (at least gracefully and earnestly) governed, has passed away.—But even for the mere Clothes-screens of rank, my Father testified no contempt: he spoke of them in public or private without acerbity; testified for them the outward deference which Custom and Convenience prescribed, and felt no degradation therein: their inward claim to regard was a thing which concerned them, not him. I love to figure him addressing these men, with bared head, by the title of 'Your Honour;' with a manner respectful yet unembarrassed; a certain manful dignity looking through his own fine face; with his noble gray head bent patiently to the (alas) unworthy. Such conduct is perhaps no longer possible.

Withal he had in general a grave natural politeness: I have seen him, when the women were perhaps all in anxiety about the disorder of the house, etc., usher men, with true hospitality, into his mean house; without any grimace of apologies, or the smallest seeming embarrassment: were the house but a cabin, it was his, and they were welcome to him and what it held. This was again the *man*. His Life was 'no idle tale,' not a Lie, but a Truth, which whoso liked was welcome to come and examine. 'An earnest toilsome life,' which also *had* a serious issue.

The more I reflect on it, the more must I admire how completely Nature had taught him; how completely he was devoted to his work, to the Task of his Life; and content to let *all* pass by unheeded that had not relation to this. It is a singular fact, for example, that though a man of such openness and clearness, he had never, I believe, read three pages of *Burns's Poems*. Not even when all about him became noisy and enthusiastic (I the loudest) on that matter did he feel it worth while to renew his investigation of it, or once turn his face towards it. The Poetry *he* liked (he did not call it Poetry) was Truth and the Wisdom of Reality. Burns indeed could have done nothing for him. As high a Greatness hung over his world, as over that of Burns (the ever-present greatness of the Infinite itself): neither was he like Burns called to rebel against the world, but to labour patiently at his Task there; 'uniting the Possible with the Necessary' to bring out the *Real* (wherein also lay an Ideal). Burns could not have in any way strengthened him in this course; and therefore was for him a phenomenon merely. Nay Rumour had been so busy with Burns, and Destiny and his own Desert had in very deed so marred his name, that the good rather avoided him. Yet it was not with aversion that my Father regarded Burns; at worst with indifference and neglect. I have heard him speak of once seeing him: standing in 'Rob Scott's Smithy' (at Ecclefechan, no doubt superintending some work) he heard one say, 'There is the Poet Burns'; he went out to look, and saw a man with boots on, like a well-dressed farmer, walking down the village on the opposite side of the burn. This was all the relation these two men ever had: they were very nearly coevals.—I know Robert Burns, and I knew my Father; yet were you to ask me which had the greater natural faculty? I might perhaps actually pause before replying! Burns had an infinitely wider Education; my Father a far wholesomer: besides the one was a man of Musical Utterance, the other wholly a man of Action, even with Speech subservient thereto. Never, of all the men I have seen, has one come personally in my way in whom the Endowment from Nature and the Arena from Fortune were so utterly out of all proportion. I have said this often; and partly *know* it. As a man of Speculation (had Culture ever unfolded him) he must have gone wild and desperate as Burns: but he was a man of Conduct, and Work keeps all right. What strange shapeable creatures we are.

My Father's Education was altogether of the worst and most limited. I believe he was never more than three months at any school: what he learned there showed what he might have learned. A solid knowledge of Arithmetic, a fine antique Handwriting; these, with other limited *practical* etceteras, were *all* the things he ever heard mentioned as excellent: he had no room to strive for more. Poetry, Fiction in general, he had universally seen treated as not only idle, but *false* and criminal. This was the spiritual element he had lived in, almost to old age. But greatly his most important culture he had gathered (and this too by his own endeavour) from the better men of the district; the Religious men, to whom as to the most excellent, his own nature gradually attached and attracted him. He was Religious with the consent of his whole faculties: without Reason he would have been nothing; indeed his habit of intellect was thoroughly free and even incredulous, and strongly enough did the daily example of this work afterwards on me. 'Putting out the natural eye of his mind to see better with a telescope:' this was no scheme for *him*. But he was in Annandale, and it was above fifty years ago; and a Gospel was still preached there to the heart of a man, in the tones of a man. Religion was the Pole-star for my Father: rude and uncultivated as he otherwise was, it made him and kept him 'in all points a man.'

Oh! when I think that all the area in Boundless Space he had seen was limited to a circle of some forty miles diameter (he never in his life was farther, or elsewhere so far, from home as at Craigenputtock); and all his knowledge of the Boundless Time was derived from his Bible, and what the oral memories of old men could give him, and his own could gather; and yet, that he was *such*,—I could take shame to myself; I feel to my Father (so great though so neglected, so generous also towards *me*) a strange tenderness, and mingled pity and reverence; peculiar to the case; infinitely soft and near my heart. Was he not a sacrifice to *me*? Had I stood in his place, could he not have stood in mine, and more? Thou good Father! well may *I* forever honour thy memory: surely that act was not without its reward.—And was not Nature great, out of such materials to make such a man?—

Though genuine and coherent, 'living and life-giving,' he was nevertheless but half developed. We had all to complain that we *durst not* freely love him. His heart seemed as if walled in; he had not the free means to unbosom himself. My Mother has owned to me that she could never understand him; that her affection, and (with all their little strifes) her admiration of him was obstructed: it seemed as if an atmosphere of Fear repelled us from him. To me it was especially so. Till late years, when he began to respect me more; and, as it were, too look up to me for instruction, for protection (a relation unspeakably beautiful), I was ever more or less awed and chilled before him: my heart and tongue played freely only with my Mother. He had an air of deepest gravity, even sternness. Yet he could laugh with his whole throat, and his whole heart. I have often seen him weep too: his voice would thicken and his lips curve while reading the Bible: he had a merciful heart to real distress, though he hated idleness, and for imbecility and fatuity had no tolerance. Once, and I think once only, I saw him in a passion of tears. It was when the remains of my Mother's fever hung upon her (in 1817), and seemed to threaten the extinction of her reason: we were all of us nigh desperate, and ourselves mad. He burst, at last, into quite a torrent of grief; cried piteously, and threw himself on the floor, and lay moaning. I wondered, and had no words, no tears. It was as if a rock of granite had melted, and was thawing into water. What unknown seas of feeling lie in man, and will from time to time break through!—

He was no niggard, but truly a wisely generous Economist. He paid his men *handsomely* and with overplus. He had known Poverty in the shape of actual want (in boyhood), and never had one penny which he knew not well how he had come by ('picked,' as he said, 'out of the hard stone'): yet he ever parted with money as a man that knew when he was getting money's worth; that could *give* also, and with a frank liberality, when the fit occasion called. I remember, with the peculiar kind of tenderness that attaches to many similar things in his life, one or I rather think two times, when he sent *me* to buy a quarter of a pound of Tobacco to give to some old women whom he had had gathering Potatoes for him: he nipt off for each a handsome leash, and handed it her by way of over-and-above. This was a common principle with him. I must have been twelve or thirteen when I fetched this Tobacco. I love to think of it. 'The little that a just man hath.' The old women are now perhaps *all* dead; he too is dead: but the gift still lives. [*Thursday night.*]

He was a man singularly free from Affectation. The feeling that he had not he could in no wise pretend to have: however ill the want of it might look, he simply would not and did not put on the show of it.

Singularly free from Envy I may reckon him too; the rather if I consider his keen temper, and the value he naturally (as a man wholly for Action) set upon *success* in life. Others that (by better fortune; none was more industrious or more prudent) had grown richer than he, did not seem to provoke the smallest grudging in him. They were going their path, he going his; one did not impede the other. He rather seemed to look at such with a kind of respect, a desire to learn from them: at lowest with indifference. In like manner, though he above all things (indeed in strictness, *solely*) admired Talent, he seemed never to have measured *himself* anxiously against anyone; was content to be taught by whosoever could teach him: one or two men (immeasurably his inferiors in faculty) he, I do believe, looked up to; and thought (with perfect composure) abler minds than himself. Complete, at the same time, was his confidence in his own judgment when it spoke to him decisively: he was one of those few that could *believe* and *know*, as well as *inquire* and *be of opinion*. When I remember how he admired Intellectual Force, how much he had of it himself, and yet how unconsciously and contentedly he gave others credit for superiority, I again see the *healthy* spirit, the genuine man. Nothing could please him better than a well-ordered Discourse of Reason; the clear Solution and Exposition of any object; and he knew well, in such cases, when the nail had been hit; and contemptuously enough recognised where it had been missed. He has said of a bad Preacher: 'He was like a fly wading among Tar.' Clearness, emphatic Clearness, was his highest category of man's thinking power: he delighted always to hear good 'Argument;' he would often say, 'I would like to hear thee argue with him:' he said this of Jeffrey and me,—with an air of such simple earnestness (not two years ago); and it was his true feeling. I have often pleased him much by arguing with men (as many years ago I was prone to do) in his presence: he rejoiced greatly in my success, at all events in my dexterity and manifested force. Others of us he admired for our 'activity,' our practical valour and skill; all of us (generally speaking) for our decent demeanour in the world. It is now one of my greatest blessings (for which I would thank Heaven from my heart) that he lived to see me, through various obstructions, attain some look of doing well. He had 'educated' me against much advice, I believe, and chiefly, if not solely, from his own noble faith: James Bell (one of our wise men) had told him: 'Educate a boy, and he grows up to despise his ignorant parents.' My Father once told me this; and added: 'Thou hast not done so. God be thanked for it!' I have reason to think my Father was proud of me (not vain, for he never, except provoked, openly bragged of us); that here too he lived to 'see the pleasure of the Lord prosper in his hands.' Oh, was it not a happiness for me! The fame of all this Planet were not henceforth so precious.—

He was thrifty, patient; careless of outward accommodation; had a Spartan indifference to all that. When he quarrelled about such things, it was rather because some human *mismanagement* seemed to look through the evil. Food and all else were simply and solely there as the means for *doing work*. We have lived for months, of old (and when he was not any longer poor), because 'by ourselves,' on porridge and potatoes with no other condiment than what our own cow yielded. Thus are we not now all beggars; as the most like us have become. Mother and Father were assiduous, abstemious, frugal without stinginess. They shall not want their reward.

Both still knew what they were doing in this world, and why they were here: 'Man's chief end,' my father could have answered from the depths of his soul, 'is to glorify God and *enjoy Him* for ever.'[1] By this light he walked, choosing his path, fitting prudence to principle with wonderful skill and manliness—through 'the ruins of a falling Era,' not once missing his footing. Go thou, whom by the hard toil of his arms and his mind he has struggled to enlighten better, go thou and do likewise!

[1] Words from the Scottish *Shorter Catechism*.

His death was 'unexpected'? Not so; every morning and every evening for perhaps sixty years, he had prayed to the great Father, in words which I shall now no more hear him impressively pronounce: 'Prepare us for these solemn events, Death, Judgment, and Eternity.' He would pray also: 'Forsake us not now when we are old, and our heads grown gray.' God did not forsake him.—

Ever since I can remember, his honoured head was gray: indeed he must have been about Forty when I was born. It was a noble head; very large; the upper part of it strikingly like that of the Poet Goethe: the mouth again bearing marks of unrefinement; shut, indeed, and significant; yet loosely compressed (as I have seen in the firmest men, if used to hard manual labour); betokening depth, passionateness, force, all in an element not of languor, yet in toil and patient perennial Endurance. A face full of meaning and earnestness.[1] A man of Strength, and a man of Toil. Jane took a profile[2] of him when she was last in Annandale: it is the only memorial we have left; and worth much to us. He was short of stature; yet shorter than usual only in the limbs: of great muscular strength, far more than even his strong-built frame gave promise of. In all things he was emphatically *temperate*: through life guilty (more than can be said of almost any man) of *no* excess.—

He was born (I think, but will inquire better) in the year 1757;[3] at a place called Brownknowe, a small farm, not far from Burnswark Hill in Annandale. I have heard him describe the anguish of mind he felt when leaving this place, and taking farewell of 'a big stone' whereon he had been wont to sit in early boyhood, tending the cattle. Perhaps there was a thorn-tree near it: his heart he said was like to burst. They were removing to Sibbaldbyside, another farm in the valley of Dryfe. —He was come to full manhood.—

[1] 'About this hour is the funeral: Irving enters—unsatisfactory.'—T. C.

[2] The profile by Mrs. Carlyle (face only) is done mechanically from the shadow.

[3] August 1758.

The family was exposed to great privations, while at Brownknowe. The Mother (Mary Gillespie: she had relatives in Dryfesdale) was left with her children, and had not always meal to make them porridge. My Father was the second son, and fourth child. My Grandfather (Thomas Carlyle, after whom I am named) was an honest, vehement, adventurous, but not an industrious man. He used to collect vigorously and rigorously a sum sufficient for his half year's rent (probably some six or five pounds); lay this by; and for the rest, leave the mother with her little ones to manage very much as they could and would; himself meanwhile amusing himself; perhaps hunting, most probably with the Laird of Bridekirk (a swashbuckler of those days, composer of 'Bridekirk's Hunting') partly in the character of kinsman, partly of attendant and henchman. I have heard my Father describe the shifts they were reduced to at home. Once, he said, meal which perhaps had been long scarce and certainly for some time wanting, arrived at last late at night,—she proceeded on the spot to make cakes of it, and had no fuel but straw that she tore from the beds (straw lies under the chaff sacks we all slept on) to do it with: the children all rose to eat. Potatoes were little in use then: a '*wecht*-ful'[1] was stored up to be eaten perhaps about Halloween. My Father often told us how he once, with a providence early manifested, got possession of four potatoes; and thinking that a time of want might come, hid them carefully against the evil day: he found them long after all grown together; they had not been needed. I think he once told us his first short-clothes were a hull made mostly or wholly of leather (?). We all only laughed; for it is now long ago. Thou dear Father! through what stern obstructions was thy way to manhood to be forced, and, for us and our travelling, made smooth.

My Grandfather, whom I can remember as a slightish wiry-looking old man, had not possessed the wisdom of his Son; yet perhaps he was more to be pitied than blamed. *His* Mother

[1] A *wecht*, large sieve for winnowing grain.

(whose name I have forgotten) was early left a Widow with two of them, in the parish, perhaps in the village, of Middlebie: Thomas the elder became a joiner, and went to work in Lancashire, perhaps in Lancaster, where he staid more than one season (he once returned home, in winter, partly by *ice*, skating along the Westmoreland and Cumberland Lakes): he was in Dumfriesshire in 1745; saw the Highlanders come through Ecclefechan (over the Cowden-heights) as they went *down*; was at Dumfries among them, as they returned back in flight: he had gone by the Lady of Bridekirk's request to look after the Laird, whom as a Whig of some note, they had taken prisoner. His whole adventures there he had minutely described to his children (I too have heard him speak, but briefly, indistinctly, of them): by my uncle Frank I once got a full account of the matter; which shall perhaps be inserted elsewhere. He worked as carpenter, I know not how long, about Middlebie (?), then laid aside that craft (except as a side-business; for he always had tools, which I myself have assisted him in grinding), and went to Brownknowe to farm. In his latter days he was chiefly supported by my Father; to whom I remember once hearing him say, with a half-choked tremulous palsied voice: 'Thou hast been a good son to me.' He died in 1804[1]: I well remember the funeral, which I was at, and that I read (being then a good reader) '*MacEwen on the Types*' (which I have not seen since, but then partially understood, and even liked for its glib smoothness) to the people sitting at the wake. The funeral was in the time of snow: all is still very clear to me. The three brothers, my Father, Frank and Tom spoke together in the dusk, on the street of Ecclefechan, I looking up and listening: Tom proposed that he would bear the whole expense as he had been 'rather backward during his Life' (the Deceased's: these were his very words); which offer was immediately rejected.—

Old Thomas Carlyle had been proud and poor; no doubt he was discontented enough: industry was perhaps more difficult in Annandale then (this I do not think very likely); at all

[1] 1806.

events, the man in honour (the *man*) of those days, in that rude Border Country, was a drinker, and hunter; above all a *striker*. My Grandfather did not drink; but his *stroke* was ever as ready as his word, and both were sharp enough. He was a fiery man; irascible, indomitable: of the toughness and springiness of steel. An old market-brawl, called 'the Ecclefechan Dog-fight,' in which he was a principal, survives in tradition there to this day. My Father who in youth too had been in quarrels, and formidable enough in them, but from manhood upwards *abhorred* all such things,—never once spoke to us of this. My Grandfather had a certain religiousness; but it could not be made dominant and paramount: his life lay in two; I figure him as very miserable, and pardon (as my Father did) all his irregularities and unreasons. My Father liked in general to speak of him, when it came in course: he told us sometimes of his once riding down to Annan (when a boy) behind him, on a sack of barley to be shipped; for which there was then no other mode of conveyance but horseback. On arriving at Annan-bridge, the people demanded three-halfpence of toll-money: this the old man would in no wise pay (for tolls then were reckoned pure impositions); got soon into argument about it; and rather than pay it, turned his horse's head aside, and swam the river (at a dangerous place) to the extreme terror of his boy. Perhaps it was on this same occasion, while the two were on the shore about Whinnyrigg, with many others on the same errand (for a 'boat had come in'—from Liverpool probably—and the country must hasten to ship) that a lad, of larger size, jeered at the little boy for his ragged coat etc.: whereupon the Father, doubtless provoked too, gave him *permission* to fight the wrongdoer,—which he did, and with victory. 'Man's inhumanity to man!'—

I must not dwell on these things: yet will mention the other Brother, my Grand-uncle Francis, still remembered by his title 'the Captain of Middlebie.' He was bred a shoemaker, and like his elder brother went to travel for work and insight. My Father once described to me, with pity and aversion, how Francis had on some occasion taken to drinking, and to gaming, 'far up in England' (at Bristol?), had lost *all* his money, and gone to bed drunk: he awoke next morning in horrors; started up (stung by the serpent of remorse), and flinging himself out of bed, broke his leg against a table standing near; and lay there sprawling,—and had to lie for weeks, with nothing to pay the shot. Perhaps this was the crisis of his life; perhaps it was to pay the bill of this very tavern, that he went and enlisted himself on board some small-craft man-of-war. A mutiny (as I have heard) took place; wherein Francis Carlyle, with great daring stood by the Captain and quelled the matter; for which service he was promoted to the command of a Revenue-ship, and sailed therein chiefly about the Solway Seas, and did feats enough—of which perhaps elsewhere. He had retired, with dignity, on half-pay to his native Middlebie before my birth. I never saw him but once, and then rather memorably. My Grandfather and he, owing to some sort of cloud and misunderstanding, had not had any intercourse for long; in which division the two families had joined: but now when old Thomas was lying on his probable, and as it proved actual Deathbed, the old rugged Sea-Captain relented, and resolved to see his Brother yet once before he died. He came in a cart to Ecclefechan (a great enterprise then, for the road was all water-cut and nigh impassable with roughness): I chanced to be standing by when he arrived. He was a grim, broad, to me almost terrible man; unwieldy so that he could not walk. (My Brother John is said to resemble him: he was my prototype of Smollett's Trunnion.) They lifted him up the steep straight stairs in a chair, to the room of the dying man. The two old Brothers saluted each other hovering over the brink of the grave (they were both above eighty): in some twenty minutes, the armchair was seen again descending (my father bore one corner of it, in front) the old man had parted with his Brother for the last time; he went away, with few words, but with a face that still dimly haunts me; and I never saw him more. The business at the moment was quite unknown to me; but I gathered it in a day or two; and its full meaning long afterwards grew clear to me. Its outward phasis, now after some twenty-eight years, is plain as I have written. Old Francis also died not long afterwards.[1]

One vague tradition I will mention: that our humble forefathers dwelt long as farmers at *Burrens*, the old Roman Station in Middlebie. Once in times of Border robbery, some Cumberland cattle had been stolen and were chased; the trace of them disappeared at Burrens, and the angry Cumbrians demanded of the poor farmer what had become of them? It was vain for him to answer and aver (truly) that he knew nothing of them, had no concern with them: he was seized by the people, and despite his own desperate protestations, despite his wife's shriekings and his children's cries, was hanged on the spot! The case even in those days was thought piteous; and a perpetual gift of the little farm was made to the poor widow as some compensation. Her children and children's children continued to possess it; till their title was questioned by 'the Duke' (of Queensberry) and they (perhaps in my great-grandfather's time, about 1727) were ousted. Date and circumstances for the Tale are all wanting. This is my remotest outlook into the Past; and itself but a cloudy half or whole hallucination: further on there is not even a hallucination. I now return: these things are secular and unsatisfactory.

Bred up in such circumstances, the Boys were accustomed to all manner of hardship; and must trust for upbringing to Nature, to the scanty precepts of their poor Mother, and to what seeds or influences of culture were hanging as it were in the *atmosphere* of their environment. Poor boys! They had to scramble ('scraffle!') for their very clothes and food. They knit, they thatched, for hire; above all they hunted. My Father had tried all these things, almost in boyhood. Every dell and *burn-gate* and *cleugh* of that district he had traversed, seeking hares and the like: he used to tell of these pilgrimages: once, I remember, his gun-flint was 'tied on with a hatband.' He was a *real* hunter, like a wild Indian, from Necessity. The hares' flesh

[1] This paragraph requires to be corrected by the following dates, viz.:—Francis died 19th August 1803 (aged 77); Thomas died 10th January 1806 (aged 84).

was food: hare-skins (at some sixpence each) would accumulate into the purchase-money of a coat. All these things he used to speak of without either boasting or complaining, not as reproaches to *us*, but as historical merely. On the whole, he never *complained*; either of the past, the present, or the future: he observed and accurately noted all, he made the most and the best of all. His hunting years were not useless to him. Misery was early training the rugged boy into a Stoic;—that, one day, there might be assurance of a Scottish Man.—

One Macleod, 'Sandy Macleod,' a wandering pensioner invalided out of some Highland Regiment (who had served in America,—I must think with General Wolfe) had strayed to Brownknowe with his old wife, and taken a Cottage of my Grandfather. He, with his wild foreign legends, and strange half-idiotic half-genial ways, was a great figure with the young ones; and I think acted not a little on their character, least of any, however, on my Father, whose early turn for the *practical* and real, made him more heedless of Macleod and his vagaries. The old Pensioner had quaint sayings, not without significance: of a lacrymose complaining man, for example, he said (or perhaps to him) 'He might be thankful he was not in Purgatory.' The quaint fashion of speaking, assumed for humour, and most noticeable in my uncle Frank, least or hardly at all in my Father,—was no doubt partly derived from this old wanderer, who was much about their house, working for his rent and so forth; and was partly laughed at partly wondered at by the young ones.—Tinkers also, nestling in out-houses, melting pot-metal, and with rude feuds and warfare, often came upon the scene. These with passing Highland Drovers were perhaps their only visitors.

Had there not been a natural goodness and indestructible force in my Father, I see not how he could have bodied himself forth from these mean impediments. I suppose, good precepts were not wanting; there was the Bible to read. Old John Orr, the Schoolmaster, used from time to time to lodge with them; he was religious and enthusiastic (though in practice irregular —with drink); in my Grandfather also there seems to have been a certain geniality: for instance, he and a neighbour, Thomas Hogg, read 'Anson's Voyage;' also the 'Arabian Nights,'—for which latter my Father (armed with zealous conviction) scrupled not to censure them openly.—By one means or another at an early age, he had acquired *principles*; lights that not only flickered but shone steadily to guide his way.

It must have been in his teens (perhaps rather early) that he and his elder brother John, with William Bell (afterwards of Wylie-hole, and a noted Drover), and *his* Brother, all met in the kiln at *Relief*[1] to play cards. The corn was dried then *at home*: there was a fire therefore, and perhaps it was both heat and light. The boys had played perhaps often enough, for trifling stakes; and always parted in good humour: one night they came to some disagreement. My Father spoke out, what was in him, about the folly, the sinfulness of quarrelling over a perhaps sinful amusement: the earnest mind persuaded other minds; they threw the cards into the fire; and (I think the younger Bell told my Brother James) no one of the four ever touched a card again through life! My father certainly never hinted at such a game, since I knew him.—I cannot remember that I, at that age, had any such force of belief; which of us can?

[*Friday night.* My Father is now in his grave; sleeping by the side of his loved ones: his face to the East, under the Hope of meeting the Lord when He shall come to Judgment—when the Times shall be fulfilled. Mysterious Life! Yes, there is a God in man. Silence! since thou hast no voice.—To imitate *him* I will pause here for the night. God comfort my Mother; God guard them all!]

Of old John Orr I must say another word: my Father, who often spoke of him, though not so much latterly, gave me copious description of that and other antiquarian matters, in one of the pleasantest days I remember; the last time but one (or perhaps two) that we talked together. A tradition of poor old Orr, as of a man of boundless love and natural worth, still

[1] Farm in Middlebie parish.

faintly lives in Annandale. If I mistake not, he worked also as a Shoemaker: he was heartily devout; yet subject to fits of irregularity; he would vanish for weeks into obscure tippling-houses, then reappear ghastly and haggard in body and mind, shattered in health, torn with gnawing remorse. Perhaps it was in some dark interval of this kind (he was already old) that he bethought him of his Father, and how he was still lying without a Stone of memorial. John had already ordered a Tombstone for him, and it was lying worked, and I suppose lettered and ready, at some mason's establishment (up the water of Mein); but never yet carried to the place. Probably Orr had not a shilling of money to hire any carter with; but he hurried off to the spot, and desperately got the Stone on his back. It was a load that had nigh killed him; he had to set it down ever and anon and rest, and get it up again. The night fell: I think some one found him desperately struggling with it near Mein Mill, and assisted him, and got it set in its place. —Should I not go and look whether it is still to be found there: in Pennersaughs Churchyard?[1]

Though far above all quackery, Orr was actually employed to exorcise a House; some house or room at Orchard in the parish of Hoddam. He entered the haunted place, was closeted in it for some time, speaking or praying: the ghost was really and truly laid, for no one heard more of it. Beautiful reverence even of the rude and ignorant for the infinite nature of Wisdom, in the infinite life of Man!–

Orr, as already said, used to come much about Brownknowe; being habitually *itinerant*, and (though Schoolmaster of Hoddam) without settled home. He commonly, my Father said, slept with some of the Boys, in a place where (as usual) there were several beds. He would call out from the bed, to my Grandfather also in his: 'Gudeman, I have found it,'—found the solution of some problem or other, perhaps arithmetical, which they had been struggling with; or: 'Gudeman, what d'ye think of this?'—I represent him to myself as a squat, pursy kind

[1] A disused churchyard, about half a mile from Ecclefechan, in which many generations of Carlyles lie buried.

of figure; grim, dusky, the blandest and most bounteous of Cynics. Also a form of the Past! He was my father's sole Teacher in 'schooling.'

It might be in the year (I think, but must inquire of my now sole surviving Aunt) 1773, that one William Brown, a Mason from Peebles came down into Annandale to do some work; perhaps boarded in my Grandfather's house; at all events married his eldest daughter and child, my now old and vehement, then young and spirited 'Aunt Fanny' ('Aunt Fann.') This worthy man, whose nephew is still Minister of Eskdalemuir (and Author of a Book on the *Jews*) proved the greatest blessing to that household; my Father could in any case have saved himself; of the other Brothers it may be doubted whether William Brown was not the primary preserver. They all learned to be Masons from him, or from one another; instead of miscellaneous labourers and hunters, became regular tradesmen; the best in all their district (the skilfullest and faithfullest) and the best rewarded—every way. Except my Father, none of them attained a decisive religiousness: but they all had prudence and earnestness; love of truth; industry and the blessings it brings. My Father, before my time, though not the eldest had become, in all senses, the head of the house. The eldest was called John. He early got asthma, and for long could not work (though he got his share of the wages still): I can faintly remember him as a pallid sickly figure, and even one or two insignificant words, and the breathless tone he uttered them in. When he seized with extreme fits of sickness, he used to gasp out: 'Bring Jamie; O send for Jamie!' He died I think in 1802.[1] I remember the funeral; and perhaps a day before it, how an ill-behaving servant-wench to some crony of hers, lifted up the coverlid from off his pale, ghastly-befilleted head to show it her: unheeding of me, who was alone with them there, and to whom the sight gave a new pang of horror.—He was the Father of two sons and a daughter, beside whom our boyhood was passed, none of whom have come to anything but

[1] Died 12th October 1801, aged 47.

insignificance. He was a well-doing man, and left them well; but their Mother was not wise, nor they decidedly so.—The youngest Brother, my 'Uncle Tom,' died next: a fiery, passionate, self-secluded warm-loving genuine soul, without fear and without guile: of whom it is recorded that he never from the first tones of speech, 'told any lie.' A true old-Roman soul, yet so marred, so stunted; who well deserves a chapter to himself, especially from me, who so lovingly admired him. He departed in my Father's house, in my presence, in the year 1815:[1] the first Death I had ever understood and laid with its whole emphasis to heart.—Frank followed next; at an interval of some five years:[2] a quaint, social, cheerful man; of less earnestness, but more openness; fond of genealogies, old histories, poems, queer sayings and all curious and *humane* things he could come at. This made him the greatest favourite: the rest were rather feared; my Father (ultimately at least) universally feared and respected. Frank left two sons, as yet young; one of whom (my namesake), gone to be a Lawyer, is rather clever, *how* clever I have not fully seen.—All these Brothers were men of evidently rather peculiar endowment: they were (censoriously) noted for their brotherly affection, and coherence; for their hard sayings, and hard *strikings* (which only my father ever grew to *heartily* detest); all of them became prosperous, got a name and possessions in their degree. It was a kindred, warmly liked, I believe, by those *near* it; by those at a distance, viewed, at worst and lowest, as something dangerous to meddle with, something *not* to be meddled with.—

What are the rich or the poor; and how do the simple Annals of the Poor differ from the complex Annals of the Rich, were they never so rich?—What is *thy* attainment compared with an Alexander's, a Mahomet's, a Napoleon's? And what was theirs? A temporary fraction of this Planetkin,—the whole round of which is but a sandgrain in the All; its whole duration but a moment in Eternity! The poor life or the rich one, are

[1] Thomas, born 1776, died 9th June 1816.
[2] Francis, born 1761, died 1819.

but the larger or smaller (*very* little smaller) *letters* in which we write the apophthegm and golden-saying of Life: it may be a False saying or it may be a True one; *there* lies it all; this is of quite *infinite* moment: the rest is verily and indeed of next to none.—

Perhaps my Father was William Brown's first Apprentice: somewhere about his sixteenth year. Early in the course of the engagement, work grew scarce in Annandale: the two 'slung their tools' (mallets and irons hung in two equipoised masses over the shoulders), and crossed the Hills into Nithsdale, to Auldgarth,[1] where a Bridge was building. This was my father's most *foreign* adventure; he never again or before saw anything so new, or (except when he came to Craigenputtock on visits) so *distant*. He loved to speak of it: that talking day we had together, I made him tell it me all over again from the beginning —as a *whole*, for the first time. He was a 'hewer,' and had some few pence a day. He could describe with the lucidest distinctness how the whole work went on; and 'headers' and 'closers' solidly massed together made an impregnable pile. He used to hear sermon in Closeburn church; sometimes too in Dunscore: the men had a refreshment of ale, for which he too used to table his twopence,—but the grown-up men generously for most part refused them. A superintendent of the work, a mason from Edinburgh, who did nothing but look on, and (rather decidedly) insist on terms of contract,—'took a great notion' of him; was for having him to Edinburgh along with him. The master-builder, pleased with his ingenious diligence, once laid a shilling on his '*banker*' (stone-bench for hewing on); which he rather ungraciously refused. A flood once carried off all the cinctures and woodwork: he saw the Master anxiously, tremulously watch through the rain as the waters rose; when they prevailed, and all went headlong, the poor man, wringing his hands together, spread them out with open palm down the river,—as if to say: There!

It was a noble moment, which I regret to have missed,

[1] Commonly spelt Auldgirth, about eight miles from Dumfries.

when my Father going to look at Craigenputtock, saw this Work, for the first time again, after a space of more than fifty years! How changed was all else, this thing yet the same. Then he was a poor boy, now he was a respected old man; increased in worldly goods; honoured in himself, and in his household. He grew alert (Jamie said) and eagerly observant: eagerly, yet with sadness. The country was all altered; broomy knowes were become seedfields; trees, then not so much as *seeds*, now waved out broad boughs: the houses, the fields, the men, were of another fashion; there was little that he could recognise. On reaching the Bridge itself, he started up to his knees (in the cart), sat wholly silent, and seemed on the point of weeping.

Well do I remember the first time I saw this Bridge: twelve years ago in the dusk of a May day; I had walked from Muirkirk, sickly, forlorn, of saddest mood (for it was then my days of darkness): a rustic answered me: 'Auldgarth'! There it lay silent, red in the red dusk. It was as if half a century of past Time had fatefully, for moments, turned back.

The Master-builder of this Bridge was one Stewart of Minnyive; who afterwards became my Uncle John Aitken's father-in-law: him I once saw. My Craigenputtock mason, James Hainning's Father, was the Smith that 'sharpened the tools.' A noble craft it is that of a mason: a good Building will last longer than most Books, than one Book of a million. The Auldgarth Bridge still spans the water, silently defies its chafing: there hangs it, and will hang, grim and strong, when of all the cunning hands that piled it together, perhaps the last now lies powerless in the sleep of death. O Time! O Time! wondrous and fearful art thou; yet there is in man what is above thee.

[*Saturday*.] Of my Father's youth and opening manhood, and with what specialties this period was marked, I have but an imperfect notion. I must inquire further what more is yet to be saved. He was now master of his own actions; possessed of means by his own earning: and had to try the world on various sides, and ascertain wherein his own 'chief end' in it actually lay. The first impulse of man is to seek for Enjoyment: he tries with more or less impetuosity, more or less irregularity, to conquer for himself a home and blessedness of a mere earthly kind; not till later (in how many cases never!) does he ascertain that on Earth there is no such home; that his true home lies beyond the world of Sense, is a celestial home.—Of these experimenting and tentative days my Father did not speak with much pleasure, not at all with exultation. He considered them days of folly, perhaps sinful days. Yet I know well that his life even then was marked by Temperance (in *all* senses); that he was abstemious, prudent, industrious, as very few.

I have a dim picture of him in his little world. In summer season diligently, cheerfully labouring with trowel and hammer; amused by grave talk, and grave humour, with the elders of the craft: building (*walling*) is an operation that beyond most other manual ones requires incessant consideration, ever-new invention; I have heard good judges say that he excelled in it all persons they had seen. In the depth of winter, I figure him with the others gathered round his father's hearth (now no longer so poor and desolate); hunting (but now happily for amusement, not necessity); present here and there at such merry meetings and social doings, as poor Annandale, for poor yet God-created men, might then offer.—Contentions occur; in these he was no man to be played with; fearless; formidable (I think to *all*). In after times, he looked back with sorrow on such things; yet to me they were not and are not other than interesting and innocent; scarcely ever, perhaps never, to be considered as *aggressions*, but always as *defences*, manful assertions of man's rights against man that would infringe them,—and victorious ones. I can faintly picture out one scene, which I got from him many years ago: perhaps it was at some 'Singing School'; a huge rude peasant was rudely defying and insulting the party my Father belonged to; the others quailed, and bore it, till he could bear it no longer; but clutches his rough adversary (who had been standing I think at some distance, on some sort of height) by the two flanks, swings him with ireful force round in the air (hitting his feet against some open door), and hurls him to a distance—supine, lamed, vanquished and utterly humbled. The whole business looks to me to have passed physically in a troublous moonlight; in the same environment and hue does it now stand in my memory, sad and stern. He would say of such things: 'I am wae to think on't'—wae from repentence: Happy who has nothing worse to repent of!—

In the vanities and gallantries of Life (though such in their way came across him) he seems to have very sparingly mingled. One Robert Henderson, a dashing projector and devotee, with a dashing daughter, came often up in conversation: this was perhaps, as it were, my Father's introduction to the 'pride of life'; from which, as his wont was, he appears to have derived little but *instruction*, but expansion, and experience. I have good reason to know that he never addressed any woman except with views that were honest pure and manly.

But happily he had been enabled very soon, in this choice of the False and Present against the True and Future, to 'choose the better part.' Happily there still existed in Annandale an influence of Goodness, pure emblems of a Religion: there were yet men living from whom a youth of earnestness might learn by example how to become a man. Old Robert Brand, my Father's maternal uncle, was probably of very great influence on him in this respect: old Robert was a rigorous Religionist, thoroughly filled with a celestial Philosophy of this earthly Life, which shone impressively through his stout decisive, and somewhat cross-grained deeds and words. Sharp sayings of his are still recollected there; not unworthy of preserving. He was a man of iron firmness, a just man and of wise insight. I think, my Father, consciously and unconsciously, may have learned more from this than from any other individual. From the time when he connected himself openly with the Religious,—became a 'Burgher' (strict, not strictest species of Presbyterian Dissenter) may be dated his spiritual majority; his earthly Life was now enlightened and overcanopied by a heavenly: he was henceforth a Man.—

Annandale had long been a lawless 'Border' Country: the people had ceased from foray-riding, but not from its effects; the 'gallant man' of those districts was still a wild, natural, almost animal man. A select few had, only of late, united themselves; they had built a little Meeting-house at Ecclefechan, thatched with heath, and chosen them a Priest by name John Johnston,—the priestliest man I ever under any ecclesiastical guise was privileged to look upon. He, in his last years, helped me well in my Latin (as he had done many); and otherwise procured me far higher benefits. This peasant union, this little heath-thatched house, this simple Evangelist, together constituted properly the 'Church' of that district: they were the blessing and the saving of many: on me too their pious heaven-sent influences still rest, and live; let me employ them well. There was, in those days, a 'Teacher of the People.' He sleeps, not far from my Father (who built his monument) in the Ecclefechan Churchyard; the Teacher and the Taught: 'Blessed,' I again say, 'are the Dead that die in the Lord. They do rest from their labours, and their works follow them.'

My Father, I think, was of the *second* race of religious men in Annandale: old Robert Brand, an ancient herdsman, old John Bretton, and some others that I have seen, were perhaps among the first. Alas, there is no third rising: Time sweeps all away with it so fast at this epoch: the Scottish Church has been short-lived, and was late in reaching thither.—

Perhaps it was in 1791 that my Father married: one Janet Carlyle, a very distant kinswoman of his own (her father yet, I believe, lives; a professor of Religion, but long since suspected to be none of the most perfect, though not without his worth): she brought him one Son; John, at present a well-doing householder at Cockermouth: she left him and this life in little more than a year. A mass of long fair woman's hair, which had belonged to her, lay long in a secret drawer at our house (perhaps still lies); the sight of it used to give me a certain faint horror. It had been cut from her head, near death, when she was in the height of fever: she was delirious, and would let none but my Father cut it. He thought himself sure of infection, nevertheless consented readily, and escaped. Many ways, I have understood he had much to suffer then: yet he never spoke of it; or only transiently, and with a historical Stoicism.

Let me here mention the reverent custom the old men had in Annandale, of treating Death even in their loosest thoughts. It is now fast passing away; with my Father was quite invariable. Had he occasion to speak in the future, he would say: I will do so and so, never failing to add (were it only against the morrow): 'if I be spared;' 'if I live.' The Dead again he spoke of with perfect freedom, only with serious gravity (perhaps a lowering of the voice), and always, even in the most trivial conversation, adding, 'that's gane:' 'my Brother John that's gane,' did so and so.—*Ernst ist das Leben.*—

He married again, in the beginning of 1795, my Mother, Margaret Aitken (a woman of to me the fairest descent, that of the pious, the just and wise): She was a faithful helpmate to him, toiling unweariedly at his side; to us the best of all Mothers, to whom for body and soul I owe endless gratitude. By God's great mercy, she is still left, as a head and centre to us all; and may yet cheer us with her pious heroism, through many toils—If God so please! I am the eldest child; and trace deeply in myself the character of both parents; also the upbringing and example of both: the inheritance of their natural *health*,—had not I and the Time together beat on it too hard.—

It must have been about the period of the first marriage that my Father and his Brothers, already Master-masons, established themselves in Ecclefechan. They all henceforth began to take on a civic existence, to 'accumulate' in all senses; to grow. They were among the best and truest men of their craft (perhaps the very best) in that whole district; and recompensed accordingly. Their gains, the honest wages of Industry, their savings were slow but constant; and in my Father's case continued (from one source or other) to the end. He was born and brought up the poorest; by his own right hand he had become wealthy, as he accounted wealth, and in all ways plentifully supplied. His household goods valued in money may perhaps somewhat exceed £1000; in real inward worth, their value was greater than that of most kingdoms,—than all Napoleon's conquests, which did not endure. He saw his children grow up round him to guard him and do him honour; he had (ultimately) a hearty respect from *all*; could look forward from the verge of this Earth, rich and increased in goods, into an Everlasting Country where through the immeasurable Deeps shone a solemn sober Hope. I must reckon my Father one of the most *prosperous* men I have ever in my life known.

Frugality and assiduity, a certain grave composure, an earnestness (not without its constraint, then felt as oppressive a little, yet which now yields its fruit) were the order of our household. We were all practically taught that *work* (temporal or spiritual) was the only thing we had to do; and incited always by precept and example to do it *well*. An inflexible element of Authority encircled us all; we felt from the first (a useful thing) that our own *wish* had often nothing to say in the matter. It was not a joyful life (what life is), yet a safe, quiet one; above most others (or any other I have witnessed) a wholesome one. We were taciturn rather than talkative; but if little were said, that little had generally a meaning. I cannot be thankful enough for my Parents.

My early, yet not my earliest recollections of my Father had in them a certain *awe*; which only now or very lately has passed into free reverence. I was parted from him in my tenth year; and never *habitually* beside him afterwards.—Of the very earliest I have saved some; and would not for money's worth lose them. All that belongs to him has become very precious to me.

I can remember his carrying me across Mein Water, over a pool some few yards below where the present Meinfoot Bridge stands. Perhaps I was in my fifth year. He was going to Luce I think to ask after some Joiner. It was the loveliest summer evening I recollect. My memory dawns (or grows light) at the first aspect of the stream, of the pool spanned by a wooden bow, without railing, and a single plank broad. He lifted me against his thigh with his right hand, and walked careless along till we were over. My face was turned rather downwards, I looked into the deep clear water, and its reflected skies, with terror yet with confidence that he could save me. Directly after, I, light of heart, asked of him what these 'little black things' were that I seemed sometimes to *create* by rubbing the palms of my hands together, and can at this moment (the mind having been doubtless excited by the past peril) remember that I described them in these words: 'like penny-rows' (rolls) 'but far less.' He explained it wholly to me: 'my hands were not *clean*.' He was very kind, and I loved him. All around this is Dusk, or Night, before and after.—It is not my *earliest* recollection, not even of him. My earliest of all is a mad passion of rage at my elder Brother John (on a visit to us likely from his grandfather's); in which my Father too figures though dimly, as a kind of cheerful comforter and soother. I had broken my little brown stool, by madly throwing it at my brother; and felt for perhaps the first time, the united pangs of Loss and of Remorse. I was perhaps hardly more than two years old; but can get no one to fix the date for me, though all is still quite legible for myself, with many of its [features]. I remember the first 'new half-pence' (brought from Dumfries by my Father and Mother for Alick and me); and words that my Uncle John said about it: this seems later (in 1799?), and might be ascertained. Backwards beyond all, are dim *ruddy* images, of deeper and deeper brown shade into the dark beginnings of being.

I remember, perhaps in my fifth year, his teaching me Arithmetical things: especially how to *divide* (of my Letters taught me by my Mother, I have no recollection whatever; of reading scarcely any): he said, 'This is the *divider* (divisor), this' etc., and gave me a quite clear notion how to do. My Mother said I would forget it all; to which he answered: Not so much as they that have never learned it.—Five years or so after, he said to me once: 'Tom, I do not grudge thy schooling, now when thy Uncle Frank owns thee to be a better Arithmetician than himself.'—

He took me down to Annan Academy on the Whitsunday morning, 1806; I trotting at his side in the way alluded to in *Teufelsdröckh.* It was a bright morning, and to me full of moment; of fluttering boundless Hopes, saddened by parting with Mother, with Home; and which afterwards were cruelly disappointed. He called once or twice in the grand schoolroom, as he chanced to have business at Annan: once sat down by me (as the master was out), and asked whether I was all well. The boys did not laugh (as I feared), perhaps durst not.

He was *always* GENEROUS to me in my school expenses; never by grudging look or word did he give me any pain. With a noble faith he launched me forth into a world which himself had never been permitted to visit: let me study to act worthily of him there.

He wrote to me duly and affectionately while I was at College; nothing that was good for me did he fail with his best ability to provide: his simple true counsels and fatherly admonitions have now first attained their fit sacredness of meaning: pity for me if they be thrown away.—

His tolerance for me, his trust in me was great. When I declined going forward into the Church (though his heart was set upon it), he respected my scruples, my volition, and patiently let me have my way. In after years, when I had peremptorily ceased from being a Schoolmaster, though he inwardly disapproved of the step as imprudent; and saw me, in successive summers, lingering beside him in sickliness of body and mind, without outlook towards any good, he had the forbearance to say at worst nothing, never once to whisper discontent with me. If my dear Mother, with the trustfulness of a Mother's heart, ministered to all my woes, outward and inward, and ever against hope kept prophesying good,—he, with whom I communicated far less, who could not approve my schemes, did nothing that was not kind and fatherly: his roof was my shelter, which a word from him (in those sour days of wounded vanity) would have deprived me of; he patiently let me have my way; helping where he could, where he could not help never hindering.—When hope again dawned for me, how hearty was his joy, yet how silent! I have been a happy Son.—

On my first return from College (in the Spring 1810) I met him in the 'Langlands Road,' walking out to try whether he would not happen to see me coming. He had a red plaid about him; was recovering from a fit of sickness (his first severe one), and there welcomed me back. It was a bright April day: *where* is it *now*?—

The great world-revolutions send in their disturbing billows to the remotest creek; and the overthrow of thrones more slowly overturns also the households of the lowly. Nevertheless in all cases the wise man adjusts himself: even in these times, the hand of the diligent maketh rich. My Father had seen the American War, the French Revolution, the rise and fall of Napoleon. The last arrested him strongly: in the Russian Campaign we bought a London Newspaper, which I read aloud to a little circle thrice weekly. He was struck with Napoleon, and would say and look pregnant things about him: empires won, and empires lost (while *his* little household held together); and now it was all vanished like a tavern brawl!—For the rest, he never meddled with Politics: he was not there to govern, but to be governed; could still *live*, and therefore did not *revolt*. I have heard him say in late years, with an impressiveness which all his perceptions carried with them: 'that the lot of a poor man was growing worse and worse; that the world could not and would not last as it was; but mighty changes, of which none saw the end, were on the way.' To him, as one about to take his departure, the whole was but of secondary moment: he was looking towards 'a city that *had* foundations.'—

In the 'dear years' (1799 and 1800), when the oatmeal was as high as ten shillings a stone, he had noticed the labourers (I have heard him tell) retire each separately to a brook, and there *drink* instead of dining,—without complaint; anxious only to hide it.—

At Langholm he once saw a heap of smuggled Tobacco publicly burnt. Dragoons were ranged round it with drawn swords; some old women stretched through their old withered arms to snatch a little of it, and the dragoons did not hinder them.—A natural artist!

The largest sum he ever earned in one year, I think, was £100; by the building of Cressfield House.

He wisely quitted the Mason trade, at the time when the character of it had changed; when universal Poverty and Vanity made *show* and *cheapness* (here as everywhere) be preferred to Substance; when as he said emphatically honest trade 'was done.' He became Farmer (of a wet clayey spot called Mainhill) in 1815; that so 'he might keep all his family about him;' struggled with his old valour, and here too prevailed. Two ears of corn are now in many places growing where he found only one: unworthy or little worthy men for the time reap the benefit; but it was a benefit done to God's Earth, and God's Mankind will year after year get the good of it.

In his contention with an unjust or perhaps only a mistaken Landlord, he behaved with prudent resolution; not like a vain braggart but like a practically brave man. It was I that innocently (by my settlement at Hoddam Hill) had involved him in it. I must admire now his *silence*, while we were all so loud and vituperative: he spoke *nothing* on that matter, except only what had practical meaning in it, and in a practical tone. His answers to unjust proposals, meanwhile, were resolute and ever-memorable for their emphasis: 'I *will* not do it,' said he once; 'I will rather go to Jerusalem, seeking farms, and die without finding one.'—'We can live without Sharpe,' said he once in my hearing (such a thing only *once*) 'and the whole Sharpe creation.'—On getting to Scotsbrig, the rest of us all triumphed; not he: he let the matter stand on its own feet; was *there* also, not to talk but to work. He even addressed a conciliatory letter to General Sharpe (which I saw right to *write* for him, since he judged prudence better than pride): but it produced no result,—except indeed the ascertainment that none could be produced; which itself was one.—

When he first entered our house at Craigenputtock he said

in his slow emphatic way, with a certain rustic dignity to my wife (I had entered introducing him): 'I am grown an *old fellow*' (never can we forget the pathetic slow earnestness of these two words) 'I am grown an old fellow; and wished to see ye all once more while I had yet opportunity.' Jane was greatly struck with him; and still further opened my eyes to the treasure I possessed in a Father.—

The last thing I gave him was a cake of Cavendish Tobacco sent down by Alick about this time twelvemonth. Through life I had given him very little; having little to give: he needed little, and from me expected nothing. Thou who wouldst give, give quickly: in the grave thy loved one can receive no kindness.—I had once bought him a pair of silver spectacles; at receipt of which and the letter that accompanied them (John told me) he was very glad, and nigh weeping. 'What I gave I have.' He read with these spectacles till his last days; and no doubt sometimes though of me in using them.—

The last time I saw him was about the first of August last, a few days before departing hither. He was very kind, seemed prouder of me than ever. What he had never done the like of before, he said, on hearing me express something which he admired: 'Man, it's surely a pity that thou should sit yonder, with nothing but the Eye of Omniscience to see thee; and thou with such a gift to speak.' His eyes were sparkling mildly, with a kind of deliberate joy.— —Strangely too he offered me on one of those mornings (knowing that I was poor) 'two sovereigns' which he had of his own; and pressed them on my acceptance. They were lying in his Desk, none knew of them: he seemed really anxious and desirous that I should take them; should take his little hoard, his *all* that he had to give. I said jokingly afterwards that surely he was *fey*. So it has proved.

I shall now no more behold my dear Father with these bodily eyes. With him a whole three-score-and-ten years of the Past has doubly died for me; it is as if a new leaf in the great Book of Time were turned over. Strange Time! Endless Time, or of which I see neither end nor beginning! All rushes on;

man follows man; his life is as a Tale that has been told. Yet under Time does there not lie Eternity? Perhaps my Father, all that essentially *was* my Father *is* even now near me, with me. Both he and I are with God. Perhaps, if it so please God, we shall in some higher state of being meet one another, recognise one another: as it is written, 'we shall be for ever with God!' The possibility, nay (in some way) the certainty of perennial existence daily grows plainer to me. 'The essence of whatever was, is, or shall be, even now *is*.' God is great; God is good: His will be done, for it will be right!—

As it is, I can think peaceably of the Departed Loved. All that was earthly harsh sinful in our relation has fallen away; all that was holy in it remains. I can see my dear Father's Life in some measure as the sunk pillar on which mine was to rise and be built; the waters of Time have now swelled up round his (as they will round mine); I can *see* it (all transfigured) though I *touch* it no longer. I might almost say his spirit seems to have entered into me (so clearly do I discern and love him); I seem to myself only the continuation, and *second volume* of my Father.—These days that I have spent thinking of him, and of his end, are the peaceablest, the only Sabbath I have had in London. One other of the universal destinies of man has overtaken me. Thank Heaven, I know and have known what it is to be a *Son*; to *love* a Father, as spirit can love spirit. God give me to live to my Father's honour, and to His!—And now beloved Father farewell, for the last time in this world of shadows! In the world of Realities may the great Father again bring us together in perfect holiness, and perfect love! Amen!

Sunday night, 29th January 1832.

JANE WELSH CARLYLE

IN MEMORIAM JANE WELSH CARLYLE

Ob. April 21, 1866

BY GERALDINE JEWSBURY

She told me that once, when she was a very little girl, there was going to be a dinner-party at home, and she was left alone with some tempting custards, ranged in their glasses upon a stand. She stood looking at them, and the thought came into her mind 'What *would* be the consequence if I should eat one of them?' A whimsical sense of the dismay it would cause took hold of her; she thought of it again, and scarcely knowing what she was about, she put forth her hand, and—took a little from the top of each! She was discovered; the sentence upon her was, to eat *all* the remaining custards, and to hear the company told the reason why there were none for them! The poor child hated custards for a long time afterwards.

THE BUBBLY JOCK

On her road to school, when a very small child, she had to pass a gate where a horrid turkey-cock was generally standing. He always ran up to her, gobbling and looking very hideous and alarming. It frightened her at first a good deal; and she dreaded having to pass the place; but after a little time she hated the thought of living in fear. The next time she passed the gate several labourers and boys were near, who seemed to enjoy the thought of the turkey running at her. She gathered herself together and made up her mind. The turkey ran at her as usual, gobbling and swelling; she suddenly darted at him and seized him by the throat and swung him round! The men clapped their hands, and shouted 'Well done, little Jeannie Welsh!' and the Bubbly Jock never molested her again.

LEARNING LATIN

She was very anxious to learn lessons like a Boy; and, when a very little thing, she asked her father to let her 'learn Latin like a boy.' Her mother did not wish her to learn so much; her father always tried to push her forwards; there was a division of opinion on the subject. Jeannie went to one of the town scholars in Haddington and made him teach her a noun of the first declension ('*Penna*, a pen,' I think it was). Armed with this, she watched her opportunity; instead of going to bed, she crept under the table, and was concealed by the cover. In a pause of conversation, a little voice was heard, '*Penna*, a pen; *pennæ*, of a pen;' etc., and as there was a pause of surprise, she crept out, and went up to her father saying, 'I want to learn Latin; please let me be a boy.' Of course she had her own way in the matter.

SCHOOL AT HADDINGTON

Boys and girls went to the same school; they were in separate rooms, except for Arithmetic and Algebra. Jeannie was the best of the girls at Algebra. Of course she had many devoted slaves among the boys; one of them especially taught her, and helped her all he knew; but he was quite a poor boy, whilst Jeannie was one of the gentry of the place; but she felt no difficulty, and they were great friends. She was fond of doing everything difficult that boys did. There was one particularly dangerous feat, to which the boys dared each other; it was to walk on a *very* narrow ledge on the outside of the bridge overhanging the water; the ledge went in an arch, and the height was considerable. One fine morning Jeannie got up early and went to the Nungate Bridge; she lay down on her face and crawled from one end of the bridge to the other, to the imminent risk of either breaking her neck or drowning.

One day in the boys' school-room, one of the boys said something to displease her. She lifted her hand, doubled it, and hit him hard; his nose began to bleed, and in the midst of the scuffle the master came in. He saw the traces of the fray, and said in an angry voice, 'You boys, you know, I have forbidden you to fight in school, and have promised that I would flog the next. Who has been fighting this time?' Nobody spoke; and the master grew angry, and threatened *tawse* all round unless the culprit were given up. Of course no boy would tell of a girl, so there was a pause; in the midst of it, Jeannie looked up and said, 'Please, I gave that black eye.' The master tried to look grave, and pursed up his mouth; but the boy was big, and Jeannie was little; so, instead of the *tawse* he burst out laughing and told her she was 'a little deevil,' and had no business there, and to go her ways back to the girls.

Her friendship with her schoolfellow-teacher came to an untimely end. An aunt who came on a visit saw her standing by a stile with him, and a book between them. She was scolded, and desired not to keep his company. This made her very sorry, for she knew how good he was to her; but she never had a notion of disobedience in any matter small or great. She did not know how to tell him or to explain; she thought it shame to tell him he was not thought good enough, so she determined he should imagine it a fit of caprice, and from that day she never spoke a word to him or took the least notice; she thought a sudden cessation would pain him less than a gradual coldness. Years and years afterwards, going back on a visit to Haddington, when she was a middle-aged woman, and he was a man married and doing well in the world, she saw him again, and then, for the first time, told him the explanation.

She was always anxious to work hard, and would sit up half the night over her lessons. One day she had been greatly perplexed by a problem in Euclid; she *could not* solve it. At last she went to bed; and in a dream got up and did it, and went to bed again. In the morning she had no consciousness of her dream; but on looking at her slate, there was the problem solved.

She was afraid of sleeping too much, and used to tie a weight to one of her ankles that she might awake. Her mother discovered it; and her father forbade her to rise before five o'clock. She was a most healthy little thing then; only she did her best to ruin her health, not knowing what she did. She always would push everything to its extreme to find out if possible the ultimate consequence. One day her mother was ill, and a bag of ice had to be applied to her head. Jeannie wanted to know the sensation, and took an opportunity when no one saw her to get hold of the bag, and put it on her own head, and kept it on till she was found lying on the ground insensible.

She made great progress in Latin, and was in Virgil when nine years old. She always loved her doll; but when she got into Virgil she thought it shame to care for a doll. On her tenth birthday she built a funeral pile of lead pencils and sticks of cinnamon, and poured some sort of perfume over all, to represent a funeral pile. She then recited the speech of Dido, stabbed her doll and let out all the sawdust; after which she consumed her to ashes, and then burst into a passion of tears.

HER APPEARANCE IN GIRLHOOD

As a child she was remarkable for her large black eyes with their long curved lashes. As a girl she was extremely pretty,—a graceful and beautifully formed figure, upright and supple,—a delicate complexion of creamy white with a pale rose tint in the cheeks, lovely eyes full of fire and softness, and with great depths of meaning. Her head was finely formed, with a noble arch, and a broad forehead. Her other features were not regular; but they did not prevent her conveying all the impression of being beautiful. Her voice was clear, and full of subtle intonations and capable of great variety of expression. She had it under full control. She danced with much grace; and she was a good musician. She was ingenious in all works that required dexterity of hand; she could draw and paint, and she was a good carpenter. She could do anything well to which she chose to give herself. She was fond of logic,—too much so; and she had a keen clear incisive faculty of seeing through things, and hating all that was make-believe or pretentious. She had good sense that amounted to genius. She loved to learn, and she cultivated all her faculties to the utmost of her power. She was always witty, with a gift for narration;—in a word she was fascinating and everybody fell in love with her. A relative of hers told me that every man who spoke to her for five minutes felt impelled to make her an offer of marriage! From which it resulted that a great many men were made unhappy. She seemed born 'for the destruction of mankind.' Another person told me that she was 'the most beautiful starry-looking creature that could be imagined,' with a peculiar grace of manner and motion that was more charming than beauty. She had a great quantity of very fine silky black hair, and she always had a natural taste for dress. The first thing I ever heard about her was that she dressed well,—an excellent gift for a woman.

Her mother was a beautiful woman, and as charming as her daughter, though not so clever. She had the gift of dressing well also. Genius is profitable for all things, and it saves expense. Once her mother was going to some grand fête, and she wanted her dress to be something specially beautiful. She did not want to spend money. Jeannie was entrusted with a secret mission to gather ivy leaves and trails of ivy of different kinds and sizes, also mosses of various kinds, and was enjoined to silence. Mrs. Welsh arranged these round her dress, and the moss formed a beautiful embossed trimming and the ivy made a graceful scrollwork; the effect was lovely; nobody could imagine of what the trimming was composed, but it was generally supposed to be a French trimming of the latest fashion and of fabulous expense.

She always spoke of her mother with deep affection and great admiration. She said she was so noble and generous that no one ever came near her without being the better. She used to make beautiful presents by saving upon herself,—she economised upon herself to be generous to others; and no one ever served her in the least without experiencing her generosity. She was almost as charming and as much adored as her daughter.

Of her *Father* she always spoke with reverence; he was the only person who had any real influence over her. But, however wilful or indulged she might be, *obedience* to her parents—unquestioning and absolute—lay at the foundation of her life. She was accustomed to say that this habit of obedience to her parents was her salvation through life,—that she owed all that was of value in her character to this habit as the foundation. Her father, from what she told me, was a man of strong and noble character,—very true and hating all that was false. She always spoke of any praise he gave her as of a precious possession. She loved him with a deep reverence; and she never spoke of him except to friends whom she valued. It was the highest token of her regard when she told any one about her father. She told me that once he was summoned to go a sudden journey to see a patient; and he took her with him. It was the greatest favour and pleasure she had ever had. They travelled at night, and were to start for their return by a very early hour in the morning. She used to speak of this journey as something that made her perfectly happy; and during that journey, her father told her he was pleased with her, that her conduct and character satisfied him. It was not often he praised her; and this unreserved flow of communication was very precious to her. Whilst he went to the sick person, she was sent to bed until it should be time to return. She had his watch that she might know the time. When the chaise came round, the landlady brought her some tea; but she was in such haste not to keep him waiting that she forgot the *watch*; and they had to return several miles to fetch it! This was the last time she was with her father; a few days afterwards he fell ill of typhus fever, and would not allow her to come into the room. She made her way once to him, and he sent her away. He died of this illness; and it was the very greatest sorrow she ever experienced. She always relapsed into a deep silence for some time after speaking of her father. [*Not very correct.* T.C.]

After her father's death they ['*they*,' *no!* T.C.] left Haddington, and went to live at *Templand*, near Thornhill, in Dumfriesshire. It was a country house, standing in its own grounds, prettily laid out. The house has been described to me as furnished with a certain elegant thrift which gave it a great charm. I do not know how old she was when her father died [*eighteen*, *just gone*, T. C.], but she was one with whom years did not signify, they conveyed no meaning as to what she was. Before she was fourteen she wrote a *tragedy* in five acts, which was greatly admired and wondered at; but she never wrote another. She used to speak of it 'as just an explosion.' I don't know what the title was; she never told me.

She had no end of ardent lovers, and she owned that some of them had reason to complain. I think it highly probable that if *flirting* were a capital crime, she would have been in danger of being hanged many times over. She told me one story that showed a good deal of character: —There was a young man who was very much in love, and I am afraid he had reason to hope she cared for him: and she only liked him. She refused him decidedly when he proposed; but he tried to turn her from her decision, which showed how little he understood her; for her *will* was very steadfast through life. She refused him peremptorily this time. He then fell ill, and took to his bed, and his mother was very miserable about her son. She was a widow, and had but the one. At last he wrote her another letter, in which he declared that unless she would marry him, he would kill himself. He was in such distraction that it was a very likely thing for him to do. Her mother was very angry indeed, and reproached her bitterly. She was very sorry for the mischief she had done, and took to her bed, and made herself ill with crying. The old servant, Betty, kept imploring her to say just one word to save the young man's mother from her misery. But though she felt horribly guilty and miserable, she was not going to be forced or frightened into anything. She took up the letter once more, which she said was very moving, but a slight point struck her; and she put down the letter, saying to her mother, 'You need not be frightened, he won't kill himself at all; look here, he has scratched out one word to substitute another. A man intending anything desperate would not have stopped to scratch out a word, he would have put his pen through it, or left it!' That was very sagacious, but the poor young man was very ill, and the doctor brought a bad report of him to the house. She suddenly said, 'We must go away, go away for some time; he will get well when we are gone.' It was as she said it would be; her going away set his mind at rest, and he began to recover. In the end he married somebody else, and what became of him I forget, though I think she told me more about him.

There was another man whom she had allowed to fall in love, and never tried to hinder him, though she refused to marry him. After many years she saw him again. He was then an elderly man; had made a fortune, and stood high as a county gentleman. He was happily married, and the father of a family. But one day he was driving her somewhere, and he slackened the pace to a walk and said: 'I once thought I would have broken my heart about you, but I think my attachment to you was the best thing that ever happened to me: it made me a better man. It is a part of my life that stands out by itself and belongs to nothing else. I have heard of you from time to time, and I know what a brilliant lot yours has been, and I have felt glad that you were in your rightful place, and I felt glad that I had suffered for your sake, and I have sometimes thought that if I had known I would not have tried to turn you into any other path.' This, as well as I can render it, is the sense of what he said gravely and gently, and I admired it very much when she told me: but it seems to me that it was *much* better as she told it to me. Nobody could help loving her, and nobody but was the better for doing so. She had the gift of calling forth the best qualities that were in people.

I don't know at what period she knew Irving, but he loved her, and wrote letters and poetry (very true and touching): but there had been some vague understanding with another person, not a definite engagement, and she insisted that he must keep to it and not go back from what had once been spoken. There had been just then some trial, and a great scandal about a Scotch minister who had broken an engagement of marriage: and she could not bear that the shadow of any similar reproach should be cast on him. Whether if she had cared for him very much she could or would have insisted on such punctilious honour, she did not know herself; but anyhow that is what she did. After Irving's marriage, years afterwards, there was not much intercourse between them; the whole course of his life had changed.

. . . .

I do not know in what year she married, nor anything connected with her marriage. I believe that she brought no money or very little at her marriage. Her father had left everything to her, but she made it over to her mother, and only had what her mother gave her. Of course people thought she was making a dreadfully bad match; they only saw the *outside* of the thing; but she had faith in her own insight. Long afterwards, when the world began to admire her husband, at the time he delivered the Lectures on 'Hero Worship,' she gave a little half-scornful laugh, and said 'they tell me things as if they were new that I found out years ago.' She knew the power of help and sympathy that lay in her; and she knew she had strength to stand the struggle and pause before he was recognised. She told me that she resolved that he should never write for money, only when he wished it, when he had a message in his heart to deliver, she determined that she would make whatever money he gave her answer for all needful purposes; and she was ever faithful to this resolve. She bent her faculties to economical problems, and she managed so well that comfort was never absent from her house, and no one looking on could have guessed whether they were rich or poor. Until she married, she had never minded household things; but she took them up when necessary, and accomplished them as she accomplished everything else she undertook, well and gracefully. Whatever she had to do she did it with a peculiar personal grace that gave a charm to the most prosaic details. No one who in later years saw her lying on the sofa in broken health, and languor, would guess the amount of energetic hard work she had done in her life. She could do everything and anything, from mending the Venetian blinds to making picture-frames or trimming a dress. Her judgment in all literary matters was thoroughly good; she could get to the very core of a thing, and her insight was like witchcraft.

Some of her stories about her servants in the early times were very amusing, but she could make a story about a broom-handle and make it entertaining. Here are some things she told me about their residence at Craigenputtock.

At first on their marriage they lived in a small pretty house in Edinburgh called Cromlech Bank [*sic*]. Whilst there her first experience of the difficulties of housekeeping began. She had never been accustomed to anything of the kind; but Mr. Carlyle was obliged to be very careful in diet. She learned to make bread partly from recollecting how she had seen an old servant set to work; and she used to say that the *first* time she attempted brown bread, it was with awe. She mixed the dough and saw it rise; and then she put it into the oven, and sat down to watch the oven-door with feelings like Benvenuto Cellini's when he watched his Perseus put into the furnace. She did not feel too sure what it would come out! But it came out a beautiful crusty loaf, very light and sweet; and proud of it she was. The first time she tried a pudding, she went into the kitchen and locked the door on herself, having got the servant out of the road. It was to be a suet pudding—not just a common suet pudding but something special—and it was good, being made with care by weight and measure with exactness. Whilst they were in Edinburgh they knew everybody worth knowing; Lord Jeffrey was a great admirer of hers, and an old friend; Chalmers, Guthrie, and many others. But Mr. Carlyle's health and work needed perfect quietness and absolute solitude. They went to live at the end of two years at Craigenputtock—a lonely farmhouse belonging to Mrs. Welsh, her mother. A house was attached to the farm, beside the regular farmhouse. The farm was let; and Mr. and Mrs. Carlyle lived in the house, which was separated from the farm-yard and buildings by a yard. A garden and outbuildings were attached to it. They had a cow, and a horse, and poultry. They were fourteen miles from Dumfries, which was the nearest town. The country was uninhabited for miles round, being all moorland, with rocks, and a high steep green hill behind the house. She used to say that the stillness was almost awful, and that when she walked out she could hear the sheep nibbling the grass, and they used to look at her with innocent wonder. The letters came in once a week, which was as often as they sent into Dumfries. All she needed had to be sent for there or done without. One day she had desired the farm-servant to bring her a bottle of yeast. The weather was very hot. The man came back looking scared; and without the yeast. He said doggedly that he would do anything lawful for her; but he begged she would never ask him to fetch such an uncanny thing again, for it had just worked and worked till it flew away with the bottle! When asked where it was, he replied, 'it had a' just gane into the ditch, and he had left it there!'

Lord Jeffrey and his family came out twice to visit her; expecting, as he said, to find that she had hanged herself upon a door-nail. But she did no such thing. It was undoubtedly a great strain upon her nerves from which she never entirely recovered; but she lived in the solitude cheerfully and willingly for six years. It was a much greater trial than it sounds at first; for Mr. Carlyle was engrossed in his work, and had to give himself up to it entirely. It was work and thought with which he had to wrestle with all his might to bring out the truths he felt, and to give them due utterance. It was his life that his work required, and it was his life that he gave, and she gave her life too, which alone made such life possible for him. All those who have been strengthened by Mr. Carlyle's written words—and they have been wells of life to more than have been numbered—owe to her a debt of gratitude no less than to him. If she had not devoted her life to him, he could not have worked; and if she had let the care for money weigh on him he could not have given his best strength to teach. Hers was no holiday task of pleasant companionship; she had to live beside him in silence that the people in the world might profit by his full strength and receive his message. She lived to see his work completed, and to see him recognised in full for what he is, and for what he has done.

Sometimes she could not send to Dumfries for butcher's meat; and then she was reduced to her poultry. She had a peculiar breed of very long-legged hens, and she used to go into the yard amongst them with a long stick and point out those that were to be killed, feeling, she said, like Fouquier Tinville pricking down his victims.

One hard winter her servant, Grace, asked leave to go home to see her parents; there was some sort of a fair held in her village. She went and was to return at night. The weather was bad and she did not return. The next morning there was nothing for it but for her to get up to light the fires and prepare breakfast. The house had beautiful and rather elaborate steel grates; it seemed a pity to let them rust, so she cleaned them carefully, and then looked round for wood to kindle the fire. There was none in the house; it all lay in a little outhouse across the yard. On trying to open the door, she found it was frozen beyond her power to open it, so Mr. Carlyle had to be roused; it took all his strength, and when opened a drift of snow six feet high fell into the hall! Mr. Carlyle had to make a path to the wood-house, and bring over a supply of wood and coal; after which he left her to her own resources.

The fire at length made, the breakfast had to be prepared; but it had to be raised from the foundation. The bread had to be made, the butter to be churned, and the coffee ground. All was at last accomplished, and the breakfast was successful! After breakfast she went about the work of the house, as there was no chance of the servant being able to return. The work fell into its natural routine. Mr. Carlyle always kept a supply of wood ready; he cut it, and piled it ready for her use inside the house; and he fetched the water, and did things she had not the strength to do. The poor cow was her greatest perplexity. She could continue to get hay down to feed it, but she had never in her life milked a cow. The first day the servant of the farmer's wife, who lived at the end of the yard, milked it for her willingly, but the next day Mrs. Carlyle heard the poor cow making an uncomfortable noise; it had not been milked. She went herself to the byre, and took the pail and sat down on the milking stool and began to try to milk the cow. It was not at first easy; but at last she had the delight of hearing the milk trickle into the can. She said she felt quite proud of her success; and talked to the cow like a human creature. The snow continued to lie thick and heavy on the ground, and it was impossible for her maid to return. Mrs. Carlyle got on easily with all the housework, and kept the whole place bright and clean except the large kitchen or house place, which grew to need scouring very much. At length she took courage to attack it. Filling up two large pans of hot water, she knelt down and began to scrub; having made a clean place round the large arm-chair by the fireside, she called Mr. Carlyle and installed him with his pipe to watch her progress. He regarded her beneficently, and gave her from time to time words of encouragement. Half the large floor had been successfully cleansed, and she felt anxious of making a good ending, when she heard a gurgling sound. For a moment or two she took no notice, but it increased and there was a sound of something falling upon the fire, and instantly a great black thick stream came down the chimney, pouring like a flood along the floor, taking precisely the lately cleaned portion first in its course, and extinguishing the fire. It was too much; she burst into tears. The large fire, made up to heat the water, had melted the snow on the top of the chimney, it came down mingling with the soot, and worked destruction to the kitchen floor. All that could be done was to dry up the flood. She had no heart to recommence her task. She rekindled the fire and got tea ready. That same night her maid came back, having done the impossible to get home. She clasped Mrs. Carlyle in her arms, crying and laughing, saying 'Oh, my dear mistress, my dear mistress, I dreamed ye were deed!'

During their residence at Craigenputtock, she had a good little horse, called 'Harry,' on which she sometimes rode long distances. She was an excellent and fearless horsewoman, and went about like the women used to do before carriages were invented. One day she received news that Lord Jeffrey and his family, with some visitors, were coming. The letter only arrived the day they were expected (for letters only came in one day in the week). She mounted 'Harry' and galloped off to Dumfries to get what was needed and galloped back, and was all ready and dressed to receive her visitors with no trace of her thirty-mile ride except the charming history she made of it. She said that 'Harry' understood all was needed of him.

She had a long and somewhat anxious ride at another time. Mr. Carlyle had gone to London, leaving her to finish winding up affairs at Craigenputtock and to follow him. The last day came. She got the money out of the bank at Dumfries, dined with a friend, and mounted her horse to ride to Ecclefechan, where she was to stay for a day or two. Whether she paid no attention to the road or did not know it I don't know; but she *lost* her way: and at dusk found herself entering Dumfries from the *other side*, having made a circuit. She alighted at the friend's house where she had dined, to give her horse a rest. She had some tea herself, and then mounted again to proceed on her journey, fearing that those to whom she was going would be alarmed if she did not appear. This time she made sure she was on the right tack. It was growing dusk, and at a joining of two roads she came upon a party of men half-tipsy, coming from a fair. They accosted her, and asked where she was going, and would she come along with them? She was rather frightened, for she had a good deal of money about her, so she imitated a broad country dialect, and said their road was not hers, and that she had 'a gey piece to ride before she got to Annan.' She whipped her horse, and took the other road, thinking she could easily return to the right track; but she had a ain lost her way and, seeing a house with a light in the lower storey, she rode up the avenue which led to it. Some women-servants had got up early, or rather late at night, to begin their washing. She knocked at the window. At first they thought it was one of their sweethearts; but when they saw a lady on a horse they thought it a ghost. After a while she got them to listen to her, and when she told them her tale they were vehement in their sympathy, and would have had her come in to refresh herself. They gave her a cup of their tea, and one of them came with her to the gate, and set her face towards the right road. She had actually come back to within a mile of Dumfries once more! The church clocks struck twelve as she set out a third time, and it was after two o'clock in the morning before she arrived, dead tired, she and her horse too, at Ecclefechan; where however she had long since been given up. The inmates had gone to bed, and it was long before she could make them hear. After a day or two of repose, she proceeded to join Mr. Carlyle in London.

At first they lived in lodgings with some people who were very kind to them and became much attached to her. They looked upon her as a superior being, of another order, to themselves. The children were brought up to think of her as a sort of fairy lady. One day, a great many years afterwards, when I had come to live in London, it was my birthday, and we resolved to celebrate it 'by doing something;' and at last we settled that she should take me to see the daughter of the people she used to lodge with, who had been an affectionate attendant upon her, and who was now very well married, and an extremely happy woman. Mrs. Carlyle said it was a good omen to go and see 'a happy woman' on such a day! So she and I, and her dog 'Nero,' who accompanied her wherever she went, set off to Dalston where the 'happy woman' lived. I forget her name, except that she was called '*Eliza*.' It was washing day, and the husband was absent; but I remember a pleasant-looking kind woman, who gave us a nice tea, and rejoiced over Mrs. Carlyle, and said she had brought up her children in the hope of seeing her some day. She lived in a house in a row, with little gardens before them. We saw the children, who were like others; and we went home by omnibus; and we had enjoyed our little outing; and Mrs. Carlyle gave me a pretty lace collar, and Bohemian-glass vase, which is still unbroken. . . .

Miss Jewsbury's Account of the Burning of the Candles

'On that miserable night, when we were preparing to receive her, Mrs. Warren came to me and said, that one time when she was very ill, she said to her, that when the last had come, she was to go upstairs into the closet of the spare room and there she would find two wax candles wrapt in paper, and that those were to be lighted, and burned. She said that after she came to live in London, she wanted to give a party. Her mother was staying with her. Her mother wished everything to be very nice, and went out and bought candles and confectionery: and set out a table, and lighted up the room quite splendidly, and called her to come and see it, when all was prepared. *She* was angry; she said people would say she was extravagant, and would ruin her husband. She took away two of the candles and some of the cakes. Her mother was hurt, and began to weep [I remember the "soirée" well; heard nothing of *this*!—T. C.] *She* was pained at once at what she had done; she tried to comfort her, and was dreadfully sorry. She took the candles and wrapped them up, and put them where they could be easily found. We found them and lighted them, and did as she had desired.

G. E. J.'

What a strange, beautiful, sublime and almost terrible little action; silently resolved on, and kept silent from all the Earth, for perhaps twenty-four years! I never heard a whisper of it, and yet see it to be *true*. The visit must have been about 1837; I remember the 'soirée' right well; the resolution, bright as with heavenly tears and lightning, was probably formed on her mother's death, February 1842. My radiant One! Must question Warren the first time I have heart (*29th May* 1866).

I have had from Mrs. Warren a clear narrative (shortly after the above date). Geraldine's report is perfectly true; fact with Mrs. Warren occurred in February or March 1866, 'perhaps a month before you went to Edinburgh, sir.' I was in the house, it seems, probably asleep upstairs, or gone out for my walk, evening about eight o'clock. My poor Darling was taken with some bad fit ('nausea,' and stomach misery perhaps), and had rung for Mrs. Warren, by whom, with some sip of warm liquid, and gentle words, she was soon gradually relieved. Being very grateful and still very miserable and low, she addressed Mrs. Warren as above, 'When the last has come, Mrs. Warren;' and gave her, with brevity, a statement of the case, and exacted her promise; which the other, with cheering counter-words ('Oh, madam, what is all this! you will see me die first!') hypothetically gave. All this was wiped clean away before I got in; I seem to myself to half recollect one evening, when she did complain of 'nausea so habitual now,' and looked extremely miserable, while I sat at tea (pour it out she always would, herself drinking only hot water, oh heavens!). The candles burnt for two whole nights, says Mrs. Warren (*24th July* 1866).

I end these 'stories told by herself,' not because there are no more. They give some slight indication of the courage and nobleness and fine qualities which lay in her who is gone. Very few women so truly great come into the world at all; and no two like her at the same time. Those who were her friends will only go on feeling their loss and their sorrow more and more every day of their own lives.

G. E. J.

Chelsea, May 20, 1866.

DEAR GERALDINE,—Few or none of these Narratives are correct in all the details; some of them, in almost all the details, are *in*correct. I have not *read* carefully beyond a certain point which is marked on the margin. Your *recognition* of the *character* is generally true and faithful; little of *portraiture* in it that satisfies me. On the whole, all tends to the *mythical*; it is very strange how much of mythical there already here is!—

As Lady Lothian set you on writing, it seems hard that she should not see what you have written: but I wish you to take *her word of honour* that none else shall; and my earnest request to you is that, directly *from* her Ladyship, you will bring the Book to me, and consign it to my keeping.

No need that an idle-gazing world should know my lost Darling's History, or mine;—nor *will* they ever, they may depend upon it! One fit service, and one only, *they* can do to Her or to Me: cease speaking of us, through all Eternity, as soon as they conveniently can.—Affectionately yours,

T. CARLYLE.

Chelsea, May 22, 1866.

25 *May* 1866. Geraldine returns me this little Book of Myths, *un*shown to anybody, and to be my own henceforth. I do not yet burn it; as I have done her kind and respectful Letter ('Narratives long ago, on our first acquaintance' etc. etc. and fermenting and agglomerating in my mind ever since!)—in fact, there is a certain mythical truth, in all or most parts of the poor scribble, and it may *wait* its doom, or execution. That of young lovers, especially that of *flirting*, is much exaggerated: if 'flirt' mean one who tries to inspire love without feeling it, I do not think she ever was a flirt. But she was very charming, full of grace, talent, clear insight, playful humour, and also of honest dignity and pride; and not a few

young fools, of her own or perhaps a slightly better station, made offers to her,—which, sometimes to their high temporary grief and astonishment, were decisively rejected. The most serious-looking of these affairs, was that of George Rennie, the Junior (not Heir but *Cadet*) of *Phantassie*, Nephew of the first Engineer Rennie; a clever, decisive, very ambitious, but quite *un*melodious young fellow; whom we knew afterwards here as sculptor, as M.P. (for a while),—finally as retired Governor of the Falkland Islands, in which latter character he died here, seven or eight years ago. She knew him thoroughly; had never loved him, but respected various qualities in him, and naturally had some peculiar interest in him to the last. In his final time he used to come pretty often down to us here, and was well worth talking to on his Falkland or other experiences: a man of sternly sound common-sense (so called), of strict veracity; who much contemned imbecility, falsity, or nonsense wherever met with; had swallowed manfully his many bitter disappointments, and silently awaited death itself for the last year or more (as I could notice), with a fine honest stoicism always complete.—My poor Jane hurried to his House; and was there for three days, zealously assisting the Widow.

The Wooer who would needs *die* for want of success, was one Fyfe M.D., an extremely conceited, limited, strutting little creature, who well deserved all he got or more. The end of him had something of tragedy in it, but is not worth recording.—*Dods* is the 'Peasant schoolfellow's' name; about seven or eight years *her* senior, son of a Nurseryman; now rich abundantly, Banker, etc. etc.; and an honest and kindly, though clumsy prosaic man. Never uttered, or could have had the remotest hope or possibility to profit by uttering, his heavy thoughts (age 17–20), of the bright young Fairy (age 10–12).

The Story of her being taken as a child of perhaps seven or eight, to drive with her Father has some truth in it; but consists of two stories rolled into one. Child of seven or eight, 'with watch forgotten,' etc., was to the 'Press Inn' (then a noted place; and to her an ever-memorable expedition beside a

Father almost her Divinity). But drive second, almost still more memorable, was for an afternoon or several hours, as a young girl of eighteen,—over some *district* of her Father's duties; she waiting in the carriage, unnoticed, while he made his visits. The usually tacit man, tacit especially about his bright Daughter's gifts and merits, took to talking with her that day, in a style quite new; told her she was a good girl, capable of being useful and precious to him and to the circle she would live in; that she must summon her utmost judgment and seriousness to choose her path, and *be* what he expected of her; that he did not think she had ever yet seen the Life-Partner that would be worthy of her (Rennie's or anybody's name he did not mention, I think);—in short that he expected her to be wise, as well as good-looking and good. All this in a tone and manner which filled her poor little heart with surprise, and a kind of sacred joy; coming from the man she of all men revered. Often she told me about this. For it was her last talk with him: on the morrow, perhaps that evening, certainly within a day or two, he caught from some poor old woman patient (who, I think, recovered of it) a typhus fever; which, under injudicious treatment, killed him in three or four days (September 1819):—and drowned the world for her in the very blackness of darkness. In effect, it was her first sorrow; and her greatest of all. It broke her health, permanently, within the next two or three years; and, in a sense, almost broke her heart. A Father so mourned and loved I have never seen: to the end of her life, his title even to me was 'He' and 'Him;' not above twice or thrice, quite in late years, did she ever mention (and then in what a sweet slow tone!), 'my Father:' nay, I have a kind of notion (beautiful to me and sad exceedingly) she was never as happy again after that sunniest youth of hers, as in the last eighteen months, and especially the last *two weeks* of her life; *when*, after wild rain-deluges and black tempests many, the *sun* shone out again, for *another's* sake, with full mild brightness, taking 'sweet farewell.' Oh it is beautiful to me; and oh it is humbling; and it is sad! Where was my Jeannie's *peer* in this world? and she fell to me, and I *could* not screen her from the bitterest distresses! God pity and forgive me; my own burden, too, might have broken a stronger back,—had not she been so loyal and loving. Enough to-day.

May 26, Saturday. (*Gone* five weeks, ah me!).—The Geraldine accounts of her Childhood are substantially correct; but without the light melodious clearness, and charm of a Fairy Tale all true, which my lost One used to give them in talking to me. She was fond of talking about her childhood; nowhere in the world did I ever hear of one more beautiful,—all sunny to her and to me, to our last years together.

That of running on the parapets of the Nungate Bridge (John Knox's old suburb), I recollect well; that of the boy with the bloody nose; many adventures about skating and leaping; that of '*Penna, pennæ*' from below the table is already in print, through Mrs. Oliphant's *Life of Irving*[1] (a loyal and clear, but feeble kind of Book, popular in late years). In all things she strove to 'be a Boy' in education; and yet by natural guidance never ceased to be the prettiest and gracefullest of little girls. Full of intelligence, of veracity, vivacity, and bright curiosity. She went into all manner of shops and workshops that were accessible; eager to see and understand what was going on. One morning (perhaps in her third or fourth year) she went into the shop of a barber, on the opposite side of the street,—*back* from which by a narrow entrance, was her own nice, elegant, quiet home. Barber's shop was empty; my Jeannie went in, silently sat down on a bench at the wall, old barber giving her a kind glance, but no word. Presently a customer came in; was soaped and lathered, in silence mainly or altogether; was getting diligently scraped and shaved, my Bonny little Bird, as attentive as possible, and all in perfect silence. Customer at length said, in a pause of the razor, 'How is John So-and-so now?' 'He's deid' (*dead*), replied Barber in a rough hollow voice, and instantly pushed on with business again. The bright little child burst into tears, and hurried out. This she told me, not half a year ago. I never saw a picture lovelier than had grown in me of her childhood.

[1] Published in 1864.

Her first school teacher was Edward Irving;[1] who also gave her private lessons in Latin etc., and became an intimate of the family; it was from him (probably in 1818) that I first heard of her Father and her; some casual mention, the loving and reverential tone of which had struck me. Of the Father he spoke always as of one of the wisest, truest, and most dignified of men; of her as a paragon of gifted young girls. Far away from me, both, and objects of distant reverence and unattainable longing, at that time! The Father, whom I never saw, died next year (Sept. 1819); her I must have seen first, I think in June 1821. Sight for ever memorable to me:—I looked up at the windows of the old room, in the desolate moonlight of my *last* visit to Haddington (*five weeks ago*, come Wednesday next); and the old summer dusk, and that bright pair of eyes, inquiringly fixed on me (as I noticed, for a moment), came up clear as yesterday, all drowned in woes and death.

Her second teacher (Irving's successor) was a Rev. James Brown, who died in India, whom also I slightly knew. The school, I believe, was and is at the hither, western, end of the Nungate Bridge; and grew famed in the neighbourhood by Irving's new methods and managements,—adopted as far as might be by Brown. A short furlong or so along paved streets, from her Father's house. Thither daily at an early hour (perhaps eight A.M. in summer) might be seen my little Jeannie tripping nimbly and daintily along; her little satchel in hand; dressed by her mother (who had a great talent that way) in tasteful simplicity,—neat bit of pelisse ('light blue,' sometimes) fastened with black belt; dainty little cap, perhaps little *beaver*kin ('with flap turned up') and I think once at least with modest 'little plume in it.' Fill that figure with *electric* intellect, ditto love, and generous vivacity of all kinds; where in Nature will you find a prettier?

At home was opulence (*without* waste), elegance, good sense, silent practical affection and manly wisdom; from thres-

[1] Preacher and visionary. Carlyle's greatest friend until his death in 1834 at the age of forty-two. There is a long memoir of Irving in the *Reminiscences*.

hold to roof-tree, no paltriness or unveracity admitted into it. I often told her how very beautiful her childhood was to me,—so authentic-looking withal, in her charmingly naïve and humorous way of telling;—and that she must have been 'the prettiest little Jenny Spinner' (Scotch name for a long-winged, long-legged, extremely bright and airy insect) that was dancing on the summer rays in her time. More enviable lot than all this was I cannot imagine to myself in any house high or low,—in the *higher* and highest still less than the other kind.

Once, I cannot say in what year, nor for how many months, —but perhaps about six or eight, her age perhaps eight or nine,—her mother thinking it good, she was sent away to another House of the Town, to *board* with some kind of Ex-Governess Person, who had married some Ex-Military ditto, and professed to be able to educate young ladies and form their *manners* ('better,' thought the mother, 'than with nothing but *men* as here at home!')—and in this place, with a Miss Something, a friend and playmate of like age, she was fixed down, for a good few months, and suffered, she and the companion manifold disgust, even hardships, even want of proper food; wholly without complaining (too proud and loyal for that); till it was, by some accident, found out, and instantly put an end to. This was the little cup of bitter; which, I suppose, sweetened into new sweetness all the other happy years of her home.—Two child *anecdotes* I will mark, as ready at this moment:

Father and mother returning from some visit (probably to Nithsdale) along with her (age, say four), at the Black Bull, Edinburgh, were ordering dinner. Waiter, rather solemn personage, inquired, 'And what will little Missie eat?' 'A roasted bumm bee' (*humming* or field bee), answered little Missie.

'Mamma, wine makes cosy!' said the little Naturalist once at home (year *before* perhaps), while sipping a drop of wine Mamma had given her.

[1][One of the prettiest stories was of the child's first Ball,

[1] This passage in square brackets is from a loose sheet written in 1868, forming part of a proposed introduction to the *Letters and Memorials of Jane Welsh Carlyle.*

'Dancing School Ball;' her first public appearance, as it were, on the theatre of the world. Of this, in the daintiest style of kind mockery, I often heard, and have the general image still vivid; but have lost the express details, or rather, in my ignorance of such things, never completely understood the details. How the evening was so great; all the higher public there, especially the maternal or paternal sections of it, to see their children dance; and Jeannie Welsh, probably then about six, had been selected to perform some *Pas seul*, beautiful and difficult, the jewel of the evening, and was privately anxious in her little heart to do it well; how she was dressed to perfection, with elegance, with simplicity, and at the due hour was carried over in a clothes-basket (streets being muddy and no carriage), and landed safe, pretty silks and pumps uninjured. Through the Ball everything went well and smoothly, nothing to be noted till the *Pas seul* came. My little woman (with a look that I can still fancy) appeared upon the scene, stood waiting for the music; music began, but alas, alas, it was the wrong music, impossible to dance that *Pas seul* to it! She shook her little head, looked or made some sign of distress. Music ceased, took counsel, scraped, began again; again wrong, hopelessly; the *Pas seul* flatly impossible. Beautiful little Jane, alone against the world, forsaken by the music but not by her presence of mind, plucked up her little skirt, flung it over her head, and curtseying in that veiled manner, withdrew from the adventure amidst general applause and admiration, as I could well believe.]

The second (properly the third) of my anecdotes is not easily intelligible except to myself: Old Walter Welsh, her maternal Grandfather, was a most picturesque, peculiar, generous-hearted, hot-tempered, abrupt and impatient old man. I guess she might be about six; and was with her mother on a visit, I know not whether at Caplegill (Moffat Water), or at Strathmilligan or Durisdeer (Nithsdale, both these; Templand was long after): old Walter, who was of few words though of very lively thought and insight, had a *burr* in pronouncing his *r*, and spoke in *old* style generally. He had taken little Jeannie out to ride on a quiet little pony; very pleasant winding ride; and at length, when far enough, old Walter said, Now we will go back by So-and-so, 'to vary the scene' (to vah-ry, properly 'to vah-*chy*' the s*ha*ne). Home at dinner, the company asked her, 'Where did you ride to, Pen?' (*Pen* was her little name there, from Paternal Grandfather's house, 'Penfillan,' to distinguish her from the other *Welshes* of Walter's household). We rode to *so*, then to *so*, answered she, punctually; then from *so*, returned by *so* 'to vah-chy the shane!' At which, I suppose, the old man himself burst into his cheeriest laugh at the mimicry of tiny little Pen.— —'Mamma, oh mamma, don't expos*ie me!*' exclaimed she once, not yet got quite the length of *speaking*, when her mother for some kind purpose was searching under her clothes.—

I will write of all this no further: the beauty of it is so steeped to me in pain. Why do I *write* at all, for that matter? Can *I* ever forget? And is not all this appointed by me rigorously to the *fire*? Somehow it solaces me to *have* written it;—and tomorrow, probably, I shall fill out these two remaining pages.[1] Ah me.—She had written at one time something of her own early life; but she gave up, and burnt it. . . . She wrote at various times in Note-books; refusing all sight of them even to me: but she has destroyed nearly every vestige of them;—one little Book, consisting of curious excerpts and jottings *not* biographic (in which she would often look practically for *Addresses*, Street and number as one item), is all that remains,—that I do not mean to burn.

Geraldine's account of *Comley Bank*[2] and Life at Edinburgh, is extremely mythic; we did grow to 'know everybody of mark,' or might have grown; but nobody except Jeffrey[3] seemed to either of us a valuable acquisition. Jeffrey much

[1] Of the Note-book in which Miss Jewsbury had written.

[2] 21 Comley Bank, Edinburgh, was the Carlyles' first home after their marriage.

[3] Francis, Lord Jeffrey, editor of the *Edinburgh Review*, and Lord Advocate in the Whig government of 1831. A separate memoir is devoted to him in the *Reminiscences*.

admired her, and was a pleasant phenomenon to both of us. . . . Wilson, a far *bigger* man, I could have loved, or fancied I could; but he would not let me try,—being already deep in *whisky-punch*, poor fellow, and apprehensive I might think less of him the better I knew him.—We had a little tea-party (never did I see a smaller or a frugaller, with the tenth part of the human grace and brightness in it) once a week;—the 'brown coffee-pot,' the feeble talk of dilettante——, pretty silly —— etc.; ah me, how she knit up all that into a shining thing! . . . Oh she was noble, very noble, in that early as in all other periods; and made the ugliest and dullest into something beautiful! I look back on it as if through rainbows, the bit of sunshine hers, the tears my own.

I was latterly beginning also to get into note and employment. 'If I could recover health!' said I always, with which view and for the sake of cheapness we moved (in May 1828) to Craigenputtock; she cheerily assenting, though our plans were surely somewhat helpless.

. . . .

May 29. We must have gone to Craigenputtock[1] early in May 1828: I remember passing our furniture carts (my Father's carts from Scotsbrig, conducted by my two farming Brothers) somewhere about Elvanfoot, as the coach brought *us* two along. I don't remember our going up to Craigenputtock (a day or two after), but do well remember what a bewildering *heap* it all was for some time after.

Geraldine's *Craigenputtock* stories are more mythical than any of the rest. Each consists of two or three, in confused exaggerated state, rolled with new confusion into one, and given wholly to *her*, when perhaps they were mainly some servant's in whom she was concerned. That of the kitchen door, which could not be closed again on the snowy morning, etc., that is a fact very visible to me yet; and how I, coming down to light my pipe, found Grace Macdonald (our Edinburgh servant, and a most clever and complete one) in tears and despair, with a

[1] The isolated farm on the Scottish moors where the Carlyles lived from May 1828 until they moved to London in 1834.

stupid farm-servant endeavouring vainly by main force to pull the door to, which, as it had a frame round it, sill and all, for keeping out the wind, could not be shut except by somebody from within (me, *e.g.*) who would first clear out the snow at the sill, and then, with his best speed, shut; which I easily did. The washing of the kitchen floor etc. (of which I can remember nothing) must have been years distant, under some quite other servant, and was probably as much of a joyous half-frolic as of anything else. I can remember very well her coming in to me, late at night (eleven or so), with her *first loaf*, looking mere triumph and quizzical gaiety: 'See!' The loaf was excellent, only the crust a little burnt; and she compared herself to Cellini and his *Perseus*, of whom we had been reading. From that hour we never wanted excellent bread. In fact, the saving charm of her life at Craigenputtock, which to another young lady of her years might have been so gloomy and vacant, was that of conquering the innumerable Practical Problems that had arisen for her there;—all of which, I think all, she triumphantly mastered. Dairy, poultry-yard, piggery; I remember one exquisite pig, which we called *Fixie* (*Quintus Fixlein* of Jean Paul), and such a little ham of it as could not be equalled. Her cow gave 24 quarts of milk daily in the two or three best months of summer; and such cream, and such butter (though oh, she had such a problem with that; owing to a bitter herb among the grass, not known of till long after by my heroic Darling, and she triumphed over that too!). That of milking with her own little hand, I think, could never have been *necessary*, even by accident (plenty of milkmaids within call), and I conclude must have had a spice of frolic or *adventure* in it, for which she had abundant spirit. Perfection of housekeeping was her clear and speedy attainment in that new scene. Strange how she made the Desert blossom for herself and me there; what a fairy palace she had made of that wild moorland home of the poor man! In my life I have seen no human intelligence that so genuinely pervaded every fibre of the human existence it belonged to. From the baking of a loaf, or the darning of a stocking, up to comporting herself in the highest scenes, or most intricate emergencies, all was insight, veracity, graceful success (if you could judge it),—*fidelity* to insight of the fact given.

We had trouble with servants, with many paltry elements and objects; and were very poor: but I do not think our days there were sad,—and certainly not *hers* in especial, but mine rather. We read together at night,—one winter, through *Don Quixote* in the original; Tasso in ditto had come before,—but that did not last very long. I was diligently writing and reading there; wrote most of 'the *Miscellanies*' there, for Foreign, Edinburgh, etc. Reviews (obliged to keep *several* strings to my bow),—and took serious thought about every part of every one of them: after finishing an Article, we used to get on horseback, or mount into our soft old Gig, and drive away, either to her Mother's (Templand, fourteen miles off), or to my Father and Mother's (Scotsbrig, seven- or six-and-thirty miles);—the pleasantest journeys I ever made, and the pleasantest visits. Stay perhaps three days; hardly ever more than four; then back to work and silence. My Father she particularly loved, and recognised all the grand rude worth and immense originality that lay in him. Her demeanour at Scotsbrig, throughout in fact, was like herself, unsurpassable; and took captive all those true souls, from oldest to youngest, who by habit and type might have been so utterly foreign to her. At Templand or there, our presence always made a sunshiny time. To Templand we sometimes rode on an evening, to return next day early enough for something of work: this was charming generally. Once I remember we had come by Barjarg, not by Auldgarth (Bridge); and were riding, the Nith then in flood, from Penfillan or Penpoint neighbourhood: she was fearlessly following or accompanying me; and there remained only one little arm to cross, which did look a thought uglier, but gave me no disturbance, when a farmer figure was seen on the farther bank or fields, earnestly waving and signalling (could not be *heard* for the floods); but for whom we should surely have had some accident, who knows how bad! Never rode that water again, at least never in flood I am sure.

May 30. We were not unhappy at Craigenputtock; perhaps these were our happiest days. Useful, continual labour, essentially successful; that makes even the moor green. I found I could do fully *twice* as much work in a given time there, as with my best effort was possible in London,—such the interruptions etc. Once, in the winter time, I remember counting that for three months, there had not any stranger, not even a beggar, called at Craigenputtock door. In summer we had sparsely visitors, now and then her Mother, or my own, once my Father; who never before had been *so far* from his birthplace as when here (and yet 'knew the world' as few of his time did, so well had he looked at what he did see!). At Auldgarth Brig, which he had assisted to build when a lad of fifteen, and which was the beginning of all good to him, and to all his Brothers (and to *me*), his emotion, after fifty-five years, was described to me as strong, conspicuous and *silent.* He delighted us, especially her, at Craigenputtock; himself evidently thinking of his *latter end*, in a most intense awe-stricken, but also quiet and altogether human way. Since my Sister Margaret's death, he had been steadily sinking in strength, though we did not then notice it.— —On the 12th of August (for the *grouse's* sake) Robert Welsh, her uncle, was pretty certain to be there; with a tag-raggery of Dumfries Writers, Dogs, etc. etc., whom, though we liked him very well, even I, and much more *she* who had to provide, find beds, etc., felt to be a nuisance. I got at last into the way of riding off, for some visit or the like, on August 12th: and unless 'Uncle Robert' came in person, she also would answer, 'not at home.'

An interesting relation to Goethe had likewise begun in Comley Bank first, and now went on increasing: 'Boxes from Weimar' (and 'to,' at least once or twice) were from time to time a most sunny event;—I remember her making for Ottilie a beautiful Highland Bonnet (bright blue velvet, with silvered thistle etc.), which gave plenty of pleasure on both hands. The *Sketch* of Craigenputtock was taken by G. Moir, Advocate (ultimately Sheriff, Professor, etc., 'little Geordie Moir' as we called him), who was once and no more with us. The visit of

Emerson from Concord, and our quiet night of clear fine talk, was also very pretty to both of us. The Jeffreys came twice, expressly, and once we went to Dumfries by appointment to meet them in passing. Their correspondence was there a steadily enlivening element. One of the visits, I forget whether first or last, but from Hazlitt, in London, there came to Jeffrey a *death-bed letter* one of the days, and instead of '£10,' £50 went by return: Jeffrey, one of the nights, young Laird of Stroquhan present, was, what with mimicry of speakers, what with other cleverness and sprightliness, the most brilliantly amusing creature I have ever chanced to see. One time we went to Craigcrook, and returned their visit;—and, as I can *now* see, staid at least *a week too long*. His health was beginning to break; he and I had, nightly, long arguments (far *too* frank and equal on my side, I can now see with penitence) about moral matters, perhaps till two or three A.M. He was a most gifted, prompt, ingenious little man (essentially a *Dramatic* Genius, say a melodious Goldoni or more, but made into a Scotch Advocate and Whig); never a deeply serious man. He discovered here, I think, that I *could* not be 'converted,' and that I was of thoughtlessly rugged rustic ways, and faultily irreverent of him (which, alas, I was). The Correspondence became mainly *hers* by degrees; but was, for years after, a cheerful, lively element,—in spite of Reform Bills and Officialities (ruinous to poor Jeffrey's health and comfort) which, before long, supervened. We were at Haddington on that Craigcrook occasion; staid with the Donaldsons at Sunnybank (*hodie* Tenterfield), who were her oldest and dearest friends (*hereditarily* and otherwise) in that region. I well remember the gloom of our arrival back to Craigenputtock: a miserable wet, windy November evening, with the yellow leaves all flying about; and the sound of Brother Alick's stithy[1] (who sometimes amused himself with smithwork, to small purpose), clink-clinking solitary through the blustering element. I said nothing, far was she from ever, in the like case, saying anything!

[1] Alexander Carlyle farmed Craigenputtock, unsuccessfully, for some time.

Indeed I think we at once readjusted ourselves; and went on diligently with the old degree of industry and satisfaction.

'Old Esther,' whose death came, one of our early winters, was a bit of memorability, in that altogether vacant scene. I forget the old woman's surname (perhaps M'George?); but well recall her lumpish heavy figure (lame of a foot), and her honest, quiet, not stupid countenance of mixed ugliness and stoicism. She lived about a mile from us in a poor Cottage of the next Farm (Corson's, of *Nether* Craigenputtock . . .); Esther had been a Laird's Daughter, riding her palfrey at one time; but had gone to wreck, Father and self,—a special 'misfortune' (so they delicately name it) being of Esther's own producing. 'Misfortune,' in the shape ultimately of a solid tall Ditcher, very good to his old mother Esther, had, just before our coming, perished miserably one night on the shoulder of Dunscore Hill (found dead there, next morning); which had driven his poor old mother up to this *thriftier* hut, and silent mode of living, in our moorland part of the Parish. She did not beg; nor had my Jeannie much to have given her of help (perhaps on occasion *milk*, old warm *clothes*, etc.), though always very sorry for her last sad bereavement of the stalwart affectionate Son. I remember one frosty kind of forenoon, while walking meditative to the top of our Hill (now a mass of bare or moorclad whinstone *Crag*, once a woody wilderness, with woody mountain in the middle of it, 'Craigen*puttock*,' or the stone-mountain, 'Craig' of the 'Puttock,'—puttock being a sort of *Hawk*, both in Galloway Speech, and in Shakspeare's old English; 'Hill-Forest of the Puttocks'), now a very bare place, the universal silence was complete, all but one click-clack, heard regularly like a far-off *spondee* or *iambus* rather, 'click-*clack*,' at regular intervals, a great way to my right. No other sound in nature. On looking sharply I discovered it to be old Esther on the highway, crippling along,—towards our house most probably. Poor old soul, thought I; what a desolation; but you *will* meet a kind face too, perhaps! Heaven is over all.

Not long afterwards, poor old Esther sank to bed; deathbed, as my Jane (who had a quick and sure eye in these things) well judged it would be. Sickness did not last above a ten days; my poor Wife zealously assiduous, and with a minimum of fuss or noise. I remember those few poor days; as full of human interest to her (and through her to me) and of a human pity, not painful, but sweet and genuine. She went, walking every morning, especially every night, to arrange the poor bed etc. (nothing but *rudish* hands, rude though kind enough, being about), the poor old woman evidently gratified by it and heart-thankful, and almost to the very *end* giving clear sign of that. Something pathetic in poor old Esther and her exit:—nay, if I rightly bethink me, that 'click-clack' pilgrimage had in fact been a last visit to Craigenputtock with some poor bit of crockery (small gray, lettered butter-plate, which I used to see) 'as a wee *memorandum* o' me, mem, when I am gane!' 'Memorandum' was her word; and I remember the poor little platter for years after. Poor old Esther had awoke, that frosty morning, with a feeling that she would soon die, that 'the bonny Leddy' had been 'unco' guid' to her, and that there was still that 'wee bit memorandum.' Nay, I think she had, or had once had, the remains, or complete *ghost* of a 'fine old riding-habit' once her own, which the curious had seen: but this she had judged it more polite to leave to the Parish. Ah me. *Sunt lachrymæ rerum!*

The gallop to Dumfries and back on 'Harry,' an excellent, well-paced, well-broken loyal little Horse of hers (thirteen hands or so, an exceeding favourite, and her *last*),—thirty good miles of swift canter, at the least,—is a fact; which I well remember, though from home at the moment. Word had come (to *her* virtually, or *properly* perhaps) that the Jeffreys, three and a servant, were to be there, day after tomorrow, perhaps morrow itself; I was at Scotsbrig; nothing ready at all (and such narrow means to get ready anything, my Darling Heroine!). She directly mounted Harry, 'who seemed to know that he must gallop, and faithfully did it;' laid her plans while galloping; ordered everything at Dumfries, sent word to me express; galloped home; and stood victoriously prepared at all points to receive the Jeffreys,—who, I think, were all there on my arrival. The night of her *express* is to me very memorable for its own sake: I had been to Burnswark (visit to good old Graham, and walk of three miles to and three from); it was ten P.M. of a most still and fine night when I arrived at my Father's door; heard him making worship, and stood meditative, gratefully, lovingly, till he had ended; thinking to myself, how good and innocently beautiful and manful on the earth, is all this:—and it was the last time I was ever to hear it. I must have been there twice or oftener [afterwards] in my Father's time; but the sound of his pious *Coleshill* (that was always his tune), pious Psalm and Prayer, I never heard again. With a noble politeness, very noble when I consider, they kept all that in a fine kind of remoteness from us, knowing (and somehow *forgiving* us completely) that we did not think of it quite as they. My Jane's express would come next morning;—and of course I made Larry ply his hoofs.

The *second* ride, in Geraldine, is nearly altogether mythical; being in reality a ride from Dumfries to Scotsbrig (two and a half miles *beyond* 'Ecclefechan,' where none of us ever passed), with *some* loss of road within the last five miles (wrong turn at Hoddam Brig, I guessed), darkness (night-time in May), money, etc.; and 'terror' enough for a commonplace young lady, but little or nothing of real danger,—and terror not an element at all, I fancy, in her courageous mind. Harry I think cannot have been her Horse (half-killed two years before in an *epidemic*, through which *she* nursed him fondly, he once 'kissing her cheek' in gratitude, she always thought) or Harry would have known the road, for we had often ridden and driven it. I was at that time gone to London, in quest of houses.

May 31. My last considerable bit of *Writing* at Craigenputtock was *Sartor Resartus*; done, I think, between January and August 1830[1] (my Sister Margaret had died while it was going on). I well remember, where and how (at Templand one morning) the *germ* of it rose above ground. 'Nine months,' I

[1] Incorrect. See prefatory note to the selection from *Sartor Resartus* in this volume.

used to say, it had cost me in writing. Had the perpetual fluctuation, the uncertainty and unintelligible whimsicality of Review Editors not proved so intolerable, we might have lingered longer at Craigenputtock,—'perfectly left alone, and able to do *more* work, beyond doubt, than elsewhere.' But a Book did seem to promise some *respite* from that, and perhaps further advantages. Teufelsdröckh was ready; and (first days of August [1831]) I decided to make for London. Night before going, how I still remember it! I was lying on my back on the sofa in the drawing-room; she sitting by the table (late at night, packing all done I suppose): her words had a guise of sport but were profoundly plaintive in meaning. 'About to part, who knows for how long; and what may have come in the interim!' this was her thought, and she was evidently much out of spirits. 'Courage, Dearie, only for a month!' I would say to her in some form or other. I went, next morning early, Alick driving: embarked at Glencaple Quay; voyage, as far as Liverpool still vivid to me; the rest, *till* arrival in London, gone mostly extinct: let it! The beggarly history of poor *Sartor among the Blockheadisms* is not worth my recording, or remembering,—least of all here!—In short, finding that whereas I had got £100 (if memory serve) for *Schiller* six or seven years before, and for *Sartor* 'at least *thrice* as good,' I could not only *not* 'get £200,' but even get no 'Murray'[1] or the like to publish it on 'half profits' (Murray, a most stupendous object to me; tumbling about, eyeless, with the evidently strong wish to say 'Yes *and* No,'—my first signal experience of that sad human predicament),—I said, 'We will make it *No*, then; wrap up our MS.; wait till this "Reform Bill" uproar abate; and see, and give our brave little Jeannie a sight of this big Babel, which is so altered since I saw it last (in 1824–25)!'— —She came right willingly; and had, in spite of her ill-health, which did not abate but the contrary, an interesting, cheery, and, in spite of our poor arrangements, a really pleasant winter here. We lodged in Ampton Street, Gray's Inn Lane, clean and decent pair of rooms, and quiet decent people (the *Daughter* is she

[1] John Murray, the publisher.

whom Geraldine speaks of as having, I might say, 'fallen in love' with her,—wanted to be our servant at Craigenputtock etc.!),—reduced from wealth to keeping lodgings, and prettily resigned to it; really good people. Visitors, etc. she had in plenty; John Mill one of the most interesting, so modest, ingenuous ingenious,—and so very fond of *me* at that time. Mrs. Basil Montagu (already a *correspondent* of hers, now accurately *seen*) was another of the distinguished. Jeffrey, Lord Advocate, often came on an afternoon;—never *could* learn his road to and from the end of Piccadilly, though I showed it him again and again. In the evening, *miscellany* of hers and mine, often dullish,—had it not been for *her*, and the light she shed on everything. I wrote *Johnson* here; just before going. News of my Father's death came here: oh, how good and tender she was, and consolatory by every kind art, in those black days! I remember our walk along Holborn forward into the City, and the *bleeding* mood I was in, she wrapping me like the softest of bandages:—in the City somewhere, two Boys fighting, with a ring of grinning Blackguards round them; I rushed passionately through, tore the fighters asunder, with some passionate rebuke ('in this world full of death'), she on my arm; and everybody silently complied. Nothing was *wanting* in her sympathy, or in the manner of it, as even from sincere people there often is. How poor we were; and yet how rich! I remember once taking her to Drury Lane Theatre (*Ticket*, from Playwright Kenny belike) along sloppy streets, in a November night (this was *before* my Father's sudden death); and how paltry the equipment looked to me, how perfectly unobjectionable to her, who was far above equipments and outer garnitures. Of the theatricality itself that night I can remember absolutely nothing.

Badams, my old Birmingham friend and physician (a most inventive, light-hearted, and genially gallant kind of man; sadly *eclipsed* within the last five years, ill-married, plunged amid grand mining speculations, which were and showed themselves *sound*, but not till they had driven him to drink brandy instead of water, and next year to die miserably overwhelmed),

—Badams with his Wife was living out at Enfield, in a big old rambling sherd of a House among waste gardens; thither I twice or thrice went, much liking the man, but never now getting any good of him; she once for three or four days, went with me: sorry enough days, had not we, and especially she, illuminated them a little. Charles Lamb and his Sister came daily once or oftener; a very sorry pair of phenomena. Insuperable proclivity to *gin*, in poor old Lamb. His talk contemptibly small, indicating wondrous ignorance and shallowness, even when it was serious and good-mannered, which it seldom was; usually *ill*-mannered (to a degree), screwed into frosty artificialities, ghastly make-believe of wit;—in fact more like 'diluted insanity' (as I defined it) than anything real of jocosity, 'humour,' or geniality. A most slender fibre of actual worth there was in that poor Charles, abundantly recognisable to me as to others, in his better times and moods; but he was Cockney to the marrow; and Cockneydom, shouting, 'Glorious, marvellous, unparalleled in Nature!' all his days, had quite bewildered his poor head, and churned nearly all the sense out of the poor man. He was the *leanest* of mankind, tiny black breeches buttoned to the knee-cap and no farther, surmounting spindle-legs also in black, face and head fineish, black, bony, lean, and of a Jew type rather; in the eyes a kind of *smoky* brightness or confused sharpness; spoke with a stutter; in walking tottered and shuffled: emblem of imbecility bodily and spiritual (something of real *insanity* I have understood), and yet something too of humane, ingenuous, pathetic, sportfully much-enduring. Poor Lamb! He was infinitely astonished at my Wife; and her quiet encounter of his too ghastly London wit by cheerful native ditto. Adieu, poor Lamb! He soon after died; as did Badams, much more to the sorrow of us both. Badams at our last parting (in Ampton Street, four or more months after this), burst into tears: 'Pressed down like *putty* under feet,' we heard him murmuring, 'and no strength more in me to rise!' We invited him to Craigenputtock, with our best temptations, next Summer; but it was too late; he answered, almost as with tears, 'No, alas,'—and shortly died.

We had come home, last days of previous March: wild journey by heavy Coach, I outside, to Liverpool: to Birmingham it was good, and Inn there good; but next day (a Sunday, I think) we were quite overloaded; and had our adventures, especially on the street in Liverpool, rescuing our luggage after dark. But at Uncle John's,[1] again, in Maryland Street, all became so bright. At mid-day, somewhere, we dined pleasantly *tête-à-tête*,—in the belly of the Coach, from my Dear One's *stores* (to save expense doubtless), but the rest of the day had been unpleasantly chaotic even to me,—though from her, as usual, there was nothing but patient goodness. Our dinners at Maryland Street I still remember, our days generally as pleasant,—our departure in the Annan Steamer; a bright sunshiny forenoon, Uncle etc. zealously helping and escorting; sick, sick my poor woman must have been; but she retired out of sight, and would suffer with her best grace in silence:—ah me, I recollect now a tight, clean, brandy-barrel she had bought; to 'hold such quantities of luggage, and be a water-barrel, for the rain at Craigenputtock!'—how touching to me at this moment!—And an excellent water-barrel it proved; the purest *tea* I ever tasted, made from the rain it stored for us.—At Whinnyrigg, I remember, Brother Alick and others of them were waiting to receive us: there were *tears* among us (my Father gone, while *we* returned); *she* wept bitterly, I recollect,—her sympathetic heart girdled in much sickness and dispiritment of her own withal: but my Mother was very kind and cordially good and respectful to her always. We returned in some days to Craigenputtock, and were again at peace there. Alick, I think, had by this time left; a new tenant there (a peaceable but dull stupid fellow); and our summers and winters for the future (1832–1834) were lonelier than ever. *Good* Servants too were hardly procurable; difficult anywhere, still more so at Craigenputtock where the choice was so limited. However, we pushed along; *writing* still brisk; *Sartor* getting published in *Fraser*, etc. etc. We had not at first any thought of leaving. And indeed would the Review Editors but

[1] John Welsh, Mrs. Carlyle's maternal uncle.

have stood *steady* (instead of for ever changeful), and domestic service gone on comfortably,—perhaps we might have continued still a good while. We went one winter (1833) to Edinburgh; the Jeffreys absent in official regions. A most dreary contemptible kind of element we found Edinburgh to be (partly by accident, or baddish behaviour of two individuals, Dr. Irving one of them, in reference to his poor kinswoman's *furnished house*): a locality and life-element never to be spoken of in comparison with London and the frank friends there. To London accordingly, in the course of next winter and its new paltry experiences of house-service etc., we determined to go. Our home-coming I remember; missed the coach in Princes Street; waited perdue till following morning; bright weather,—but my poor Jeannie so ill by the ride, that she could not drive from Thornhill to Templand (half a mile), but had to go or stagger hanging on my arm, and instantly took to bed with one of her terrible headaches. Such headaches I never witnessed in my life; agony of retching (never anything but phlegm) and of spasmodic writhing, that would last from twenty-four to sixty hours, never the smallest help affordable. Oh, what of pain, *pain*, my poor Jeannie had to bear in this thorny pilgrimage of life; the unwitnessed Heroine, or witnessed only by me,—who never till now *see* it *wholly*!

She was very hearty for London, when I spoke of it, though *till* then her voice on the subject had never been heard. 'Burn our ships!' she gaily said, one day,—i.e. dismantle our House; carry all our furniture with us. And accordingly here it still is (mostly all of it her Father's furniture; whose character of solidly noble is visibly written on it: 'respect what is *truly* made to its purpose; detest what is *falsely*, and have no concern with it!'). My own heart could not have been more emphatic on that subject; honour to him for its worth to me, not as furniture alone. My Writing-table, solid mahogany, well devised, always *handy*, yet *steady* as the *rocks*, is the best I ever saw: 'no Book could be too good for being written here,' it has often mutely told me. *His* Watch, commissioned by him in Clerkenwell, has measured my time, for forty years;—and would still guide you to the *longitude*, could anybody now take the trouble of completely regulating it (but old Whitelaw in Edinburgh, perhaps thirty-five years ago, was the last that did). Repeatedly have upholsterers asked, 'Who made these chairs, ma'am?' In Cockneydom, nobody in our day; 'unexampled prosperity' makes another kind. Abhorrence, quite equal to my own, of *cheap and nasty*, I have nowhere seen, certainly nowhere else seen completely accomplished, as poor mine could never manage almost in the least degree to be. My *pride*, fierce and sore as it might be, was never hurt by that furniture of his in the house called mine; on the contrary my *piety* was touched; and ever and anon have this *Table* etc. been a silent solemn sermon to me. Oh, shall not victory at last be to the Handful of Brave; in spite of the rotten multitudinous canaille, who *seem* to inherit all the world and its forces and steel-weapons and culinary and stage properties? Courage; and be true to one another!

June 3. I remember well my departure (middle of May, 1834), she staying to superintend packing and settling; in gig, I, for the last time; with many thoughts (forgotten these); Brother Alick *voluntarily* waiting at Shillahill Bridge with a *fresh* horse for me; night at Scotsbrig; ride to Annan (through a kind of May series of slight showers); pretty breakfast waiting us in poor good Mary's (ah me, how strange is all that now, 'Mother, you *shall* see me once yearly, and regularly hear from me, while we live!' etc. etc.): embarkation at Annan-water Foot, Ben Nelson and James Stuart; our lifting hawser, and steaming off,—my two dear Brothers (Alick and Jamie) standing silent, apart, feeling I well knew what;—self-resolute enough, and striving (not *quite* honestly) to feel more so! Ride to London, all night and all day (I think),—Trades-Union people out processioning ('Help *us*; what is your sublime Reform Bill else?' thought they,—and I, gravely saluting one body of them, I remember, and getting grave response from the leader of them). At sight of London I remember humming to myself a ballad-stanza of *Johnnie o' Braidislea* which my dear old Mother used to sing,

'For there's seven Foresters in yon Forest;
And them I want to see, see,
And them I want to *see*' (and shoot down)!

Lodged at Ampton Street again; immense stretches of walking in search of houses. Camden Town once; Primrose Hill and its bright dwarfed population in the distance; Chelsea; Leigh Hunt's huggermugger, etc. etc.—What is the use of recollecting all that?

Her arrival I best of all remember: ah me! She was clear for *this* poor house[1] (which she gradually, as poverty a little withdrew after long years of pushing, has made so beautiful and comfortable) in preference to all my other samples: and *here* we spent our two-and-thirty years of hard battle against Fate; hard but not quite unvictorious, when she left me, as in her car of heaven's fire. My noble one! I say deliberately *her* part in the stern battle, and except myself none knows how stern, was brighter, and braver than my own. Thanks, Darling, for your shining words and acts, which were continual in my eyes, and in no other mortal's. Worthless I was your divinity; wrapt in your perpetual love of me and pride in me, in defiance of all men and things. Oh was it not beautiful, all this that I have lost forever! And I was Thomas the *Doubter*, the Unhoping; till now the only Half-believing, in myself and my priceless opulences!—At my return from Annandale, after *French Revolution*, she so cheerily recounted to me all the good 'items;' item after item, 'Oh, it has had a great success, Dear!'—to no purpose; and at length beautifully lost patience with me for my incredulous humour. My life has not wanted at any time what I used to call '*desperate* hope' to all lengths; but of common '*hoping* hope' it has had but little; and has been shrouded since youthhood (almost since boyhood, for my school-years, at Annan, were very miserable, harsh, barren and worse) in continual gloom and grimness, as of a man set too nakedly *versus* the Devil and all men. Could I be easy to live with? She flickered round me, like perpetual radiance; and in spite of my glooms

[1] 5, Great Cheyne Row.

and my misdoings, would at no moment cease to love me and help me. What of bounty too is in Heaven!

Monday, June 4, 1866. Yesterday all spent against my will in foreign talk: 'National Portrait Exhibition' (Tyndall's kindness), American Pike (Belgian Minister), Mazzini (kind and sad) etc. etc.: At midnight, alone upon the streets, I felt only gloomier and sorer than ever,—as if *she* had been defrauded of my thoughts every instant they had been away from her.

We proceeded all through Belgrave Square hither, with our Servant, our looser luggage, ourselves and a little canary bird ('Chico' which she had brought with her from Craigenputtock); one hackney coach rumbling on with us all. Chico, in Belgrave Square, burst into singing, which we took as a good omen. We were all of us striving to be cheerful (she needed no effort of striving): but we 'had burnt our ships,' and at bottom the case was grave. I don't remember our arriving at this door; but I do the cheerful Gipsy life we had here among the litter and carpenters, for three incipient days. Leigh Hunt was in the next street, sending kind *un*practical messages; in the evenings, I think, personally coming in; we had made acquaintance with him (properly he with us), just before leaving in Spring 1832. Huggermugger was the type of his Economics, in all respects, financial and other; but he was himself a pretty man, in clean cotton nightgown, and with the airiest kindly style of sparkling talk,—wanting only wisdom of a sound kind, and true insight into fact. A great want!

I remember going with my Dear One (and Eliza Miles, the 'Daughter' of Ampton Street, as escort), to some dim ironmonger's shop, to buy kettles and pans, on the thriftiest of fair terms. How noble and more than royal is the look of that to me now, and of my Royal One then! California is dross and dirt to the experiences I have had.— —A tinderbox with steel and flint was part of our outfit (incredible as it may seem at this date): I could myself burn rags into tinder; and I have groped my way to the kitchen, in sleepless nights, to strike a light, for my pipe, in that manner. . . . *Chico* got a Wife by and by (Oh the wit there was about that and its sequels), produced two bright yellow ones, who, so soon as they were fledged, got out into the trees of the garden, and vanished towards swift destruction; upon which, villain Chico, finding his poor wife fallen so tattery and ugly, took to pecking a hole in her head; pecked it, and killed her: by and by ending his own disreputable life. I had begun *The French Revolution* (trees at that time before our window—a tale by these too on her part): infinitesimal little matters of that kind hovered round me like bright fireflies, irradiated by *her* light! Breakfast, early, was in the back part of this ground-floor room; details of gradual intentions etc. as to *French Revolution*, advices, approval or criticism, always beautifully wise, and so soft and loving, had they even been foolish!

We were not at all unhappy during those three years of *French Revolution*; at least she was not; her health perhaps being better than mine, which latter was in a strangely painful, and as if conflagrated condition towards the end. She had made the house 'a little Eden round her' (so neat and graceful in its simplicity and thrifty poverty); 'little Paradise round you,'—those were Edward Irving's words to her, on his visit to us; short affectionate visit, the first and the last (October 1834); on horseback, just about setting off for Glasgow, where he died, December following: I watched him till at the corner of Cook's Grounds, he vanished, and we never saw him more. Much consulting about him we had already had: a *Letter* to Henry Drummond (about delivering him from the fools and fanatics that were agitating him to death, as I clearly saw) lay on the mantelpiece here for some days, in doubt, and was then burnt. Brother, Father, rational Friend, I could not think of, except Henry; and him I had seen only once, not without clear view of his unsoundness too. Practically we had long ago had to take leave of poor Irving: but we both knew him well, and all his *brotherhoods* to us first and last, and mourned him in our hearts as a lost Hero. Nobler men I have seen few if any, till the foul gulfs of London Pulpit-Popularity sucked him in, and tragically swallowed him.

We were beginning to find a 'friend' or two here; that is, an eligible acquaintance,—none as yet very dear to us, though several brought a certain pleasure. Leigh Hunt was here almost nightly, three or four times a week, I should reckon;—he came always neatly dressed, was thoroughly courteous, friendly of spirit, and talked—like a singing bird. Good insight, plenty of a kind of humour too;—I remember little *warbles* in the turns of his fine voice which were full of fun and charm. We gave him Scotch Porridge to supper ('nothing in nature so interesting and delightful'): *she* played him Scotch tunes; a man he to understand and feel them well. His talk was often enough (perhaps at first oftenest) Literary-Biographical, Autobiographical, wandering into Criticism, *Reform of Society*, Progress, etc. etc.,—on which latter points he gradually found me very shocking (I believe,—so fatal to his rose-coloured visions on the subject). An innocent-hearted, but misguided, in fact rather foolish, *un*practical and often much-suffering man. John Mill was another steady visitor (had by this time introduced his Mrs. Taylor[1] too,—a very Will-o'-wispish 'Iridescence' of a creature; meaning nothing bad either). She at first considered my Jane to be a rustic spirit fit for rather tutoring and twirling about when the humour took her; but got taught better (to her lasting memory) before long. Mill was very useful about *French Revolution*; lent me all his Books, which were quite a Collection on that subject; gave me, frankly, clearly and with zeal, all his better knowledge than my own (which was pretty frequently of some use in this or the other detail): being full of eagerness for such an advocate in that cause as he felt I should be. His evenings here were sensibly agreeable for most part. Talk rather wintry ('*sawdust*'-ish, as old Sterling[2] once called it); but always well-informed and sincere. The Mrs. Taylor business was becoming more and more of questionable benefit to him (we could see), but on that subject we were strictly silent; and he was very pretty still.

[1] Harriet Taylor, Platonica Taylor as Carlyle called her in reference to her relations with Mill. After the death of her husband, Mrs. John Stuart Mill.

[2] Edward Sterling, editor of *The Times*.

For several years he came hither, and walked with me every Sunday,—Dialogues fallen all dim, except that they were never in the least genial to me, and that I took them as one would wine where no nectar is to be had,—or even thin ale where no wine. *Her* view of him was very kindly, though precisely to the same effect. How well do I still remember that night when he came to tell us, pale as Hector's ghost, that my unfortunate First Volume was burnt! It was like *half* sentence of death to us both; and we had to pretend to take it lightly, so dismal and ghastly was *his* horror at it, and try to talk of other matters. He staid three mortal hours or so; his departure quite a relief to us. Oh the burst of sympathy my poor Darling then gave me; flinging her arms round my neck, and openly lamenting, condoling, and encouraging like a nobler second self! Under Heaven is nothing beautifuller. We sat talking till late; '*shall* be written again,' my fixed word and resolution to her. Which proved to be such a task as I never tried before or since. I wrote out *Feast of Pikes* (vol. ii.), and then went at it,—found it fairly *impossible* for about a fortnight; passed three weeks (reading Marryat's novels), tried, cautious-cautiously, as on ice paper-thin, once more; and in short had a job more like breaking my heart than any other in my experience. Jeannie, alone of beings, burnt like a steady lamp beside me. I forget how much of money we still had: I think there was at first something like £300; perhaps £280 to front London with. Nor can I in the least remember where we had gathered such a sum;—except that it was our own, no part of it borrowed or *given* us by anybody. 'Fit to last till *French Revolution* is ready!'—and she had no misgivings at all. Mill was penitently liberal: sent me £200 (in a day or two), of which I kept £100 (actual cost of house while I had written burnt volume); upon which he bought me *Biographie Universelle*, which I got bound, and still have. Wish I could find a way of getting the now much macerated, changed, and fanaticised 'John Stuart Mill' to take that £100 back; but I fear there is no way!

How my Incomparable One contrived to beat out these exiguous resources into covering the appointed space I cannot now see, nor did I then know: but in the like of that, as in her other tasks, she was silently successful always, and never, that I saw, had a misgiving about success. There would be some trifling increments from *Fraser's Magazine*, perhaps (*Diamond Necklace*, etc. were probably of those years); but the *guess* stated above is the nearest I can now come to, and I don't think is in defect of the actuality.—I was very diligent, very desperate ('desperate *hope*!'),—wrote my two (folio) pages (perhaps four or five of print) day by day: then about two P.M. walked out; always heavy-laden, grim of mood; sometimes with a feeling not rebellious or impious against God Most High, but otherwise too similar to Satan's stepping the burning marle. Some conviction I had that the Book was worth something,—a pretty constant persuasion that it was not I that could make it better. Once or twice among the flood of equipages at Hyde-Park Corner, I recollect sternly thinking: 'Yes; and perhaps none of *you* could do what I am at!' But generally my feeling was, 'I will finish this Book, throw it at your feet; buy a rifle and spade, and withdraw to the Trans-atlantic Wildernesses,—far from human beggaries and basenesses!' This had a kind of comfort to me; yet I always knew too, in the background, that this would not practically do. In short, my nervous-system had got dreadfully irritated and inflamed before I quite ended; and my desire was *intense*, beyond words, to have done with it. The *last* paragraph I well remember writing: upstairs in the drawing-room that now is, which was then my writing-room; beside *her* there, in a gray evening (summer, I suppose), soon after tea perhaps;—and thereupon, with her dear blessing on me, going out to walk. I had said before going out, 'What they will do with this Book, none knows, my Jeannie, lass; but they have not had, for a two hundred years, any Book that came more truly from a man's very heart; and so let them trample it under foot and hoof as *they* see best!' 'Pooh, pooh; they cannot trample that!' she would cheerily answer; for her own approval (I think she had read always regularly behind me), especially in vol. iii., was strong and decided.

We knew the Sterlings by this time, John, and all of them. Old Sterling very often here; knew Henry Taylor,[1] etc., the Wilsons of Eccleston Street, Rev. Mr. Dunn, etc. etc.; and the waste wilderness of London was becoming a peopled garden to us, in some measure, especially to *her*, who had a frank welcome to every sort of worth and even kindly-singularity in her fellow-creatures, such as I could at no time rival.

Sprinklings of Foreigners, 'Political Refugees,' had already begun to come about us; to me seldom of any interest, except for the foreign instruction to be gathered from them (if any), and the curiosity attached to their foreign ways. Only two of them had the least charm to me as men: Mazzini whom, I remember, Mr. Taylor, Mrs. Taylor's (ultimately Mrs. Mill's) *then* Husband, an innocent dull good man, brought in to me one evening; and Godefroi Cavaignac, whom my Jane had met somewhere, and thought worth inviting. Mazzini I once or twice talked with; recognisably a most valiant, faithful, considerably gifted and noble soul; but hopelessly given up to his Republicism, his 'Progress,' and other Rousseau fanaticism, for which I had at no time the least credence, or any considerable respect amid my pity. We soon tired of one another, Mazzini and I; and he fell mainly to *her* share; off and on, for a good many years, yielding her the charm of a sincere mutual esteem, and withal a good deal of occasional amusement from his curious bits of Exile London- and Foreign-life, and his singular Italian-English modes of locution now and then. For example,—Petrucci having quenched his own fiery chimney one day, and escaped the fine (as he hoped), 'there *came to pass* a Sweep,' with finer nose in the solitary street, who involved him again. Or, '*Ma, mio caro, non v'è ci un morto!*' which, I see, she has copied into her poor little book of *notabilia*. Her reports of these things to me, as we sat at breakfast or otherwise, had a tinkle of the finest mirth in them, and in short a beauty and

[1] Not Harriet Taylor's husband, but a Civil Servant, important in the Colonial Office; author of a once-famous drama named *Philip van Artevelde.*

felicity I have never seen surpassed. Ah me, ah me, *whither* fled?

Cavaignac was considerably more interesting to both of us. A fine Bayard soul (with figure to correspond), a man full of seriousness and of genial gaiety withal; of really fine faculties, and of a politeness (especially towards women) which was curiously elaborated into punctiliousness, yet sprang everywhere from frank nature. A man very pleasant to converse with, walk with, or see drop in on an evening, and lead you or follow you far and wide over the world of intellect and humanly recorded fact. A Republican to the bone, but a 'Bayard' in that vesture (if only Bayard had wit and fancy at command). We had many dialogues while *French Revolution* struggled through its last two volumes; Cavaignac freely discussing with me, accepting kindly my innumerable dissents from him, and on the whole elucidating many little points to me. Punctually on the *jour de l'an,* came some little gift to her, frugal yet elegant; and I have heard him say with a mantling joyous humour overspreading that sternly sad French face, '*Vous n'êtes pas Écossaise, Madame; désormais vous serez Française!*' I think he must have left us in 1843; he and I rode, one summer forenoon, to Richmond and back (some old *Bonapartist* Colonel married out there, dull ignorant loud fellow to my feeling); country was beautiful, air balmy, ride altogether *ditto ditto* I don't remember speaking with him again; 'going to Paris this week' or so, he (on unconditional amnesty, not on conditional like all the others) He returned once, or indeed twice, during the three years he still lived: but I was from home the last time, both of us the first (at Newby Cottage, Annan, oh dear!)—and I saw him no more. The younger Brother ('*President*' in 1849 etc.) I had often heard of from him, and learned to esteem on evidence given, but never saw. I take him to have been a second *Godefroi* probably with less gift of social utterance, but with a soldier's breeding in return.

One autumn, and perhaps another, I recollect her making a tour with the elder Sterlings (Thunderer and Wife), which, in spite of the hardships to one so delicate, she rather enjoyed.

Thunderer she had at her apron-string, and brought many a comical pirouette out of him from time to time. Good Mrs. Sterling really loved her, and *vice versâ*; a luminous household circle that to us:—as may be seen in *Life of Sterling*, more at large.

Of money from *French Revolution* I had *here* as yet got absolutely nothing; Emerson in America, by an edition of his *there*, sent me £150 ('pathetic!' was her fine word about it; 'but never mind, Dear'); after some three years grateful England (through poor scrubby but correctly arithmetical Fraser) £100; and I don't remember when, some similar munificence: but I now (and indeed not till recent years do I) see it had been, as *she* called it, 'a great *success*,' and greatish of its kind. Money I did get somewhere honestly, Articles in *Fraser*, in poor Mill's (considerably hidebound) *London Review*; *Edinburgh* I think was *out* for me before this time. *London Review* was at last due to the charitable faith of young Sir William Molesworth, a poorish narrow creature, but an ardent believer in Mill *Père* (James) and Mill *Fils*: 'How much will your Review take to launch it then?' asked he (all other Radical believers being so close of fist)—'Say £4000,' answered Mill. 'Here, then,' writing a cheque for that amount, rejoined the other. My private (altogether private) feeling, I remember, was, that they could, with profit, have employed me much more extensively in it; perhaps even (though of this I was candid enough to doubt) made me Editor of it, let me *try* it for a couple of years,—worse I could not have succeeded than poor Mill himself did as Editor (*sawdust* to the masthead, and a croakery of crawling things, instead of a speaking by men); but I whispered to none but *her* the least hint of all this: and oh, how glad am I now, and for long years back, that apparently nothing of it ever came to the thoughts or the dreams of Mill and Co.! For I should surely have accepted of it, had the terms been at all tolerable. I had plenty of *Radicalism*, and have, and to all appearance shall have; but the opposite hemisphere (which never was wanting either, nor will be, as it miserably is in Mill and Co.) had not yet found itself summoned by the trumpet of Time and his Events (1848: study of *Oliver* etc.) into practical emergence, and emphasis and prominence as now. 'Ill luck,' take it quietly; you never are sure but it may be *good* and the *best*.

Our main revenue for perhaps three, or four years (?) now was *Lectures*; in Edward Street, Portman Square, the only free *room* there was; earnestly forwarded by Miss and Thomas Wilson, of Eccleston Street (who still live and are good), by Miss Martineau, by Henry Taylor, Frederick Elliot, etc. etc. Brought in, on the average, perhaps £200, for a month's labour: first of them must have been in 1838, I think,—Willis's Rooms, this. 'Detestable mixture of Prophecy and Play-actorism,' as I sorrowfully defined it: nothing could well be hatefuller to me; but I was obliged. And she, oh she was my Angel, and unwearied helper and comforter in all that; how we drove together, poor Two, to our place of execution; she with a little drop of brandy to give me at the very last,—and shone round me like a bright *aureola*, when all else was black and chaos! God reward thee, Dear One; now when I cannot even own my debt. Oh why do we *delay* so much, till Death makes it impossible? And don't I continue it still with others? Fools, fools; we forget that it *has* to end; lo this *has* ended, and it is such an astonishment to me; so sternly undeniable, yet as it were incredible!—

It must have been in this 1838 that her Mother first came to see us here.[1] I remember giving each of them a sovereign, from a pocketful of *odd* which I had brought home,—greatly to satisfaction especially of Mrs. Welsh, who I doubt not bought something pretty and symbolic with it. She came perhaps three times: on one of the later times was that of the 'One Soirée,' with the wax-candles on Mother's part,—and subsequent remorse on Daughter's. 'Burn these last two, on the night when I lie dead!' Like a stroke of lightning this has gone through my heart, cutting and yet healing. *Sacred* be the name of it; its praise *silent*. Did I elsewhere meet in the world a soul so direct from the Empyrean? My dear old Mother was

[1] In September 1835.

perhaps equally pious, in the Roman sense, in the British she was much more so: but starry flashes of this kind she had not, —from her education etc., could not.

June 6. Surely this is very idle work,—the rather if it is all to be burnt! But nothing else yields me any solace at all, in those days. I will continue it to-morrow. Poor Tablet or memorial due to me from the lapidary, this day fortnight, at farthest, surely.

June 7. By this time we were getting noticed by select individuals of the Aristocracy; and were what is called 'rather rising in society.' Ambition that way my Jane never had; but she took it always as a something of honour done to *me*, and had her various bits of satisfaction in it. The Spring-Rices (Lords Monteagle afterwards) were probably the first of their class that ever asked me out as a distinguished thing. I remember their flunkey arriving here with an express while we were at dinner; I remember, too, their Soirée itself in Downing Street, and the καλοὶ and καλαὶ (as I called them) with their state and their effulgences, as something new and entertaining to me. The Stanleys (of Alderley), through the Bullers, we had long since known, and still know; but that I suppose was still mostly *theoretic*,—or perhaps I *had* dined there, and seen the Hollands (Lord and Lady), the etc. (as I certainly did ultimately), but not been judged eligible, or both catchable and eligible? To me I can recollect (except what of snob ambition there might be in me, which I hope was not very much, though for certain it was not quite wanting either!), there was nothing of charm in any of them: old Lady Holland I viewed even with aversion, as a kind of hungry 'ornamented witch,' looking over me with merely carnivorous views (and always questioning her Dr. Allen, when I said anything); nor was it till years after (Husband, Allen, etc. all dead) that I discovered remains of beauty in her, a pathetic situation, and distinguished qualities. My Jane I think knew still less of her: in her house neither my Jane nor I ever was. At Marshall's (millionaire of Leeds, and an excellent man, who much esteemed me, and once gave me a horse for health's sake) we had ample assemblages, shining enough in their kind;—but *she*, I somehow think, probably for saving the cost of 'fly' (oh my Queen, *mine* and a true one!), was not so often there as I. On the whole, that too was a thing to be gone through in our career; and it had its bits of benefits, bits of instructions etc. etc.; but also its temptations, intricacies, tendencies to vanity etc., to waste of time and faculty; and in a better sphere of arrangement, would have been a 'game not worth the candle.' Certain of the Aristocracy, however, did seem to me still very *noble*; and, with due elimination of the grossly worthless (none of whom had we to do with), I should vote at present that, of *classes* known to me in England, the Aristocracy (with its perfection of human politeness, its continual grace of bearing and of acting, steadfast 'honour', light address and cheery *stoicism*, if you see *well* into it), is actually yet the best of English Classes. Deep in it *we* never were, promenaders on the shore rather; but I have known it too, and formed deliberate judgment as above. My Dear One, in theory, did not go so far (I think) in that direction,—in fact was not at the pains to form much 'theory;' but no eye in the world was quicker than hers for individual specimens;—and to the last she had a great pleasure in consorting more or less with the select of these: Lady William Russell, Dowager Lady Sandwich, Lady etc. etc. (and not in over-quantity). I remember, at first sight of the *first* Lady Ashburton[1] (who was far from regularly *beautiful*, but was probably the *chief* of all these great ladies), she said of her to me, 'Something in her like a Heathen Goddess!'—which was a true reading, and in a case not plain at all, but oftener mistaken than rightly taken.

Our first visit to Addiscombe together: a bright summer Sunday; we walked (*thrift*, I daresay, ah me!) from the near Railway Station; and my poor Jeannie grew very tired and disheartened, though nothing ill came; I had been there several times, and she had seen the Lady here (and called her 'Heathen Goddess' to me): this time I had at once joined the company under the shady trees, on their beautiful lawn; and

[1] Formerly Lady Harriet Baring; the woman whose platonic friendship with Carlyle caused Jane Welsh Carlyle so much mental torment.

my little woman, in few minutes, her dress all adjusted, came stepping out, round the corner of the house,—with such a look of lovely innocency, modesty, ingenuousness, gracefully suppressed timidity, and radiancy of native cleverness, intelligence, and dignity, towards the great ladies and great gentlemen; it seems to me at this moment, I have never seen a more beautiful expression of a human face. Oh my Dearest; my Dearest that cannot now know how dear! There are glimpses of Heaven too given us on this Earth, though sorely drowned in terrestrial vulgarities, and sorely 'flamed-on from the Hell beneath' too. This must have been about 1843 or so?

A year or two before, going to see her Mother, she had landed in total wreck of sea-sickness (miserable always at sea, but had taken it as cheapest doubtless)—and been brought up almost speechless, and set down at the Queensberry Arms Inn, Annan. Having no maid, no sign but of trouble and (unprofitable) ladyhood, they took her to a remote bedroom, and left her to her solitary shifts there. Very painful to me, yet beautiful and with a noble pathos in it, to look back upon (from her narrative of it) here and now! How Mary, my poor but ever faithful 'Sister Mary,' came to her (on notice), *her* resources few, but her heart overflowing; could hardly get admittance to the Flunkey House of Entertainment at all; got it, however, had a 'pint of sherry' with her, had this and that, and perhaps on the third day, got her released from the base place; of which that is my main recollection now, when I chance to pass it, in its now dim enough condition. Perhaps this was about 1840; Mary's husband (now Farmer at the Gill, not a clever man, but a diligent and good-natured) was then a 'Carter with two Horses' in Annan,—gradually becoming unable to live in that poor capacity there. They had both been Craigenputtock figures. . . . She loved Mary for her kind-heartedness; admired and respected her skill and industry in Domestic management of all kinds; and often contrasted to me her perfect talent in that way, compared to Sister Jean's, who intellectually was far the superior (and had once been her own Pupil and Protégée, about the time we left Comley Bank; always very kind and grateful to her since, too, but never such a favourite as the other). Mary's Cottage was well known to me too, as I came home by the Steamer, on my visits, and was often riding down to bathe etc. These visits, 'once a year to my Mother,' were pretty faithfully paid; and did my *heart* always some good; but for the rest were unpleasantly chaotic (especially when my poor old Mother, worthiest and dearest of simple hearts, became incapable of management by her own strength, and of almost all enjoyment even from me): I persisted in them to the last, as did my Woman; but I think they comprised for both of us (such skinless creatures), in respect of outward *physical* hardship, an amount larger than all the other items of our then life put together.

How well I remember the dismal evening, when we had got word of her Mother's dangerous crisis of illness (a *Stroke*, in fact, which ended it); and her wildly impressive look, laden as if with resolution, affection and prophetic woe, while she sat in the railway carriage and rolled away from me into the dark. 'Poor, poor Jeannie' thought I; and yet my sympathy how paltry and imperfect was it to what hers would have been for me! Stony-hearted; shame on me! She was stopped at Liverpool, by news of the *worst*; I found her sharply wretched, on my following,—and had a strange two or three months, slowly settling everything at Templand; the 'last Country Spring,' and my *first* for many long years. Bright, sad, solitary (letters from Lockhart etc.), nocturnal mountain heather-burning, by day the courses of the hail-storms from the mountains, how they come pouring down their respective valleys, deluge-like, and blotted out the sunshine etc. Spring of 1842.

I ought to have copied my Mother-in-law's *epitaph* at least, or to send for it now to the Minister of Crawford in Clydesdale. Stop to-day; or even altogether? No; can't.

I find it was in 1842 (20th February) that my poor Mother-in-law died. Wild night for me from Liverpool, through Dumfries (Sister Jean out with tea, etc.), arrival at waste Templand (only John Welsh etc. there; funeral quite over): all this and the lonesome, sad, but not unblessed three months almost which I spent there, is still vividly in my mind. I was for trying to keep Templand once, as a summer refuge for us,—one of the most picturesque of locations; but *her* filial heart abhorred the notion; and I have never seen more than the chimney-tops of Templand since. Her grief, at my return and for months afterwards, was still poignant, constant:—and oh how inferior my sympathy with her, to what hers would have been with me; woe on my dull hard ways in comparison! To her Mother she had been the kindest of Daughters; life-rent of Craigenputtock settled frankly on her (and such effort to make it practically good to the letter when needful);—I recollect one gallop of hers, which Geraldine has not mentioned, gallop from Craigenputtock to Dumfries Bank, and thence to Templand at a stretch, with the half-year's rent, which our procrastinating Brother Alick seldom could or would be punctual with: ah me, gallop which pierces my heart at this moment, and clothes my Darling with a sad radiancy to me. But she had many *remorses*, and indeed had been obliged to have manifold little collisions with her fine high-minded, but often fanciful and fitful Mother, —who was always a Beauty, too, and had whims and thin-skinned ways, distasteful enough to such a Daughter. All which, in cruel aggravation (for all were really small, and had been ridiculous rather than deep or important), now came remorsefully to mind, and many of them, I doubt not, *staid*.—Craigenputtock lapsed to *her*, in 1842, therefore;—to me she had left the fee-simple of it by will (in 1824, two years before our marriage),—as I remember she once told me *then*abouts, and never but once: Will found, the other day, after some difficulty, since her own departure, and the death of any Welsh to whom she could have wished me to bequeath it. To my kindred it has no relation, nor shall it go to them: it is much a problem with me how I shall leave it settled ('Bursaries for Edinburgh College;' or *what* were best?) after my poor interest in it is over. Considerably a problem;—and what her wish in it would have actually been? 'Bursaries' had come into my own head, when we heard that poor *final* young Welsh was in consumption; but to her I never mentioned it ('wait till the young man's *decease* do suggest it!')—and now I have only hypothesis and guess.[1] She never liked to speak of the thing, even on question (which hardly once or twice ever rose);—and except on question, a stone was not more silent. Beautiful queenlike woman: I did admire her complete perfection on this head of the actual 'dowry' she had now brought; £200 yearly or so,—which to us was a highly considerable sum,—and how she absolutely ignored it, and as it were had not done it at all. Once or so I can dimly remember telling her as much (thank God I did so), to which she answered scarcely by a look, and certainly without word, except perhaps 'Tut!'

Thus, from this date onward, we were a little richer, easier in circumstances; and the *pinch* of Poverty, which had been relaxing latterly, changed itself into a gentle *pressure*, or into a *limit* and little more. We did not change our habits in any point, but the grim collar round my neck was sensibly slackened. Slackened, not removed at all,—for almost twenty years yet. My Books were not, nor ever will be 'popular,' productive of money to any but a contemptible degree: I had lost by the death of Bookseller Fraser and change to Chapman and Hall; —in short, to judge by the running after me by *owls* of Minerva in those times, and then to hear what day's-wages my Books brought me, would have astonished the owl mind! I do not think my literary income was above £200 a year in those decades,—in spite of my continual diligence day by day. *Cromwell* I must have *written*, I think, in 1844; but for four years prior it had been a continual toil and misery to me. I forget what was the price of *Cromwell*, greater considerably than in any previous case;—but the *annual* income was still somewhat as above. I had always £200 or £300 in bank, and continually forgot all about money. My Darling rolled it all over upon *me*; cared not one straw about it; only asked for assurance or promissory engagement from me, '*How* little,

[1] In fact Carlyle bequeathed Craigenputtock to the University of Edinburgh; the income derived from it to be expended in Scholarships called 'The John Welsh Bursaries'.

then?' and never failed to make it liberally and handsomely do. Honour to her (beyond the ownership of California, I say now); and thanks to Poverty that showed me how noble, worshipful and dear she was.

In 1850, after an interval of deep gloom and bottomless dubitation, came *Latter-Day Pamphlets*, which unpleasantly astonished everybody; set the world upon the strangest suppositions ('Carlyle got deep into whisky!' said some), ruined my 'reputation' (according to the friendliest voices), and, in effect, divided me altogether from the mob of 'Progress-of-the-Species' and other vulgar,—but were a great relief to my own *conscience* as a faithful citizen, and have been ever since. My Darling gaily approved; and we left the thing to take its own sweet will, with great indifferency and loyalty on our part. This did not help our incomings; in fact I suppose it effectually hindered, and has done so *till quite recently*, any 'progress' of ours in that desirable direction, though I did not find that the small steady sale of my Books was sensibly altered from year to year, but quietly stood where it used to be. Chapman (hard-fisted cautious Bibliopole) would not, for about ten years farther, go into any edition of my 'Collected Works;' I did once transiently propose it, once only;—and remember being sometimes privately a good deal sulky towards the poor man for his judgment on that matter, though decided to leave him strictly to his own light in regard to it, and indeed to avoid him altogether when I had not clear business with him. The 'recent return of popularity greater than ever,' which I hear of, seems due alone to that late Edinburgh affair;[1] especially to the Edinburgh *Address*; and affords new proof of the singularly dark and feeble condition of 'Public Judgment' at this time. No idea, or shadow of an idea, is in that Address, but what had been set forth by me tens of times before: and the poor gaping sea of Prurient Blockheadism receives it as a kind of inspired revelation,—and runs to buy my Books (it is said) now when I have got quite done with their buying or refusing to

[1] Carlyle's installation as Lord Rector of Edinburgh University, and his very successful inaugural address.

buy. If they would give me £10,000 a year, and bray unanimously their *hosannahs* heaven-high for the rest of my life, —who *now* would there be to get the smallest joy or profit from it? To *me* I feel as if it would be a silent sorrow rather, and would bring me painful retrospections, nothing else.—— On the whole, I feel often, as if poor England had really done its very kindest to me, after all. Friends not a few I do at last begin to see that I have had all along; and these have all, or all but two or three, been decorously silent: enemies I cannot strictly find that I have had any (only blind blockheads running athwart me on their own errand);—and as for the speaking and criticising multitude, who regulate the paying ditto, I perceive that their labours on me have had a two-fold result: 1°. That, after so much nonsense said, in all dialects, and so very little sense or real understanding of the matter, I have arrived at a point of indifferency towards all that, which is really very desirable to a human soul that will do well; and 2°. That, in regard to money, and payment etc. in the money kind, it is essentially the same. To a degree which, under *both* heads (if it were safe for me to estimate it), I should say was really a far nearer than common approach to completeness. And which, under both heads, so far as it *is* complete, means *victory*, and the very highest kind of 'success'! Thanks to poor anarchic crippled and bewildered England, then; hasn't it done its very *best* for me, under disguised forms; and seeming occasionally to do its *worst*? Enough of all that. I had to say only that my dear little Helpmate, in regard to these things also, has been throughout as one sent from Heaven to me. Never for a moment did she take to blaming England or the world on my behalf; rather to quizzing my *despondencies* (if any) on that head, and the grotesque stupidities of England and the world: she cared little about Criticisms of me, good or bad; but I have known her read, when such came to hand, the unfriendliest specimens with real amusement, if their stupidity was of the readable or amusing kind to bystanders. *Her* opinion of me, it was curiously unalterable from the first! In Edinburgh for example, in 1826 still, Bookseller Tait (a foolish goosey, innocent but very vulgar kind of mortal), 'Oh Mrs. Carlyle, fine criticism in *The Scotsman*; you will find it at, I think you will find it at——.' 'But what good will it do me?' answered Mrs. Carlyle, with great good humour; to the miraculous collapse of Tait, who stood (I dare say) with eyes staring!

In 1844, late Autumn, I was first at the Grange for a few days (doing d'Ewes's *Election to the Long Parliament*, I recollect); she with me next year, I think; and there, or at Addiscombe, Alverstoke, Bath House,[1] saw on frequent enough occasions, for twelve years coming, or indeed for nineteen (till the second Lord Ashburton's death), the choicest specimens of English Aristocracy; and had no difficulty in living with them on free and altogether human terms, and learning from them by degrees whatever *they* had to teach us. *Something* actually, though perhaps not very much, and surely *not* the best. To me, I should say, more than to her, came what lessons there were; human friendships we also had; and she too was a favourite with the better kind,—Lord Lansdowne, for example, had at last discovered what she was; not without some amazement in his old retrospective mind, I dare say! But to her the charm of such circles was at all times insignificant; *human* was what she looked at, and what she was, in all circles. *Ay de mi:* it is a mingled yarn, all that of our 'Aristocratic' History; and I need not enter on it here. One evening, at Bath House, I saw her, in a grand soirée, softly step up, and (unnoticed, as she thought, by anybody) *kiss* the old Duke of Wellington's shoulder! That perhaps was one of the prettiest things I ever saw there. Duke was then very old, and hitched languidly about, speaking only when spoken to, some 'Wow-*wow*,' which perhaps had little real meaning in it: he had on his Garter-order, his gold-buckle stock, and was very clean and trim; but except making appearance in certain evening parties, half an hour in each, perhaps hardly knew what he was doing. From Bath House, we saw his Funeral Procession, a while after; and, to our disgust, in one of the Mourning Coaches, some Official

[1] Residences of the Ashburtons.

or Dignitary reading a Newspaper. The hearse (seventeen tons of bronze), the arrangements generally, were vulgar and disgusting: but the *fact* itself impressed everybody; the street rows all silently doffed hat as the Body passed;—and London, altogether, seemed to be holding its breath. A dim, almost wet kind of day. Adieu, adieu.—With Wellington I don't think either of us had ever spoken; though we both esteemed him heartily: I had known his face for nearly thirty years; he also, I think had grown to know mine, as that of somebody who wished him well, not otherwise, I dare say, or the proprietor's name at all; but I have seen him gaze at me a little as we passed on the streets. To speak *to* him, with my notions of his ways of thinking, and of his *articulate* endowments, was not among my longings. I went once to the House of Lords, expressly to hear the sound of his voice, and so complete my little private Physiognomic Portrait of him: a fine *aquiline* voice, I found it, quite like the face of him;—and got a great instruction and lesson, which has staid with me, out of his little speech itself (Lord Ellenborough's 'Gates of Somnauth' the subject, about which I cared nothing); speech of the most *haggly*, hawky, pinched and meagre kind, so far as utterance and 'eloquence' went; but potent for *conviction* beyond any other, nay, I may say, quite exclusively of all the others that night, which were mere 'melodious wind' to me (Brougham's, Derby's, etc. etc.), while *this* hitching, stunted, haggling discourse of ten or fifteen minutes had made the Duke's opinion completely mine too. I thought of O. Cromwell withal. And have often since, oftener than ever before, said to myself, 'Is not this (to make your opinion mine) the aim of all 'eloquence,' rhetoric, and Demosthenic artillery practice?' And what is it good for? Fools: get a *true* insight and belief of your own as to the matter; that is the way to get your belief into me, and it is the only way!—

One of the days while I was first at The Grange (in 1844) was John Sterling's *death*-day: I had well marked it, with a sad almost remorseful contrast;—we were at St. Cross and Winchester Cathedral that day.—I think my Wife's latest favourites, and in a sense friends and intimates, among the Aristocracy were the old Dowager Lady Sandwich (died about four years ago, or three); *young* Lady Lothian (recent acquaintance); and the (Dowager) Lady William Russell, whom I think she had something of real love to, and in a growing condition for the last two or three years. This a clever, high-mannered, massive-minded old lady, now seventy-two. . . .

Sunday, 10*th June;* weather fiercely hot; health suffering visibly last week; *must* take new courses; form new resolutely definite *plans*,—which requires (or *would* require) a great deal more of strength and calmness than I have at present! Quiet I am, avoiding almost everybody, and far preferring *silence* to most words I can hear: but clear of vision, *calm* of judgment I am far from being!—Ought I to *quit* this 'work' here, which I feel to be very idleness? I sit in great gloom of heart, but it is gloom all drenched in soft pity (as if *she* were to be 'pitied!') in benign affection: really it is like a kind of religious course of worship to me, this of 'Sitting by her Grave,' as I daily do. Oh my Loved one, must I quit even that, then? Dost *thou*, as if it were *thou*, bid me Rise, go hence, and work at something? Patience; yet a little, yet a little!—At least I will quit these vague provinces; and try to write something more specifically *historical*, on this Paper of *her* providing!—Stop to-day.

11*th June;* Very mournful little hour: 'Parting of her raiment' (I somehow call it), sad *sanction* of what Maggie Welsh[1] had done in it! Have read the (Dumfries) Copy of her Will, too; a beautiful *Letter* to her Mother, and other *Deed* ('of Life-rent'),—all gone, *gone* into the vacant Past:—and have reposited both Documents. Intend to put down something about her Parentage etc., *now*;—and what of reminiscence most lives with me on that head. Little *Tablet* is not due for ten days yet; feel it too sad to quit my daily companionship, idle though it be, and almost blamable—no, it is not *blamable*, no!

John Welsh, Farmer of Penfillan, near Thornhill, Nithsdale,

[1] Jane's cousin, who stayed at Cheyne Row for a short time after Jane's death.

for the greater part of his life, was born, I believe at Craigenputtock, 9th December 1757; and was sole Heir of that place, and of many ancestors there; my Wife's paternal Grandfather,—of whom she had many pretty things to report, in her pleasant interesting way; genuine affection blending so beautifully with perfect candour, and with arch recognition of whatever was, comically or otherwise, singular in the subject matter. Her Father's name was also John; which from of old had specially been that of the *Laird*, or of his First-born, as her Father was. This is *one* of the probabilities they used to quote in claiming to come from John Knox's youngest daughter and her husband, the once famous John Welsh, minister of Ayr, etc.: a better probability perhaps is the topographical one that Craigenputtock, which, by site and watershed would belong to Galloway, is still part of Dumfriesshire, and did apparently form part of Collieston, fertile little farm still extant, which probably was an important estate when the antique 'John Welsh's Father' had it in Knox's day: (see the *Biographies*),—to which Collieston, Craigenputtock, as moorland, extending from the head of the Glenessland Valley, and a two miles farther southward (quite over the slope and down to Orr, the next river), does seem to have been an appendage. My Jeannie cared little or nothing about these genealogies, but seeing them interest *me*, took some interest in them. Within the last three months (*à propos* of a new Life of the famed John Welsh), she mentioned to me some to me new, and still livelier spark of likelihood, which her 'Uncle Robert' (an expert Edinburgh lawyer) had derived from reading the old Craigenputtock law-papers: what this new 'spark' of light on the matter was (quite forgotten by me at that time, and looking 'new') I in vain strive to recall; and have *again* forgotten it (swallowed in the sad Edinburgh hurlyburlies of 'three months ago,' which have now had such an issue!). To my present judgement there is really good likelihood of the genealogy, and likelihood all going that way; but no certainty attained or perhaps ever attainable. That 'famed John Welsh' lies buried (since the end of James I's reign) in some churchyard of Eastern

London, name of it known, but nothing more. His Grandson was minister of Erncray ('Irongray' they please to spell it) near by, in Claver'se's bloody time; and there all certainty ends.— —By her Mother's *mother*, who was a Baillie, of somewhat noted kindred in Biggar country, my Jeannie was further said to be descended from 'Sir William Wallace' (the great); but this seemed to rest on nothing but air and vague fireside rumour of obsolete date; and she herself, I think, except perhaps in quizzical allusion, never spoke of it to me at all. Edward Irving once did (1822 or so) in his half-laughing Grandison way, as we three sat together talking: 'From Wallace and from Knox,' said he, with a wave of the hands: 'there's a Scottish Pedigree for you!' The good Irving: so guileless, loyal always, and so hoping and so generous!

My wife's Grandfather, I can still recollect, died 20 September 1823, aged near sixty-six;—I was at Kinnaird (Buller's in Perthshire), and had it in a Letter from *her*: Letters from her were almost the sole light-points in my dreary miseries there (fruit of *miserable health* mainly, and of a future blank and barred to me, as I felt). Trustfully she gave me details: how he was sixty-three, near sixty-six (in fact); hair still raven-black, only within a year *eyebrows* had grown quite white; which had so softened and sweetened the look of his bright glancing black eyes, etc. etc. A still grief lay in the dear Letter, too, and much affection and respect for her old Grandfather just gone. Sweet and soft to *me* to look back upon; and very sad now, from the threshold of our own grave. My bonnie Darling, *ja*; I shall follow thee very soon, and then—!—

Grandfather's youngest years had been passed at Craigenputtock; mother had been left a widow there, and could not bear to part with him; elder sisters there were, he the only boy. Jane always thought him to have fine faculty, a beautiful clearness, decision, and integrity of character; but all this had grown up in solitude and vacancy, under the silent skies on the wild moors for most part. She sometimes spoke of his (and her) ulterior ancestors; 'several blackguards among them,' her old Grandfather used to say; 'but not one blockhead that I heard of!' Of one, flourishing in 1745, there is a story still current among the country people thereabouts: how, though this Laird of Craigenputtock had not himself gone at all into the Rebellion, he received with his best welcome certain other Lairds or gentlemen of his acquaintance who *had*, and who were now flying for their life; kept them there, as in a seclusion lonelier almost than any other in Scotland;—heard timefully that Dragoons were coming for them; shot them thereupon instantly away by various well-contrived routes and equipments; and waited his Dragoon Guests as if nothing were wrong. 'Such and such men here with you; aren't they, you——!' said they. 'Truly they were, till three hours ago; and they are *rebels*, say you? Fie, the villains, had I but known or dreamt of that! But come, let us *chase* immediately: once across the Orr yonder (and the swamps on this side, which look green enough from here), you find firm road, and will soon catch the dogs!' Welsh mounting his galloway, undertook to guide the Dragoons through that swamp or 'bottom' (still a place that needed guiding in our time, though there did come at last a 'solid road and bridge'); Welsh, trotting cheerily along on his light galloway, guided the Dragoons in such way that their heavy animals sank mostly or altogether, in the treacherous element, safe only for a native galloway and man; and with much pretended lamentation, seeing them provided with work that would last till darkness had fallen, rode his ways again. I believe this was *true* in substance; but never heard any of the saved rebels named. Maxwells etc., who are of Roman-Catholic Jacobite type, abound in those parts: a Maxwell, I think, is feudal superior of Craigenputtock. This Welsh, I gather, must have been *grandfather* of my wife's grandfather: she had strange stories of his wives (three in succession, married perhaps all, especially the second and third, for money); and how he kept the last of them, a decrepit ill-natured creature, *in*visible in some corner of his house; and used gravely to introduce visitors to her 'gown and bonnet' hanging on a stick as 'Mrs. Welsh III.' *Him* his Grandson doubtless ranked among the 'blackguard' section of ancestry: I suppose his immediate heir may have died shortly after him and been an unexceptionable man.

In or about 1773, friends persuaded the widow of this latter that she absolutely must send her Boy away for some kind of *schooling*, his age now fourteen: to which she sorrowfully consenting, he was despatched to Tynron school (notable at that time) about twelve miles over the hills Nithsdale way, and consigned to a farmer named Hunter, whose kin are now well risen in the world thereabouts, and who was thought to be a safe person for boarding and supervising the young moorland Laird. The young Laird must have learned well at school, for he wrote a fine hand (which I have seen) and had acquired the ordinary elements of country education in a respectable way, —in the course of one year as turned out. Within one year, 16th February 1774, these Hunters had married him to their eldest Girl (about sixteen, three months *younger* than himself), and his school-days were suddenly completed! This young girl was my Jeannie's Grandmother; had fourteen children, mostly men (of whom, or of whose male posterity, none now survive, except the three Edinburgh Aunts, youngest of them a month *younger* than my Jane was); and thus held the poor Laird's face considerably to the grindstone all his days! I have seen the Grandmother, in her old age and widowhood; a respectable-looking old person (lived then with her three daughters in a house they had purchased at Dumfries); silently my woman never much liked her or hers (a palpably rather tricky, cunning set these, with a turn for ostentation and hypocrisy in them);—and was accustomed to divide her uncles (not without some ground, as I could see) into 'Welshes,' and 'Welshes with a cross of Hunter,' traceable oftenest (not always though) in their very physiognomy and complexion. They are now all gone; the kindred as good as *out*, only their works following them, *talia qualia!*—

This imprudent marriage reduced the poor young man to pecuniary straits (had to *sell* first *Nether* Craigenputtock, a minor part, in order to pay his Sisters' portions; then long years afterwards, in the multitude of his children, *Upper*

Craigenputtock, or Craigenputtock Proper, to my Wife's Father this *latter* sale); and though, being a thrifty vigorous and solid manager, he prospered handsomely in his farming, first of Milton, then ditto of Penfillan, the best thing he could try in the circumstances, and got completely above all *money*-difficulties; the same 'circumstances' kept him all his days a mere '*Terræ Filius*,' restricted to Nithsdale and his own eye-sight (which indeed was excellent) for all the knowledge he could get of this Universe; and on the whole had made him, such the contrast between native vigour of faculty and accidental contraction of arena, a singular and even interesting man, a Scottish Nithsdale Son of Nature. Highly interesting to his bright young Grand-daughter, with the clear eyesight and valiant true heart like his own, when she came to look into him in her childhood and girlhood. He was solidly devout, truth's own self in what he said and did; had dignity of manners too, in fact a really brave sincere and honourable soul (reverent of talent, honesty, and sound sense, beyond all things); and was silently a good deal respected and honourably esteemed (though with a grin here and there) in the district where he lived. For chief or almost sole intimate he had the neighbouring (biggish) Laird, 'old Hogan of Waterside,' almost close by Penfillan, whose peremptory ways and regularities of mind and conduct, are still remembered in that region,—sorrowfully and strangely as his sons, grandsons, and now great-grandson, have distinguished themselves in the other direction there. It was delightful to hear my Bright One talk of this old Grandfather; so kindly yet so playfully, with a vein of fond affection, yet with the justest insight. In his Last Will (owing to Hunterian artifices and unkind whisperings, as she thought) he had omitted *her*, though her Father had been such a Second Father to all the rest:—£1000 apiece might be the share of each son and each daughter in this Deed of the old man's; and my Jane's name was not found there, as if she too had been dead like her beneficent Father. Less care for the *money* no creature in the world could have had; but the neglect had sensibly grieved her; though she never at all blamed the old man himself, and before long, as was visible, had forgiven the suspected Hunterian parties themselves,—'Poor souls, so earnest about their paltry bits of interests, which are the vitallest and highest *they* have! or perhaps it was some whim of the old man himself? Never mind, never mind!' And so, as I could perceive, it actually *was abolished* in that generous heart, and not there any longer, before much time had passed. Here are two pictures, a wise and an absurd, two of very many she used to give me of the loved old Grandfather;—with which surely I may *end*:

1°. 'Never hire as servant a very poor person's daughter or son: *they* have seen nothing but confusion, waste, and hugger-mugger, mere *want* of thrift or method.' This was a very wise opinion surely. On the other hand,—

He was himself a tall man, perhaps six feet or more, and stood erect as a column. And he had got gradually into his head, supported by such observation as the arena of Keir Parish and neighbouring localities afforded, the astonishing opinion—

2°. That small people, especially short people, were good for nothing; and in fine that a man's bodily stature was a correctish sign of his spiritual! Actually so; and would often make new people, aspiring to be acquaintances, stand up and be measured, that he might have their inches first of all. Nothing could drive this out of him; nothing till he went down once to sit on a jury at Dumfries; and for pleader to him had Francis Jeffrey, a man little above five feet, and evidently the cleverest Advocate one had ever heard or dreamed of!—Ah me, these were such histories and portrayings as I shall never hear again, nor I think did ever hear, for some of the qualities they had.

June 13. John Welsh, my Wife's Father, was born at *Craigenputtock* (I now find, which gives the place a new interest to me), 4th April 1776,'—little more than eighteen years younger than his father, or than his mother. His first three years or so (probably till 26th May 1779, when the Parents may have moved to Milton, in Tynron) must have been passed in those solitudes. At Milton he would see his poor young Sister die,—

wonted Playmate sadly vanish from the new hearth;—and would no doubt have his thoughts about it (my own little Sister Jenny in a similar stage, and my dear Mother's tears about her, I can vividly remember; the strangely silent white-sheeted room; white-sheeted linen-curtained bed, and small piece of elevation there, which the joiner was about measuring; and my own outburst into weeping thereupon, I hardly knew why, —my first passing glance at the Spectre Death!)—more we know not of the Boy's biography there; except that it seems to have lasted about seven years at Milton; and that, no doubt, he had been for three or four years at school there (Tynron School, we may well guess) when (1785 or 6) the family shifted with him to Penfillan. There probably he spent some four or three years more; Tynron still his school, to which he could walk; and where I conclude he must have got what Latin and other education he had. Very imperfect he himself, as I have evidence, considered it; and in his busiest time he never ceased to struggle for improvement of it. Touching to know,—and how superlatively well, in other far more important respects, Nature and his own reflections and inspirations had 'educated' him. Better than one of many thousands, as I do perceive! *Closeburn* (a school still of fame) lay on the other side of Nith River, and would be inaccessible to him, though daily visible.

What year he first went to Edinburgh, or entered the University, I do not know;—I think he was first a kind of apprentice to a famous Joseph or Charles Bell . . . and with this famed Bell he was a favourite;—probably I think attending the classes etc., while still learning from Bell. I rather believe he never took an M.D. degree; but was, and had to be, content with his Diploma as Surgeon: very necessary to get out of his Father's way, and shift for himself in some honest form! Went, I should dimly guess, as Assistant to some old Doctor at Haddington on Bell's recommendation,—I know not in what year (say about 1796, his twentieth year, my first in this world). Went first, I clearly find, as Regimental Surgeon, 10th August 1796, into the 'Perthshire Fencible Cavalry,' and served there some three years. Carefully tied up and reposited by pious hands (seemingly in 1819), I find three old 'Commissions' on parchment, with their stamps, seals, signatures, etc. (Surgeon, 10th August 1796; Cornet, 15th September 1796; and Lieutenant, 5th April 1799) which testify to this;—after which there could have been no 'assistantship' with Somers, but *purchase* and full *practice* at once;—marriage itself having followed in 1800, the next year after that 'Lieutenancy' promotion. The old Doctor's name, if I mistake not, was Somers. Somers finding his Assistant able for everything, a man fast gaining knowledge, and acceptable to all the better Public, or to the Public altogether, agreed in a year or two, to demit, withdraw to country retirement, and declare his assistant successor, on condition, which soon proved easy and easier, of being paid (I know not for how long, possibly for life of self and wife, but it did not last long) an annuity of £200. Of which I find trace in that poor Account Book of his; piously preserved by his Daughter ever since his death.

Dr. Welsh's success appears to have been, henceforth and formerly, swift and constant; till, before long, the whole sphere, or section of life he was placed in had in all senses, pecuniary and other, become his own, and there remained nothing more to conquer in it, only very much to retain by the methods that had acquired it, and to be extremely thankful for as an allotment in this world. A truly superior man, according to all the evidence I from all quarters have. A 'very valiant man,' Edward Irving once called him in my hearing. His medical sagacity was reckoned at a higher and higher rate, medical and other *honesty* as well; for it was by no means as a wise Physician only, but as an honourable exact and quietly dignified man, punctual, faithful in all points, that he was esteemed over the County. It was three years after his death when I first came into the circle which had been his; and nowhere have I met with a posthumous reputation that seemed to be higher or more unanimous, among all ranks of men. The brave man himself I never saw: but my poor Jeannie, in her best moments, often said to me, about this or that, 'Yes, *he* would have done it so!' 'Ah, *he* would have liked you!' as her highest praise. 'Punctuality' Irving described as a thing he much insisted on. Many miles daily of riding ('three strong horses in saddle' always, with inventions against frost etc.): he had appointed the minute everywhere; and insisted calmly on having it kept by all interested parties, high or low. Gravely inflexible, wherever right was concerned; and 'very independent' where mere rank etc. attempted to avail upon him. Story of some old valetudinarian Nabal of eminence (Nisbet of Dirleton, immensely rich, continually cockering himself, and suffering); grudging audibly once at the many fees he had to pay (from his annual £30,000):—'Daresay I have to pay you [£160] a year, Dr. Welsh!'—'Nearly or fully that, I should say; all of it accurately for work done.'—'It's a great deal of money, though!'—'Work not demanded, drain of payment will cease; of course, *not* otherwise,' answered the Doctor; and came home with the full understanding that his Dirleton practice and connection had ended. My Jeannie recollected his quiet report of it to Mamma and her, with that corollary:—however, after some short experience (or re-experience of London Doctors) Nabal Nisbet (who had 'butter churned *daily* for breakfast,' as one item of expenditure) came back, with the necessary *Peccavi* expressed or understood.

One anecdote I always remember, of the *per contra* kind. Riding along one day, on his multifarious business, he noticed a poor wounded partridge, fluttering and struggling about, wing or leg, or both, broken by some sportman's lead. He alighted, in his haste, or made the groom alight if he had one; gathered up the poor partridge, looped it gently in his handkerchief; brought it home; and, by careful splint and salve and other treatment, had it soon on wing again, and sent it forth healed. This, in so grave and practical a man, had always in it a fine expressiveness to me:—*she* never told it me but once, long ago; and perhaps we never spoke of it again.— —

Some time in Autumn 1800 (I think) the young Haddington Doctor married: my Wife, his first and only child, was born 14*th July* ('Bastille-day,' as we often called it) 1801;—sixty-four and a half years old when she died. The Bride was Grace Welsh of Caplegill (head of Moffat Water in Annandale); her Father an opulent store-farmer up there, native of Nithsdale; her Mother, a Baillie from Biggar region, already deceased. Grace was beautiful,—must have been; she continued what might be called beautiful till the very end, in or beyond her sixtieth year. *Her* Welshes were Nithsdale people of good condition, though beyond her grandfather and uncles, big farmers in Thornhill Parish (the 'Welshes of Morton-Mains' for I know not what length of time before, nor exactly what after, only that it ceased some thirty or perhaps almost fifty years ago, in a tragic kind of way); I can learn nothing certain of them from Rev. Walter of Auchtertool, nor from his sister Maggie here, who are of that genealogy, children of my Mother-in-law's brother John; concerning whom perhaps a word afterwards.—When the young Haddington Doctor and his beautiful Grace had first made acquaintance I know not; probably on visits of hers to Morton-Mains, which is but a short step from Penfillan: acquainted they evidently were, to the degree of mutually saying, 'Be it for life then;' and, I believe, were and continued deeply attached to one another. Sadder widow than my Mother-in-law, modestly, delicately, yet discernibly was, I have seldom or never seen; and my poor Jeannie has told me, he had great love of her, though obliged to keep it rather secret or undemonstrative, being well aware of her too sensitive, fanciful, and capricious ways.

June 15. Mrs. Welsh when I first saw her (1821) must have been in the [second] year of her widowhood. I think, when Irving and I entered, she was sitting in the room with Benjamin[1] and my Jane, but soon went away. An air of deep sadness lay on her, and on everybody, except on poor dying Benjamin, who affected to be very sprightly, though overwhelmed as he must have felt himself. His spirit, as I afterwards learned from his Niece, who did not love him, or feel grateful to him, was extraordinary, in the worldly-wise kind. Mrs. Welsh, though beauti-

[1] Dr. Welsh's youngest brother, who died in the following year at the age of 26.

ful, a tall *aquiline* figure, of elegant carriage and air, was not of intellectual or specially distinguished physiognomy; and, in her severe costume and air, rather repelled me than otherwise at that time. A day or so after, next evening perhaps, both Irving and I were in her Drawing-room, with her Daughter and her, both very humane to me, especially the former, which I noticed with true joy for the moment. I was miserably ill in health; miserable every way more than enough, in my lonely imprisonment, *such* it was, which lasted many years. The Drawing-room seemed to me the finest apartment I had ever sat or stood in:—in fact it was a room of large and fine proportions, looking out on a garden, on mere gardens or garden walls and sprinkling of trees, across the valley or plain of the Tyne (which lay hidden),—house quite at the back of the Town, facing towards Lethington etc. the best rooms of it; and everywhere bearing stamp of the late owner's solid temper. Clean, all of it, as spring water; solid and correct as well as pertinently ornamented: in the Drawing-room, on the tables there, perhaps rather a superfluity of elegant whimwhams. The summer twilight, I remember, was pouring in rich and soft; I felt as one walking transiently in upper spheres, where I had little right even to make transit. Ah me! They did not *know* of its *former* tenants when I went to the house again in April last. I remember our all sitting, another evening, in a little parlour off the dining-room (downstairs), and talking a long time; Irving mainly, and bringing out *me*, the two ladies benevolently listening with not much of speech, but the younger with lively apprehension of all meanings and shades of meaning. Above this parlour I used to sleep, in my visits in after years, while the house was still unsold. Mrs. W. left it at once, autumn 1826, the instant her Jeannie had gone with me; went to Templand, Nithsdale, to her Father;—and turned out to have decided never to behold Haddington more.

She was of a most generous, honourable, affectionate turn of mind; had consummate skill in administering a household; a goodish well-tending intellect,—something of real drollery in it; from which my Jeannie, I thought, might have inherited that beautiful lambency and brilliancy of soft genial *humour*, which illuminated her perceptions and discoursings so often to a singular degree, like pure soft morning radiance falling upon a perfect picture, *true* to the facts. Indeed, I once said, 'Your mother, my Dear, has narrowly missed being a woman of genius.' Which doubtless was reported by and by in a quizzical manner, and received with pleasure. For the rest, Mrs. Welsh, as above said, was far too sensitive; her beauty, too, had brought flatteries, conceits perhaps; she was very variable of humour, flew off or on upon slight reasons, and, as already said, was not easy to live with for one wiser than herself, though very easy for one more foolish, if especially a touch of hypocrisy and perfect assentation were superadded. The married life at Haddington, I always understood, was loyal and happy, sunnier than most; but it was so by the Husband's softly and steadily *taking* the command, I fancy, and knowing how to keep it in a silent and noble manner. Old Penfillan (I have heard the three Aunts say) reported once, on returning from a visit to Haddington, 'He had seen her one evening in fifteen different humours' as the night wore on. This, probably, was in his own youngish years (as well as hers and his son's), and might have a good deal of satirical exaggeration in it. She was the most exemplary nurse to her Husband's Brother William, and to other of the Penfillan sons who were brought there for help or furtherance. William's stay lasted five years, three of them involving two hours daily upon the 'spring-deal' (a stout elastic plank of twenty or thirty feet long, on which the weak patient gets himself shaken and secures exercise), she herself, day after day, doing the part of trampler;—which perhaps was judged useful, or as good as necessary, for her own health. William was not in all points a patient one *could* not have quarrelled with; and my Mother-in-law's quiet obedience I cannot reckon other than *exemplary*,—even supposing it was partly for her own health too. This I suppose was actually the case. She had much weak health, more and more towards the end of life. Her husband had often signally helped her by his skill and zeal; once, for six months long, he, and visibly he alone, had been the means of keeping her alive. It was a bad inflammation or other disorder of the liver; liver disorder was cured, but power of digestion had ceased; Doctors from Edinburgh etc. unanimously gave her up, food of no kind would stay a moment on the stomach, 'What can any mortal of us do?' Husband persisted; found food that would stay (arrowroot perfectly pure; if by chance, your pure stock being out, you tried *shop* arrowroot, the least of starch in it declared it futile); for six months kept her alive and gathering strength on those terms, till she rose again to her feet. 'He much loved her,' said my Jeannie; 'but none could less love what of *follies* she had,'—not a few, though none of them deep at all, the good and even noble soul! How sadly I remember now, and often before now, the time when she vanished from her kind Jane's sight and mine, never more to meet us in this world. It must have been in autumn 1841; she had attended Jane down from Templand, [to Dumfries] probably I was up from Scotsbrig (but don't remember); I was, at any rate, to *conduct* to Scotsbrig that night, and on the morrow or so, thence for London. Mrs. Welsh was unusually beautiful, but strangely sad too,—eyes bright, and as if with many tears behind them. Her Daughter too was sad; so was I, at the sadness of both, and at the evidently boundless feeling of affection which knew not how to be kind enough. Into shops etc. for last gifts, and later than last: at length we had got all done; and withdrew to Sister Jean's, to order the gig and go. She went with us still; but feeling what would not be the kindest, heroically rose (still not weeping), and said Adieu there. We watched her, sorrowful both of us, from the end window; stepping, tall and graceful, feather in bonnet, etc., down Lochmaben Gate, casting no glance *back*; then vanishing to rightward, into High Street (bonnet feather perhaps, the last thing), and she was gone for ever. *Ay de mi, Ay de mi.* What a thing is Life; bounded thus by Death! I do not think we ever spoke of this; but how could either of us ever forget it at all?—

Old Walter Welsh, my Wife's maternal Grandfather, I had seen twice or thrice, at Templand, before our marriage; and for the next six or seven years, especially after our removal to Craigenputtock, he was naturally a principal figure in our small circle. He liked his Granddaughter cordially well; she had been much about him on visits and so forth, from her early childhood; a bright merry little grig, always pleasant, in the troubled atmosphere of the old Grandfather. 'Pen' (*Penfillan* Jeannie, for there was another) he used to call her to the last; Mother's name in the family was 'Grizzie' (Grace). A perfect true affection ran through all branches, my poor little 'Pen' well included and returning it well. She was very fond of old Walter (as he privately was of her); and got a great deal of affectionate amusement out of him. Me too he found much to like in, though practically we discorded commonly on two points: 1°, that I did and would smoke tobacco; 2°, that I could not and would not drink, with any freedom, whisky punch, or other liquid stimulants; a thing breathing the utmost poltroonery in some section of one's mind, thought Walter always. He for himself cared nothing about drink; but had the rooted idea (common in his *old* circles) that it belonged in some indissoluble way to good fellowship. We used to presently knit up the peace again; but tiffs of reproach from him on this score would always arise from time to time; and had always to be laughed away by me, which was very easy, for I really liked old Walter heartily; and he was a continual genial study to me over and above: *microcosm* of old Scottish Life as it *had* been; and man of much singularity, originality and real worth of character, and even of intellect too if you saw well. He abounded in contrasts; glaring oppositions, contradictions, you would have said in every element of him,—yet all springing from a single centre (you might observe) and honestly uniting themselves there. No better-*natured* man (sympathy, sociality, honest loving-kindness towards all innocent people); and yet of men I have hardly seen one of hotter, more impatient *temper*. Sudden, vehement; breaking out into fierce flashes as of lightning when you touched him the wrong way. Yet they were flashes only, never bolts, and were gone again in a moment; and the fine old face beaming quietly on you as before. Face uncommonly fine: serious, yet laughing eyes, as if inviting you *in*; bushy eyebrows, face which you might have called picturesquely shaggy, under its plenty of gray hair, beard itself imperfectly shaved here and there; features massive yet soft (almost with a tendency to pendulous or flabby in parts): and nothing but honesty, quick ingenuity, kindliness, and frank manhood as the general expression. He was a most simple man, of stunted utterance, *burred* with his *r* and had a *chewing* kind of way with his words, which, rapid, and few, seemed to be forcing their way through laziness or phlegm, and were not extremely distinct till you attended a little (and then, aided by the face etc., they *were* extremely and memorably,—brave old Walter's words, so true too; as honest almost as my own Father's though in a strain so different!). Clever things Walter never said or attempted to say; nor wise things either in any sphere beyond that of sincerely accepted commonplace; but he very well knew when such were said by others and glanced with a bright look on them, a bright dimpling chuckle sometimes (*smudge* of laughter, the Scotch call it, one of the prettiest words and ditto things); and on the whole, hated no kind of talk but the unwise kind. He was serious, pensive, not morose or sad, in these old times. He had the prettiest laugh (once or at most twice, in my presence) that I can remember to have heard,—not the loudest, my own Father's still rarer laugh was louder far, though perhaps not more complete; but his was all of artillery-thunder, *feu de joie* from all guns as the main element; while in Walter's there was audible something as of infinite flutes and harps, as if the vanquished themselves were invited (or compelled) to partake in the triumph. I remember one such laugh (quite forget about what), and how the old face looked suddenly so beautiful and young again. 'Radiant ever-young Apollo' etc. of Teufelsdröckh's laugh is a reminiscence of that. Now when I think of it, Walter must have had an immense fund of inarticulate gaiety in his composition, a truly fine sense of the ridiculous (excellent *sense* in a man, especially if he never cultivate it, or be conscious of it, as was Walter's case): and it must have been from him, then, that my Jane derived that beautiful light of humour (*never* going into folly, yet full of tacit fun) which spontaneously illuminated all her best hours. Thanks to Walter; *she* was of him in this respect: my Father's laugh, too, is mainly mine (a grimmer and inferior kind); of my Mother's beautifully sportive vein (which was a *third* kind,—also hereditary I am told) I seem to have inherited less, though not nothing either, nay, perhaps at bottom not even less, had my life chanced to be easier or joyfuller. 'Sense of the ridiculous' (worth calling such; i.e. 'brotherly sympathy with the *downward* side') is withal very indispensable to a man:—Hebrews have it not; hardly any Jew creature (not even blackguard Heine, to any real length),—hence various *mis*qualities of theirs, perhaps most of their qualities too which have become *Historical.* This is an old remark of mine, though not yet written anywhere.

Walter had been a Buck in his youth, a high-prancing horseman etc.: I forget what image there was of him, in buckskins, pipe hair-dressings, grand equipments; riding somewhither (with John Welsh of Penfillan I almost think?)—bright air-image, from some transient discourse I need not say of *whom.* He had married a good and beautiful Miss Baillie (of whom already); and settled with her at Caplegill, in the Moffat region; where all his children were born,—and left with him young; the mother having died, still in the flower of her age; ever tenderly remembered by Walter to his last day (as was well understood, though mention was avoided). From her my Jeannie was called 'Jane Baillie Welsh' at the time of our marriage; but after a good few years, when she took to signing 'Jane *Welsh* Carlyle,' in which I never hindered her, dropped the 'Baillie,' I suppose as too long. I have heard her quiz about the 'unfortunate Miss Baillie' of the song at a still earlier time. Whether Grace Welsh was married from Caplegill I do not know. Walter had been altogether prosperous in Caplegill; and all of the Family that I knew (John a merchant in Liverpool, the one remaining of the sons, and Jeannie the one other daughter, a beautiful 'Aunt Jeannie' of whom a word by and by) continued warmly attached to it as their real home in this earth: but at the renewal of leases (1801 or so) had lost it in a quite provoking way. By the treachery of a so-called Friend, namely: Friend a neighbouring farmer perhaps, but with an inferior farm, came to *advise* with Walter about rents, probably his own rent first, in this general time of leasing: 'I am thinking to offer so-and-so, what say you? what are *you* going to offer by the bye?' Walter, the very soul of fidelity himself, made no scruple to answer;—found by and by that this precious individual had thereupon himself gone and offered for Caplegill the requisite few pounds *more*, and that, according to fixed customs of the Estate, he and not Walter, was declared tenant of Caplegill henceforth. Disdain of such scandalous conduct, astonishment and *quasi* horror at it, could have been stronger in few men than in Walter; a feeling shared in heartily and irrevocably by all the Family; who, for the rest, seldom spoke of it, or hardly ever, in my time; and did not seem to hate the man at all, but to have cut him off as non-extant and left him unmentioned thenceforth. Perhaps some Welsh he too, of a different stock? There were Moffat country Welshes, I observed, with whom thay rather eagerly (John of Liverpool eagerly) disclaimed all kinship but it might be on other grounds: this individual's name I never once heard. Nor was the story touched upon except by rare chance and in the lightest way.

After Caplegill, Walter had no more farming prosperity: I believe he was unskilful in the *arable* kind of business, certainly he was unlucky; shifted about to various places (all in Nithsdale, and I think on a smaller and smaller scale, Castlehill in Durisdeer, Strathmilligan in Tynron, ultimately Templand), and had gradually lost nearly all his capital, which at one time was of an opulent extent (actual number of thousands quite unknown to me) and felt himself becoming old and frail, and as it were thrown out of the game. His Family meanwhile had been scattered abroad, seeking their various fortune: son John to Liverpool (where he had one or perhaps more uncles of mercantile distinction), son William to the West Indies (?) and to early death, whom I often heard lamented by my Mother-in-law; these and possibly others who were not known to me. John, by this time, had, recovering out of one bit of very bad luck, got into a solid way of business; and was, he alone of the Brothers, capable of helping his Father a little on the pecuniary side. Right willing to do it, to the utmost of his power or further! A most munificent, affectionate, and nobly honourable kind of man; much esteemed by both my Jane and me, foreign as his way of life was to us.

Besides these there was the youngest Daughter, now a woman of thirty or so, the excellent 'Aunt Jeannie,' so lovable to both of us; who was said to resemble her Mother ('nearly *as* beautiful, all but the golden hair,'—Jeannie's was fine flaxen, complexion of the fairest); who had watched over and waited on her Father, through all his vicissitudes, and everywhere kept a comfortable, frugally effective and even elegant house round him,—and in fact let no wind visit him too roughly. She was a beautifully patient, ingenious and practically thoughtful creature; always cheerful of face, *suppressing* herself and her sorrows, of which I understood there had been enough,—in order to screen her Father, and make life still soft to him. By aid of John, perhaps slightly of my Mother-in-law, the little Farm of Templand (Queensberry farm, with a strong but gaunt and inconvenient old stone house on it) was leased and equipped for the old man: house thoroughly repaired, garden etc.; that he might still feel himself an active citizen, and have a civilised habitation, in his weak years. Nothing could be neater, trimmer, in all essential particulars more complete than house and environment, under Aunt Jeannie's fine managing, had in a year or two grown to be. Fine sheltered beautiful and useful garden in front, with trellises, flower-work, and strip of the cleanest river shingle between porch and it: House all clean and complete like a new coin; steadily kept dry (by industry), bedroom, and every part; old furniture (of Caplegill) really interesting to the eye, as well as perfect for its duties. Dairy, kitchen etc.: nothing that was fairly needful or useful could you find to be wanting:—the whole matter had the air, to a visitor like myself, as of a rustic Idyl (the seamy side of it all strictly hidden by clever Aunt Jeannie);—I think she must have been, what I often heard, one of the best Housekeepers in the world. Dear good little Beauty: it appears too she had met with her tragedies in life, —one tragedy hardest of all upon a woman, betrothed Lover flying off into infamous treason, not against her specially, but against her Brother and his own honour and conscience (Brother's Partner he was, if I recollect rightly, and fled with all the funds, leaving £12,000 of *minus*); which annihilated *him* for her, and closed her poor heart against hopes of that kind, at an early period of her life. Much lying on her mind, I always understood, while she was so cheery, diligent and helpful to everybody round her!—I forget, or never knew what time they had come to Templand but guess it may have been in 1822 or shortly after: dates of Castlehill and Strathmilligan I never knew, even *order* of dates:—last summer, I could so easily have known (Deaf-and-Dumb 'Mr. Turner,' an old Strathmilligan acquaintance, recognised by *her* in the Dumfries Railway Station, and made to *speak* by paper and pencil, I writing for *her* because she could not,—oh me, oh me, *where is* now that summer Evening, so beautiful, so infinitely sad and strange! The train rolled off with her to Thornhill, Holm Hill, and that too, with its setting sun, is gone).—I almost think Durisdeer (Castlehill) must have been *last* before Templand; I remember passing that quaint old Kirk (with village hidden) on my left, one April Evening, on the top of a Dumfries Coach from Edinburgh, with reveries and pensive reflections, which must have belonged to 1822 or 1823. Once, long after, on one of our London visits, I drove thither sitting by her, in an afternoon; and *saw* the Gypsy Village for the first time; and looked in with her, at the fine Italian Sculptures on the Queensberry Tomb through a gap in the old kirk wall. Again a pensive Evening, now so beautiful and sad.

From Childhood upwards she seemed to have been much about these Homes of old Walter; summer visits almost yearly; and, after her Father's death, likely to be of longer continuance. They must have been a quiet, welcome, and right wholesome element for her young heart and vividly growing mind: beautiful simplicity and rural Scottish Nature in its very finest form: frugal, elegant, true and kindly; *simplex munditiis* nowhere more descriptive both for men and things. To myself, summing up what I experienced of them, there was a real gain from them as well as pleasure. Rough nature I knew well already, or perhaps too well; but here it was reduced to cosmic, and had a victorious character which was new, and grateful to me, well nigh poetical. The old Norse Kings, the Homeric *grazier* sovereigns of men: I have felt in reading of them, as if their ways had a kinship with these (*un*sung) Nithsdale ones. Poor 'Aunt Jeannie' sickened visibly the Summer after our Marriage; Summer 1827, while we were there on visit. My own little Jeannie, whom nothing could escape that she had the interest to fix her lynx-eyed scrutiny upon, discovered just before our leaving, that her dear Aunt was dangerously ill, and indeed had long been,—a tumour, now evidently cancerous, growing on her breast for twelve years past; which, after effort, she at last made the poor Aunt confess to! We were all (I myself by sympathy, had there been nothing more) thrown into consternation; made the matter known, at Liverpool etc., to everybody but old Walter; and had no need to insist on immediate steps being taken. My Mother-in-law was an inmate there, and probably in chief command (had moved thither, quitting Haddington for good, directly on our marriage): she at once took measures; having indeed a turn herself for *medicining*, and some skill withal. That autumn Aunt Jeannie and she came to Edinburgh, had a furnished house close by us, in Comley Bank; and then the dismal operation; successfully, the Doctors all said,—but alas! Dim sorrow rests on those weeks to me. Aunt Jeannie showed her old Heroism; and my Wife herself strove to hope: but it was painful, oppressive, sad;—twice or so I recollect being in the sick-room; and the pale yet smiling face, more excitation in the eyes than usual: one of the times she was giving us the earnest counsel (my Jane having been consulting), 'To *go* to London, clearly, if I could,—if they would give me the Professorship there!'

(Some Professorship in Gower Street, perhaps of 'Literature,' which I had hoped vaguely [for], not strongly at all, nor ever formally declaring myself, through Jeffrey from his friend Brougham and consorts,—which they were kind enough to dispose of *otherwise*). My own poor little Jeannie; my poor *pair* of kind little Jeannies! Poor Templand Jeannie went home again, striving to hope; but sickened in winter; worsened when the spring came; and *summer* 1828 was still some weeks off when she had departed. Or *were* we at Craigenputtock by that time? I cannot think so. No it must have been in April or March of 1828. The Funeral, at Crawfurd, I remember sadly well; old Walter, John and two Sons (Walter of Auchtertool, and Alick now successor in Liverpool), with various old Moffat people etc. etc. at the Inn of Crawfurd; Pass of Dalveen with Dr. Russell in the dark (holding candles, both of us, inside the chaise): and old Walter's silent sorrow and my own as we sat together in the vacant parlour after getting home. 'Hah, we'll no see *her* nae mair!' murmured the old man; and that was all I heard from him, I think.

Old Walter now fell entirely to the care of Daughter 'Grizzie,' who was unweariedly attentive to him, a most affectionate Daughter, an excellent housewife too, and had money enough to support herself and him in their quiet, neat and frugal way. Templand continued, in all points, as trim and beautiful as ever; the old man made no kind of complaint, and in economics there was even an improvement: but the old cheery patience of Daughter 'Jeannie,' magnanimously effacing herself, and returning all his little spurts of smoke in the form of lambent kindly flame and radiant light upon him, was no longer there; and we did not doubt but he sometimes felt the change. Templand has a very fine situation; old Walter's walk, at the south end of the house, was one of the most picturesque and pretty to be found in the world. Nith valley (river half a mile off, winding through green holms, now in its borders of clean shingle, now lost in pleasant woods and bushes) lay patent to the south, the country sinking perhaps a hundred feet, rather suddenly, just beyond Templand; Keir,

Penpont, Tynron lying spread, across the river, all as in a map, full of cheerful habitations, gentlemen's mansions, well-cultivated Farms and their cottages and appendages; spreading up in irregular slopes and gorges against the finest range of hills, Barjarg with its trees and mansion atop, to your left hand; Tynron Doon, a grand massive lowland mountain (you might call it) with its white village at the base (behind which, in summer time was the setting of the sun for you); one big pass (Glen-shinnel, with the clearest river-water I ever saw out of Cumberland) bisecting this expanse of heights, and leading you by the Clone ('cloven?') of Maxwellton, into Glencairn valley, and over the Black Craig of Dunscore (*Dun-scoir* = Black Hill) and to Craigenputtock if you chose. Westward of Tynron, rose Drumlanrig Castle and woods; and the view, if you quite turned your *back* to Dumfries, ended in the Lowthers, Leadhills, and other lofty mountains, watershed and boundary of Lanarkshire and Dumfriesshire: rugged, beautifully piled *sierra*, winding round into the eastern heights (very pretty too) which part Annandale from Nithsdale. [Alas, what is the use of all this, here and now?] Closeburn, mansion, woods and greeneries, backed by brown steep masses, was on the south-eastern side, house etc. hiding it from Walter's walk. Walk where you liked, the view you could reckon unsurpassable,—not the least needing to be 'surpassed.' Walter's walk *special* (it never had any name of that kind; but from the garden he glided mostly into it, in fine days, a small green seat at each end of it, and a small ditto gate, easy to open and shut) was not above 150 yards long: but he sauntered and walked [in] it as fancy bade him (not with an *eye* to 'regimen,' except so far as 'fancy' herself might unconsciously point that way); took his newspapers (*Liverpool*, sent by John) to read there in the sunny seasons, or sat, silent, but with a quietly alert look, contemplating the glorious panorama of 'sky-covered earth' in that part, and mildly reaping his poor bit of harvest from it without needing to pay rent!

We went over often; were always a most welcome arrival, surprise oftenest; and our bits of visits, which could never be prolonged, were uniformly pleasant on both sides. One of *our* chief pleasures, I think almost our chief, during those moorland years. Oh those pleasant gig-drives, in fine leafy twilight, or deep in the night sometimes, ourselves two alone in the world, the good 'Harry' *faring* us (rather too light for the job, but always soft and willing), how they rise on me now, benignantly luminous from the bosom of the grim dead night! What would I give for *one*, the very worst of them, at this moment! Once we had gone to Dumfries, in a soft misty December day (for a Portrait which my darling wanted, not of *herself!*)—a bridge was found broken as we went down; brook unsafe by night; we had to try 'Clyden (*Lower-Cairn*)-Water' road, as all was mist and pitch-darkness, on our return, road unknown to me except in general,—and drive like no other in my memory. Cairn hoarsely roaring on the left (my Darling's side); Harry, with but one lamp-candle (for we had put out the other, lest both might fall done), bending always to be straight in the light of that; I really anxious, though speaking only hopefully; my Darling so full of trust in me, really *happy* and opulently interested in these equipments, in these poor and dangerous circumstances,—how opulent is a nobly royal heart. She had the worthless 'Portrait' (pencil-sketch by a wandering German, announced to us by poor and hospitable Mrs. Richardson, once a 'Novelist' of mark, much a gentlewoman and well loved by us both) safe in her reticule; 'better far than none,' she cheerfully said of it, and the price, I think, had been 5s., fruit of her thrift too:—well, could California have made me and her so rich, had *I* known it (sorry gloomy mortal) just as she did? To noble hearts such wealth is there in Poverty itself, and impossible without Poverty! I saw ahead, high in the mist, the minarets of Dunscore Kirk, at last, glad sight; at Mrs. Broatch's cosy rough inn, we got Harry fed, ourselves dried and refreshed (still seven miles to do, but road all plain), and got home safe, after a pleasant day, in spite of all.—Then the drive to Boreland once (George Welsh's, 'Uncle George,' youngest of the Penfillans), heart of winter, intense calm frost, and through Dumfries, at least thirty-five miles for poor

Harry and us; very beautiful, that too, and very strange; past the base of towering New Abbey, huge ruins, piercing grandly into the silent frosty sunset, on this hand, despicable cowhouse of Presbyterian Kirk on that hand (sad new contrast to Devorgilla's *old* bounty) etc. etc.:—of our drive home again I recollect only *her* invincible contentment, and the poor old Cowar-woman offering to warm us with a flame of dry broom, 'A'll licht a bruim couw, if ye'll please to come in!' Another time we had gone to 'Dumfries Cattle Show' (*first* of its race, which are many since): a kind of *lark*, on our part; and really entertaining, though the day proved shockingly wet and muddy; saw various notabilities there, Sir James Grahame (baddish, proud man, we both thought by physiognomy, and did not afterwards *alter* our opinion much), Ramsay Macculloch (in sky-blue coat, shiningly on visit from London) etc. etc., with none of whom, or few, had we right (or wish) to speak, abundantly occupied with seeing so many fine specimens, biped and quadruped: in afternoon we suddenly determined to take Templand for the night (nearer by some miles, and weather still so wet and muddy); and did so, with the best success, a right glad surprise there. Poor Huskisson had perished near Liverpool, in first trial of the railway, I think, the very day before; at any rate we heard the news, or at least the full particulars there,—the tragedy (spectacular mostly, but not quite, or inhumanly in any sense) of our bright glad evening there. But I must quit these things.

June 18; day wet and muddy. . . . Sad; quiet and sad;—'*drowned* in soft regrets and loving sorrow,' so I define my common mood at present,—and sometimes estimate it as a kind of *religious* worship (course of devotional exercises) I have got into,—driven by Fate, at the long last!

The Liverpool children first, then 'Uncle John' himself for a fortnight or so, used to come every summer; and stir up Templand's quietude,—to us bystanders, in a purely agreeable way. Of the children I recollect nothing almost; nothing that was not cheerful and auroral or matutinal. The two Boys, Walter and Alick, came once on visit to us, perhaps oftener, but once

I recollect their lying quiet in their big bed till eleven A.M., with exemplary politeness,—for fear of awakening me, who had been up for two hours, though everybody had forgotten to announce it to them. We ran across to Templand rather oftener than usual on these occasions, and I suppose staid a shorter time.

My Jeannie had a great love and regard for her 'Uncle John,' whose faults she knew well enough, but knew to be of the surface all, while his worth of many fine kinds ran in the blood, and never once failed to show in the conduct when called for. He had all his Father's *veracity*, integrity, abhorrence of dishonourable behaviour; was kind, munificent, frank; and had more than his Father's impetuosity, vehemence, and violence, or perhaps was only more provoked (in his way of life) to exhibit these qualities now and then. He was cheerful, musical, politely conversible; truly a genial harmonious, loving nature; but there was a roar in him too like a lion's. He had had great misfortunes and provocations; his way of life, in dusty, sooty, ever noisy Liverpool, with its dinnerings, wine-drinkings, dull evening parties issuing in whist, was not *his* element, few men's less, though he made not the least complaint of it (even to himself, I think): but his heart, and all his pleasant memories and thoughts, were in the breezy Hills of Moffatdale, with the rustic natives there, and their shepherdings, huntings (brock and fox), and solitary fishings in the clear streams. It was beautiful to see how he made some pilgriming into those ot the kindred localities; never failed to search out all his Father's old herdsmen (with a sovereign or two for each, punctual as fate); and had a few days' fishing as one item. He had got his schooling at Closeburn; was, if no very learned, a very intelligent inquiring kind of man; could talk to you instructively about all manner of practical things; and loved to talk with the intelligent, though nearly all his life was doomed to pass itself with the stupid or commonplace sort, who were intent upon nothing but 'getting-on,' and giving dinners or getting them. Rarely did he burst out into brief fiery recognition of all this; yet once at least, before my time, I heard of his doing so in his own drawing-room, with brevity, but with memorable emphasis and fury. He was studiously polite in general, *always* so to those who deserved it, not quite always to those who didn't.

His demeanour in his bankruptcy, his and his Wife's . . . when the villain of a partner eloped, and left him possessor of a *minus* £12,000, with other still painfuller items (Sister Jeannie's incurable heart, for example), was admitted to be beautiful. Creditors had been handsome and gentle, aware how the case stood; household with all its properties and ornaments left intact, etc.: Wife rigorously locked all her plate away; Husband laboriously looked out for a new course of business; ingeniously found or created one, prospered in it, saving every penny possible;—then, after perhaps seven or eight years, had a great dinner: all the plate out again; all the creditors there—and under every man's cover punctual sum due, payment complete to every creditor, 'Pocket your cheques, Gentlemen, with our poor warmest thanks;—and let us drink Better Luck for time coming!' He prospered always afterwards; but never saved much money; too hospitable, far too open-handed, for that; all his dinners, ever since I knew him, were *given* (never dined out, he); and in more than one instance, to our knowledge, ruined people were lifted up by him (one widow *Cousin*, one orphan, young daughter of an acquaintance e.g.) as if they had been his own; sank possibly enough mainly or altogether into his hands, and were triumphantly (with patience and in silence) brought through. No wonder my Darling liked this Uncle; nor had I the least difficulty in liking him!—

Once I remember mounting early, almost with the sun (a kind hand expediting, perhaps sending me), to breakfast at Templand, and spend the day with him there. I rode by the shoulder of the Black Craig (Dunscore Hill), might see Dumfries with its cap of early kitchen-smoke, all shrunk to the size of one's hat, though there were 11,000 souls in it, far away to the right; descended then by Cairn, by the Clone of Maxwellton (where at length came roads), through fragrant grassy or bushy solitudes; at the Bridge of Shinnel, looked down into the pellucid glassy pool rushing through its rock chasms, and at a young peasant woman, peeling potatoes by the brink, chubby infant at her knee,—one of the finest mornings, one of the pleasantest rides; and arrived at Templand in good time and in good time and trim for my hosts. The day I forget; would be spent wholesomely wandering about, in rational talk on indifferent matters.—Another time, long after, new from London then, I had wandered out with him, his two pretty Daughters, and a poor good Cousin called Robert Macqueen attending; we gradually strolled into Crichop Linn (a strange high-lying chasmy place, near Closeburn); there pausing, well aloft, and shaded from the noon sun, the two Girls, with their Father for *octave* accompaniment, sang us 'The Birks of Aberfeldy' so as I have seldom heard a song; voices excellent and true, especially his voice and native expression given; which stirred my poor London-fevered heart almost to tears.—One earlier visit from London, I had driven up, latish, from Dumfries, to see my own little Woman who was there among them all. No wink could I sleep; at length about three A.M., reflecting how miserable I should be all day, and cause only misery to the others—(with leave had) rose, yoked my gig, and drove away the road I had come. Morning cold and surly, all mortals still quiet, except unhappy self; I remember seeing towards Auldgarth, within few yards of my road, a vigilant industrious heron, mid-leg deep in the Nith-stream, diligently fishing, dabbing its long bill and hungry eyes down into the rushing water (tail up stream), and paying no regard to my wheels or me. The only time I ever saw a hernshaw ('herrin-shouw' the Annandalers call it) actually fishing. *Cætera desunt*; of Dumfries, of the day there, and its sequences, all trace is gone. It must have been soon after *French Revolution* Book; nerves all inflamed and torn up, body and mind in a hag-ridden condition (too much their normal one those many London years).

Of visits *from* Templand there were not so many; but my Darling (hampered and gyved as we were by the *genius loci* and its difficulties) always triumphantly made them do. She had the genius of a Field-marshal, not to be taken by surprise, or weight of odds, in these cases! Oh my beautiful little Guardian Spirit! Twice at least there was visit from Uncle John in person and the Liverpool strangers, escorted by Mother;—*my* Mother, too, was there one of the times. Warning I suppose had been given; night-quarters etc. all arranged. Uncle John and boys went down to Orr Water, I attending without rod, to fish. Tramping about on the mossy brink, Uncle and I awoke an adder; we had just passed its underground hole; alarm rose,—looking round, we saw the vile sooty-looking fatal abominable wretch, towering up above a yard high (the only time I ever saw an adder): one of the boys snatched a stray branch, hurried up from behind, and with a good hearty switch or two, broke the creature's back.

Another of these dinner days, I was in the throes of a Review Article (*Characteristics*, was it?), and could not attend the sports; but sauntered about, much on the strain, to small purpose; *dinner* all the time that I could afford. Smoking outside at the dining-room window,—'Is not every *Day* the conflux of Two Eternities,' thought I, 'for every man?' Lines of influence from all the Past, and stretching onwards into all the Future, do intersect there. That little thoughtkin stands in some of my Books: I recollect being thankful (scraggily thankful) for the day of small things.

Oh my Darling, how dark and sad am I, and seem to have been defrauding *Thee* all this while, and speaking only about others! I will stop; and go out.

22d June . . . The London bits of *memorabilia* do not disengage themselves from the general mass, as the earlier Craigenputtock ones did; the years here, *I* still struggling *in* them, lie as a confused heap, *un*beautiful in comparison. Let me pick out (and be speedier) what comes to hand.

She liked London constantly; and stood in defence of it against me and my atrabilious censures of it; never had for herself the least wish to quit it again, though I was often talking of that, and her *practice* would have been loyal compliance for my behoof. I well remember my first walking her up to Hyde Park Corner in the summer evening, and her fine interest in everything. At the corner of the Green Park, I found something for her to sit on; 'Hah, there is John Mill coming!' I said; and her joyful ingenuous blush is still very beautiful to me. The good Child! It did not prove to be John Mill (whom she knew since 1831, and liked for my sake): but probably I showed her the Duke of Wellington, whom one often used to see there, striding deliberately along, as if home from his work, about that hour: him (I almost rather think, that same evening), and at any rate, other figures of distinction or notoriety. And we said to one another, 'How strange to be in big London here; isn't it?'—Our purchase of household kettles and saucepans etc. in the mean Ironmongery, so noble in its poverty and loyalty on her part, is sad and infinitely lovely to me at this moment.

We had plenty of 'company' from the very first: John Mill, down from Kensington once a week or oftener; the 'Mrs. Austin' of those days, so popular and almost famous, on such exiguous basis (Translations from the German, rather poorly done, and of original nothing that rose far above the rank of twaddle): '*femme alors célèbre*,' as we used to term the phenomenon, parodying some phrase I had found in Thiers: Mrs. Austin affected much sisterhood with us (*affected* mainly, though in *kind* wise); and was a cheery, sanguine, and generally acceptable member of society,—already *up* to the Marquis of Lansdowne (in a slight sense), much more to all the Radical Officials and notables: Charles Buller, Sir W. Molesworth, etc. etc. of '*alors*.' She still lives, this Mrs. Austin, in quiet though eclipsed condition: spring last she was in Town for a couple of weeks; and my Dear One went twice to see her, though I couldn't manage quite.—Erasmus Darwin, a most diverse kind of mortal, came to seek us out very soon ('had heard of Carlyle in Germany' etc.); and continues ever since to be a quiet house-friend, honestly attached; though his visits latterly have been rarer and rarer, health so poor, I so occupied, etc. etc. He has something of original and sarcastically ingenious in him; one of the sincerest, naturally truest, and most modest of men. Elder brother of Charles Darwin (the famed *Darwin on Species* of these days), to whom I rather prefer him for intellect, had not his health quite doomed him to silence and patient idleness;—Grandsons, both, of the first *famed* Erasmus ('Botanic Garden' etc.), who also seems to have gone upon 'species' questions; '*Omnia ex Conchis*' (all from Oysters) being a *dictum* of his (even a *stamp* he sealed with, still extant), as the *present* Erasmus once told me, many long years before this of 'Darwin on Species' came up among us! Wonderful to me, as indicating the *capricious* stupidity of mankind; never could *read* a page of it, or waste the least thought upon it. Erasmus Darwin it was who named the late Whewell, seeing him sit, all ear (not all *assent*) at some of my Lectures, 'The Harmonious Blacksmith;' a really descriptive title. My Dear One had a great favour for this honest Darwin always; many a road, to shops and the like, he drove her in his Cab ('*Darwingium Cabbum*,' comparable to *Georgium Sidus*), in those early days, when even the charge of Omnibuses was a consideration; and his sparse utterances, *sardonic* often, were a great amusement to her. 'A perfect *gentleman*,' she at once discerned him to be; and of sound worth, and kindliness, in the most unaffected form. 'Take me now to *Oxygen* Street; a dyer's shop there!' Darwin, without a wrinkle or remark, made for Oxenden Street and drew up at the required door. Amusingly admirable to us both, when she came home.

Our commonest evening sitter, for a good while, was Leigh Hunt, who lived close by, and delighted to sit talking with us (free, cheery, *idly* melodious as bird on bough), or listening, with real feeling, to her old Scotch tunes on the Piano, and winding up with a frugal morsel of Scotch Porridge (endlessly admirable to Hunt)—I think I spoke of this above? Hunt was always accurately dressed, these evenings, and had a fine chivalrous gentlemanly carriage, polite, affectionate, respectful (especially to her) and yet so free and natural. Her brilliancy and faculty he at once recognised, none better; but there rose gradually in it, to his astonished eye, something of positive, of practically steadfast, which scared him off, a good deal; the like in my own case too, still more;—which he would call

'Scotch,' 'Presbyterian,' who knows what; and which gradually repelled him, in sorrow, not in anger, quite away from us, with rare exceptions, which, in his last years, were almost pathetic to us both. Long before this, he had gone to live in Kensington;—and we scarcely saw him except by accident. His Household, while in '4 *Upper* Cheyne Row,' within few steps of us here, almost at once disclosed itself to be huggermugger, *un*-thrift, and sordid collapse, once for all; and had to be associated with on cautious terms;—while he himself emerged out of it in the chivalrous figure I describe. Dark complexion (a trace of the African, I believe), copious clean strong black hair, beautifully-shaped head, fine beaming serious hazel eyes; *seriousness* and intellect the main expression of the face (to our surprise at first),—he would lean on his elbow against the mantelpiece (fine clean, elastic figure too he had, five feet ten or more), and look round him nearly in silence, before taking leave for the night: 'as if I were a *Lar*,' said he once, 'or permanent Household God here!' (such his polite *Ariel*-like way). Another time, rising from his *Lar* attitude, he repeated (voice very fine) as if in sport of parody, yet with something of very sad perceptible: 'While I to sulphurous and penal fire'—as the last thing before vanishing. Poor Hunt! no more of him. She, I remember, was almost in *tears*, during some last visit of his, and kind and pitying as a Daughter to the now weak and time-worn old man.

23d June 1866, Saturday; *hot*, and weary of heart. Allan Cunningham, living in Pimlico, was well within walking distance; and failed not to come down, now and then; always friendly, smooth and fond of pleasing: 'a solid Dumfries Stonemason at any rate!' *she* would define him. He had very smooth manners, much practical shrewdness, some real tone of *melody* lodged in him, *item* a twinkle of bright mockery where he judged it safe: culture only superficial (of the *surface*, truly), reading, information, ways of thinking, all mainly ditto ditto. Had a good will to us evidently; not an unwelcome face, when he entered, at rare intervals,—always rather *rarer*, as they proved to be:—he got at once into *Nithsdale*, recalled old rustic comicalities (seemed habitually to *dwell* there); and had not much of instruction either to give or receive. His resort seemed to be much among Scotch City people; who presented him with punchbowls etc.; and in his own house that was chiefly the (unprofitable) people to be met. We admired always his shrewd sense for managing himself in strange London; his stalwart healthy figure and ways (bright hazel eyes, bald open brow, sonorous hearty tone of voice; a tall, perpendicular, quietly manful-looking figure); and were sorry sincerely to lose him, as we suddenly did. His widow too is now gone; some of the sons (especially Colonel Frank, the youngest, and a daughter, who lives with Frank), have still a friendly though far-off relation to this house.

Harriet Martineau had for some years a much more lively intercourse here;—introduced by Darwin possibly, I forget by whom; on her return from America, her *Book* upon which was now in progress. Harriet had started into lionhood since our first visit to London; and was still much run after, by a rather feeble set of persons chiefly. She was not unpleasant to talk with for a little, though through an ear-trumpet, without which she was totally deaf. To admire her literary genius, or even her solidity of common sense, was never possible for either of us: but she had a sharp eye, an imperturbable self-possession, and in all things a swiftness of positive decision, which, joined to her evident loyalty of *intention*, and her frank, guileless, easy ways, we both liked. Her adorers, principally, not exclusively, 'poor *whinnering* old moneyed women in their well-hung broughams, otherwise idle,' did her a great deal of mischief, and indeed as it proved were gradually turning her fine clear head (so to speak), and leading to sad issues for her. Her talent, which in that sense was very considerable, I used to think, would have made her a quite shining Matron of some big Female Establishment, mistress of some immense Dress-Shop, for instance (if she *had* a dressing-faculty, which perhaps she hadn't); but was totally inadequate to grapple with deep spiritual and social questions,—into which she launched at all turns, nothing doubting. However, she was very fond of us, *me* chiefly, at first, though gradually of both, and I was considerably the *first* that *tired* of her: she was much in the world, we little or hardly at all; and her frank friendly countenance, eager for practical help had it been possible, was obliging and agreeable in the circumstances, and gratefully acknowledged by us. For the rest, she was full of Nigger fanaticisms; admirations (e.g.) for her Brother James (a Socinian preacher of due quality). The 'exchange of ideas' with her was seldom of behoof in our poor sphere. But she was practically very good. I remember her coming down, on the sudden when it struck her, to demand dinner from us; and dining pleasantly, with praise of the frugal terms. Her Soirées were frequent and crowded (small house in Fludyer Street full to the door); and we, for sake of the notabilities or notorieties wandering about there, were willing to attend. Gradually learning how *in*significant such notabilities nearly all were. Ah me, the thing which it is now touching to reflect on, was the thrift we had to exercise, my little Heroine and I! My Darling was always dressed to modest perfection (talent conspicuous in that way, I have always understood and heard confirmed); but the expense of 10s. 6d. for a 'neat fly' was never to be thought of: omnibus, with clogs and the best of care; that was always our resource. Painful at this moment is the recollection I have of one time: muddy night, between Regent Street and our goal in Fludyer Street, one of her clogs came loose; I had to clasp it,—with what impatience compared to her fine tolerance, stings me with remorse just now. Surely, even I might have taken a Cab *from Regent Street;* 1s., 1s. 6d. and there could have been no '*quarrel* about fare' (which was always my horror in such cases): she, beautiful high soul, never whispered or dreamt of such a thing, possibly may have expressly forbidden it, though I cannot recollect that it was proposed in this case. Shame on me! However, I cleaned perfectly my dirty fingers again (probably in some handy little rain-pool in the Park, with diligent wiping); *she* entered faultless into the illumination (I need not doubt): and all still went well enough.

24th June . . . In a couple of years or so, our poor Harriet, nerves all torn by this racket, of 'fame' so-called, fell seriously ill; threatening of tumour, or I know not what; removed from London (never has resided there since, except for temporary periods); took shelter at Tynemouth, 'to be near her brother-in-law, an expert surgeon in Newcastle, and have solitude, and the pure sea air.' Solitude she only sometimes had; and, in perfection, never: for it soon became evident she was constantly in spectacle there, to herself and to the sympathetic adorers (who refreshed themselves with frequent personal visits and continual correspondings), and had, in sad effect, so far as could be managed, the whole world, along with self and company, for a theatre to gaze upon her. *Life in the Sickroom*, with 'Christus Consolator' (a paltry print then much canted of), etc. etc.: this, and other sad Books, and actions full of ostentation, done there, gave painful evidence; followed always by painfuller, till the *Atheism* etc. etc., which I heard described (by the first Lady Ashburton once) as 'a stripping of yourself naked, not to the skin only, but to the bone, and walking about in that guise!' (*clever*, of its kind).

Once in the earliest stage of all this, we made her a visit, my Jane and I; returning out of Scotland by that route. We were very sorry for her; not *censorious* in any measure, though the aspects were already questionable, to both of us (as I surmise). We had our lodging in the principal street (rather noisy by night); and staid about a week,—not with much profit I think, either to her or ourselves; I at least with none.

25th June. There had been, before this, some small note or two of correspondence; with little hope on my part; and now I saw it to be hopeless. My hopefuller and kindlier little Darling continued it yet awhile; and I remember scrubbyish (lively enough, but 'sawdustish') Socinian *didactic* little notes from Tynemouth for a year or two hence; but the vapidly didactic etc. vein continuing more and more, even she, I could perceive, was getting tired of it: and at length, our poor good Harriet, taking the sublime terror 'that her letters might be laid hold of by improper parties in future generations,' and demanding them all back that she herself might burn them, produced, after perhaps some retiring pass or two, a complete cessation. We never quarrelled in the least; we saw the honest ever self-sufficient Harriet, in the company of common friends, still once or twice; with pleasure rather than otherwise; but never had more to do with her or say to her. A soul clean as river sand; but which would evidently grow no *flowers* of *our* planting!—I remember our return home from that week at Tynemouth; the yelling flight through some detestable smoky chaos, and midnight witch-dance of base-looking nameless dirty towns (or was this some other time, and Lancashire the scene?). I remember *she* was with me: and her bright laugh (long after, perhaps towards Rugby now) in the face of some innocent young gentleman opposite, who had ingeniously made a *nightcap* for himself of his pocket-handkerchief, and looked really strange (an improvised 'Camus crowned with sedge'),—but was very good-humoured too. *During* the week, I also recollect reading one Play (never any since or before) of Knight's *Edition of Shakespeare*; and making my reflections on that fatal brood of people, and the nature of 'fame' etc.: Sweet friends, for Jesus' sake forbear!

26th June . . . In those first years, probably from about 1839, we had got acquainted with the Leeds Marshall family; especially with old Mr. (John) Marshall, the head and founder of it, and the most or really almost only interesting item of it. He had made immense moneys ('wealth now no object to him,' Darwin told us in the name of everybody), by skilful, faithful and altogether human conduct in his flax and linen manufactory at Leeds; and was now settled in opulently shining circumstances in London; endeavouring to *enjoy* the victory gained. Certain of his sons were carrying on the Leeds 'business,' in high, quasi-'patriotic' and 'morally exemplary,' though still prudent and successful style; the eldest was in Parliament, 'a landed gentleman' etc. etc.: wife and daughters were the old man's London household, with sons often incidentally present there. None of them was entertaining to speak with, though all were honest wholesome people. The old man himself, a pale, sorrow-stricken ,modest, yet dignified-looking person, full of respect for intellect, wisdom and worth (as he understood the terms); low voiced, almost timidly inarticulate (you would have said),—yet with a definite and mildly precise imperativeness to his subalterns, as I have noticed once or twice,—was an amiable, humane and thoroughly respectable phenomenon to me. The house (Grosvenor Street, western division) was resplendent, not gaudy or offensive, with wealth and its fruits and furnishings; the dinners large, and splendidly served; guests of distinction (especially on the Whig or Radical side) were to be met with there, and a good sprinkling of promising younger people of the same, or a superior type. Soirées extensive, and sumptuously *illuminated* in all senses; but generally *not* entertaining. My astonishment at the 'Reform' M.P.'s whom I met there, and the notions they seemed to have of 'reforming' (and *radical*ling, and quarrelling with their superiors) upon! We went pretty often (I think I myself far the oftener, as in such cases; my loyal little Darling taking no manner of offence *not* to participate in my *lionings*; but behaving like the royal soul she was,—I, dullard egoist, taking no special recognition of such nobleness, till the bar was quite passed, or even not fully then! Alas, I see it *now*, perhaps better than I ever did!), but we seldom had much real profit, or even real enjoyment for the hour. We never made out together that often-urged 'visit to Hallsteads' (grand Mansion and Establishment, near Greystoke, head of Ullswater in Cumberland); I myself, partly by accident, and under convoy of James Spedding, was there once, long after, for one night; and felt very dull and wretched, though the old man and his good old wife etc. were so good. Old Mr. Marshall was a man worth having known; evidently a great deal of human worth and wisdom lying funded in him. And the world's resources even when he had victory over it to the full, were so exiguous, and perhaps to himself almost contemptible! I remember well always, he gave me the first *Horse* I ever had in London, and with what noble simplicity of unaffected politeness he did it. 'Son William' (the gentleman son, out near Watford) 'will be *glad* to take it off your hands through winter; and in summer it will help your health, you *know*!' And in this way it continued two summers (most part of two), till in the second winter William brought it down; and it had to be sold, for a trifle—£17, if I recollect, which William would not give to the Anti-Corn-Law Fund (then struggling in the shallows) as I urged, but insisted on handing over to me. And so it ended. I was at Headingley (by Leeds) with James Marshall, just wedded to Spring-Rice's daughter, a languishing patroness of mine; staid till third day; and never happened to return. And this was about the sum of my share in the Marshall adventure. It is well known the Marshall daughters were all married off (each of them had £50,000) and what intricate intermarrying with the Spring-Rices there was.... My Jeannie quarrelled with nothing in Marshalldom; quite the contrary; formed a kind of friendship (conquest I believe it was on her side, generously converted into something of friendship) with Cordelia Marshall, ... who became, shortly after, wife, first wife of the late big Whewell, and aided his position and advancement towards Mastership of Trinity, etc. I recollect seeing them both here, and Cordelia's adoration of her 'Harmonious Blacksmith,' with friendly enough assent, and some amusement, from us two; and I don't think I ever saw Cordelia again. She soon ceased to write hither; we transiently heard ... that she was very unhappy (Poor innocent Cordelia!) and transiently, after certain years, that she was dead, and Whewell had married again.

I am weary, writing down all this; so little has my Lost One to do with it, which alone could be its interest for me! I believe I should stop short. The London years are not definite, or fertile in disengaged remembrances, like the Scotch ones: dusty, dim, unbeautiful they still seem to me in comparison; and my poor Jeannie's 'Problem' (which I believe was sorer, perhaps far sorer, than ever of old, but in which she again proved not to be vanquishable, and at length to be triumphant!) is so mixed with confusing intricacies to me that I cannot sort it out into clear articulation at all, or give the features of it, as before. The general type of it is shiningly clear to me: A noble fight at my side; a valiant strangling of serpents day after day

—done gaily by her (for most part), as I had to do it angrily and gloomily; thus we went on together: *Ay de mi, Ay de mi!*—

June 27. Note from Dods yesterday that the *Tablet*[1] was not come, nor indeed had been expected; note to-day that it did come yesterday: at this hour probably the mason is hewing out a bed for it; in the silence of the Abbey Kirk yonder, as completion of her Father's Tomb. The Eternities looking down on him, and on us poor Sons of Time! Peace, Peace!

June 28. By much the tenderest and beautifullest reminiscence to me out of those years is that of the Lecturer times. The vilest welter of odious confusions, horrors and repugnancies; to which, meanwhile, there was compulsion absolute; —and to which she was the one irradiation; noble loving soul, not to be quenched in any chaos that might come. Oh, her love to me; her cheering, unaffected, useful practicality of help: was not I *rich*, after all? She had a steady hope in me, too, while I myself had habitually none (except of the 'desperate' kind); nay a steady contentment with me, and with our lot together, let hope be as it might. 'Never mind him, my Dear,' whispered Miss Wilson to her, one day, as I stood wriggling in my agony of incipiency, 'people like it; the more of that, the better does the Lecture prove!' Which was a truth; though the poor *Sympathiser* might, at the moment, feel it harsh. This Miss Wilson and her brother still live; opulent, fine, Church of England people (scrupulously orthodox to the secularities not less than the spiritualities of that creed), and Miss Wilson very

[1] The tablet on Jane Welsh Carlyle's tombstone at Haddington bears the following inscription:

'Here likewise now rests

'JANE WELSH CARLYLE,

'Spouse of Thomas Carlyle, Chelsea, London.

'She was born at Haddington, 14th July 1801: only child of the above John Welsh, and of Grace Welsh, Caplegill, Dumfriesshire, his Wife. In her bright existence she had more sorrows than are common; but also a soft invincibility, a clearness of discernment, and a noble loyalty of heart, which are rare. For forty years she was the true and ever-loving Helpmate of her Husband; and, by act and word, unweariedly forwarded him, as none else could, in all of worthy that he did or attempted.

'She died at London, 21st April 1866; suddenly snatched away from him, and the light of his life as if gone out.'

clever too (i.e. full of strong just insight in her way);—who had from the first taken to us, and had us much about them (Spedding, Maurice, etc. attending) then and for some years afterwards; very desirous to help us, if that could have much done it (for indeed, to me, it was always mainly an indigestion purchased by a loyal kind of weariness). I have seen Sir James Stephen[1] there, but did not then understand him, or that *he* could be a 'clever man,' as reported by Henry Taylor and other good judges. 'He shuts his eyes on you,' said the elder Spring-Rice (Lord Monteagle), 'and talks as if he were dictating a Colonial Despatch' (most true;—'teaching you How *Not* to do it,' as Dickens defined afterwards): one of the pattest things I ever heard from Spring-Rice, who had rather a turn for such. Stephen, ultimately, when on half-pay and a Cambridge Professor, used to come down hither pretty often on an evening; and we heard a great deal of talk from him, recognisably serious and able, though always in that Colonial-Office style, more or less. Colonial-Office *being* an Impotency (as Stephen inarticulately, though he never said or whispered it, well knew), what *could* an earnest and honest kind of man do, but try and teach you How *not* to do it? Stephen seemed to me a master in that art.—

The *Lecture* time fell in the earlier part of the Sterling Period,—which latter must have lasted in all, counting till John's death, about ten years (Autumn 1844 when John died). To my Jeannie, I think, this was clearly the sunniest and wholesomest element in her then outer life. All the Household loved her; and she had virtually, by her sense, by her felt *loyalty*, expressed oftenest in a gay mildly quizzing manner, a real influence, a kind of light *command* one might almost call it, willingly yielded her among them. Details of this are in print (as I said above).—In the same years, Mrs. Buller (Charles's mother) was a very cheerful item to her. Mrs. Buller (a whilom Indian Beauty, Wit and finest Fine Lady), who had, at all times a very recognising eye for talent, and a real reverence for it, very soon made out something of my little woman; and took more

[1] Father of Fitzjames and Leslie Stephen.

and more to her, all the time she lived after. Mrs. Buller's circle was gay and populous at this time (Radical, chiefly Radical, lions of every complexion), and we had as much of it as we would consent to. I remember being at Leatherhead too;—and, after that, a pleasant rustic week at Troston Parsonage (in Suffolk, where Mrs. Buller's youngest son 'served,' and serves); which Mrs. Buller contrived very well to make the best of, sending me to ride for three days in Oliver Cromwell's country, that she might have the Wife more to herself. My Jane must have been there altogether, I dare say, near a month (had gone before me, returned after me); and I regretted never to have seen the place again. This must have been in September or October 1842; Mrs. Welsh's death in early Spring past. I remember well my feelings in Ely Cathedral, in the close of sunset or dusk; the place was open, free to me without witnesses; people seemed to be tuning the organ, which went in solemn gusts far aloft; the thought of Oliver, and his 'Leave off your fooling, and come down, Sir!' was almost as if audible to me. Sleepless night, owing to Cathedral bells; and strange ride next day to St. Ives, to Hinchinbrook, etc., and thence to Cambridge, with thunder-cloud and lightning dogging me to rear, and bursting into torrents few minutes after I got into The Hoop Inn.—

My poor Darling had, for constant accompaniment to all her bits of satisfactions, an altogether weak state of health, continually breaking down, into violent fits of headache in her best times, and in winter-season into cough, etc., in lingering forms of a quite sad and exhausting sort. Wonderful to me how she, so sensitive a creature, maintained her hoping cheerful humour to such a degree, amidst all that; and, except the pain of inevitable sympathy, and vague flitting fears, gave me no pain. Careful always to screen me from pain, as I by no means always reciprocally was; alas, no; miserable egoist in comparison! At this time, I must have been in the thick of *Cromwell*; 'four years' of abstruse toil, obscure tentations, futile wrestling, and misery, I used to count it had cost me, before I took to editing the *Letters and Speeches* ('to have *them* out of my way');

which rapidly drained off the sour swamp water bodily, and left me, beyond all first expectations, quite free of the matter. Often I have thought how miserable my Books must have been to *her*; and how, though they were none of her choosing, and had come upon her like ill weather or ill health, she at no instant (never once, I do believe) made the least complaint of me or my behaviour (often bad, or at least thoughtless and weak) under them! Always some quizzing little lesson, the purport and effect of which was to encourage me; never once anything *worse*. Oh it was noble;—and I see it so well now, when it is gone from me, and no return possible!

Cromwell was by much the worst Book-time; till this of *Friedrich*; which indeed was infinitely worse; in the dregs of our strength too;—and lasted for about thirteen years. She was generally in quite weak health, too; and was often for long weeks or months, miserably ill.

28th June. Interruption here yesterday; to-day likewise, the whole morning gone, in extraneous fiddle-faddle, and not so much as one word here! Shame on *me*; for (though 'the world' is a most intrusive, useless, nay plunderous and obstructive affair to me at present), the blame is not chiefly 'the world's' but my own! Froude is now coming; and with remorse, I must put this away. News of Craik's death, at Belfast, 27th ult., came last night.

29th June. It was strange how she contrived to sift out of such a troublous forlorn day as hers, in such case, was, all the available little items; as she was sure to do,—and to have them ready for me in the evening when my work was done; in the prettiest little narrative anybody could have given of such things. Never again shall I have such melodious, humanly beautiful Half-hours; they were the *rainbow* of my poor dripping *day*,—and reminded me that there otherwise *was* a Sun. At this time, and all along, she 'did all the society;' was all brightness to the one or two (oftenest rather dull and prosaic fellows, for all the *better* sort respected my seclusion, especially during that last *Friedrich* time), whom I *needed* to see on my affairs in hand, or who, with more of *brass* than others, managed to intrude upon me: for these she did, in their several kinds, her very best; all of her own people, whom I might be apt to feel wearisome (dislike any of them I never did, or his or her *discharge from service* would have swiftly followed), she kept beautifully out of my way, saving my 'politeness' withal: a very perfect skill she had in all this. And *took* my dark toiling periods, however long sullen and severe they might be, with a loyalty and heart-acquiescence that never failed. The heroic little soul!

Latter-Day Pamphlet time, and especially the time that preceded it (1848 etc.) must have been very sore and heavy: my heart was long overloaded with the meanings at length uttered there, and no way of getting them set forth would answer. I forget what ways I tried, or thought of; *Times* Newspaper was one (alert, airy, rather vacant editorial gentleman I remember going to once, in Printing House Square); but this way, of course, proved *hypothetical* merely,—as all others did, till we, as last shift, gave the rough MSS. to Chapman (in Forster's[1] company one winter Sunday). About *half* of the ultimately *printed* might be in Chapman's hands; but there was much manipulation as well as addition needed. Forster soon fell away, I could perceive, into terror and surprise;—as indeed everybody did: 'A lost man!' thought everybody. Not she at any moment; much amused by the outside pother, she; and glad to see me getting delivered of my black electricities and consuming fires, in that way. Strange letters came to us, during those nine months of pamphleteering; strange visitors (of moonstruck unprofitable type for most part), who had, for one reason or another, been each of them wearing himself half-mad on some *one* of the public scandals I was recognising and denouncing. I still remember some of their faces, and the look their paper bundles had. She got a considerable entertainment out of all that; went along with me in everything (probably *counselling* a little here and there; a censorship well worth my regarding, and generally *adoptable*, here as everywhere); and

[1] John Forster, the minuscule Dr. Johnson of the Victorian age, remembered now for his biography of Dickens.

minded no whit any results that might follow this evident *speaking of the truth.* Somebody, writing from India I think, and clearly meaning kindness, 'did hope' (some time afterwards) 'the tide would turn, and this lamentable Hostility of the Press die away into friendship again:' at which I remember our innocent laughter,—ignorant till then what 'The Press's' feelings were, and leaving 'The Press' very welcome to them then. Neuberg[1] helped me zealously, as volunteer amanuensis etc., through all this business; but I know not that even he approved it all, or any of it *to the bottom.* In the whole world I had one complete Approver; in that, as in other cases, *one*; and it was worth all.

On the back of *Latter-Day Pamphlets* followed *Life of Sterling*; a very quiet thing; but considerably disapproved of too, as I learned; and utterly revolting to the *Religious people* in particular (to my surprise rather than otherwise): 'Doesn't believe in *us*, then, either?' Not he, for certain; *can't*, if you *will* know! Others urged disdainfully, 'What has Sterling done that he should have a *Life*?' '*Induced* Carlyle *somehow* to write him one!' answered she once (to the Ferguses, I think) in an arch airy way, which I can well fancy; and which shut up the question there. The book was afterwards greatly praised,—again, on rather weak terms, I doubt. What now will please me best in it, and alone *will*, was then an accidental quality,—the authentic light, under the due conditions, that is thrown by it on *her*. Oh my Dear One; sad is my soul for the loss of Thee, and will to the end be, as I compute! *Lonelier* creature there is not henceforth in this world ;neither person, work, or thing going on in it that is of any value, in comparison, or even at all. Death I feel almost daily in express fact, Death is the one haven; and have occasionally a kind of *kingship*, sorrowful, but sublime, almost godlike, in the feeling that that is nigh. Sometimes the image of Her, gone in her car of victory (in that beautiful death), and as if nodding to me with a smile, 'I am gone, loved one; work a little longer, if thou still canst; if not, follow! There

[1] Joseph Neuberg, Carlyle's principal helper with the book on Frederick the Great.

is no baseness, and no misery *here*. Courage, courage to the last!'—that, sometimes, as in this moment, is inexpressibly beautiful to me, and comes nearer to bringing *tears* than it once did. Stop for to-day.

June 30. In 1852 had come the new-modelling of our House;—attended with infinite dusty confusion (head-carpenter stupid, though honest, fell ill, etc. etc.); confusion falling upon *her* more than me, and at length upon her altogether. *She* was the architect, guiding and directing and contriving genius, in all that enterprise, seemingly so foreign to her. But indeed she was ardent in it; and she had a talent that way which was altogether unique in my experience. An 'eye' first of all, equal in correctness to a joiner's square,—this, up almost from her childhood, as I understood. Then a sense of order, sense of beauty, of wise and thrifty convenience;—sense of *wisdom* altogether in fact; for that was it! A human intellect shining luminous in every direction, the highest and the lowest (as I remarked above); in childhood she used to be sent to seek when things fell lost; 'the best seeker of us all,' her Father would say, or look (as she thought): for me also she *sought* everything, with such success as I never saw elsewhere. It was she who widened our poor drawing-room (as if by a stroke of genius) and made it (zealously, at the partial expense of three feet from *her own* bedroom) into what it now is, one of the prettiest little drawing-rooms I ever saw, and made the whole house into what it now is. How frugal, too, and how modest about it! House was hardly finished, when there arose that of the 'Demon-Fowls,'—as she appropriately named them: macaws, Cochin-chinas, endless concert of crowing, cackling, shrieking roosters (from a bad or misled neighbour, next door) which cut us off from sleep or peace, at times altogether, and were like to drive me mad, and her through me, through sympathy with me. From which also she was my deliverer,—had delivered and continued to deliver me from hundreds of such things (Oh my beautiful little *Alcides*, in these new days of Anarchy and the Mud-gods, threatening to crush down a poor man, and kill him with his work still on hand!) I remember well her setting off, one winter morning, from the Grange on this enterprise;—probably having thought of it most of the night (sleep denied), she said to me next morning the first thing: 'Dear, we *must* extinguish those Demon-Fowls, or they will extinguish us! Rent the house (No. 6, proprietor mad etc. etc.) ourselves; it is but some £40 a year,—pack away those vile people, and let it stand empty. I will go this very day upon it, if you assent!' And she went accordingly; and slew altogether this *Lerna Hydra*; at far less expense than taking the house, nay almost at no expense at all, except by her fine intellect, tact, just discernment, swiftness of decision, and general nobleness of mind (in short). Oh, my bonny little woman; mine only in memory now!—

I left the Grange two days after her, on this occasion; hastening through London, gloomy of mind; to see my dear old Mother yet once (if I might) before she died. She had, for many months before, been evidently and painfully sinking away,—under no disease, but the ever-increasing infirmities of eighty-three years of time. She had expressed no desire to see me; but her love from my birth upwards, under all scenes and circumstances, I knew to be emphatically a Mother's. I walked from the Kirtlebridge ('Galls') Station that dim winter morning; my one thought, 'Shall I see her yet alive?' She was still there; weary, very weary, and wishing to be at rest. I think she only at times knew me; so bewildering were her continual distresses; once she entirely forgot me; then, in a minute or two, asked my pardon—ah me, ah me! It was my Mother, and not my Mother; the last pale *rim* or sickle of the moon, which had once been *full*, now sinking in the dark seas. This lasted only three days. Saturday night she had her full faculties, but was in nearly unendurable misery; not breath sufficient etc., etc.: John tried various reliefs, had at last to give a few drops of laudanum, which eased the misery, and in an hour or two brought sleep. All next day she lay asleep, breathing equably but heavily,—her face grand and solemn, almost severe, like a marble statue; about four P.M. the breathing suddenly halted; recommenced for half an instant, then fluttered,—ceased. 'All the days of my appointed time,' she had often said, 'will I wait, *till my change come.*' The most beautifully *religious* soul I ever knew. Proud enough she was, too, though piously humble; and full of native intellect, humour, etc., though all undeveloped. On the *religious* side, looking into the very heart of the matter, I always reckon her rather *superior* to my Jane, who in other shapes and with far different exemplars and conditions, had a great deal of noble religion too. Her death filled me with a kind of *dim amazement*, and crush of *confused* sorrows, which were very painful, but not so sharply pathetic as I might have expected. It was the earliest terror of my childhood that I 'might lose my Mother;' and it had gone with me all my days:—But, and that is probably the whole account of it, I was then sunk in the miseries of *Friedrich* etc. etc., in many miseries; and was then fifty-eight years of age.—It is strange to me, in these very days, how *peaceable*, though still sacred and tender, the memory of my Mother now lies in me. (This very morning, I got into dreaming confused *nightmare* stuff about some *funeral* and her; not hers, nor obviously my Jane's, seemingly my Father's rather, and she *sending* me on it,—the saddest bewildered stuff. What a dismal debasing and confusing element is that of a *sick body* on the human soul or *thinking* part!)—

It was in 1852 (September-October, for about a month) that I had first seen Germany,—gone on my first errand as to *Friedrich*: there was a second, five years afterwards; this time it was to *inquire* (of Preuss and Co.); to look about me, search for books, portraits, etc. etc. I went from Scotsbrig (my dear old Mother painfully weak, though I had no thought it would be the *last* time I should see her *afoot*);—from Scotsbrig by Leith for Rotterdam, Köln, Bonn (Neuberg's);—and on the whole never had nearly so (outwardly) unpleasant a journey in my life; till the second and last I made thither. But the Chelsea establishment was under carpenters, painters; till those disappeared, no *work* possible, scarcely any *living* possible (though my brave woman did make it possible without complaint): 'Stay so many weeks, all painting at least shall then be off!' I returned, near broken-down utterly, at the set time; and, alas, was met by a foul dabblement of paint oozing downstairs: the painters had proved treacherous to her; time could not be kept! It was the one instance of such a thing here; and except the first sick surprise, I now recollect no more of it.

Sunday, 1st July. 'Mamma, *wine* makes cosy!' said the bright little one, perhaps between two and three years old, her Mother, after some walk with sprinkling of wet or the like, having given her a dram-glass of wine on their getting home: 'Mamma, wine makes *cosy*!' said the small silver voice, gaily sipping, getting its new bits of insight into natural philosophy! What 'pictures' has my Beautiful One left me;—what joys can surround every well-ordered human hearth. I said long since, I never knew so beautiful a childhood. Her little bit of a first chair, its wee wee arms etc., visible to me in the closet at this moment, is still here, and always was; I have looked at it hundreds of times; from of *old*, with many thoughts. No daughter or son of *hers* was to sit there; so it had been appointed us, my Darling. I have no *Book* thousandth-part so beautiful as Thou; but these were *our* only 'Children,'—and, in a true sense, these *were* verily OURS; and will perhaps live some time in the world, after we are both gone;—and be of no damage to the poor brute chaos of a world, let us hope! The Will of the Supreme shall be accomplished: *Amen*. But to proceed.

Shortly after my return from Germany (next summer, I think, while the *Cochin-chinas* were at work, and we could not quit the house, having spent so much on it, and got a long lease), there began a new still worse hurlyburly of the building kind; that of the new top-story,—whole area of the house to be thrown into one sublime garret-room, lighted from above, thirty feet by thirty say, and at least eleven feet high; double-doored, double-windowed; impervious to sound, to—in short, to everything but self and work! I had my grave doubts about all this; but John Chorley, in his friendly zeal, warmly urged it on; pushed, superintended;—and was a good deal disgusted with my dismal experience of the *result*. Something really good might have come of it in a scene where good and faithful work was to be had on the part of all, from *architect* downwards; but here, from all (except one good young man of the carpenter trade, whom I at length noticed thankfully in small matters), the 'work,' of planning to begin with, and then of executing, in all its details, was mere work of Belial, i.e. of the Father of LIES; such 'work' as I had not conceived the possibility of among the sons of Adam till *then*. By degrees, I perceived it to be the ordinary English 'work' of this epoch;—and, with manifold reflections, deep as Tophet, on the outlooks *this* offered for us all, endeavoured to be silent as to my own little failure. My new illustrious 'Study' was definable as the *least* inhabitable, and most entirely detestable and despicable bit of human workmanship in that kind. Sad and odious to me *very*. But by many and long-continued efforts, with endless botherations which lasted for two or three years after (one winter starved by 'Arnott's improved *grate*,' I recollect), I did get it patched together into something of supportability; and continued, though under protest, to inhabit it during all working hours, as I had indeed from the first done. The whole of the now printed *Friedrich* was written there (or in summer in the back court and garden, when driven down by baking heat); much rawer matter, I think, was tentatively on paper, *before* this sublime new 'Study.' *Friedrich* once done, I quitted the place for ever; and it is now a bedroom for the servants. The 'architect' for this beautiful bit of masonry and carpentry was one 'Parsons,' really a clever creature, I could see, but swimming as for dear life in a mere 'Mother of Dead Dogs' (ultimately did become bankrupt); his *men* of all types, Irish hodmen and upwards, for real *mendacity* of hand, for drunkenness, greediness, mutinous nomadism, and anarchic malfeasance throughout, excelled all experience or conception. Shut the *lid* on their 'unexampled prosperity' and them, for evermore.

The sufferings of my poor little woman, throughout all this, must have been great, though she whispered nothing of them, —the rather, as this was my enterprise (both the *Friedrich* and it);—indeed it was by her address and invention that I got my sooterkin of a 'study' improved out of its worst blotches; it was she, for example, that went silently to Bramah's smith people, and got me a fireplace, of merely human sort, which actually warmed the room, and sent Arnott's miracle about its business. But undoubtedly that *Friedrich* affair, with its many bad adjuncts, was much the *worst* we ever had; and sorely tried us both. It lasted thirteen years or more. To me a desperate dead-lift pull at that time; my whole strength devoted to it; alone, withdrawn from all the world (except some bores who would take no hint, almost nobody came to see me, nor did I wish almost anybody then left living for me), all the world withdrawing from me; I desperate of ever *getting through* (not to speak of 'succeeding'); left solitary 'with the nightmares' (as I sometimes expressed it), 'hugging unclean creatures' (Prussian Blockheadisms) 'to my bosom, trying to caress and flatter their secret out of them!' Why do I speak of all this? It is now become *coprolith* to me, insignificant as the dung of a thousand centuries ago: I did get through, thank God; let it now wander into the belly of oblivion for ever. But what I do still, and shall more and more, remember with loving admiration is her behaviour in it. She was habitually in the feeblest health; often, for long whiles, grievously ill. Yet by an alchemy all her own, she had extracted grains as of gold out of every day, and seldom or never failed to have something bright and pleasant to tell me, when I reached home after my evening ride, the most foredone of men. In all, I rode, during that book, some 30,000 miles, much of it (all the winter part of it) under cloud of night, sun just setting when I mounted. All the rest of the day, I sat silent aloft; insisting upon work, and *such* work, *invitissimâ Minervâ* for that matter. Home between five and six with mud mackintoshes off, and, the nightmares locked up for a while, I tried for an hour's sleep before my (solitary, *dietetic*, altogether simple, simple) bit of dinner; but first *always*, came up for half an hour to the drawing-room and Her; where a bright kindly fire was sure to be burning (candles hardly lit, all in trustful *chiaroscuro*), and a spoonful of brandy in water, with a pipe of tobacco (which I had learned to take sitting on the rug, with my back to the jamb, and door never so little *open*, so that all the smoke, if I was careful, went up the chimney): this was the one bright portion of my black day. Oh those evening half-hours, how beautiful and blessed they were, —*not* awaiting me now on my home-coming, for the last ten weeks! She was oftenest reclining on the sofa; wearied enough, she too, with her day's doings and endurings. But her history, even of what was bad, had such grace and truth, and spontaneous tinkling melody of a naturally cheerful and loving heart, I never anywhere enjoyed the like. Her courage, patience, silent heroism, meanwhile, must often have been immense. Within the last two years or so she has told me about my talk to her of the Battle of Mollwitz on these occasions, while that was on the anvil. She was lying on the sofa; weak, but I knew little how weak, and patient, kind, quiet and good as ever. After tugging and wriggling through what inextricable labyrinth and Sloughs-of-despond, I still well remember, it appears I had at last *conquered* Mollwitz, saw it all clear ahead and round me, and took to telling her about it, in my poor bit of joy, night after night. I recollect she answered little, though kindly always. Privately, she at that time felt convinced she was dying:—dark winter, and such the weight of misery, and utter decay of strength;—and, night after night, my theme to her, *Mollwitz!* This she owned to me, within the last year or two;—which how could I listen to without shame and abasement? Never in my pretended-superior kind of life, have I done, for love of any creature, so supreme a kind of thing. It touches me at this moment with penitence and humiliation, yet with a kind of soft *religious* blessedness too.—She *read* the first two volumes of *Friedrich*, much of it in printer's sheets (while on visit to the aged Misses Donaldson at Haddington); her applause (should not I collect her fine Notekins and reposit them here?) was beautiful and as sunlight to me,—for I knew it was sincere withal, and unerringly straight upon the blot, however exaggerated by her great love of me. The other volumes (hardly even the third, I think) she never read,—I knew too well why; and submitted without murmur, save once or twice perhaps a little quiz on the subject, which did not afflict her, either. Too weak, too weak by far, for a dismal enterprise of that kind, as I knew too well! But those Haddington visits were very beautiful to her (and to me through her letters and her); and by that time, we were over the hill and 'the worst of our days were *past*' (as poor Irving used to give for *toast*, long ago),—worst of them past, though we did not yet quite know it.

July 3. Volumes One, Two of *Friedrich* were published, I find, in 1858. Probably about two years before that was the *nadir* of my poor Wife's sufferings;—internal sufferings and dispiritments; for outward *fortunes* etc. had now, for about ten years, been on a quite tolerable footing, and indeed evidently fast on the improving hand: nor had *they*, at any worst time, ever disheartened her, or darkened her feelings. But in 1856, owing to many circumstances,—my *engrossment* otherwise (sunk in *Friedrich*, in etc. etc.; far *less* exclusively, very far *less*, than she supposed, poor soul!);—and owing *chiefly*, one may fancy, to the deeper downbreak of her own poor health, which from this time, as I now see better, continued its advance upon the *citadel*, or nervous system, and intrinsically grew worse and worse:—in 1856, too evidently, to whatever owing, my poor little Darling was extremely miserable! Of that year there is a bit of private diary, by chance, left unburnt; found by me since her death, and not to be destroyed, however tragical and sternly sad are parts of it. She had written, I sometimes knew (though she would never show to me or to mortal any word of them), at different times, various bits of diary; and was even, at one time, upon a kind of autobiography (had not —— stept into it with swine's foot, most intrusively, though without ill intention—finding it unlocked one day;—and produced thereby an instantaneous burning of it; and of all like it which existed at that time). Certain enough, she wrote various bits of diary and private record, unknown to me: but never anything so sore, downhearted, harshly distressed and sad as this (right sure am I!)—which alone remains as specimen! The rest are all burnt; no trace of them, seek where I may.

[Here followed Mrs. Carlyle's melancholy private diary;

at the end of which Carlyle has written: 'A very sad record! We went to Scotland soon after;' (*i.e.* after the date of the last entry in it, 5th July 1856) 'she to Auchtertool (cousin Walter's), I to the Gill (sister Mary's).']

In July 1856, as marked in her sad record, may have been about the middle of month, we went to Edinburgh; a blazing day full of dust and tumult,—which I still very well remember! Lady Ashburton had got for herself a grand 'Queen's saloon' or *ne-plus-ultra* of railway carriages (made for the Queen some time before) costing no end of money; Lady sat, or lay, in the 'saloon;' a common six-seat carriage, immediately contiguous, was accessible from it; in this the Lady had insisted *we* should ride, with her doctor and her maid; a mere partition, with a door, dividing us from her. The Lady was very good, cheerful though much unwell; bore all her difficulties and disappointments with an admirable equanimity and magnanimity: but it was physically almost the uncomfortablest journey I ever made. At Peterborough, the *Ne-plus-ultra* was found to have its axletree *on fire*; at every station afterwards *buckets* were copiously dashed and poured (the magnanimous Lady saying never a syllable to it); and at Newcastle-on-Tyne, they flung the humbug *Ne-plus* away altogether, and our whole party into common carriages. Apart from the burning axle, we had suffered much from dust and even from foul air,—so that, at last, I got the door opened, and sat with my head and shoulders stretched out backward, into the wind. This had alarmed my poor Woman, lest I should tumble out altogether; and she angrily forbade it, dear loving Woman; and I complied, not at first knowing why she was angry. This and Lady Ashburton's opening her door to tell us, 'Here is Hinchinbrook!' (a long time before, and with something of pathos traceable in her cheery voice) are nearly all that I now remember of the base and dirty hurlyburly. Lord Ashburton had preceded by some days; and was waiting for our train, at Edinburgh, 9.30 P.M.—hurlyburly greater and dirtier than ever. They went for Barry's Hotel at once, servants and all,—no time to *inform* us (officially), that *we* too were their guests. But that, too, passed well. We ordered apartments, refreshments of our own there (first of all *baths*, inside of my shirt-collar was as black as ink!) —and before the refreshments were ready, we had a gay and cordial invitation etc. etc.; found the 'Old Bear' (Ellice) in their rooms, I remember, and Lord Ashburton and he with a great deal to say about Edinburgh and its people and phenomena. Next morning, the Ashburtons went for Kinloch-Luichart (fine hunting-seat in Ross-shire); and my dear little Woman to her Cousins at Auchtertool; where, I remember, she was much soothed by their kindness, and improved considerably in health, for the time. The day after seeing her settled there, I made for Annandale, and my Sister Mary's at the Gill. (Maggie Welsh, now here with me, has *helped* in adjusting into clearness the recollection of all this.)—I remember working on final corrections of Books ii. and iii. of *Friedrich*, and reading in *Plato* (Translation, and not my first trial of him) while there. My Darling's Letters I remember too (am on search for them just now); also visits from Sister Jean and *to* Dumfries and her,—silent nocturnal rides from that town etc., and generally much riding on the (Priestside) Solway Sands, and plenty of sombre occupation to my thoughts.

Late on in Autumn, I met my Jeannie at Kirkcaldy again; uncomfortably lodged, both of us, and did not loiter (though the people very *kind* . . .); I was bound for Ross-shire and the Ashburtons (miserable journey thither, sombre, miserable stay there, wet weather, sickly, solitary mostly, etc. etc.);—my Wife had gone to her Aunts in Edinburgh, for a night or two, to the Haddington Miss Donaldsons, and in both places, the *latter* especially, had much to please her, and came away with the resolution to go again.

Next year, 1857, she went accordingly; staid with the Donaldsons (eldest of these old ladies, now well above eighty. and gone stone-blind, was her 'godmother,' had been at Craigenputtock to see us, the dearest of old friends my wife now had). She was at Auchtertool too, at Edinburgh with her Aunts, once and again; but the chief element was 'Sunny Bank, Haddington,' which she began with and ended with; a stay of some length, each time. Happy to her, and heart-interesting to a high degree, though sorrowfully involved in almost constant bodily pain. It was a Tour for *Health*; urged on her by me for that end;—and the poor little Darling seemed inwardly to grudge all along the expense on herself (generous soul!) as if *she* were not worth money spent,—though money was in no scarcity with us now! I was printing *Friedrich*, volumes i. and ii. here; totally solitary; and recollect her Letters of that Tour as altogether genial and delightful,—sad and miserable as the view is which they *now* give me of her endless bodily distresses and even torments, now when I read them again, after nine years, and what has befallen me eleven weeks ago!

Sunday, July 8. Began writing again at the second line of this page; the intermediate time has been spent in a strenuous search for, and collection of all her letters now discoverable (by Maggie Welsh and me),—which is now completed, or nearly so,—1842–3 the earliest found (though surely there ought to be others, of 1837 etc.?), and some of almost every year onward to the last. They are exceedingly difficult to arrange; not having in general any *date*; so that place often enough, and day and even year throughout, are mainly to be got by the *Post Office Stamp*, supported by inference and inquiry such as is still possible, at least to me.

The whole of yesterday I spent in reading and arranging the *letters* of 1857; such a day's *reading* as I perhaps never had in my life before. What a piercing radiancy of meaning to me in those dear records, hastily thrown off, full of misery, yet of bright eternal love; all as if on wings of lightning, tingling through one's very heart of hearts! Oh, I was blind not to see how *brittle* was that thread of noble celestial (almost more than terrestrial) life; how much it was all in all to me, and how impossible it should long be left with me. Her sufferings seem little short of those in an hospital fever-ward, as she painfully drags herself about; and yet constantly there is such an electric shower of all-illuminating brilliancy, penetration, recognition, wise discernment, just enthusiasm, humour, grace, patience, courage, love,—and in fine of spontaneous nobleness of mind and intellect,—as I know not where to parallel! I have asked myself, Ought all this to be lost, or kept for myself, and the brief time that now belongs to *me*? Can *nothing* of it be saved, then, for the worthy that still remain among these roaring myriads of profane unworthy? I really must consider it further; and already I feel it to have become uncertain to me whether at least this poor Notebook ought to be burnt ere my decease, or left to its chances among my survivors? As to 'talent,' epistolary and other, these *Letters*, I perceive, equal and surpass whatever of best I know to exist in that kind; for 'talent,' 'genius,' or whatever we may call it, what an evidence, if my little woman needed that to me! Not all the *Sands* and *Eliots* and babbling *cohue* of 'celebrated scribbling women' that have strutted over the world, in my time, could, it seems to me, if all boiled down and distilled to essence, make one such woman. But it is difficult to make these Letters fairly legible; except myself there is nobody at all that can completely *read* them, as they now are. They abound in allusions, very full of meaning in this circle, but perfectly dark and void in all others: '*Coterie-sprache*,' as the Germans call it, 'family-circle dialect,' occurs every line or two; nobody ever so *rich* in that kind as she; ready to pick up every diamond-spark, out of the common floor-dust, and keep it brightly available; so that hardly, I think in any house, was there *more* of 'Coterie-speech,' shining innocently, with a perpetual expressiveness and twinkle generally of quiz and real humour about it, than in ours. She mainly was the creatress of all this; unmatchable for quickness (and trueness) in regard to it;—and in her letters it is continually recurring; shedding such a lambency of 'own fireside' over everything, if you are in the secret. Ah me, ah me!—At least, I have tied up that bundle (the *two* letters touching on *Friedrich* have a paper round them; the first written in Edinburgh, it appears *how!*) *Enter* Froude; almost the only man I care to speak with, in these weeks. Out with him to Battersea Park; day gray, temperate and windy.

July 9. Day again all spent in searching and sorting: a box of *hers*, full of strange and sad memorials of her Mother, with a few of Father and infant Self (put up in 1842)—full of poignant meanings to her then and to me now. Her own *christening cap* is there (e.g.), the *lancet* they took her Father's blood with (and so *killed* him, as she always thought); Father's door-plate; 'commission in Perth Fencibles,' etc.: two or three Christmas notes of mine; which I could not read without almost sheer weeping. . . .

July 13. . . . On the whole two days of absence from my little 'Shrine of pious Memory' here, where alone it is best for me to be, at present!—I will write down my reminiscence of the 'Accident in Cheapside' (1863); the opening of what has proved to be the last act of all. Hand sadly shaky, weather extremely hot.

It must have been near the end of October 1863, when I returned home from my ride, weather soft and muddy, humour dreary and oppressed as usual (nightmare *Friedrich* still pressing heavily as ever), but as usual also, a bright little hope in me that now I was *across* the muddy element, and the lucid twenty minutes of my day were again at hand. To my disappointment, my Jeannie was *not* here; 'had gone to see her Cousin in the City,'—a Mrs. Godby, widow of an important Post-Official, once in Edinburgh, where he had wedded this cousin, and died leaving children; and in virtue of whom she and they had been brought to London a year or two ago, to a fine situation as 'Matron of the Post-office Establishment' ('forty maids under her etc. etc., and well managed by her') in St. Martin's-le-Grand. She was a good enough creature, this Mrs. Godby (Binnie had been her Scotch name; she is now Mrs. Something-else, and very prosperous):—my Jeannie, in those early times, was anxious to be kind to her in the new scene, and had her often here (as often as, for my convenience, seemed to the loyal heart permissible); and was herself, on calls and little tea-visits, perhaps still oftener there. A perfectly harmless Scotch cousin, polite and prudent; almost prettyish . . . ; with good wise instincts; but no developed intelligence in the articulate kind. Her mother, I think, was my mother-in-law's cousin or connection; and the young widow and her London friend were always well together. This was, I believe, the last visit my poor wife ever made her, and the last but two she ever received from her, so miserably unexpected were the issues on this side of the matter!

We had been at The Grange for perhaps four or five weeks that autumn; utterly quiet, nobody there besides ourselves; Lord Ashburton being in the weakest state, health and life visibly decaying;—I was permitted to keep *perdu* till three o'clock daily; and sat writing about Poland I remember. Mournful, but composed and dignifiedly placid the time was to us all. My Jeannie did not complain of health beyond wont, except on one point: that her right arm was strangely lame, getting lamer and lamer, so that at last she could not '*do her hair herself*,' but had to call in a maid to fasten the hind part for her. I remember her sadly dispirited looks, when I came in to her in the mornings with my inquiries; 'No sleep,' too often the response; and this lameness, though little was said of it, a most discouraging thing. Oh, what discouragements, continual distresses, pains and miseries my poor little Darling had to bear, remedy for them nowhere, speech about them useless, best to be avoided,—as, except on pressure from myself, it always nobly was! This part of her life-history was always sad to me; but it is tenfold more now, as I read in her old *Letters*, and gradually realise, as never before, the continual grinding wretchedness of it, and how, like a winged Psyche, she so soared above it, and refused to be chained or degraded by it.—'Neuralgic rheumatism,' the Doctors called this thing; 'neuralgia' by itself, as if confessing that they knew not what to do with it. Some kind of hot half-corrosive ointment was the thing prescribed;—which did, for a little while each time, remove the pain mostly, the lameness not;—and I remember to have once seen her beautiful arm (still so beautiful) all stained with spots of *burning*, so zealous had she been in trying, though with small faith in the prescription. This lasted all the time we were at The Grange; it had begun before, and things rather seemed to be worsening after we returned. Alas, I suppose it was the Siege of the *Citadel* that was now going on; disease and pain had for thirty or more years been trampling down the *outworks*; were now got to the *nerves*, to the citadel, and were bent on storming that.

14*th July*, *twelfth* Saturday *since*. I was disappointed, but not sorry at the miss of my 'twenty minutes;' that my little Woman, in her weak languid state, had gone out for exercise, was glad news; and I considered that the 'twenty minutes' was only postponed, not lost, but would be repaid me presently with interest. After sleep and dinner (all forgotten now), I remember still to have been patient, cheerfully hopeful, 'she *is* coming, for certain; and will have something nice to tell me of news etc., as she always has!' In that mood I lay on the sofa, not sleeping, quietly waiting, perhaps for an hour-and-half more. She had gone in an omnibus, and was to return in one; at this time, she had no carriage: with great difficulty I had got her induced, persuaded and commanded, to take two drives weekly in a hired brougham ('more difficulty in persuading *you* to go into expense, than other men have to persuade their wives to keep out of it!'): on these terms she had agreed to the two drives weekly, and found a great benefit in them;—but, on no terms, could I get her consent to go, *herself*, into the adventure of purchasing a brougham etc., though she knew it to be a fixed purpose, and only delayed by absolute want of time on my part. She could have done it, too, employed the right people to do it, right well; and knew how beneficial to her health it would, likely, be: but no, there was a refined delicacy which would have perpetually prevented *her*;—and my 'time,' literally, was *zero*; I believe, for the last seven years of that nightmare *Friedrich*, I did not write the smallest message to friends, or undertake the least business, except upon plain *compulsion* of necessity. How lucky that, next autumn, I did actually, in spite of *Friedrich*, undertake this of the brougham: it is a mercy of Heaven to me for the rest of my life! And oh why was it not undertaken, in spite of all *Friedrichs* and nightmares, years before! That had been still luckier; perhaps endlessly so? But this was not to be.

The visit to Mrs. Godby had been pleasant, and gone all

well; but now, dusk falling, it had to end,—again by omnibus, as ill-luck would have it. Mrs. Godby sent one of her maids as escort; at the corner of Cheapside, the omnibus was waited for (some excavations going on near by, as for many years past they seldom cease to do); Chelsea omnibus came; my Darling was in the act of stepping in (maid stupid, and of no assistance), —when a cab came rapidly from behind, and, forced by the near excavation, seemed as if it would drive over her, such her frailty, and want of *speed*. She desperately determined to get on the flag pavement again; desperately leaped, and did get upon the curbstone; but found she was falling over upon the flags, and that she would alight on her right or neuralgic arm, which would be ruin; spasmodically struggled against this for an instant or two (maid nor nobody assisting), and *had* to fall on the neuralgic arm,—ruined *otherwise* far worse. For, as afterwards appeared, the muscles of the thigh-bone or sinews attaching them had been torn in that spasmodic instant or two; and, for three days coming, the torment was excessive, while in the right arm there was no neuralgia perceptible during that time, nor any very manifest new injury afterwards either. The calamity had happened, however; and in that condition, my poor Darling, 'put into a cab' by the humane people, as her one request to them, arrived at this door,—'later' than I expected; and after such a 'drive from Cheapside' as may be imagined!

I remember well my joy at the sound of her wheels ending in a knock; then my surprise at the *delay* in her coming up; at the singular silence of the maids when questioned as to that: thereupon my rushing down; finding her in the hands of Larkin[1] and them; in the greatest agony of pain and helplessness I had ever seen her in. The noble little soul, she had determined I was not to be shocked by it; Larkin then lived next door; assiduous to serve us in all things (did *maps*, *indexes*, even *joinerings* etc. etc.): him she had resolved to charge with it,— alas, alas, as if you *could* have saved me, noble heroine and

[1] Henry Larkin, who made elaborate indexes for all of Carlyle's works.

martyr! Poor Larkin was standing helpless; he and I carried her upstairs in an armchair to the side of her bed; into which she crept by aid of her hands: in few minutes, Barnes (her wise old doctor) was here,—assured me there were no bones broken, no joint out; applied his bandagings and remedies; and seemed to think the matter was slighter than it proved to be,—the spasmodic *tearing of sinews* being still a secret to him.

For fifty hours the pain was excruciating; after that it rapidly abated; and soon altogether ceased, except when the wounded limb was meddled with never so little. The poor Patient was heroic, and had throughout been. Within a week, she had begun contriving rope-machineries, leverages; and could not only pull her bell, but lift and shift herself about, by means of her arms, into any coveted posture; and was, as it were, *mistress* of the mischance. She had her poor little room arranged, under her eye, to a perfection of beauty and convenience; nothing that was possible to her had been omitted (I remember one little thing the apothecary had furnished; an artificial *champagne-cork*; turn a screw, and your champagne spurted up, and when you had a spoonful, could be instantly closed down: with what a bright face she would show me this in action!)—in fact her sick-room *looked* pleasanter than many a drawing-room (all the weakness and suffering of it nobly veiled away); the select of her lady-friends were admitted for short whiles, and liked it well: to me, whenever I entered, all spoke of cheerfully patient *hope*;—the bright side of the cloud always assiduously turned out for *me*, in my dreary labours! I might have known, too, better than I did, that it had a dark side withal, sleeplessness, sickliness, utter weakness;—and that 'the silver lining' was due to my Darling's self mainly, and to the inextinguishable loyalty and hope that dwelt in her. But I merely thought, 'How lucky beyond all my calculations!'

I still right well remember the night when her bedroom door (double-door) suddenly opened upon me into the drawing-room, and she came limping and stooping on her staff, so gracefully, and with such a childlike joy and triumph, to irradiate my solitude. Never again will any such bright vision of gladdening surprise illuminate the darkness for me in that room or any other! She was in her Indian dressing-gown; absolutely beautiful, leaning on her *nibby* staff (a fine hazel, cut and polished from the Drumlanrig woods, by some friend for *my* service); and with such a kindly brilliancy and loving innocence of expression, like that of a little child, unconquerable by weakness and years! A hot-tempered creature, too; few hotter, on momentary provocation: but what a fund of soft affection, hope, and melodious innocence and goodness, to temper all that lightning:—I doubt, candidly, if I ever saw a nobler human soul than this which (alas, alas, never *rightly* valued till now!) accompanied all my steps for forty years. Blind and deaf that we are: oh think, if thou yet love anybody living, wait not till *Death* sweep down the paltry little dust-clouds and idle dissonances of the moment; and all be at last so mournfully clear and beautiful, when it is too late!

We thought all was now come or fast coming right again; and that, in spite of that fearful mischance, we should have a good winter, and get our dismal 'misery of a book' *done*, or almost done. My own hope and prayer was and had long been continually that; *hers* too, I could not doubt, though hint never came from *her* to that effect; no hint or look, much less the smallest word, at any time, by any accident. But I felt well enough how it was crushing down her existence, as it was crushing down my own,—and the thought that *she* had *not* been at the choosing of it, and yet must suffer so for it, was occasionally bitter to me. But the practical conclusion always was, 'Get done with it, get done with it! For the saving of us both, that is the one outlook.' And, sure enough, I did stand by the dismal task with all my time and all my means; day and night, wrestling with it, as with the ugliest dragon, which blotted out the daylight and the rest of the world to me, till I should get it slain. There was perhaps some merit in this; but also, I fear, a *de*merit. Well, well; I could do no better. Sitting smoking upstairs, on nights when sleep was impossible, I had thoughts enough; not permitted to rustle amid my rugs and wrappages lest I awoke *her*, and startled all *chance* of sleep away from her. Weak little Darling, thy sleep is now unbroken; still and serene in the Eternities (as the Most High God has ordered for us); and nobody more in this world will wake for my wakefulness, but for some other reason!—

My poor Woman was what we called 'getting well' for several weeks still; she could walk very little, indeed she never more walked much in this world:—but it seems she was out driving, and again out, hopefully for some time (I cannot now remember at all how long); considered to be steadily mending of her accident. Interruption from Ruskin, *July* 16, must stop again for this day.

Towards the end of November (perhaps it was in December), she caught some whiff of cold; which, for a day or two, we hoped would pass, as many such had done: but on the contrary, it began to get worse, soon rapidly worse, and developed itself into that frightful universal 'neuralgia,' under which, it seemed as if no force of human vitality would be able long to stand. 'Disease of the nerves' (poisoning of the very *channels* of sensation): such was the *name* the doctors gave it; and for the rest, could *do* nothing further with it; well had they only attempted nothing! I used to compute that *they*, poor souls, had at least *reinforced* the disease to *twice* its natural amount; such the pernicious effect of all their 'remedies' and appliances, opiates, etc. etc.; which every new one of them (and there came many) applied anew,—and always with the like *inverse* result. Oh, what a sea of agony my Darling was immersed in; and had to plunge and toss and desperately struggle in, month after month. Sleep had fled. A hideous pain of which she used to say that 'common honest pain, were it cutting of one's flesh or sawing of one's bones would be a luxury in comparison,'—seemed to have begirdled her, at all moments and on every side. Her intellect was clear as starlight, and continued so; the clearest *intellect* among us all; but she dreaded that this too must give way. 'Dear,' said she to me, on two occasions, with such a look and tone as I shall never forget, '*promise* me that you will not put me into a mad-house, however this go. Do you *promise* me, now?' I solemnly did. 'Not if I do quite lose my wits?' 'Never, my Darling; oh compose thy poor terrified heart!' Another time, she punctually directed me about her *burial*; how her poor bits of possessions were to be distributed, this to one friend, that to another (in help of their necessities, for it was the *poor* sort she had chosen, old indigent Haddington figures),—what employment in the solitary night watches, on her bed of pain: ah me, ah me!

The house, by day especially, was full of confusion: Maggie Welsh had come at my solicitation; and took a great deal of patient trouble (herself of an almost obstinate placidity); doing her best among the crowd of doctors, sick-nurses, visitors:—I mostly sat aloft, sunk, or endeavouring to be sunk, in *work*; and till evening, only visited the sick-room at intervals,—first thing in the morning, perhaps about noon again, and always (if permissible) at three P.M., when riding time came, etc. etc.;—*if* permissible, for sometimes she was reported as 'asleep' when I passed, though it oftenest proved to have been quiescence of exhaustion, not real sleep. To this hour it is inconceivable to me how I could continue 'working;' as I nevertheless certainly for much the most part did! About three times or so, on a morning it struck me, with a cold shudder as of conviction, that here did lie death; that my world must go to shivers, down to the abyss; and that 'victory' never so complete, up in my garret, would not save *her*, nor indeed be possible without her. I remember my morning walks, three of them or so, crushed under that ghastly spell. But again I said to myself, 'No man, doctor or other, *knows* anything about it. There is still what *appetite* there was; that I can myself understand:'—and generally, before the day was done, I had decided to *hope* again, to keep hoping and working. The *after*-cast of the Doctors' futile opiates were generally the worst phenomena: I remember her once coming out to the drawing-room sofa, perhaps about midnight; decided for trying that—ah me, in vain, palpably in vain; and what a look in those bonny eyes, vividly present to me yet; unaidable, and like to break one's heart!

One scene with a Catholic sick-nurse I also remember well. A year or two before this time, she had gone with some acquaintance who was in quest of sick-nurses to an establishment under Catholic auspices, in Brompton somewhere (the acquaintance, a Protestant herself, expressing her 'certain knowledge' that this Catholic was the one good kind);—where accordingly the aspect of matters, and especially the manner of the old French lady who was matron and manager, produced such a favourable impression, that I recollect my little Woman saying, 'If I need a sick-nurse, that is the place I will apply at.' Appliance now was made; a nun duly sent, in consequence:—this was in the early weeks of the illness; *household* sick-nursing (Maggie's and that of the maids alternately) having sufficed till now. The nurse was a good-natured young Irish nun; with a good deal of brogue, a tolerable share of blarney too, all varnished to the due extent; and, for three nights or so, she answered very well. On the fourth night, to our surprise, though we found afterwards it was the common usage, there appeared a new Nun; new and very different,—an *elderly* French *young lady*, with broken English enough for her occasions, and a look of rigid earnestness, in fact, with the air of a life broken down into settled despondency, and abandonment of all hope that was not *ultra*-secular. An unfavourable change;—though the poor lady seemed intelligent, well-intentioned; and her heart-broken aspect inspired pity and good-wishes, if no attraction. She commenced by rather ostentatious performance of her nocturnal Prayers, '*Beata Maria*', or I know not what other Latin stuff; which her poor Patient regarded with great vigilance, though still with what charity and tolerance were possible. 'You won't understand what I am saying or doing,' said the Nun; 'don't mind me.' 'Perhaps I understand it better than yourself,' said the other (who had *Latin* from of old), and did 'mind' more than was expected. The dreary hours, no sleep, as usual, went on; and we heard nothing,—till about three A.M. I was awakened (I, what never happened before or after, though my door was always left slightly ajar, and I was right above, usually a deep sleeper),—awakened by a vehement continuous ringing of my poor Darling's bell. I flung on my dressing-gown, awoke Maggie by a word, and hurried down.

'Put away that woman!' cried my poor Jeannie vehemently; 'away, not to come back!' I opened the door into the drawing-room; pointed to the sofa there, which had wraps and pillows plenty; and the poor Nun at once withdrew, looking and murmuring her regrets and apologies. 'What was she doing to thee, my own poor little Woman?' No very distinct answer was to be had then (and afterwards there was always a dislike to speak of that hideous bit of time at all, except on necessity); but I learned in general, that during the heavy hours loaded, every moment of them, with its misery, the Nun had gradually come forward with ghostly consolations, ill received, no doubt; and at length, with something more express, about 'Blessed Virgin,' '*Agnus Dei*,' or whatever it might be; to which the answer had been: 'Hold your tongue, I tell you; or I will ring the bell!' Upon which the Nun had rushed forward with her dreadfullest supernal admonitions, '*im*penitent sinner,' etc., and a practical attempt to *prevent* the ringing. Which only made it more immediate and more decisive. The poor woman expressed to Miss Welsh much regret, disappointment, real vexation and self-blame; lay silent, after that, amid her rugs; and disappeared, next morning, in a polite and soft manner: never to reappear, she or any consort of hers. I was really sorry for this heavy-laden, pious or quasi-pious and almost broken-hearted Frenchwoman,—though we could perceive she was under the foul tutelage and guidance, probably, of some dirty muddy-minded semi-*felonious* Proselytising Irish Priest:—but there was no help for her, in this instance; probably, in all England, she could not have found an agonised human soul more nobly and hopelessly superior to her and her *poisoned-gingerbread* 'consolations.'—This incident threw suddenly a glare of strange and far from pleasant light over the sublime Popish 'Sisters of Charity' movement;—and none of us had the least notion to apply there henceforth.

The doctors were many; Dr. Quain (who would take no fees) the most assiduous; Dr. Blakiston (ditto), from St. Leonard's, express, one time;—speaking hope, always, both of these, and most industrious to help;—with many more, whom I did not even see. When any *new* miraculous kind of Doctor was recommended as such, my poor struggling martyr, conscious too of grasping at mere straws, could not but wish to see him; and he came, did his mischief, and went away. We had even (by sanction of Barnes, and indeed of sound sense never so sceptical) a trial of 'Animal Magnetism;' two magnetisers, first a man, then a *quack* woman (evidently a conscious quack I perceived her to be),—who at least did no ill, *except* entirely disappoint (if that were much an exception). By everybody it had been agreed that a 'change of scene' (as usual, when all else has failed) was the thing to be looked to: 'St. Leonard's so soon as the weather will permit!' said Dr. Quain and everybody,—especially Dr. Blakiston, who generously offered his house withal, 'Infinitely more room than we need!' said the sanguine Blakiston always; and we dimly understood too, from his wife ('Bessie Barnet,' an old inmate here,[1] and of distinguished qualities and fortunes), that the doctor would accept 'remuneration;' though this proved quite a mistake.... Money for the use of two rooms in his house, we might have anticipated, but did not altogether, he would regard with sovereign superiority.

It was early in March, perhaps 2d March 1864, a cold blowing damp and occasionally raining day, when the flitting thither took effect. Never shall I see again so sad and dispiriting a scene; hardly was the day of her last departure for Haddington, departure of what had once been She (the *instant* of *which*, they contrived to hide from me here) so miserable; for *she* at least was now suffering nothing, but safe in victorious rest for evermore—though then beyond expression suffering. There was a railway 'invalid carriage,' so expressly adapted, so etc.,—and evidently costing some ten or twelve times the common expense:—this drove up to the door; Maggie and she to go in this. Well do I recollect her look as they bore her downstairs: full of nameless sorrow, yet of clearness, practical management, steady resolution; in a low small voice she gave her direction, once or twice, as the process went on, and prac-

[1] At one time a servant at Cheyne Row.

tically it was under her wise management. The 'invalid carriage' was hideous to look upon; black, low, base-looking,—and you entered it by window, as if it *were* a hearse: I knew well what she was thinking; but her eye never quailed, she gave her directions as heretofore; and, in a minute or two, we were all away. Twice or oftener in the journey, I visited Maggie and her in their prison: no complaint; but the 'invalid carriage,' in which I doubt if you could actually sit upright (if you were of *man's* stature or of tall woman's), was evidently a catch-penny humbug; and she freely admitted afterwards that she would never enter it again, and that in a 'coupé to ourselves' she would have been far better. At St. Leonard's, I remember, there was considerable waiting for 'the horses' that should have been ready; a thrice bleak and dreary scene to all of us (*She* silent as a child); the arrival, the dismounting, the ascent of her quasi-bier up Blakiston's long stairs, etc., etc.: ah me! Dr. Blakiston was really kind. The sea was hoarsely moaning at our hand, the bleared skies sinking into darkness overhead. Within doors, however, all was really nice and well-provided (thanks to the skilful Mrs. Blakiston); excellent drawing-room, and sitting-room, with bed for *her*; bedroom upstairs for Maggie, ditto for servant, within call, etc. etc.; all clean and quiet: a kind of hope did rise, perhaps even in her, at sight of all this. My mood, when I bethink me, was that of deep misery frozen *torpid*; singularly dark and stony,—strange to me now; due in part to the *Friedrich* incubus then. I had to be home again that night, by the last train;—miscalculated the distance, found no vehicle; and never in my life saved a train by so infinitesimally small a miss. I had taken mournfully tender leave of my poor much-suffering Heroine (speaking hope to her, when I could more readily have 'lifted up my voice and wept'). I was to return in so many days, if nothing went wrong; *at once*, if anything did;—I lost nothing by that hurried ride, except at London Station, or in the final cab, a velvet Cap, of her old making; which I much regretted, and still regret. 'I will make you another cap, if I get better,' said she lovingly, at our next meeting; but she never did, or perhaps well could. What matter? That would have made me still sorrier, had I had it by me now. *Wae's me, wae's me! Wae* is the Scotch *adjective*, too: '*wae, wae,*'—there is no word in English that will express what is my habitual mood in these months.

I was twice or perhaps thrice at St. Leonard's (Warrior Square, Blakiston's house, *right* end of it to the sea). Once I recollect being taken by Forster, who was going on a kind of birthday Holiday with his Wife. Blakiston spoke always in a swaggering tone of hope, and there really was some improvement; but, alas, it was small and slow; deep misery and pain still too visible: and all we could say was, 'We must try St. Leonard's further; I shall be able to shift down to you in May!' My little Darling looked sweet gratitude upon me (so thankful always for 'the day of small things!')—but heaviness, sorrow, and *want* of hope was written on her face; the sight filling me with sadness, though I always strove to be of Blakiston's opinion. One of my volumes (fourth, I conclude) was coming out at that time;—during the Forster visit, I remember there was some *review* of this volume, seemingly of a shallow impudent description, concerning which I privately applauded Forster's silent demeanour, and not Blakiston's vocal, one evening at Forster's inn. The dates, or even the number, of these sad preliminary visits, I do not now recollect: they were all of a sad and ambiguous complexion: at home, too, there daily came a letter from Maggie; but this in general, though it strove to look hopeful, was *ambiguity's* own self. Much driving in the open air, appetite where it was, sleep at least ditto: all this, I kept saying to myself, must lead to something good.

Dr. Blakiston, it turned out, would accept no payment for his rooms; 'a small furnished house of our own' became the only outlook, therefore;—and was got, and entered into, some time in April, some weeks before my arrival in May. Brother John, before this, had come to visit me here; ran down to St. Leonard's one day, and, I could perceive, was silently intending to pass the summer with us at St. Leonard's. He did so, in an innocent, self-soothing, kindly and harmless way (the good soul, if good wishes would always suffice!)—and occasionally was of some benefit to us, though occasionally also not. It was a quiet sunny day of May when we went down together;—I read most of 'Sterne's Life' (just out, by some Irishman, named Fitz-something); looked out on the old *Wilhelmus Conquestor* localities; on Lewes, for one thing (de '*Le Ouse*,'—Ouse the dirty river there is *still* named); on Pevensey, Bexhill etc., with no unmixed feeling, yet not with absolute misery, as we rolled along. I forget if Maggie Welsh was still there at St. Leonard's. My Darling, certain enough, came down to meet us, attempting to sit at dinner (by my request, or wish already signified); but too evidently it would not do. Mary Craik was sent for (from Belfast) instead of Maggie Welsh who 'was wanted' at Liverpool, and did then or a few days afterwards return thither,—Mary Craik succeeding, who was very gentle, quiet, prudent, and did well in her post. . . . Miss Jewsbury had *offered* 'for a fortnight,'—'say No, and write to Mary Craik,' was my poor Jane's direction to me (more practical sense in her sick head, than in all the sound ones together!—So it was with her *throughout*) . . .

I had settled all my Book affairs the best I could: I got at once installed into a poor closet on the ground-floor, with window to the north (keep that open and the door ajar, there will be fresh air!)—Book box was at once converted into Book press (of rough deal, but covered with newspaper *veneering* where necessary), and fairly held and kept at hand the main books I wanted; camp-desk, table or two, drawer or two, were put in immediate seasonablest use: in this closet there was hardly room to turn; and I felt as if crushed, all my apparatus and I, into a stocking, and *there* bidden *work*. But I really did it withal, to a respectable degree, Printer never pausing for me, work daily going on; and this doubtless was my real anchorage in that sea of trouble, sadness and confusion, for the two months it endured. I have spoken elsewhere of my poor Darling's hopeless wretchedness, which daily cut my heart, and might have cut a very stranger's: those drives with her ('daily, one of your drives, is with *me*,'—and I saw her gratitude, poor soul, looking out through her despair; and sometimes she would *try* to talk to me, about street sights, persons etc.; and it was like a bright lamp flickering out into extinction again), drives mainly on the streets, to escape the dust, or still dismaller if we did venture into the haggard, parched lanes, and their vile whirlwinds: Oh my Darling, I would have cut the Universe in two for thee,—and *this* was all I had to share with thee, as we were!—

St. Leonard's, now that I look back upon it, is very odious to my fancy, yet not without points of interest. I rode a great deal too,—two hours and a half daily my lowest stint; bathed also, and remember the bright morning air, bright Beachy Head and everlasting Sea, as things of blessing to me; the *old* lanes of Sussex too, old cottages, peasants, old vanishing ways of life, were abundantly touching: but the *new* part, and it was all getting 'new,' was uniformly detestable and even horrible to me. Nothing but dust, noise, squalor, and the universal tearing and digging as if of gigantic human *swine*, *not* finding any worms or roots that would be useful to them! The very 'houses' they were building, each 'a congeries of rotten band-boxes' (as our own poor 'furnished house' had taught me, if I still needed teaching), were 'built' as if for nomad apes, not for men. The 'moneys' to be realised, the etc. etc.: does or can God's *blessing* rest on all that? My dialogues with the dusty sceneries there (Fairlight, Crowhurst, Battle, Rye even, and Winchelsea), with the novelties and the antiquities, were very sad for most part, and very grim,—here and there with a kind of wild interest too. Battle I did arrive at, one evening, through the chaotic roads; Battle, in the rustle or silence of incipient dusk, was really affecting to me;—and I saw it to be a good post of fence for King Harold, and wondered if the Bastard did 'land at Pevensey,' or not near Hastings somewhere (Bex-hill or so?) and what the marchings and preliminaries had really been. (Faithful study, continued for long years or decades, upon the old Norman romances etc., and upon the ground, would still tell some fit person, I believe.) But there shrieks the railway, 'shares' at such and such a premium; let us make for home! My Brother, for a few times at first, used to accompany me on those rides; but soon gave in (not being bound to it like me); and Noggs and I had nothing for it but solitary contemplation and what mute 'dialogues' with Nature and Art we could each get up for himself. I usually got home towards nine P.M. (half-past eight the rigorous rule); and in a gray dusty evening, from some windy hill-top, or in the intricate old narrow lanes of a thousand years ago, one's reflections were apt to be of a sombre sort.—My poor little Jeannie (thanks to her, the loving one) would not fail to be waiting for me, and sit trying to talk or listen, while I had tea; trying her best, sick and weary as she was; but always very soon withdrew after that; quite worn down, and longing for solitary *silence*, and even a *sleepless* bed, as was her likeliest prospect for most part. How utterly sad is all that! yes; and there is a kind of devout blessing in it too (so nobly was it borne, and conquered in a sort); and I would not have it altered now, after what has come, if I even could.

Sunday, 22d July. We lived in the place called 'Marina' (what a name!) almost quite at the west end of St. Leonard's; a new house (bearing marks of thrifty, wise, and modestly-elegant habits in the old-lady owners just gone from it); and for the rest, decidedly the *worst*-built house I have ever been within. A scandal to human nature, it and its fellows; which are everywhere, and are not objected to by an enlightened public, as appears! No more of *it*,—except our farewell malison; and pity for the poor Old Ladies who perhaps are still there!

My poor suffering woman had at first, for some weeks, a vestige of improvement, or at least of new hope and alleviation thereby: she 'slept' (or tried for sleep) in the one tolerable bedroom; second floor, fronting the sea; darkened and ventilated, made the tidiest we could; Miss Craik slept close by. I remember our settlings for the night; my last journey up, to sit a few minutes, and see that the adjustments *were* complete, —a 'Nun's lamp' was left glimmering within reach; my poor little woman *strove* to look as contented as she could, and to exchange a few friendly words with me as our last for the night. Then in the morning, there sometimes *had* been an hour or two of sleep; what news for us all! And even brother John, for a while, was admitted to step up and congratulate, after breakfast. But this didn't last; hardly into June, even in that slight degree. And the days were always heavy; so sad to her, so painful, dreary, without hope: what a time, even in my *reflex* of it! Dante's *Purgatory* I could now liken it to; both of us, especially my Loved One by me, 'bent like corbels,' under our unbearable loads as we wended on,—yet in me always with a kind of steadily glimmering hope! Dante's *Purgatory*; not his *Hell*, for there was a sacred blessedness in it withal; not wholly the society of devils, but among *their* hootings and tormentings something still pointing afar off towards Heaven withal. Thank God!

At the *beginning* of June, she still had the feeling we were better here than elsewhere; by her direction, I warned the people we would not quit at 'the end of June,' as had been bargained, but 'of July,' as was also within our option, on due notice given. End of *June* proved to be the time, all the same; the Old Ladies (justly) refusing to *revoke*, and taking their full claim of money, poor old souls, very polite otherwise. Middle of June had not come when that bedroom became impossible: 'roaring of the sea,' once a lullaby, now a little too loud, on some high-tide or west wind, kept her entirely awake: I exchanged bedrooms with her; 'sea always a lullaby to *me*,'—but, that night, even I did not sleep one wink; upon which John exchanged with me, who lay to rearward, as I till then had done. Rearward we looked over a Mews (from this room); from her now room, into the paltry little 'garden;' overhead of both were clay cliffs, multifarious dog and cock establishments (unquenchable by bribes paid), now and then stray troops of asses, etc. etc.: what a lodging for my poor sufferer! Sleep became worse and worse; we spoke of shifting to Bexhill; 'fine airy house to be let there' (fable when we went to look); then some quiet old country Inn? She drove one day (John etc. escorting) to Battle, to examine; nothing there, or less than nothing. Chelsea home was at least quiet, wholesomely aired and clean: but she had an absolute horror of her old *home* bedroom and drawing-room, where she had endured such torments latterly. 'We will new-*paper* them, rearrange them,' said Miss Bromley; and this was actually done in August following (not by Miss Bromley). That 'new-*papering*' was somehow to me the saddest of speculations: 'Alas, Darling, is that all we can do for thee?' The weak *weakest* of resources; and yet what other had we! As June went on, things became worse and worse. The sequel is mentioned elsewhere: I will here put down only the successive steps and approximate dates of it.

June 29, after nine nights totally without sleep, she announced to us, with a fixity and with a clearness all her own, That she would leave this place to-morrow for London; try there, not in her own house, but in Mrs. Forster's (Palace-Gate House, Kensington), which was not yet horrible to her. June 30 (John escorting), she set off by the noon train; Miss Bromley had come down to see her,—*could* only be allowed to see her in stepping into the train, so desperate was the situation, the mood so *adequate* to it: a moment never to be forgotten by me! How I 'worked' afterwards that day is not on record. I dimly remember walking back with Miss Bromley and her lady-friend to their hotel; talking to them (as out of the heart of icebergs); and painfully somehow sinking into icy or stony rest, worthy of oblivion.

At Forster's there could hardly be a more dubious problem. My poor wandering martyr did get snatches of sleep there; but found the room so noisy, the scene so foreign etc., she took a further resolution in the course of the night and its watchings; sent for John, the first thing in the morning; bade him get places in the night-train for Annandale (my Sister Mary's, all kindness poor Mary, whom she always liked): 'The Gill; we are not yet at the *end: there;*—and Nithsdale too is that way!' John failed not, I dare say, in representations, counter-considerations; but she was coldly positive;—and go they did, express of about 330 miles. Poor Mary was loyal kindness itself; poor means made noble and more than opulent by the wealth of love and ready will and invention:—I was seldom so agreeably surprised as by a letter in my Darling's own hand, narrating the heads of the adventure, briefly, with a kind of defiant satisfaction, and informing me that she *had* slept, that first Gill night, for almost nine hours! Whose joy like ours, durst we have hoped it would last, or even though we durst *not*! She staid about a week still there; Mary and kindred eager to get her carriages (rather helplessly in that particular), to do and attempt for her whatever was possible; but the success, in sleep especially, grew less and less: in about a week, she went on to Nithsdale, to Dr. and Mrs. Russell, and there slowly improving continued. Improvement pretty constant; fresh air, driving, silence, kindness; by the time Mary Craik had got me flitted home to Chelsea, and herself went for Belfast, all this had steadily begun; and there were regular *letters* from her, etc.; and I could work here with such an alleviation of spirits as had long been a stranger to me. In August (rooms all 'new-*papered*,' poor little Jeannie) she came back to me; actually there in the cab (John settling) when I ran downstairs; looking out on me with the old kind face, a little graver, I might have thought, but as quiet, as composed and wise and good as ever. This was the *end*, I might say, of by far the most *tragic* part of our Tragedy. Act Fifth, though there lay Death in it, was nothing like so unhappy.

July 23. The last epoch of my Darling's life is to be defined as almost *happy*, in comparison! It was still loaded with infirmities; bodily weakness, sleeplessness, continual or almost continual pain, and weary misery, so far as *body* was concerned; but her noble spirit seemed as if it now had its wings *free*; and rose above all that to a really singular degree. The Battle was over, and *we* were sore wounded; but the Battle was over, and *well*. It was remarked by everybody that she had never been observed so cheerful and bright of mind as in this last period. The poor *bodily* department, I constantly hoped this too was slowly recovering; and that there would remain to us a 'sweet farewell' of sunshine after such a day of rains and storms, that would still last a blessed while, all *my* time at least, before the end came. And, alas, it lasted only about twenty months; and ended as I have seen. It is beautiful still, all that period, the *death* very beautiful to me, and will continue so: let me not repine, but patiently bear what I have got!—While the autumn weather continued good, she kept improving; I remember mornings when I found her quite wonderfully cheerful, as I looked in upon her bedroom in passing down; a bright ray of *mirth* in what she would say to me; inexpressibly pathetic, shining through the wreck of such storms as there had been. How could I but hope?—It was an inestimable mercy to me (as I often remark) that I did at last throw aside everything for a few days, and actually get her that poor Brougham. Never was soul more grateful for so small a kindness; which seemed to illuminate, in some sort, all her remaining days for her. It was indeed useful, and necessary, as a means of health; but still more precious, I doubt not, as a mark of *my* regard for her,—ah me, she never knew fully, nor could I show her in my heavy-laden miserable life, how *much* I had, at all times, regarded, loved and admired her. No telling of her now;—'five minutes *more* of your dear company in this world; oh that I had you yet for but five minutes, to tell you *all*!' this is often my thought since April 21.

Friedrich ended in January 1865, as above written; and we went to Devonshire together; still prospering and happy, she chiefly, though she was so weak. And her talk with me, and with others there; nobody had such a charming tongue, for truth, discernment, graceful humour and ingenuity; ever patient too, and smiling over her many pains and sorrows. In May, while I had gone to Scotland, she took to refitting my room here (in the ground floor, and shifting me down from the garret); which she has done, how admirably, and with what labour, the noble loving unwearied little soul! Bad days, especially bad nights overtook her; and she fled, out of the *paint* etc. (I could guess, though all remonstrances of mine were useless, about paint or whatever difficulty); and for a month I had her within reach of me, she in Nithsdale, I at The Gill in Annandale (my Sister Mary's poor little rustic farm-place); within an hour or so of her, by train; and we met (in spite of some disappointments) about weekly; I some three visits which

I recollect; met *twice* at Dumfries at least,—and the last time I rode with her in the railway carriage to Annan; express for London she, with a new Maid she had acquired; I not to follow till the 'room' were ready. She was the charm of everybody, my poor weak Darling; especially good to *me* unworthy. Oh my own, my own, now lost for ever! The stir and eager curiosities of the poor ignorant people about 'T. Carlyle,' in our old native land, I could see, were interesting and amusing to her, though she knew their folly and inanity as well as I. Thanks to fate for that too. There has been a great deal more of that since, and far too much of it on any ground it had; but except as pleasure to her, which it really was, as nothing else could have been (my own little Jeannie, loyal to me when there was none else loyal), it had as good as no value to me;—and has now absolutely none, or almost the reverse of one.

She was surely very feeble in the Devonshire time (March, etc., 1865); but I remember her as wonderfully happy; she had long dialogues with Lady Ashburton;[1] used to talk so prettily with me, when I called, in passing up to bed and down from it; she made no complaint; when driving daily through the lanes —sometimes regretted her own poor Brougham and 'Bellona' (as 'still more one's own'), and contrasted her situation as to *carriage* convenience, with that of far richer ladies. 'They have £30,000 a year; cannot command a decent or comfortable vehicle here (*their* vehicles all locked up, 400 miles off, in these wanderings); while *we—!*' The Lady Ashburton was kindness itself to her; and we all came up to Town together, rather in improved health she, I not visibly so, being now *vacant* and on the *collapse*,—which is yet hardly over, or fairly on the turn. Will it ever be? I have sometimes thought this dreadful unexpected stroke might perhaps be *providential* withal upon me and that there lay some other little *work* to do, under changed conditions, before I died. God enable me, if so: God knows.

In Nithsdale, last year, it is yet only fourteen months ago

[1] The second Lady Ashburton, formerly Miss Louisa Stuart Mackenzie, with whom both the Carlyles became very friendly.

(ah me) how beautiful she was; our three or four half or *quarter* days together, how unique in their sad charm as I now recall them from beyond the grave! That day at Russell's, in the garden etc. at Holmhill; so poorly she, forlorn of outlook (one would have said; one outlook ahead, that of *getting me this room trimmed up*,—the darling ever-loving soul!)—and yet so lively, sprightly even, for my poor sake; 'Sir William Gomm' (old Peninsular and Indian General, who had been reading *Friedrich* when she left), what a sparkle that was, her little slap on the table, and arch look, when telling us of him and it! And her own *right* hand was lame; she had only her left to slap with: I cut the meat for her, on her plate, that day at dinner. And our drive to the station at seven P.M.; so sweet, so pure and sad: 'We must retrench, Dear!' (in my telling her of some foolish *Bank*-adventure with the *draft* I had left her; 'retrench!' oh dear, oh dear!)—Among the last things, she told me that evening was, with deep sympathy, 'Mr. Thomson' (a Virginian who sometimes came) 'called, one night; he says there is little doubt they will *hang* President Davis!' Upon which I almost resolved to write a Pamphlet upon it,—had not I myself been so ignorant about the matter, so foreign to the whole abominable fratricidal 'War' (as they called it; 'self-murder of a million brother Englishmen, for the sake of sheer *phantasms*, and totally *false* theories upon the Nigger,' as I had reckoned it). In a day or two I found I could not enter upon that thrice-abject Nigger-delirium (viler to me than old witchcraft, or the ravings of John of Münster; considerably viler); and that probably I should do poor Davis nothing but harm.

The second day, at good old Mrs. Ewart's, of Nithbank, is still finer to me. Waiting for me with the carriage; 'Better, Dear, fairly better since I shifted to Nithbank!'—the 'dinner' ahead there (to my horror), her cautious charming preparation of me for it; our calls at Thornhill (new servant 'Jessie,' admiring old tailor women,—no, *they* were not of the Shankland kind,—wearisome old women, whom *she* had such an interest in, almost wholly for *my* sake); then our long drive through the Drumlanrig woods, with such talk from her (careless of the shower that fell, battering on our hood and apron); in spite of my habitual dispiritment, and helpless gloom all that summer, I too was cheered for the time. And then the dinner itself, and the bustling rustic company, all this, too, was saved by her, with a quiet little touch here and there, she actually turned it into something of *artistic*, and it was pleasant to everybody.—I was at two or perhaps three dinners, after this, along with her, in London: I partly remarked, what is now clearer to me, with what easy perfection she had taken her position in these things; that of a person *recognised* for quietly *superior* if she cared to be so; and also of a suffering aged woman, accepting her age, and feebleness, with such a grace, polite composure and simplicity as—as all of you might imitate, impartial by-standers would have said! The Minister's Assistant, poor young fellow, was gently ordered out by her, to sing *me*, 'Hame cam our gudeman at e'en,'—which made him completely happy, and set the dull drawing-room all into illumination till tea entered. He, the assistant, took me to the station (too late for *her* that evening).

The third day was at Dumfries; Sister Jean's and the Railway Station: more hampered and obstructed, but still good,—beautiful as ever on her part. *Dumb* Turner, at the Station, etc.; evening falling, ruddy opulence of sky,—how beautiful, how brief and *wae!*—The fourth time was only a ride from Dumfries to Annan, as she went home: sad and afflictive to me, seeing such a journey ahead for her (and nothing but the new 'Jessie,' as attendant, some carriages off); I little thought it was to be the *last* bit of railwaying we did together. These, I believe, were all our meetings in the Scotland of last year. One day I stood watching 'her train' at The Gill, as appointed; Brother Jamie too had been summoned over by her desire: but at Dumfries she felt so weak, in the hot day, she could only lie down on the sofa, and sadly send John in her stead. Brother Jamie, whose rustic equipoise, fidelity and sharp vernacular sense, she specially loved, was not to behold her at this time or evermore.

25th July. . . . Have to go into my writing-case, and sort and reposit her *last* Letters, and the rings and a *buckle*;—*could* not yesterday.

She was waiting for me the night I returned hither; she had hurried back from her little visit to Miss Bromley (after the 'room' operation); must and would be here to receive *me*. She stood there, bright of face and of soul, her drawing-room all bright; and everything to the last film of it in order; had arrived only two or three hours before; and here again *we* were. Such welcome, after my vile day of railwaying, like Jonah in the whale's belly! That was always her way; bright home, with its bright face, full of love, and victorious over all disorder, always shone on me like a star as I journeyed and jumbled along amid the shriekeries and miseries. Such welcomes could not await me for ever; I little knew this was the last of them on Earth. My *next*,—for a thousand years, I should never forget the next (of April 23, 1866)! which now was lying only some six months away. I might have seen she was very feeble, that; but I noticed only [how] refinedly beautiful she was, and thought of no sorrow ahead;—did not even think, as I now do, how it was that she was beautifuller than ever; as if years and sorrows had only 'worn' the noble texture of her being into greater *fineness*, the colour and tissue still all complete!—That night she said nothing of the room here (down below); but next morning, after breakfast, led me down, with a quiet smile, expecting her little triumph,—and contentedly had it; though I knew not at first the tenth part of her merits in regard to that poor enterprise, or how consummately it had been *done* to the bottom, in spite of her weakness (the noble heart!); and I think (remorsefully) I *never* praised her *enough* for her efforts and successes in regard to it. Too late now!

My return was about the middle of September; *she* never travelled more, except daily up and down among her widish circle of friends, of whom she seemed to grow fonder and fonder, though generally their qualities were of the *affectionate* and faithfully *honest* kind, and not of the *distinguished*, as a requisite. She was always very cheerful, and had businesses enough,—though I recollect some mornings, one in particular, when the sight of her dear face (haggard from the miseries of the past night) was a kind of shock to me. Thoughtless mortal: —she rallied always so soon, and veiled her miseries away:—I was myself the most collapsed of men; and had no sunshine in my life but what came from *her*. Our old laundress, Mrs. Cook, a very meritorious and very poor and courageous woman, age eighty or more, had fairly fallen useless that Autumn, and gone into the Workhouse. I remember a great deal of trouble taken about her, and the search for her, and settlement of her,—such driving and abstruse inquiry in the slums of Westminster, and to the Workhouses indicated; discovery of her at length, in the *chaos* of some Kensington Union (a truly *cosmic* body, herself, this poor old Cook); with instantaneous stir in all directions (consulting with Rector Blunt, interviews with Poor-Law Guardians etc., etc.),—and no rest till the poor old Mrs. Cook was got promoted into some quiet *cosmic* arrangement; small cell or 'cottage' of your own somewhere, with liberty to read, to be clean, and to accept a packet of tea, if any friend gave you one, etc., etc.: a *good* little 'triumph' to my Darling;—I think perhaps the best she had that spring or winter, and the last *till* my business and the final one. Of our Rectorship, and what came of *it*, there is already some record given (*Own* Notebook, marked 'Notebook III.,' last pages there).[1]

We were peaceable and happy (comparatively) through autumn and winter—especially she was; wonderfully bearing her sleepless nights and thousandfold infirmities, and gently picking out of them (my beautiful little heroine!) more bright fragments for herself and me than many a one in perfect health and overflowing prosperity could have done. She had one or two select quality friends among her many others;—Dowager Lady William Russell is the only one I will name, who loved her like a daughter, and was charmed with her talents and graces; often astonishing certain quality *snobs* by the way she treated *her*, the *un*titled queen. 'Mr. Carlyle a great man, yes; but Mrs. Carlyle, let me inform you, is no less

[1] What follows, on to p. 695 (see footnote there), is taken from the Notebook here referred to, and runs consecutively.

great as a woman.' Which used to amuse my little Darling;—not that she needed protection in such circles; from the first, her self-possession there, as everywhere, was complete; though her modesty and graceful bashfulness were also great. For timid modesty, with perfect simplicity, composure, veracity and grace of demeanour, in entering such scenes, I have never seen her equal. One or two such *entrances* of hers I remember yet (with my very heart), as surpassingly beautiful! Lady William's pretty little 'dinners of three' were every week or two an agreeable and beneficial event,—to me also, who heard the *report* of them given with such lucidity and charm.

End of October came somebody about the Edinburgh Rectorship (to which she gently advised me); beginning of November I was elected; and an inane though rather amusing hurlyburly of empty congratulations, imaginary businesses, etc. etc., began,—the *end* of which has been so fatally tragical! Many were our plans and speculations about her going with *me*; to lodge at Newbattle, at etc.; the heaps of frivolous letters lying every morning at breakfast, and which did not entirely cease all winter, were a kind of entertainment to her; and then, onwards into March, when the *Address* and Journey had to be thought of as practical and close at hand. She decided, *un*willingly, and with various hesitations, *not* to go with me to Edinburgh, in the inclement weather; not to go even to Fryston (Lord Houghton's, Richard Milnes's); as to Edinburgh, she said one day, 'You are to speak extempore' (this she more than once clearly advised, and with sound insight); 'now if anything should happen you, I find on any sudden alarm there is a sharp twinge comes into my back, which is like to cut my breath, and seems to stop the heart almost; I should take some fit in the crowded House;—it will never do, really!' Alas, the doctors now tell me, this meant an affection in some ganglion near the spine; and was a most serious thing, though I did not attach importance to it; but only assented to her practical conclusion as perfectly just. She lovingly bantered and beautifully encouraged me about my Speech, and its hateful ceremonials and empty botherations; which for a couple of weeks were giving me, and her through me, considerable trouble, interruption of sleep, etc.: so beautifully borne by her (for my sake),—so much less so by me for hers. In fact I was very miserable (angry with myself for getting into such a coil of vanity, sadly ill in health), and her noble example did not teach me as it should. Sorrow to me now, when too late!

Thursday—But I will give over; no end to paltry interruptions; and poor trivialities bursting in upon my most sacred thoughts (*Monday, 7th May,* $2\frac{1}{2}$ P.M.)—Thursday 29th March, about nine A.M., all was ready here (she softly regulating and forwarding, as her wont was); and Professor Tyndall,[1] full of good spirits, appeared with a cab for King's Cross Station,—Fryston Hall to be our lodging till Saturday and Edinburgh. I was in the saddest sickly mood, full of gloom and misery, but striving to hide it; she too looked very pale and ill, but seemed intent only on forgetting nothing that could further me. A little flask, holding perhaps two glasses, of fine brandy, shc brought me as a thought of her own:—I did keep a little drop of that brandy (*hers*, such was a supersition I had), and mixed it in a tumbler of water in that wild scene of the Address,—and afterwards told her I had done so: thank Heaven that I remembered that in one of my hurried Notes. The last I saw of her was as she stood with her back to the Parlour-door to bid me her good-bye. She kissed me twice (she me once, I her a second time); and—oh blind mortals, my one wish and hope was to get back to her again, and be in peace under her bright welcome,—for the rest of my days, as it were!

Tyndall was kind, cheery, inventive, helpful; the loyalest *Son* could not have more faithfully striven to support his father, under every difficulty that rose. And they were many. At Fryston, no sleep was to be had for *railways* etc.; I had two nights, the *first* and the *last*, that were totally hideous;—and the terror lay in them that speaking would be impossible; that I should utterly break down,—to which, indeed, I had in my mind said, 'Well then,' and was preparing to treat it with the best *contempt* I could. Tyndall wrote daily to her, and kept up

[1] The scientist John Tyndall.

better hopes; by a long gallop with me the second day, he did get me one good six hours of sleep, and to her made doubtless the most of it: I knew dismally what her anxieties would be, but trust well he reduced them to their *minimum.* Lord Houghton's and Lady's, kindness to me was unbounded; *she* also was to have been there, but I was thankful not.—Saturday (to *York* etc. with Houghton; thence, after long wet loiterings to Edinburgh with Tyndall and Huxley) was the *acme* of the three road-days,—my own comfort was that there could be no post to her;—and I arrived at Edinburgh, the forlornest of all physical wretches; and had it not been for the kindness of the good Erskines and of their people too, I should have had no sleep there either, and have gone probably from bad to worse. But Tyndall's letter of Sunday would be comforting; and my poor little Darling would still be in hope, that Monday morning; though of course in the painfullest anxiety (Tyndall's *telegram* to come to her in the afternoon),—and I know she had quite 'gone off her sleep,' in those five days since I had left.

Monday at Edinburgh was to me the gloomiest chaotic day, nearly intolerable for confusion, crowding, noisy inanity and misery,—till once I got done. My Speech was delivered as if in a mood of defiant despair, and under the pressure of nightmares. Some feeling that I was *not* speaking lies, alone sustained me. The applause etc., I took for empty noise, which it really was not altogether: the instant I found myself loose, I hurried joyfully out of it, over to my Brother's Lodging (73 George Street, near by); to the Students all crowding and shouting round me, I waved my hand prohibitively at the door, perhaps lifted my hat; and they gave but one cheer more,—something in the tone of *it,* which did for the first time go into my heart: 'Poor young men; so well affected to the poor old brother or grandfather here; and in such a black whirlpool of a world here, all of us!'—Brother Jamie, and Son, etc., were sitting within; Erskine and I went silently walking through the streets, and at night was a kind but wearing and wearying congratulatory dinner. Followed by others such; unwholesome to me, not joyful to me; and endured as duties, little more.—But that same afternoon, Tyndall's telegram, emphatic to the uttermost ('A perfect triumph,' the three words of it) arrived here; a joy of joys to my own little Heroine (so beautiful her description of it to me),—which was its one value to me; nearly *naught* otherwise (in very truth); and the *last* of such that could henceforth have any such addition made to it. Alas all 'additions' are now ended; and the thing added to has become only a pain. But I do thank Heaven for this last favour to her that so loved me; and it will remain a joy to me, if my last in this world. She had to dine with Forster and Dickens that evening, and their way of receiving her good news seemed to have charmed her as much almost as the news itself. From that day forward her little heart appears to have been fuller and fuller of joy, newspapers, etc. etc. making such a jubilation (foolish people, as if 'the Address' were anything, or had contained the least thing in it which had not been told you already!) She went out for a two days to Mrs. Oliphant at Windsor; recovered her sleep, to the old poor average, or nearly so; and by every testimony, and all the evidence I myself have, was not for many years, if ever, seen in such fine spirits and so hopeful and joyfully serene and victorious frame of mind,—till the last moment. Noble little Heart; her painful, much enduring, much endeavouring little History now at last crowned with plain victory, in sight of her own people, and of all the world; everybody now obliged to say my Jeannie was not wrong, she was right, and has made it good! Surely for this I should be grateful to Heaven; for this, amid the immeasurable wreck that was preparing for us. She had from an early period formed her own little opinion about *me* (what an Eldorado to me, ungrateful being, blind, ungrateful, condemnable, and heavy-laden, and crushed down into blindness by great misery, as I oftenest was!)—and she never flinched from it an instant, I think, or cared or counted what the world said *to the contrary* (very brave, magnanimous, and noble, truly, she was in all this); but to have the world confirm her in it was always a sensible pleasure, which she took no pains to hide, especially from me.

She lived nineteen days after that Edinburgh Monday; on the nineteenth (April 21, 1866, between three and four P.M., as near as I can gather and sift), suddenly as by a thunderbolt from skies all blue, she was snatched from me: a 'death from the gods,' the old Romans would have called it; the kind of death she many a time expressed her wish for: and in all my life (as I feel ever since) there fell on me no misfortune like it; —which has smitten my whole world into universal wreck (unless I can repair it in some small measure), and extinguished whatever light of cheerfulness, and loving hopefulness life still had in it to me.

The paragraph in *The Times* (Monday, 23d April), which I believe is by Dr. Quain (a most kind Physician of hers), contains in briefest compass the true Narrative of her Death,— which I have searched into all the items of, but have no wish or need to record here *on paper*, as if *they* were liable to be forgotten, or erased from the poor heart of me while I live here. She had 'lunched' (dined, for *her*) with the Forsters that day, who noticed her especial cheerfulness and well-being, 'Carlyle coming home the day after to-morrow!' She drove away, perhaps towards three P.M.; walked (about a hundred and fifty yards) in Kensington Gardens; got in again south end of Serpentine Bridge; set out that wretched little dog to run by her near 'Victoria Gate' (north-east corner of the Park); swift brougham hurting its foot, instant spring out to help *it* (though she little loved it, and had taken it only by charity; woe to it!), return of the swift-brougham Lady to apologise (*in* the footpath out [of the brougham], this, opposite Stanhope Place), re-ascent into her carriage, and Sylvester driving on: this was the last act of her to me inestimable life! She had laid off her bonnet, taken out two combs (that sharp prick in the back stopping heart and lungs), laid her hands on her lap, right-hand back uppermost, left-hand palm uppermost; and leaning in the left-hand corner of her carriage, she lay dead! Death, they tell me, must have followed almost instantly;—her last brief thought, if she had any, must have been a pang of sorrow about *me*. God be gracious to her through Eternity—and oh to be joined with her again, if that is not too fond a thought; free both of us from sin, for evermore; that were indeed a Heaven!— —Silvester seems to have spent still about three-quarters of an hour, suspecting nothing wrong; drove down by the Big Drive, then up by the Serpentine, and down by the Victoria Gate and Big Drive once more; at the bottom of that, he half paused for orders; getting none, looked back over the blinds, saw the two hands; turned up by the Serpentine again, but after a few yards, looking back, saw the dear little hands again,—drove towards an elderly Lady near by, in the path *beyond* Rotten Row; begged her to look in; she half did, elderly Gentleman near her wholly did; pronounced it death to all appearance, and recommended him to hasten over to St. George's Hospital, which he in a moment did. All in vain, in vain! Her look of peace, of beautiful absolute repose had struck them much; very kind, very helpful to *me*, if to no other,—everybody was. For, as I learned ultimately, had it not been for their and John Forster's, and Dr. Quain's and everybody's mercy on me, there must have been, by rule, a Coroner's Inquest held,—which would have been a blotch upon my memory intolerable then, and discordantly ugly for all time coming. It is to Forster's unwearied and invincible efforts, that I am indebted for escape from this sad defilement of my feelings. Indeed *his* kindness then, and all through, in every particular and detail was *un*exampled, of a cordiality and assiduity almost painful to me: thanks to him and perpetual recollection.

Saturday night about half-past nine, I was sitting in Sister Jean's at Dumfries; thinking of my Railway to Chelsea on Monday, and perhaps of a sprained ankle I had got at Scotsbrig two weeks or so before,—when the fatal telegram (two of them in succession) came; it had a kind of *stunning* effect upon me; not for above two days could I estimate the immeasurable depth of it, or the infinite sorrow which had peeled my life all bare, and, in one moment, shattered my poor world to universal ruin. They took me out next day, to wander (as was medically needful) in the green sunny Sabbath fields; and ever and anon there rose from my sick heart the ejaculation 'My poor little Woman!'—but no full gush of tears came to my relief, nor has yet come; will it ever? A stony 'Woe's me, woe's me!' sometimes with infinite tenderness, and pity not for myself, is my habitual mood hitherto. I had been hitching lamely about in the Terregles quarter, my company the green solitudes and fresh Spring breezes,—quietly but far from happily,—about the hour she died. Sixteen hours *after* the telegram,—(Sunday about two P.M.) there came to me a *Letter* from her, written on Saturday before going out; the cheeriest and merriest of all her several prior ones;—a Note for *her* written at Scotsbrig, Friday morning, and which *should* have been a pleasure to her at breakfast that morning was not put in till *after* six at Ecclefechan (negligence of ———, excusable, but unforgettable); had not left Ecclefechan till ten P.M., nor arrived till two P.M. next day, and lay *un*opened here.

Monday morning, John set off with me for London;—never, for a thousand years, should I forget that arrival here of ours,—my first *un*welcomed by her; *she* lay in her coffin, lovely in death; I kissed her cold brow . . . pale Death and things not mine or *ours* had possession of our poor dwelling. Next day wander over the fatal localities in Hyde Park; Forster and Brother John settling, apart from me, everything for the morrow. Morrow, Wednesday morning, we were under way with our sacred burden; John and Forster kindly did not speak to me (good Twisleton too was in the train without consulting me): I looked out upon the Spring fields, the everlasting Skies, in silence; and had for most part a more endurable day,—till Haddington where Dods etc. were waiting with hospitalities, with etc. etc. which almost drove me openly wild. I went out to walk in the moonlit silent streets; *not* suffered to go alone: I looked up at the windows of the old Room where I had first seen her,—1821 on a Summer evening after Sunset,—five and forty years ago. Edward Irving had brought me out, walking, to Haddington; *she* the first thing I had to see there. The beautifullest young creature I had ever beheld; sparkling with grace and talent, though sunk in sorrow (for loss of her Father), and speaking little. I noticed her once looking at me,—Oh Heaven, to think of that now!—

The Dodses (excellent people in their honest homely way) had great pity for me, patience with me; I retired to my room, slept none all night,—little sleep to me since that telegram night;—but lay silent in the great Silence. Thursday (26th April 1866), wandered out into the Churchyard etc.: at one P.M. came the Funeral; silent, small (only twelve old friends, and two *volunteer*, besides us three), very beautiful and noble to me: and I laid her head in the grave of her Father (according to covenant of forty years back); and all was ended. In the nave of the old Abbey Kirk, long a ruin, now being saved from further decay, with the skies looking down on her, there sleeps my little Jeannie, and the light of her face will never shine on me more. One other time,—after the *Inscription* is put on,—I have promised myself to be in Haddington. We withdrew, that afternoon; posted up (by Edinburgh with its many confusions) towards London all night, and about ten or eleven A.M. were shovelled out here; where I am hitching and wandering about, best off in strict solitude (were it only possible); my one solace and employment that of doing all which I can imagine *she* would have liked me to do. Maggie Welsh and my Brother are still with me.—I suppose it to be useless to continue these jottings (Book probably to be *burnt* from all other eyes, and to myself painful!)—but perhaps will add something to-morrow still. 8*th May* 1866; 9*th* I find!

Thursday, *May* 10. (Days all dim to me; yesterday I was *wrong* in date). . . . My one solace and employment hitherto is that of sorting up, and setting as I judge *she* would have wished, all that pertained to her beautiful existence and her: *her* advice on it all, how *that* wish starts out on me strangely at many a turn; and the sharp twinge that reminds me, 'No!' One's first *awakening* in the morning, the reality all stript so *bare* before one, and the puddle of confused dreams at once gone, is the ghastliest half-hour of the day;—as I have heard others remark. On the whole there is no use in writing here. There is even a lack of *sincerity* in what I write (strange but true). The thing I *would* say, I cannot. All words are idle.[1] . . .

The paper of this poor Notebook of hers is done; all I had to say, too (though there lie such volumes yet unsaid), seems to be almost done: and I must sorrowfully end it, and seek for something else. Very sorrowfully still; for it has been my sacred shrine, and *religious* city of refuge from the *bitterness* of these sorrows, during all the doleful weeks that are past since I took it up: a kind of *devotional* thing (as I once already said), which *softens* all grief into tenderness and infinite pity and repentant love; one's whole sad *life* drowned as if in *tears* for one, and all the wrath and scorn and other grim elements silently melted away. And now, am I to *leave* it; to take farewell of *Her* a second time? Right silent and serene is *She*, my lost Darling yonder, as I often think in my gloom; no sorrow more for *Her*,—nor will there long be for me. . . .

Everything admonishes me to *end* here my poor scrawlings and weak reminiscences of days that are no more.

I still mainly mean to *burn* this Book before my own departure; but feel that I shall always have a kind of grudge to do it, and an indolent excuse, 'Not *yet*; wait, any day that can be done!'—and that it *is* possible the thing *may* be left behind me, legible to interested survivors,—*friends* only, I will hope, and with *worthy* curiosity, not *un*worthy!

In which event, I solemnly forbid them, each and all, to *publish* this Bit of Writing *as it stands here*; and warn them that *without fit editing* no *part* of it should be printed (nor so far as I can order, *shall* ever be);—and that the '*fit* editing' of perhaps nine-tenths of it will, after I am gone, have become *impossible*.

T. C. (Saturday, 28th July 1866).

[1] The extract from Notebook III. ends here.

Selected Letters

The selections from letters that follow are taken from *The Love Letters of Thomas Carlyle and Jane Welsh* edited by Alexander Carlyle, M.A. (Bodley Head, 1909); *New Letters of Thomas Carlyle*, edited and annotated by Alexander Carlyle (Bodley Head, 1904); and the *Letters of Thomas Carlyle to John Stuart Mill, John Sterling and Robert Browning*, edited by Alexander Carlyle, M.A. (T. Fisher Unwin, 1923). The letter to John Carlyle about Coleridge and the letter to Disraeli do not appear in any collection, and I have taken the texts from Froude's biography. The three letters to Lady Harriet Baring, later Lady Ashburton, are printed by the kind permission of the Marquess of Northampton. A few of the notes appeared in the original editions; most of them, and all the prefatory remarks to letters, are mine.

Selected Letters

TO JANE BAILLIE WELSH

This is a typical example of the letters written by Carlyle to Jane Welsh during their long courtship by correspondence, in which Carlyle blended awkwardly enough the part of suitor with that of literary instructor and guide.

3, MORAY STREET, WEDNESDAY-NIGHT,
[26 MARCH, 1823.]

MY DEAR FRIEND,—You have not done a more beneficial action for a long time than writing to me last Monday. I had already spent too much of the preceding week in the delightful exercise of *that Christian virtue*, for which both of us are so remarkable; I had wearied myself in the region of conjecture, and found little comfort within its ample domain. On the evening in question, I had just brought out my papers, and was sitting down to begin that weary Life of Schiller[1]—in the most vinegar humour that a man could well be in—with a head empty of ideas, and a heart oppressed by as many chagrins as might have served a dozen hearts—when her Serene Lowness, the Dowager Wilkie,[2] came gliding in, with—'a parcel Sir!' I felt myself grow half a hundred-weight lighter whenever I saw it. Your Letter wrought upon me as if by art magic: I was another man when I had read it. To use a Slawkenbergian figure, it was as if you had lit up a blazing fire in the dark damp haunted chamber of some old ruined Gothic pile, scattering the ghosts and spectres into the shades of Erebus and tinging the grim walls once more with the colours of jovial life and warm substantial cheer. I declared within myself that you were the very best of all the daughters of Eve: I proceeded to

[1] Carlyle's first published book, which appeared in 1825.
[2] Mrs. Wilkie, Carlyle's landlady, at 3, Moray Street.

my work as if I had grown young again.—It is pity that this magical force will not always continue; pity that the *fire* at last goes out, and leaves the poor mind's chamber cold and dark, and haunted by the Devil as before! Yet after all, we should be thankful for our mercies: there are parts of life too fine to be the general material of it; and virtue itself, they say, is nothing but the victory, often fiercely struggled for, of freewill over fate. Let it be so.

I know not how I felt when I read of these marryings and givings in marriage. It seems to me as if our destiny were yet long to be intermingled, as if we were yet to walk side by side thro' many bright scenes, to assist each other in many a noble purpose; and Oh! what a pitiful conclusion to all this would a vulgar wedding make! It is true they manage it otherwise in the common world: there the great object of a young woman's existence is to get a rich Husband, and a fine house, and give dinners; just as it is the great object of ravens to find carrion, or of pawn-brokers to amass a *plum*; and the sooner they attain their respective destinations it is surely the better. But if each creature ought to follow the good its nature aims at, then *you* are right to take another path—right to press forward towards the golden summit of mental eminence, and to shrink at no sacrifice which you believe that elevation will repay you for. The time *will* come indeed, when you must 'fall in love' and be wedded as others have been; it is the general law, and must be fulfilled: but I fear not that I shall ever have the pain of seeing your happiness entrusted to one unworthy however desirous of the charge, or the high ambitions of your youth given up for anything less sacred than the feelings of the heart, if these unhappily should come to oppose them. I say *unhappily*; for the love of knowledge is a passion which, once in possession of the mind, can hardly ever be extinguished; it is noble in its nature too, and like other noble passions elevates itself into a kindred with all the virtues of the character: if stinted, and still more if checked, in its gratification, it leaves a painful hankering behind it, which is inconsistent with true peace of mind, and often, I imagine, with the free exercise of the moral faculties.

In the mean time, therefore, you must just continue on your way. If I had my way you should not be married till—not till a considerable period after this. Literary women have many things to suffer, but they have likewise something to enjoy. I confess it appears to me more enviable to be a sister of Madame de Staël's for half a year, than 'to suckle fools and chronicle small beer' for half a century.

But I must cease to preach, for the text is plain without commentary, and I have other things to do. You are right to keep by Gibbon, since you have begun it: there is no other tolerable history of those times and nations, within the reach of such readers as we are; it is a kind of bridge that connects the antique with the modern ages. And how gorgeously does it swing across the gloomy and tumultuous chasm of those barbarous centuries! Gibbon is a man whom one never forgets—unless oneself deserving to be forgotten; the perusal of his work forms an epoch in the history of one's mind. I know you will admire Gibbon, yet I do not expect or wish that you should love him. He has but a coarse and vulgar heart, with all his keen logic and glowing imagination and lordly irony: he worships power and splendour; and suffering virtue, the most heroic devotedness if unsuccessful, unarrayed in the pomp and circumstance of outward glory, has little of his sympathy. To the Christians he is frequently very unfair: if he had lived now, he would have written differently on these points. I would not have you love him; I am sure you will not. Have you any notion what an *ugly* thief he was? Jack[1] brought down his *Life* today, and it has a profile of his whole person—alas for Mlle. Curchod! Alas for her daughter Wilhelmina Necker who wished to marry him, when she was thirteen—not out of love to him but to her Mother! I would have sent you this *Life*, but it is a large quarto—and I knew not if you would receive it patiently. Should you wish it, write to me tomorrow and I will send it out. There is some amusement in it, but you will relish it more, when you know more fully and think more highly of the studied labours of the mind which it shows you in *déshabille*.

[1] Carlyle's brother, John.

I am also glad that you like my thrice illustrious Goethe, and can *not* understand him. What expounding and reading and chit-chatting we shall have together when you come! I beg only that you do not disappoint me again. At first I was rather disconcerted at this postponement: I had calculated on your arrival as a perfect certainty ; nay it was only on Monday, that I got into the most wonderful flurry at what I conceived to be the actual sight of you! The small divine who was with me on Princes Street might as well have spoken to the winds, I could answer his prosing statements but by monosyllables which I daresay had no connection oftener than once with the 'subject matter of his discourse': the lady before us seemed to have your very dress and form and gait, and I heard not what he said.—Alas! we overtook this beatific vision and she had a nose about the length of a moderate *dibble!*[1] So abrupt is often the transition from the height of poetry to the depth of prose.

On second thoughts, however, I am satisfied. By the time you arrive, I shall have finished Schiller; I shall see more of you, and be more at leisure to see you. It will be absolutely cruel, if you do not come about the very beginning of the month. We could be so happy, I often think, wandering at large beneath these clear Spring skies, talking over all our plans and hopes, arguing or discussing—or doing nothing at all beside each other! You *must* come in less than a fortnight. You will write to me just once before that time, and the next message will be that 'Miss Welsh condescends to allow the dyspeptical Philosopher to behold the light of her countenance tomorrow-morning about ten.' Said Philosopher will be punctual to the hour, and promises to conduct himself with great submissiveness and propriety. If you have any heart—which I sometimes do believe is the case, in spite of all your sinful indifference and manifold railleries—you will think of this and do it. I look forward to April as to a *white month.*

You do not say a word about *composition* this time—because I suppose you have had other things to mind. We will settle all that when we meet. Bring *Götz* with you also, and we will

[1] A gardener's tool for planting cabbages, etc.

decipher it, tho' it were as dark as the *Linen Books*. I like you better for dismissing that ancient sinner Giovan Boccaccio: he is a wicked knave with all his talents, and intellectual pleasure may be dearly purchased at such a risk. You are yourself throughout, my own noble Jane in everything....

Now have I not tired you enough for once? There is poor Schiller lying too, at whom I must have a hit or two before I sleep. It will be an invaluable Life this of Schiller's, were it once completed: so splendid and profound and full of *unction*—Oh! I could beat my brains out, when I think what a miserable pithless ninny I am! Would it were in my power either to write like a man or honestly to give up the attempt forever. Chained to the earth by native gravitation and a thousand wretched fetters, I am miserable unless I be soaring in the empyrean; and thus between the lofty will and the powerless deed, I have no peace, no peace. Sometimes I could almost run distracted; my wearied soul seems as if it were hunted round within its narrow enclosure by a whole legion of the dogs of Tartarus, which sleep not, night or day. In fact I am never happy except when *full* of business, and *nothing more*. The secret of all is 'I have no genius,' and like Andrew Irving's horse, I *have* 'a *dibbil* of a temper.' We must just submit!

Boyd the pursy Bookseller wishes me to translate Goethe's *Wilhelm Meister*, which I have told him is very clever. It will not be determined for some weeks—not till I see where I am to be and how, during Summer. Come, my dear Jane, and let us consider all these matters! Come! Come! I am vehemently longing to see you.—Write at any rate when your Mother has finished *Delphine*—sooner if you want Gibbon. My 'Amplification' greets you most respectfully. My best compliments to your Mother....

Yours, *Mia Cara, per sempre*,

THOMAS CARLYLE

Excuse this crumpled paper; I knew not how to fold it, and have much more to say than it would hold. Write to me immediately—and *come*, if you would make me happy.

TO JANE BAILLIE WELSH

This letter was written in response to one from Jane Welsh giving the simple address of 'Hell', in which she expressed her pleasure that '*One* in the world loves me—will love me ever, ever,—and tells me more boldly than Hope that my future *may* yet be glorious and happy.' Carlyle misinterpreted these phrases, not surprisingly, as a personal declaration of love. He was sharply undeceived by Jane Welsh's next letter, in which she repeated that she loved him—as a Friend. 'Your Friend I will be, your truest most devoted Friend, while I breathe the breath of life; but your Wife! Never, never!' Carlyle's pretence that she had put their concerns '*on the very footing where I wished them to stand*' has its own pathos.

KINNAIRD HOUSE, 31 AUG., 1823.

MY DEAR JANE,—I have longed for the arrival of this day, as the reward of a week's disquietude and toil: I determined not to write, till I should have it in my power to say that I was settled at my tasks, and doing something, however small. The miserable weather kept me four days later in arriving than I had expected: your Letter (with a heap of meaner scrolls) was waiting to welcome me. And such a welcome! I felt in reading it and reading it again, as if it were more to me than the charter to all the metal of Potosi. What a frank and true and noble spirit is my Jane's! No artifice, no vulgar management; her sentiments come warm and fearless from her heart, because they are pure and honest as herself, and the friend whom she trusts, she trusts without reserve. I often ask myself: 'Is not all this a dream? Is it true that the most enchanting creature I have ever seen does actually love me? No! thank God it is not a dream: Jane loves me! she loves me! and I swear by the Immortal Powers that she shall yet be mine, as I am hers, thro' life and death and all the dark vicissitudes that await us here or hereafter.' In more reasonable moments, I perceive that I am very selfish and almost mad. Alas! my fate is dreary and obscure and perilous: is it fit that you, whom I honour as among the fairest of God's works, whom I love more dearly than my own soul, should partake in it? No, my own best of Maidens, I will not deceive you. Think of me as of one that will live and die to do you service; whose good will if his good deeds cannot, may perhaps deserve some gratitude; but whom it is dangerous and useless to love. If I were intellectual sovereign of all the world, if I were—But it is vain to speculate: I know that I am nothing. I know not that I shall not always be so. The only thing I know is that you are the most delightful, enthusiastic, contemptuous, affectionate, sarcastic, capricious, warm-hearted, lofty-minded, half-devil, half-angel of a woman that ever ruled over the heart of a man; that I will love you, must love you, whatever may betide, till the last moment of my existence; and that if we both act rightly our lot *may* be the happiest of a thousand mortal lots. So let us cling to one another (if you dare when thus forewarned)—forever and ever! Let us put faith in one another, and live in hope that prospects so glorious and heavenly will not end in darkness and despair. If your happiness be shipwrecked by my means, then woe, woe is to me without end! But it will not: no, you will yet be blessed yourself in making me more blessed than man has right to look for being upon earth. God bless you, my heart's Darling; and grant that our honest purposes may prosper in our hands!

All these incoherent inconsistent things you have often heard already: but you will bear with me in uttering them yet again. For me no subject connected with our correspondence and affection for each other needs the charm of novelty to make it interesting. If it were repeated to me fifty times a-day, that you loved me, I should still desire to hear it oftener. For the present, however, I must let you go.

How is it that you have lost all influence with your Mother, that she will not return and let you be at rest? I declare even I am beginning to get vexed at these delays. No wonder that you murmur, that you have given patience to the winds, and become determined to look on Templand only as a place of torment. That 'strenuous idleness' was not made for minds like yours. Yet what is to be done? You have forsworn the under-strapping virtue of submissive endurance; cannot you betake yourself to the more profitable resources of activity? Might you not write to the little Doctor to send you down Musäus (can you read it now?) from the coach-office; and then bolt your chamber-door, and sit down to *render* it, in Nithsdale as in Lothian? If you are not to depart in a week or two, I do think you should try this. These *Volksmährchen* are a promising enough kind of task for you: you will translate them excellently, I have no fear; and Boyd to whom I talked on the subject, as I last went thro' Edinburgh, is all in trim to have them published. I think they will make a very pretty volume, and a fair commencement of your intellectual labours. About your talents and ultimate success I have less doubt every day. No soul so vehement, no heart so fine as yours, but must ultimately come to light, to full development and full reward, in spite of difficulties far weightier than yours. Be restless, then, but not unhappy at your present isolation. I would ride their horses to death, and dispute every word they said, till they let me go. Long before October, when I see you, you will have advanced far into Musäus; full of ardent thoughts and cheered by gleams of celestial promise, you will have exchanged the residence of 'Hell' for a region that stretches to the neighbourhood of Heaven. If you are so delicious in *that* ugly abode, what will you be in the other! Be at peace, then, if you can, till the hour of freedom arrive. There is a long and brilliant life before you: trust in yourself and me, my best beloved Jane; and fear nothing. For you I am still a prophet of good not of evil. Stand to your task, and there is no danger.

You ask me what are my employments and my plans; you speak to me like my guardian Angel as you are. My feelings you seem perfectly to understand; I thank you a thousand times for your encouragements and sympathy; and I still hope however feebly that a day will come when you will say that they have not been in vain. Alas! no! I am not satisfied: my mind is a prey to everlasting strife when I contrast what I would be with what I am. There is a restless ardour in my heart as in yours. Like you I am ambitious, far too much so, tho' I phrase it otherwise; but the root of my inquietude lies far deeper than yours. My character is full of contradictions; outwardly, on the surface as it were, I am timid as a leveret; while within there are feelings that might suit a tiger—fierce, desperate, deep tormenting feelings! Hence a perpetual inconsistency in my conduct; hence my habit is less to act than to endure; hence the great principle that moves me is little better than a kind of—desperation! Poor Gentleman! I wonder what is to be done with him at last. A difficulty harder than all and partly peculiar I have yet to mention. O how often, when sicker than I am now, have I prayed that I might but be broken on the wheel every morning, and then have nothing more to do with pain! O! thrice and four times accursed 'physical disease'; Tophet has not in its recesses such a tremendous scourge as thou! But what avails it to speculate? This evil also is but another element in the chaos of materials out of which the intellect and the will (if any) are to create a glorious and manly history. This evil too I will overcome. I have brought a horse out with me hither; I am trying every precaution to keep myself in tolerable health; in three weeks, if I find that I *cannot* live here without the loss of that priceless blessing, I shall return to Mainhill—where a single month had almost made me whole. Meanwhile too I am not unemployed: after long re-deliberations, I have been decided (by the Bookseller) to go on with Goethe. Ten pages a day is my task: with riding, and teaching and other drivelling, I seldom get begun till six at night. Some parts of *Meister* are very stupid, and it is all very difficult to translate. But 'let us not despise the day of small things!' All experience tells us that *mountains may be removed by faith*. Yes! I swear it, my noble Jane, you and I *shall* yet vanquish all these mean impediments, and shine together in the degree of brilliancy which *is* ours by nature, whatever that may be. If *not*—then woe to that man, it were good for him that he had never been born! In November they expect to begin printing *Meister*; when will *Musäus* be ready? Work, work, my heroine! There is nothing but toil, toil, toil,—till we reach the golden glowing summit,—and then!—!— But I must cease, tho' the thousandth part has not been told. O do write to me constantly, and often, often: let *no week* pass without writing to me: we are *one* heart and soul forever, and each of us has none but the other to love and look to. Adieu my ever-dearest!

I am always yours,

T. CARLYLE

Write to me without any delay, if you love me. I have millions of things to say, and boundless desire to say them. I *will* see you in October, if both of us are this side Hades. Be diligent and good and love me with all your heart as I do you.

TO JANE BAILLIE WELSH

KINNAIRD HOUSE, 18TH SEPTEMBER, 1823.

MY DEAR JANE,—If I were not a fool of some standing, I should not have vexed you on this occasion, or given you this fresh opportunity of testifying how true is the affection which you bear me. Your Letter has set me a-thinking about matters which, with my accustomed heedlessness, I was letting take their course without accurate investigation, tho' conscious that a right understanding of them was of vital importance to both of us. I honour your wisdom and decision: you have put our concerns *on the very footing where I wished them to stand*. So be of good cheer, for no harm is done.

When I placed the management of our intercourse and whatever mutual interests we had or might have, entirely at your own disposal, making you sole queen and arbitress of the 'commonweal,' I stipulated for myself as much freedom of speech as you could conveniently grant, leaving to you an unbounded power of acting, then and in all time coming. It is to the terms of this *compact* that I still adhere in their widest acceptation. I know very well you will never be my wife. Never! Never!—I never believed it above five minutes at a time all my days. 'T is all one as I should love a bright particular star, and think to wed it.' My fancy can form scenes, indeed, which with you to share them were worthy of a place in the heaven above; but there are items wanting, without which all these blessings were a curse, and which not your consent (if that were ever to be dreamed of) nor any influence of man can assure me of realizing. Such illusions do in truth haunt me, nor am I very sedulous to banish them. The harsh hand of Time will do it speedily enough without help of mine, and leave no truth behind that will ever give me half the pleasure. I grant it is absurd, and might be more than absurd, to utter them so freely: but what then? They give a momentary pleasure to myself, and do harm to no one. Strip life of all its baseless hopes and beautiful chimeras; it seems to me there would be little left worth having.

Thus then it stands: You love me as a sister, and will not wed; I love you in all possible senses of the word, and will not wed, any more than you. Does this reassure you? If so, let us return to our old position: let me continue writing what comes into my head, and do you continue acting now or forever after just as you judge best. I seek no engagement, I will make none. By God's blessing, I will love you with all my heart and all my soul, while the blood continues warm within me; I will reverence you as the fairest living emblem of all that is most exalted and engaging in my conceptions of human nature; I will help you according to my slender power, and stand by you closer than a brother: but these feelings are entertained for myself alone; let them be their own reward, or go unrewarded —that is *my* concern. So long as you have charity to hear me talk about affections that must end in nothingness, and plans which seem destined to be all abortive, I will speak and listen; when you tire of this, when you marry, or cast me off in any of the thousand ways that fortune is ever offering, I shall of course cease to correspond with you, I shall cease to love Mrs. ——, but not Jane Welsh; the image she will have left in my mind I shall always love, for even this tho' the original is gone forever, will still have more reality than mere fantasies that would replace it. In all this I see no blame; and if there were, I cannot help it. Had it pleased Providence to plant some other standard of excellence in me, or make you different from what you are, then I should have felt and acted otherwise: but as it is, I am no free agent. For the rest, do not fear the consequence so far as I am concerned. My heart is too old by almost half a score of years, and made of sterner stuff than to break in junctures of that kind. Had it not been harder than the nether millstone it must have shivered into fragments very long ago. I have no idea of dying in the Arcadian shepherd style, for the disappointment of hopes which I never seriously entertained, or had no right to entertain seriously.

Now, in the name of the ever blessed Trinity, have I done with these preliminaries? Ass that I was in forcing you to ask them! I confess it grieves me to address you in this cold formal style, as if writing to my Tailor for a suit of clothes, and directing him where to cut and where to spare; not to my own best Jane, the friend of my soul, from whom I have no secrets or separate interests, and whom I love because she has no secrets from me. Let us forget it altogether, and be as we were! If you *will* part with me, do it; but not for *my* sake! For my sake, I call God to witness, you never shall. Again I say, let us forget it utterly, forever and ever!

These woful explanations I judged it right to send without a moment's delay: your comfort seemed to be concerned in their being given you instantly. You must not count this as *any Letter* or your last as any: but write to me again in your own careless style, *about Musäus and all that*, just as if this thing had never happened. I long to be again introduced to your home at Haddington, to share in all your tasks and difficulties, to cherish your fainting hopes, and tell you a thousand times without stint or fear of reproof that you are dearer to me than aught in life, and that united we will conquer every difficulty, and be glorious characters—if it so please the Fates.

This last proviso seems a needful one for me at present, tho' in your case I esteem it little. I appear to be fast going to the devil here; my health is getting worse every week; I sleep at the easy rate of three or four hours per night, and feel throughout the day in the most beatific humour! If it had not been that the people are kind to me as if I were their son, I had been gone ere now. They design staying here all Winter: I will try it another month; and if without improvement, I mount the horse Bardolph, and turn my face back again to the plain country. I was looking out, while there, in the valley of Milk, for some cottage among trees, beside the still waters; some bright little place, with a stable behind it, a garden and a rood of green,—where I might fairly commence housekeeping, and the writing of books! They laughed at me, and said it was a joke. Well! I swear it is a lovely world this, after all. What a pity that we had not *five* score years and ten of it!

Meanwhile I go on with Goethe's *Wilhelm Meister*: a book which I love not, and which I am sure will never sell, but which I am determined to print and finish. There are touches of the very highest and most ethereal genius in it; but diluted with floods of insipidity, which even *I* would not have written for the world. I sit down to it every night at six, with the ferocity of a hyæna; and in spite of all obstructions my keep-lesson is more than half thro' the first volume, and travelling over poetry and prose, slowly but surely to the end. Some of the poetry is very bad, some of it rather good. The following is mediocre—the worst kind!

> Who never ate his bread in sorrow,
> Who never spent the darksome hours
> Weeping and watching for the morrow,
> He knows you not, ye gloomy Powers.
>
> To earth, the weary Earth, ye bring us,
> To guilt ye let us heedlesss go,
> Then leave repentance fierce to wring us:
> A moment's guilt, an age of woe!

And now, my own best Jane, before leaving you, what more have I to ask? That you would love me forever, in any way, on any terms you please; that you continue while we both live to make me the confidant of all your sorrows and enjoyments great and small; and above all that you would find me means of doing you some essential service—something that might make our intercourse and affection more than a pleasing dream, when God shall see meet to put an end to it forever. Shew me, O shew me how I may benefit you. . . . Write to me *instantly*, to 'reassure *me*.' Tell me all things that concern you—*all things*. God bless you my Dearest! Do write me as you like, I am ever yours with all my soul!—

T. CARLYLE

TO DR. CARLYLE

24 JUNE 1824.

. . . I have seen many curiosities; not the least of them I reckon Coleridge, the Kantian metaphysician and quondam Lake poet. I will tell you all about our interview when we meet. Figure a fat, flabby, incurvated personage, at once short, rotund, and relaxed, with a watery mouth, a snuffy nose, a pair of strange brown, timid, yet earnest-looking eyes, a high tapering brow, and a great bush of grey hair; and you have some faint idea of Coleridge. He is a kind good soul, full of religion and affection and poetry and animal magnetism. His cardinal sin is that he wants *will*. He has no resolution. He shrinks from pain or labour in any of its shapes. His very attitude bespeaks this. He never straightens his knee-joints. He stoops with his fat, ill-shapen shoulders, and in walking he does not tread, but shovel and slide. My father would call it 'skluiffing.' He is also always busied to keep, by strong and frequent inhalations, the water of his mouth from overflowing, and his eyes have a look of anxious impotence. He *would* do with all his heart, but he knows he dares not. The conversation of the man is much as I anticipated—a forest of thoughts, some true, many false, more part dubious, all of them ingenious in some degree, often in a high degree. But there is no method in his talk: he wanders like a man sailing among many currents, whithersoever his lazy mind directs him; and, what is more unpleasant, he preaches, or rather soliloquises. He cannot speak, he can only *tal-k* (so he names it). Hence I found him unprofitable, even tedious; but we parted very good friends, I promising to go back and see him some evening—a promise which I fully intend to keep. I sent him a copy of 'Meister,' about which he had some friendly talk. I reckon him a man of great and useless genius: a strange, not at all a great man. . . .

T. CARLYLE

TO JANE BAILLIE WELSH

This letter is written in reply to one from Jane Welsh, in which she light-heartedly and rashly said that, although she had promised to marry Carlyle, they were not, after all, married yet. Perhaps they should both change their minds? Carlyle's reply shows that she should have known better than to joke with him on such a subject; it shows also his consciousness of having attained domination over her mind.

HODDAM HILL, 26 FEBRUARY, 1826.

MY DEAREST,—I received your Letter on Friday, after asking for it many times in vain. The cause of your unwonted silence afflicts me doubly, as it came unexpected; John told me he had seen you in Edinburgh, and that you were 'in good health.' Alas, my good kind Jane! It is a hard fate for thee to lie in prison in a sick frame, with little entertainment for thy vehement spirit but doleful meditations on the gross folly and perverseness of the man thou has loved above all others. I grieve that I cannot better it; for in all likelihood this Letter will at first vex you still more; yet, on more serious reflexion, I hope it will not fail to produce some peaceable fruit.

I have already noticed oftener than once that in unguarded moments you let indications escape you of a judgement existing in the bottom of your mind by no means favourable to my present walk and conversation. You seem in your secret soul to think that I am but a whimsical unstable person, that I might do well if I liked, that my chief distress at present is idleness and a diseased imagination. To these criticisms of 'good-natured friends' I am already so much accustomed that I can estimate them in my own mind at something like their just value; but from you, I will confess it, they affect me with a sharp distress. When my heart is opening towards you in trustful Husband-like communion, they shut it with a harsh hostile violence; I thought we were *one*, and I find that we are still *two*; that far from sympathising with me, by helpful encouragement, in my great enterprise (and every man's enterprise appears great in his own little eyes) you scarcely approve of it, you do not even seem to know with any accuracy what it is. Allow me to speak in all plainness; for there are many mistakes here.

I can by no means engage, in the space of one short Letter, to vindicate the whole course of my late history; but so much I may say in clear words: that I do in no wise accuse myself of fluctuations and change of purpose; that on the contrary ever since I became master of my own movements I seem to have walked forward in one path with more and more steadiness; and can even tell myself at some moments that I am distinctly advancing towards my highest and most desirable objects, and in spite of all impediments, and well or ill meant counter advices, shaping my own dismembered life again into a whole; by means of my own; peculiar as the case they were to meet is peculiar. A little more than a twelvemonth ago, when it had become too apparent to be longer denied that unless I could devise for myself a more self-regulated existence I must soon sink to utter destruction both of soul and body; having at last acquired calmness and seclusion for meditating the aspect of my ship-wrecked fortune, I first bethought me of *you* as of one to whom I was dearer than to almost any other; and with such knowledge as I had of your circumstances and intentions, I called on you for help in my extreme need. Your love of me, I knew, was great, your nobleness of mind I had also reason to know; and the sacrifice I required of you was such as to put both to the utmost proof. I asked of you no less than yourself and all that you had and were, your heart your hand and your worldly resources; *you* were to have the happiness of snatching the immortal Mr. Carlyle from the jaws of perdition which were ready to swallow him forever; to you he was to owe a home, and the peace and kind ministrations of a home; your angel hand was to lift him from the abyss, your true bosom to be the resting-place of his marred and wearied soul; and all this you were to do for him *on trust*, in the hope that as he grew again to life and strength, he would more and more repay your celestial helpfulness, and, become what he might, would be yours and utterly and wholly thro' time and eternity;—or else, such was my view of it, you were to do for yourself the kindness of forthwith ejecting him from the place he had too long unworthily occupied in your hopes and interest. These things you could not do, your fortune was called from you by a higher duty; from you I was not to receive a home. Next month I had procured one for myself. In due time I took possession of it; and here commenced, on my own poor resources, that mode of life which my own best judgement had more and more loudly declared to be essential not for my happiness but for my existence as a man deserving to exist. In this course I have continued to persevere with at least no *thought* of fluctuation; I am still persevering in it; and by God's blessing I intend to continue so till my aim is attained; till I am strong and collected enough in body and spirit to mingle, in something like my own form, with the tumultuous floods of living business, and cut my little way in it with unshackled limbs. That circumstances are not unchangeable, that wilful squirelets and unjust stewards respect not even the cottage of a German Philosopher, is no blame of mine:[1] nor does it behove me when such squirelets and stewards have pulled down my hut about my ears, to sit down and bewail or vituperate their injustice and wilfulness, but to go forth and seek myself another dwelling. This very thing is now in progress: I must have another house; in the country, if I can, for a while longer; in Edinburgh, if I cannot. In twelve days hence the possibility or impossibility of the first scheme will have been determined; and far from the other being abandoned, I understand my brother to have been out just yesterday, surveying the environs of Edinburgh to meet that contingency. Now in all this, my kind, but overhasty Love, there appears no inconsistency to me: there is one purpose, and the means of attaining it change as the accidents on which they depend. As to my ulterior views, my

[1] Carlyle was to leave the farm rented at Hoddam, because of a disagreement between his father and the landlord.

hopes of employing myself profitably in this interval, and gradually working my way into a more natural condition of activity and domestic accommodation, by your permission I have told you all the fancies of my head without reserve, as they rose there; but these were transitory visions rather than fixed prospects. No man, I avow it proudly, had ever more reason to praise a woman for compliance in his schemes than I have towards you; and the thought of this has often been as water to my thirsty spirit: but really, since the first great project[1] which you were forced to reject, I do not find that I have formed any practical plan with even an approach to determination, to which your assistance was necessary or even possible. With regard to my treatment of *your* purposes, the reception this last proposal met with ought not to mislead you. I regarded it only as brief whim, one night old when dispatched to me, and probably dead of a natural death before I received it. To this hour I am not sure that I understand it fully. What house were you providing for me in Edinburgh? Unless indeed you meant me to live, with my Wife, in your Mother's house; a generous proposal, which, had I so taken up your meaning, would have merited a more serious deliberation, and at the very least a more courteous refusal. But this it could not be.

O Jane, Jane! Your half-jesting enumeration of your wooers does anything but make me laugh. A thousand and a thousand times have I thought the same thing in deepest earnest. That you have the power of making many good matches is no secret to me; nay it would be a piece of news for me to learn that I am not the very *worst* you ever thought of. And you add with the same tearful smile: 'Alas! we are married already.' Let me now cut off the interjection, and say simply what is true that we are *not* married already; and do you hereby receive further my distinct and deliberate declaration that it depends on yourself, and shall always depend on yourself whether we ever be married or not. God knows I do not say this in a vulgar spirit of defiance; which in our present relation were coarse and cruel; but I say it in the spirit of dis-

[1] The idea of living at Craigenputtock, which was later carried out.

interested affection for you, and of fear for the reproaches of my own conscience should your fair destiny be marred by me, and you wounded in the house of your friends. Can you believe it with the good nature which I declare it deserves? It would absolutely give me satisfaction to know that you thought yourself entirely free of all ties to me, but those, such as they might be, of your own still-renewed election. It is reasonable and right that you should be concerned for your future establishment: Look round with calm eyes on the persons you mention or may hereafter so mention; and if there is any one among them whose Wife you had rather be—I do not mean whom you love better than me—but whose Wife, *all* things considered, you had rather be than mine, then *I* call upon you, I your Brother and Husband and friend thro' every fortune, to accept that man and leave me to my destiny. But if, on the contrary, my heart and my hand with the barren and perplexed destiny which promises to attend them, shall after all appear the *best* that this poor world can offer you, then take me and be content with me, and do not vex yourself with struggling to alter what is unalterable; to make a man who is poor and sick suddenly become rich and healthy. You tell me that you often weep when you think what is to become of us. It is unwise in you to weep: if you are reconciled to be *my* Wife (not the Wife of an ideal *me*, but the simple actual prosaic *me*), there is nothing frightful in the future. I look into it with more and more confidence and composure. Alas! Jane, you do not know me: it is not the poor, unknown, rejected Thomas Carlyle that you know, but the prospective rich, known and admired. I am reconciled to my fate as it stands or promises to stand ere long; I have pronounced the word *unpraised* in all its cases and numbers; and find nothing terrific in it, even when it means *unmonied*, and by the mass of his Majesty's subjects *neglected* or even partially *contemned*. I thank Heaven I have other objects in my eye than either *their* pudding or their breath. This comes of the circumstance that my Apprenticeship is ending, and yours still going on. O Jane! Jane! I could weep too; for I love you in my deepest heart.

These are hard sayings, my beloved Child; but I cannot spare them; and I hope, tho' bitter at first, they may not remain without wholesome influence. Do not get angry with me! Do not! I swear I deserve it not! Consider this as a true glimpse into my heart, which it is good that you contemplate with the gentleness and tolerance you have often shown me. I do not love you? If you judge it fit, I will clasp you to my bosom and my heart, as my wedded Wife, this very week: if you judge it fit, I will this very week forswear you forever. More I cannot do; but all this, when I compare myself with you, it is my duty to do.—Now think if I long for your answer! Yet not in my time, but in yours. I have lived as a *widower* from you these two days, I must live so till I hear from you again. *Till* I hear from you? Good God! Perhaps, first rightly, *when* I hear from you!—Adieu, my heart's Darling! God bless you and have you always in His keeping! I am yours, at your own disposal, forever and ever,

T. CARLYLE

TO JANE BAILLIE WELSH

The last letter written before their marriage on 17 October 1826.

SCOTSBRIG, MONDAY-NIGHT, [9 OCTOBER, 1826.]

'THE Last Speech and *marrying* words of that unfortunate young woman Jane Baillie *Welsh*,'[1] I received on Friday-morning; and truly a most delightful and swan-like melody was in them; a tenderness and warm devoted trust, worthy of such a maiden bidding farewell to the (unmarried) Earth, of which she was the fairest ornament. Dear little Child! How is it that I have deserved thee; deserved a purer and nobler heart than falls to the lot of millions? I swear I will love thee with *my* whole heart, and think my life well spent if it can make thine happy.

[1] This phrase contains two literary references—one to an article by Swift entitled 'The last Speech and dying Words of Ebenezer Elliston, who was executed the 2nd May, 1722', and another to an old ballad called 'The unfortunate Miss Bailey'

In fine, these preliminaries are in the way towards adjustment. After some vain galloping and consultation, I have at length got that certificate which the Closeburn Session in their sapience deem necessary; I have ordered the Proclaiming of Banns in this Parish of Middlebie, and written out a Note giving order for it in your Parish of Closeburn. Pity, by the way, that there is no man in the Closeburn Church possessed of any little fraction of vulgar earthly logic! It might have saved me a ride to Hoddam Manse this morning (the good Yorstoun my native Parson was away), and a most absurd application to the 'glass Minister' my neighbour. One would think that after fair *crying* three times through the organs of Archibald Blacklock, this certificate of celibacy would be like gilding refined gold, or adding a perfume to the violet: for would not my existing wife, in case I had one, forthwith, at the first hum from Archibald's windpipe, start up in her place, and state aloud that *she* had 'objections'?—But I will not quarrel with these Reverend men; *laissez les faire*, they will buckle us fast enough at length, and for the *How* I care not.

Your own day, Tuesday, as was fitting, I have made mine. Jack and I will surely call on Monday evening at Templand, most likely *after* tea; but I think it will be more commodious for all parties that we sleep at the Inn. You will not see me on Monday-night? I bet two to one you will! At all events I hope you will on Tuesday; so, as Jack says, 'it is much the same.'

All hands are sorting, packing, rummaging and rioting here. To Jane[1] I read her part of your Letter; she will accompany us in our Edinburgh sojourn with all the pleasure in the world. Jack will bring her out, when we want her: she may try the household for awhile; if it suit she will have cause to love her Sister for her life long.

Your Mother will take down this Note to the Minister, and appoint the hour? I think, it should be an early one, for we have far to go. Perhaps also she might do something towards engaging post-horses at the Inn; but I suppose there is little fear of failure in that point.

[1] One of Carlyle's sisters.

Do you know aught of wedding-gloves? I must leave all that to you; for except a vague tradition of some such thing I am profoundly ignorant concerning the whole matter. Or will you give *any? Ach du guter Gott!* Would we were off and away, three months before all these observances of the Ceremonial Law!

Yet fear not, Darling; for it must and will be all accomplished, and I admitted to thy bosom and thy heart, and we two made *one life* in the sight of God and man! O my own Jane! I could say much; and what were words to the sea of thoughts that rolls thro' my heart, when I feel that thou art mine, that I am thine, that henceforth we live not for ourselves but for each other! Let us pray to God that our holy purposes be not frustrated; let us trust in Him and in each other, and fear no evil that can befall us. My last blessing as a Lover is with you; this is my last Letter to Jane Welsh: my first blessing as a Husband, my first kiss to Jane Carlyle is at hand! O my Darling! I will always love thee.

Good night, then, for the last time we have to part! In a week I see you, in a week you are my own! Adieu *Meine Eigene!*

In haste, I am forever yours,

T. Carlyle

TO MARGARET CARLYLE

5 GREAT CHEYNE ROW, CHELSEA, LONDON,
THURSDAY, 12TH JUNE 1834.

My Dear Mother,—I promised you that the first frank I filled from our new House should be for you; and here I am, in the middle of a most miscellaneous collection of operative men and women, accomplishing that promise. It is not only the first Letter I have written, but the first time I have put pen to paper. However, I have for the present (while the Bell-hangers are absent) a room to myself; I have my old *firm* writing-table, firm as a rock; my old inkbottle and penholder; and the quietest outlook, through an open window, into green fields and trees; I have even my old Highland bonnet on: so I will tell you the completest story I can, with moderate composure after all.

Jane gave me, in a Letter from Liverpool, a sad tale of your parting at Annan, and how you stood waving your handkerchief to her, in front of a great crowd of people, to make amends for your tears, and keep up her heart. All *that* is past, and too sad to dwell on. Carlyle of Waterbeck was abundantly civil to the poor Traveller; as indeed all people had been and continued to be helpful and civil: so finally, on, I think, the Wednesday afternoon, as I returned to Frederick Street from Mrs. Austin's (where they had kept me to dinner), I was met by the *chirling* of a little Canary-bird (the same as I hear even now, from the under-story), and in the next room, safe in bed, and already well-rested, lay my little Wife, 'actually' engaged in drinking tea! She was well, she assured me, and all was well. Let us be thankful; and trust that the rest, too, will be well!

With our renewed house-huntings, and how we dashed up and down for three or four days, in all manner of conveyances, where such were to be had cheap, and on our legs where not,—I need not detain you here. We saw various Houses; but the Chelsea House (though our Dame did not think so at first, but thought and thinks *doubly* so afterwards) seemed nearly *twice* as good as any other we could get at the money: so on Saturday afternoon we finally fixed; and moved hither, according to appointment, on Tuesday forenoon. Bessy Barnet[1] had joined us from Birmingham the night before; and we came all down in a Hackney Coach, loaded with luggage, and *Chico* (the Canary-bird) singing on Bessy's knee. Jane says the little atom put great heart into her frequently through the journey: *he* sang aloud, wherever he might be; praising, in his way, the Maker that gave him Life and Food and fine weather. How much more should we!

. . . The House, which we have now inhabited (in the *Gillha'*[2] style) for two days and nights, is certainly by many degrees the suitablest I could find far or near. . . . We lie safe down in a little bend of the river, away from all the great roads; have air

[1] Their servant. [2] Makeshift.

and quiet hardly inferior to Craigenputtock, an outlook from the back-windows into mere leafy regions, with here and there a red high-peaked old roof looking through; and see nothing of London, except by day the summits of St. Paul's Cathedral and Westminster Abbey, and by night the gleam of the great Babylon affronting the peaceful skies. Yet in *half an hour* (for it is under two miles to Piccadilly) we can be, with a pair of stout legs, in the most crowded part of the whole habitable Earth; and, even without legs, every quarter of an hour, from sun to sun, a Coach will take you for sixpence from your own threshold, and set you down there again for another. We are south-west *from* the smoke; so during great part of the year we shall have no more to do with it than you. Nay even, in East winds, we are near *five* miles from the old, manufacturing part of London, and the smoke is all but gone before it reaches us.—As for the House itself, it is probably the *best* we ever lived in: a right old strong roomy brick house, built near one hundred and [thirty] years ago, and likely to see *three* races of their modern fashionables fall before it come down: it has all been put in perfect repair, and has closets and conveniences without end. Our furniture suits it too; being all of a strong *weighty* sort. . . . In addition to the many properties of our House, I should have mentioned a little Garden behind; where all is as yet barren or weedy, except a cherry-tree with almost *ripe* cherries on it, and two miserable rose-bushes: however, I have got a new set of Garden-tools(for six shillings), and will soon give it at least a clean face. It is of admirable comfort to me, in the *smoking* way: I can wander about in dressing-gown and straw hat in it, as of old, and take my pipe in peace. I think, were the Railways done, you must see it all with your own eyes, my dear Mother; that were the shortest way.

Of Bessy Barnet I dare not yet say much: we have seen so little of her; and that little seems so *very* favourable. She is by far the orderliest, cleverest worker we ever had in the house (hardly even excepting Grace Macdonald), and has manners and an appearance of character totally beyond the servant class: if she go on as we hope, and as she has begun, it will be our duty and pleasure to treat her not as a servant but as a friend. On this side too, therefore, we have as yet *great* reason to be thankful.

You see all things painted here in the colours of Hope: there is no doubt but by and by we shall have them (House, Place, Servant and all) painted in the dingier colours of Reality: nevertheless I think and calculate there will still be much more than Tolerability to boast of; much which, with grateful hearts, we should thank the Giver for, and above all study to improve by welldoing, which is the acceptablest sort of thanks. —I write all to you; because I know there is not *any*thing (down to our very water-barrel) that you do not feel a motherly interest in for our sake.

The Literary craft is bad, though hardly *so* bad as I expected. I find I shall get my Book (on the French Revolution) *printed* without cost; but probably nothing more. In the meantime I have some Magazine things in my eye, of a slight kind, to work at, and keep '*mall in shaft*' by; and then if my Book were *well* written, and out, I shall have a better name to start Lecturing, etc., with; and so, on the whole, we *shall* make it out, by God's help, better or worse. If to 'His glory and my own eternal good,' all else will be as dust on the balance, and an exceeding little thing. 'They cannot hinder thee of God's Providence:' that is the beautiful part of it.

For the rest, my Friends here continue all very kind, and do more for me than I had any right to expect, or even to wish; I who profess to depend on no friend, but only on God and myself. Hunt who lives close by, is not only the kindest but the politest of men; has never yet been near us (which we reckon very civil), but will always be delighted when I go and rouse *him* for a walk; and indeed a sprightly sensible talker he is, and very pleasant company for a stroll. Jane greatly preferred his 'poetical Tinkerdom' to any of the unpoetical Gigmandoms (even Mrs. Austin's) which I showed her. The Hunts, I think, will not trouble us, and indeed be a pleasure so far as they go.

And now, my dear Mother, here surely is enough about London and me for once. As for you and Scotsbrig, I begin to feel exceedingly disheartened about my prospects of news thence. Not one *scrape of a pen* have I yet realised from any of you; not so much as a Newspaper: the very *Courier* has not come, I think, for three weeks. You really must not treat me so; nay I know it is not *you*, dear Mother: but do you, if none else will, get the *Courier* Newspaper yourself, and in your own hand, as you can, write our address upon it: that, with *two strokes*[1] (if happily you can still send them) will be a great comfort to me. But, indeed, I do wrong to accuse the rest of negligence; for surely there is some mistake in it: they are too much occupied otherwise, or perhaps had not rightly understood how to direct to me. Give my love to them all; and not reproaches but entreaties. . . .

Oh my dear Mother! how much there was to say, which there is now no time for! May the Almighty Father of us all bless you, and guide all your footsteps! Through Time and through Eternity.—Blessings with you all! Ever your affectionate,

T. CARLYLE

[Postscript by Mrs. Carlyle.]

Is not all this very satisfactory, my dear Mother, and have we not great cause of thankfulness? I declare to you I could not have made myself a better house if I had had money at command; and for my servant, I expect she will be sister to me as well as servant.—No fear but we shall get a living, and my Husband will be healthier and happier than he has been for long years.—I will write you a long letter 'with my own hand' when I am a little settled, at present I am so busy *fettling* up things! but Bessy is equal to all, and Eliza Miles is come to help me besides. Everybody is kind to me—and *has been* kind to me. I shall ever remember you all with gratitude as well as love. God be with you every one.—Your affectionate,

JANE

[1] The Carlyle code indicating that all was well, which saved the expense of a letter.

TO DR. CARLYLE, Naples

5 GREAT CHEYNE ROW, CHELSEA,
15TH AUGUST, 1834.

. . . As for myself, I go on here almost without adventure of any kind. All of us have tolerable health: Jane generally better than before; I certainly not worse, and now more in the ancient accustomed fashion. I am diligent with the Showerbath; my pilgrimages to the Museum and on other Town-errands keep me in walking enough; once or twice weekly, on an evening, Jane and I stroll out along the Bank of the River, or about 'the College,' and see white-shirted Cockneys in their green canoes, or old Pensioners pensively smoking tobacco. I long much for a *hill*, but unhappily there is no such thing; only knolls, and these with difficulty, are attainable. The London street tumult has become a kind of marching music to me: I walk along, following my own meditations, without thinking of it. Company comes in desirable quantity, not deficient, not excessive, and there is talk enough from time to time: I myself however, when I consider it, find the whole all-too *thin*, unnutritive, unavailing, and that I am *alone* still under the high vault. All London-born men without exception seem to me narrow-built, considerably perverted men, rather fractions of a man. Hunt, by nature a *very* clever man, is one instance; Mill, in quite another manner, is another. These and others continue to come about me, as with the cheering sound of temporary *music*, and are right welcome so: a higher co-operation will perhaps somewhere else or sometime hence disclose itself.

'There was a Piper had a Cow
And he had nought to give her;
He took his pipes and play'd a spring
And *bade the Cow consider!*'[1]

---

[1] The next verse supplies the meaning:

'The Cow considered wi' hersel',
That music ne'er wad fill her:
Gie me a pickle pease strae
And sell your wind for siller.'

Allan Cunningham was here two nights ago; very friendly, very full of Nithsdale, a pleasant *Naturmensch.* Mill gives me logical developments of *how* men act (chiefly in Politics); Hunt tricksy devices, and crotchety whimsicalities on the same theme: *what* they act is a thing neither of them much sympathises in, much seems to know. I sometimes long greatly for Irving, for the old Irving of fifteen years ago: nay the poor actual gift-of-tongues Irving has seemed desirable to me; and I have actually, as you shall hear, made my way through to him again. We dined with Mrs. (Platonica) Taylor and the Unitarian Fox (of the *Repository,* if you know it), one day: Mill also was of the party, and the Husband, an obtuse most joyous-natured man, the pink of social hospitality. Fox is a little thickset bushy-locked man of five-and-forty, with bright sympathetic-thoughtful eyes (the whole face reminded me of Æneas Rait's, compressed, and well buttressed out into broadness), with a tendency to pot-belly, and *snuffiness*: from these hints you can construe him; the best *Socinian Philosophist* going, but not a whit more. I shall like well enough to meet the man again; but I doubt he will not me. . . . We walked home however, even Jane did, all the way from the Regent's Park, and felt that we had done a duty. For me, from the Socinians, as I take it, *wird Nichts.* Here too let me wind up the Radical-Periodical Editorship,[1] which your last Letter naturally speculates on. Mill I seem to discern has given it to this same Fox (who has just quitted his Preachership, and will, like myself be out on the world); partly I should fancy by Mrs. Taylor's influence, partly as himself thinking him the safer man. *Ebbene*! I can already picture to myself the Radical Periodical, and even prophesy its destiny: with myself it had not been so; the only thing certain would have been difficulty, pain and contradiction; which I should probably have undertaken; which I am far from breaking my heart that I have missed. I may mention too that Mill is so taken with the *Diamond Necklace,* he in a covert way offered the other night

[1] Editorship of the short-lived *London Review,* which Carlyle thought might be given to him.

to print it at his own expense, if I would give it him, that he might have the pleasure and profit of reviewing it! Mill likes me well; and on his embarrassed face when Fox happened to be talked of, I read both that Editorship business, and also that Mill had *known* my want of it; which latter was all that I desired to read. As you well say, disappointment on disappointment only simplifies one's course; your possibilities become diminished, your choice is rendered easier. In general I bate no jot of confidence in myself and in my cause. Nay it often seems to me as if the extremity of suffering, if such were appointed me, might bring out an extremity of energy as yet unknown to myself. God grant me faith; clearness and peaceableness of heart! I make no other prayer.

As to Literary work there is still no offer made that promises to bring in a penny; though I foresee that probably such will come, and, as they often do, all in a rush. Mill will want if his Fox concern go on; nay poor Heraud was here the other day endeavouring to bespeak me for a Periodical of his; for even he is to have a dud of a Periodical. Cheeriest and emptiest of all the sons of men ! Yet in his emptiness, as in that of a dried bladder, he keeps triumphantly jingling his Coleridgean long-gnawed metaphysical cherry-stones, and even 'makes a kind of martial music' for himself thereby. I do not remember that I ever met a more ridiculous-harmless froth-lather of a creature in all my travels. He lets you tumble him hither and thither, and cut him in two as you like; but in the cheerfullest way joins again, and is brisk froth-lather as before. One should surely learn by him.—The *Diamond Necklace*, I should have told you, has been refused by Moxon: shall I *let* Mill print it? I do not know, and really hardly care. . . .

. . . I told you I had seen Irving. It was but yesterday, in Newman Street, after *four* prior ineffectual attempts. William Hamilton, who with his wife was here on Saturday, told me Irving had grown worse again, and Mrs. Irving had been extremely ill: he too seemed to think my Cards had been withheld. Much grieved with this news I called once more on Monday: a new failure. Yesterday I went again with an unsuppressible indignation mixed with my pity: after some shying, I was admitted! Poor Irving! he lay there on a sofa, begged my pardon for not rising; his Wife, who also did not and probably could not well rise, sat at his feet, and watched all the time I was there, miserable, haggard. . . . Irving once lovingly ordered her away; but she lovingly excused herself, and sat still. He complains of biliousness, of a pain at his right short-rib; has a short thick cough which comes on at the smallest irritation. Poor fellow! I brought a short gleam of old Scottish laughter into his face, into his voice, and that too set him coughing. He said it was the Lord's will; looked weak, dispirited, partly embarrassed. He continues toiling daily, though the Doctor (Darling) says, rest only can cure him. Is it not mournful, hyper-tragical? There are moments when I determine on sweeping in upon all Tongue-work and Martin-doms and accursed choking Cobwebberies, and snatching away my old best Friend, to save him from Death and the Grave! It seems too likely he will die there. At lowest I will go again soon and often: I cannot think of it with patience. . . .

T. Carlyle

TO MARGARET CARLYLE

Chelsea, 17th February 1835.

My Dear Mother—I am afraid I do not keep my promise and purpose to you so well as I ought in the writing way; it is the weakness of the ability not of the will. I sit here of late so very motionless over my task-sheet, that the world is almost foreign to me: I take no note of its ways; the flight of days and of weeks goes on unmarked, and I am astonished to find them departed. You get the Newspaper, happily still with its *two strokes*; and will not be uneasy about me. Besides I think you know so much of my old punctuality as to be pretty sure that if anything really bad were happening, I would not keep you in ignorance. As to the *fash* of putting the Newspaper into the Post-office, that is literally nothing; I go out to walk daily, and nearly always from choice go up towards the press of the

Town (close *past* the Post-office); the tumult of these, my brethren, sons of Adam, amuses me. How different from the lone musing stroll along the Glaisters Hill-side! I never think of that now without a kind of shudder at it; of thankfulness that I am away from it.—But indeed I ought to write to you more deliberately, and will (were this villainous Book once done): nay, there is hope that I shall see you again before very long, which will be far better!

Jack's letter when it came in reminded me that I had heard nothing from Annandale since the last time of writing to him; also that I had not written to you again as I meant.—He is well, the worthy Doctor, and talks of home-coming! That late illness of Lady Clare's[1] seems to have been a trying kind of predicament for him; and I think he managed with great honesty and discretion, really very *well*. The 'Homœopathic Medicine' he talks of is a thing the poor *Gomerals* are making a noise about here too: it is probably among the most perfect delusions of its day, as far as I can see into it. Neither for love nor for money let a man have *any*thing to do with delusions in any place or at any time! Jack, I trust, will come back to us *grown* in many respects; I hope we shall all meet again, for the better and not for the worse.

As to my own proceedings here, they amount to almost nothing, except the slow but determined progress my poor Book is making. I *cannot* write it fast; I could write it fast enough, if I would write it ill: but that I have determined not to do—wilfully. It will be bad enough *against* one's will. O that I were done with it! But Patience! Patience! One must *go* on,—as we did at the Cressfield shearing: were it but a sheaf cut, it will not '*loup in again*.' Hurry after all is of no use; one does nothing of any weight by *hurrying*. Many a time I think of my good Father's method of working, how he went on 'without haste, without rest;' and did in that way the very most, I must believe, that he *could* do. I am not so wise in my trade; which, indeed, is more difficult to manage wisely.

[1] Dr. Carlyle had been appointed physician to Lady Clare, and travelled about Europe with her.

However, you are not to suppose that I work myself into ill health. No; I really am not under my usual condition in that particular; rather above, I should say; for I take *no* drugs now; and, for example, yesterday I walked upwards of eight miles . . . before dinner, and was not a whit exhausted. I am still in a *new* sort of health, not as I used to be; nay I sometimes think, I shall get heartily healthy once more, and be a young brisk man—turned of forty! In my mind, I feel quite young yet; and *growing*, as when I was eighteen: this is the greatest blessing. As to my outlooks here, and indeed as to the world and the ways of it, and *its* usage of me better or worse, I cannot say that my heart is distressed, or will distress itself about it: it is God's world, and I am God's worker in it; well for me if I can *be* that! I seem to see better and better that I have not wholly mistaken my calling, in that point of view; and as to the rest—*Good* is our Maker; He will give us strength according to our burden.—Hitherto the look of Literature as a trade is full of the wretchedest contradictions; nor do I see how any man that has more than meat to look for, and would *keep*, not a carriage, but a conscience, can do much good in it as a getter of money. I have not found it very blessed in the way of *ease* either as I worked at it: on the whole, if it do not show a fairer side, I will fling it from me, and seek bread *otherwise*: there is bread to be had elsewhere; and I will think my thought, and write it down (as the Heavens enable me), and ask only Heaven's permission to do that. Accordingly, I question if there is any man in London with as small a 'fixed capital,' who carries his head as free, and will take fewer *dunts* from man or thing than 'one Carl*y*le[1] of Craigenputtock,' worthy man,—one of whose *toes* is sore at this moment; which is his grand grievance. The truth is, dear Mother, I am *full* of my task, and see it getting on; and think that is more than perhaps His Majesty can say: for me it ought to be enough. The Book will probably bring me no money; but I can do without that; and were it done and my hands free, I can write an 'Article' or two again.

[1] Carlyle objected to this pronunciation of his name. He emphasised the first syllable.

They say it is going to be a tolerable enough Book; a queer Book, yes, a *very* queer Book.—Jane's foot is quite whole, and her health, I think, as good as it has been for long. We go on very quietly here: 'indulge' in a cup of hot coffee at eight o'clock by way of breakfast: she then goes downstairs, and leaves me the room to scribble in till one or two; then I walk or dig till four: dinner next of simple mutton chop and *'tatie*; a little music, reading, or by a time some solid friendly visitor (no *quack* is at the pains to come so far), and so at ten our porridge comes in, and 'all is by' in a very innocent manner. . . .

Now, when is the ruled sheet to come? I long to know all about you, how you are, what you are doing. . . . O what a blessing that you are still able to go on so well. That you have a reasonable, acquiescing, hoping spirit! I thank you, dear Mother, a thousand times for the lessons you and my Father taught me; they are more precious than fine gold. . . . Jane's love to you all. Good-night, dear Mother.—Ever your affectionate,

T. CARLYLE

TO JOHN STUART MILL

It was on the evening of March 6 that Mill had come to tell Carlyle of the burning of the *French Revolution* manuscript.

SATURDAY [7TH MARCH 1835].

MY DEAR MILL,—How are you? You left me last night with a look which I shall not soon forget. Is there anything that I could do or suffer or say to alleviate you? For I feel that your sorrow must be far sharper than mine; yours bound to be a *passive* one. How true is this of Richter: '*All* Evil is like a nightmare; the instant you begin to *stir* under it, it is *gone*.'

I have ordered a *Biographie Universelle*, this morning; and a better sort of paper. Thus, far from giving up the game, you see, I am risking another £10 on it. Courage, my Friend!

That I can never write *that* Volume again is indubitable: singular enough, the whole Earth could not get *it* back; but only a better or a worse one. There is the strangest dimness over it. A figure thrown into the melting-pot; but the metal (all that was golden or gold-like of that,—and *copper*, can be gathered) is there; the model also *is*, in my head. O my Friend, how easily might the bursting of some puny ligament or filament have abolished all light *there* too!

That I *can* write a Book on the French Revolution is (God be thanked for it) as clear to me as ever; also that if life be given me so long, I will. To it again, therefore! *Andar con Dios!*

I think you once said you could borrow me a *Campan*? Have you any more of *Lacretelle's* things; his 18me *Siècle*? (that is of almost no moment). The first vol. of *Genlis's Mém.*? &c. But I find *Campan* (if I get the *Biographie*) is the only one I shall really want much. Had I been a *trained* Compiler, I should not have wanted that. To make some search for it, I know, will be a kind of solace to you.

Thanks to Mrs. Taylor for her kind sympathies. May God guide, and bless you both! That is my true prayer.

Ever your affectionate Friend,

T. CARLYLE

TO JOHN STUART MILL

Mill had asked to be allowed to reimburse Carlyle for his merely financial loss in the burning of the manuscript. He wanted Carlyle to accept £200.

MONDAY [9TH MARCH 1835].

MY FRIEND,—You shall do the thing you so earnestly entreat for: it is not unreasonable; *ungigmanic* it may either be or not be. How lucky, in this as in other instances, that neither of us has money for the lifting; that neither of us wealthy, and one of us poor! It has positively hereby become a case which money can remedy. For my own share I find that the thought of my having got day's wages for my labour will give a new face to the whole matter: what more do I ever expect (so often not finding it) but day's wages for my work? It is likely enough this may prove the only portion of the Book I may ever get so much for. I can attack the thing again, with unabated cheerfulness; and certainly, one may hope, do it better and not worse.

For you again: the smart of having in so simple a way, forfeited so much money (which you also had to work for) may well burn out the other smart; and so, the precious feeling of a satisfied conscience succeeding to great pain, the whole business be healed, and even be made *wholer* than ever. Let us believe firmly that, to those who take them wisely, *all* things whatsoever are *good*.

I am to be out tonight, at tea with Allan Cunningham. The following nights we are at home: on Thursday night I could even hope to give you the completed *Fête des Piques* (if I get on well),—provided you durst take it: with me it were no daring; for I think of all men living you are henceforth the least likely to commit such an oversight again. I mean also by the first good opportunity to let you see a little farther into my actual economic position here than you have yet done: these confusions, I feel, have thrown us still closer together than we were; and I hope in that sense too will be blessed.

One thing I forgot to mention on Saturday: That we will not *speak* of the misfortune, to any new unconcerned person; at least not till it is made good again, or made better. I had to impart it in general terms to the Bookseller Fraser, but only in general; as 'an accident' chargeable on no one; and he has promised me to maintain perfect silence. My Brother John and my Mother must know of it; but no other has right to do so.

Among the Books needful one of the needfullest, as I now bethink me, is on your own shelves: Condorcet's *Life of Turgot*. Pray bring it in your pocket. I will also have de Staël's *Considerations*; but this I think I can procure perhaps more readily than you.—The thing must be made *better* than it was, or we shall never be able, not to forget it, but to laugh victorious in remembering it.

And so, now for the *Champ de Mars!* And with you be all good!

Your affectionate,

T. Carlyle

TO JOHN STUART MILL

TUESDAY [17TH MARCH 1835].

My Dear Mill,—You are right in this matter, and yet also wrong; and have sent me just *twice* the sum due. By the correctest computation I can institute, I find the writing of that thing to have cost me in money wages not £200 but £100: more than the latter sum, accepted on such grounds, were a *defrauding of the revenue.* It was among the *slowest* feats of writing I ever executed; and tho' the rewriting of it is new and very singular work (for I have been at it these two days), it surely cannot prove slower.

Will you therefore cancel this little Document, and make out another for half the amount.

One hundred Pounds thrown away as in a whiff of smoke is damage enough! It is a distracted wasteful world,—where the Devil is busy.—But we are not to speak of it, till the whole is made good again.

On Thursday night your Books will be welcome, and yourself welcomer.

Ever faithfully yours,

T. Carlyle

TO DR. CARLYLE, Rome

CHEYNE ROW, CHELSEA, LONDON, 23D MARCH 1835.

My Dear Brother—Your Letter came in this morning (after sixteen days from Rome); and, to-morrow being post-day, I have shoved my writing-table into the corner, and sit (with my back to the fire and Jane, who is busy sewing at my old jupe of a Dressing-gown), forthwith making answer. It was somewhat longed for; yet I felt, in other respects, that it was better you had not written sooner; for I had a thing to dilate upon, of a most ravelled character, that was better to be knit up a little first. You shall hear. But do not be alarmed; for it is 'neither death nor men's lives': we are all well, and I heard out of

Annandale within these three weeks, nay, Jane's Newspaper came with the customary 'two strokes,' only five days ago. I meant to write to our Mother last night; but shall now do it to-morrow.

Mill had borrowed that first Volume of my poor *French Revolution* (pieces of it more than *once*) that he might have it all before him, and write down some observations on it, which perhaps I might print as Notes. I was busy meanwhile with Volume Second; toiling along like a *Nigger*, but with the heart of a free Roman: indeed, I know not how it was, I had not felt so clear and independent, sure of myself and of my task for many long years. Well, one night about three weeks ago, we sat at tea, and Mill's short rap was heard at the door: Jane rose to welcome him; but he stood there unresponsive, pale, the very picture of despair; said, half-articulately gasping, that she must go down and speak to 'Mrs. Taylor.' . . . After some considerable additional gasping, I learned from Mill this fact: that my poor Manuscript, all except some four tattered leaves, was *annihilated!* He had left it out (too carelessly); it had been taken for waste-paper: and so five months of as tough labour as I could remember of, were as good as vanished, gone like a whiff of smoke.—There never in my life had come upon me any other *accident* of such moment; but this I could not but feel to be a sore one. The thing was *lost*, and perhaps worse; for I had not only forgotten all the structure of it, but the spirit it was written with was past; only the general impression seemed to remain, and the recollection that I was on the whole well satisfied with that, and could now hardly hope to equal it. Mill whom I had to comfort and speak peace to remained injudiciously enough till almost midnight, and my poor Dame and I had to sit talking of indifferent matters; and could not till then get our lament freely uttered. *She* was very good to me; and the thing did not beat us. I felt in general that I was as a little Schoolboy, who had laboriously written out his *Copy* as he could, and was showing it not without satisfaction to the Master: but lo! the Master had suddenly torn it, saying: 'No, boy, thou must go and write it *better*.' What could I do but sorrowing go and try to obey. That night was a hard one; something from time to time tying me tight as it were all round the region of the heart, and strange dreams haunting me: however, I was not without good thoughts too that came like healing life into me; and I got it somewhat reasonably crushed down, not abolished, yet subjected to me with the resolution and prophecy of abolishing. Next morning accordingly I wrote to Fraser (who had *advertised* the Book as 'preparing for publication') that it was all gone back; that he must not *speak of it* to any one (till it was made good again); finally that he must send me some *better paper*, and also a *Biographie Universelle*, for I was determined to risk ten pounds more upon it. Poor Fraser was very assiduous: I got Bookshelves put up (for the whole House was *flowing* with Books), where the *Biographie* (not Fraser's, however, which was countermanded, but Mill's), with much else stands all ready, much readier than before: and so, having first finished out the Piece I was actually upon, I began *again* at the beginning. Early the day after to-morrow (after a hard and quite novel kind of battle) I count on having the First Chapter on paper a second time, no worse than it was, though considerably different. The bitterness of the business is past therefore; and you must conceive me toiling along in that new way for many weeks to come. As for Mill I must yet tell you the best side of him. Next day after the accident he writes me a passionate Letter requesting with boundless earnestness to be allowed to make the loss good as far as *money* was concerned in it. I answered: Yes, since he so desired it; for in our circumstances it was not unreasonable: in about a week he accordingly transmits me a draft for £200; I had computed that my five months' housekeeping, etc., had cost me £100; which sum therefore and not two hundred was the one, I told him, I could take. He has been here since then; but has not sent the £100, though I suppose he will soon do it, and so the thing will end,—more handsomely than one could have expected. I ought to draw from it various practical 'uses of improvement' (among others not to lend manuscripts again); and above all things try to do the work *better* than it was; in which case I shall never grudge the labour, but reckon it a goodhap.—It really seemed to me a Book of considerable significance; and not unlikely even to be of some interest at present: but that latter, and indeed all economical and other the like considerations had become profoundly indifferent to me; I felt that I was honestly writing down and delineating a World-Fact (which the Almighty had brought to pass in the world); that it was an *honest* work for me, and all men might do and say of it simply what seemed good to *them*.—Nay I have got back my spirits again (after this first Chapter), and hope I shall go on tolerably. I will struggle assiduously to be done with it by the time you are to be looked for (which meeting may God bring happily to pass); and in that case I will cheerfully throw the business down a while, and walk off with you to Scotland; hoping to be ready for the *next* publishing season.—This is my ravelled concern, dear Jack; which you see is in the way to knit itself up again, before I am called to tell you of it And now for something else. I was for writing to you of it next day after it happened: but Jane suggested, it would only grieve you, till I could say it was in the way towards adjustment; which counsel I saw to be right. Let us hope assuredly that the whole will be for *good*. . . .

T. Carlyle

TO JOHN STERLING

Written in reply to Sterling's criticism of the style of *Sartor Resartus.*

4th June 1835.

My Dear Sterling,—I said to Mill the other day that your Name was hopeful; of which truth surely this copious refreshing shower of really kind and genial criticism you have bestowed on the hardened, kiln-burnt, altogether contradictory Professor Teufelsdröckh, is new proof. Greater faith I have not found in Israel! Neither here shall faith and hope wholly fail: know, my Friend, that your shower does not fall as on mere barren bricks, like water spilt on the ground; that

I take it hopefully in, with great desire (knowing what spirit it is of) to *assimilate* such portion of it as the nature of things will allow. So much, on this sheet, I must announce to you, were it at full gallop, and in the most imperfect words.

Your objections as to phraseology and style have good grounds to stand on; many of them indeed are considerations to which I myself was not blind; which there (unluckily) were no means of doing more than nodding to as one passed. A man has but a certain strength; imperfections cling to him, which if he wait till he have brushed off entirely, he will spin forever on his axis, advancing nowhither. Know thy thought, *believe* it; front Heaven and Earth with it,— in whatsoever *words* Nature and Art have made readiest for thee! If one has thoughts not hitherto uttered in English Books, I see nothing for it but that you must use words not found there, must *make* words,—with moderation and discretion, of course. That I have not always done it *so*, proves only that I was not strong enough; an accusation to which I for one will never plead not guilty. For the rest, pray that I may have more and more strength! Surely too, as I said, all these *coal-marks* of yours shall be duly considered, for the first and even for the second time, and help me on my way. With unspeakable cheerfulness I give up '*Talented*': indeed, but for the plain statement you make, I could have sworn such word had never, except for parodistic, ironical purposes, risen from my inkhorn, or passed my lips. Too much evil can hardly be said of *it*: while speech of it at all is necessary.—But finally, do you reckon this really a time for Purism of Style; or that Style (mere dictionary Style) has much to do with the worth or unworth of a Book? I do not: with whole ragged battalions of Scott's-Novel Scotch, with Irish, German, French, and even Newspaper Cockney (when 'Literature' is little other than a Newspaper) storming in on us, and the whole structure of our Johnsonian English breaking up from its foundations,—revolution there as visible as anywhere else!

You ask, How it comes that none of the 'leading minds' of this country (if one knew where to find them) have given the

'Clothes-Philosophy' any response? Why, my good friend, not one of them has had the happiness of seeing it! It issued thro' one of the main *cloacas* of Periodical Literature, where no leading mind, I fancy, looks, if he can help it: the poor Book cannot be destroyed by fire or other violence now, but solely by the *general* law of Destiny; and *I* have nothing more to do with it henceforth. How it chanced that no Bookseller would print it (in an epoch when Satan Montgomery runs, or seems to run, thro' thirteen editions), and the morning Papers (on its issuing thro' the *cloaca*) sang together in mere discord over such a creation: this truly is a question, but a different one. Meanwhile, do not suppose the poor Book has *not* been responded to; for the historical fact is, I could show very curious response to it here; not ungratifying, and fully three times as much as I counted on, as the wretched farrago itself deserved.

You say finally, as the key to the whole mystery, that Teufelsdröckh does not believe in a 'personal God'. It is frankly said, with a friendly honesty for which I love you. A grave charge nevertheless, an *awful* charge: to which, If I mistake not, the Professor, laying his hand on his heart, will reply with some gesture expressing the solemnest *denial*. In gesture, rather than in speech; for 'the Highest *cannot* be spoken of in words.' '*Personal*', 'impersonal,' One, Three, *what* meaning can any mortal (after all) attach to them in reference to such an object? *Wer dark ihn NENNEN?* I dare not, and do not. That you dare and do (to some greater extent) is a matter I am far from taking offence at: nay, with all sincerity, I can rejoice that you have a creed of that kind, which gives you happy thoughts, nerves you for good actions, brings you into readier communion with many good men; my true wish is that such creed may long hold compactly together in you, and be 'a covert from the heat, a shelter from the storm, as the shadow of a great rock in a weary land.' Well is it if we have a printed Litany to pray from; and yet not ill if we *can* pray even in *silence*, for silence too is audible *there*. Finally, assure yourself, I am neither Pagan nor Turk, not circumcised Jew, but an unfortunate Christian individual resident at Chelsea in *this* year of Grace; neither Pantheist nor Pottheist, nor any Theist or *ist* whatsoever, having the most decided contempt for all manner of Systembuilders and Sectfounders—so far as contempt may be compatible with so mild a nature; feeling well beforehand (taught by experience) that all such are and even must be *wrong*. By God's blessing, one has got two eyes to look with; and also a mind capable of knowing, or believing: that is all the creed I will at this time insist on. And now may I beg one thing: that whenever in my thoughts or your own you fall on any dogma that tends to estrange you from me, pray believe *that* to be *false*;—false as Beelzebub till you get clearer evidence. . . .

I remain always,

Yours with great sincerity,

T. Carlyle

TO DR. CARLYLE, Munich

CHELSEA, 23D SEPTEMBER 1835.

You are doubtless longing, my dear Brother, to have another Letter from me; and will open this at Munich, I hope, safe and sound, with considerable impatience. I have not delayed wilfully; but only till I could send you decisive news. This is literally the first day, in which I could have specified my future whereabout in Time and Space, for the nearest Future, with any kind of completeness.

Though you are a sharp-tempered man, Jack, like the rest of us; yet I know you certainly for the placablest of *all* men: so I doubt not whatsoever of natural wrath you felt went fairly up the chimney with that sacrificed Letter, and there was again peace between us, nay better peace than before. Well when a small holocaust of that kind will do the business!—I did not write in irritation against Her Ladyship[1] or indeed anybody so far as I remember; but expressed in such words as came readiest the deliberate permanent opinion I had been led to form of her from such imperfect data as I had. If my

[1] The Countess of Clare.

reading was wrong, I recant it not only willingly but joyfully. To you at any rate such defence of your rather skittish and peculiar co-partner in this wayward business is very creditable: continue forever to take the *best* view of all mortals which your understanding will admit; nay it is often also *truer* than the surly one. But, for myself, all buckram grows more and more a kind of weariness to me: there perhaps has not been these two thousand years or thereby any mortal to whom man stood more completely as an *unclothed animal* than he (unluckily and luckily) does to me. It makes a strange world of it for one; and gives and will give one work enough: for often the buckram *crackles* amazingly when you treat it like mere cloth.—However let me tell you my history.

First then, by the real blessing and favour of Heaven, I got *done* with that unutterable Manuscript, on Monday last. . . . The work does not seem to myself to be *very* much worse than it was; it is worse in the style of expression, but better compacted in the thought: as it goes through the Press I may help it somewhat. On the whole I feel like a man that had 'nearly killed himself accomplishing *zero.*' But *zero* or not *zero*, what a deliverance! I shall never without a kind of sacred shudder look back at the detestable state of enchantment I have worked in for these six months, and am now blessedly delivered from. The rest of the Book shall go on quite like child's play in comparison: also I do think it will be a *queer* Book; one of the *queerest* published in this century, and *can*, though it cannot be popular, be better than that. My Teufelsdröckh humour, no *voluntary* one, of looking 'through the clothes' finds singular scope in this subject. Remarkable also is the 'still death-defiance' I have settled into; equivalent to the most absolute sovereignty conceivable by the mind. I say 'still death-defiance;' yet it is not unblended with a Greek-fire of Hope, *un*quenchable, which glows up silent, steady, brighter and brighter. My one thought is to be done with this Book. Innumerable things point all that way: my whole destiny seems as if it lost itself in chaos there (for my money also gets done then, etc. etc.); *in chaos, which I am to re-create*, or to perish miserably,—an arrangement which I really regard as blessed comparatively. So I sit here and write, composed in mood; responsible to no man or to no thing; only to God and my own conscience: with publishers, reviewers, hawkers, bill-stickers, indeed, on the Earth round me; but with the stars and the azure Eternities above me in the Heaven. Let us be thankful! —On the whole, I am rather stupid; or rather I am not stupid (for I feel a fierce glare of insight in me into many things); not stupid,—but I have *no sleight of hand*. A raw untrained savage; for every trained civilised man *has* that sleight, and is a bred workman by having it: the bricklayer with his trowel, the painter with his brush, the writer with his pen. The result of the whole is: 'one must just do the best he can for a living, Boy.' Or in my Mother's phrase, never 'tine heart,'—or even *get* provoked heart, which likewise is a danger. . . .

T. CARLYLE

TO MARGARET CARLYLE

CHELSEA, 15 MAY 1836.

MY DEAR MOTHER,—I am afraid you begin to think us rather negligent: at all events you have good right to be impatient to get some news from us; for since Jack's Letter, announcing hastily nothing or little more than that he was arrived, you have not received the smallest scrape of a pen from us,—if it were not the two strokes on the back of the Newspaper. It should not have been so. But the matter went as matters often go: I thought Jack would write, having less to do than I; Jack thought probably I would write: and thus, as the old Proverb teaches, 'between two stools the unfortunate sitter came to the floor.' Whether Jack will write today, I cannot tell, tho' I have urged him; but one thing I can tell, that I will write. None of us are going to Church, and it seems to me I could not readily find better employment.

The truth is, there was hitherto almost nothing definite to be written. Jack has been flying about here as you can fancy him: entirely uncertain this day what he would do the next; speaking about doing all things under the moon and above it; but with no means of forming any positive plan for the future. It is to a good degree the like case with us all. . . .

As to myself, for the last three weeks I have been going what you call *bane*-idle. I finished my Second Volume then, and determined to have a rest for one week; it was very grand: Jack and I went swashing far and near. . . .

I often think it is a great malady and madness this poor Book of mine, which wears me so, and has been so unlucky: yet rather I should say, it is a great happiness, and gives me the completest indifference towards all fretting of fortune, towards much that has haunted me like pale spectres all my life long. With little in my purse, little in my hope, and no very fixed landmark in this Earth, I stand serene under the sky, and really have the peaceablest fearlessness towards all men and things. Such blessing I owe to the poor Book; and therefore will not abuse it, but speak well of it. In some few months it will be printed and done, and the world all round me once again,—much more homelike than it ever before was. The people are exceedingly good and kind to me, the better and kinder, that I depend little on that, or not at all on it, and could do quite tolerably, with their badness and indifference. . . .

I will not be so long in writing again. Take care of yourself, dear Mother. Jane sends her love to all of you, as we all do.

Ever your affectionate

T. Carlyle

TO JANE WELSH CARLYLE, Templand

CHELSEA, SUNDAY, 24TH JULY 1836.

My Dear Womannie,—I promised on a Newspaper that I would write so soon as my Chapter was finished; and that great event having happened yesterday at two o'clock, I with right goodwill proceed to fulfilment. . . .

There has nothing gone wrong since you went away; and

now that I have news of your safe resting beside your Mother, all is well. It was a sad shaking that of the long Coach-ride and whirling on Railways for a poor weak Goody, and would shatter her terribly; neither, I fancy, is the Country at its best, this rainy season: but still it is the country; it is your Mother; and the infinite fret and tumult of this place is far behind you. Splash away in the shower-bath; drink new milk (with a little brandy in it); tolerate the Country gossips; possess your wearied soul in patience; and come back to me rested and well, and *all* will be well. Hast thou recovered any hope? O thou of little faith!—Your Uncle never did a more judicious thing in his life than buying you that shawl, for which I thank him with all my heart. I hope you delivered my '*special* compliments': it is a cheering kind of thing for me to remember a broad brave Annandale Man of that figure: how greatly different from the Formulas of Men one meets with, here and elsewhere!—Have you *got* baked Bread yet? I advise you to heat the oven with *coals*, and on the whole to realize Bread. Have you Cavaignac's Manuscript, or any kind of work? Be not solitary, be not idle. . . .

Since that Saturday Night, I have had the most private, speechless, life of perhaps all men in London. . . . Hardly two or three mortals (always, too, at times when I was out) have come to stir the knocker. The French are occupied with *Ma Mère et Ma Soeur*; Cavaignac,[1] tho' he had made an appointment with his Dornet (the Advocate), and volunteered to that effect, did not make it out till three days after the time; and I have never seen him since, or got up yet to see his women, tho' I meant to do it,—last night, if Jack had not come. . . . But before quitting Cavaignac, I must tell you a thing I *saw* at Mrs. Buller's rout, but did not *discern* till a day or two after. Charles Buller led Cavaignac away to introduce him to a large lady, whom I afterwards perceived to be Mrs. G——: Cavaignac went, without struggling, tho' verily like a sheep to the slaughter; the presentation performed, he made I think *five*

[1] Godefroi Cavaignac, a French Republican exile, friend of the Carlyles.

successive low bows to Mrs. G—— (a very shower of rapid bows); then, without uttering a word, reeled back, like a sheep *from* the slaughter (or a *calf*, for you know how he *goes*), and landing in a very elegant attitude, stood, five paces off, with his hat behind his back, looking out into space, and the general movement of the rout,—*this* while Introduction, Acquaintance, Friendship being begun, carried on, finished and abolished with such incredible brevity as I describe! It was two days before this phenomenon presented itself rightly before me; and it has tickled me ever since. . . .

One night also, being determined to *order* myself a pair of shoes[1] (*trash* beyond utterance; ugly and *dear*, are my late pairs), I called on Allan Cunningham to ask: Not in. Then forward to Willis to ask: Not in. Wherefore, home;—and the shoes are still unordered. Jack has offered me an old pair; which I think I shall accept. By the bye, James Aitken has a pair of lasts lying ready, and a *cast* of my foot; will you take down these lasts, that image of the foot ('roots of trieys'[2] and all), and considering it deeply, and consulting with James who is a judicious man, see if you cannot order me a pair of shoes to be made off them? See if you cannot, Goody with that *hellen Blick* of yours! Poor James[3] has sent me two pounds of Mundell's Tobacco by Jack; a sort of thing which, I know not why, almost made me *greet*: it was in huge coarse paper; the poor Brother had earned it by the toil of his right-hand: I remembered him a tow-headed judicious herd-boy; and so many chancings and changings had gone on since then. Thank him *heartily* from me (but not in the sad mood).—I believe you had also better choose me a pair of winter trousers; you: and set Shankland on them, if he have the measure: wide enough, long enough: not too heavy, and of a dim colour! I shall then have nothing to do with Cockney snips for another blessed Winter, —perhaps never more in Time? . . .

As for the *Chapter* entitled *September*, the poor Goody knows

[1] That is, order them from Scotland, through a Scottish friend.

[2] His brother Alick remarked that Carlyle's toes were so long that they were 'like the roots of *trieys*'.

[3] James Carlyle, not the shoemaker James Aitken.

with satisfaction that it is *done*. I worked all day, not all night; indeed oftenest, not at night at all: but went out, and had long swift-striding walks (till ten) under the stars. I also slept in general tolerably: for the last two days, however, I have been poisoned again with *veal-soup* (beef being unattainable); I *will* know again! The Chapter is some thirty-six close pages: not at all a bad Chapter;—would the Goody had it to read! A hundred pages more, and this cursed Book is flung out from me. I mean to write with the force of fire till that consummation,—above all, with the speed of fire; still taking natural *intervals*, of course, and resting myself; the unrested horse or writer *cannot* work. But a despicability of a thing that has so long held me and held us both down to the grindstone is a thing I could almost swear at, and kick out of doors; at least, most swiftly equip for *walking* out of doors. *Speranza*, thou 'Spairkin Goody; *Hope*, my little Lassie, it will all be better than thou thinkest.'—For two or three days I am to have the most perfect rest now. Then Louis is to be tried and guillotined; then the Gironde, etc. etc.: it all stands pretty fair in my head; nor do I mean to *investigate* much more about it, but to splash down what I know, in large masses of colours; that it may look like a smoke-and-flame conflagration in the distance, —which it is. . . .

My dear little Janekin! I must leave thee now. Write a long Letter: they are all very pleasant, very good for me; but the 'reposing humour' would give me most pleasure of all. *Behab' Dich wohl! Sey hold mir; hoffe, zweifle nicht!* Kiss your kind Mother for me; say I wear her brown waistcoat, not without remembrances, daily: it is the respectablest piece in my suit. . . .

Ever affectionately thine,

T. Carlyle

TO JOHN STERLING

Chelsea, 29th September 1839.

My Dear Sterling,—Your good Letter, after some detours, found me at my Mother's in Annandale; most languid, vacant, not to say altogether torpid and closed up in melancholy remembrances, sad aspects, sad prospects, and continual deluges of wet weather. Solitude is indispensable to my existence now and then; it is very miserable, yet a kind of blessed misery, with a wholesomeness in it, the beginning of a time more wholesome than the past was.

Your Welsh excursion, and child's idyll with your Brother, came like a sunny place into that dim Hades of mine. You take those matters more wisely than I.

The reason of my not writing answer was mainly a grand scheme I had of soon speaking an answer. It was among our projects that my Wife, who in her sail from Liverpool to Annan nearly gave up the ghost and altogether declared she would never go to sea again, should proceed homeward by Carlisle and the Preston Railway; leaving me to come at a week's distance, round by Dublin, Bristol, Clifton, and so see Sterling, and find the dilapidated Chelsea establishment somewhat set up again first. But the poor Dame gave in, when it came to the point; would like *so* much better, if, &c.: whereupon we got together into the huge Steam mystery, and it snorted off with us (under cloud of night) like an enormous diabolic fire-dragon as it is, and in the most unintelligible yet unerring way, set us down at Chelsea next morning, *without* any sight of Sterling. I have waited since then, a fortnight or more now, till the suspicious *Sterling Article*[1] should appear, that I might see whether I was to excommunicate the man, or what I was to do with him. Mill, the day before yesterday, gave me unexpectedly a copy, which I have read, which I have even sent off into Scotland; and now I write—the excommunication that is needed.

Mill says this is the best thing you ever wrote; and truly so should I, if you had not shut my mouth. It is a thing all glowing and boiling, like a furnace of molten metal. A brave thing, nay a rash and headlong; full of generosity, passionate insight, lightning, extravagance and Sterlingism: such an 'article' as we have not read for some time past! It will be talked of, it

[1] Sterling's article, 'On the Writings of Thomas Carlyle', appeared in the *London and Westminster Review*, Autumn 1839.

will be admired, condemned, and create astonishment and give offence far and near. My friend, what a notion you have got of *me*! I discern certain natural features, the general outline of shape; but it is as one would in the Air-giant of the Harz, huge as Ophiuchus; painted there, as one finds, by sunrise and early vapour, that is, by Sterling's heart impinging on you between himself and the *Westminster Review*! I do not thank you; for I know not whether such things are good, nay whether they are not bad and a poison to one: but I will say there has no man in these Islands been so reviewed in my time; it is the most magnanimous eulogy I ever knew one man utter of another man whom he knew face to face, and saw go grumbling about there, in coat and breeches, as a poor concrete reality—very offensive now and then. And so we will let it lie there; incredible to all men, incrediblest of all to me; yet sweet in the highest degree, for very obvious reasons, notwithstanding.

I admire the ingenuity with which this Reviewer contrives withal to introduce the quarrels he has against me. Not a crow we have ever had to pluck together but he plucks it here, and scatters the limbs of it triumphantly to the winds. I swear honestly I like him all the better. 'Consciousness,' 'Silence,' &c., &c. I tell you, my dear fellow, you are right; and yet I myself am perfectly right too, and know not well yet how I could find terms to express myself in, less liable to contradiction. It is the fault, as Shandy said, of 'the auxiliary verbs.' Goethe's saying comes often in my mind: 'We begin to err, the first *word* we utter.' For Nature is solid, with six sides; Language is superficial, nay linear. I believe you have me, however, in regard to Mother Cagliostro and the gold ounces; I had read that passage wrong, and yet, as I remember, not without some misgiving as to the truth.[1] With regard to *September Massacring*, again, *you* are wrong, and I will prove it —by silence at present. Wrong indeed! Where are you *right*, if one come to that? God help you, my man, with such a huge Brocken-Spectre 'Chimera' and lot of 'Cub chimeras' sucking at her! I would not be in your shoes for something.

[1] A reference to a passage in Carlyle's essay on Cagliostro.

Mill, whom I had not seen till that day at the India House, was looking but indifferently; he professed not to be sensibly better at all by his last-year's journeying. Mrs. Taylor, he farther volunteered to tell me, is living not at the old abode in the Regent's Park, but in Wilton Place, a street where as I conjecture there are mainly wont to be *Lodgings*. Can it be possible? Or if so, what does it betoken? I am truly sorry for Mill: he has been a most luckless man since I came hither, seeming to himself all the way to be a lucky one rather. He seems to fear that the Review will have to cease; a thing I regret but do not wonder at. . . . He has no skill in 'concrete realities,' or less than I ever saw in a man so skilful about abstractions. Nature and Fact, as you remarked, first tell a man the truth about his philosophy. Sow real wheat on the honest earth, you reap real wheat; sow chaff ever so *like* wheat, the earth receives it, but says nothing about it next year.

As for me, I have been busy daily, revising *Wilhelm Meister*, which they are reprinting (*Apprenticeship* and *Travels* together) as rapidly as they can. I dissent greatly from much that I find; yet everywhere there is truth, real truth even in what you hate, and it is good for you to see it; there is real talent, to me the infallible symptom of all other sorts of reality, sorts of worth, for no real thing is not worthy—you know! Fraser has got to hand the American *Miscellanies*, and sold 100 of them; regrets immensely that he has got so few still to sell. I sent your Mother a copy, not you one; I intend for you a better *English* copy, such as seems possible and probable by and by. What I am to do for the winter is all uncertain. This *Meister* business will keep me busy for three weeks yet. I am far from ready to write on anything. My Brother, in Scotland at present, is coming soon; *unbestimmt* he too. We see your people as often and gladly as ever; that is to say, therefore *more* gladly, so precious is *continuance*, in a world like ours. Your Father had bad news from you yesterday: nothing serious we *will* hope. Take care of yourself, do not wear yourself to pieces. You are too vehement, mind that always. My Wife is charmed, as the female character may well be, with your review. She salutes you a hundred times; you, and your better half and household. Good be always with you all!

T. CARLYLE

I have heard twice from Emerson, mainly about books and shipments, the good Emerson. He is getting forward with something of his own to be published soon. In one of his Letters he says: 'I have only time to say that I love Sterling's poetry, that I admire his prose with reservations here and there. What he knows he writes manfully and well. All our readers here take *Blackwood* for his sake, and latterly seek him in vain.'—This you see was not designed for you, but I cabbage it.

TO JOHN STERLING

CHELSEA, 12TH NOVEMBER 1840.

MY DEAR STERLING,—Your Poem is full of talent, and full of faults. I wish to Heaven I could give you some wise word of advice about it:—but indeed, would you have the smallest chance to follow such advice if given? I have read this *Election* with much more entertainment than I ever before read any Poem of yours. Nay, at bottom, it is perhaps almost the only Piece, especially of such length, that I could, independently of my regard for the writer, have read *with* real entertainment. In spite of the rhyme, in spite of the afflictive snakishly ambiguous hand (the *s* not knowing whether it will turn out an *n* or an *m* or a *u*!), I found the reading of this thing not a duty but a pleasure. So much from me, you will admit, is a great deal.

I do not yet find a *musical tune* in either the soul or the body of this Piece; but the rhyme flows evenly along, does not *much* obstruct the grammatical perspicacity; and in the burlesque parts the jingle of it at the end of the lines has a gratifying effect on me. I, even I, find some benefit in rhymes on such occasions. The serious passages again, which in themselves are the truest as well as far the worthiest, I could have liked better to see still in prose,—if it were Sterlingian prose. This is the naked truth; tho' you will not believe much of it, but will only believe that I believed it. For the rest, I like the burlesque too, think it good of its kind, and that, as I said, the rhyme has a good effect on it. But in the *serious* there struggles a great meaning, seizable here only in straggling glimpses, obstructed altogether by the form of the composition, and generally out of place when you do seize it.

The Master-fault of the Piece, hear it my Friend with a frown is, as ever, that it *is too easily born*. Could I enwrap *you* in *one* of the thick atrabiliary cloaks-of-darkness that envelop my poor self, cloak above cloak, till my light seems quenched for most part as in London fog, and all utterance of myself is so inexpressibly difficult, inexpressibly hateful,—what a fellow I should make of you! I would sink this Piece down into the *Orcus* of your soul, and it should not spring up but with a fight at every step; and arise at last a shorter and wiser Poem! But it may not be. Who knows how much of your gift were inconsistent with such wrappages and practices, and might expire in such handling?

As it stands, your *Story* in this *Election* is eminently loose-jointed, improbable, not to say incredible; your *earnest* does not cohere with your *sport* (indeed they would be terribly difficult to make cohere well), the *earnest* is too long, and nothing to the purpose in hand, for most part;—in short, the whole thing coheres very loosely, or is incoherent; and only by natural worth of material *forces* some pleasure on you,—no inconsiderable pleasure. . . .

On the whole, and this is the sum of my advice, take *deep* and ever deeper counsel with yourself, what it is that will really give *you* most satisfaction in the ordering of this business (to print or not to print); and account that a greater fact than any other,—if you can once ascertain it well. Do you really from the heart like this thing; or do you merely think and hope that others may like, &c.? Doctors say the *real* voice of the appetite is the best rule in Dietetics; but it has to be carefully discriminated from the superficial, transient, fallacious voice, which declares for gingerbread, peppercake, comfits and the like!

You see what a pen I have; in what impetuous velocity I must write! You have the rudest thoughts of my heart; all the truer for that, if you can read them. Adieu, my friend; and a *wise* decision to you, be it in my sense or not in mine.

Yours ever,

T. Carlyle

P.S.—Do you mean to entitle yourself *the Revd.* J. Sterling still! It is awfully heterodox much of that quizzing; tho' to me all the welcomer.

TO JOHN STERLING

Chelsea, 4th December 1843.

My Dear Sterling,—I received your kind Note, written in the hour of your departure; I received your Irish Newspaper from Ventnor, and understood it as a monition that I had permission to write to you,—which I wished to do, but alas, could not! In truth I am very miserable at present; or call it heavy-laden with fruitless toil; which will have much the same meaning. My abode is, and has been, figuratively speaking, in the centre of chaos: onwards there is no moving, in any yet discovered line, and where I am is no abiding:—miserable enough! The fact is, without any figure, I am doomed to write some Book about that unblessed Commonwealth; and as yet there will no Book show itself possible. The whole stagnancy of the English genius, two hundred years thick, lies heavy on me; dead Heroes, buried under two centuries of Atheism, seem to whimper pitifully, 'Deliver us, canst thou not deliver us!'—and alas, what am I, or what is my father's house? Confound it, I have lost four years of good labour in the business; and still the more I expend on it, it is like throwing good labour after bad! On the whole, you ought to pity me. Is thy servant a dead dog, that these things have fallen on him?—My only consolation is that I am struggling to be the most conservative man in England, or one of the most conservative. If the Past

Time, only two centuries back, lie wholly as a torpedo Darkness and Dulness, freezing as with Medusa-glance all souls of men that look on it, where are our foundations gone? If the Past Time cannot become *melodious*, it must be forgotten, as good as annihilated; and we rove like aimless exiles that *have* no ancestors,—whose world began only yesterday! That must be my consolation, such as it is.

I see almost nobody, I avoid sight rather, and study at least to consume my own smoke. I wish among your buildings, you would build me some small Prophet's Chamber, fifteen feet square, with a separate garret and flue for smoking; within a furlong of your big house; sacred from all noises, of dogs, cocks, pianofortes and insipid men;—engaging some dumb old woman to light a fire for me daily and boil some kind of kettle: a man might write there all day to some purpose, and cheer himself by talk all evening! But it cannot be. There is no such city of refuge, I am told, till once we get beyond the Zodiac; so, in the meantime, we must study to go on without it.

Of men or new books or things, I cannot say a word: dwelling myself so deep, with mere Chaos and old Nox. I have only seen Mill transiently once, Lockhart transiently once, and hardly any other person whose existence is of any moment to you. A man from Chancery Lane, anonymous hitherto, sent me a Pamphlet about the necessity of an *Authors' Publishing Society*, in which project, I hear, he still persists, tho' not entirely a fool; I also purchased for sixpence lately the first No. of an *Authors' Institution Circular*, or some such thing, worth less than any known coin:—indeed there is everywhere a bodeful premonition heard that Bookselling, in our sense of the business, draws to a close; that *it* is due some time since to Chaos again, —and that something else must follow it.

Did you see an American of the name of James[1] who went towards you? An estimable man, full of sense and honest manfulness, when you get acquainted with him. My regards to him, if he is near you.

My Wife is gone this evening with your Father to drink tea

[1] Henry James, Senior.

with Darwin; a notable lark! The articles in the *Times* do the writer of them an immense good, besides what they infallibly do or tend towards doing to the world. Adieu, dear Sterling, best friend! Be not angry with me, be patient with me; write when you have charity, and so, *Vale, vale.*

T. CARLYLE

TO JOHN STERLING

These last two letters were written when Sterling was manifestly near to death; a fact which Carlyle characteristically refused to recognize. On 10 August, 1844, Sterling wrote to Carlyle that he was treading 'the common road into the great darkness. . . . With regard to You and Me I cannot begin to write; . . . Towards me, it is still more true than towards England, that no man has been and done like you.' The poem that follows the last of these letters was written by Sterling four days before his death on 18 September, 1844.

CHELSEA, 9TH JUNE 1844.

MY DEAR STERLING,—I hear almost daily of you, and think of you oftener than daily this long while, tho' I write nothing. Sometimes I have said to myself: 'You should write. He knows your feeling, and it is something to him;—and in dark hours, now and then, such silence may seem doubtful to him.' Perhaps I should. But indeed all words of mine seemed little other than an impertinence in that solemn situation. Many of my thoughts continue silent, incapable of being written, on this as on other subjects! The longer I live, I think it grows the more so. My much-loved Friend —— I really can write nothing! It all lies in *these three words*;—and these, if they are of any use to you, you are authorized to write in ineffaceable characters in your very heart.

Except for some days during the darkest part of the crisis, I have never, in spite of all your own sad utterances, seriously feared that I was to lose you. Perhaps I am wrapping myself in mere cowardly delusions; preparing for myself, at a future day, a frightful awakening: but such is the fact. I have, in spite of all Doctors, a great confidence in your vitality of structure; the fibres of the man tho' diseased, are those of a lion! My Brother too speaks always hopefully; says, he has seen men lying to all appearance at the verge of death in that disorder, pale, with their eyes and being all aglow in speechless still excitement; who nevertheless rose up again, and were well. He says, if you can live to five-and-forty, this disordered condition of the lungs will abate of itself. My constant hope is, That your last terrible crisis may be a *warning* to you, more impressive than any of the others were. They have all come, I think, out of some rash liberty, permitted to other men, but to you forbidden. You have in all things been too hot and hasty, my Friend,—in all things, that generous infirmity cleaves to you. Lay it aside; learn by these stern teachings, to recognise the adamantine limits that so bound you, as such do bound us all. Within these, if it please God, there is yet a most fruitful and noble existence in store for you.—'Let us be still,' as the Old Hebrews and Old Puritans used to say; 'let us be still, and call on God.' There is yet no other wisdom, and will be none other, for the son of Adam on this Earth.

I have been looking forward to the West wind, which we now have, as the best of all medicines for you. It seems you again were a little hasty; went out too rashly, and have got a little check. *Canny, canny!* as the Scotch say; use as not abusing!—On the whole, you must get well again: you must *fast* get a little better again,—that I may come and see you. I will come certainly whenever I can hear conclusively that it will not be a mere burden to you, hurtful and not profitable.

All Spring and Summer, hitherto, I have, for my own share, been abundantly miserable; plunging thro' Chaos, as I call it, —the Rushworth Dryasdust chaos; unable to find north or south in it, bottom or shore in it! Really, as I said somewhere, it *is* 'like walking hand in hand with mere *Madness*'; trying whether you shall make it sane, or it shall make you mad! No labour for the present is joyous but grievous.—I have seen your Father, your Son and your Brother today; all well. *Wir heissen euch HOFFEN!*

Auf ewig,

T. Carlyle

TO JOHN STERLING

CHELSEA, 27TH AUGUST 1844.

MY FRIEND,—Today another little Note from you makes the hearts start within us. On Sunday morning gone a fortnight there came another; which will dwell in my memory, I think, while I have any memory left. Ever since, it mingles with every thought, or is itself my thought; neither do I wish to exclude it, if I could. To me there is a tone in it as of Sphere-music, of the Eternal Melodies which we know well to be sacred,—sadder than any tears, and yet withal more beautiful than any joy. My Friend, my brave Sterling! A right valiant man; very beautiful, very dear to me; whose like I shall not see again in this world!

We are journeying towards the Grand Silence; what lies beyond it earthly man has never known, nor will know: but all brave men have known that it was Godlike, that it was right GOOD,--that the name of it was GOD. *Wir heissen euch hoffen.* What is right and best for us will full surely be. Tho' He slay me, yet will I trust in Him. 'ETERNO AMORE'; that is the ultimate significance of this wild clashing whirlwind which is named Life, where the Sons of Adam flicker painfully for an hour.

My Wife is all in tears: no tear of mine, dear Sterling, shall, if I can help it, deface a scene so sacred. The memory of the Brother that is gone, like a brave one, shall be divine to us; and, if it please the Supreme Wisdom, we shall—O my friend, my friend!

In some moods it strikes me, with a reproachful emphasis, that there would be a kind of satisfaction for me could I see you with these eyes yet again. But you are in great suffering; perhaps I should be but a disturbance? There is a natural longing that way; but perhaps it is a false pusillanimous one: I have, at bottom, no speech for you which could be so eloquent as my silence is. And yet I could be silent there too; silent and quiet. . . .

Adieu, my brave and dear one.

Yours evermore,

T. CARLYLE

TO THOMAS CARLYLE

O! Carlyle, could I find a word
  Before I leave this earthly shore
Of greater orb than e'er was heard
  By kinsman or by friend before,

To thee that word I'd surely breathe;
  For thou wouldst guard it in a cell
Deep-built as central caves beneath,
  And Silence is the sentinel.

There long thy Thoughts are steeped in flame
  And in the thrice-locked fount of tears,
Till, sounded forth, at once they shame
  And move a host with tingling ears.

For not as in a bounded bay
  Thy billows roll unripe and weak,
But from a thousand leagues away
  The long vast waters booming speak.

Such roar on crags and sands of earth
  I ne'er have heard, nor felt the soul
So startled into throes of birth
  By piercing clang or awful toll.

But greater e'en than this the right
  Of him who knows thee friend to friend,
To whom laugh, groan and maddest flight
  More than the Sage the Man commend.

That I shall leave behind me here
  A greater soul below the sky
I know not, knowing none more dear
  For me sometimes will pause and sigh.

SEPTEMBER 14TH, 1844. JOHN STERLING

TO LADY HARRIET BARING

The wholly platonic love affair which Carlyle carried on with Lady Harriet Baring, later Lady Ashburton, caused much distress to Mrs. Carlyle.

CHELSEA, 20 FEB. 1845.

Sunday, yes my Beneficent, it shall be then: the dark man shall again see the daughter of the Sun, for a little while; and be illuminated, as if he were not dark! Which he very justly reckons among the highest privileges he has at present. Poor creature!

My wife will follow, on Monday or on Tuesday, according to your will. But you must do a little German—you must. And I will come in the rear to see whether you are right. And, on the whole, you are going to be wise, and we are all going to be wise, now that the Corn Laws are abolished? It would well become us. . . .

Adieu my sovereign Lady. Take care of these ugly foggy evenings; we cannot quite afford to have you unwell! Also be patient with the dark man, who is forever loyal to you.

Yours to command,

T. C.

TO LADY HARRIET BARING

CHELSEA, 11 JAN. 1847.

You are good and wise, and beautiful and brave; and in fact have no fault to speak of except a tendency to sore-throat; which I hope you will abandon by and by! Your letter is here: and we are to hope to come, *both* of us, next Monday, this day week. That is the prophecy at present. My wife hopes she will be well enough by that time; is really anxious to come, if able; and indeed I think it might actually do her good. By myself I could not get away till Saturday; and then, it seems, I should have to return again on Monday, owing to the course of Political Affairs. Better wait till Monday, and then come altogether! If my wife be *not* able for the expedition on Monday, then I am to wait till Mr. Baring's 'two or three days' are over, and come down along with him. You shall put me away again, when it becomes necessary—will not that do? What a pity we could not all serve God, and be 'happy' in this world (as Miss Martineau and the Unitarians prescribe); instead of partly serving the Devil, and being unhappy! Really it were cheap at the money, one would say. Alas, alas!

Today there is sunshine; which, tho' coupled with hoar frost, looks far cheerfuller. Take care of yourself; be not you unwell! This, we can hope, will be the last frost of the season; be patient with this.

The maid at Stanhope Street, I think, will not send the Book till you send for it. I have nailed up a map of Ireland on the wall here; and today am busy with St. Patrick's Purgatory and the ancient Annals of that country. Once a week also I have to read an Irish newspaper. There never was, surely, under the sun such a spectacle as that wretched island now exhibits! The land, it seems to me inevitable, will all or nearly all be confiscated; the whole frame of society is not unlike trembling to pieces. The *Potatoe* breaking down, all manner of Impostures tremble rapidly together; and Nature, very audibly indeed, declares to that people: 'Wretched People, unless you can find more sense and faithfulness among you, you shall not any longer subsist on the earth! Your Importer Aristocracy shall go and beg, your Importer Populace shall starve to death: of *you* at last the world shall be quit!'—Is not this an awful prophecy to terminate with? Adieu, best lady.

T. C.

TO LADY ASHBURTON

The 'sad tragedy' was the death of Charles Buller, Carlyle's friend and former pupil, and one of the brightest stars in Lady Ashburton's constellation.

CHELSEA, 29 NOV. 1848.

Alas, alas, what sad tragedy is this—the saddest, I think, that ever befel among friends of mine! 'Five minutes to six':

about the very moment I awoke, this morning, with the thought of him painfully blazing in me. And it was all over. And we shall never see that blithe face more; for the rest of our pilgrimage, never more!

That Monday you went away, the last time I saw him, he was unusually cheerful; spoke of his operation for the morrow as a thing of no significance, like the mere drawing of a tooth or less; and invited me to come and talk with him 'next Wednesday'—I privately believe, it is the *chloroform* that has done it, but alas, of what moment is that now?

To all of us his death is a sore loss; not to any living creatures, I think, could it seem a gain: for his presence was cheering and beneficent to all, and hurtful or afflictive to none that lived. But to you, dear friend, alas, it is a loss which I fear none of us can ever repair! In his own form he was by far the brightest soul in your circle; or indeed in all the world, that I know of. A great blank indeed to you; and who can console you? For himself it is perhaps happy: he passes away in the flower of his years, with the love of all the world following him; had he lived to see old age, perhaps its austerities, sadnesses, and sterner duties might have less suited him. The Eternal Power has willed it *so*.

I do not forbid you to weep. Nature will have its due; and an immense unexpected loss, one is permitted to bewail it. But you will not indulge in grief; no, you will rouse your better heart to conquer grief, to transform it into heroic determination. For us it is appointed still to *live*; and Destiny is striking as with an iron hammer on our hearts to say 'Remember to live *well*!' That is the one way of conquering grief. All pious thoughts be near you, dear lady!

It was soon after nine when our messenger returned, this morning; my wife went off directly after to attend poor Mrs. Buller. What in the world will become of that poor bereaved old mother, already at the point of death! Her calmness yesterday, Jane said, was almost frightful. . . .

God be merciful to us all. We ought to be *silent*; and accept, with pious submission, with profitable thoughts, unknown in these times, whatever bitter cup is sent us. May God bless you evermore, dear lady, and make *all* turn to good for you! That is the prayer of those still left.

T. C.

TO MRS. AITKEN[1]

CHELSEA, 26 JANUARY 1850.

DEAR JEAN—. . . After long tumbling and wrestling about with a mass of confused written-stuff here, which has been oppressing me for months and years past,—I have decided at last to give vent to myself in a Series of Pamphlets; 'Latter-day Pamphlets' is the name I have given them, as significant of the ruinous overwhelmed and almost dying condition in which the world paints itself to me. The First, about what they call the 'New Era,' is to come out at the beginning of February now instant: it is quite gone from *me*; they are printing the *Second* even (which is for March); and I have begun this day to turn the *Third* over in my mind. A questionable enterprise; but I could not help it! I think there will be perhaps a dozen Pamphlets in all,—two volumes when completed;—and it is to be expected they will occasion loud astonishment, condemnation, and a universal barking of 'Whaf-thaf? Bow-wow!' from all the dogs of the Parish.—A Paper I published in *Fraser* about *Niggers* has raised no end of clamour; poor scraggy critics, of the 'benevolent' school, giving vent to their amazement, and uttering their 'Whaf-thaf? Bow-wow!' in a great variety of dialects up and down all the country, as I am informed. That will be neither chaff nor sand to what they will hear in these 'Latter-day' Discourses, poor souls! All the twaddling *sects* of the country, from Swedenborgians to Jesuits, have for the last ten years been laying claim to 'T. Carlyle,' each for itself; and now they will all find that the said 'T.' belongs to a sect of his own, which is worthy of instant damnation. All which is precisely as it must be, and as it should be. Nay, we have a considerable amusement over it here; being, I do suppose, about as well situated for speaking what is our own mind on occasion

[1] Carlyle's sister, Jean.

as perhaps any 'free king' of these parts, or these times! A much more questionable consideration is that of one's *bodily health* holding out thro' the job:—but that too we must risk; trying to take all precautions as we go. . . .

Your affectionate Brother,

T. CARLYLE

TO MARGARET CARLYLE

CHELSEA, 29 MARCH 1850.

MY DEAR MOTHER,—Nobody can well be *busier* than I at present: but here is a little message for you. I am just about fairly *thro'* my No. 4 (which comes out on the 15th of April); and I mean to have *one* silent day, walking out among the heaths, before I begin No. 5. This is fine sunny weather (tho' with frost still) and most agreeably *silent*, to-day being what they call 'Good Friday,'—an old festival of the Church, now chiefly employed by the mass of the English population in taking jaunts into the Country, comforting their souls with beer, and eating a kind of puffy butter-*scons* called 'cross-buns,' *cookies* with a cross stamped on them,—sacred to this good day! Not sleeping well, I went out for a walk this morning; all was grey, dim, and *snell* as winter: but at the 'Original Chelsea Bunhouse' (for we pique ourselves on our fame for buns), there was a gathering as of people about the drawing of a lottery; I stept near, it was poor souls crowding forward for their *buns*, and Baker and Wife serving them eagerly out of door and window: all *silent* too,—an affair of real business, and no mistake. At richer doors, as I walked along, Bakers' men were delivering the same sacred very edible article; at one particular door, it seemed to me as if the maid were taking about five dozen or so;—many children, and their bits of appetites good! 'Got your *buns*, old boy?' the workmen said to one another as they hurriedly saluted. A fine *well-living* people this,—after all!

The noise about those Pamphlets is very great, and not very *musical*,—but indeed I take care not to hear it, so don't care.

Chapman is about printing the fourth thousand of No. One, which he thinks naturally is good work. What he means to give *me*, I do not yet ascertain; but have decided that he shall let me know accurately in black on white within a week,—while I have the hank in my own hand!—A certain *second* Chapman[1] here (John knows him) called the other morning with an offer of £4 10s. for a copy of each No., '*one steamer* before it was published.' I instantly said, 'done!' He has got the First accordingly, and paid me for it; the second he will get in about a week, and pay me for it;—and I decide to give these two American first windfalls, one of them to Jane, and the other to my good old Mother by way of gratification to myself. Jane has got hers; and here is yours, dear Mother,—buy yourself something you may like with it, or make some loved soul a gift out of it, let me have that little pleasure to myself in secret! . . . Poor Jane has caught a kind of real *cold* at last; but it seems fast going again, tho' she is still a prisoner.

Adieu, dear Mother,

Ever your affectionate,

T. Carlyle

TO LEIGH HUNT

Chelsea, 17th June 1850.

Dear Hunt,—I have just finished your *Autobiography*, which has been most pleasantly occupying all my leisure these three days; and you must permit me to write you a word upon it, out of the fulness of my heart, while the impulse is still fresh to thank you. This good Book, in every sense one of the *best* I have read this long while, has awakened many old thoughts, which never were extinct, or even properly *asleep*, but which (like so much else) have had to fall silent amid the tempests of an evil time,—Heaven mend it! A word from me, once more, I know, will not be unwelcome, while the world is talking of you.

[1] John Chapman, bookseller; the *first* Chapman being Frederick, the publisher.

Well, I call this an excellent good Book; by far the best of the autobiographic kind I remember to have read in the English language; and indeed, except it be Boswell's of Johnson, I do not know where we have such a Picture drawn of a human Life as in these three volumes. A pious, ingenious, altogether *human* and worthy Book; imaging, with graceful honesty and free felicity, many interesting objects and persons on your life-path,—and imaging throughout, what is best of all, a gifted, gentle, patient and valiant human soul, as it buffets its way thro' the billows of time, and will not drown, tho' often in danger; *cannot* be drowned, but conquers, and leaves a track of radiance behind it: that, I think, comes out more clearly to me than in any other of your Books;—and that I can venture to assure you is the best of all results to realize in a Book or written record. In fact this Book has been like an exercise of *devotion* to me: I have not assisted at any sermon, liturgy or litany, this long while, that has had so *religious* an effect on me. Thanks in the name of all men. And believe along with me that this Book will be welcome to other generations as well as ours. And long may you live to write more Books for us; and may the evening sun be softer on you (and on me) than the morn sometimes was!

Adieu dear Hunt (you must let me use this familiarity, for I am an old fellow too now as well as you). I have often thought of coming up to see you once more; and perhaps I shall one of these days (tho' horribly sick and lonely, and beset with spectral lions, go whitherward I may): but whether I do or not, believe forever in my regard. And so God bless you,—prays heartily

T. Carlyle

TO DR. CARLYLE

CHELSEA, 8 JULY 1852.

My Dear Brother,—We are in a furious uproar here, nothing but bricklayers, dust and tumult over all the house; a 'thorough repair' going actually on! I am banished up to my little dressing-closet here, behind the bedroom; here stands my desk, with a few books; the *rest* are all now mere *stacks* of books, or pinned in their shelves with curtains, to keep off the unspeakable dust: it is truly a hot case we are in. For, besides there has come a blazing heat (physically speaking too) within these four days, very horrible for human creatures among bricks; and if thunder and rain don't come soon, it will be bad times with us, I perceive. Meanwhile it is not quite so unendurable as I expected; I have off all the carpets here; I keep a watering-pot beside me, and fearlessly moisten both floors and walls; so that with windows down, and plenty of wind blowing, and almost no clothes at all, I contrive to get along. Want of sleep is the worst; but it raises us at a far thriftier hour, and makes a nice long day, for one thing,—so is not without its advantages too.

The chief 'repairs' contemplated are an enlargement of the Library,—conversion of the Library into a kind of Drawing room, according to the modern ideas. They are taking back the fireplace (*two feet* of that great tower of brickwork are gone out of the way); new proper windows with a great increase of light; lastly three feet additional width to be taken off Jane's bedroom,—Jane will shift to the top front room, which used to be yours, which, with this of mine, she has undertaken to make 'very handsome.' We are also to get water into the house, etc., etc. There will remain always behind the Drawing room, a *guest's bedroom*, tho' contracted in size,—where we hope to see you one day, our first guest in it if we are in luck!—. . . . We have got a 'lease of 31 years,' and fair basis for changing the house into our own image as nearly as it will come: so *En avant!* The place too is very cheap:[1] and on the present terms (whatever become of *us*) an outlay of £200 or £250 is considered a perfectly safe investment. . . .

T. CARLYLE

[1] The rent was £35 *per annum*.

TO G. REMINGTON, 6 Cheyne Row

CHELSEA, 12 NOVEMBER 1852.

DEAR SIR,—It is with great reluctance that I venture to trouble you in any way; but a kind of necessity compels me; and I trust your good nature will excuse it in a distressed neighbour.

We have the misfortune to be people of weak health in this house; bad sleepers in particular; and exceedingly sensible in the night hours to disturbances from sound. On your premises for some time past there is a Cock, by no means particularly loud or discordant; whose crowing would of course be indifferent or insignificant to persons of sound health and nerves; but, alas, it often enough keeps us unwillingly awake here, and on the whole gives a degree of annoyance which, except to the unhealthy, is not easily conceivable.

If you would have the goodness to remove that small animal or in any way render him inaudible from midnight to breakfast time, such charity would work a notable relief to certain persons here, and be thankfully acknowledged by them as an act of good neighbourship.

With many apologies, and neighbourly respects,

I remain, Yours sincerely,

T. CARLYLE

TO MRS. AITKEN

CHELSEA, 23 DECEMBER 1852.

MY DEAR SISTER—. . . 'Frederick the Great' continues very questionable: nobody yet could say, I should ever fairly *try* to write a Book about him! The sight of actual Germany, with its flat-soled puddlings in the slough of nonsense (quite a different kind of nonsense from ours, but not a whit less genuine) has hurt poor *Fritz* (Freddy) very much in my mind; poor fellow, he too lies deep-buried in the *middenstank* even as Cromwell did; and then he is not half or tenth-part such a man as Cromwell, that one should swim and dive for him in that manner! In fact tho' I have not yet quitted the neighbourhood of Fritz and his cocked-hat, his fate is very uncertain with me; and every new German *Book* I read about him, my feeling is, All up with Fritz. In Germany I could not even get a good Portrait of him,—tho' they spend the year round in singing dull insincere praises to him in every key; and have built a huge bronze and granite monument to him, in Berlin, as big as your Midsteeple, at the cost of perhaps half a million, which is worth next to nothing [*Letter torn*]. They have the mask of his dead face, however; a fiercely shrivelled plaster cast; lips and chin and bottom of the nose I recollect as perfectly the image of old —— ——, if you remember her, in those features! The face of a *lean lion*, or else partly, alas! of a ditto *cat!* The lips are thin, and closed like pincers; a face that never yielded;—not the beautifullest kind of face. In fine why should *I* torment my domestic soul writing his foreign history? He may go to France for me!

All people are getting ready their Christmas eatables here; determined upon doing a good stroke of work that way. Such walls of beef, such wildernesses of plucked turkeys, eyes never saw: 'all from the country, ma'am!' The poor people, who cannot buy, stand in crowds in speechless approval and generous admiration of those who can. . . . Likewise all the world is busy baking a new Ministry; which is to be laid upon the peel, and go into the oven, they say, this very night. A 'Coalition' of Whigs and Grahamites, or I know not what: not good, but compared with the late Derby swindle, and *its* abominable Stump-Orator and 'Impenitent Thief,'[1] it will be lovely for a season, and a relief to all eyes! Poor Protectionists, there never were men so 'sold,' since Judas concluded his trade. *This* Jew however will not hang himself; no, I calculate he has a great deal more of evil work to do in the world yet, if he live. Whatever brutish Infatuation has money in its purse, votes in its pocket, and no tongue in its head, here is the man to be a ton ue for it (rather than be *nothing*, which *is* his func-

[1] Disraeli.

tion, could he believe it) and to use all his 'fine intellect' to put words in its mouth. In fact, he is not a beautiful man to me at all, that one;—and so we will leave him, in a plight, for the present, that is rather suitable to him. . . .

T. Carlyle

TO ALEXANDER CARLYLE, Brantford, Canada

SCOTSBRIG, 28 DECEMBER 1853.

My Dear Brother,—To-day comes the saddest news I ever sent you from this place; the sorrow you have no doubt long been anticipating: our good and beloved old Mother is gone from us; on this Earth we have no Mother. She died on Sunday last (the 25th) at ten minutes past four in the afternoon; nothing else had been expected for many weeks and months; she had endured much suffering too (tho' without any disease except old age), and was spent to the last thread of weakness, hardly could you fancy a weaker creature with life, with clear intellect and generous affection still left. The good Doctor was unwearied in his attendance, coming from Moffat once or twice a week this long while, and lately staying here nearly altogether. Jean and Mary alternated in their attendance for several months; for almost the last two, it had been chiefly Jean alone whom our Mother seemed to prefer, and who indeed alone of the two had strength sufficient either of body or mind: Jean *refused* to be worn out, and has indeed stood with faithful, almost heroic affection to her task, in a loving manner well rewarded with love; looks greatly fatigued and excited, but I think will recover herself gradually without damage. I came from Chelsea hither only on Friday morning last, after great uncertainties as to what I ought to do,—for I could ill move, and felt that I should be in the way here. It had long been signified expressly to our dear Mother that if she gave the least sign of wish to me I could be with her in one day; but she was too magnanimous ever to express such a wish; and it was not till last week that I could fairly see I ought to go without delay. During the journey it became frightfully uncertain to me whether I should still find her alive; walking from Kirtlebridge where the morning train had set me down, I durst ask nobody; I learned with certainty only when half-way up this stair-case. Thank God (as I may do for the rest of my life), my dear old Mother was still alive, still able with a perceptible joy to recognize me: her mind tho' occasionally clouded with pain and extreme weakness, was there, as it had always been, and as it continued still more conspicuously to the end, clear, quietly nobly patient, simple and composed: her spirit, her very form of character and humour (for she occasionally spoke with a faint touch of *jocosity*, in her old fashion even in late weeks) continued *entire* to the very last, to a most singular degree; I likened it to a bit of sharp steel ground now to the very back, yet still the same steel in all respects, and with the same edge. Her weakness that Friday, after all I had heard so long, was almost beyond my expectation; she had a restless weary day, asleep and awake from minute to minute; —mistook us several times; me once, 'did not know me at all,' yet sent Jane out directly after (the good generous ever-loving Mother!) to bring me back with apologies, 'That I was Tom, that she knew me right weel.' After midnight when I was retiring, she said as in old healthy days, 'Tell us how thou sleeps!' Ah me, ah me! On the morrow, especially towards dusk and afterwards, she was visibly weaker; but her mind was steady and clear as it had ever been, indeed to a degree that still astonishes me. Struggling for breath (for she had not strength to take half an ordinary fill of the lungs, as John explained to us), she was in great suffering and distress for some hours; little sips of a kind of drink ('give me a *spark* of that thing'), shifting of her posture; restlessly struggling (as seemed evident then) with the last enemy, in this condition she asked for Jean; heard that she was 'seeking up coals' (from the old shed you will remember), and thereupon ordered John to 'hold the candle to the Window' for light to Jean! Such a trait I never witnessed from any creature before; and there were others of the like which I shall remember with satisfaction as long as I live.—Jean said she nightly heard her whispering her prayers all along; forgetting none of us, 'going round by America too now' (as she sometimes would say, when speaking of it), nay not forgetting any public or general interest fit for prayer; and thinking only of herself and her own grandest interests as *subject* and posterior to these. Oh my Brother, we are to be forever thankful to such a Mother! A pious dignity, a truth, affection, generosity, and simple valour and invincibility were in her, such as are given to only very few; and are a high and noble treasure, far above this world's wealth, to all connected with them.—About midnight of Saturday, there being no relief visible anywhere, John ventured not without apprehension, on a small appliance (half her former quantity) of laudanum, in two portions; this very soon brought abatement. A little after midnight, John said to her, 'Here's Tom come to bid you goodnight.' She looked kindly at me, as she had done even in the worst pain, and she was now somewhat easier; I kissed her cold lips; and she took leave of me in these words, 'I'm muckle obliged t'ye,' audibly whispered; which are forever memorable to me,—which except a 'yes' and a 'no' in answer to questions from John about one and about four o'clock, were the last she spoke in this world. For shortly after midnight, she fell asleep, slept ever deeper for sixteen hours; her look on Sunday morning and all day pointing grandly towards death as we sat by her: about 3.45 P.M. the breathing rather suddenly sank fainter (it had never been harsh, nor was there any phlegm),—paused once or twice, and then gently ceased; and she was with God. Amen, amen.—My only consolation ever since is, the thought that she is freed forevermore from great bodily suffering; that she finished a life full of sorrows, but also full of worth, and such as only a few whom God loves can lead.—This is what I had to write, dear Brother, not in good circumstances for imparting in a proper way such news to you. Please send the Letter forward to Jenny, to whom I will now write only the bare fact. The Funeral is to be to-morrow (Monday); the weather is frosty with some snow.

You will, after that, hear some humbler details about business, and have your consent asked to what the other three parties here shall think wisest to be done in that respect. . . . I hope to write you soon again; and now bid God bless you!

Your affectionate Brother,

T. Carlyle

TO MRS. AITKEN

CHELSEA, 10 NOVEMBER 1854.

My Dear Sister—. . . The day before yesterday I went to Windsor; for the sake of innumerable Portraits, Engravings, Miniatures, etc., which I had got access to there. It is some twenty and odd miles off: one of the beautifullest Palaces,—for situation, etc., much the beautifullest I ever saw. Built on a short steep hill (high for those parts, and beautifully *clothed*); commanding an immense plain, the richest in the Island; with oak forests, with the River, with etc., etc., to all lengths. I regarded little or nothing of that; but proceeded straight to my Print rooms, where a Mr. Glover, the 'Librarian' of the place, was extremely kind to me, and I saw really a great many things that may be useful in my operations; and had four diligent and goodish hours out of a day. I mean to go back when the weather is brighter (for Pictures and old eyes), and when the 'Court' is not there. Towards four o'clock, while I was busy with a hundred Prints of Frederick, there came a soft step to the door; I did not look up till Glover said, 'Prince Albert!'—and there in truth was the handsome young gentleman, very jolly and handsome in his loose greyish clothes, standing in the door; not advancing till I bowed. His figure and general face were well known to me, well-built figure of near my own height, florid *blond* face (with fair hair); but the *eyes* were much better than I had fancied; a pair of strong steady eyes, with a good healthy briskness in them. He was civility itself, and in a fine simple fashion: a sensible man withal. We talked first of Frederick's Portraits; then went, by a step or two, into the Saxon genealogy line, into the Wartburg, Coburg, Luther, Frederick the Wise (that is the Prince who caught up Luther, put him safe into the Wartburg; he is *Ancestor* of Albert); we had there abundant scope of talk, and went on very well, the Prince shewing me a Portrait he had copied of 'Frederick the Wise' (not ill done), telling of a Luther Autograph he had (from Coburg, and a joke appended to the getting of it there),—when a *domestic* glided in upon us, murmured something, of which I heard, 'gone out to the Terrace! (Queen out, wants you,—he had been in Town all morning)—whereupon, in a minute or two, our Dialogue winding itself up in some tolerable way, Prince Albert (prince of courtesy) bowed himself out, back foremost and with some indistinct mention of 'your *Works*,' which did not much affect me; and so ended our interview. I had had an indistinct questionable anticipation of some such thing all day; but thought too I was safe, having *met* his carriage on the railway as I came. However, it was managed as you hear; and I was not ill pleased with it, nor had any reason,—but *well pleased* to have it over as you may fancy. Not a word more, dear Jean.

Your affectionate Brother,

T. Carlyle

TO DR. CARLYLE

CHELSEA, 4 MAY 1859.

My Dear Brother—. . . Did not I *send* you Mill's Essay on *Liberty*? I meant it; and do not now find the Book here. In my life I never read a serious, ingenious, clear, logical Essay with more perfect and profound dissent from the basis it rests upon, and most of the conclusions it arrives at. Very strange to me indeed; a curious monition to me what a world we are in! As if it were a sin to control, or coerce into better methods, human swine in any way;—as if the greater and the more universal the 'liberty' of human creatures of the *Swine* genus, the more fatal all-destructive and intolerable were not the 'slavery' the few human creatures of the *Man* genus are thereby thrown into, and kept groaning powerless under. *Ach Gott im Himmel!* . . .

Adieu, in hot *haste*,

T. Carlyle

TO MRS. AITKEN

The four extracts from letters that follow were written during the time of Mrs. Carlyle's accident and subsequent illness (see *Reminiscences*, this edition, pp. 666–680.)

CHELSEA, 10 JANUARY 1864.

Dear Jean,—You, and those dear to me, and to whom I am dear, ought to at once be made partakers of my little gleam of good luck!—

The poor Soul had at last two hours of good sleep last night, and generally a 'much quieter' night; she admits this morning (she for the *first time*, and dare not yet without *buts* and doubts, poor creature) that she is a *kenning* better! The rest of us all hope now that we are fairly *round*,—tho' taught by former experience, we will not anticipate *un*interrupted progress, and will be content with the slowest rate of *speed*. . . .

TO JANE WELSH CARLYLE,
Care of Dr. Blakiston, St. Leonards

CHELSEA, 9 MARCH 1864.

Oh My Poor Little Darling!—You behaved like a heroine yesterday, firm to your purpose; and surely it was a blessing you got the journey done, instead of waiting,—till to-day, for instance. How quiet you were, and clear and calm: my dear little suffering woman!—

I *saved* my train by probably the nearest miss even I ever made. Two seconds more would have been fatal to it! I saw no carriage or omnibus; missed the road a little (quite at the end); and had to come in at a *run*, shouting like 'stop thief!'—I got home in good time; found a good fire, etc.: but, alas, a house *too* silent, and gone all into the *gaunt* mood to one's poor sunk heart. If I could have burst into a passion of tears, it would have been some relief. I finished off my Proof; and went timefully to bed. For Maggie [Welsh] there was the enclosed Letter; and this morning for self the enclosed Mrs. Kemble's: I have not asked *her* to call on you.

Oh if I could hear some good news of my poor Jeannie's *sleep* to-morrow morning! I try to live in hope. Surely, surely the *shaking* and the change will do something for us.—I think perhaps you will have to get a house of your own? But you need do nothing rashly.—God keep my Darling for me. Amen.

T. C.

TO JANE WELSH CARLYLE,
St. Leonards

CHELSEA, 13 MAY 1864.

My poor little Jeannie, I hope, has slept *better* last night; and if so, this good May day may be further of benefit,—at least, pleasanter to drive in. I got John's Letter last night, but not till eleven o'clock, our oblivious maid having left it in the letter-box till then. Of course I am very glad that you have got a Craik settlement on the favourable terms.[1] Maggie [Welsh] waits your permission to attend me to-morrow, and stay till *Wednesday*:—I hope you will let her come? She is abundantly diligent here; and keeps the gloom of the House from settling on me.

For the rest we are up to the chin in wreck and pother; the Books are all packed,—Larkin to ascertain if *they* cannot be sent this night, and got to arrive on Saturday as soon as *we*! To-morrow at 12 we actually vanish hence (unless something occur), and shall be with you at the hour John and I arrived. Oh poor Darling, I wish I could do you any good by my coming! But at least you will have the comfort, as I shall, of our being all together again: that is always something. . . .

[1] *I.e.*, arranged satisfactorily with Miss Mary Craik to stay as companion, etc.

Thank John for his two Notes; let him have the groom waiting to-morrow! Good bye Dearest, till then.—Your T. C.

TO JANE WELSH CARLYLE,
Care of Dr. Russell, Thornhill

CHELSEA, 3 AUGUST 1864.

Oh my poor little Woman, it is indeed terrible. Night after night, the 'wakeful sleep' itself gone, nothing but miserable vigilance, and the desperate unrest you have been so long used to! Would I might hope to-morrow for news of a *second* sleep following: but I dare not hope yet;—tho' every circumstance as you say is in your favour, were it not for your own poor nervous system ruined (for the present), not by these late months only, but by long years of more or less the like. . . . Nevertheless, I by no means permit you or myself to despair. No; I seem even to discern some rays of fluctuating hope (real tho' fitful) even in your present state: Hold on, hold on! Try all that you can by diet, by study to your *best* of what hurts and what answers;—that clearly is the one strength we have; but that also is a thrice important. The *centre* of all: consider it so. Dr. Russell will do and forbear what the kindest and wisest of Doctors attainable on the Earth would! Quinine (or Jesuits' Bark simple) is the hopefullest drug I ever heard of to you: so too, I daresay, he thinks; but gives it over too, while you object (which also I reckon wise altogether). Perhaps you may come back on it again.—Oh what is my poor Woman doing at this hour (this warm, still August day,—which *here* would be very hot for horses and her at 3 P.M.)? Oh that I might *believe* that you have had some sleep, driving through those old scenes, so full of *prophetic* and supernal thoughts looking behind and before! I will pray for a Letter. I have not answered Froude; I shudder to answer anybody, on a subject so indifferent to *him* in comparison. Indeed I have not spoke an word to anybody these three days.

Geraldine has and shall have nothing to do with the

'Papering' or any of our affairs.[1] Indeed she handsomely keeps silent and away.

I am better than yesterday; still not quite up to par. The noises have considerably increased about me; but I care much less about them, in general: Night always brings her coolness, her silence deep as could be,—which is an infinite solace to me, body and *soul*. . . . My work has been *intense* to-day; but far from brilliantly successful. But I do make progress, nearly daily,—*altogether* daily, I may say, tho' not always visible daily. Oh if I but had my Jeannie again! But Patience, there too, and Hope, hope! *At spes infracta.* God bless thee, Darling.

T. C.

TO DR. CARLYLE

CHELSEA, 24 SEPTEMBER 1864.

MY DEAR BROTHER,—I yesterday sent your Letter to Jane; I find to-day she decides to accept your proffered assistance,[2]—which is a bit of very comfortable news, among the others she sends which are rather below average to-day.

I can give no advice about the Trains, the Night-or-Day question, or any practical point at all: of course she, you and Dr. Russell will with your best light consider all these things;—and I need not advise you (what will double and treble the kindness, and is perhaps really the difficult part) to be gentle, *patient*, and *soft* and yielding in all respects, as towards a creature *without skin*, in a manner! This you already well know, I am aware; and will, without counsel of mine, do your very best in: it will be the greatest favour I can get at present from any-body living.

I shall not grudge much your troublesome journey, if you *are* really for the Continent. A day or two of you here will be a great treat to me, and I shall not grudge a little loss of time; —before winter quite some (before December *end*, surely!) I

[1] Mrs. Carlyle had written (2nd August), 'Above all, do not let Geraldine interfere,—*she* has the least taste of any woman I know.'

[2] In convoying Mrs. Carlyle home.

shall be ready for any amount of roving and recreating, if things only go well! . . .

Your affectionate Brother,

T. CARLYLE

TO MRS. AITKEN

CHELSEA, 28 APRIL 1866.

DEAR SISTER,—You will read these three Letters with a very melancholy interest;—especially the *one* of them I wrote from Scotsbrig the morning we left for Dumfries; and will regret with me to the end of your life that she did not see it;[1] alas, no; it was *not* posted at Ecclefechan by 6 P.M. in time for the morning mail at London; would come about 2 P.M. by which time she was gone *out*, never to return more. Oh why didn't I post it myself at Blackburn as I rode past; why did I wait for anything,—why did Jamie [Carlyle] junior make any delay in posting! But alas what is the use of such reflexions:—was not her own death caused by the hurt toe of a miserable little scraping of a *dog* hardly even hers? That wretched animalcule has done *me* more mischief than all the men and animals that have ever lived in my time! We must take these paltrinesses to us, also; they are part of our bitter cup.

The Letter she wrote, after that of Scotsbrig *should* have arrived, you will never forget reading with me last Sunday; after writing so, she lunched with the Forsters (old friends), was never seen more brilliantly cheerful, *well* beyond wont, and seemed to *eat* better than usual: 'my Friend coming home to me, day after to-morrow!'—and within half or three-quarters of an hour, she sat dead. Oh, that Monday night, oh this week in general, the *black* week of my poor life.—But *she* died happy and victorious, in the way she had always wished to do.—No more; this is my first writing, and my hand is as you see.

In a few days I will write again. Day by day I am getting bits of order introduced into this great overturn of my past

[1] Mrs. Carlyle died on the 21st of April

existence; that is the only thing *she* would have wished as a consolation to me. I saw her dead face twice: beautiful as Eternity, soft as an angel's or as a babe's. Put in these four Letters into the Miss Welsh's cover,—and dispatch to them by *Monday's* mail, that you may have *time* for reading them (yourself only).—I will walk all day; my sleep only half come back: well otherwise. God bless you, dear Sister, and reward your sympathy and kindness for me. Ever yours,

T. C.

TO MRS. AITKEN

CHELSEA, 11 MARCH 1869.

DEAR JEAN—. . . 'Interview'[1] took place this day gone a week; nearly a week before that, the Dean and Dean*ess* (who is called Lady Augusta Stanley, once *Bruce*, an active hard and busy little woman) drove up here, and, in a solemnly mysterious, though half quizzical manner, invited me for Thursday, 4th, 5 P.M.:—Must come, a very 'high or indeed highest person has long been desirous,' etc., etc. I saw well enough it was the Queen incognita; and briefly agreed to come. 'Half past 4 come *you!*" and then went their ways.

Walking up at the set time, I was there ushered into a long Drawingroom in their monastic edifice. I found no Stanley there; only at the farther end, a tall old *Gearpole* of a Mrs. Grote,—the most wooden woman I know in London or the world, who thinks herself very clever,etc.,—the sight of whom taught me to expect others; as accordingly, in a few minutes, fell out. Grote and Wife, Sir Charles Lyell and ditto, Browning and myself, these I saw were to be our party. 'Better than bargain!' 'These will take the edge off the thing, if edge it have!'—which it hadn't, nor threatened to have.

The Stanleys and we were all in a flow of talk, and some flunkies had done setting coffee-pots, tea-cups of sublime patterns, when Her Majesty, punctual to the minute, glided softly in, escorted by her Dame in waiting (a Dowager

[1] With Queen Victoria.

Duchess of Athol), and by the Princess Louise, decidedly a very pretty young lady, and *clever* too, as I found in speaking to her afterwards.

The Queen came softly forward, a kindly little smile on her face; gently shook hands with all three women, gently acknowledged with a nod the silent deep bow of us male monsters; and directly in her presence everybody was as if at ease again. She is a comely little lady, with a pair of kind clear and intelligent grey eyes; still looks plump and almost young (in spite of one broad wrinkle that shows in each cheek *occasionally*); has a fine soft low voice; soft indeed her whole manner is and melodiously perfect; it is impossible to imagine a *politer* little woman. Nothing the least imperious; all gentle, all *sincere*-looking, unembarrassing, rather atractive even;—*makes* you feel too (if you have sense in you) that she is Queen.

After a little word to each of us in succession as we stood,—to me it was, 'Sorry you did not see my Daughter,' Princess of Prussia (or 'she sorry,' perhaps?), which led us into Potsdam, Berlin, etc., for an instant or two; to Sir Charles Lyell I heard her say, 'Gold in Sutherland,' but quickly and delicately cut him *short* in responding; to Browning, 'Are you writing anything?' (he has just been publishing the absurdest of things!); to Grote I did not hear what she said: but it was touch-and-go with everybody; Majesty visibly *without* interest or nearly so of her *own*. This done, Coffee (very black and muddy) was handed round; Queen and Three women taking seats (Queen in the corner of a sofa, Lady Deaness in opposite corner, Mrs. Grote in a chair *intrusively close* to Majesty, Lady Lyell modestly at the *diagonal* corner); we others obliged to stand, and hover within call. Coffee fairly done, Lady Augusta called me gently to 'come and speak with Her Majesty.' I obeyed, first asking, as an old infirmish man, Majesty's permission to *sit*, which was graciously conceded. Nothing of the least significance was said, nor *needed*; however my bit of dialogue went very well. 'What part of Scotland I came from?' 'Dumfriesshire (where Majesty might as well go some time); Carlisle, *i.e.*, '*Caer-Lewel*, a place about the antiquity of King

Solomon (according to Milton, whereat Majesty smiled); Border-Ballads (and even old Jamie Pool slightly alluded to, —not by name!); Glasgow, and even Grandfather's ride thither,—ending in mere *psalms* and streets *vacant* at half-past nine P.M.;—hard sound and genuine Presbyterian *root* of what has now shot up to be such a monstrously ugly Cabbage-tree and Hemlock-tree!' All which Her Majesty seemed to take rather well.

Whereupon Mrs. Grote rose, and good-naturedly brought forward her Husband to her own chair, *cheek by jowl* with Her Majesty, who evidently did not care a straw for him; but kindly asked, 'Writing anything?' and one heard 'Aristotle, now that I have done with Plato,' etc., etc.—but only for a minimum of time. Majesty herself (I think àpropos of some question of my *shaking hand*) said something about her own difficulty in writing by dictation, which brought forward Lady Lyell and Husband, mutually used to the operation. After which, talk becoming trivial, Majesty gracefully retired,— Lady Augusta with her,—and in ten minutes more, returned to receive our farewell bows; which, too, she did very prettily; and sailed out as if moving on skates, and bending her head towards us with a smile. By the Underground Railway I was home before seven, and out of the adventure, with only a headache of little moment.

Froude tells me there are foolish *myths* about the poor business; especially about my share of it; but this is the real truth;—*worth* to me, in strict speech all but nothing; the *myths* even less than nothing. . . .

T. CARLYLE

TO THE RIGHT HON. B. DISRAELI

Disraeli, who had been persistently vilified by Carlyle, had written to offer him a baronetcy, the Grand Cross of the Bath, and a pension.

5, CHEYNE ROW, CHELSEA: DECEMBER 29 1874.

SIR,—Yesterday, to my great surprise, I had the honour to receive your letter containing a magnificent proposal for my benefit, which will be memorable to me for the rest of my life. Allow me to say that the letter, both in purport and expression, is worthy to be called magnanimous and noble, that it is without example in my own poor history; and I think it is unexampled, too, in the history of governing persons towards men of letters at the present, or at any time; and that I will carefully preserve it as one of the things precious to memory and heart A real treasure or benefit *it*, independent of all results from it.

This said to yourself and reposited with many feelings in my own grateful mind, I have only to add that your splendid and generous proposals for my practical behoof, must not any of them take effect; that titles of honour are, in all degrees of them, out of keeping with the tenour of my own poor existence hitherto in this epoch of the world, and would be an encumbrance, not a furtherance to me; that as to money, it has, after long years of rigorous and frugal, but also (thank God, and those that are gone before me) not degrading poverty, become in this latter time amply abundant, even superabundant; more of it, too, now a hindrance, not a help to me; so that royal or other bounty would be more than thrown away in my case; and in brief, that except the feeling of your fine and noble conduct on this occasion, which is a real and permanent possession, there cannot anything be done that would not now be a sorrow rather than a pleasure.

With thanks more than usually sincere,
I have the honour to be, Sir,
Your obliged and obedient servant,
T. Carlyle

TO DR. CARLYLE

CHELSEA, 4TH DEC. 1875.

My Dear Brother,—There has been this day a complete whirlwind of Birthday Gifts and congratulations, about the poor arrival of my 80th, and probably last 4th of Decr,—from the whole of which Mary and Jean, with the good sense of the senders, have mercifully delivered me; so that I have got little harm from them, which is a mercy. All this ended, there has come down a dark sleety cloud, more suitable for midnight, in regard to which, I have set down Mary with two candles, to write a word or two to you, generally announcing the thing and copying the two most remarkable of these Birthday documents, both of them from Berlin, with purpose to send you at least, a *selection* from the others, were a new day, with visible, or presumable, sun once come. Prince Bismarck, you will observe, thinks it is my 70*th* Birthday, which is enough to quench any vanity one might have on a Missive from such a man: but I own to being truly pleased with the word or two he says about *Friedrich*, which seems to me a valuable memorial and certificate of the pains I took in that matter,—not unwelcome in the circumstances.

Besides German Documents, more or less remarkable, there is an Edinburgh Affair, got up, I think, by Masson, which has issued in a fine Gold Medal, done by Boehm, and an Address with many signatures appended; of which you shall hear more specially by and by. Let this, with the copies accompanying, suffice at present on that head. . . . There has come a Letter from Canada Tom, yesterday morning; which distresses us all, announcing the great frailty and constant suffering of poor Alick, who perhaps will not survive me, as by nature he should. God bless him and me and all of us! Mary has much to do, and Forster has positively, by the most obstinate persistence, managed to have us all to dine to-night; so at present I will not add another word.—God's blessing on you all.

T. CARLYLE.

TO PRINCE BISMARCK

CHELSEA, 10TH DECEMBER 1875.

SIR,—On Saturday morning, which was my eightieth, and probably enough my last, Birthday, I was honoured with a

Letter, by far the remarkablest, the least expected and the most agreeable that came to me on that occasion. This is the noble, wise, sincere and generous Letter which you have been pleased to write, and which I read with very great surprise and very great and lasting pleasure. Permit me to say that no honour could have been done to me, which I should have valued so much, or which shall live more brightly in my thoughts for the rest of my time in this world. What you deign to say of my poor History of your great King Friedrich seems to me the most pertinent and flattering utterance I have yet anywhere heard on that subject; and I am truly proud of it from such a quarter.

With very great sincerity, I warmly thank you for your goodness; and shall continue to wish for you, as I have long done, every prosperity in your great and noble career, and that God may grant you years and strength to fulfil, or carry beyond risk of failure, the grand and salutary enterprise in which you have already gone so far, in sight of all the world.

I have the honour to be and remain,

Sir,

Your obliged and obedient servant,

T. Carlyle

TO DR. CARLYLE

CHELSEA, 15 NOV. 1878.

My Dear Brother,—Thanks for your punctual Letter, which lay waiting me when I got in from my poor cripply walk half way down the Embankment. I am not now able to get to the bottom of the Embankment, but have to stop half way and rest a little and return. My limbs getting quite lame about the middle of the back part of the thighs, reminding me daily of old Ziethen's description to Friedrich: *Die Füsse wollen nicht fort.* I have been thinking even more constantly than ever of your imprisonment during these wild mornings, while even with us the weather has been so bad; and certainly, as I daily considered, it would be worse with you. I am not sure that you take the best plan in keeping your fire alight all night. Would it not be better to go to bed with a good warm fire and then to have it lighted again in the morning near rising time? There is an excellent recipe against cold, in down quilts to cover the feet or even the whole body if necessary, but probably, as Mary says, you already have one of these. The thick night socks are also very useful on the feet. I have these and also a soft red-flannel night-shirt (on the top of my ordinary night-shirt) coming down to my heels, which Mary has provided for me, and which I feel to be a great comfort. . . .

I have tried the Russian Pushkin, as I mentioned, already, without any fruit. I have been reading a Life of Magliabecchi,—which contains a hirsute portrait of him, one of the ruggedest and ugliest conceivable, and a good many details that seemed to me incredible. I have even been thinking to try and read again either Shakespear or the Bible, but have for the present a new French Book on Russian Literature which I must first dispatch, or dismiss. These are all my poor adventures, dear Brother, not worth detailing except to yourself. God grant us patience, is my constant prayer. The end surely is near and then all these troubles will have vanished. My kindest continual regards to Sister Jean. My blessing to all of you.

I am ever, Your affectionate Brother,

T. Carlyle